Business Law

John Ellison Jim Bedingfield Tom Harrison

The authors are all Senior Lecturers in Law at New College Durham

BUSINESS EDUCATION PUBLISHERS LTD

1991

ISBN 0 907679 39 0
Published in Great Britain by Business Education Publishers Ltd.

Sales Office
Leighton House 10 Grange Crescent Stockton Road Sunderland
Tyne and Wear SR2 7BN
Telephone 091 567 4963 Fax 091 514 3277
Editorial Office
4 Vine Place The Broadway Houghton-le-Spring
Tyne and Wear DH4 5AS
Telephone 091 5120151 Fax 091 512 0145

First edition 1987
Reprinted 1989, 1990
Second edition 1991

A CIP catalogue record for this book is available from the British Library

Printed in Great Britain by M & A Thomson Litho Ltd East Kilbride Glasgow

PREFACE

This book has been written to provide comprehensive coverage of Business Law for students studying on BTEC and professional courses. It assumes no previous legal knowledge on the part of the reader. The text has been structured to take the student on a logical journey through the legal environment in which the business community operates, beginning with the nature of the legal system and its significance to business activity. The text covers in depth the internal and external legal framework of business: its aquisition and use of resources; the nature of its transactions and its rights and obligations.

In addition to updating and overhauling the original text, the second edition includes new chapters dealing with all the major areas of employment law. The rate of legal change has continued unabated since the publication of the first edition, and this is reflected in the general expansion of the book.

The inclusion of a range of practical, work related problem based assignments provides an opportunity for students to engage in an active learning process. It also provides a basis for the BTEC in-course assessment programmes.

For ease of expression the book adopts the practice of using 'he' for 'he or she', and 'his' for 'his or hers'.

The book complements the main text 'Core Studies for BTEC' by the same publisher. A tutor's guide is available from the publishers for colleges which adopt the book.

Acknowledgements

We would like to thank Caroline, Moira and Paul at Business Education Publishers for all the assistance they have provided in the production of this book. Most especially we must record our thanks to our tolerant and long suffering wives and children.

All errors and omissions remain the responsibility of the authors.

The law is stated as at 1 July 1991.

Durham
July 1991

JE JB TH

Table of Contents

Chapter 1 *An Introduction to Business Law*

Chapter 2 *The Resolution of Business Disputes*

Chapter 3 *Establishment and Operation of Business Organisations*

Chapter 4 *The Termination of Business Organisations*

Chapter 5 *The Nature and Formation of Contracts*

Chapter 6 *Validity and Content of Contracts*

Chapter 7 *Discharge and Remedies*

Chapter 8 *Sale of Goods and Related Transactions*

Chapter 11 *Employment Relationships*

Chapter 12 *The Contract of Employment*

Chapter 13 *Health and Safety at Work*

Chapter 14 *The Termination of Employment*

Table of Cases

C

D

E

F

G

H

I

J

K

L

R

S

T

Table of Statutes, Statutory Instruments and Treaties

Chapter 1

An Introduction to Business Law

The Nature and Purpose of Law

The principal objective of a legal system is the establishment of rules which in the broadest sense are designed to regulate relationships. Human societies are highly complex social structures. Without systems of rules or codes of conduct to control them, such societies would find it difficult to maintain their cohesion, and would gradually break up. The interdependence of each member of the community with its other members brings people into constant contact and this contact sometimes leads to disagreement and conflict. It is unrealistic to expect in a Western culture like ours which recognises that people should have the freedom to express their individualism, there will never be occasions when the activities of one person interfere with those of another. Someone operating a commercial enterprise by selling second hand cars in the street outside his house, or building an extension, or holding regular all night parties may regard these activities as the exercise of his personal freedoms. They may however give rise to conflict if his neighbours resent the street being turned into a used vehicle lot, or find the light to their windows and gardens cut out by the new building, or that they cannot sleep at night for the noise. What the law seeks to do in circumstances where interests conflict in this way is to attempt to reconcile differences by referring their solution to established principles and rules which have been developed to clarify individual rights and obligations. The relationships between neighbours are of course but a small part of the complex pattern of relationships most people are involved in and which the law attempts to regulate. A book devoted to the study of business law focuses specifically on the particular legal relationships that are a product of business activity.

The task of defining what is meant by business activity is dealt with in some detail later in Chapter 3, but we can note at this initial stage that essentially businesses are provider organisations, selling goods and services to anyone who requires them. The customers of a business are usually referred to as consumers. They may be other businesses themselves, but they also include of course individuals, ultimate consumers, who use the goods and services for their own private benefit. Once we begin to examine the business world in any detail we encounter far more complex legal relationships than the simple neighbour example given above. We find an environment in which an enormously diverse range of transactions are constantly taking place, resources of labour, capital, and land are being acquired and disposed of, all kinds of property are being bought and sold, information and advice is being given and sought, and decisions are regularly being made which have an impact on the owners, managers and customers of the organisations with which they are associated. In short we are seeing a sophisticated market economy conducting its operations.

The business environment is not however an area of commercial activity of importance to the business community alone. All of us are involved in it in one way or another. The most obvious illustration of how this occurs comes from when we look at ourselves in our role as consumers, that is as users of products and services. Whether we are buying clothes, household goods, holidays, shares, having the car repaired, opening a bank account, taking a job or renting a flat we will be engaging in a business relationship. It does not always have to be a formal matter, and usually will not be. But all these activities are carried on within a legal framework which, as we shall see in this book, attempts to set out the responsibilities of the participants.

A useful starting point for our study is to simplify the types of relationship that most business organisations are likely to be engaged in by setting them out diagrammatically. In this way it is possible to obtain an overview of the business environment (Figure 1.2). As well as the external dimension of a business organisations' relationships, it will also have an internal dimension to its activities which is equally important to it. Figure 1.1 provides a simple illustration of the internal shape of a business organisation, indicating the relationships which exist inside a business. The example used is that of a registered company.

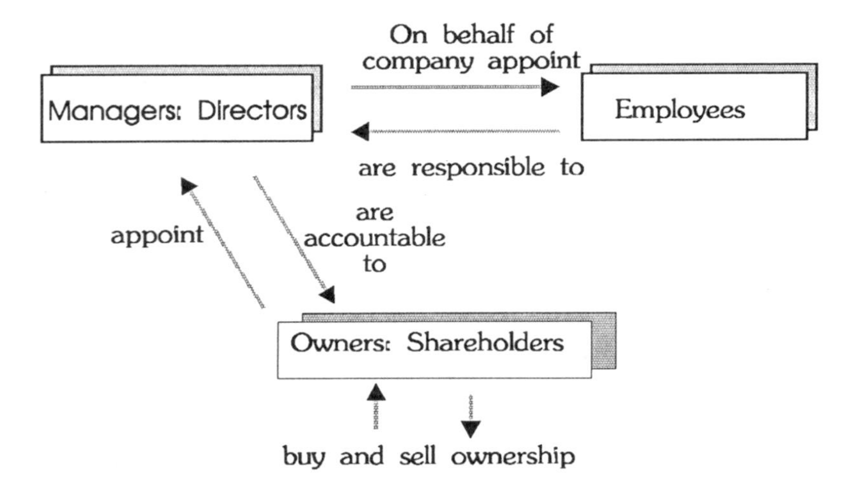

Fig 1.1 The internal dimensions of a business organisation - the limited company

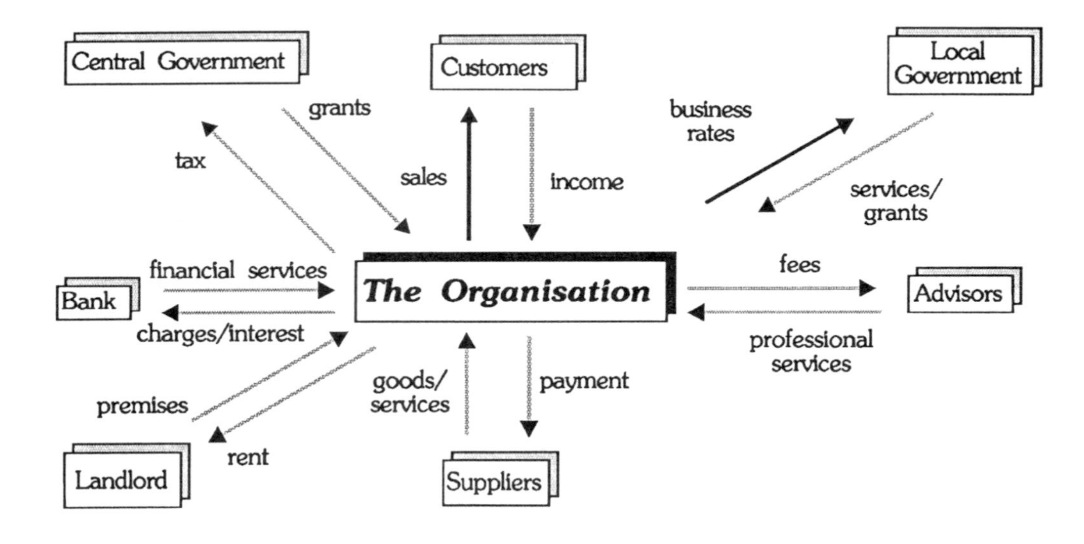

Fig. 1.2 The external dimensions of a business organisation

Even at the superficial level of analysis provided by these models, they enable us to see that business organisations are at the centre of a web of relationships all of which have a strong legal dimension to them. For instance, a business may take decisions on the basis of expert advice provided by a professional advisor in return for payment of a fee or charge. Inaccurate or incomplete advice relied upon by the business may cause it to suffer commercial damage. If this occurs the business may have a legal remedy against the advisor, and will seek to recover any losses it has sustained. Similarly, within the organisation legal relationships exist between managers, owners and staff, thus for example, directors of a limited company are accountable to the shareholders in general meeting, and can be dismissed from their office by a company resolution in circumstances where they have been guilty of commercial incompetence or malpractice. An exploration of the law as it applies to business thus involves examining the legal framework within which all businesses, from the multinational corporations to the one man businesses, pursue their commercial objectives. We have noted that this framework has to do with the relationships their business activity creates. What we must next do is to ascertain more precisely the purposes which underpin the legal regulation of business affairs.

The Purpose of a System of Business Law

Complex, affluent, property owning societies develop detailed and sophisticated rules to regulate themselves, and in the United Kingdom as in most modern states almost every aspect of human activity is either directly or indirectly affected by law. These laws seek to achieve different purposes. One major classification in any legal system involves distinguishing between those legal rules which are concerned with private rights and obligations, a branch of law referred to as *civil* law, and those whose primary purpose is the welfare of society generally, and its protection by means of rules that seek to prevent anti-social forms of behaviour, supported by the power to punish those who break them. This is the *criminal* law.

Legal rules in the field of business are designed to fulfil certain primary purposes. These include the remedying of private grievances, the control of anti-social activities and the regulation of harmful activities.

The remedying of private grievances

Various branches of law are concerned with recognising personal rights which can be enforced by means of legal proceedings if they are infringed, or even where there is simply a threat to infringe them. One of these branches is the law of tort. It is based upon the existence of a set of obligations referred to as torts, or civil wrongs, which have been evolved by the courts as a response to the need for established codes of conduct to protect people from certain types of harm. Tortious obligations are imposed by law, rather than arising by agreement between the parties as is the case with contractual obligations. In effect the law of tort recognises legal rights, which entitle anyone whose rights have been infringed to sue the wrongdoer for compensation. Examples of torts include those of trespass, nuisance and defamation. The tort of negligence, which is considered in detail further on in the book is probably the most important of all the torts which affect business operations.

The law of contract is a further example of a branch of law dealing in private rights and obligations. Contractual agreements involve the making of promises which are legally enforceable. A party to a contract therefore has the right to take legal action against the other party to the agreement in the event of that person being in breach of his contractual obligations.

Both the law of contract and the law of tort are crucial to the effective functioning of the business environment. Without the ability to enter into binding agreements businesses would be left fully exposed to the risk of their transactions being unilaterally terminated by the other contracting party. Such vulnerability would seriously undermine business confidence and would hamper economic activity generally, and without the ability to seek compensation and redress for wrongs committed against them businesses could suffer significant economic harm. Consider for instance, a situation where a small under-insured business could obtain no compensation following the total destruction of its stock and premises due to negligent repair work carried out to an adjoining gas main by the gas company.

The control of anti-social activities

This is essentially the task of the criminal law. Whilst it is not possible to prevent crimes from being committed, the presence of penal sanctions, such as imprisonment and fines, which are used to support the criminal code, can act as a deterrent to the commission of an offence.

There is no adequate definition of a crime. Lord Diplock in *Knuller v. Director of Public Prosecutions* 1972 attempted to pinpoint the essential differences between civil and criminal law when he said, *"Civil liability is concerned with the relationship of one citizen to another; criminal liability is concerned with the relationship of a citizen to society organised as a state."*

Businesses, like individuals, are subject to the criminal law. Of the wide range of offences that an organisation might commit in the course of its business, the following provide some illustrations:

(a) **offences in the field of consumer protection.** These are many and varied. They include offences connected with false trade descriptions applied to goods and services, consumer credit arrangements such as engaging in activities requiring a licence but where no licence has been granted, and safety obligations for certain manufactured items, for instance oil heaters and electric blankets, which must meet standards laid down under government regulations;

(b) **offences in the field of employment**, such as a contravention of the obligations owed to employees under health and safety legislation;

(c) **offences connected with the operation of registered companies,** such as failure to file accounts or the insertion of untrue statements in a prospectus;

(d) **offences in relation to tax liability**, such as the making of false returns.

The regulation of harmful activities

Methods of legal regulation include licensing, registration and inspection. These are useful mechanisms for exercising effective control over a range of activities, which, if uncontrolled, could be physically, economically and socially harmful. Thus powers of inspection, supported by enforcement mechanisms, are granted to factory inspectors working for the Health and Safety Executive. The inspection of work places such as factories and building sites enables inspectors to ascertain whether safety legislation is being complied with, and that employee's physical requirements are thus being met. Certain types of trading practices which are potentially anti-competitive can only be pursued legitimately if the agreements in which they are contained are registered with the Director General of Fair Trading, under the Restrictive Trade Practices Act 1976. Even then they are only legally permissible if they are approved by the Restrictive Trade Practices Court. Additionally anyone in the business of providing credit facilities is obliged to register under the Consumer Credit Act 1974 with the Director General of Fair Trading before being legally permitted to lend money. The aim is to eliminate unscrupulous finance dealers from the credit market, overcoming the social problems which arise when poorer members of society borrow at high rates of interest which they are unable to afford, often in an effort to extricate themselves from other debts. And in cases of alleged malpractice in the management of registered companies the Department of Trade and Industry has the power to carry out investigations into the affairs of companies, for instance to establish the true ownership of shares in a company.

The Importance of Law to Business

The legal system affects businesses just as it does individuals. Every aspect of business life, from formation and operation to dissolution is conducted within an environment of legal regulation. As we have seen above, many purposes are being served in applying legal regulation to business activity. In broad terms the underlying characteristics of business law may be seen as the dual aims of:

(a) providing a practical and comprehensive framework of legal rules and principles to assist the organisation in its commercial affairs, whilst at the same time

(b) ensuring a sufficient level of protection for the legitimate interests of those who come into direct contact with it. This includes not only members of the public in their capacity as consumers, but also business creditors and the employees and owners of business enterprises.

There appears to be one fundamental and compelling reason why business organisations are likely to seek to comply with the law. If they fail to do so it will cost them money, either directly or indirectly. A business which is in breach of law, whether the civil law or the criminal law, will in most cases suffer from the breach commercially.

The commercial consequences to an organisation which has been found to have broken or otherwise failed to comply with the law includes the possibility of:

(i) an action for damages against the business, brought by someone seeking financial compensation from it. Such an action may be the result of a breach of contract committed by the business, or be in respect of some form of tortious liability it has incurred. An alternative claim brought against it could be for an injunction restraining it from pursuing a particular course of action;

(ii) a claim that the action of the business is devoid of legal effect because it has failed to follow procedures which bind it. For instance, a limited company cannot act unless it has correctly followed the registration procedures laid down by statute, and has received a certificate of incorporation. Nor can it alter its own constitution, its memorandum and articles of association, unless this is done in accordance with relevant statutory procedures regarding notice periods, the holding of a meeting and the need to secure an appropriate majority of votes cast;

(iii) the loss of an opportunity to take some form of legal action, because the time limit for doing so has passed, for instance bringing a late appeal against an unfavourable planning decision;

(iv) a prosecution brought against it alleging breach of the criminal law, resulting in a fine, or in certain circumstances the seizure of assets;

(v) the exercise of enforcement action against it for its failure to comply with some legal requirement, for example to take steps to remedy a serious hazard to health, as a result of which its business operations are suspended;

(vi) the bringing of a petition to have the organisation brought to an end. A registered company can for example be wound up compulsorily by its unpaid creditors.

Thus there are sound commercial reasons for keeping properly informed about the law and complying with it as it affects business, quite apart from any moral or social responsibility for doing so. Moreover, legal proceedings often attract public attention and result in adverse publicity to the organisations involved, whilst at a personal level individuals engaged in managing a business may find themselves dismissed and facing civil and/or criminal liability if they are responsible for serious errors of judgment which carry legal consequences, such as negligent or dishonest performance in handling a company's financial affairs. The problems involving the Guinness Company, its managing director Ernest Saunders and some of his business associates provides a striking example in recent times.

Developing Legal Knowledge and Skills

Usually it is not possible for people in business to find the time or develop the skills to cope with all the legal demands of operating a business, however there will remain strong reasons for acquiring at least a basic level of legal knowledge and skills and devoting some time to legal issues as and when they arise. This is because:

(a) many straightforward legal problems can be resolved simply by means of a letter or a telephone call to the other party involved. Legal advice has to be paid for, and in some situations will be both an unnecessary expense, and a time consuming activity;

(b) certain legal problems require immediate action, for example, what rights the employer has to dismiss an employee against whom an allegation of sexual misconduct has been made; or what rights a buyer has to reject goods delivered late by the seller;

(c) the daily routine of a business involves frequent encounters with matters of a legal nature, such as examining contracts, signing cheques, negotiating deals and organising the workforce. It would be impractical to seek professional advice regularly in these routine areas;

(d) many business activities are closely legally regulated, and a working knowledge of them is essential if the business is to function effectively. For example a business providing credit facilities needs to employ staff who are fully aware of the strict legal requirements regulating such transactions;

(e) when expert advice and assistance is being sought the effectiveness of the process of consultation is assisted if the precise issues can be identified from the outset, and relevant records and materials can be presented at the time. In addition, when the advice is given it will be of little value in the possession of someone who can make no real sense of it;

(f) managing a business effectively demands a working knowledge of the legal implications not only of what is being decided, but also of the processes by which it is decided. For instance company directors ought to be familiar with the basic principles of the law of company meetings, since it is by means of such meetings that important decision making is achieved.

Obtaining and Using Legal Information

Having established the importance of legal rules and procedures in the running of a business, the next question which emerges is how to obtain and apply relevant legal principles, so that the process of business decision making and practical operation is informed and guided by the legal environment in which it functions. Large organisations employ their own professional advisors. Public companies and local authorities will have departments specialising in legal, financial and other areas of professional work. In such organisations it will be the role of staff in the legal department to deal with the routine legal aspects of the work of the business, and it may be expected of them to produce and distribute to relevant personnel details of legal changes which are likely to have an effect on the way in which the business works. For example, following the introduction of the Health and Safety at Work Act 1974, employers were required to fulfil a number of general duties set out by the Act to ensure the health, safety and welfare of their employees whilst at work. The Act specifically stated that these duties were to include providing staff with any necessary information, instruction, training and supervision. Smaller organisations, whose scale of business operations is insufficient to make the employment of a full time lawyer financially viable will instead rely for their legal needs on the services of a law firm, which will probably be locally based, to deal with legal matters as and when they arise. The nature of such an arrangement makes it unlikely that legal changes affecting the business will always be picked up by their legal advisers and fed into the business in advance of the change. Most of the legal work performed will be as a response to matters which are routinely passed on to the firm, such as the renewal of the business lease, actions for the recovery of debts and financial borrowing by means of the use of a security such as a mortgage or debenture.

In the smallest organisations, such as one man businesses, there may be reluctance to seek legal services at all, unless it is absolutely necessary for the business to do so. Professional advice costs money, and time is taken up in meetings with professional advisors. Whilst this may be a short-sighted view, and one which can result in the organisation getting itself into greater difficulty in the long term, it is nevertheless the case that such organisations will occasionally try to 'go it alone'.

It is clear that the nature of advice and assistance that organisations have need of to operate satisfactorily, is often of a detailed and technical kind which only accountants, lawyers and other professionals are capable of providing. However, it would be quite wrong to assume that in consequence there is little value to be gained from employing staff who have a basic knowledge and appreciation of principles of bookkeeping, or how the Sale of Goods Act 1979 works. Daily, practical business operations raise a range of issues, many of which, whilst broadly located in areas of technical expertise of which staff have no deep knowledge, can be easily dealt with by people with only a general level of knowledge. There is no reason why a small trading organisation should not be able to cope with most of the contractual disagreements that will arise from time to time between it and its suppliers and customers in the ordinary course of business.

Whatever method a business uses to obtain legal support, it is obvious that business managers are not doing their jobs properly if they are ignorant of the legal implications inherent in the daily activities carried out by their organisations. How they manage their premises, their staff, their financial affairs and their trading operations should be guided by their business ability, and part of this ability involves recognising the legal implications inherent in pursuing different courses of action. Certainly the failure of management to identify and respond to changes in the law which directly affects the business will prevent it from adapting its operations to accommodate and comply with these changes. How significant such a failure might be can be usefully illustrated by referring to many modern statutes, Take for example the Consumer Protection Act 1987. This legislative enactment is of considerable importance to any business which is a producer of goods that will ultimately be purchased by consumers. The Act significantly alters the basis of a producers liability for defective products, and as is the case in respect of many contemporary legal changes, the failure of the organisation to recognise the change and reassess its operational activity in the light of it, can result in the payment of large sums by way of compensation. Legal changes can produce immediate alterations to the extent of an organisation's liabilities, affecting the very heart of its commercial activities. In these circumstances it is essential that information is fed into the organisation to enable appropriate action to be taken. Given the dynamic nature of modern business, the capacity of an organisation to respond to change, of whatever kind it might be, is often crucial to its continued commercial survival. In the case of law essentially there are two stages involved in reacting to a legal change; obtaining the relevant information, and applying it.

Obtaining legal information and being able to understand and apply it effectively requires us to examine the various sources of English law.

Sources of English Law

The expression 'source of law' carries with it a number of different meanings, but we only need to concentrate on two of them. They are:

(a) source of law as a way of describing where the law is located, that is where one can obtain legal source materials; and

(b) source of law in the sense of where the law comes from, in other words who makes it.

As we shall see these two apparently separate ideas are very closely linked.

Legal source materials

To operate a detailed system of law it is essential that the law be recorded. The effective development of English law as a coherent and uniform body of established rules and principles dates back to the thirteenth century, by which time it was already possible to find comprehensive written accounts of the law. The recording of the law in a written form means that, as far as possible, the ambiguity, inconsistency and lack of precision that comes about when rules are merely passed on by word of mouth is eliminated. In practice, as we shall see, expressing the law by means of the written word is no guarantee of achieving absolute certainty as to meaning, although it does usually seem to achieve a satisfactory and workable framework within which individuals and organisations can conduct their affairs in confidence.

There are two forms of written law:

(a) the reports of court proceedings in which the judgments delivered by the court contain the statements of principle which express the relevant law; and

(b) the publication of UK and EC legislation. This includes subordinate legislation, and the various forms of EC legislation.

Both these legal sources are publicly available. Major academic libraries usually hold an extensive range of law reports covering the decisions of all the superior courts, as well as keeping volumes of statutes. In such libraries the statutes are usually held in bound volumes chronologically, the main series being published under the title Current Law Statutes Annotated, but also by subject title. Statutes published in this format are under the title Halsburys Statutes, and both these series include annotations, notes, to assist the reader in understanding and applying the law concerned. Individual Acts of Parliament can also be purchased from branches of HMSO.

Law reports are of various kinds. Some concentrate upon specific areas of law, such as local government (Knights Reports), whilst others report all the leading cases decided by a particular court or set of courts, whatever the subject matter of the case happens to be. Two major sets of law reports of this kind are the All England Law Reports, and the Weekly Law Reports. Law reports share at least one common characteristic in that they are published on a chronological basis, so that year by year they build up, volume by volume. Given the large number of annually reported cases there may be two or even three volumes of a particular set of reports covering a single year. In common with any large body of written material, and the English law reports must rank as one of the largest in existence, with approximately half a million decided cases on record, it is essential to have a workable reference system by which a particular decision, or statutory provision for that matter, can be located quickly and simply. The reference system used for law reports uses the case name, followed by a reference to the year, the volume, an abbreviation of the particular series of law report involved, and finally the page reference. Thus a reference to *Smith v. Brown* 1991 2 WLR 551, would enable a person to easily access the case involving the parties Smith and Brown, whose case is reported in the second volume of the Weekly Law Reports for 1991, at page 551. The table of cases at the beginning of the book includes all the case references for the cases referred to in the text. The corresponding table of statutes lists them all in alphabetical rather than chronological order, but breaks down each statute where appropriate into individual parts, or sections as they are referred to. Usually a section is drafted so that it is further broken down into sub-sections, and maybe further sub-divided into an (a), (b), (c) and so on. It is not uncommon to find that even the (a), (b) or (c) is subdivided into (i), (ii), (iii) etc. Obviously such a way of drafting can make it difficult to understand what the legislature is actually saying without careful attention to detail and examination of how each part of a section relates to the rest of the section, and to the Act itself. For instance the Companies Act 1989 contains provisions dealing with the requirement that at the end of each financial year the directors of a parent company are to produce group accounts representing the financial health of all the companies controlled by the parent company. Section 228 contains certain exemptions. It reads as follows:

"s.228(1) A company is exempt from the requirement to prepare group accounts if it is itself a subsidiary undertaking and its immediate parent undertaking is established under the law of a member State of the European Economic Community, in the following cases–

(a) where the company is a wholly-owned subsidiary of that parent undertaking;

(b) where that parent undertaking holds more than 50 per cent of the shares in the company and notice requesting the preparation of group accounts has not been served on the company by shareholders holding in aggregate–

(i) more than half of the remaining shares in the company, or

(ii) 5 per cent of the total shares in the company.

Such notice must be served not later than six months after the end of the financial year before that to which it relates."

Here we see an illustration of how detailed statutory provisions can sometimes be. But often they are very straightforward. A little further on in the same Act section 233 sub-section 1, which is expressed as S.233(1), states, *"A company's annual accounts shall be approved by the board of directors and signed on behalf of the board by a director of the company."* A provision of this kind expresses a simple idea in a straightforward sentence using clear language.

Law Making Institutions

Until the 1st January 1973 English law was created by two separate law making institutions, the courts and Parliament. However in 1973 the United Kingdom became a member of the European Economic Community (the EEC - but usually referred to more simply now as the EC), the effect of which in legal terms was to introduce a new, third, law making source. The impact of this fundamental change has been considerable, although there are many areas of activity which remain outside the jurisdiction of the law making bodies of the EC. Business operations however fall within the remit of the work of the Community and we will need to examine in some detail the ways in which the Community is structured and performs its functions, looking particularly at its lawmaking functions. Before doing so it is appropriate to look at our own domestic law makers, and examine the methods by which they create the laws which we will be encountering throughout this book. In an historical context it was the courts which originally developed our law, and so we shall consider the courts first.

The Courts of England and Wales

For the purpose of the administration of justice in England and Wales two separate court structures exist, one dealing with civil law matters and the other criminal matters. Some courts exercise both a civil and criminal jurisdiction. An example is provided by the Magistrates courts, which are primarily criminal courts but which also exercise a limited but nevertheless important civil jurisdiction in family matters.

An appeals structure gives the parties involved in any form of legal proceedings the opportunity to appeal against the trial court on points of law or fact. The trial court is the court in which the case is first tried, and in which evidence is given on oath to the court by witnesses appearing for the parties involved, in an attempt at enabling the court to establish for the purposes of the case the relevant material facts. The court in which a case is first tried is known as a court of *first instance*. Usually *leave to appeal* must be granted either by the trial court or the appellate court although certain appeals are available as of right.

The civil courts

In a civil court an action is commenced by a *plaintiff* who sues the other party, called the *defendant*. If either party takes the case before a higher court on appeal that party is known as the *appellant* and the other as the *respondent*.

Before commencing proceedings the plaintiff must decide whether the case is worth bringing. This is likely to involve a number of considerations including costs, time, the complexity of the action, and the resources of the defendant. We will return to look at these considerations in more detail later in the chapter.

A diagram of the structure of the civil courts is shown in Figure 1.3. Each court has a particular *jurisdiction*, a word which signifies the court's competence to hear a particular action. Civil cases are tried at first instance either before the County Court or before the High Court of Justice. Appeals from either of these courts are heard before the Court of Appeal (Civil Division). The highest appellate court is the House of Lords. A litigant, that is a person bringing legal proceedings, is thus faced with the choice of whether to bring the claim in the County Court or the High Court.

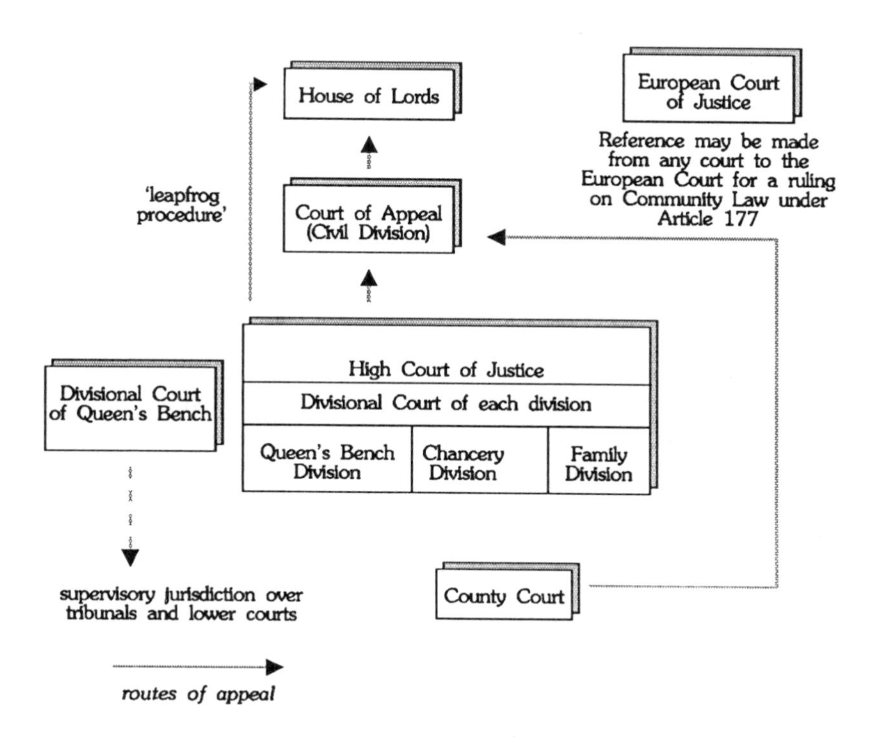

Fig. 1.3 The Civil Court System

County Court or High Court?

The decision as to whether to bring proceedings in the County Court or the High Court will be based upon a number of factors:

(i) **Convenience.** There are over 400 County Courts in England and Wales. This means they are readily accessible to plaintiffs. A County Court can usually hear those cases where the cause of action arose in its own district, or where the defendant either resides or carries on his business. Thus it is possible that a plaintiff might have the choice of three courts in which to commence proceedings. By contrast the High Court sits in London, and only rarely hears civil cases outside London.

(ii) **Costs.** Court costs are much cheaper in the County Court than the High Court. Bringing a High Court action may involve the payment of additional lawyers, for instance a firm of solicitors acting as the London agents for the local firm who originally handled the case. Lawyers' professional charges, like those of other professionals, vary not only according to the nature of the work involved but also according to where they carry out their work. Legal charges in London and other major cities for example are generally much higher than those of lawyers working elsewhere.

(iii) **Quality.** It is very dangerous to make comparisons about the quality or standard of justice as between courts. Sometimes it may be felt that the complexity of a case makes it a more suitable candidate for consideration before a High Court judge than before a circuit judge in a County Court. Equally it may be the case that a plaintiff's lawyer is entirely confident that the case should go before the local County Court. It is worth bearing in mind that the legal complexity of a case is not necessarily related to the amount of the claim involved.

(iv) **Jurisdictional limitations.** As we saw above because of the geographical distribution of County Courts there are jurisdictional rules as to which court can hear the case. No such limitations apply to the High Court. However there are further jurisdictional considerations that need to be borne in mind. These concern the type of action that is being dealt with and the financial value of the claim involved. Over certain kinds of action the County Court has exclusive jurisdiction, such as applications for the renewal of a business lease and in consumer credit cases such as the repossession of goods subject to a hire purchase agreement. With respect to the financial value of a claim, regulations introduced under the Courts and Legal Services Act 1990 have made it possible for the County Courts to deal with many more actions than was previously the case. To cope with the increased workload there are now 72 continuous trial centres. In general cases with a value of below £25,000 will be heard in the County Court, and with a value of more than £50,000 in the High Court. For those between £25,000 and £50,000 the case will be allocated to either the County Court or the High Court on the basis of financial substance, complexity, importance and the need for the matter to be dealt with as quickly as possible. When a legal claim is brought it is, of course, not always possible to quantify in advance the amount the plaintiff is claiming. A claim for compensation for personal injuries will be for an unspecified sum, or in legal terminology an unliquidated amount, it being left to the court to decide on the evidence the figure which should be awarded. A claim for loss of profits on the other hand can be expressed in a quantified or liquidated form. In the past plaintiffs would often seek to overcome financial allocation requirements by overvaluation of claims. The value to be attached to such claims is now to be the amount in money which the plaintiff could reasonably state the case to be worth to him.

For the purpose of determining small claims, that is those claims not exceeding £1,000 rules made under the County Courts Act 1984 require that the matter must be referred to the arbitration procedure operated by the County Courts. In brief this provides for a relatively informal method for considering the claim, which will usually be heard before a district judge (previously known as a Registrar) rather than a circuit judge, the title given to the senior judge attached to the Court. Although the parties may be legally represented they must normally pay for their own lawyers' fees themselves, whatever the outcome of the case. Thus a successful plaintiff cannot recover from the defendant the costs of being legally represented. Arbitration arrangements are considered in more depth in the next chapter.

The Organisation and work of the Supreme Court of Judicature

The Supreme Court of judicature is the collective title given to two superior civil courts, the High Court of Justice and the Court of Appeal (Civil Division). These courts sit in London at the Royal Courts of Justice.

The High Court of Justice

The High Court of Justice is for administrative convenience separated into three divisions, each with its own particular jurisdiction. These are the Queen's Bench Division, the Chancery Division and the Family Division. In addition to the cases which are heard in London, High Court cases are also heard at certain centres outside London. These centres are known as High Court and Crown Court Centres, and they include Birmingham, Bristol, Manchester, Leeds and Cardiff.

The Queen's Bench Division hears contractual and tortious actions and any claim not specifically allocated to the other divisions. This makes it the busiest division of the High Court. There is no financial upper limit on its jurisdiction, so it is competent to deal with claims for any amount, though it does not normally try matters which the county court is competent to hear. Two specialised courts within the Queen's Bench Division are the Admiralty Court, which has jurisdiction over shipping matters, and the Commercial Court, which hears only commercial actions and has the advantage for businesses of using a simplified form of procedure. The Queen's Bench Division is headed by the Lord Chief Justice, abbreviated to LCJ.

The Chancery Division has as its nominal head the Lord Chancellor (who is also the head of the Judiciary); however, in practice, the organisation of the work of the court is carried out by the Vice-Chancellor. The jurisdiction of the division includes company law and partnership matters, mortgages, trusts and revenue disputes.

When the High Court deals with a case at first instance exercising what is known as its *'original jurisdiction'* a single judge is competent to try the case. Such a judge is known by the title 'Mr. Justice' or 'Mrs. Justice' in the case of a woman judge, married or unmarried, so a reference to Smith J is a reference to Justice Smith, a High Court judge.

Each division possesses an appellate jurisdiction which is exercised by three judges (sometimes only two) sitting together, and when it is being exercised the court is known, rather confusingly, as a Divisional Court. The work of the Divisional Courts of the Queen's Bench Division is of considerable importance, and covers the following matters:

(i) Hearing criminal appeals from Magistrates Courts and the Crown Court by means of a *case stated*. This is a statement of the lower courts' findings of fact which is used by the Divisional Court for redetermining a disputed point of law.

(ii) Hearing civil appeals from certain tribunals.

(iii) Exercising a supervisory jurisdiction over inferior courts and tribunals. This is carried out by means of applications made to the court for the issue of the prerogative orders. These orders provide remedies to protect people and organisations from various forms of injustice. There are three of them; certiorari, prohibition and mandamus.
Certiorari brings before the court cases from inferior courts and tribunals that have already been decided, or are still being heard, to determine whether the inferior body has exceeded its jurisdiction or denied the rules of natural justice. (An example of these rules is one which provides that both parties in a case must be given the opportunity to be heard.) If such an injustice has occurred the earlier decision will be quashed.
Prohibition is used to prevent inferior courts, tribunals and other judicial and quasi-judicial bodies from exceeding their jurisdiction.
Mandamus is a command used to compel performance of a legal duty owed by some person or body. It may be used against a government department, a local authority, or a tribunal which is unlawfully refusing to hear a case.

The Divisional Courts of Chancery hear appeals on bankruptcy matters from County Courts with bankruptcy jurisdiction.

The Court of Appeal (Civil Division)

Acting in its civil capacity this court has the Master of the Rolls as its president (referred to in written form as MR). Its judges are called Lord Justices of Appeal (referred to as LJ or LJJ in plural), and the quorum of the court is three.

The court can hear appeals from all three divisions of the High Court and appeals from the County Courts. It also deals with appeals from certain tribunals, such as the Employment Appeals Tribunal.

The appeal is dealt with by way of a rehearing, which involves reviewing the case from the transcript of the trial and of the judges' notes. The court may uphold or reverse the whole or any part of the decision of the lower court, alter the damages awarded, or make a different order concerning costs.

The House of Lords

The House of Lords fulfils two functions, for it is not only the upper chamber of Parliament, but also the final appellate court within the United Kingdom. When it sits as a court its judges are those peers who hold or have held high judicial office. By convention lay peers do not sit. The judges are known as Lords of Appeal in Ordinary or, more commonly, Law Lords, and they are presided over by the Lord Chancellor. Although the quorum of the court is three, usually five judges sit. Majority decisions prevail in cases of disagreement.

The House of Lords hears appeals from the Court of Appeal, but only if that court or the Appeals Committee of the House has granted leave.

The Administration of Justice Act 1969 enables certain appeals from the High Court to be heard by the House of Lords without first passing through the Court of Appeal. This is known as the *leapfrog* procedure, and it is available only where the appeal involves a point of general public importance, for example on a question of the interpretation of a statutory provision, and then only if the parties consent, and if the House of Lords grants leave for the appeal. It has been used only rarely.

The Criminal Courts

The structure of the criminal courts under the criminal justice system within England and Wales is shown in Figure 1.4 . Business organisations are less likely to find themselves involved in legal proceedings within the criminal courts than in the civil courts, and the following account provides merely a brief outline of the way in which criminal cases are dealt with.

In the criminal court proceedings are normally brought in the name of the Crown against the accused (commonly called the defendant). The proceedings are known as prosecutions and if the defendant is found guilty of the offence for which a charge or charges have been brought against him, the defendant is said to be convicted. The court will then determine the appropriate punishment. Most prosecutions are brought by the Crown Prosecution Service, although there are many other agencies involved in the enforcement of the criminal code, including local authorities under trading standards and public health legislation, the Inland Revenue, Customs and Excise, the Health and Safety Executive and the Equal Opportunities Commission and the Commission for Racial Equality. The range of agencies involved provides a clear illustration of the extent to which the criminal law infiltrates all aspects of life.

Organisations, just as they may sue or be sued, may institute criminal proceedings, such as a theft charge brought by a department store against an alleged shoplifter, or be prosecuted themselves. Corporate bodies, such as registered companies, which are regarded as legal persons in their own right, usually incur criminal liability through the acts of their human agents, normally their employees. It is important to appreciate that a corporation will not be responsible for the acts of every employee, but only for the acts of a person, *"who is in actual control of the operations of a company or part of them and who is not responsible to another person in the company for the manner in which he discharges his duties in the sense of being under his orders."* Lord Reid, in *Tesco Supermarkets Ltd. v. Natrass* 1972.

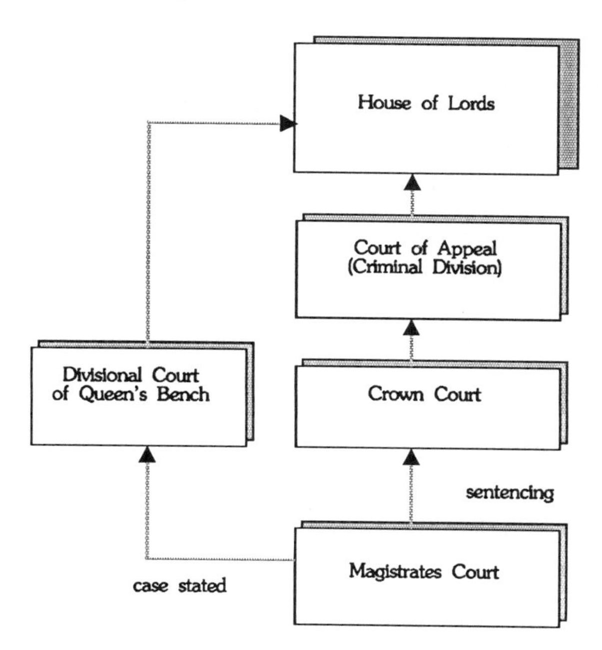

Fig. 1.4 The Criminal Court System

Corporate liability arising through the misconduct of an employee is said to be vicarious, or substituted liability, and such liability is considered thoroughly in Chapter 13. In the case of criminal liability, a corporation is generally only vicariously liable if the offence is one of strict liability, meaning an offence where liability can arise without fault on the part of the wrongdoer. A corporation can also be *directly* liable under the criminal law for any offence except murder. It could not be convicted of murder since this offence carries a mandatory life sentence, and a corporation cannot be imprisoned. Direct or primary liability for criminal acts has only been recognised by the courts in more modern times.

> In *Lennard's Carrying Company Co. Ltd. v. Asiatic Petroleum Co. Ltd.* 1915, Viscount Haldane remarked that , *'A corporation is an abstraction. It has no mind of its own any more than it has a body of its own; its active and directing will must consequently be sought in the person of somebody who...is really the directing mind and will of the personality of the corporation.'* This suggests someone at the very top of the organisation, someone who, in Viscount Haldane's words is in effect the corporation itself since, *"his action is the very action of the company itself."*

It was upon this basis of legal reasoning that the charge of manslaughter was brought against P&O in respect of the deaths resulting from the Zeebrugge disaster in 1987. Although the company was not convicted it is apparent that there is no technical bar to the bringing of a prosecution for 'corporate crimes' of this kind.

The classification of criminal offences

There are various ways in which it is possible to classify criminal offences. Here we shall note two of them.

(i) Traditionally a crime consists of two elements, both of which must be proved before a conviction is possible. These elements are the *actus reus* of the offence, and the *mens rea* of the offence. The actus reus consists of the definition of the particular prohibited conduct, which may be either an action or a failure to act. The mens rea, or guilty mind, is the accompanying state of mind which is required for the offence. Thus such words as *wilfully*, *knowingly*, *with intent*, and *permitting* are all concerned with defining particular states of mind. As an illustration the Theft Act 1968 defines theft by stating that, *"A person is guilty of theft if he dishonestly appropriates property belonging to another with the intention of permanently depriving the other of it;"*. Here the words "dishonestly" and "intention" provide the *mens rea* of the offence.

For reasons of policy some offences do not require a *mens rea*. They are referred to as absolute offences and cover cases where the offence is contained in a statute and where effective enforcement would be difficult if *mens rea* were required, for instance in cases of environmental pollution. Even in these cases however the courts will usually imply the existence of a *mens rea* requirement on the grounds that this is what Parliament intended, since, in Lord Reid's words in *Sweet v. Parsley* 1969 *"... there has for centuries been a presumption that Parliament did not intend to make criminals of persons who were in no way blameworthy in what they did."*.

(ii) The distinction which is drawn between serious and less serious offences. *Indictable* offences, the most serious, can only be tried before a judge and jury, whilst *summary* offences, the less serious, are dealt with in the Magistrates Courts. Jury trials are conducted in Crown Courts. The seriousness of an offence is obviously associated with its potential threat to society; in crude terms this is measurable by looking at the level of punishment that can be meted out to a person convicted of the offence. Some offences for instance are only punishable by a fine, and these are dealt with by Magistrates Courts. Others will carry the possibility of a prison sentence up to a specified maximum. Magistrates powers are limited to imposing fines of up to £2,000 and/or sentences of up to 6 months' imprisonment. In many cases where a custodial sentence can be imposed by a Magistrates Court the accused is given the choice of being tried summarily before the Magistrates, or on indictment before the Crown Court. Magistrates Courts hear 98% of all criminal cases.

It is possible to appeal against the decision of a criminal trial court, and the potential possible appeal routes are shown in Figure 1.4. Unlike the appellate system for the civil courts however, criminal appeals rarely reach the House of Lords.

Law Making by the Courts

As we have already seen the two major domestic sources of lawmaking are the courts and the legislature. Whilst the legislature creates law through the introduction of statutes, the law making role of the courts is very different. Parliament enjoys a virtually unlimited lawmaking capacity. The courts on the other hand are subject to very significant restrictions in their role as lawmakers. This is entirely proper since the courts are manned by members of the judiciary, the judges, who are neither elected by the public to this office nor are accountable to the public for the way in which they discharge their responsibilities.

The primary role of the courts, and the various tribunals which supplement the courts system, is the resolution of legal disputes which are brought before them. This process has a history dating back to Norman times.

In order to resolve a dispute it is necessary to have a reference point; some identifiable rule or principle which can be applied in order to solve the problem. One approach is simply to treat each case on its own merits, but such a system would hardly be just for decisions would turn on the character of the individual judge, whose values, prejudices, qualities of analysis and reasoning power would dominate the decision making process. Such a system would be unpredictable and capricious. English law, in common with other law making systems, adopted an approach that sought to achieve a level of certainty and consistency. It did this by means of a process referred to as *stare decisis*, literally 'standing by the decision'. Today we talk of the doctrine of judicial precedent. Under the doctrine of judicial precedent, the successor to the stare decisis system, judges when deciding cases must take into account relevant precedents, that is earlier cases based upon materially similar sets of facts. Whether a court is bound to follow an earlier case of a similar kind can be a matter of considerable complexity, however the general rule is that the decisions of higher courts are binding on lower courts within the hierarchical courts structure that can be seen in diagrams contained in Figures 1.3 and 1.4

English law became enshrined in the precedent system, and much of our modern law is still found in the decisions of the courts arrived at by resolving the cases brought before them. Not surprisingly this body of law is often referred to as case law. It is these cases, or precedents, which make up the contents of the law reports which were considered earlier in the chapter. The bulk of the law of contract and the law of tort is judge made law, or as it is more usually known, the common law.

In addition to developing and refining the common law, the judges in modern times have played an increasingly important role in the task of interpreting and applying statutory provisions, and we need to consider in outline the way in which they have fulfilled responsibility.

Statutory Interpretation

When a dispute comes before a court it is the task of the court to hear the evidence, identify the relevant law and apply it. The legal principles which the court has to apply may be common law principles. Often however they will be principles, or rules, which are contained in statutes. Where this is so, the court has to ascertain the meaning of the statute in order to apply it, and sometimes this can cause problems for a court because it discovers that the language of the statute is not entirely clear. The courts take the view that their responsibility is to discern Parliament's will or intention from the legislation under consideration, and in cases of difficulty the courts apply certain principles of construction or interpretation to aid them in this task These are usually referred to as the rules of statutory interpretation, although it seems doubtful that the courts regard them as rules in the ordinary sense. There are three main rules.

(a) *The literal rule* Applying this approach a court will give the words of a statute their ordinary natural grammatical meaning, that is they will be applied literally provided there is no ambiguity.

In *R. v. Hinchy* the House of Lords used this approach in a tax case. The defendant had incorrectly completed a tax return for which the penalty under statute was *'treble the tax that ought to be charged'*. This presumably meant three times the excess owed. However the Court construed "tax" to mean the whole tax bill for the year, the difference between £42 and £418.

(b) *The golden rule* This is used to overcome the problems which occur when the application of the literal rule produces so absurd a result that Parliament could not be taken as having intended it. It simply provides that an interpretation be given which best overcomes the absurdity.

(c) *the mischief or purposive rule* This rule involves the court in interpreting the statute in accordance with the apparent purpose for which it has been passed, so that its purpose is as far as possible fulfilled. An illustration can be seen in the case of *Mandla v. Dowell Lee* 1983 which involved an alleged offence of discrimination by the headmaster of a school who required of a fee paying Sikh pupil that he remove his turban and cut his hair short to meet the school's uniform regulations. This he refused to do on grounds of his religion. It is an offence to discriminate against a person under the Race Relations Act 1976 *"on grounds of his race, colour, ethnic or national origin"*. The Court of Appeal, on the basis that the statute makes no reference to religion took the view that the action of the school was not discriminatory. The House of Lords took an alternative view, regarding the Act as designed to protect people like Sikhs, and finding that the Sikhs could arguably be regarded as a group identifiable by a common ethnic origin.

Other aids to interpretation include certain sub-rules, the most important of which is the *ejusdem generis* rule which requires that if in a statute, general words are preceded by two or more specific words, the general words should be treated as being of the same kind *(ejusdem generis)* as the specific words. For instance in *Lane v. London Electricity Board* 1955, the words *"shock, burn or other injury"* were used in statutory regulations regarding safety in electrical installations. The plaintiff, who broke his leg as a result of inadequate lighting in an electricity sub-station had not, in the court's opinion, suffered an " other injury" since the specific words, if properly construed, suggested injuries arising from direct contact with electricity.

Most statutes also contain an interpretation section which provides specific definitions for words and phrases which are contained in the statute and in addition the Interpretation Act 1978, which is incorporated into many statutes, gives presumptive interpretations to common words and phrases, for instance that the expression 'man' when used in a statute should include 'woman', and vice versa, unless some contrary intention appears.

The meaning of 'common law'

In its modern day usage the expression *common law* has come to mean all law other than that contained in statutory provisions. Thus common law in this sense means judge made law embodied in case decisions. The expression common law is also sometimes used to describe, in a broader sense, the *type* of legal system that operates in England and Wales, and indeed has been adopted by countries all over the world and particularly in the Commonwealth.

The common law of England dates back as far as the Norman Conquest and has its origins in the decisions of the royal judges who attempted to develop and apply principles of law 'common' to the whole country. This they did by modifying and adapting rules of Norman law, and rules contained in Saxon local custom. The development of the common law was a long process evolving over hundreds of years. When the process had been completed England and Wales was in possession of a unified and coherent body of law which remains even today the foundation upon which larger and significant areas of our law,such as the law of contract and torts are based.

The judgment of the court

Whatever the nature of a case coming before a court the most vital legal aspect of the legal proceedings comes at the end of the case when judgment is delivered. Certain parts of the judgment will be binding for the future, whilst the remainder of the judgment will have merely persuasive authority whenever it is considered by a court in the future. These ideas need further explanation.

The binding element of a judgment

When a decision is reached on a dispute before a superior court, the judges will make their decision known by making speeches known as judgments. Within a judgment, the judges will refer to numerous matters, such as the relevant legal principles which are drawn from existing cases or statutes, a review of the facts of the case, their opinion on the relevant law, their actual decision and the reasons for it. As far as the parties to a dispute are concerned the matter they are most concerned with is the actual decision, that is who has won the case. The main matter of relevance to the law, however, is the reason for the decision. This is known as the *ratio decidendi* of the case (the reason for deciding). The *ratio* expresses the underlying legal principle relied on in reaching the decision and it is this which constitutes the binding precedent. As we have seen this means that if a lower court in a later case is faced with a similar dispute it will in general be bound to apply the earlier *ratio decidendi.*

The persuasive element of a judgment

All other matters referred to in a judgment are termed *obiter dicta* (things said by the way). The *obiter* forms persuasive precedent and is likely to be taken into account by a lower court in a later similar case, although a lower court is not bound to follow it.

The Legislature: Parliament

The legislature, Parliament, sits as Westminster. It consists of a lower house, the Commons, in which M.P.s sit and an upper house, the Lords, which has a non elected membership that includes hereditary and life peers, law Lords and the Archbishop and Bishops of the Church of England. The primary responsibility of Parliament is the enactment of legislation, which in broad terms extends to the granting of consent to the spending of public revenue, and the guardianship of the interests of the nation, which involves controlling the activities of the government when they are believed to conflict with the national interest. This control mechanism relies upon the accountability of Ministers to Parliament. They can be called upon to provide public answers during question time and during debates on proposed legislation. Furthermore they can be summoned to appear before Parliamentary Select Committees for more detailed and rigorous questioning. Undoubtedly the broadcasting on radio and television of Parliamentary proceedings has increased the public awareness of the role of the legislature. Nowadays when the Government faces a severe test during Prime Minister's question time the occasion is built up into a significant media event.

What is legislation?

Technically, legislation is defined as the formulation of law by the Queen in Parliament, thus the Monarch and both Houses are involved in creating it. The Monarch's role is limited to the granting of assent which is a formality and no longer involves the Monarch personally; the real legislative power lies with the two Houses of Parliament of whom the House of Commons is constitutionally the most powerful. During this century two Acts, the Parliament Acts of 1911 and 1949, have reduced the power of the House of Lords. The 1911 Act provides that a money Bill (e.g. the Finance Bill) must be passed through the Lords without amendment, within one month following its passage through the Commons, whilst under the 1949 provisions the Lords are unable to 'block' any public Bill which has passed the Commons in two successive sessions. A Bill is the name given to legislation whilst it proceeds through the various stages which culminate in it becoming an Act after the Royal Assent is given.

Figure 1.5 The Classification of Parliamentary Bills

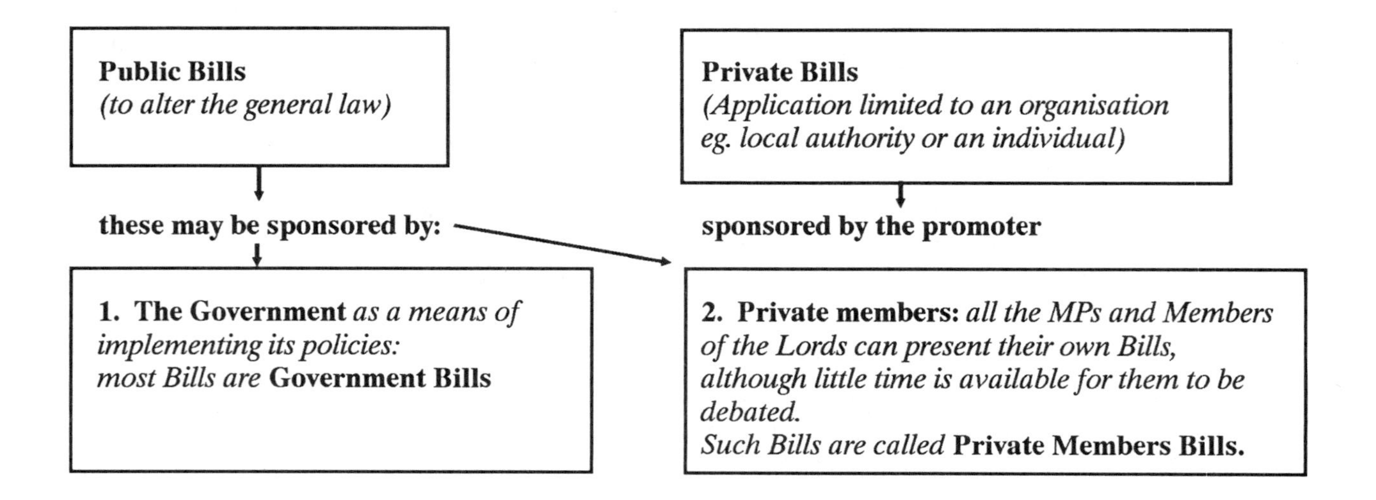

A classification of Bills showing their scope is contained in Figure 1.5.

Something in the region of sixty to eighty Bills become law annually. Creating legislation is the most obvious way in which governments are able to implement their policies, whether they be fiscal, economic or social. The process by which governments arrive at reaching legislative proposals which are put to Parliament is beyond the scope of this book, but it is certainly possible to note some of the most significant factors which influence legislation. These include:

(a) the reports of Royal Commissions, and other enquiries which are government inspired;

(b) the activities of pressure and cause groups, such as the RSPCA, and Friends of the Earth;

(c) UK membership of international organisations, such as the EC. EC policy decisions have a direct impact upon legislative activity in the United Kingdom. For instance the Companies Act 1989 which we will be considering in Chapter 3, was passed as a response to Community requirements;

(d) public opinion and the media;

(e) government reports; and

(f) lobby groups such as local authority associations, trade unions and employees associations.

Thus before a bill is presented to Parliament many events may have occurred leading to its promotion. One possibility is given in Figure 1.6

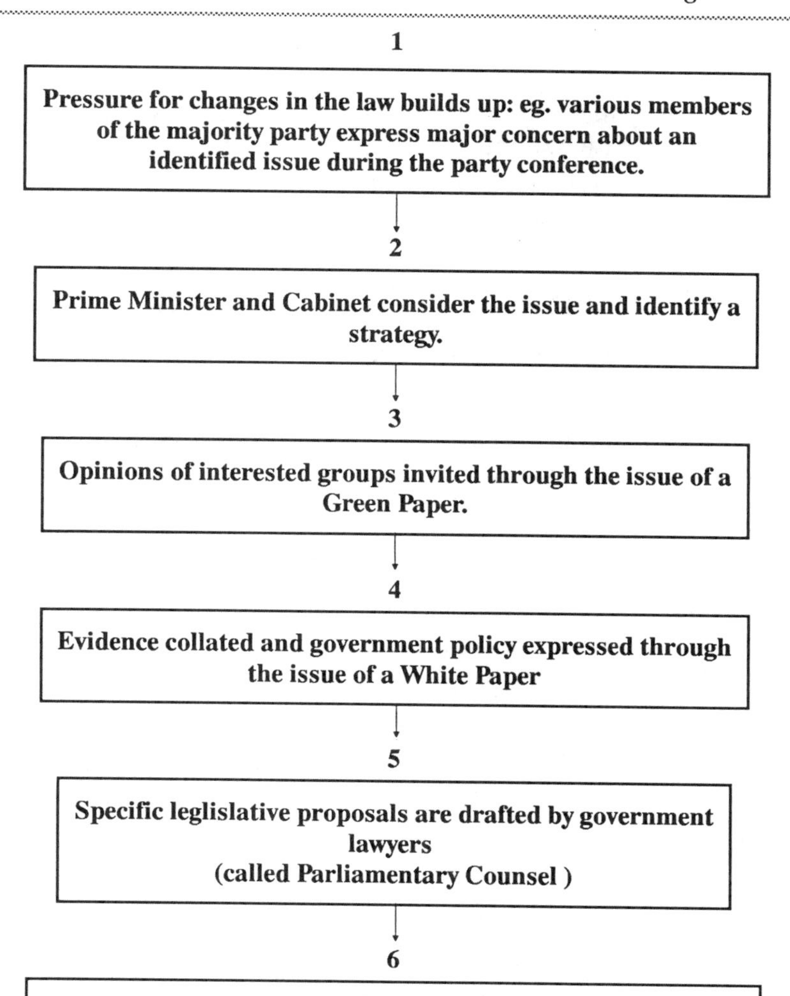

Figure 1.6 *The stages leading to the Proposal of Legislation*

The process by which legislation is subsequently created is illustrated in Figure 1.7.

The procedure followed in both Houses is the same where public bills are being considered.

Delegated or subordinate legislation

It is not possible for Parliament to cope with all the legislative demands placed upon it. One reason is that it lacks time due to its slow procedures; another is that it does not always possess the technical expertise necessary to create detailed rules in specialised fields of knowledge. A further difficulty lies in anticipating, in the legislation being enacted today, what might develop in the future.

Parliament overcomes these inadequacies by delegating law making power to subordinates. These include organisations - local authorities are a prime example - as well as individuals, most notably the various Secretaries of State who head government departments. Thus much of our statute law merely lays down general principles, while specifically granting the power to a Minister, in liaison with his or her department, to "finish the job" by legislatively filling in the details by means of statutory instruments and regulations. Without such a system effective government could not be carried out in a state as complex as ours, but this does not mean that this method of legislating escapes criticism. Constitutionally the role of Parliament is weakened, as the executive obtains a law making capacity for itself. Moreover delegated legislation does not attract publicity and sometimes the subordinate can legislate on matters principle. These criticism are dealt with by control mechanisms which seek to maintain a proper balance between effective government on the one hand and accountability on the other. The courts can be resorted to where it is believed that the delegated powers have been exceeded and, if this is established, the action taken by the subordinate will be declared ultra vires (beyond the powers) and void. Additionally Parliament has its own 'Scrutiny Committee' which examines statutory instruments (one form of delegated legislation) in order to report to Parliament on any matters requiring special attention such as lack of clarity in the instrument.

First reading
a formal notification of the bill to the House

Second reading
a general debate on the principles of the bill

Committee stage
detailed discussion of the bills in committee, amendments are proposed

Report stage
bill as amended, passed back to whole House for consideration

Third reading
a formal final debate, only verbal amendments permitted

House of Lords
(or the House of Commons), if the bill began in the Lords

The Royal Assent
the bill is now an Act of Parliament and enforceable by the Courts

Figure 1.7 *The Passage of Legislation*

European Community Law

The United Kingdom has been a member of the European Communities since 1972. There are in fact three Communities, the European Coal and Steel Community (ECSC), the European Economic Community (EEC) and the European Atomic Energy Community (Euratom). Since 1965 the three communities have been managed by common institutions, and it is usual to refer to them collectively as the European Community or EC. As a member state, the UK is bound by EC law. The impact of EC law is particularly significant in the field of business law as the EC is essentially economic in nature, having as a major concern the harmonisation of legal rules governing trade between member states.

Primacy of Community Law

An important feature of EC law is that it overrides any conflicting provisions in the national laws of member states. This was acknowledged by the European Court of Justice in the case *Costa v. ENEL* 1964 in which it was stated:

> *"the law stemming from the Treaty, an independent source of law, could not, because of its special and original nature, be overridden by domestic legal provisions, however framed, without being deprived of its character as Community Law and without the legal basis of the Community itself being called into question."*

The pervasive nature of EC law was described by Lord Denning MR in *Bulmer Ltd. v. Bollinger SA* 1974 in a much-quoted passage:

> *"... when we come to matters with a European element, the Treaty is like an incoming tide. It flows into the estuaries and up the rivers. It cannot be held back. Parliament has decreed that the Treaty is henceforward to be part of our law. It is equal in force to any statute..."*

A fundamental shift in the powers of the UK parliament is effected by s.2 of the European Communities Act 1972, which gives legal force in the UK to EC law and provides for the supremacy of EC law. The effect of s.2 is simply that EC law *is* UK law, and indeed the highest form of UK law.

Types of EC Law

EC law derives from three major sources: the treaties, secondary legislation of the Community and unwritten general principles of law.

The treaties

The so-called *primary legislation* of the EC consists of the treaties and associated documents which have been agreed between the member states. These include the Treaty of Paris 1951 which established the ECSC; the Treaty of Rome 1957 which established the EEC; the Euratom Treaty 1957 which established Euratom; the Merger Treaty 1965 which established common institutions for all three Communities; various Treaties of Accession on the admission of new members to the Community; a number of Association Agreements with non members; and the Single European Act 1986 which extended the areas of competence of the EC, introduced the co-operation procedure and a programme for the completion of the single market by the end of 1992.

The treaties set out the framework of EC law, create the institutions which operate the Community and lay down procedures for making secondary legislation on an ongoing basis. As primary sources of law, certain provisions of the treaties are directly enforceable in the UK courts, for example art. 119 of the Treaty of Rome which creates an *enforceable community right* in relation to equal pay as between men and women. Article 119 provides:

"Each Member State shall ensure and subsequently maintain the application of the principle that men and women should receive equal pay for equal work".

Secondary legislation of the Community

The institutions of the Community have significant powers to make new laws under the treaties, although it should be appreciated that these law making powers extend only to areas in which the Community has competence to act. Some areas remain within the exclusive domain of the national sovereignty of member states. Article 189 empowers the Council of Ministers and the Commission to make *regulations*, issue *directives* and take *decisions*.

Regulations are binding in their entirety and directly applicable throughout the EC. They operate in a similar fashion to UK legislation and no steps need to be taken at national level to give them effect.

Directives are binding as to the result to be achieved and leave to member states the choice of form and method of implementation. Directives are the major instrument for achieving the harmonisation of national laws as between member states. They operate by setting out the objectives which the proposed new laws must achieve, giving a time limit within which member state governments must introduce them. In the UK directives are implemented either by a new Act of Parliament or by delegated legislation using the enabling powers in s.2 of the European Communities Act 1972. Many examples of this process can be seen throughout this text, for instance the implementation of the Product Liability Directive by Part 1 of the Consumer Protection Act 1987, which is discussed on page 357 in Chapter 10.

Decisions may be addressed to one or more member states, business organisations or private individuals and are binding on those to whom they are addressed.

In addition to these formal law making powers, the Council of Ministers and the Commission are able to promote their views on policies and practice by issuing recommendations and opinions although under art. 189 these have no binding force.

General principles of law

These are an unwritten source of EC law whose validity and existence derives from art. 215 of the Treaty of Rome which recognises as part of EC law *the general principles common to the laws of member states* and art. 164 which mandates the European Court of Justice to ensure that *in the interpretation and application of this Treaty the law is observed*. These provisions enable the Court to draw from the legal traditions of member states in deciding upon the interpretation and application of EC law.

The Institutions of the Community

The four principal EC institutions are:

(a) the Commission

(b) the Council of Ministers

(c) the European Parliament

(d) the European Court of Justice

The Commission

The Commission has the duty to initiate proposals for measures likely to advance the development of Community policy. It is also the executive arm of the EC, with responsibility for the implementation of agreed policies. As the guardian of the Treaties it must ensure full compliance by member states, companies and individuals with Community obligations in accordance with EC law. It has power to impose fines, for example for breach of competition law, and to bring before the Court of Justice any member state which fails to comply with its obligations.

The Council of Ministers

The Council of Ministers is the Community's principal decision-making body and member states are represented by appropriate Ministers at Council meetings. The Presidency of the Council is held by each member state in rotation for a six month term. Proposals for secondary legislation are discussed at permanent working parties set up by the Council and attended by civil servants from the appropriate government department in each member state. The proposals are initiated by the Commission and undergo a consultation process carried out by the appropriate department in each member state.

The UK Parliament has the opportunity to assess the legal and political implications of a proposal. This is carried out by the Scrutiny Committees of the Commons and the Lords who are given a copy of the proposals with an explanatory memorandum. The Scrutiny Committees have power to call for written or oral evidence, consult with government departments, call for a debate and if necessary request that amendments to the proposal be negotiated. Once the Scrutiny Committee has cleared a proposal then the Minister is free to accept it in the Council of Ministers.

The European Parliament

The European Parliament is the public forum for debating issues of interest to the Community, and often a source of ideas which provide the basis for policies initiated formally by the Commission. In terms of law making power, the Parliament is markedly different from the UK parliament. The European Parliament has no final say in the enactment of secondary Community legislation, and only a subsidiary role in the legislative process. This is still the case, despite the increase in its powers brought about by the introduction of the *co-operation procedure* following the Single European Act. Although these increased powers have widened the influence of the Parliament, the Council of Ministers still has the final word in the making of EC law.

The Parliament has an important function in relation to the budget of the EC. Its power to reject a proposed budget, which it has exercised on a number of occasions, gives considerable influence on the direction of policy. In addition it has the power, not yet used, to dismiss the whole of the Commission on a motion of censure by a two-thirds majority, although it cannot dismiss individual Commissioners.

The European Court of Justice

The European Court of Justice sits in Luxembourg and deals principally with two types of cases. The first relate to acts done or measures adopted by member states, the commission or the council of ministers, the validity of which is challenged on the grounds of incompatibility with treaty obligations. The second type of case results from a request for a preliminary ruling on the meaning or interpretation of an aspect of Community law. Such a request may be made, under art. 177, by a court or tribunal in an individual member state, where the ruling is required to enable that court or tribunal to give judgment in the case before it. Where there is no appeal from the decision of the court or tribunal, it must, under art. 177, request a preliminary ruling.

Under the Single European Act, a new court of first instance was created with power to hear certain types of cases, for example in the field of competition law.

Change and the Law

Legal rules are not made simply for their own sake. They are made because there is a need for them. It may not always be easy to recognise why particular areas of law, or specific legal rules have become necessary. Nor will people always agree that a particular need has been properly established, or that legal rule making is the best way to respond to an identified problem or issue. However it remains true that all laws originate out of some sense of need for formal regulation or control of a particular situation. We have already seen the variety of purposes these legal rules are designed to fulfil, each purpose being an area of need for rule creation. One way of expressing these ideas is to say that legal rules are an effect rather than a cause.

Although certain fundamental needs are constant, such as food and shelter, others are more variable. Whilst our need for law to regulate human conduct is always present the form and content of the law varies over time, altering and adapting to take account of the dynamic nature of modern society. We have always had a need for laws to provide for order in society, and the criminal law is the outcome. Crimes have been recognised since earliest times as offences against the well-being of society, which if allowed to pass unchecked would undermine the fabric of society. Criminal laws have thus been created to protect the individual and property. However whilst crimes such as murder and theft have always been regarded as an essential part of the criminal code, the means by which we define these crimes today, and the legal penalties that are attached to them are not exactly as they were a hundred years ago, or even thirty years ago. Law evolves as society evolves, and this is entirely appropriate for law is the servant of society rather than its master.

It is possible to identify certain general causes of legal change, and the following list indicates what these may be:

(a) *Social Causes*

For example to provide tenants with legal protection from unscrupulous landlords who threaten eviction if the tenant refuses to pay unjustifiable rent increases.

(b) *Economic Causes*

Within a free market economy trading practices often develop which may be harmful to general economic needs. For example, dominant suppliers who use their market dominance to restrict competition in the supply of such goods are distorting market conditions. Governments may find it necessary to intervene by means of legislation to curb the growth of dominant market suppliers.

(c) *Political Causes*

For instance a government may feel it appropriate to introduce legislation to penalise councils who overspend.

(d) *Technological and Scientific Developments*

Technological change has from time to time created problems which require legal regulations to control. The growth in the use of computers over the past twenty years as a means of storing personal data, has given rise to concern over the apparent loss of rights of individuals whose lives are recorded in this way and who may have little or no control over the use to which such information is put. Legislation now seeks to provide a measure of security for individuals in this situation.

In reality the change factors we have listed here overlap to a considerable extent. For example, the decision to join the European Economic Community was both political and economic. Legally it was achieved by passing the European Communities Act 1972. Potentially it also had social implications, since for example, the Community was pledged to move towards enabling a free movement of labour between the member states. A more specific example of the overlap is provided by various aspects of modern employment legislation. The creation of the right of employees not to be unfairly dismissed by their employers, which is at present contained in the Employment Protection (Consolidation) Act 1978 (as amended) illustrates the use of a legal device (statute) to achieve a social objective (job security), which has political implications (electorally popular) and includes an economic dimension (restriction on employers' freedom to reduce the size of the workforce).

The protection of the interests of the buying public has produced a spate of legal change over the past two decades. It is a recognition by Parliament that consumers' rights are a matter of national interest and debate, making them a part of the political agenda. Increases in the spending power of the nation, together with great technological advances in the production of consumer durables from compact discs to microwave ovens have led to an enormous growth in the demand for goods from consumers, and producers have responded accordingly. As 'consumerism' has expanded, and the demand for consumer rights has increased, so the law has been invoked as the means of achieving an appropriate level of consumer protection. Statutory changes have sought to regulate this particular market.

An illuminating illustration of the change process in operation is provided by one facet of modern consumer law. Back in 1893, the Sale of Goods Act was passed as a means of codifying the law of sale. Codification involves bringing all the law in a specific field together in a single statute. It is a way of clarifying the law, and it assists the task of discovering the law on a particular subject if it is primarily contained in a single statute. The rules that were expressed in the Act were based upon the need for a clear legal framework within which trade could be effectively conducted between businesses. At that time the interests of private consumers of goods were given little consideration. One of the provisions of the Act stipulated that in any sale of goods transaction between a buyer and a business seller, the seller would be treated as impliedly promising the buyer that the goods were of a certain standard, known technically as the standard of 'merchantable quality'. The seller was however at liberty to exclude this implied promise if he did so clearly, a right eagerly grasped by most sellers, who had no desire to increase their liabilities unnecessarily. At this time the predominant business philosophy was *caveat emptor*, let the buyer beware. It was essentially the buyer's task to satisfy himself that what he was buying was suitable and fit.

By the 1970s it was felt that the interests of private consumers were being largely overridden by the majority of sellers, who simply avoided their legal obligations to provide merchantable goods by the use of contractual clauses excluding liability. This, of course, they were perfectly legally entitled to do, but it was felt that consumers were being treated harshly by being denied the opportunity to reject defective goods, from whose sale the seller had made a profit. In 1973 legislation was introduced which invalidated any attempt by a seller to exclude liability for breach of the merchantable quality provisions in such transactions.

Sellers however continued to exclude, confident that private consumers were largely unaware of their rights, and that in any event attempting to exclude was not unlawful, simply invalid. This subsequently lead to further statutory intervention, so that since 1978 an attempt to exclude liability has constituted a criminal offence, under the Consumer Transactions (Restrictions on Statements) Order. The order has proved an effective deterrent to most traders, and consumer rights have been fully secured in this field.

One other cause of legal change requires brief mention, that of legal clarity. Legislation is introduced from time to time as an attempt at simply clarifying legal rules, rather than creating new ones. The codified Sale of Goods Act mentioned above provides an example.

As you consider the various aspects of business law covered in this book it will soon become apparent to you through an examination of legislative and case law developments just how dynamic our legal system is. This in turn is simply a reflection of a way in which as a society we evolve through change.

Chapter 2

The Resolution of Business Disputes

Introduction

In this chapter we shall be examining in more detail the machinery which exists for resolving legal conflict in the business world. While the High Court has an important role to play in hearing civil disputes concerning large sums of money the vast majority of civil legal actions which go to Court are dealt with at County Court level. Changes in the jurisdiction of the County Courts, which we considered in Chapter 1, has increased their workload by taking cases which previously would have been heard before the High Court.

Not all civil disputes however are resolved by means of court proceedings. Many cases are dealt with instead before tribunals. We will explore more thoroughly later in the chapter the nature of tribunals. One important field in which they are used is in the handling of employment disputes. These are dealt with before industrial tribunals.

The chapter therefore looks at the way in which a legal dispute is dealt with before (a) the County Court and (b) an Industrial Tribunal, and concludes by considering the use of arbitration as a means of resolving business disputes without recourse to the Courts.

Sources of Legal Advice and Information

Many sources of legal advice and information are available to a trader who has a legal problem. He may be able to research it himself by looking at law books in a library, but more usually he will seek outside help. If he is a member of a trade or professional association or trade union it is probable that he will be able to obtain legal guidance from such a body, particularly if the question is one which is closely associated with the operation or regulation of his business.

In relation to legal enquiries of a general nature, the Citizen's Advice Bureau may be able to point the trader in the right direction, or provide the information which he requires. In addition, there are a number of law centres which provide a similar, though more specialist, role in giving legal advice and acting on behalf of clients. Law centres, however, tend to deal with legal problems arising in relation to social issues such as housing, immigration, consumer and employee rights. They do not usually take on the role of advising businessmen in relation to commercial matters.

Lawyers

The most obvious source of advice and legal information is the solicitor. Larger business organisations may have their own legal department or in-house solicitor to provide a comprehensive legal service for the business, by dealing with such matters as conveyancing, drawing up contracts, registering intellectual property rights, advising management on day to day legal matters, designing procedures to ensure compliance by the business with its legal requirements and conducting litigation on its behalf.

Smaller business organisations cannot usually justify the expense of a legal department and will use solicitors in private practice to deal with their legal affairs. Solicitors are the general practitioners of the law, although within any particular firm individual solicitors will usually specialise in one or two areas of law. If a businessman refers a legal problem to solicitor and the solicitor requires further specialist help or advice in order to deal with it, the solicitor can obtain the opinion of a barrister. The barrister, or counsel, usually specialises in a much narrower field of law than the solicitor. A businessman cannot approach a barrister directly for legal help but must first use a solicitor. The solicitor can refer the matter to a barrister if he feels that it is necessary. The main functions of the barrister are to provide legal opinions, to draw pleadings in preparation for litigation, and to act as an advocate in court. A solicitor cannot always act as an advocate without a barrister because the solicitor has only limited rights of audience before the courts. He is allowed to appear before a Magistrates Court, a County Court and, in certain circumstances, a Crown Court without a barrister. He is unable to appear in the High Court or any of the appeal courts and must use a barrister if he intends to conduct a case in one of these courts.

Communications between a client and a solicitor or barrister are subject to legal professional privilege. This means that the lawyer is duty bound not to disclose the communication to any other party without the authority of the client. In practice the effect of legal professional privilege is that the client can disclose all of the information which is relevant to his legal problem without fear that the information may be used against him at some later stage. The purpose of the rule is to ensure that the client does not hold back information which might be relevant to the legal problems which has arisen. This allows the lawyer to have all of the facts and to make a proper decision as to the course of action which is in the client's best interests.

Legal aid

Under the Legal Aid Scheme an individual may be entitled to receive help with his legal problem. Depending upon his financial circumstances, all or part of the cost of legal help will be paid by the state. This can extend to representation before a court. In order to qualify for free legal aid the individual's resources must be very low, both in terms of capital and income. If he is not entitled to free legal aid because he has more than the minimum resources he may still get some help from the legal aid scheme but he will have to make a contribution towards his own costs. If the individual has capital assets or average income, however, he may be caught in the "middle income trap". This is described as a trap because he will be too well off to obtain legal aid but will not be sufficiently well off to be able to afford the costs of litigation himself. He may therefore have to decide not to take legal action in the courts.

Suing in the County Court

Before the businessman takes a decision to sue in the County Court, for example for an outstanding debt, there are a number of matters which he must consider carefully. Probably the most important factor will be that of cost, both in terms of money and in terms of the time and resources which must be invested in legal proceedings. Most of the plaintiff's costs will eventually be payable by the defendant if the plaintiff wins his case. However the plaintiff has a contract with his solicitor and is bound under that contract to pay the solicitors fees, and disbursements such as court fees, regardless of the outcome of the case. The plaintiff must therefore spend all of this money himself in the hope of later recovering it from the defendant. Even if the plaintiff is successful, he may not be able to obtain an order that the defendant pays all of his legal costs because a defendant can challenge the amount of a successful plaintiff's legal bill. This is done in a *taxation of costs* in which the court will require the defendant to pay only those costs which were reasonably and necessarily incurred by the plaintiff in the action. After a taxation, the plaintiff will usually have to pay some part of his own legal costs. These in effect are deducted from whatever damages he has recovered from the defendant.

Another important consideration, closely associated with the question of costs, is whether the defendant will actually be able to satisfy any judgment which is eventually made against him. If the defendant is a "man of straw", and has no resources, the plaintiff will be wasting his money by pursuing him in the courts. He may end up by having to pay all of his own legal costs and by getting them back from the defendant by instalments of one a month, or by not getting them back at all. For this reason it is essential that the financial circumstances of the potential defendant are investigated before proceedings are issued against him. There is no formal procedure for this type of investigation, so the plaintiff will simply have to conduct it in the best way that he can.

In making the decision to sue someone, the businessman must also be aware that the legal process is slow. It may take 1 to 4 years to obtain judgment against a defendant, depending on the complexity of the case and its particular circumstances. In extreme cases, litigants have suffered mental illness or depression as a result of involvement with litigation. There is recognised mental condition called litigation neurosis. Involvement in litigation over a long period of time is certainly a drain on the resources of the parties in terms of time, money and mental energy.

Publicity is another important factor. Proceedings before the courts are held in public and can be attended by anyone, including the press. Depending on the circumstances, the businessman may be inviting adverse publicity and a loss of goodwill by taking legal proceedings. If the legal action is being taken against an important customer, the damage to ongoing business relationships can be considerable.

In addition to these factors, it almost goes without saying that the plaintiff must have a sound legal basis for his claim and sufficient evidence to support it. This evidence may be documentary or may be provided by witnesses. In the case of the verbal evidence by witnesses, the credibility of the witnesses will be an important consideration. It may also be necessary to employ expert witnesses if the subject matter of the dispute is technical in nature, for example if it centres around a mechanical or electrical problem.

Negotiation, compromise and settlement

For one or more of the reasons given above, the parties to a dispute will usually try to reach a settlement without the necessity of taking legal proceedings. Negotiations will take place before legal proceedings are issued and will usually continue as an ongoing process right up to the date of the trial. If both parties are prepared to litigate, this is probably an indication that there is some merit in the case that each of them is arguing. If a compromise can be agreed this will probably result in the saving of costs, time and adverse publicity.

County Court Procedure

Once the decision to sue has been taken, the plaintiff must decide in which court to issue proceedings. We considered in Chapter 1 the basis up on which this decision will be made. The procedures in both the County Court and the High Court are broadly similar, although in the High Court the procedure tends to be more complicated. We shall examine County Court procedures only.

Assuming that the case is to be brought in the County Court, the plaintiff must decide which County Court to use. The claim must usually be brought in the district in which the defendant lives or carries on business or in the district in which the cause of action arose (for example where the contract was made).

The procedure for the conduct of the action is laid down in the County Court Rules. These are designed to ensure fairness between the parties. This is achieved by ensuring that the matter in dispute is understood by the parties and by the court, and that neither party is taken by surprise at the trial by the introduction of any new matter which ought to have been disclosed to him before the trial. The rules also give time limits within which procedural steps must be taken by each party. These are designed to ensure that there is no unnecessary delay in the conduct of the case.

Letter before action

The first step which must be taken by the plaintiff is to send a *letter before action* to the defendant. In it the plaintiff will state his claim, invite the defendant to comply with his demands within 7 days, and inform him that court proceedings will be taken if he fails to do so. A letter before action gives the defendant the opportunity to meet the plaintiff's claim without incurring legal costs, or to state any legitimate grounds of defence which are available to him, and which may give rise to negotiations for settlement of the claim. If the plaintiff does not send a letter before action, and the defendant meets his demands as soon as proceedings are issued, the plaintiff will be unable to recover costs from him.

Issuing a summons

Within a fortnight of sending a letter before action, if there is no positive response to it, the plaintiff may request the court to issue a summons against the defendant. A *default summons* is used whenever the plaintiff is claiming a fixed sum of money. A *fixed date summons* is used either when there is a claim for money which includes an element of damges to be assessed by the court, or a non-money remedy, such as an injunction, the possession of land or the recovery of goods. In this text we shall be examining the procedure which applies to a default summons, because this type of summons is most often used by the businessman. (See Figure 2.1) The procedure for a fixed date summons is broadly similar.

The plaintiff must file a request for the issue of a default summons, together with the summons itself at the County Court office. In addition he must provide two copies of the particulars of claim, one for the court and one for the defendant. In the particulars of claim the plaintiff must specify the legal basis of his claim and remedy which he seeks. He will also include a brief description of the material facts surrounding his claim. The particulars of the claim and summons will be served on the defendant by the court together with forms on which the defendant can either make an admission and a proposal for payment or put forward a defence and/or a counterclaim.

Judgment in default

If the defendant fails to respond within 14 days of receiving the summons the plaintiff may request the court to enter judgment against him. The plaintiff has in effect won his case by default, and can enforce the judgment against the defendant if he fails to pay.

Admission and offer of payment

On receiving the summons however the defendant may have decided to admit the claim in part or in full, and make an offer to pay the amount due either immediately or by instalments. If the defendant requests time to pay, he must provide the court with details of his financial circumstances and the exact terms of his proposals for payment. These will be forwarded by the court to the plaintiff, who will decide whether or not to accept the offer of payment. If he accepts, judgment will be entered in the terms of the agreement. If the plaintiff does not accept the defendant's proposals, the court will fix a date for a hearing before the district judge for a decision on the terms of payment. The decision of the district judge will be binding on both parties and judgment will be entered.

If the defendant fails to keep up payment, enforcement action may be taken against him by the plaintiff.

Defence

If the defendant believes he has a valid defence to the plaintiff's claim, he must file particulars of the defence in the County Court Office within 14 days of receiving the summons, in order to prevent judgment being entered against him in default.

If he feels that he has insufficient information about the plaintiff's claim to set out his defence in full or if he does not have time to prepare a full defence, but still wishes to defend the action, he may lodge a *holding defence* with the court within the time period and give *further and better particulars* of his defence at a later date when he is requested to do so by the plaintiff. A holding defence is simply a statement denying any indebtedness to the plaintiff.

Counterclaim

A counterclaim may be made by the defendant at the same time as he lodges his defence with the court. In a counterclaim he is making a separate claim for damages against the plaintiff, which will survive as a separate action if the original claim by the plaintiff is withdrawn. Where circumstances permit, a counterclaim should be made as it provides a useful bargaining tool in negotiations for settlement.

Further and better particulars

If either of the parties feels that he has insufficient information relating to the claim or defence of the other, he may, within prescribed time, request further and better particulars of the other party's claim or defence. The other party must then supply the information. The County Court Rules make provision for this so that each party may know the exact case which he has to answer, and neither may be taken by surprise at a late stage in the proceedings. In this way the process helps to narrow down the issues and highlight the points of difference between the parties.

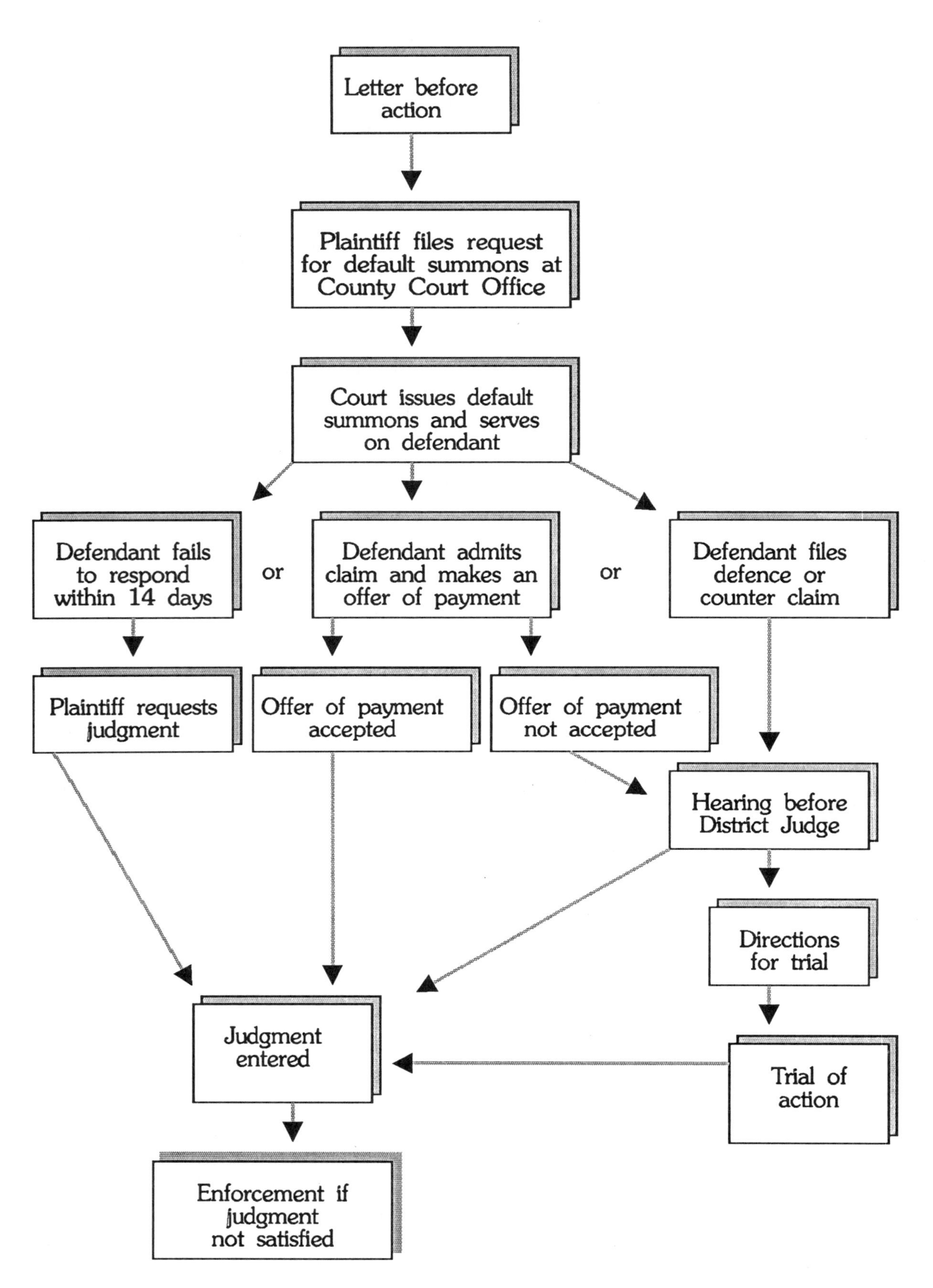

Fig.2.1 Main Steps in a Default Action in the County Court

Pre-trial review

Once the initial exchange of information about each party's side of the case has taken place, the court will fix a date for a pre-trial review. This will be held in private before the district judge. If the plaintiff fails to attend, the action may be struck out or discontinued on the order of the court. If the defendant does not attend the plaintiff may be able to obtain judgment if he can prove his case.

If both parties are present the district judge will seek to clarify the points at issue, if there is any doubt about them. He may also explore the possibility of a settlement at this stage. If the action is to go to trial, the district judge will give directions to the parties as to the things that they must do in order to prepare the case for trial. Directions given by the district judge at the pre-trial review may include orders that:

(i) further and better particulars of the claim or the defence must be given;

(ii) each party prepare a list of the documents in their possession relating to the case and give it to the other;

(iii) each party allow the other to inspect the listed documents, and take copies of them, a process known as *discovery of documents;*

(iv) the parties try to agree matters which are not disputed, to save the necessity and expense of proving them in court; and

(v) the parties produce plans, photographs or experts reports, and agree on their contents if possible.

Setting the case down for trial

When the directions given by the district judge at the pre trial review have been complied with, either party may apply to the court to fix a date for the trial. Once this has been fixed, the court will notify the parties, who must then complete their final preparations.

The trial

Many cases are settled on the doorstep of the courtroom before a trial takes place. This is because the pressure for settlement builds up to a peak when the parties are faced with the reality of a trial. They may be aware of some weakness in their case, or may doubt the ability of a key witness to appear credible and resolute in the face of cross examination. Even at this late stage considerable savings of costs can be made by settling the case.

The proceedings in a County Court trial are conducted in a formal manner. The plaintiff will have to present his evidence first, and any witnesses may be cross examined by the defence, or questioned by the judge. The plaintiff's lawyers can re-examine any of his witnesses, but must confine their questioning to matters already raised by them. Thus they could, for example, clarify any points which may have become confused in cross examination, or emphasise any important points which may have been obscured. Next it is the turn of the defence to present its evidence, and again there may be cross examination and re-examination.

Legal argument may then take place, followed by a summing up of each party's case. The judge will usually deliver judgment at the end of the trial, but may reserve judgment, particularly if there are difficult points of law to consider. If judgment is reserved the parties will have to attend court at a later date when judgment will be given.

Costs

As we noted above, the party who loses the case will have to pay the winner's costs, in addition to his own. He can however, challenge the amount of the other party's bill by applying to the court for a taxation of costs.

Appeal

An appeal can be made from a decision of the County Court to the Court of Appeal. The appeal may be on a question of law or a question of fact, and must be lodged within specified time limits. The costs involved in making an appeal will be very high and careful thought should be given before this step is taken.

Enforcement of a Judgment

If judgment is given against a defendant, payment is due immediately unless the court has made an order for payment by instalments or has otherwise postponed payment. If the judgment debtor does not make payment when it is due, steps can be taken to enforce the judgment. There are a number of alternative methods of enforcement, and it will be important to choose a method which will bear fruit having regard to the particular circumstances of the judgment debtor.

Oral examination

To assist in making an informed choice as to the method of enforcement, the party entitled to payment may make an application to the court for an order that the judgment debtor be orally examined before the court as to his means. The order may include provision for the production of books, accounts or other documents. The judgment debtor will be liable to imprisonment if he fails to attend. At the oral examination he will be cross examined on oath, as to his means and resources, by the judge and the applicant. It can be established, for example, whether he has any investments, bank accounts, savings or other assets such as a house or a car; or if he is working, the name and address of his employer and details of his salary and any other source of income. Armed with this information, a decision can be taken as to the most effective method of enforcement. The following are the principal methods.

Warrant of execution

A warrant of execution directs the County Court bailiff to seize any goods belonging to the judgment debtor, and to sell them to raise money to pay the creditor. It will be useful, at the oral examination, to establish what goods belong to the debtor and where they are located, in preparation for the issue of a warrant of execution.

Attachment of earnings

If it has been established that the judgment debtor has regular employment, the plaintiff can apply for an order under the Attachment of Earnings Act 1971. This is in effect a direction to the employer to deduct a specified sum from the debtor's wages each week, and pay it direct to the court, which will forward the money to the plaintiff.

Garnishee orders

If the plaintiff discovers, at the end of the oral examination, that the debtor is owed money by a third party, he may apply for a garnishee order. The effect of the order is to require the third party to pay the money direct to the plaintiff, or at least so much of it as will satisfy the judgment debt and costs. This type of order is particularly useful where, for example, the judgment debtor has money in a bank account or some other similar form of savings.

Charging orders

The plaintiff can apply for a charging order on land held by the debtor or on any shares owned by him in a company. This gives him security for the judgment debt which can ultimately be enforced by the sale of the property in question.

Bankruptcy proceedings

A creditor will have grounds to petition for the bankruptcy of the debtor if a judgment debt of £750 or more remains outstanding after a warrant of execution has been issued but returned unsatisfied. In practice the threat of bankruptcy proceedings is a powerful stimulus to make a defaulting debtor find the money to pay the debt.

Bringing a Claim Before an Industrial Tribunal

Tribunals are an alternative method to the Courts which are used to handle certain types of specific disputes. In general they tend to be quicker, cheaper and less formal than the ordinary courts. The vast majority of individual employment rights and duties are legally enforceable by mean of presenting a complaint before an Industrial Tribunal. Originating under the Industrial Training Act 1964 with only a restricted function, the Industrial Tribunal is now the focus for dealing with statutory employment law disputes. Industrial Tribunals have a jurisdiction extending to unfair dismissal, redundancy, employment status, trade union rights and documentation all of which considered later in the book in the context of employing the workforce. The Tribunal is composed of three members, a legally qualified chairman and two lay members, one of whom is usually a nominee of an employer's organisation, and the other the nominee of a trade union. Its role has been described as acting as "an industrial jury" and as such it is the final arbiter on questions of fact. While the aim of conferring jurisdiction on a Tribunal is to encourage decision-making which is both inexpensive and speedy, the reality is that there has been increasing legal complexity introduced into Tribunal proceedings. The procedure of Tribunals is regulated by the Industrial Tribunal (Rules of Procedure) Regulations 1985.

Submitting the claim

It is of crucial importance that a complainant to an Industrial Tribunal presents the claim within the appropriate time limits. In a complaint involving unfair dismissal the claim must be presented within three months of the effective date of the termination of employment. The Tribunal does have a discretion to allow an application out of time where it was not reasonably practicable to present if before the end of three month period. In practice Tribunals rarely hear applications presented out of time however and in *Swainston v. Hetton Victory Club Ltd.* 1983 the fact that the complainant was only one day late was sufficient for the Tribunal to refuse to hear the complaint. To present a claim it is usual to complete and submit an Industrial

Tribunal 1 (IT1) form to the Regional Office of Industrial Tribunals (ROIT), although the use of that particular form is not a statutory requirement and another form of writing could suffice. The ROIT acknowledges receipt of the IT1 by sending the complainant a form which confirms that copies of the complaint have been sent to the employer and passed on to the Advisory Conciliation and Arbitration Services (ACAS). The form also informs the employee that notice of the hearing will be sent at a future date. The employer (respondent), having received a copy of the IT1 and also a formal notice that the application has been made, has then fourteen days to *enter an appearance*. It is at this stage that the respondent should attempt to clarify the legal position, consider the evidence and, if necessary, apply to the ROIT for an extension of time before entering an appearance. If he requires further clarification of the complainant's grounds for the claim he can make a request for further particulars. Whether or not the respondent wishes to resist the claim, he must complete the notice of appearance and return it to the ROIT. If, in the notice, the respondent fails to provide sufficient particulars of his ground for resisting the claim, he can be required to do so by the Tribunal.

A copy of the notice of appearance is sent to the complainant and to ACAS. It is then in the hands of the ROIT to set a date for the hearing but in practice a postponement can be applied for in writing and is normally granted when requested. It may be that the respondent disputes that the applicant is qualified to bring the claim, perhaps on the ground that the employee has insufficient continuous employment for the purposes of a complaint of unfair dismissal. In these circumstances it is usual to request a preliminary hearing to determine the issue.

Conciliation

One of the functions of ACAS is in relation to conciliation when a complaint is presented alleging that a statutory right has been infringed. The role of a conciliation officer in an unfair dismissal claim for instance, is to endeavour to promote a settlement of the complaint without the dispute having to go before an Industrial Tribunal. The officer is required to promote a settlement if requested to do so by either party or if he feels that he could act with a reasonable prospect of success. For this purpose an officer could seek to promote the reinstatement or re- engagement of a dismissed employee on equitable terms or if this is not practicable, attempt to persuade the employer to agree to make the employee a compensation payment. His function is not to negotiate with the parties but rather to act as a channel of communication through which the parties do their bargaining. The conciliation officer will have considerable experience of this type of conflict and if asked to do so can draw on his experience to give an impartial opinion on the legal position. If a settlement is needed, and this happens in over fifty percent of cases, it is usual for it to be arranged through the conciliation officer. Such a settlement is enforceable in the same way as an award from an Industrial Tribunal, if necessary by action in the county court.

It is an important feature of employment law that an employee cannot opt out of his statutory rights so that if a private settlement is reached, which is not approved by an ACAS conciliation officer, either party could still present a complaint to an Industrial Tribunal. Any sum of money agreed as compensation in a private settlement would however be taken account of in determining a Tribunal award. The relevant statutory provision is contained in s.140(1) of the Employment Protection (Consolidation) Act 1978 (EPCA 78); *"Except as provided by the following provisions of the section, any provision in an agreement (whether a contract of employment or not) shall be void in so far as it purports -*

(a) to exclude or limit the operation of any provision of this Act; or

(b) to preclude any person from presenting a complaint to, or bringing any proceedings under this Act before, an industrial tribunal."

While there are a number of exceptions to the general rule, for instance fixed term contracts of employment of one year or more which exclude unfair dismissal rights, it would be prudent to call in a conciliation officer to give his stamp of approval to any private settlement.

Figure 2.2 *Main Steps in an Application Brought Before an Industrial Tribunal*

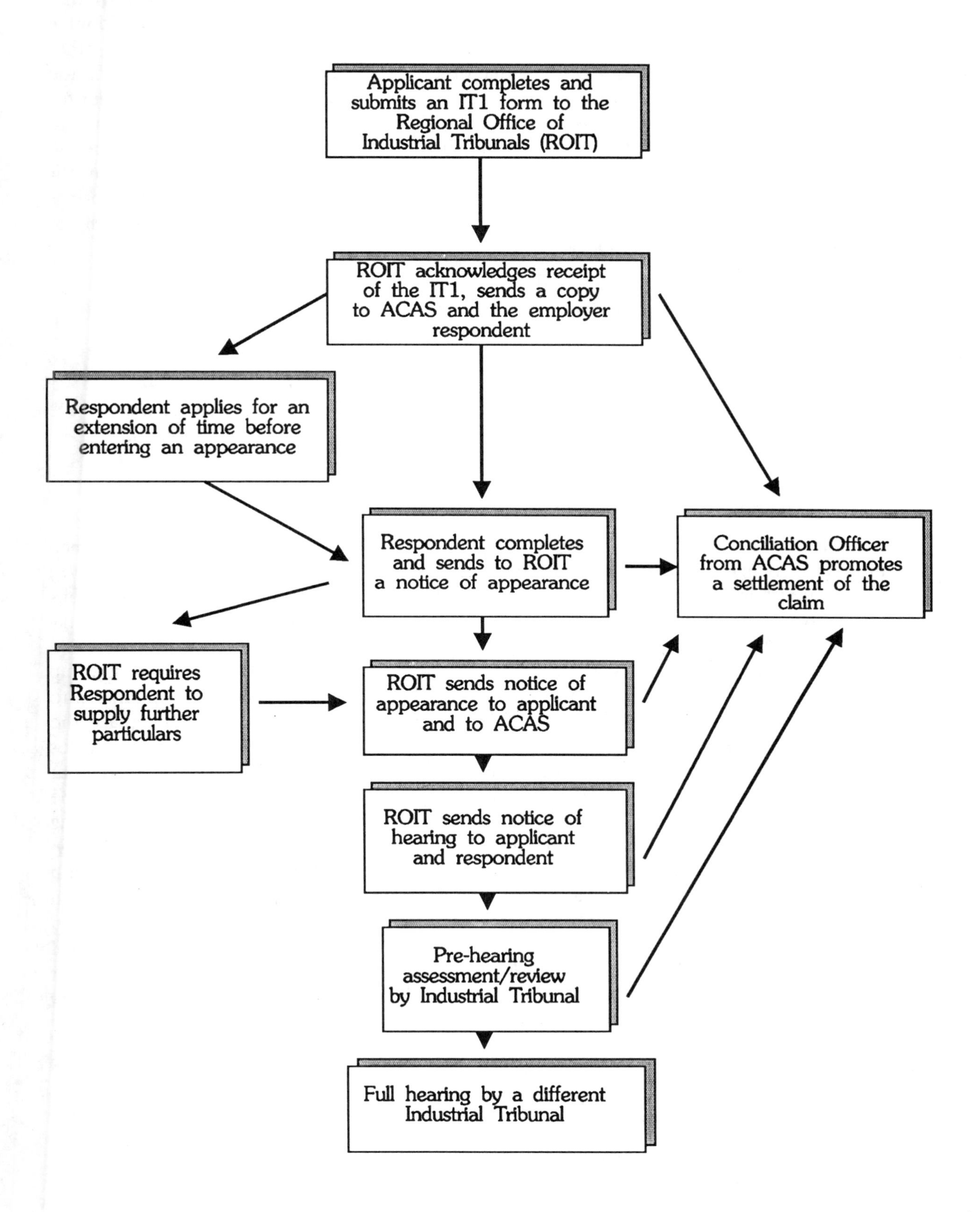

Before the hearing

Either party may apply for a pre-hearing assessment to take place, or the Tribunal may arrange an assessment in the absence of an application. The pre-hearing assessment is carried out by a full Tribunal examining the papers, assessing the strength of the claim and deciding whether the respondent's defence has any merit. No evidence from witnesses is heard but the Tribunal may take account of any written applications and the argument of the parties or other representatives. If an opinion is reached that other party's case is particularly weak then the Tribunal will issue a warning that if the party concerned proceeds to a full trial, an order for costs may be made against him. While the Tribunal rarely awards costs, it has a discretion to do so where a party, in bringing the proceedings, has acted frivolously, vexatiously or otherwise unreasonably. By proceeding with a claim after a pre-trial assessment has decided that it is particularly weak, a party would be regarded as acting unreasonably. An employee who brings a claim without any substance with the aim of harassing the employer, acts frivolously or vexatiously and could have costs awarded against him.

> In *Ferodo Ltd. v. Bradbury and Mycock* 1990 the purpose of a pre-hearing assessment was referred to by the President of the Employment Appeal Tribunal. *"The industrial members of this court bear in mind the purpose of a pre-hearing assessment namely: to eliminate those cases which have little or no prospect of success, thus to save not only the costs of the respondent employer but also of those representing applicants, who may or may not have received the full picture in their instructions; to identify relevant issues and to discard those issues which are really incapable of being pursued; to shorten the full hearings of originating applications before the tribunal; and lastly, to avoid improper use of industrial tribunal procedures."*

One of the most controversial sections of the Employment Act 1989 (EA 89) is s.20 which inserts into Schedule 9 of the Employment Protection (Consolidation) Act 1978 (EPCA 78) a new paragraph which empowers the Secretary of State for Employment to make regulations which provide for *pre-hearing reviews* in Industrial Tribunal proceedings. The regulation may provide for a review by a single person (the Tribunal chairman) or the full Tribunal and significantly, at that review, a party to the proceedings may be required to pay a deposit of up to £150 if he wishes to continue to participate in the proceedings. The aim of course is to discourage unmeritorious or ill founded claims. The pre-hearing reviews will replace the pre-hearing assessment where the present possible warning as to costs, if the Tribunal decides that a party has no reasonable prospect of success, has been of limited success in weeding out ill founded complaints. The danger of introducing a system of deposit which may not be returnable and possibly paid over to another party is that it may have the effect of discouraging applicants of limited means from approaching a Tribunal at all. It has been called *"a tax on justice"*. The availability of a sum such as £150 to a complainant who has just lost his/her job should not be assumed. Bear in mind also that as yet, legal aid does not extend to representation before an Industrial Tribunal despite the obvious need. The 1987 White Paper on Legal Aid suggested that legal aid should be extended to Tribunals and the Annual Report of the Council on Tribunals for 1987/88 stated that: *"The policy of providing tribunals to resolve disputes is undermined unless potential users are aware of their rights and are capable of putting their cases effectively. We emphasise our long held view that publicly funded advice, and where appropriate, representation, should be available to those of modest means who appear before them."*

The hearing

An Industrial Tribunal hearing is not conducted with the same degree of formality as a trial in a court of law and the rules of procedure make it clear that a Tribunal may conduct a hearing in a manner most suitable to clarify the issues, without the need to comply strictly to the normal rules relating to the admissibility of evidence. This makes it possible for lay representation which may put the complainant under a disadvantage, particularly if the employer is legally represented. In an attempt to speed up Tribunal proceedings there is no longer a requirement to provide full reasons for a decision except in cases involving discrimination. the reasons must be recorded in a written document signed by the chairman but they could be recorded in a *full* or *summary* form.

> In relation to summary reasons, Lord Donaldson MR in the Court of Appeal hearing of *William Hill Organisation Ltd. v. Gavas* 1990 said that *"It is the practice for Industrial Tribunals to give summary reasons and then, if asked, to amplify them as full reasons. It may be convenient to say that, certainly in my experience...we are getting into the position... in which summary reasons have grown and grown until they are scarcely distinguishable from full reasons"*. He went on to suggest that guidance should be given by the Employment Appeal Tribunal to get Tribunals *"back to first principles"* so that the applicant and respondent are given no more than in essence what is the reason for the decision when summary reasons are given.

The various remedies that are available to a Tribunal will depend upon the nature of the claim but they range from compensation awards to orders requiring a course of action such as reinstatement, declarations and recommendations. An Industrial Tribunal has no power to enforce its own remedies so that if a mandatory order such as reinstatement is not complied with, it can be reduced to a compensation award and if necessary enforced in the county court.

The Employment Appeal Tribunal (EAT)

An appeal from the Industrial Tribunal on a question of law or a mixed question of law and fact with usually lie to the Employment Appeal Tribunal. First established in 1975, the EAT is regulated by s.135 of the Employment Protection (Consolidation) Act 1978 (EPCA 78). The President of the EAT will be a High Court judge or a Lord Justice of Appeal who will normally sit with two lay members drawn from a panel of persons who have proven industrial relations experience. The procedure of the EAT is regulated by the Employment Appeal Tribunal Rules 1980 (as amended). The time limit for submitting an appeal from a Tribunal decision is 42 days and this involves submitting a notice of appeal together with the reasons for it and a copy of the Tribunal decision. Even without the full reasons the EAT can authorise an appeal if it considers that it would lead to the *"more expeditious or economic disposal of any proceedings or would otherwise be desirable in the interests of justice"*. Appeal from the decision of the EAT lies to the ordinary courts, namely the Court of Appeal and from there, in rare cases, an appeal lies to the House of Lords.

Arbitration

Arbitration is a means of resolving a dispute without recourse to the courts. An arbitrator is a person to whom both sides of the dispute put their case. He will consider the evidence and make a decision by applying ordinary rules of law to the facts before him. The decision of an arbitrator can be enforced in the courts, if necessary.

The legal framework within which arbitration operates is contained in the Arbitration Act 1950. This deals with matters such as the effect of arbitration agreements, awards, costs and enforcement. The Act does not lay down procedures for the conduct of arbitration, however, as these will vary according to the nature of the dispute and the way in which the parties wish it to be handled. In this respect, as we shall see, arbitration provides a more flexible method of resolving a dispute than proceedings in the ordinary courts.

Arbitration under codes of practice

The Director General of Fair Trading has a duty to encourage trade associations to promote voluntary codes of practice. The aim of these codes is the improvement of standards of service in particular sectors of business; and the laying down of methods for handling complaints about goods or services. Many codes set up low cost independent arbitration schemes for dealing with consumer complaints against traders who are members of the trade association which adopted the code. A free booklet entitled *"I am going to take it further!: Arbitration under Codes of Practice"*, which outlines a number of arbitration schemes available for various types of product, can be obtained from the Office of Fair Trading, Room 310, Field House, Bream's Buildings, London EC4A 1PR

Arbitration schemes sponsored by professional bodies

Many professional associations sponsor arbitration schemes as a substitute for litigation in relation to complaints against their members.

Arbitration in the County Court

A claim for £1000 or less in the County Court, if defended, will automatically be referred to arbitration under the small claims procedure. Under this procedure the deterrent of being saddled with the opposing party's costs in the event of losing the case does not apply. The Court has only limited power to award costs, for example where the unreasonable conduct of one party causes expense to the other.

A County Court arbitration hearing usually takes place in private before an arbitrator without the formalities associated with a full trial. The arbitrator will usually be the County Court district judge but any other suitable person may be appointed if both parties agree. The procedure is designed to encourage people making small claims to handle their own cases without the assistance of a lawyer.

If the amount in dispute exceeds £1000, the matter can still be dealt with as an arbitration if both parties agree or if the court so orders on the application of one of the parties. It is possible to object to the use of arbitration, even for claims under £1000, in any of the following circumstances:

(a) where the case involves a difficult question of law or an exceptionally complex question of fact;

(b) where one of the parties is accused of fraud or deliberate dishonesty;

(c) where the parties both agree that normal court proceedings shall apply;

(d) where it would be unreasonable for the claim to be heard as an arbitration having regard to its subject matter or the interests of any other person likely to be affected, for example where the decision will, in practice, create a precedent which will be followed in a number of similar cases.

Where a dispute is dealt with by way of arbitration in the County Court, the hearing will usually be informal and strict rules of evidence will not apply. The arbitrator may adopt any method of proceeding which he considers to be convenient, so long as it affords a fair and equal opportunity to each party to present his case. The case could be dealt with by an exchange of documents for example rather than a hearing with the parties present in person.

Arbitration clauses in contracts

Many standard from contracts contain an arbitration clause. This is an agreement to submit any differences or disputes which may arise in relation to the contract to arbitration. An example of such a clause can be found in the standard form contract contained in Chapter 8. Condition 14 of the agreement gives the parties the power to choose arbitration as a means of resolving any dispute. Some standard form contracts contain conditions under which any dispute must be submitted to arbitration. This can be done by adopting the wording of an arbitration clause which was held to be valid in the case of *Scott v. Avery* 1856. Under such a clause the right of action in court only arises after an award has been made by an arbitrator. The use of arbitration clauses in consumer transactions is looked at in Chapter 5.

Subsequent agreement to arbitration

Even where there is no arbitration clause in the contract, parties to a dispute can agree at any time to submit the dispute to arbitration. The agreement may be made after the dispute has arisen and any agreement to submit to arbitration operates as a binding contract.

An arbitration agreement comes into being where two or more persons agree that an existing or potential dispute between them shall be resolved in a legally binding way by one or more persons in a judicial manner. Under s. 32 of the Arbitration Act 1950 an arbitration agreement must be in writing. If an arbitrator is appointed under a verbal agreement he will usually invite the parties to enter into a written agreement, in order to bring the arbitration within the 1950 Act. The arbitration agreement may incorporate such matters as the method of appointment of the arbitrator and the procedural rules governing the conduct of the arbitration.

The unique features of arbitration

Where the parties have not laid out in advance any particular procedure, there is a large degree of flexibility in the way in which the arbitration can be concluded. With the agreement of the parties the arbitrator can adopt whatever procedure appears most appropriate. The case may be decided upon documentary evidence alone; or documents and written representations; or a site visit; or the examination of any goods which are at the centre of a dispute. Alternatively there could be a formal hearing of the case with expert witnesses and lawyers in attendance.

In addition to the flexibility of choosing an appropriate procedure, there is flexibility in relation to the location and time of any hearing. The arbitration can be heard at any place which the parties choose. This could, for example, be in a location near the site of the dispute, and take place at the weekend thereby avoiding the loss of working hours.

In a dispute involving matters of a technical nature, an appropriately qualified independent expert could be appointed as arbitrator. This may enable a swifter conclusion to be reached in the case.

Probably the single most important factor in the mind of a businessman who chooses to refer a dispute to arbitration is that the proceedings are totally private. Adverse publicity can therefore be avoided, and so can the public disclosure of confidential information or trade secrets. The advantage of privacy may be lost, however, if there is an appeal against the decision of the arbitrator.

Appeal against the decision of an arbitrator can be made on the grounds either that the proceedings were not conducted fairly, or that the decision contains an error of law. An arbitration award will only be set aside on grounds of unfairness if the arbitrator has failed to comply with the rules of natural justice. These are that he must be, and be seen to be, impartial and unbiased; and that each party to the dispute must be given a fair opportunity to present his own case and to answer the case put forward by his opponent.

One of the parties may suspect that the arbitrator has made an error of law in reaching his decision, but be unable to confirm that suspicion because the arbitrator has not given full reasons for his decision. In such a case that party can apply, under s.1 of the Arbitration Act 1979, to the High Court for an order requiring the arbitrator to give full reasons.

Arbitration is often a less expensive method of resolving business disputes than litigation in the ordinary courts. In some cases, however, where formal procedures are adopted, arbitration may actually be more expensive than litigation. One reason for this is that the cost of the actual hearing must be borne by the parties. This will include, for example, the arbitrator's fee, the cost of accommodation for the hearing, and of recording evidence. In most cases these costs are more than compensated for by the speed with which a case can be dealt with, the informality of procedures and the fact that the arbitrators award is final and cannot, except in the limited circumstances discussed above, be the subject of an appeal.

One of the disadvantages of arbitration is that an arbitrator, having reached a decision and made an award, in unable to enforce that award. In the event that the award is not complied with, it can only be enforced by taking action in the courts. The agreement to submit a claim to arbitration is a binding contract and failure to comply with an arbitrator's award is a breach of contract which can be the subject of proceedings in the County Court or the High Court. A simple procedure for enforcement is provided for in s.26 of the 1950 Act. Under this the award may be enforced in the same way as a court order with the permission of the High Court. This involves an application to the High Court for the enforcement of the arbitration award. If the court is satisfied that the award is valid it will enter judgment in favour of the successful party. The award can then be enforced in the same way as any other judgment of the court.

Assignment *To Sue or not to Sue*

David Adams and Frank Bartlett are partners in a firm of accountants which carries on business in Dartley, a small market town in the North West. Their work is almost exclusively confined to preparing accounts and advising on tax matters for clients who operate small businesses in the local area. The business has a clientele of between seventy and eighty, providing a turnover of around £195,000. When you bear in mind that the firm has a staff of three employees, an accounting assistant and two secretaries, it is not difficult to appreciate that bad debts are to be avoided at all costs. Unfortunately the firm has had an unpaid bill of £2,340 on its books for the past eighteen months. The bill relates to work done in 1990 for a new client, Andrew Davies, a building merchant in Dartley. Despite three reminders from the firm and a solicitor's letter threatening legal action no payment has yet been received. This is despite the fact that Davies is expanding into bigger premises. Frank Bartlett has also heard on the grapevine that Davies is now using a rival firm of accountants.

Six months ago the accountancy firm purchased an electronic typewriter with a memory and visual display facility from Bilton Office Supplies Ltd. for £454. The typewriter developed an electronic fault which has rendered the display facility unreliable. The firm sought to reject the machine when the fault was discovered, however the supplier refused to take it back, and offered instead to deliver the typewriter to the manufacturer for repair under the terms of the manufacturer's guarantee. David Adams wrote to the supplier and rejected this suggestion pointing out that Bolton Office Supplies Ltd. were legally responsible for the defects in the typewriter. He again demanded a full refund of the purchase price and requested the supplier to take the machine back. The letter was posted three weeks ago and no response has been made by the supplier.

Yesterday Frank Bartlett, the senior partner, received a letter from a firm of solicitors requesting a statutory statement of the reason or reasons for dismissing Sarah Tindley an ex-employee. Sarah had worked as a secretary for the firm for the past eleven years but three weeks ago was summarily dismissed with wages paid in lieu of the three months notice that she was entitled to. The reason for dismissal was that she admitted that she had "borrowed" money from the firm's petty cash to purchase a pair of shoes which were on sale.

Task

In the role of James Morris, a trainee accountant at the firm you are required to prepare an informal report in which you indicate:

1. Whether legal proceedings to recover the debt are worthwhile and the legal process involved in taking county court action for debt recovery.

2. Whether the firm is within its contractual rights to repudiate the contract for the typewriter and if legal proceedings are taken how they differ from the debt action.

3. If Sarah decides to pursue a claim for unfair dismissal indicate the steps which the firm would need to take should they decide to defend the claim.

Chapter 3

Establishment and Operation of Business Organisations

Introduction

The logical starting point in a study of business law is to examine the business organisations which are involved in conducting business activity. To do so we need to be clear about what the expression "business organisations" means. The problem this raises is that business is an economic concept rather than a legal one. The law does on occasion find it necessary to define the meaning of business, but only in specific situations limited to the context of a particular problem. For instance tax liability may depend upon deciding whether a person who has bought and sold a certain number of cars during the year is trading, and is thus in business as a car dealer. But the answer to such questions would tell us very little about the nature and quality of businesses in general, even though it would provide a solution to the particular case.

In order then to appreciate fully the law as it applies to business organisations it is helpful to draw briefly from economics, and summarise what an economist sees as making up a business organisation. It should be remembered that the decision to form a business is a commercial rather than a legal one, and that those who set up businesses will treat the legal form the business is to take as a secondary rather than a primary consideration. First you decide your business aims and objectives. Then you decide on the form of business appropriate to achieve them. As we shall see, examining the general economic background to business organisations is also useful because it helps to explain why substantial parts of business law have evolved, either as an aid to the business community in achieving commercial aims, or as a means of regulating business activities and curbing undesirable practices.

Characteristics Common to Business Organisations

Most business organisations will display the following characteristics:

(a) They will establish their business aims. In general organisations are set up for a specific purpose; selling particular products, providing a service, and so on. Of course businesses are also likely to evolve as the commercial environment changes and new commercial opportunities present themselves.

(b) The identity of the organisations will be distinct. It will, for example, be possible to establish who owns the organisation, and who is employed by it.

(c) There will be some form of leadership in the organisation. Leadership will be provided in the form of a system of management within it.

(d) There will be accountability within the organisation. The organisation itself will possess accountability. It will be accountable to those who own it, those whom it employs, and those with whom it trades.

It is the commercial aim of the business enterprise which distinguishes this type of organisation from others. For instance some organisations have scientific, educational, or social goals, and are not primarily concerned with the profit motive in the same way as commercial businesses; examples include charitable organisations such as Oxfam and the National Trust, educational bodies like the GCSE and GCE examining boards and BTEC, and a broad spectrum of other bodies such as local chambers of trade, and sports and social clubs. Local authorities are not commercial organisations either although as incidental activities they may operate profit making ventures such as sports and leisure centres. The expression 'business' is however a wide one, and used in some senses would certainly apply to the organisations just mentioned even though they are non-commercial. The expression is often used in a general sense to describe the way in which an organisation is run, a 'business-like operation', meaning it is run efficiently. It is also used to characterise the type of organisational activity being carried out, thus someone may loosely describe Greenpeace as being 'in the environment business'. For our purposes we will be using business in its commercial sense, looking at organisations which aim to make a profit for their owners, and which are owned privately, rather than by the state.

The Classification of Business Organisations

It is easy to get bogged down in charts and diagrams which classify business organisations in different ways, but it is helpful to take a birds-eye view of how these organisations relate to each other. Figure 3.1 below provides a broad classification, which distinguishes organisations according to ownership and then breaks down private sector business organisations which form the subject matter of this chapter, into their specific legal categories.

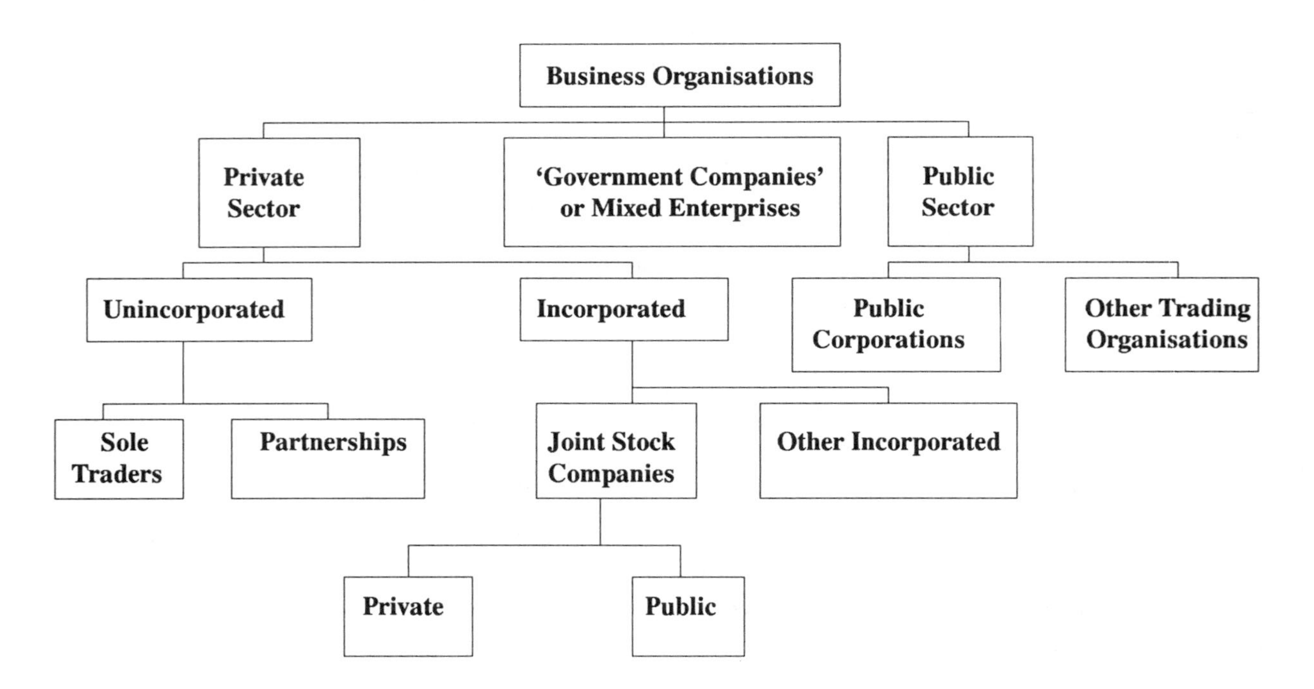

Figure 3.1 *Classification of Business Organisations*

Two features of the figure above require special attention. These are the distinctions between

(a) corporate and unincorporated bodies, and

(b) private and public sector organisations.

It is outside the scope of this book to examine the differences between public and private sector organisations in any detail, however it is important to be clear as to the significance of the distinction. Essentially what distinguishes a public sector from a private sector organisation is who owns, and therefore controls it. In the case of the public sector this will be the state; in the private sector it will be private individuals and organisations. Most of the work carried out by organisations in the public sector is not principally concerned with commercial trading, but rather with the provision of public services such as health, education and housing, and the management of a wide range of social welfare benefits such as pensions. The state does however engage in commercial trading in certain areas. British Rail is a state trading organisation; so too is Her Majesty's Stationery Office (HMSO). Much of the law contained in this book is as applicable to these state organisations as to those trading in the private sector.

A further distinguishing feature is the method used to create public sector organisation. Usually they are created by a specific Act of Parliament, thus British Coal, which is state owned, was created by the Coal Industry Nationalisation Act, 1946. The use of an Act of Parliament to create a private sector organisation, whilst not unknown, is most unusual nowadays.

Corporate and Unincorporated Bodies

Under English Law all business enterprises can be classified into two basic legal forms. They are either corporate bodies or unincorporated bodies. An unincorporated body is either an individual or more usually a group of individuals, who have joined together to pursue a common business purpose. The body and the individuals who compose it are not separate from each other under the law, even though they may trade under a business name, rather than using their own names, thereby creating the appearance that the business is a separate entity. A corporate body, or corporation, is also made up of a group of individuals who have joined together for a common purpose, but by the process of legal incorporation they have created an artificial legal person which has a separate legal identity from the members who compose it. The distinction between corporate and non-corporate bodies is thus fundamental to an understanding of the law as it applies to organisations.

Corporate Bodies

The corporation has proved itself to be a significant business form in the pursuit of commercial activity in the United Kingdom, for reasons that are explained below. Two basic types of corporation exist, the corporation sole and the corporation aggregate.

Corporations Sole

These consist of a single person and all the successors of that person. The bishops are corporations sole and so is the Crown. The Bishop of Durham is not only an individual but an office, and the office itself continues to exist despite one bishop being replaced by another. This is known as perpetual succession and can be a useful legal device because it can mean, for example, that property held by the office of the Bishop of Durham does not have to be transferred from one holder of the office to the next. Corporations sole are not primarily commercial organisations.

Corporations Aggregate

These are by far the most numerous type of corporation, and they consist of a number of people who combine to form or constitute the corporation, such as the elected members of a county or district council or the shareholders of a limited company.

Corporations may be created in the following ways:

(a) by Royal Charter. Charter, or common law corporations, are rarely created today, although many of the early trading organisations such as the Hudson's Bay Company were created in this way. The charter is granted by the Monarch acting under the royal prerogative upon the advice of the Privy Council. Examples of twentieth century charter corporations include the BBC and the more modern universities, and professional bodies such as the Institute of Housing;

(b) by a particular statute. Here an Act of Parliament creates and grants powers to the corporation. Public corporations such as the Independent Broadcasting Authority have been created in this way, and outside London, the corporate status and powers of all local authorities in England and Wales are contained in the Local Government Act 1972;

(c) by registration under the Companies Act 1985. The 1985 Act recognises two basic forms of registered company, public limited companies and private companies. The distinction between public and private companies is examined later in the chapter.

The liability of the members of a registered company may be limited either by shares or guarantee, or in rare cases be unlimited. This is provided for by s.1(2) of the Companies Act 1985 which states that a company may be:

(i) limited by shares, where the liability of the company members, the shareholders, is limited to any amount as yet unpaid on their shares; or

(ii) limited by guarantee, where the members' liability is limited to an amount they have guaranteed to contribute in the event of the company being brought to an end, a process known technically as winding up; or

(iii) unlimited, where the members are fully liable for the debts of the company, in the event of it being wound up.

At the time of writing there are approximately 6,000 public companies and 816,000 private companies in England and Wales. Unlimited companies can only operate as private companies, and there are around 4,000 of them. They operate primarily as service and investment companies. Although the number of public limited companies is relatively small, they are certainly of great commercial importance. They include the major banks, and multinational organisations such as I.C.I., British Airways and Lloyds Bank. It is usual to find that public companies have begun life as private companies which have become sufficiently successful commercially to warrant *going public*, that is offering their shares to the general public.

The classification of companies registerable under the Companies Act 1985 is contained in Figure 3.2.

Public Limited Companies	**Private Companies**
limited by shares	limited by shares
limited by guarantee (with a share capital)	limited by guarantee
	unlimited

Figure 3.2 *Classification of Registered Companies Under the Companies Act 1985*

Certain other statutes allow for incorporation by registration, for example working mens' clubs and organisations such as workers' co-operatives, can incorporate by registration under the Industrial and Provident Society Acts 1965-1975. The latter group, which have grown in number over recent years and now total about 1,000, can also be registered as companies limited by guarantee, or may operate as partnerships (see later).

Statutory registration was first introduced under the Companies Act 1844, to provide a method of forming corporations which was less expensive and cumbersome than obtaining a charter or sponsoring legislation through Parliament. The system of statutory registration proved immediately popular and helped to provide the capital which the growth of business activity at that time urgently needed. Capital was provided by investors attracted not only by the investment prospects offered by newly formed registered companies but also by the financial protection available through limited liability. The registered company remains just as popular with investors today, and has been further stimulated by the privatisation programme of the Thatcher and Major Governments, under which many previously state owned businesses have been sold off to the public for example Jaguar Cars, British Telecom, British Airways, and the Electricity Companies.

Later we will consider in more detail the legal implications of trading as a corporate body, but before so doing, it is helpful to look first at business organisations which function as unincorporated bodies, and examine their legal status. As we shall see, the legal status of a business is a matter of considerable importance to its members, not least because it is largely responsible for describing what their rights and responsibilities are, and hence their relationship to the organisation and to each other.

Unincorporated Bodies

The two types of unincorporated businesses we need to consider are the sole trader and the partnership.

Sole Traders

The term "sole trader" is an expression used to describe an individual who is self employed operating a business alone and who has sole responsibility for its management. In practice, of course, sole traders rarely work alone and will usually employ staff to assist them in the operation of the business. There are no specific legal formalities relating to the creation of such businesses. However operating as a sole trader will necessarily involve the owner in buying and selling, employing staff and acquiring business premises. As an employer, a sole trader is subject to the law relating to employment contained in the common law, (that is law defined by the courts) and numerous statutes, (law determined by Parliament), the most important of which is the Employment Protection (Consolidation) Act 1978 (as amended). In addition, as a supplier of goods or services, a sole trader must comply with the law relating to consumer protection, for example the Sale of Goods Act 1979, the Trade Descriptions Act 1968 and the Supply of Goods and Services Act 1982. Some types of business enterprise must also acquire a licence to permit them to operate. For example a publican requires a licence to sell intoxicating drinks and a turf accountant a betting and gaming licence.

A sole trader's business will normally be financed by the owner himself, which means that the opportunities for raising business capital are necessarily restricted. Whilst the sole owner is entitled to all the profits of the business, he has unlimited liability in relation to its losses and so must bear them personally. The sole trader form of business is therefore most suitable for an individual who wishes to retain absolute control of the sort of business enterprise which requires only a modest amount of financial investment. Obvious examples include retail shops and service trades such as plumbing and hairdressing. Collectively, sole traders provide a valuable service to the community by making a wide range of goods and services available in a personal way, meeting needs which might otherwise be unfulfilled.

The responsibility for decision making in such a business rests with the owner, and there is no individual or group to which he is made directly accountable. This is very attractive to those who wish to 'be their own boss'. Of course there are groups who will be affected by the owner's actions such as the customers or clients, the creditors to whom the business owes money, and especially the employees of the business. Such groups have a valid interest in the decisions made by the sole trader and may ultimately seek to hold him accountable for his actions. For instance an employee may complain that employment rights have been infringed, or a customer that consumer rights have been abused. Accountability is perhaps at its most extreme level in the event of the sole trader becoming insolvent.

Over recent years there has been a substantial increase in the number of one-man businesses being established and this trend has been encouraged by the government by giving grants and tax advantages to small businesses. The present climate of unemployment has resulted in large numbers of skilled and unskilled workers losing their jobs and many receive lump sum payments as compensation. There is evidence that increasing numbers of such individuals have been willing to use their redundancy payments as initial capital to set up a business in which they will be their own employer.

Partnerships

The other major form of unincorporated business organisation is the partnership. Partnerships are commonly referred to as 'firms' and the Partnership Act 1890 states under s.4 that: *"Persons who have entered into a partnership with one another for the purposes of this Act are called collectively 'a firm', and the name under which their business is carried on is called the firm-name"*. There are no detailed legal formalities required when individuals agree to operate a business together and thus form a partnership, and the advantages to a business enterprise of forming a partnership are somewhat similar to those enjoyed by the sole trader. The partners are capable of managing their own firm as they see fit, of sharing the profits and being able to deal directly with their customers or clients.

The partnership provides the compromise of allowing an extension of skill and expertise and the possible influx of additional capital by the introduction of extra partners. This extra potential for capital allows many partnerships to grow to become substantial business enterprises.

Although it has always tended to be overshadowed by the limited company, the partnership remains a significant form of business organisation in the United Kingdom, and is the choice of many people either setting up a new business or modifying an existing one. There are in fact over two million businesses operated either as partnerships or under sole trader arrangements, a clear indication of their popularity as a business form.

An agreement between two or more persons to form a partnership will constitute a contract but there is no legal requirement as to its specific form. It may be oral, in writing, contained in a deed, or even implied by the law from the surrounding circumstances. The Partnership Act 1890, which contains most of the legal rules relating to partnerships, defines a partnership under s.1 simply as the *"relation which subsists between persons carrying on business in common with a view of profit"*. It follows from this definition that it is quite possible for a business to be run as a joint venture without the participants ever being aware that their business is in law a partnership. Whilst this may be of no consequence to them for as long as they are able to work together in harmony, in the event of a dispute it is important to them to ascertain whether their relationship constitutes a partnership. If it does the provisions of the 1890 Act will apply, and as we shall see the effect of this statute on the partnership business in terms of the rights and obligations it lays down is substantial.

The main risk in operating a business as a firm is that if the business should get into financial difficulties, the liability of the partners is not limited in any way. The individual members are liable to the extent of their personal wealth to pay off partnership debts.

Partnership formalities

As noted earlier, a partnership agreement can be created in many ways. The 1890 Act lays down no formalities. It is of course commercially desirable, and common practice for partners to execute a deed of partnership, in which they provide for matters such as the capital contribution required from each member of the firm, and how profits and losses are to be divided. If the partners do not agree such details then the rights and duties laid down under the Act will apply to the partnership.

By s.716 Companies Act 1985, a partnership cannot validly consist of more than twenty members. An exception is made however for certain professions, such as accountants and solicitors, who are prevented by statute from practising as limited companies. No restriction is placed upon the size of such firms. Some of the larger firms of lawyers and accountants now have in excess of a hundred partners.

The partners may choose any name they please for the firm provided it is not similar to an existing name and therefore not likely to mislead others. Also, there is a legal restriction that the last name must not be the word 'limited' or any abbreviation of it, for this would indicate that the organisation is a company having limited liability. The words 'and Co' at the end of the partnership name refers to the fact that there are partners in the firm whose names do not appear in the firm name. Under the Business Names Act 1985 when a firm carries on business using a trading name which does not consist of the surnames of all the partners then their names must appear on their business stationery, and their true names and addresses must be prominently displayed at their business premises in a place to which the public have access. Non-compliance with these statutory provisions is a criminal offence.

The definition of partnership

It will be recalled that the definition of a partnership under s.1 requires there to be

(i) a business,

(ii) carried on in common by its members,

(iii) with a view to making a profit.

Under the Act *"business"* includes every trade, occupation or profession. Although business is a broad term it does seem that it involves the carrying on of some form of commercial activity. This may be for a single purpose.

> In *Spicer (Keith) Ltd. v. Mansell* 1970 the Court of Appeal held that two persons who were working together for the purpose of forming a limited company, and had opened a bank account and ordered goods in this connection were not in partnership prior to the incorporation of the company (which in fact was never formed). The reason was that at that time, they were preparing for business, rather than operating an existing one.

Further examples of how the courts have approached the question of determining whether a business exists are provided by the following two cases. They in fact involve individuals rather than firms, but they provide a useful illustration of the thin line that often exists between a mere hobby and a business.

> In *Eiman v. London Borough of Waltham Forest* 1982 the issue was whether the defendant had been rightly convicted in the Crown Court of the offence of making a demand for unsolicited goods *"in the course of a trade or business"*, contrary to the Unsolicited Goods and Services Act 1971. As a full time employee of the local authority the accused had, as a hobby, composed and published a book of verse. He had then sent out copies of the book to local libraries and made a demand for payment. The High Court held that the Crown Court was entitled to convict the defendant as what had started as a hobby, had become a 'business' as defined by the Act and therefore the Unsolicited Goods and Services Act did apply. The court found it possible to reach such a conclusion despite the fact that this was an isolated incident without any intention to make a profit.

> In *Blakemore v. Bellamy* 1983 the question was whether the accused's spare time activity of buying and selling motor cars through advertisements, contravened the Fair Trading Act 1973, and the Business Advertisements (Disclosure) Order 1977. This is because in the course of a business it is an offence to *"advertise goods for sale"* without making it clear that the goods were sold in the course of a business. Offences under the Trade Descriptions Act, 1968 were also alleged which involved applying false trade descriptions to two of the vehicles in the course of a business. Despite the number of transactions involved, eight in all, the High Court agreed with the Magistrates' finding that the defendant's activity was merely a hobby rather than a business. Accordingly the statutory provisions had not been infringed, for the sales were merely private bargains. This was despite the fact that the defendant's objective in making the sales was to achieve gain or reward and as a seller he had clearly demonstrated skill and expertise in the business of buying and selling cars.

The business must be a joint venture, which implies mutual rights and obligations existing between the members of it. There may still be a joint venture even though one (or more) of its members is a *sleeping partner* who does not take an active part in the management of the business but simply contributes capital.

There must be a profit motive underlying the business. It will be a question of fact whether the partners aim to make a profit.

Help in determining when a business may be treated as a partnership is provided by s.2. It states that where a person receives a share in the profits of a business, this will be prima facie evidence that he is a partner, although the presumption can be shifted by other conflicting evidence. The section goes on to state a list of situations which do not, of themselves, make a person a partner, namely where a person:

(i) receives a debt or other liquidated amount out of the profits of a business, whether or not by instalments;

(ii) being a servant or agent is paid out of a share of the profits of the business;

(iii) being the widow or child of a deceased partner receives an annuity (an annual set payment) out of a portion of the profits of the business in which the deceased was a partner;

(iv) lends money to a person engaged or about to engage in business, on a written contract signed by, or on behalf of the parties to it that the lender shall be repaid either at a rate of interest varying with the profits, or as a share of the profits;

(v) receives by way of annuity or otherwise a portion of the profits of a business in consideration of the sale by that person of the goodwill of the business.

> In *Pratt v. Strick* 1932 a situation of the kind described in (v) above occurred. A doctor sold his medical practice together with its goodwill, on terms that for the following three months he would remain living at the practice, introducing patients, and sharing profits and losses equally with the purchaser. It was held that the practice was the purchaser's as soon as he bought it.

Two further situations are specified by s.2 which it indicates do not automatically give rise to a partnership. Firstly co-ownership of land, even where profits are shared from the use of the land. Secondly the sharing of gross returns even if the people sharing the returns have a common right or interest in the property which is yielding the income. This draws a distinction between returns and profit. A return is the revenue obtained by some business activity, such as the receipts obtained from the sale of a book over a fixed period, whilst the profit is the sum left after deducting costs from revenue. In the example these would include printing and transport costs.

A partner's authority to bind the firm

There are obvious problems inherent in attempting to reach the sort of joint decisions which are necessary to successfully manage a partnership and it is not uncommon for partners to disagree. There are also risks involved, both in having unlimited liability and in the fact that individual partners may be responsible for the acts and defaults of their co-partners. Each partner is an agent of the co-partners and as such has an agent's power to bind the partnership by his acts undertaken within the ordinary course of the business. It is crucial therefore that each partner has trust and confidence in his co-partners, the relationship being one of the utmost good faith. This is sometimes given its latin name and is known as a relationship of *uberrimae fidei*. Each partner is therefore under a duty to make a full and frank disclosure to the firm of any matters affecting it that come to the partner's attention.

The power of a partner to bind the other members of the firm by his actions illustrates how important it is that each partner should trust and have confidence in his co-partners, not only in regard to their business ability but also as to their business ethics. In *Helmore v Smith* 1886

Bacon V-C remarked that, *"mutual confidence is the life-blood"* of the firm, whilst in *Baird's Case* 1870 James LJ stated:

> *"Ordinary partnerships are by the law assumed and presumed to be based upon the mutual trust and confidence of each partner in the skill, knowledge and integrity of every other partner. As between the partners and the outside world (whatever may be their private arrangements between themselves), each partner is the unlimited agent of every other in every matter connected with the partnership business, or which he represents as the partnership business, and not being in its nature beyond the scope of the partnership".*

In the course of business, partnerships enter into transactions with other organisations and individuals and inevitably such transactions are negotiated and executed for the partnership by individual partners, rather than by the firm as a whole. It has already been noted that each partner is an agent of his co-partners. *"In English law a firm as such has no existence; partners carry on business both as principals and as agents for each other within the scope of the partnership business; the firm-name is a mere expression, not a legal entity"*, stated Lord Justice Farwell in *Sadler v. Whiteman* 1910.

Under the law of agency, an agent will bind the principal (i.e. the person who has appointed the agent to act) by contracts made within the agent's actual and apparent authority. If the agent acts within either of these two spheres the contract concluded between the agent and the third party becomes the principal's contract, and hence it is the principal and the third party who become bound to each other. The *actual* authority of an agent is the express power given by the principal. A firm may for instance expressly resolve in a partnership meeting that each partner shall have the power to employ staff. Authority may also arise where the agent's power to make a particular contract or class of contracts can be implied from the conduct of the parties or the circumstances of the case. The *apparent*, or *ostensible* authority of an agent is the power which the agent appears to others to hold. Of a partner's apparent authority s.5 Partnership Act, 1890, says:

> *"Every partner is an agent of the firm and his other partners for the purpose of the business of the partnership; and the acts of every partner who does any act for the carrying on in the usual way business of the kind carried on by the firm of which he is a member bind the firm and his partners, unless the partner so acting has in fact no authority to act for the firm in the particular matter, and the person with whom he is dealing either knows that he has not authority, or does not know or believe him to be a partner".*

Whether a particular contract is one carrying on in the usual way business of the kind carried on by the firm is a question of fact.

> In *Mercantile Credit Co. Ltd. v. Garrod* 1962 the court had to decide what would be considered as an act of a *"like kind"* to the business of persons who ran a garage. It was held that the sale of a car to a third party by one of the partners bound the other partners. This was despite an agreement between them that provided for the carrying out of repair work, and the letting of garages, but expressly excluded car sales.

The agency position of a partnership is contained diagrammatically in Figures 3.3 and 3.4.

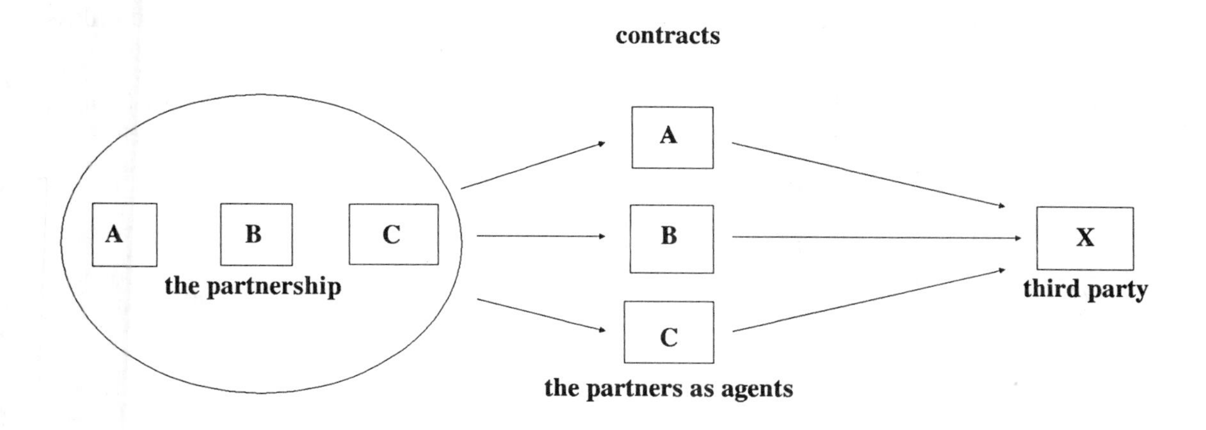

Figure 3.3 *Ability of Each Partner to Bind the Firm*

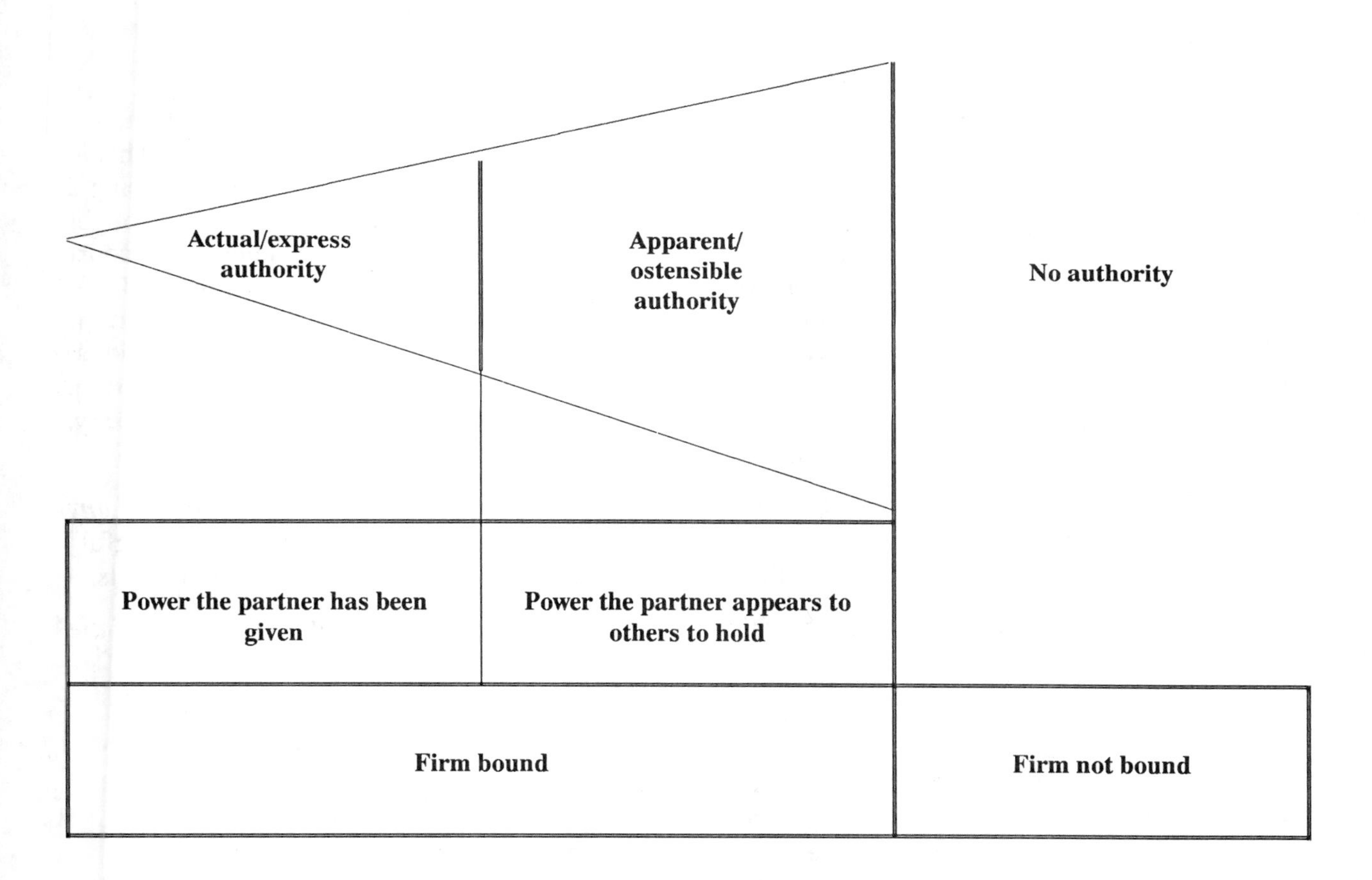

Figure 3.4 *Capacity of a Partner to Bind the Firm*

A private limitation of the powers of an agent is not an effective way to bring the restriction to the notice of an outsider dealing with the agent, and the law recognises this. But if, for example, a partner has acted as an agent for his firm in the past with a particular third party, and he carries out a further transaction of a similar kind with the third party after the firm has taken away his express authority, the third party can nevertheless hold the firm bound unless he knew at the time of contracting of the partner's lack of authority.

The exact scope of an agent's apparent authority under s.5 has been the subject of much litigation, and the following powers will usually fall within the agent's apparent authority:

(a) in the case of all types of partnership the power to:

  (i) sell the goods or personal property of the firm;

  (ii) purchase in the firm's name goods usually or necessarily used in the firm's business;

  (iii) receive payments due to the firm;

  (iv) employ staff to work for the firm.

(b) in the case of a partnership whose business is the buying and selling of goods (i.e. a trading partnership), the following additional powers are within the partner's authority:

  (i) to borrow money for a purpose connected with the business of the firm;

  (ii) to deal with payments to and from the firm.

A partnership has no separate legal identity so it is the individual partners who are ultimately accountable for all the firm's debts. Under the Partnership Act every partner is jointly liable with the other partners for all the debts and obligations of the firm incurred whilst being a partner. A legal action by a creditor seeking to recover money owed to him may be brought against any one or more of the firm's partners. However if the judgment obtained in the court does not satisfy the creditor he cannot then sue the remaining partners for, having sued one partner, he is precluded from suing the others for the same debt. Nevertheless the creditor, if he had chosen to do so, could have sued the firm in its own name rather than suing an individual partner of the firm. This has the effect of automatically joining all the partners in the action, and means that the judgment will be met out of assets of the firm as a whole and, if necessary, out of the property of the individual partners.

The Act goes on to provide that the firm is liable for the *"wrongful act or omission of any partner"* committed within the ordinary course of the firm's business. The term "wrongful" certainly embraces tortious acts although it appears that it does not extend to criminal acts.

An exception however occurs in relation to fraudulent acts carried out within the scope of the firm's business.

> In *Hamlyn v. Houston & Co.* 1903 the defendant firm was run by two partners as a grain merchants. One of the partners bribed the clerk of a rival grain merchant, and obtained information from him which enabled the firm to compete at greater advantage. The Court of Appeal held that both partners were liable for this tortious act. Obtaining information about rivals was within the general scope of the partners's authority, and therefore it did not matter that the method used to obtain it was unlawful. In the words of Lord Collins, M.R:
>
> *"It is too well established by the authorities to be now disputed that a principal may be liable for the fraud or other illegal act committed by his agent within the general scope of the authority given to him, and even the fact that the act of the agent is criminal does not necessarily take it out of the scope of his authority".*

It is no defence for a firm to show that it did not benefit from the unlawful act of its agent.

> The House of Lords in *Lloyd v. Grace, Smith & Co.* 1912 held a solicitor's firm liable for the fraud of its managing clerk who induced one of the firm's clients to transfer certain properties into his name. In advising the client the clerk was acting within the scope of his authority, and that alone made the firm liable for his acts.

Although the Act does not apply to criminal matters two points should be noted. Firstly, there may be occasions when one partner may be held vicariously liable for an offence committed by another (see Chapter 13). Secondly, a partner may be a party to an offence committed by another simply because it is in the nature of that partnership that they work together.

> In *Parsons v. Barnes* 1973 where two partners worked together in a roof-repairing business, one of them was convicted of an offence under the Trade Descriptions Act 1968, by being present when his co-partner made a false statement to a customer.

If a partner acting within the scope of his apparent authority receives and misapplies the property of a third person while it is in the firm's custody the firm is liable to meet the third person's loss. Similarly when the firm has received property of a third person in the course of its business, and the property has been misapplied by a partner while in the firm's custody, it must make good the loss. The liability of partners for misapplications of property, or wrongs of the firm, is stated by the Act to be joint and several. This means that if a judgment is obtained by a plaintiff against one partner, this does not operate as bar to bringing a further action against all or any of the others if the judgment remains unsatisfied. Where liability is merely joint this is not possible.

> In *Plumer v. Gregory* 1874 two of the partners in a firm consisting of three solicitors accepted on the firm's behalf and subsequently misappropriated money entrusted to them by the plaintiff, a client of the firm. The third member of the firm was unaware of these events, which only came to light after the other partners had died. The plaintiff's action against the remaining partner succeeded, for the firm was liable to make good the loss, and liability of the members was joint and several.

Changes in membership

The membership of a firm will normally alter from time to time. It may wish to expand its business by bringing in new partners to provide the benefit of additional capital or fresh expertise. Existing partners may leave the partnership to join a new business, or to retire. A changing membership poses the question of the extent to which incoming and outgoing partners are responsible for the debts and liabilities of the firm. Although partners are responsible for any matters arising during their membership of the firm, incoming partners are not liable for the debts incurred before they joined, nor outgoing partners for those incurred after they leave, provided the retiring partner advertises the fact that he is no longer a member of the firm. This involves sending notice to all customers of the firm while that person was a partner, and advertising the retirement in a publication known as the London Gazette. If this is not done a person dealing with the firm after a change in its membership can treat all apparent members of the old firm as still being members of the firm. With regard to existing liabilities the partner may be discharged from them when he retires through the agreement of the new firm and the creditors.

Rights and duties of the partners

Ideally the partnership relationship should be regulated by a comprehensive partnership agreement. If it is not, the provisions of the Partnership Act will apply when the parties are in dispute as to the nature of their duties and are unable to reach agreement amongst themselves, but in a business enterprise of this sort, where a member's entire wealth lies at stake, it is clearly of great value to execute a detailed agreement setting out in precise form the powers and responsibilities of the members. For instance it would be prudent for the agreement to provide grounds for the removal of partners, since the Act makes no such provision. Because the members of the firm have the freedom to make their own agreement, without the statutory controls imposed upon other forms of business organisation, such as the registered company, the partnership stands out as a most flexible form of organisation.

The duties that the Act sets out are based upon a single foundation of fundamental importance to all partnerships, namely that the relationship between the parties is of the utmost good faith.

> This principle can be seen in *Law v. Law* 1905. A partner sold his share in the business to another partner for £21,000, but the purchasing partner failed to disclose to his co-partner certain facts about the partnership assets, of which he alone was aware. When the vendor realised that he had sold his share at below its true value he sought to have the sale set aside. The Court of Appeal held that in such circumstances the sale was voidable, and could be set aside.

A partner is under a duty to his co-partners to render true accounts and full information of all things affecting the partnership. Personal benefits can only be retained with the consent of the other partners.

> In *Bentley v. Craven* 1853 one of the partners in a firm of sugar refiners, who acted as the firm's buyer, was able to purchase a large quantity of sugar at below market price. He resold it to the firm at the true market price. His co-partners were unaware that he was selling on his own account. When they discovered this they sued him for the profit he had made, and were held to be entitled to it. It was a 'secret profit' and belonged to the firm.

A partner is under a duty not to compete with his firm by carrying on another business of the same nature unless the other partners have consented. If a partner is in breach of this duty he must account to the firm for all the profits made and pay them over. If the partnership agreement prohibits the carrying on of a competing business, the court may grant an injunction to stop a partner who disregards the limitation.

Further rights and duties are set out in the Act which states that, in the absence of a contrary agreement:

(i) all partners are entitled to take part in the management of the partnership business;

(ii) any differences arising as to ordinary matters connected with the partnership business are to be decided by a majority of the partners, but no change can be made in the nature of the partnership business without the consent of all the partners;

(iii) no person may be introduced as a partner without the consent of all existing partners;

(iv) all partners are entitled to share equally in the profits of the business irrespective of the amount of time they have given to it, and must contribute equally towards any losses. The Act does not require the firm to keep books of account, although this will normally be provided for in the partnership agreement, together with specific reference to the proportions of the profit each partner is entitled to. If however there are partnership books they have to be kept at the principal place of business, where every partner is entitled to have access to them for the purpose of inspection and copying;

(v) if a partner makes a payment or advance beyond the agreed capital contribution he is entitled to interest at 5% p.a.;

(vi) a partner is not entitled to payment of interest on his capital until profits have been ascertained;

(vii) the firm must indemnify a partner in respect of payments made and personal liabilities incurred in the ordinary and proper conduct of the business of the firm, or in or about anything necessarily done for the preservation of the business or property of the firm (e.g. paying an insurance premium);

(viii) a partner is not entitled to remuneration for acting in the partnership business.

In cases where the firm consists of active and sleeping partners the partnership agreement will often provide that as well as taking a share of the profits the active partners shall be entitled to the payment of a salary.

If any of the terms of the partnership agreement are broken, damages will be available as a remedy, and where appropriate an injunction may be granted.

Partnership property

It can be of importance, particularly to the partners themselves, to establish which assets used by the partnership actually belong to the firm itself, rather than to an individual partner. Mere use of property for partnership purposes does not automatically transfer ownership in it to the business.

> In *Miles v. Clarke* 1953 the defendant started up a photography business which involved him in acquiring a lease and photographic equipment. After trading unsuccessfully he was joined by the plaintiff, a free-lance photographer, who brought into the firm his business connection which was of considerable value. The partners traded profitably for some time, on the basis of equal profit sharing. Later, as a result of personal difficulties, it became necessary to wind up the firm. The plaintiff claimed a share in all the assets of the business. The Court held that the assets of the business other than the stock-in-trade which had become partnership property, belonged to the particular partner who had brought them in.

The Act provides that all property and rights and interests in property originally brought into the partnership or subsequently acquired by purchase or otherwise on account of the firm, must be held and applied by the partners exclusively for the purpose of the partnership and in accordance with the partnership agreement. Such property is called 'partnership property' and will normally be jointly owned by the partners. Because a partner is a co-owner of partnership property, rather than a sole owner of any particular part of the partnership's assets, he may be guilty of theft of partnership property if it can be established that his intention was to permanently deprive the other partners of their share.

Under the Act property bought with money belonging to the firm is deemed to have been bought on account of the firm, unless a contrary intention appears. There is nothing to prevent an individual partner taking out of the partnership a particular asset, provided the co-partners' consent is obtained. The asset may be purchased by the partner either by making payment, or by accepting a reduction in his capital. However if at the time of the transaction the firm is insolvent then the removal of the asset will not affect the interests of the firm's creditors, for they can require the asset to be returned.

Limited Partnerships

Unlike the liability of members of a limited company for its debts, the liability of partners for partnership debts is unlimited. If the partnership assets are insufficient to meet them, the personal property of the partners can be legitimately realised by the firm's creditors to meet the liability. It is however possible to trade using a business organisation known as a limited partnership, which is a cross between the ordinary partnership we have considered so far, and the limited companies which are examined later in the chapter.

Limited partnerships are permitted under the Limited Partnership Act 1907 and must consist of:

(a) one or more persons called general partners, who are liable for all the debts and obligations of the firm in the ordinary way; and

(b) one or more persons, called limited partners, who have contributed at the time of entering into the partnership a sum or sums as capital or property of a stated value who are not liable for the debts or obligations of the firm beyond the amount contributed.

The Act allows a limited partner to be a body corporate. Once the limited partner has made the capital contribution he cannot withdraw any part of it, either directly or indirectly, without becoming liable for the firm's debts and liabilities up to the amount withdrawn.

Limited partnerships must be registered with the Registrar of Companies. This is achieved by sending to the Registrar a statement signed by the partners containing details of the firm's name, the general nature of its business, the principal place of business, the full name of each partner, the date of commencement and length of term of the partnership (if any), a statement that the partnership is limited, and particulars of each limited partner and the amount contributed by each whether in cash or otherwise. The registered statement is available for public inspection. If the partnership fails to register the limited partner becomes fully liable as a general partner. It will be appreciated that the principal difference between a limited partnership and a general partnership lies in the accountability of the partners of these respective organisations for the debts and liabilities of the firm. In a general partnership each partner has an unlimited liability for the debts and other liabilities for the firm, whereas in a limited partnership there must by definition be at least one member who, like a shareholder in a limited company, has a fixed or limited liability. Unlike a shareholder, however, the limited partner has no right to take part in the management of the organisation; a partner who does so becomes fully responsible for all liabilities incurred by the firm while acting as its manager. Nor does the limited partner have power to bind the firm. The limited partner is however granted the right to inspect the firm's books.

The limited partnership has been an unsuccessful rival to the private limited company largely, it would seem because of its non-corporate status. The total number of partnerships registered in this way numbers approximately 4,000 whereas there are almost $\frac{3}{4}$ million private limited companies.

Registered Companies

As we have already seen the registered company limited by shares is a corporate body, an artificial person recognised by the law, which has an identity separate and distinct from the members which compose it. The members of such an organisation are referred to as its shareholders. The limited company is the most common type of business enterprise operated as a corporation, although there are of course many other types of corporation in existence. These were considered earlier in the chapter.

Many thousands of registered limited companies operate in this country and between them they employ the majority of the nation's workforce and comprise about two thirds of the income made by the private sector. Companies can be formed which have only two members. They can also develop into massive multi-national UK registered enterprises which have thousands of shareholders. Such is the diversity of these organisations that it is difficult to generalise on their structure and behaviour but most have been formed with the expectation of future expansion financed by the raising of capital through the issue of shares. As separate legal entities they also give the owners the protection of limited liability and it is this feature more than any other that has contributed to their popularity. Another appealing feature is that ownership can be divorced from management, thus an investor can stake capital in a company without having to be involved in the actual running of it whilst maintaining control over the managers by means of their accountability in the general meeting.

Limited liability means that in the event of the company facing financial difficulty the shareholders' legal liability to contribute to the payment of debts is limited to the amount, if any, unpaid on their shares. For instance, if an individual purchases 20 £1 shares in the company and pays 25p on each share (these are called partly paid shares) he is only liable to contribute the amount of the share value remaining unpaid, in this case 20 x 75p, a total of £15.

Companies can expand and diversify by raising additional capital when it is needed, through the issue of more shares, and hence large scale commercial organisations have evolved with thousands of shareholders holding between them millions of shares. The growth of this form of business enterprise and the recognition of the company as a separate legal entity has however posed many problems and led to many abuses. The law has recognised these difficulties. Various Companies Acts, now consolidated in the Companies Act 1985, have attempted to regulate corporate behaviour, bearing in mind not only the interests of the shareholders themselves but also the interests of outsiders who trade with them.

The concept of corporate personality

As we have seen the limited company is an artificial legal person, and has some although not all the powers and responsibilities of a natural person. It is capable therefore of owning property, entering into contracts such as trading contracts and contracts of employment, and of suing or being sued in its own name. But its artificial nature imposes some obvious limitations upon its legal capacity. It cannot generally be held liable for criminal acts, since most crimes involve proving a mental element such as intention or recklessness and a corporation has as such no mind. Nevertheless there may occur circumstances in which the collective intention of the Board of Directors can be regarded as expressing the will of the corporation. Lord Denning has spoken of the company as having a human body, the employees being the hands that carry out its work while *"others are directors and managers who represent the directing mind and will of the company and control what it does"*.

Since the membership of a company is distinct from the corporate body this means that the company shareholders are separate from the company which has a legal personality of its own. Changes in its membership, including the death or bankruptcy of members ,will have no effect upon the company, which may have an almost perpetual life span if there remain investors willing to become or to remain members of it.

> The separation of a company from its members was confirmed in the leading case of *Salomon v. Salomon & Co.* 1897. Salomon owned a boot and shoe business. His sons worked in the business and they were anxious to have a stake in it so Salomon formed a registered company with himself as managing director, in which his wife, daughter and each son held a share. The company's nominal capital was £40,000 consisting of 40,000 £1 shares.
>
> The company resolved to purchase the business at a price of £39,000. Salomon had arrived at this figure himself. It was an honest but optimistic valuation of its real worth. The company paid him by alloting him 20,000 shares treated as fully paid, £10,000 worth of debentures (a secured loan repayable before unsecured loans) and the balance in cash. Within a year of trading the company went into insolvent liquidation owing £8,000 to ordinary creditors and having only £6,000 worth of assets. The plaintiff claimed that as a debenture holder with £10,000 worth of debentures he was a secured creditor and entitled to repayment before the ordinary unsecured creditors. The unsecured creditors did not agree. The House of Lords held that despite the fact that following the company's formation, Salomon had continued to run the business in the same manner and with the same control as he had done when it was unincorporated, the company formed was a separate person from Salomon himself. When the company was liquidated therefore, and in the absence of any fraud on the creditors and shareholders, Salomon, like any other debenture holder, was a secured creditor and entitled to repayment before ordinary creditors. The Court thus upheld the principle that a company has a separate legal existence from its membership even where one individual holds the majority of shares and effectively runs the company as his own.

A company is also the owner of its own property in which its members have no legal interest, although clearly they have a financial interest.

> In *Macaura v. Northern Assurance Co. Ltd.* 1925 it was held that a majority shareholder has no insurable interest in the company's property. A fire insurance policy over the company's timber estate was therefore invalid as it had been issued in the plaintiff shareholder's name and not the company's name.

Both the Courts and Parliament have accepted that situations may arise in which it is right and proper to prevent the members from escaping liability by hiding behind the company. The result has been the creation of a number of exceptions to the principle of limited liability. These exceptions seem to be based broadly upon public policy considerations, and many of them are associated with fraudulent practices.

So for example if a company is wound up and the court is satisfied that the directors have carried on the business with an intention to defraud the creditors, they may be made personally liable for all the company's debts. This would cover trading and incurring debts, where they knew that there was no reasonable prospect that the creditors would be paid.

In special cases, the courts will disregard the separate legal personality of a company because it was formed or used to facilitate the evasion of legal obligations. This is sometimes referred to as 'lifting the veil of incorporation', meaning that the court is able to look behind the corporate, formal identity of the organisation to the shareholders which make it up. Clearly this is a very significant step, since it is effectively denying the protection which the members have sought to obtain by incorporation.

> In *Gilford Motor Co. Ltd. v. Horne* 1933 the defendant had been employed by the plaintiff motor company and had entered into a valid agreement not to solicit the plaintiff's customers or to compete with it for a certain time after leaving the company's employment. Shortly after leaving the employment of the motor company, the defendant formed a new company to carry on a similar business to that of his former employers and sent out circulars to the customers he had previously dealt with whilst working for the old business. In an action to enforce the restraint clause against the new company the court held that as the defendant in fact controlled the new company, its formation was a mere "cloak or sham" to enable him to break the restraint clause. Accordingly an injunction was granted against the defendant and against the company he had formed, to enforce the restraint clause.

> Similarly in *Jones v. Lipman* 1962 the defendant agreed to sell land to the plaintiff and then decided not to complete the contract. To avoid the possibility of an order to specific performance to enforce the sale the defendant purchased a majority shareholding in an existing company to which he then sold the land. The plaintiff applied to the court for an order against the defendant and the company to enforce the sale. It was held that the formation of the company was a mere sham to avoid a contract of sale, and specific performance was ordered against the vendor and the company.

The courts are also prepared to lift the veil in order to discover the relationship within groups of companies. It is a common commercial practice for one company to acquire shares in another, often holding sufficient shares to give it total control over the other. In these circumstances the controlling company is referred to as a holding company, and the other company its subsidiary. In appropriate cases a holding company can be regarded as an agent of its subsidiary, although it is more usual to find the subsidiary acting as an agent for the holding company.

> In *DHN Food Distributors Ltd. v. Tower Hamlets LBC. 1976 an arrangement under which two subsidiaries of the holding company were wholly owned by it and had no separate business operations from it, was held by the court to constitute a single corporate body rather than three separate ones.*

> In Re: *Bugle Press Ltd.* 1961 the company consisted of three shareholders. Two of them, who together had controlling interest, wanted to buy the shares of the third, but he was not willing to sell so the two of them formed a new company which then made a 'take-over bid' for the shares of the first company. Not surprisingly the two shareholders who had formed the new company accepted the bid. The third did not. However since he only held 1/10 of the total shareholding, under what is now s.428 Companies Act 1985, the new company was able to compulsorily acquire the shares. The Court of Appeal however held that this represented an abuse of the section. The minority shareholder was in effect being evicted from the company. The veil of the new company was lifted and, in the words of Harman LJ: this revealed a

"hollow sham", for it was *"nothing but a little hut built round"* the majority shareholders.

In *Firestone Tyre & Rubber Co. Ltd. v. Llewellin (Inspector of Taxes)* 1957 the appellant company was a subsidiary of an American company which made and sold branded tyres and had a world-wide organisation. The British subsidiary manufactured and sold tyres in Europe. The House of Lords held that the appellant company was in fact not trading on its own behalf but as agent of the parent company and the parent company was consequently liable to pay United Kingdom income tax.

In some cases the courts have disregarded the separate legal personality of a company and have in the public interest investigated the personal qualities of the shareholders. It is in the public interest that an enemy alien is unable to sue in British courts.

In *Daimler Co. Ltd. v. Continental Tyre and Rubber Co. (Gt. Britain) Ltd.* 1916 the tyre company, which was registered in England, and had its registered office there, sued Daimler for debts incurred before the war with Germany had been declared. Daimler claimed that as all the members of the tyre company except one were German nationals and the directors were German nationals resident in Germany the claim should be struck out because to pay the debt would be to trade with the enemy. The House of Lords held that although the nationality of a company is normally decided by where it is incorporated, in some cases the court has power to consider who was in control of the company's business and assets in order that it might determine its status. Here, those in control of the company were enemy aliens and the action was struck out.

In addition there are a number of provisions contained in the Companies Act 1985 which have the effect of lifting the veil. They include the following:

(a) a fall in the membership of a company to below 2, under s.24. In these circumstances the sole shareholder becomes personally liable for the company's debts. Note that to be a member of a company it is only necessary to hold a single share.

(b) Under s.349(4) if an officer of a company or any person on its behalf:

  (i) uses the company seal and the company name is not engraved on it;

  (ii) issues or authorises the issue of a business letter or signs a negotiable instrument and the company name is not mentioned;

  (iii) issues or authorises the issue of any invoice, receipt or letter of credit of the company and again the company name is not mentioned;

  that person shall be personally liable for debts incurred unless they are paid by the company.

  In *Penrose v. Martyr* 1858 a bill of exchange was drawn up with the word 'limited' omitted after the company's name and the company secretary who had signed the bill on the company's behalf was held to be personally liable for it.

(c) Under powers granted to the Department of Trade and Industry to investigate the affairs of any company within the same group as one primarily under investigation by a DTI Inspector. S442(1) provides that where there appears to be good reason to do so, the Department may appoint inspectors to investigate and report on the membership of any company in order to determine the true identity of the persons financially interested in its success or failure, or able to control or materially influence its policy.

(d) Under sections 213 and 214 Insolvency Act 1986. These important provisions, which need to be carefully considered, are invoked in the course of the winding up of a company. We shall be looking closely at the winding up process at the end of the chapter, but it is appropriate to discuss ss 213 and 214 at this stage because in cases where the sections apply they have the effect of lifting the corporate veil, exposing those who have been engaged in the running of the company to personal liability, and they therefore represent a significant inroad to the principle of limited liability and the separation of the company from its members. Indeed s.214 has been described as one of the most important modifications to the principle of limited liability this century. S.213 deals with cases of fraudulent trading, and s.214 with cases of wrongful trading.

Fraudulent and Wrongful Trading

The concept of fraudulent trading is a well known one in company law. It is a crime under the Companies Act 1985, and gives rise to civil liability under the Insolvency Act 1986. Civil liability can only occur when the company is being wound up. If in the course of the liquidation it appears to the liquidator that the company's business has been carried on with intent to defraud creditors or for any fraudulent purpose, the liquidator may apply to the court for an order that any person who has knowingly been a party to such conduct be liable to contribute to the assets of the company. The court can order such a contribution as it thinks proper in the circumstances. In this way the creditors as a whole are compensated in the winding up for any serious wrongdoing committed by the directors, or any other party, in their management of or dealings with the company. The expression *fraudulent* is not defined by statute, however the courts have provided some indication of what must be established.

> In Re: *William C. Leitch Brass Ltd.* 1932 it was said that a company will be acting fraudulently by incurring debts either knowing it will be unable to meet them when they fall due, or reckless as to whether it will be able to pay them at such time. An important qualification to liability was given in Re: *Patrick & Lyon Ltd.* 1933 where it was said that the behaviour of the directors had to demonstrate real moral blame, and it is this feature of fraudulent trading which presents the major limitation upon its effectiveness as a civil remedy. So long as the directors can satisfy the court that, even when the company was in an insolvent situation, they genuinely and honestly believed that the company would be able to meet its debts when they fell due, then it is unlikely that they will be held personally accountable. Clearly the less business competence and experience they possess the easier it will be for them to avoid liability.

It was because of this difficulty in establishing fraudulent trading that the Cork Committee, in the course of examining the reform of the insolvency laws in the early 1980's, recommended the introduction of an additional head of civil liability, which could be established by proving negligence. This recommendation was implemented by the wrongful trading provisions contained in s.214 Insolvency Act 1986. Only a director can incur liability for wrongful trading, and as with s.213 action can only be taken by the liquidator of the company. The liquidator needs to establish that the person was at the time a director, that the company had gone into insolvent liquidation, and that at some time before the proceedings to wind up commenced the person against whom they were being brought knew or ought to have concluded that there was no reasonable prospect the company would avoid going into insolvent liquidation. If these criteria are met the court may declare the person concerned liable to contribute to the assets of the company. The section is particularly harsh on directors in a number of aspects. Insolvent liquidation means, in the context of s.214, that the assets as realised in the liquidation are insufficient to meet not only the company's debts and other liabilities, but also the costs of the winding up itself, which are generally substantial. The standard of skill expected of the director is based upon two sets of criteria, that is not only the general knowledge skill and experience which that particular director holds, but also the skill and experience that can be reasonably expected from a reasonably diligent director. The test is an objective rather than a subjective one. Even the defence available under the section operates in a harsh fashion towards directors. It provides that no order may be made by the court if it is satisfied that the person in question took every step with a view to minimising the potential loss to the company's creditors as he ought to have taken. The expression 'every step' is clearly very stringent.

> The wrongful trading provisions were applied in Re: *Produce Marketing Consortium Ltd.* 1989 where two directors had continued to trade when the accounts showed their company to be insolvent, in the honest but unrealistically optimistic belief that the company's fortunes would change. They were ordered by the court to contribute £75,000 plus interest to the assets of the company.

It seems that s.214 is a more potent weapon in the hands of liquidators than s.213. Establishing fraud is more difficult than establishing negligence, and this together with the rigorous standards demanded by s.214 suggests that wrongful trading is likely to be regarded increasingly by liquidators as a more attractive remedy than fraudulent trading. Even so there may still be reasons why a claim under s.213 may be brought by a liquidator. Perhaps the most significant is where a contribution is being sought from someone other than a director, for unlike s.214, s.213 catches anyone 'knowingly' a party to the fraud.

> In Re: *Gerald Cooper Chemicals Ltd.* 1978 the court held that a creditor who accepts money from the company knowing it has been procured by carrying on business with the intent to defraud other creditors by the act of paying him, will be liable under s.213. Templeman, J. stated *"A man who warms himself with the fire of fraud cannot complain if he is singed"*.

Classification of Companies

S1 Companies Act 1985 provides that a registered company limited by shares may be either a public or a private one. The most significant distinction between them is that a public limited company is permitted to advertise publicly to invite investors to take shares in it. Once purchased these shares can then be freely disposed of by the shareholder to anyone else who is willing to buy them. By contrast private companies commonly issue shares on terms that if the member wishes to dispose of them they must first be offered to the existing members. Where such rights are available to members they are known as pre-emption rights.

Before 1980 all companies were treated as being public ones, unless the company's articles of association contained specific provisions which enabled it to acquire private company status. Legislation passed in 1980, and now contained in the Companies Act 1985, completely reversed this situation, making private companies the residual class. Thus all companies are now treated as though they are private ones, unless certain requirements have been met which allow the company to be registered as a public limited company. This change was introduced to make it easier to define public companies for the purpose of complying with EC company law directives applicable to public companies.

Registration as a public limited company

This can be achieved by satisfying the following requirements:

(i) stating both in the company name, and in its memorandum that it is a public company. Thus its name must end in the works "public limited company" or the more convenient form "plc." The name of a private company will end with the word "limited" or "ltd.";

(ii) registering a memorandum of association which is in the form contained in Table F of the Companies (Tables A to F) Regulations 1985;

(iii) meeting the requirements of s.11 of the 1985 Act, which states that the company must have an authorised share capital figure of at least £50,000. The memorandum of association always contains a capital clause stating the amount of capital a company can raise by issuing shares, and it is in this clause that the authorised share capital amount appears. At least one quarter of this amount must be paid up before the company can commence trading, or exercise its borrowing powers, and the company must have allotted shares up to the authorised minimum (ss.101 and 107) Consequently a plc. must have at least £12,500 paid up share capital before it starts trading, and be able to call for an additional £37,500 from its members.

It may be useful here to explain these terms regarding company capital.

The *nominal share capital* is the amount that the company is legally authorised to raise by the issue of shares, the *paid-up share capital* is the amount the company has received from the shares it has issued, and the *uncalled capital* is the amount remaining unpaid by shareholders for the shares they hold; e.g. a company may issue £1 shares but require those to whom they are allotted to pay only 50p per share for the present.

The expression *allotment of shares* describes the notification by the company, usually in the form of a letter, that it has accepted the offer for the shares, and that the shareholders name will be entered on the register of shareholders.

A registered company which does not meet the three requirements listed above will be treated as a private company. Private companies differ from public companies in a number of respects, and an examination of these differences is a way of gaining an appreciation of the nature of these two forms of registered company. We can carry out the examination by considering the advantages and disadvantages of a private company over a public one.

The advantages of a private company

In contrast to a public company a private company enjoys the following advantages:

(i) it does not require a minimum level of share capital either to register or to commence trading. Its share capital could legitimately comprise of £1 made up of two 50 pence shares, the members holding a share each;

(ii) it can avoid s.89 Companies Act 1985, which provides that ordinary shares issued for cash by the company must first be offered to existing ordinary shareholders in proportion to the nominal value of their existing holdings - a "rights issue". S.91 provides that s.89 can be excluded by a private company in its articles;

(iii) it has a much greater freedom to issue shares in return for assets other than cash than a public company has;

(iv) the directors have more freedom in their financial dealings with the company and need not disclose as much information about such dealings in the company accounts as is the case for directors of public companies;

(v) subject to its size it may be excluded from publication of some or all of its accounts;

(vi) no special qualifications are required of the company secretary;

(vii) it has power to purchase its own shares, and may do so out of capital;

(viii) it can use procedures to avoid the need to hold meetings and satisfy various other statutory obligations. These procedures were introduced by provisions contained in the Companies Act 1989, designed to make it easier for private companies to comply with the substantial level of statutory regulation imposed upon registered companies. The objective has been to further deregulate the private company, thereby assisting it in the conduct of its business affairs. What the Act does is to permit private companies to *deregulate* themselves by means of the use of two types of resolution, the written resolution and the elective resolution.

The written resolution

By using the written resolution procedure a private company is able to do anything which would otherwise require a resolution of the members in a general meeting of the company. The written resolution must be signed by or on behalf of all the members of the company, who, at the date of the resolution, would be entitled to attend and vote at the meeting which would otherwise have to be held to conduct the business. If their approval is obtained a copy of the proposed resolution has to be sent to the company auditors, who must decide whether it concerns them in their capacity as the auditors. If it does they must then indicate whether they are willing to give it their approval. If they approve it the resolution is effective as if it had been passed in general meeting, but if it is not granted the company must hold a general meeting to conduct the business in the ordinary way. This procedure is not available in certain circumstances eg: to remove a director, and in other cases there are further formalities which must be complied with.

The elective resolution

An elective resolution can be used by a private company as a means of avoiding a number of formalities that it would otherwise have to observe under company legislation. Such a resolution can dispense with the need to obtain the authority of the members before the company issues shares, the need to lay accounts and reports before the general meeting, the need to hold an annual general meeting, and to reappoint auditors annually. Like the written resolution, the elective resolution requires the unanimous approval of all the company members entitled to attend and vote at a general meeting. There are certain qualifications attached to the use of an elective resolution. For instance if it is used to dispense with the need to hold an annual general meeting, a member may serve written notice on the company no later than three months before the end of the year to which the meeting relates, requiring that it be held.

In addition an elective resolution can be revoked by means of an ordinary resolution (which requires a simple majority) passed by the members in general meeting.

The disadvantages of a private company

The only major disadvantage it suffers is that it cannot advertise its securities to the public through the issue of a prospectus or other advertising device. S.170 Financial Services Act 1986 however does enable the Secretary of State to make regulations allowing for purely private advertisements between the issuer and the recipient. This lack of capacity to raise capital through the public issue of shares can really only be regarded as a disadvantage if the growth of the business needs to be financed in this way, when the company faces a choice between remaining privately owned and seeking finance by other means, or of going public and reducing the level of control exercisable by the original members over the new business as new members are brought in.

The meaning of the expression 'public company'

As we have seen a public limited company is one which satisfies certain statutory criteria, however the expression public company is sometimes used in a commercial rather than a legal sense to denote companies whose shares are dealt with on the Stock Exchange; major United Kingdom organisations such as ICI and Marks and Spencer are examples. Technically such companies are 'listed' or 'market' companies. Not all public limited companies are quoted i.e. listed on the Stock Exchange, but only the largest ones which are able to meet the stringent entry requirements the Stock Exchange demands. Those public limited companies which are not quoted on the Stock Exchange will offer their securities in one of the intermediate securities markets, such as the Unlisted Securities Market (the USM) a 'junior league' of the Stock Exchange set up in 1980. The other intermediate securities markets are the Over the

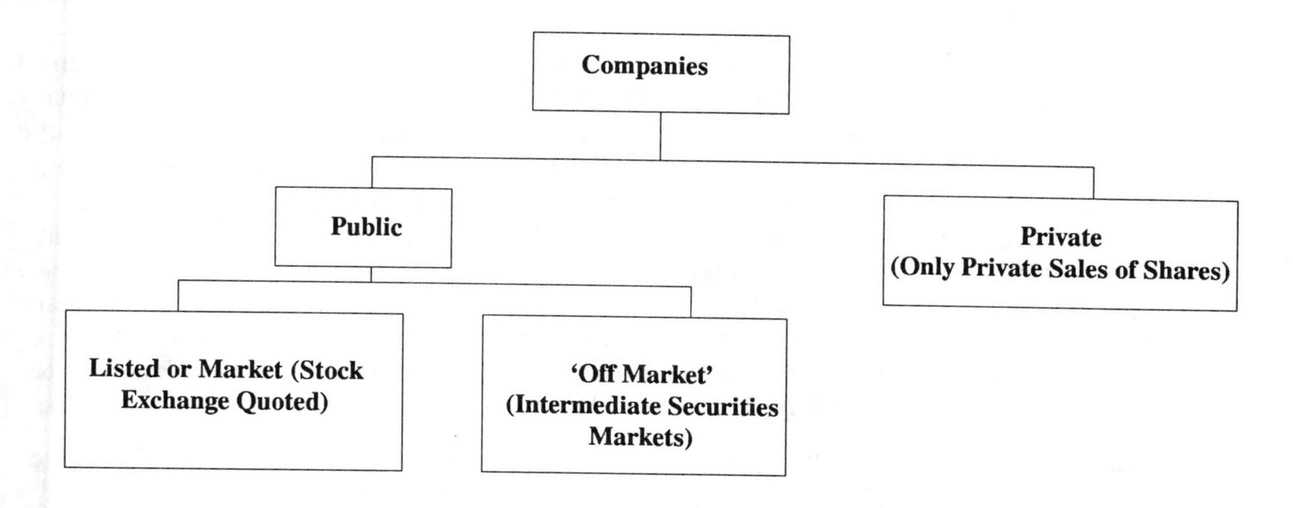

Figure 3.5 *Classification of Companies by Market*

Counter Market and the Third Market. Thus public and private companies can be classified by reference to the method by which their shares can be issued.

Formation of a Registered Company

A company is incorporated and so comes into being when the Registrar of Companies issues it with a document called the certificate of incorporation. This certificate is issued following an application by the persons who wish to form the company. They are known as the company's promoters. The two main documents which must be included in the application are the memorandum of association and the articles of association. Once the certificate of incorporation has been granted a private company can commence trading immediately however a public company must be issued with a further document, a trading certificate, before it is authorised to start trading.

The Memorandum of Association

The memorandum of association and the articles of association set out the constitution of a registered company. They are the two major documents within a group of documents to be sent to the Registrar of Companies prior to incorporation. A memorandum is required by the Companies Act 1985 which specifies that it must include the following matters:

(i) the name of the company with 'limited' as the last word in the case of a private company, or 'public limited company' in the case of a public company;

(ii) the situation of the registered office identifying whether the company is situated in England or Scotland;

(iii) the objects of the company;

(iv) the liability of the members;

(v) the nominal capital of the company and its division into numbers of shares and denominations.

The Registrar of Companies maintains a file for all registered companies, which is open to public inspection on payment of a fee. The file for each company includes the company memorandum. The contents of the memorandum are of importance to the members of the company itself (the shareholders), and especially to those who deal with the company commercially. The indication that the company has limited liability shown by the inclusion of the word 'limited', serves as a warning to outsiders that in the event of the company being unable to meet its financial liabilities at any time, its shareholders, as we have previously seen, can only be called upon to make good any loss up to the value which remains unpaid to the company on their shares. Once however the shares have been fully paid the shareholders' financial liability ceases. Of course the liability of the company, as opposed to its members, is not limited in any way and if it is wound up all its assets will be used to meet the claims of the creditors.

Stating the country in which the company is situated determines whether it is an English or Scottish company. Usually a Notice of Situation of Registered Office, giving the company's full address is sent to the Registrar together with the Memorandum. It must, in any event, be sent to him within fourteen days of incorporation of the company. The registered office is important since documents must be effectively served on the company by posting or delivering them to this address. Thus a writ (a document used to commence legal proceedings) served on the company will be effectively served if delivered to the registered office.

The objects clause sets the contractual limits within which the company can validly operate. The need to state the company's objects may be seen as a protection to shareholders by giving them some reassurance as to the ways in which their capital may be used by the directors. A company, can, however, resolve to alter its objects, and in any event it is usual to draft the objects clause very widely. Furthermore even if a company acts outside its objects clause the transaction will in most cases be binding on it, although the members may seek to censure the authorising directors. This matter is considered in more detail below.

The liability clause is a formality which merely states the nature of the shareholders' liability, that is whether it is limited by shares, by guarantee, or unlimited.

The capital clause sets out the amount of capital the company is authorised to raise by the issue of shares, and the way in which the shares are to be divided. This amount can be raised by the agreement of the shareholders without difficulty, although a reduction in the share capital, whilst possible, is more of a problem to achieve. It is a basic principle of company law that share capital should be maintained to protect the interests of the company's creditors.

The subscribers for the shares in the memorandum will often be appointed as directors. As the statutory minimum membership of a company is two, two subscribers to the memorandum will suffice to form the company. Each subscriber will agree to take a certain number of shares on incorporation of the company, and the subscribers are therefore the first members of the company. Subsequently new members will join the company when it allots shares to them and their names are entered on the register of members which every company must maintain, and which is open to public inspection. Usually the subscribers will have been the promoters - the people engaged in setting up the company.

Company name

Generally a company is free to choose the name it wishes to adopt, although as we have seen the word 'limited' for a private company or 'plc' for a public company must be inserted at the end of the company name. This is required by s.26 Companies Act 1985. The section also provides that the name cannot be the same as one already held on the index of company names kept by the Registrar. Nor can a name be used which would in the opinion of the Secretary of State constitute a criminal offence or be offensive.

It is a tort for a person to represent his business as that of another and thereby obtain profit from that other's business goodwill. In such circumstances the injured business can claim under the tort of passing off against the business guilty of the deception and recover damages and obtain an injunction, by way of a remedy.

> In *Ewing v. Buttercup Margarine Co. Ltd.* 1917 the plaintiff, who carried on business using the name Buttercup Dairy Co. obtained an injunction against the defendant company on the grounds that the public might be confused as to the identity of the two organisations.

It makes no difference whether the name is real or invented.

> In *Exxon Corporation v. Exxon Insurance Consultants International Ltd.* 1981 the plaintiffs obtained an injunction to prevent the defendants from passing off its goods as the defendant's by the use of the word 'Exxon'. The plaintiffs, formerly the Esso Company,had invented the word Exxon as a replacement name. They were however unsuccessful in seeking an injunction for breach of copyright. The court held that the word 'Exxon' was not an *"original literary work"* under the Copyright Act 1956, since, in the words of Stephenson LJ a *"literary work is something intended to afford either information and instruction or pleasure in the form of literary enjoyment"*.

The objects clause and the ultra vires doctrine

The background to ultra vires

Being a corporate body the registered company can only lawfully do those things which its constitution allows it to do. This is a feature of corporate status which we have already considered. It is a direct consequence of the artificiality of corporations which, being purely creations of the law, only possess a restricted capacity. As a condition of incorporation every registered company must include a statement in its memorandum which sets out what the company has been formed to do. The scope or extent of this statement, known as the company's *objects clause*, is initially decided by the people setting up the company, its promoters. They will often become the company's first directors following its incorporation.

The details contained in the objects clause provide shareholders with a description of the range of activities their company can legitimately undertake. It is right that as investors, a company's shareholders should know the purpose for which their financial contribution can be used. A rational investor will want to establish how well the board of directors manages the company, something which can be achieved by looking at the company's trading performance in its particular line of business. An investor may be less willing to put money into an enterprise where the board has a wide freedom under the company's objects clause to pursue diverse commercial activities, some of which may fall well outside their experience as managers. This is particularly likely in the smaller private companies, for whereas the boards, handling the affairs of public companies will include executive directors having wide commercial experience, in small private limited companies directors will sometimes have at best only a rudimentary knowledge of business management, and at worst none at all.

If a company acts outside the limits of its permissible activities as expressed in the objects clause it is said to be acting *ultra vires*, that is beyond its powers. At common law an ultra vires transaction has always been treated as a nullity, consequently an ultra vires contract entered into by a company was neither enforceable by it or against it. Even if the other contracting party was unaware that the company was exceeding its powers as expressed in the memorandum this would provide no relief, for under the doctrine of *constructive notice* a person dealing with a company was deemed to be aware of its public documents and hence of any restrictions on the company's capacity contained in them. Nor could the company subsequently ratify in general meeting an ultra vires transaction made on its behalf by the directors. Ratification has the effect of retrospectively validating a transaction, but in the case of an ultra vires contract this is not possible since the contract is a nullity.

> The application of these principles is seen in *Ashbury Railway Carriage Co. Ltd. v. Riche* 1875. The company's objects included the power to manufacture or sell rail rolling stock and carry on business as mechanical engineers and general contractors. The company purchased a concession to finance the building of a railway in Belgium, but later the directors repudiated the contract. In an action for breach of contract against the company, the House of Lords held that the contract was ultra vires and void from the outset. Lord Cairns expressed the law when he said, *"This contract was entirely beyond the objects in the memorandum ... If it was a contract void at its beginning, it was void because the company could not make the contract".*

During the nineteenth century and early part of the twentieth century the ultra vires doctrine operated in an oppressive manner. The courts took the view that in the drafting of an objects clause only a single principal object could be included. The powers necessary to achieve the stated object would be implied if they were not specifically stated, but essentially the company could only pursue one main object. This became known as the *main objects rule*. It was not commercially very satisfactory for it severely restricted diversification of a company's trading activities, as and when the opportunity arose. The drafters of objects clauses tried to overcome the limitations imposed by the main objects rule through the device of setting out more than one main object in the memorandum, supported by a statement that each object was to by regarded as independent and separate from the others. By 1918 the courts were accepting that with suitable wording clauses containing independent main objects would be upheld as valid.

> In *Cotman v. Brougham* 1918 the memorandum clearly stated that each of a rubber company's many objects were to be regarded as independent. The main clause was to develop rubber estates abroad but another subclause authorised the company to deal with the shares of any company. When the company underwrote shares in an oil company the action was challenged as ultra vires. The House of Lords held that the power to underwrite was clearly provided for in the memorandum and the action was therefore intra vires and valid.

By 1966 even greater freedom was being permitted by allowing clauses giving a wider discretion to the board of directors.

> In *Bell Houses Ltd. v. City Wall Properties Ltd.* 1966 the main object of the company was to develop housing estates, but another clause allowed the company to carry on 'any other trade or business whatsoever which can, in the opinion of the board of directors, be advantageously carried on by the company with, or as ancillary to, any of the above businesses or the general business of the company'. The Court of Appeal held that such a clause was valid provided that the directors in forming their opinion acted in good faith.

When the United Kingdom became a member of the European Community on 1st January, 1973, the European Communities Act 1972, by which entry was effected, in a hurried attempt at providing for some measure of harmonisation between english company law and company law as it applied in the other member states, introduced an important statutory modification to the ultra vires doctrine. This modification which was contained in s.9(1), and was subsequently incorporated unchanged into the Companies Act 1985 as s.35, provided that in favour of a person acting in good faith with a company, any transaction decided on by its directors was deemed to be within the capacity of the company to make. Whilst not eliminating the doctrine of ultra vires s.35 went some way towards reducing its impact. The Companies Act 1989, which implements more fully the first EC directive on company law, has introduced a new s.35 which goes much further towards eliminating ultra vires as it affects the registered company. As we shall see however the doctrine is still not completely dead.

The present law

The new s.35 states that, *"The validity of an act done by a company shall not be called into question on the ground of lack of capacity by reason on anything in the company's memorandum."* In other words it validates transactions which would otherwise be void on the grounds of breaching the company's constitution as expressed in the memorandum. The section goes on to say that anyone making a transaction with the company is not obliged to check the memorandum to ascertain whether it authorises the transaction. A further provision, s.711A, abolishes the doctrine of constructive notice of matters which would be disclosed by a company search. Previously, as we have seen, a person dealing with a company was in some circumstances deemed to have knowledge of information contained in the public file of the company held at the Companies Registry. This principle no longer applies.

The changes introduced under the Companies Act 1989 do not however completely eliminate the application of ultra vires to registered companies. In this context three matters need to be noted:

(i) a shareholder still retains the power to seek an injunction to restrain the company from entering into an ultra vires transaction, although this opportunity is lost once the transaction has been made, whether or not it has been carried out;

(ii) directors are still obliged to act within their company's constitution. S.35(3) says, *"it remains the duty of the directors to observe any limitations on their powers flowing from the company's memorandum"*. The company can now ratify action taken by directors in excess of their powers by means of a special resolution, thus reversing the position in the Ashbury Railway Carriage case, and an additional special resolution may be passed to relieve the directors of any liability they may have incurred for breach of duty as a result of exceeding the company's powers;

(iii) as a result of s.109 Companies Act 1989 if a director exceeds his powers and the other party to the contract is a director of the company or the holding company, the company can if it chooses avoid the contract. The section is an attempt at preventing directors defrauding the company using the provisions of the new s.35.

s.35 and the rule in Turquand's Case

Whilst the powers of a company are found in its memorandum, the rules regulating the way in which these powers should be exercised are usually contained in the articles of association. Articles may, for example, cut down on the general powers enjoyed by directors to make contracts within the company's authorised areas of business, by requiring that transactions involving more than a certain amount of money be approved by the members through an ordinary resolution passed at a meeting of the company. This can give rise to circumstances where an outsider enters into a transaction with a company which its memorandum authorises, but where the company's internal rules have not been complied with. Internal rules contained in a company's articles of association, being contained in its public file, came within the doctrine of constructive notice: the outsider was deemed to be aware of them. What he could not know was whether they had in fact been complied with when a company decision was made.

For instance, he would have no way of discovering whether a resolution required to be passed by the company under the articles had been passed. As a response to this difficulty the rule in *Royal British Bank v. Turquand* 1856 provided that an outsider was entitled to assume that the necessary rules of internal management had been complied with.

The rule in *Turquand's Case* is affected by the Companies Act 1989. It provides that a third party dealing in good faith with a company can treat the company's constitution as imposing no restrictions on the power of the board of directors or persons authorised by them to bind the company. This provision thus supersedes the rule in *Turquand's Case*. A third party is assumed to be acting in good faith, unless the contrary can be shown. Knowledge that the directors are acting beyond their powers does not, in itself, amount to bad faith.

Alteration of the objects clause

By virtue of s.4 Companies Act 1985, a company may by means of a special resolution alter its object clause at any time and for any reason. The alteration is effective so long as no application is made to the court to cancel it within 21 days of the special resolution, and the company sends the Registrar within a further 15 days a copy of the altered memorandum. An application to cancel can be made by the holders of at least 15% of the issued share capital of any class, and the alteration is only effective in these circumstances where the court confirms it. It is relevant to point out in connection with the alteration of objects that a company can now adopt a single object to carry on business as a general commercial company (s.3A). A company formed with such an object will be able to carry on any business or trade, and do anything incidental or conducive to such a business or trade.

The Articles of Association

The articles of association of a registered company must be supplied to the Registrar of Companies prior to incorporation. Like the memorandum of association the articles will then be included in the company's file kept at Companies House in Cardiff.

The articles are concerned with the internal administration of the company, and it is for those setting up the company (its promoters) to determine the rules they consider appropriate for inclusion within the articles. The Companies Act 1985 does however provide a set of model articles which a company can adopt in whole or in part if it wishes. If a company fails to provide a set of articles then the model articles contained in the 1985 Act automatically apply to the company. They are known as *Table A* Articles. Matters which are normally dealt with in the Articles include the appointment and powers of the board of directors, the rules in relation to members' meetings and voting and the types of shares and rights attaching to the share categories.

Alteration of the Articles

Once the company has been incorporated the articles may be altered or added to by means of a special resolution which requires a 75% majority of the members voting in favour of it. No such resolution is necessary if there is unanimous agreement of the members to the proposed alteration: *Cane v. Jones* 1980. Alterations must however be made *bona fide*, that is in good faith, and for the benefit of the company as a whole. This is an important aspect of the law regulating companies, for articles constitute a contract between the company and its members and identify members' rights, such as the right to vote. Clearly the ability of the company to change the terms of this contract at some future time may have the effect of placing individual members who might be harmed by such changes, in a disadvantageous position. Thus the courts reserve the power to refuse an alteration to the articles which has such an effect, unless there is a benefit to the company as a whole and the alteration has been made in good faith. This principle is best appreciated by looking at some of the caselaw on the subject.

> In the leading case, *Allen v. Gold Reefs of West Africa* 1900 the articles of the company which already granted it a lien on partly paid shares to cover any liabilities owed to it by a member, were altered by extending the lien to holders of fully paid shares as well. A lien is simply a charge on shares, enabling the company to sell the shares in order to meet the debts owed to it by the members. Here a shareholder who at the time of his death held both fully and partly paid shares in the company and owed the company money for the partly paid shares, was also the only holder of fully paid shares. His executors challenged the alteration on the grounds of bad faith, but the court upheld the alteration. There was no evidence that the company was attempting to discriminate against the deceased personally; it was simply

chance that he was the only holder of fully paid shares. In the words of Lord Lindley, *"The altered articles applied to all holders of fully paid shares and made no distinction between them."*

It seems that the test which should be applied is whether the proposal is in the honest opinion of those voting for it, for the benefit of the members. An alteration may be challenged if it is, *"so oppressive as to cast suspicion on the honesty of the persons responsible for it, or so extravagant that no reasonable men could really consider it for the benefit of the company."* (Bankes L.J. in *Shuttleworth v. Cox Bros. & Co. (Maidenhead) Ltd.* 1927). If it can be established that the alteration has the effect of discriminating between members, granting advantages to the majority which are denied to the minority then a challenge will normally be successful, although an alteration may be upheld as bona fide even though the members voting for it are improving their own personal prospects.

In *Greenhalgh v. Arderne Cinemas Ltd.* 1951 the articles of company, which prohibited the transfer of shares to a non member as long as an existing member was willing to pay a fair price for them, were altered to enable a transfer of shares to anyone by means of an ordinary resolution passed in a general meeting. The alteration was made because the majority shareholder wished to transfer his shares to a non member. This was held to be a valid alteration.

The courts will also uphold alterations which cause direct prejudice to individual members, as long as they are shown to be alterations made in good faith, and in the company's interest.

In *Sidebottom v. Kershaw Leese & Co.* 1920 an alteration was made enabling the directors, who were the majority shareholders, to request the transfer to their nominees at a fair value the shares of any member competing with the company's business. The court found this to be a valid and proper alteration for, in the words of Lord Sterndale M R, *"it is for the benefit of the company that they should not be obliged to have amongst them as members, persons who are competing with them in business and who may get knowledge from their membership which would enable them to compete better."*

By way of contrast in *Brown v. British Abrasive Wheel Co.* 1919 a majority of the shareholders (98%) were willing to provide the company with much needed extra capital if they could buy the 2% minority interest. As the minority were unwilling to sell, the majority proposed to alter the articles so as to enable nine-tenths of the shareholders to buy out any other shareholders. The plaintiff, representing the minority, brought an action to restrain the majority. It was held by the Court that the alteration would be restrained as it was not for the benefit of the company as a whole but rather for the benefit of the majority shareholding, and was in any case too wide a power and was therefore unlawful as constituting a potential fraud on the members.

In addition the following common law and statutory conditions apply to an alteration:

(i) it must be lawful, that is not be in conflict with the Act or with the general law;

(ii) it must not create a conflict between the memorandum and the articles. If this does occur the provisions of the memorandum will prevail for it is the superior document;

(iii) it will require the leave of the court in certain circumstances. These are where a minority of members have applied to the court for the cancellation of an alteration to the objects clause (s.5), where there has been an application for the cancellation of a resolution of a public company to re-register as a private company (s.54), or where a petition has been presented to the court on the ground that the affairs of the company are being conducted in a manner unfairly prejudicial to some part of the membership (s.461);

(iv) if it involves an increase in a members liability it will only be valid if the member has given a written consent (s.16);

(v) if it affects the rights attached to a particular class of shares (i.e. *class rights*) it is subject to the capacity of dissentient members - those disagreeing with the change - to apply to the court for a cancellation. This power is available to 15% or more of the holders of the shares who did not give their consent, and it must be exercised within 21 days.

The Statutory Contract

The rule that the articles and the memorandum of a company constitute a binding contract between the company and its members is contained in s.14 of the 1985 Act. It is a provision which has caused some difficulty for the courts in the past, in their attempts at precisely identifying its effects. The section states that the company and its members are bound to each other as though each shareholder has covenanted to observe the provisions of the memorandum and articles, the *statutory contract.* It also provides that any money owed by a member to the company is a speciality debt. This means the company has twelve years in which to recover the debt. In the case of debts arising from a simple contract the period would otherwise be six years.

The effect of the articles can be summarised as follows:

(a) The company is bound to the members in their capacity as members, and they are bound to it in the same way.

An illustration of this principle is provided by *Salmon v. Quin & Axtens Ltd.* 1909. Here the articles gave directors full management powers, but prevented the directors from purchasing or letting any premises if the managing director dissented. The directors however resolved to deal in premises, despite the dissent of the managing director, and an extraordinary meeting of shareholders affirmed this action by a simple majority. The managing director sought an order from the court that the resolutions were invalid. The Court of Appeal agreed. The resolutions conflicted with the articles, and the company was bound by the articles. It could be restrained from its proposed action.

In *Hickman v. Kent or Romney Marsh Sheepbreeders Association* 1915 the articles of the association stipulated that disputes between itself and its members should be referred to arbitration. The plaintiff, a member, brought court action against the association in relation to a number of matters. It was held that in accordance with the articles these matters must be referred to arbitration.

(b) The members are contractually bound to each other, under the terms of the articles.

Generally it is not possible for an individual member to enforce the contract in his own name against another member, although exceptionally this may be possible if the articles grant him a personal right.

The position is illustrated in the case of *Rayfield v. Hands* 1960. A clause in the articles of a private company stated, *"Every member who intends to transfer shares shall inform the directors who will take the said shares equally between them at a fair value."* The plaintiff notified the defendant directors of his intention to transfer his shares, however they denied any liability to take and pay for them. The court held they were obliged to do so, firstly because of their binding obligation indicated by the word "will" and secondly because the clause was a term of the contractual relationship between the plaintiff and the directors as company members.

The position regarding the contractual position as between the members themselves is dealt with more fully later (see *Foss v. Harbottle* 1834).

Controlling the company

It is relevant to point out in the context of alteration of the articles that a company has two principal sources of control over its affairs. These are the shareholders in general meeting and the directors. The most important matters affecting the company, for example changes in its constitution, rest with the shareholders in general meeting. Decisions reached at such meetings are arrived at through the putting of resolutions, which are then voted on. Generally a simple majority vote is sufficient to carry them, although some matters of special significance require a 75% majority. Since voting power plays such an important role in company matters the type of shares the company has issued is of considerable significance. Some shares, for example ordinary shares, usually carry full voting rights.

However other classes of share, such as preference shares, may carry no voting rights at all and therefore exclude shareholders of that class from effectively influencing the company in its decision making.

Since all public companies and many private companies consist of numerous members it is impractical to operate the company on a daily basis by means of general meetings. The articles will therefore provide for directors to be responsible for the daily running of the company and usually grant them the right to exercise all the powers of the company. They will remain answerable to the members in a general meeting although acts carried out by the directors within the powers delegated to them under the articles cannot be affected by decisions of a general meeting. So, if the directors have acted contrary to the wishes of the members, the ultimate sanction is to dismiss them or to change the articles and so bring in provisions that restrict the powers of the directors. In small companies the directors will often be the principal or only shareholders, so that such considerations will not be relevant.

Other registration documents

In addition to the memorandum and articles of association there are certain other documents which must be supplied to the Registrar prior to incorporation. These include a Statutory Declaration that all the requirements of the Act have been complied with. Fees must also be paid.

Having examined all the documents filed and ensured that they are in order, the Registrar then issues a certificate under official seal which certifies that the company is incorporated. The certificate is conclusive evidence that all the requirements of the Companies Act 1985 have been complied with and that the company is a company authorised to be registered and duly registered under the Act. A private company can enter into contracts, borrow money, and carry on business immediately on incorporation. However a public limited company registered under the 1985 Act cannot commence business until a certificate is issued by the Registrar that the share capital of the company is not less than the authorised minimum (i.e. £50,000 with at least one-quarter paid up). If more than a year after the incorporation of a public company it has not been issued with such a certificate the Secretary of State may petition the court for the company to be wound up.

The Holding of Company Meetings and the Maintenance of Records

Meetings

We have seen that a partnership is subject to few statutory regulations and the partners are free to decide for themselves such matters as the conduct of meetings, the keeping of records and accounting methods.

Registered companies limited by shares however, are different. The fundamental principle of accountability of the directors to the members necessarily involves stricter regulation of the company's operation. The Companies Act 1985 provides therefore that every company must, in each year, hold an annual general meeting and that every member is entitled to notice of this meeting. In addition, the holders of one-tenth or more of paid-up shares with voting rights may at any time compel the directors to call an extra-ordinary general meeting. The articles usually regulate the procedures to be adopted at these meetings, but in any case the minutes of all meetings must be strictly recorded.

Decisions at general meetings are usually taken by ordinary resolution, that is a simple majority of voting members present. For some types of business, usually related to the company's constitution such as the alteration of the articles or objects of the company, a special resolution is necessary which requires a three-quarter majority of voting members.

Types	Business	When called	Notice
Annual General Meeting	**Declaring dividends, Directors'and Auditors' Reports, Appointment of Directors**	**Within 18 months of incorporation then once a year with no more than 15 months between each**	**At least 21 days Items of ordinary business need not be mentioned in notice**
Extraordinary General Meeting	**All business is 'special' eg. alteration of articles, memorandum, removal of Directors**	**Whenever Directors think fit, or if demanded by holders of one tenth or more of paid up shares.**	**At least 14 days If called by members, they must state why they want it**

Figure 3.6 *Form of Meetings*

Type	Majority	Notice	Use
Ordinary	**Simple ie over 50%**	**At the meeting**	**For matters not covered below**
Extraordinary	**75% of votes cast**	**At the time the meeting was called**	**Where required by the Companies Act or the articles**
Special	**75% of votes cast**	**21 days**	**Where required by law**
Elective and written	**Unanimous approval**		**For deregulation purposes**

Figure 3.7 *Resolutions*

Maintaining records

Each year a company must submit an annual report to the Registrar of Companies which has to include details of the company's share capital, share division, debts secured by mortgages, and a list of members and directors. Also company legislation contains detailed provisions relating to the preparation of accounts, the information to be included in these accounts, and the need for submission of annual accounts to the general meeting and the Registrar of Companies. Generally the accounting records must be kept at the registered office of the company and must be available for inspection by shareholders. Company accounts must also be audited, and the auditor's report must be read out to the company in general meeting, and must be open to inspection by any member. Other documents which a company is obliged to keep include a register of the interests of directors and their service contracts, a register of the company members and debenture holders, and a register of members who have substantial interests in the company, that is, of those who have one-tenth or more of the share capital of the company.

These requirements not only ensure the members are kept informed, but also assist outsiders in assessing the strength of the company prior to investing in it or doing business with it. Investment in a company can be undertaken in two ways:

(a) By lending money to the company in return for an issue of debentures. A debenture holder is a secured creditor of the company who is entitled to a fixed rate of interest on the investment.

(b) By taking up shares and becoming a company member. The rights of a shareholder depend upon the type of shares involved but generally a shareholder has the right to receive a proportion of the profits of a company, vote in general meetings and share in the capital of the company if it is wound up.

Financing a Limited Company

There are various methods used by companies to raise capital, the issue of shares and debentures being two of the most significant methods. Before considering them in more detail, it will be helpful to recap and expand upon the meaning of the expression 'capital' which we encountered earlier in the chapter whilst examining the contents of the memorandum of association. Capital is unfortunately a broad expression carrying a number of meanings, however in relation to limited companies the following are the most common uses of the expression:

(i) *Nominal (or authorised) capital*
This expression refers to the value of shares that a company is authorised to issue, and is included in the capital clause of its memorandum of association.

(ii) *Issued capital*
This refers to the value of capital in the form of shares which have been actually issued to the shareholders.

(iii) *Paid-up capital*
This is the amount of capital which has actually been paid up on the shares issued, or the amount of capital that the company has actually raised and received. Under s.351 Companies Act 1985 if a company makes a reference to share capital on its business stationery or order forms, it must refer to its paid-up capital.

(iv) *Unpaid capital*
If shares which have been issued are not fully paid for, the amount outstanding is referred to as unpaid capital, e.g. if 5,000 shares issued have a nominal value of £1 each and only 50p has been paid up on them, then the paid up capital is £2,500 and the unpaid capital is £2,500. Shareholders may be required to pay up the unpaid amount on their shares by the company making a 'call' on them to do so.

(v) *Reserve capital*
A company, by special resolution (75% majority vote) may declare that any portion of its unpaid capital shall not be called up except if the company is being brought to an end by a winding up. This is called reserve capital and cannot be converted into ordinary capital for use in the operation of the company without the court's permission.

It is important to remember that the references to capital being made here are to share capital. The law regards capital as something positive, a financial contribution to the company which it can use for the purpose of its business. For instance it purchases business premises, which are then regarded as fixed capital, and stock, which becomes circulating capital. Accountants see capital in a different way. They regard it as something the company owes: the members are owed the company's share capital; the debenture holders are owed the loan capital. To the economist capital again has a different meaning. In the context of any discussion concerning capital it is clearly important to establish in which sense the term is being used. Here we are using the term in the legal sense.

Shares

The nature of shares has been considered both by Parliament and the courts. Thus s.182 Companies Act 1985 provides that shares are personal property and that they are transferrable in accordance with the provisions in the articles, whilst in *Borland's Trustee v. Steel Bros. & Co. Ltd.* 1901 Farwell J stated that; *"A share is the interest of a shareholder in the company measured by a sum of money, for the purpose of liability in the first place, and of interest in the second".* This is a helpful definition. It indicates that a member:

(i) has a liability to pay the company, which arises when he applies for the shares, or when they are allotted to him, or when having received them he is called upon to pay for them; and

(ii) has an interest in the company which grants him rights. These rights are determined by the class or type of shares he acquires and what the articles identify as the rights attached to the class, such as voting rights, and rights to dividends. Whatever these rights may be the shareholder is a part owner of the company. It is of course impossible to say which part is owned. The shareholders collectively own the undertaking of the company, and the company is a single person, thus the company is in effect the agent of the shareholders. It is they who ultimately determine the actions of the company through shareholders' meetings. Invariably the company will appoint directors to carry out the management of the company. The directors will be responsible to the shareholders for their actions,and in carrying out the business of the company will themselves be agents of it (see Figure 3.8). A private company must have at least one director, and a public company at least two.

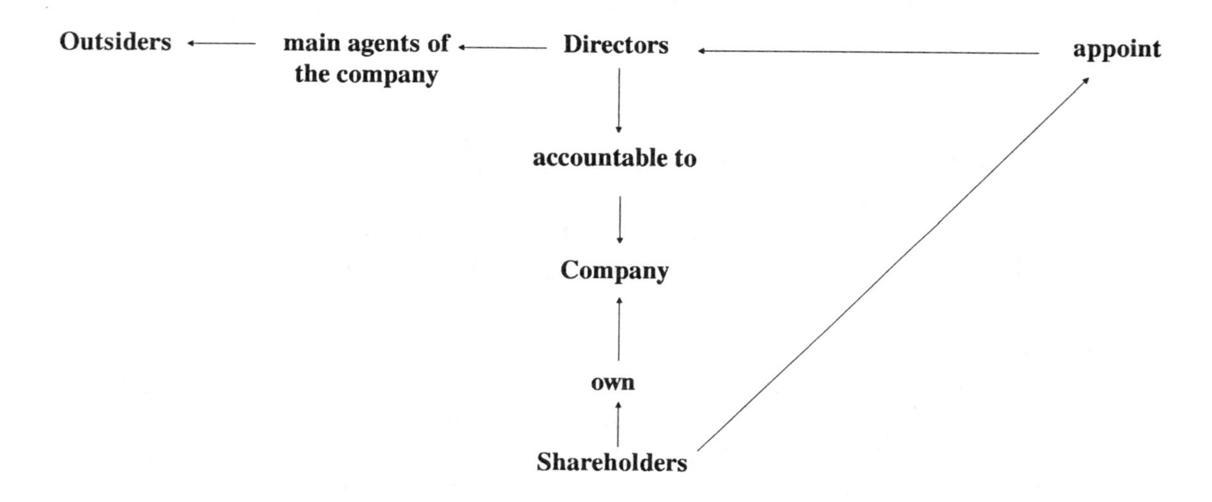

Figure 3.8 *Shareholders as Company Controllers*

A shareholder can transfer his shares by selling them or giving them away, for instance as a gift during his lifetime or under his will after his death. S.183 Companies Act 1985 requires a *"proper instrument of transfer"* to be delivered to the company for a valid assignment of ownership to occur. All this means is that a written document is necessary. It does not need to be a deed unless the articles require one. The shareholders' document of title to the shares is a share certificate, issued by the company. The shareholder obtains legal title to the shares when his name is entered by the company onto its register of shareholders. The share certificate is a document of considerable importance. Although physically transferring it from one person to another does not pass legal ownership in the shares (registration is required), s.186 of the 1985 Act states that the certificate is prima facie evidence of the shareholder's ownership in the shares. It is in other words a statement by the company that at the time it was issued the person named on it was the owner, and had paid for the shares to the extent stated. The company is bound by this statement in respect of those who have relied upon its accuracy.

Classes of shares

There is nothing to prevent a registered company limited by shares from issuing one class of shares with equal rights. Usually, however, different classes of shares are issued with varying rights attaching to them relating to such matters as voting, payment of dividends and return of capital on liquidation. The three main types of shares are:

(a) *Preference shares*
The main characteristic of a preference share is that it will have the right to a preferred fixed dividend. This means that the holder of a preference share is entitled to a fixed amount of dividend, e.g. 6% on the value of each share, before other shareholders are paid any dividend. They are presumed to be cumulative which means that if in any year the company fails to declare a dividend, the shortfall must be made up out of profits of subsequent years. A preference share is therefore a safe investment with fixed interest, no matter how small or large is the company's profit. As far as return of capital on a winding up is concerned, the preference shareholder will rank equally with ordinary shareholders for any payment due, unless the preference shares are made 'preferential as to capital'. Normally, preference shares do not carry voting rights and therefore the preference shareholder has little influence over the company's activities.

(b) *Ordinary shares*
Ordinary shares are often referred to as the *equity share capital* of a company. When a company declares a dividend and the preference shareholders have been paid, the holders of ordinary shares are entitled to the remainder.It follows therefore that an ordinary shareholder in a well-managed company making high profits will receive a good return on his investment and consequently the value of his shares will rise, e.g. a £1 ordinary share could have a market value of £1.25. Unfortunately, the reverse is also true and they may fall in market value so that ordinary shares inevitably involve a certain risk. This risk is reflected in the amount of control that an ordinary shareholder has over the company's business. While voting rights are not normally attached to preference shares, they are attached to ordinary shares enabling the ordinary shareholder to voice an opinion in a general meeting and vote on major issues involving the running of the company. Ordinary shareholders will thus have the capacity to remove directors who have mismanaged the business of the company. An ordinary resolution is required in order to do so.

(c) *Founders shares (or deferred ordinary shares)*
Such shares are now uncommon but were originally granted to the founders of a company, the company promoters. Their main characteristics was to confer on the holder the right to the remainder of the distributed profit after a dividend had been paid on the ordinary shares.

A private company, it will be recalled, is unable to issue its shares publicly. If it does so it loses its status as a private company. A public limited company can publicly advertise its shares which it may do either to acquire initial capital or more commonly to increase its existing capital. The methods used by a public limited company to raise capital from the public are:

(i) through direct invitation to the public, through the issue of a prospectus;

(ii) by an offer for sale. This involves the company selling the total number of shares it hopes to issue to an organisation which specialises in financial transactions of this kind. Such organisations are known, not surprisingly, as 'issuing houses'. They resell to the public at a higher price, by publishing a document called an 'offer for sale', which contains an application form for the prospective shareholder to complete and return to the issuing house; and

(iii) by placing. Again an issuing house is involved. It may subscribe for the share issued itself, reselling as in (ii) usually inviting its own clients to purchase the shares, or it may simply seek persons interested in purchasing the shares acting merely as an agent for the company, which will pay a fee for the service provided. This is called 'brokerage'. The most common method used is (ii) above.

There are detailed legal provisions dealing with the public sale of shares. They are designed to protect the investing public, and are contained in the Financial Services Act 1986. One of the most important features of this statutory protection relates to the obligation on the company to disclose specific information of relevance to investors in reaching a decision as to whether to buy. Aspects of this protection are considered in Chapter 6.

Shareholders' rights - majority rule, minority protection

As we have already seen the rights enjoyed by a member of a company are primarily contractual, arising from the class of shares acquired and the rights attached to them as specified in the articles. Unlike a partner, who will always possess the right to take part in the management of the firm, a shareholder will not always be involved in the daily management of the company, unless the organisation has a very small membership and its shareholders are also its directors. Companies' articles usually confer power on directors to operate the business, which they will perform on behalf of the members. The effect of such an arrangement is that ownership and management are separated. Nevertheless, ultimate control of the business is in the hands of the shareholders by the exercise of voting power in the general meeting. Where appropriate they can vote to remove a director.

In any vote which does not produce a unanimous outcome there will be two groups, the majority shareholders and the minority shareholders. In effect it is the majority that make the company decisions. If the minority have a grievance, legally there is little they can do to redress it. The courts have been reluctant to assist minority shareholders who are claiming they have been oppressed or have had their interests prejudiced by the majority. Since it is the majority who rule the company it is not for the court to thwart their actions. If the minority are arguing that the majority have acted in breach of the memorandum or the articles, then it is a wrong which has been done to the company. The proper plaintiff is the company itself, not the minority shareholders. Of course they will find it impossible to pass a resolution that the company sue the majority, for the voting strength of the majority will be sufficient to block such a move. This leaves the minority in a very vunerable position.

The case of *Foss v. Harbottle* 1843 laid down as a general principle that the courts will not interfere in the internal management of a company at the insistence of the minority shareholders. Here an action had been brought by the minority alleging that the directors were responsible for losses that had occurred when they sold some of their own land to the company,at what was alleged to be an over valuation. The Court held that the action must fail as the proper plaintiff in such circumstances was the company itself. As the action to which the minority shareholders objected could have been ratified by the majority then it was the majority shareholders who should decide whether an action should be brought in the company name. The Court saw no merit in interfering in the internal management of a company by passing judgment on its commercial decisions.

In *Pavlides v. Jenson and others* 1956, a company sold an asbestos mine for £182,000 when its real value was close to £1,000,000. A minority shareholder brought an action for damages against three directors who were responsible for the sale and against the company, alleging gross negligence. The Court held that the action could not be brought by a minority shareholder because it was the company itself which should decide whether to redress the wrong that had been committed.

Thus the process of incorporation, having invested a company with a separate legal personality, dictates that the company and individual members are separate. If a wrong is committed against the company it is the company, by virtue of a decision made by the Board of Directors that should seek redress for it.

The rule in *Foss v. Harbottle* does not however apply to every type of action taken by the majority. In certain situations the court will hear a claim brought by minority shareholders, even though the majority do not wish it. Thus:

(a) proposed ultra vires activities can be restrained, even by a member holding a single share;

(b) where directors attempt to do something requiring a special resolution (i.e. a $\frac{3}{4}$ majority and prior notice) which they do not obtain, then action cannot be ratified by an ordinary resolution (i.e. a simple majority). Were this to be otherwise, the protection for minorities granted in circumstances where a $\frac{3}{4}$ majority is needed would be avoided;

(c) where a wrong is suffered to a member in his personal capacity, through the action of the directors.

For instance in *Pender v. Lushington* 1877 the company chairman wrongfully refused to accept the votes cast by certain shareholders. The resolution they opposed was in consequence able to be carried. The Court held that the company could be restrained from carrying out the proposed resolution;

(d) when a fraud has been committed against the minority. This does not mean fraud in the criminal sense, rather conduct which is grossly unfair.

An example is provided by *Daniels v. Daniels* 1978. Here two company directors, in 1970, instructed the company to sell land to one of them for £4,250. In 1974 the land was resold for £120,000 and a minority shareholder brought an action claiming that damages should be payable to the company. The Court held that despite no allegation of fraud the action by the individual shareholders should be allowed to proceed.

In addition to the common law, the Companies Act 1985 confers certain statutory rights on minority shareholders.

An important example of this is s.459 which gives a member the right to apply to the court for an order on the ground that the affairs of the company are being or have been conducted in a manner which is unfairly prejudicial to some members (including at least himself), or that any actual or proposed act or omission of the company is or would be prejudicial.

If the case is proved the court may issue an order to:

(i) regulate the company's affairs for the future;

(ii) require the company to act or refrain from acting in a particular way;

(iii) authorise civil proceedings in the name and on behalf of the company by a person; or

(iv) require the purchase of any member's shares by the company or by other members.

> An example of a court order regulating a company's future affairs is seen in Re: *H R Harmer Limited* 1959. The company was run by an elderly father acting as chairman and his two sons as directors. The father had voting control. He largely ignored the wishes of the board of directors and ran the business as his own. On an application by the sons as minority shareholders, alleging oppression, the Court held that relief should be granted. The father was appointed life president of the company without rights, duties or powers and was ordered not to interfere with the company's affairs.

Debentures

A trading company may, as an alternative to a share issue, raise money by means of issuing a debenture or series of debentures. These may be secured by a charge or be unsecured. The definition of 'debenture' is very wide and includes all forms of securities (undertakings to repay money borrowed) which may or may not be secured by a charge on the company's assets. Indeed a mortgage of the company's property to a single individual may be regarded as a debenture within the definition. Debentures are usually made by means of a trust deed which will create a *fixed* charge over specific company property by mortgage and/or a *floating* charge over the rest of the company assets. The distinction between a fixed and floating charge is essentially that a company is not free to deal with assets subject to a fixed charge, i.e. by selling or mortgaging, but is free to deal with any of its assets covered by a floating charge. However, on the occurrence of a particular event, a floating charge is said to crystallise and is then converted into a fixed charge. Such an event occurs when money becomes payable under a condition in the debenture such as repayment of interest, and the debenture holder takes some steps to enforce his security because the interest due is unpaid.

The principal rights of a debenture holder are contained in the debenture deed. They will include:

(i) the date of repayment of the loan and the rate of interest;

(ii) a statement of the assets of the company which are subject to fixed or floating charges;

(iii) the rights of the company to redeem the whole or part of the monies owing;

(iv) the circumstances in which the loan becomes immediately repayable, i.e. if the company defaults in repayment of interest;

(v) the powers of the debenture holder to appoint a receiver and manager of the assets charged.

Other Forms of Financing

Loans

All trading companies have an implied power to borrow finance for the purposes of their business activities. In the case of non-trading companies, there is no such power unless expressly provided for in the memorandum of association. Power to borrow money is usually conferred on the company directors in the articles of association. However there is nothing to prevent a company from restricting its own borrowing powers to a specific amount stated in the memorandum, e.g. borrow an amount which is no more than two-thirds of the value of the company's paid-up capital. If a power to borrow has been conferred, then this will also carry with it an implied power to offer company property as security for a loan. If a company has power to borrow money, the lender is under no obligation to discover the purpose for which the money is to be used.

In the short term, registered companies make use of overdraft facilities offered by the commercial banks to finance a temporary cash flow difficulty. This type of borrowing is increasingly used during temporary financial and economic recession, when the cash receipts of the company are anticipated to rise in the future.

Longer term loans may be borrowed either through the commercial banks or on the capital market and are normally secured against some collateral offered by the company which may be realised by the lender in the event of a default on the loan.

Factoring

A further means of raising capital open to organisations facing a cash flow problem is factoring. Essentially this means that an organisation with outstanding monies owed to it, sells the right to this money to a factor (an organisation willing to provide immediate cash in return for the right to collect and keep the monies owed from the organisation's debtors). The factor will usually pay the organisation less than the face value of the debts and so if the debt can be collected in full, this percentage is the factor's profit on the transaction.

The acquisition of assets

It may be briefly noted here that a limited company is able to acquire property and property rights in the same way as an individual. As well as purchasing property outright, companies frequently take leased property such as vehicles and land under which they acquire limited rights of ownership. They also obtain goods on credit terms, for example by hiring equipment. The legal considerations applying to such arrangements are examined in detail later in the book.

Management of the Company

The position of directors

The management of a registered company is carried on by the directors who are responsible for policy making, contract making and supervising the company property. Company directors are normally appointed in a manner prescribed in the articles of association, for example by the company in general meeting or by the existing directors. The Companies Act 1985 (s 303) specifically provides, however, that despite anything in the articles to the contrary, a director may be removed by an ordinary resolution. There is nothing to prevent the articles conferring special voting rights on certain occasions.

> In *Bushell v. Faith* 1970 the company had an issued share capital of £300 equally divided between three members. Each share carried one vote. The articles provided, however, that on a resolution to remove a director, the directors' individual shares should carry three votes per share. Two of the members voted to remove the third from his position as director but were defeated because their 200 votes were cancelled by the individual director's 300 votes. The Court held this to be in order.

Directors' powers and duties

The specific powers of directors are stated in the articles but in addition to this actual authority to carry out functions, the directors will also have an authority to act which is implied under the law. This is because the director is an agent of the company and can bind it whether he acts within his actual or apparent authority.

It is important to be aware of the two issues which emerge here:

(a) what the contractual capacity of the company is; and

(b) what the agency powers of the directors are.

As we have previously seen, at one time there was no question in law of a director, or indeed the full board, being able legitimately to make a contract outside the objects of the company, even if the company itself had attempted to authorise such action. It was ultra vires and beyond the company's, and therefore the directors', powers. Since the Companies Act 1989, other than in special circumstances, a company will be held bound by an ultra vires contract. It is within the capacity of directors to bind the company to an outsider in this way. However in such circumstances the directors will be responsible to the company for such action. They should know the limitations imposed upon their own company's contractual capacity by its constitution. Indeed the 1989 Act specifically states that it is the duty of directors to observe such limitations. Thus the company may seek a remedy against a director for a breach of such a duty, and perhaps seek to remove the director from the board.

> In addition the rule in *Royal British Bank v. Turquand* 1856 which was discussed earlier in the chapter, established that where a company acting through its board has failed to comply with its own internal rules, this will not invalidate the transaction. Here a company conferred power on the directors to borrow such sums as were authorised by an ordinary resolution of the general meeting. The directors borrowed money without such a resolution being passed. The Court held that the company was bound by the loan and laid down the following basic principles:

(i) An outsider who is dealing with a company is not bound to inquire whether the internal regulations of the company have been complied with, such as passing resolutions to authorise specific acts. Basically, therefore, an outsider is entitled to assume that the directors have acted properly.

(ii) An outsider is not entitled to rely on this presumption if he is aware of the irregularity or ought in the circumstances to have made inquiries.

Turquand is now replaced by the provisions of the 1989 Act which indicate that an outsider is deemed to be acting in good faith. Thus as an agent a director will not be capable of binding the company where he acts outside his actual or apparent authority and the outsider is or ought reasonably to be aware that he has exceeded his authority.

This aspect of the principle can be seen operating in the following cases.

> In *Howard v. Patent Ivory Manufacturing Co.* 1888 the directors of the company had power to borrow up to £1,000, with larger amounts having to be authorised by the general meeting. The company borrowed £3,500 from the directors without a resolution being passed. The court held that as the directors were aware of the procedural irregularity the borrowing was only valid up to £1,000.

> In *Underwood Ltd. v. Bank of Liverpool* 1924 the director of a company paid cheques, made payable to the company, into his personal account. An action was brought against the bank to recover the sums paid. The court held that the bank was not entitled to assume that the director was acting properly, as the circumstances were so unusual that the bank ought to have been suspicious.

Even if an individual has not been actually appointed as director or managing director, should the company, through the directors, expressly or impliedly represent him as such, then as far as the outsider is concerned the individual will have all the apparent authority of a director.

> In *Freeman Lockyer v. Buckhurst Properties* 1964 an individual director, with the consent of his fellow directors, employed the plaintiff architects to do some work. The director had been held out as managing director although he had not been appointed to this post, and the contract of employment was held to be binding. To enter into such a contract was within the apparent scope of a managing director's power.

Since it is the directors who are responsible for managing the company, it is of great concern to establish what they are legally capable of carrying out in the company's name, and to what extent they are accountable to the company for their actions.

Their powers are conferred on them by the articles, and in general these powers cannot be removed from them by resolution in a general meeting. Alteration of the articles themselves will be necessary.

The Companies Act 1985 does not define the term 'director' in a way which is very helpful. It says simply, a director is *"any person occupying the position of director, by whatever name called"*. This is contained in s. 741. The courts however have provided some useful indications as to the nature of the director, variously describing such a person as a trustee, agent and managing partner.

> However Lord Jessel stated in Re: *Forest of Dean Coal Mining Co.* 1878, *"It does not matter much what you call them, so long as you understand what their true position is which is that they are merely commercial men, managing a trading concern for the benefit of themselves and all other shareholders in it"*.

It is clear that a director stands in a fiduciary capacity to the company, and like an agent for a principal, must act in good faith and not make personal use of his position. The nature of a director's fiduciary duty can be broken down into the following components:

(a) A director must act bona fide in what he considers is the interest of the company

The powers that are invested in directors are to be used for the benefit of the company as a whole, that is all the shareholders, rather than some sectional interest such as a class of shareholders, the company employees, the directors, a holding or subsidiary company. Thus a breach of duty will occur where the directors:

(i) issue new shares to themselves, not because the company needs more capital but merely to increase their voting power.

In *Piercy v. S. Mills & Co. Ltd.* 1920 the directors used their powers to issue new voting shares to themselves, solely to acquire majority voting power. The Court held that the directors had abused their powers and the allotment was declared void;

(ii) approve a transfer of their own partly-paid shares to escape liability for a call they intend to make. A call is a request for payment on the shares.

In *Alexander v. Automatic Telephone Co.* 1900 the directors used their position to require all shareholders to pay 3s 6d on each share excluding themselves. The Court held that his was a clear abuse of power and the directors were required to pay to the company the same amount;

(iii) negotiate a new service agreement between the company and its managing director simply in order to confer additional benefits on him or his dependents.

In Re: *W and M Roith* 1967 it was held that a new service contract negotiated between a managing director and his company was unlawful as it was solely to make a pension provision for his widow and that no regard had been taken as to whether this was for the benefit of the company;

(iv) abdicate responsibility for the running of the company and appoint a manager with full powers (i.e. no board control), or obey the majority shareholder without exercising their own judgment or discretion;

(v) being directors of a subsidiary company use their powers exclusively in the interests of the holding company to the detriment of the minority shareholders of the subsidiary.

(b) A director must not place himself in a position where there is likely to be conflict between personal interests and duty to the company.

Directors act as agents on behalf of the company they represent and in such a capacity they must not enter into engagements where there is, or is likely to be, a conflict between the interests of the company and their own personal interests. The Companies Act therefore requires a director to give notice at the board meeting of a personal interest - direct or indirect - in any contracts or proposed contracts in which the company is involved. Failure to disclose such an interest can result in fines being imposed. In addition any director who uses position to make personal profit may be made to account for such a profit to the company.

In *Cook v. Deeks* 1916 the directors of a railway company having negotiated a contract on behalf of the company decided to make the contract in their own names. The Court held that the benefit of the contract belonged to the company and the directors should account to the company for any profit made. The extent of the duty is also illustrated by the case of *Regal Hastings v. Gulliver* 1942. Here the company owned a cinema and decided to purchase two others with the intention of selling the whole undertaking as a going concern. A subsidiary company was formed which acquired the other cinemas, however the shares of the subsidiary were allocated between the company and its directors. Following a sale of the whole undertaking, involving a transfer of the shares of the company and its subsidiary the purchasers brought an action to recover the profit on the sale by the directors of their shares in the subsidiary. Despite the fact that the purchasers had freely agreed to pay the share price, the House of Lords held that the former directors must deliver up to the company the profit they had made. It was by the use of their special knowledge and opportunities as directors that they had made the profit.

If a director uses his position to make a secret profit for himself, he will be in breach of his contract of employment, and may also be made to hand over such profit to the company.

In *Boston Deep Sea Fishing & Ice Co. v. Ansell* 1888 the managing director of a trawling business received a secret commission on placing an order for the construction of fishing boats. The Court held that the company was entitled to the commission.

It seems that a director will remain accountable even where the company has not sustained a loss.

In *Industrial Development Consultants and Cooley* 1972 the defendant acted as the managing director of a design company. In this capacity he tried to obtain some design work for the company from the Eastern Gas Board. The Board indicated to him that they were not prepared to give his company the work. Realising he might gain a contract for himself he left his company on the pretence of being close to a nervous breakdown. He set up his own company and secured the gas board contract. It was held that he must account to his former company for the profit he had made, despite the fact that it was most unlikely the company would ever have obtained the work for itself.

The Financial Services Act 1986 makes it a criminal offence for an *"insider"*, that is an individual connected with a company as a director, officer, employee or someone having a professional or business relationship with it, to deal on a recognised stock exchange in the company's shares in prescribed circumstances. These are that the insider has information obtained through his connection with the company which it would be reasonable to expect him not to disclose and which he knows to be price sensitive unpublished information. Obviously many people who deal with and work in companies are ideally placed to either purchase or dispose of shares having obtained confidential information about such matters as possible takeovers, trading difficulties and so on. A person who receives information from an insider, a *tippee*, may also commit an offence if it has been knowingly obtained.

In Re: *Attorney General's Reference (No1 of 1988)* 1989 the Court decided that a person can be said to have 'obtained' insider information regarding a company even where it has been volunteered to him, without him seeking it out. If such a person goes on to deal an offence is committed under the 1986 Act.

The Criminal Justice Act 1988 provides for a maximum penalty of seven years and/or an unlimited fine. To eliminate needless prosecutions proceedings can only be brought by the Secretary of State, or someone authorised by the Secretary of State such as the Stock Exchange. A prosecution may also be brought by or with the consent of the Director of Public Prosecutions.

A further duty imposed upon a director is the common law obligation to exercise care and skill in performing his work. This duty is variable one. In Re: *City Equitable Fire Insurance Co. Ltd.* 1925 Romer J commented:

> *"The position of a director of a company carrying on a small retail business is very different from that of a director of a railway company. The duties of a bank director may differ widely from those of an insurance director, and the duties of a director of one insurance company may differ from those of another ... The larger the business carried on by the Company the more numerous, and the more important the matters that must of necessity be left to the managers, the accountants and the rest of the staff".*

Provided the directors act honestly this will normally be sufficient to fulfil the duty.

> In Re: *New Marshonaland Exploration Co.* 1892 the directors approved a loan of £1,250 and failed to ensure that security was given. The Court held that in the absence of fraud the directors were not liable for this *"error of judgment"*.

> In Re: *Denham & Co.* 1883 a situation had arisen where, for four years, a company's dividend was negligently paid out of capital. As the powers of management of the company had been vested in one individual, another director who rarely attended board meetings and had no reason to suspect misconduct, was held not liable for the negligence.

Clearly however there are circumstances in which a director can fall short of what the law expects. The standard of care is a subjective one that is of a variable standard based upon the skill and knowledge of the individual in question. A highly paid professional director of a public limited company is expected to demonstrate a high level of business acumen.

Even non executive directors with experience or qualifications in areas of relevance to the work of their company may find high objective standards appropriate to their specialism being expected of them in law.

> In *Dorchester Finance Co. Ltd. v. Stebbing* 1989 the company lost money as the result of gross negligence committed by the company's sole executive director. He had failed to take out adequate securities on loans made by the company, as a result of which it found itself unable to recover the money advanced. The two non executive directors, who had little to do with the company, had signed cheques in blank at the executive directors request. All three men had considerable financial experience. The Court held the two non executive directors equally liable with the executive director to the company in damages.

Persons who may not be appointed

Table A contains no restrictions on who may be appointed as a director, although articles may be drafted to include such restrictions. For instance the company may seek to exclude minors from acting as directors, or perhaps another company.

Under statute, as we have seen, a person cannot be a company's sole director and secretary at the same time, nor its sole director and auditor. In addition statute provides that no person shall be appointed as a director of a public company, or of a private company which is the subsidiary of a public company, if at the time of his appointment he has reached the age of 70. This provision may be varied or excluded altogether under the articles, and in any case such a person may be appointed by the members in general meeting by an ordinary resolution of which special notice (of 28 days) has been given.

Under the Company Directors Disqualification Act 1986 it is an offence for an undischarged bankrupt to act as a director without permission of the court. Articles may provide that anyone who has been bankrupt shall not be appointed as a director, and Table A more specifically states that a directors office becomes vacant on his bankruptcy. The 1986 Act also empowers the court to make a disqualification order against a named person, preventing him for the duration of the order, without leave of the court, from being a director of a company, or being concerned with or taking part in, directly or indirectly, the promotion, formation or management of a company (s.1).

Grounds for a disqualification order

Under the 1986 Act a number of grounds are identified under which the court may grant a disqualification order. Breach of an order renders the disqualified person liable to criminal proceedings carrying a maximum penalty of six months imprisonment, and it also renders the person personally liable for the company's debts. These are formidable penalties, and certainly the imposition of personal liability, with its effect of lifting the corporate veil, is seen as an appropriate way to deal with someone who has had a disqualification order made against him, because he has shown himself not fit to be a director, yet has continued in breach of the order to manage a company.

The grounds are:

(a) conviction of an indictable offence (s.2). An indictable offence is one which can be tried before a Crown Court, however such an offence may be dealt with summarily before Magistrates. The Crown Court can on conviction disqualify for up to 15 years, the Magistrates Court up to 5 years. There is no minimum disqualification period.

One of the most common offences associated with company affairs is fraud. In *R v. Corbin* 1984 the defendant ran a business selling yachts through companies he owned. He was convicted of various fraudulent practices including borrowing from finance companies to buy yachts, falsely stating he had paid a deposit on them. He received two a half years imprisonment and a disqualification order for five years;

(b) persistent breaches of company law (s.3);

Under s.3 the breaches in question involve the failure to provide any return account or documents required to be filed with the Registrar of Companies. There is a presumption that a person has been persistently in default if he has been convicted of a default three times in the past five years. The maximum period for disqualification is five years;

(c) fraud, fraudulent trading or breach of duty revealed in a winding up (s.4);

The Court may make an order following the offence of fraudulent trading under s.458 Companies Act 1985, or where the person has otherwise been guilty of any fraud in relation to the company or breach of duty, in his capacity as an officer, liquidator, receiver or manager. The maximum period for disqualification is fifteen years;

(d) unfitness (ss 5,6,7 and 9);

When a company becomes insolvent the person involved in administering the insolvency such as the liquidator or administrative receiver must make a return to the Secretary of State regarding the conduct of the company's directors. On the basis of this information the Secretary of State may apply to the Court for a disqualification order against an individual director on the grounds of his unfitness as evidenced in the return. The Court must then satisfy itself as to the unfitness before it can make an order. Schedule 1 of the 1986 Act lists the factors to be considered by the Court in reaching its decision. In broad terms these factors share a common feature, namely the way the directors have managed the company. The list is a long one, and it includes the following:

(i) any misfeasance or breach of duty by the director in relation to the company;

(ii) any misapplication or retention of company money or property by the director;

(iii) the directors responsibility for the company entering into transactions liable to be set aside by a liquidation;

(iv) the directors failure to keep proper company records, or prepare or file annual company accounts;

(v) the directors responsibility for the company becoming insolvent;

(vi) the directors responsibility for any failure by the company to supply goods or services which have already been paid for;

(vii) the directors responsibility for failing to call a creditors meeting in a creditors voluntary winding up;

(viii) any failure by the director to produce a statement of affairs as required in any insolvency proceedings concerning the company.

A disqualification order can only be made if the company is insolvent, which in this context means either that an administration order has been made against it, or an administrative receiver has been appointed, or at the time of the liquidation its assets are insufficient to pay its debts or other liabilities. An order made on grounds of unfitness must be for a minimum of two years, and may be up to a maximum of fifteen years;

(ix) following a DTI investigation (s.8). If the DTI has investigated the affairs of the company and following an inspectors report, or information or documents obtained under powers to require production of documents and enter and search premises (s.447 and s.448 Companies Act 1985 respectively), it appears to the Secretary of State that a disqualification order should be made in the public interest, he may apply to the Court. The maximum period for disqualification is fifteen years.

Director disqualification statistics

The number of company director disqualifications in Great Britain for the past three years, together with the period of disqualification, is shown opposite.

Director Disqualifications in Great Britain - 1988-90

	Total	up to 1	1-2	2-3	3-4	4-5	5-10	10-15
1988	**332**	0	39	80	49	100	53	11
1989	**303**	6	36	91	39	64	58	9
1990	**309**	8	35	78	45	80	52	11

Source: *Department of Trade and Industry*

Removal of directors

If the directors have voting control of the company they cannot be removed. Where this does not occur s.303 of the 1985 Act provides that a company may by means of an ordinary resolution remove a director before his term of office expires, despite anything in the articles or in any agreement made between the company and the director. The section does not deprive the director of his right to sue for breach of contract on removal, if he has this right.

A public company must have at least two directors, a private company must have at least one. Directors of public companies must normally retire at 70, although the articles may provide otherwise. It is not a legal requirement that directors hold shares in the company, although articles commonly specify that such 'qualification' shares be held.

A common provision in articles is that directors hold office for three years, after which time they must either retire or offer themselves for re-election. Any changes in the directors must be notified to the Registrar of Companies. The company must keep a register at its office, available for public inspection, containing a list of the directors and the company secretary. Directors are also required by statute to disclose to the company and its members matters such as their financial interests in the company and connected companies.

Auditors

The auditing of company accounts is a process by which the company auditors carry out an annual investigation into the financial affairs of the company, so that they can confirm, primarily for the shareholders benefit, that the companies books reflect the actual position of the company's finances.

All registered companies must appoint auditors, unless the company is a dormant one, that is a *"small"* company which has had no *"significant accounting transaction"* since the end of the previous financial year. Appointment is made at each general meeting at which accounts in respect of an accounting reference period are laid. It is thus the members who make the appointment. The first auditors may be appointed by the directors, and casual vacancies may be filled either by the directors, or by the company in general meeting. A private company may now, by means of an elective resolution, opt out of annual appointment arrangements, so that the appointed auditors will continue in office until either side choose to terminate the appointment.

It is clearly important that auditors be both independent from the company, and suitably qualified to perform their functions. Only a "registered auditor" can carry out company auditing work, and a registered auditor is someone who is regarded as qualified by the Chartered Institutes of Accountants, or the Chartered Association of Certified Accountants, or the Department of Trade and Industry as having the appropriate overseas or other professional qualifications. Education, training and other matters affecting the work of auditors has now been brought under general statutory control. Certain persons are not permitted to act as auditors. These include an officer or servant of the company, a person employed by them, officers and servants of the company's holding or subsidiary companies or persons who have a *'connection'* with the company. A body corporate may act as an auditor.

A company may remove an auditor by means of an ordinary resolution under s.391. The provisions relating to such a removal are identical to those contained in s.303 for the removal of directors. An auditor may also resign from office, by depositing a notice to that effect at the company's registered office. The resignation is ineffective unless it either states that there are no circumstances connected with the resignation that should be brought to the attention of the members or creditors or alternatively it contains a statement outlining what those circumstances are. If such a statement is made a copy of it must be sent within fourteen days to all members, debenture holders, and every person entitled to receive notices of general meetings of the company. In such cases the auditor may also require the directors to convene an extraordinary general meeting of the company for the purpose of considering the resignation, a very powerful if rarely used threat.

Payment of auditors is determined by the company in general meeting.

Duties

Auditors duties are examined in detail in Chapter 10. The principal duties are (i) to audit the company accounts, and (ii) report to the members of the company on the accounts.

> In *Caparo Industries plc v. Dickman* 1990 the House of Lords was required to consider the extent of an auditor's liability for negligently audited accounts. The auditors in question had verified accounts which showed a pre-tax profit of £1.2M, when the company had in fact sustained a loss of over £400,000. Caparo Industries, who already held shares in the audited company, took more of its shares and later made a take-over bid for it on the strength of the inaccurate accounts. Caparo sued the auditors when the true position was discovered. The action was unsuccessful. The Court took the view that auditors of a public limited company owe no duty of care either to a potential investor or to an existing member who takes more shares in the company. To allow otherwise would be to create an unlimited liability on the part of auditors. On the facts there was not a sufficient relationship of proximity between the parties. The audited accounts went into general circulation and might foreseeably have been relied on by strangers for many different purposes. The duty of the auditors was a statutory duty owed to the company as a whole, to enable the members as a body to exercise proper control over it. A duty of care could however arise in cases when auditors have provided accounts with the intention or knowledge that they would be supplied by the company to a particular person or class of people, for example a specific bank, or banks generally, even though the precise purpose for which the accounts will be used is not known by the auditors.

Assignment *Westborough Rock Concert*

During the summer Westborough City Council organised a series of rock concerts over a three day period. The concerts were very successful, however the event has given rise to certain legal issues, and the file dealing with them has been passed to the City Solicitor. You work in the City's Legal Department and the file has been referred to you from the City solicitor with a covering internal memorandum from him. The letters are included below:

"The Chief Executive
Westborough City Council
City Hall
WESTBOROUGH

Dear Sir,

Westborough Rock Concert

I am the managing director of Starburst Enterprises Limited, and I am writing to you regarding the contract under which we agreed to provide you with a supporting band, The Roadcrash, for each of the three performances organised by you at the concert. The agreement was negotiated on our side by Ralph Jacobs, a director of the company, for a fee of £6,000. Ralph informs me that due to the non appearance of the band for the first night's performance, you are seeking to invoke clause 8 of our agreement with you which states:

> "In the event of the artists failing to perform on stage for any one or more of the agreed performances, the council shall have the right, at its absolute discretion, to claim damages of an amount not to exceed one and a half times the total appearance fee due to the company."

I must point out to you that my company intends to strenuously resist any attempt by you to realise this sum. It is indeed the company's view that the agreement itself is invalid since the company's articles of association require all contracts over £5,000 to be agreed by the full board, and Mr. Jacobs neither sought nor received such approval.

Yours faithfully,

Jack Soames

JACK SOAMES
Managing Director."

A S GILBERT ACCA
Chartered Accountant

Breams Buildings
West End
Denton Grove
Westborough WH1 2AC

The Chief Executive
Westborough City Council
City Hall
Westborough BM1 1AA

Dear Sir,

I have been appointed as Liquidator of Happy Jack Records Ltd. I understand that you are owed the sum of £400 by the company for a licence you granted to it to operate a small sales unit at the Westborough Rock Concert, from which it sold teeshirts, badges and similar items.

It is my view that the company lacked the authority to enter into this licence agreement. Its object clause provides that:

> "The objects for which the company is established are: to carry on and undertake the business of phonographic materials retailers; and to carry on any trade, business or mercantile operation which in the opinion of the directors may be incident, auxiliary or conductive to the above objects."

In these circumstances I must reject all liability for the licence fee due.

Yours faithfully,

A.S. Gilbert

A S Gilbert
Liquidator

Tasks

1. (a) Draft a letter of reply to the managing Director of Starburst Enterprises in which you argue the legal merits of the council's claim against the Company;

   (b) Produce notes to append to the file which identify any weakness in the Council's claim.

2. Draft an internal memorandum to the City Solicitor indicating whether , in your view, the liquidator's denial of liability for payment of the licence fee is a valid one.

Chapter 4

The Termination of Business Organisations

Introduction

The life of a business organisation can come to an end for many reasons. It may have achieved what its members required of it, so that it no longer has any useful value. It is not, for instance, unknown for a group of people to form a limited company for the purpose of carrying out a specific business venture, and insert a provision in the company's articles of association making it clear that the business is to last for a fixed period, or that it will expire on the happening of a certain event. A group of businessmen may contribute capital to a company they have formed, with the aim that the company will purchase, renovate and then sell certain industrial premises, or buy and then resell some other substantial asset. The company will end when the sale takes place if its sole purpose was the making of the sale.

A business may also come to an end because the commercial foundations upon which it was based have ceased to exist, or it has become no longer commercially viable to continue. If this occurs there is nothing to prevent the organisation from diversifying if this is acceptable to the members, thus prolonging the life of the business.

> An interesting illustration of this process, and the legal consequences which can attach to it, is provided by *Prudential Assurance Co. v. Chatterley-Whitfield Collieries Ltd.* 1949. The colliery company's main business interest was in coal mining, although it had other business interests as well. Following the nationalisation of the coal industry in 1946, the company, in common with other colliery companies, received a large payment by way of compensation. It decided to continue to operate its other business activities, but had more capital than it needed for these, and so it passed a special resolution to repay all its preference shareholders. Under the articles they had the right to priority of repayment of capital in the event of the company being brought to an end. The preference shareholders objected, claiming they would lose the opportunity to share in future profit.
>
> Company legislation strictly controls the power of a company to reduce its capital, in order to protect creditors, shareholders and the public. The court must sanction the reductions, which it will not do if the reduction is not fair and equitable as between different classes of shareholders. The House of Lords nevertheless held that this reduction was fair and equitable on the basis that surplus capital should first be returned to the class of shareholders having priority to repayment in the event of the company being brought to an end.

Most business which are terminated however, do not end their own lives out of choice, but because such action has been forced on them by their creditors. This occurs when the creditors lose confidence in the capacity of the organisation to repay them. It is a common feature of commercial life that when a business develops financial ill-health, its creditors will seek to reduce their losses by dissolving the business whilst there are still assets remaining in it.

Thus in considering the law as it affects the dissolution of businesses it is helpful to bear in mind the health of the organisation at the time it is being dissolved. The law, quite understandably, exerts far greater control over business which are terminated in circumstances of financial failure, than in cases where they are brought to an end fit and healthy, and nobody will lose money. Dissolution is important to the members of the business, who will be concerned as to what share of the assets they are entitled to, and for much the same reason it will be of concern to the creditors; they will want to know what the assets of the business are, and how they are to be distributed.

The process of dissolution

The process laid down for terminating or dissolving a business depends upon two factors:

(a) what the type of business is; and

(b) what its financial condition is.

We have previously seen that business organisations can be classified according to their legal status. Some are corporate bodies, some are unincorporated associations, whilst others are simple one man businesses. By now it should be clear that there are significant differences between these alternative business forms. This is reflected in the procedures for dissolving them. In the case of a limited company the procedure by which it is dissolved is referred to as a winding-up. Bankruptcy is the term used to describe the process by which an insolvent individual's assets are collected in, converted into money and distributed between his creditors. There is no technical term to describe the process for terminating a partnership. It is simply referred to as dissolution.

Dissolution of a Partnership

When the commercial activity of a partnership ceases so does the business itself, for it is no longer being "carried on" as required under the Partnership Act 1890. In such circumstances the partnership will be dissolved, and its assets disposed of to those legally entitled to them. Alternatively a partnership which is still in operation, may be dissolved on any one of a number of different grounds.

Dissolution can occur either with or without the intervention of the court. Under the Partnership Act 1890 a partnership is dissolved *without* the intervention of the court, in any of the following circumstances:

(a) if it was entered into for a fixed term, when that term expires;

(b) if it was entered into for a single venture, when that venture has been completed, for example, where the aim of the business is to acquire a single piece of property and resell it;

(c) if entered into for an undefined time, by any partner giving notice to the other or others of his intention to dissolve the partnership. If such a notice is served then the partnership is dissolved from the date mentioned in the notice as the date of dissolution. If no date has been given dissolution operates from the time the notice was received, subject to its articles providing for some other date;

(d) by the death or bankruptcy of any partner. Partnership articles will often provide that in such an event the partnership will continue to be run by the remaining partners. In the case of the death of a partner the articles may provide that the surviving partners will continue to run the business in partnership with the personal representative of the deceased;

(e) if a partner's share of the business is charged to secure a separate judgment debt, the other partners may dissolve the business;

(f) by the happening of an event which makes it unlawful for the business of the firm to be carried on, or for the members of the firm to carry it on in partnership. This may occur, for example, where there is a partnership between a British partner and a foreign partner, the business is carried on in the United Kingdom, and war breaks out between the countries of the respective partners.

Dissolution can be granted by *the court* on an application to dissolve, made by a partner, in any of the following cases:

(a) where a partner is suffering from a mental disorder;

(b) where a partner other than the partner petitioning

  (i) becomes in any way permanently incapable of performing their part of the partnership contract, e.g. through physical illness, or

  (ii) has been guilty of misconduct in business or private life, as in the opinion of the court, bearing in mind the nature of the partnership business, is calculated to be prejudicial to the carrying on of the business, or

  (iii) wilfully or persistently commits a breach of the partnership agreement, or otherwise behaves in a way in matters relating to the partnership business that it is impractical for the other partners to carry on in business with that partner.

  Cases on dissolution on these grounds have included a refusal to meet for discussions on business matters, the keeping of erroneous accounts, persistent disagreement between the parties, and in *Anderson v. Anderson* 1857 where a father and son were in partnership together, by the opening by the father of all his son's correspondence;

  (iv) where the business of the partnership can only be carried on at a loss;

  (v) if circumstances have arisen which, in the opinion of the court, render it just and equitable that the partnership be dissolved.

  In Re: *Yenidje Tobacco Co. Ltd.*. 1916 although the company was trading profitably the court held that it was just and equitable to wind it up, on the basis that its two directors had become so hostile towards each other that they would only communicate by means of messages passed to each other via the Secretary, and that this amounted to a position of deadlock. It was pointed out that a private limited company is similar to a partnership, and that had the directors been partners in a partnership, there would have been sufficient grounds for dissolution. Lord Justice Warrington stated:

"... I am prepared to say that in a case like the present, where there are only two persons interested, and there are no shareholders other than those two, where there are no means of over-ruling by the action of a general meeting of shareholders the trouble which is occasioned by the quarrels of the two directors and shareholders, the company ought to be wound up if there exists such a ground as would be sufficient for the dissolution of a private partnership at the suit of one of the partners against the other. Such grounds exist in the present case."

The partnership and bankruptcy

Two distinct insolvency situations may arise which affect the partnership:

(a) one of the partners is declared personally bankrupt, whilst the remaining partners are personally solvent. This automatically brings the partnership to an end, although a new one may well be formed, without the bankrupt partner. The reason the firm automatically dissolves in such circumstances is because the bankrupt party's share passes to his trustee in bankruptcy, and thus in effect he is withdrawing his contribution and his stake in the business;

(b) the partnership itself is insolvent. If this is so, all the partners will normally have bankruptcy proceedings brought against them. It should be remembered that since a partnership does not grant limited liability to its members, they become personally liable for the debts which cannot be met by the assets of the firm.

The administration and distribution of assets

If the partnership is dissolved its property is gathered in, and used to pay all debts and liabilities. If after this is done a surplus is left it is distributed between the partners. What they receive will depend upon what their partnership agreement says. If it makes no provision for such a situation, the following rules are laid down by the 1890 Act:

(a) If there is no loss suffered by the firm, the surplus is used firstly to repay the capital contribution of the partners, and then to the partners in equal shares. Thus if the firm has three partners, A, B, and C, whose respective capital contributions were £2,000, £1,000 and £500, and on dissolution the firm has debts of £3,000 and assets of £8,000, the distribution to the partners will be as follows:

	£
Assets available for distribution	**8 000**
Firm's debts	**3 000**
Surplus assets available for distribution	**5 000**
Repayment of capital contributions: A	**2000**
B	**1000**
C	**500**
	3 500
Remaining surplus to be equally distributed	**1 500**

The share of net assets taken by each partner will be
A £2 500, B £1 500, C £1 000

(b) If there are losses these are met in the following order:

  (i) out of profits;

  (ii) out of capital;

  (iii) by the partners individually according to the proportions by which they shared profits.

Using the example of A, B and C above, if the partnership assets on dissolution were £5,000 and the debts £3,000, then assuming profits were shared equally, the distribution to each partner would be as follows:

	£
Assets available for distribution	5 000
Firm's debts	3 000
Surplus assets available for distribution	2 000
Repayment of total capital contribution	3 500
Shortfall	1 500
Losses shared equally	500

A receives £2 000 - £500 = £1 500
B receives £1 000 - £500 = £500
C receives £500 - £500 = £0

Where there has been a bankruptcy situation with either a partner or the firm itself being adjudicated bankrupt, there will be two groups of creditors; those of the partners personally, and those of the firm itself. It is important therefore that the personal debts and property of the partners can be kept separate from those of the partnership itself.

Dissolution of a Registered Company

We have already seen that the process by which a registered company can be brought to an end is known as a winding up or a liquidation. The process is a detailed and complex one. It is regulated by the Insolvency Act 1986, a statute based upon the report of Sir Kenneth Cork. Shortly before the Royal Assent was granted, the Insolvency Bill as it then was, came back to the House of Lords for approval, where Lord Denning remarked, *"In 1977 Sir Kenneth Cork and his committee entered upon a review of the insolvency law. They sat for five years and heard the most expert evidence. It is the most technical subject you can imagine. Both lawyers and accountants hate it. Most of them know nothing about it."*

The main aspects of it will be examined shortly, but before doing so two further points need to be made regarding dissolution. The first is that there are other methods by which a company can be dissolved that do not involve winding up procedures. The second is that where the threat of dissolution is based upon company insolvency, alternatives to the drastic step of terminating the company by sending it up and realising its assets are available to creditors. A creditors composition may be entered into, or an administration order may be order may be by the court. These points are considered below.

Methods of dissolution

A company is created by incorporation through registration. It can therefore only come to an end when the registration is discharged. Once this happens the contractual relationship between the company and its members, based upon the memorandum and articles of the company, also comes to an end.

A company can be dissolved:

(a) by proceedings brought by the Attorney-General for cancellation of the registration, on the grounds that the company's objects are illegal.

> In *Attorney-General v. Lindi St. Claire (Personal Services) Ltd.*. 1980 a lady, Miss St. Claire, formed the defendant company for the purposes of prostitution. The Registrar had granted it a certificate of incorporation, after refusing to register it under various names submitted by Miss St. Claire, including Hookers Ltd., Prostitutes Ltd. and even Lindi St. Claire French Lessons Ltd. The Court however granted the cancellation on the grounds that the objects of the company were illegal;

(b) by an order of the court where the company is transferring its undertaking to another company under a scheme of reconstruction or reorganisation;

(c) by the Registrar, who under s.652 Companies Act 1985 may strike off the register a company that is defunct. A defunct company is one which is no longer carrying on business. The section lays down a procedure to be followed by the Registrar before he can validly exercise the power to remove the company from the register. This has become a very common method of dissolution, for it is cheap and easy; and

(d) by being wound-up, which may be either voluntary or compulsory. The legal provisions relating to company liquidations are contained in the Insolvency Act 1986. The title of this statute is perhaps rather misleading, since it contains provisions which regulate not only companies which are being dissolved on the basis of their insolvency, but also companies which, for a variety of reasons, are being wound up fully able to meet their liabilities.

The process of winding up

Like a partnership, a limited company can be wound up as mentioned above either *voluntarily*, or *compulsorily* by order of the court. The grounds for winding up, whether on a voluntary or compulsory basis, are set out in the Insolvency Act 1986. They recognise that winding up is a step which may become necessary not only in cases of financial instability, but also because the company, which is of course a creature of statute, has failed to comply with the statutory provisions which bind it, or simply because the members no longer wish to trade together. When examining the operation of the limited company it is common to draw an analogy with natural persons. Thus the company is said to be born when its certificate of incorporation is granted, and henceforth its brain, the board of directors, guides its actions and formulates it decision, which are executed through those it employs. Following this analogy through to its conclusion the process of winding up is akin to the process of administering the estate of a deceased person. Assets are collected and used to satisfy debts owing, after which any property remaining can be distributed to those lawfully entitled to them. In the case of a company this will be to its members. However the process of administering the estate of a deceased person commences with death, whereas winding up is a process which culminates in the dissolution of the company, the administration being completed before the life of the company ends.

Terminology

A number of technical expressions are used in liquidation and it is helpful to briefly identify and describe them before proceeding further.

A *petition* is an application to the court requesting the court to exercise its jurisdiction over company liquidations. A petition is presented where the liquidation is compulsory. In such cases the court has a major role to play. This is not so however in voluntary liquidations, where the liquidation is under the control of either the members or the creditors of the company.

A *contributory* is a person liable to contribute to the assets of a company if it is wound up. Existing members whose shares have not been fully paid fall within the definition of a contributory, and so to do similarly placed past members, whose shareholding ceased within the year preceding the winding up. However a past member is not liable in respect of any debt contracted after his membership ceased. Nor is he required to make a contribution if the existing members are able to satisfy the contributions required of them.

A *liquidator* is a person appointed to take control of the company, collect its assets, pay its debts, and distribute any surplus to the members according to their rights as shareholders. The liquidator therefore holds a position of great responsibility, and it is important to ensure that only individuals of integrity are qualified to hold such a post. In recent years some disquiet has been felt as a result of company liquidations in which the liquidator has been found to be conducting the winding up for the benefit of directors, rather than the company's creditors. The Insolvency Act 1986 copes with this by requiring that only an *insolvency practitioner*, a term covering liquidators, can act in a winding up. He must be authorised to do so by his own professional body (these include accountancy bodies and the Law Society), or by the Department of Trade and Industry. Certain people are completely excluded. An applicant must be shown to be a fit and proper person, and must provide security, to become an insolvency practitioner.

The *Official Receiver* is appointed by the Department of Trade, and is concerned both with personal insolvency and with corporate insolvency. Official receivers are attached to courts with insolvency jurisdiction, and they act in the capacity of liquidators in the case of compulsory liquidations, being appointed automatically when a *winding up order* is made, that is when the court issues an order that the company be wound up. The Official Receiver (OR) remains in this office until another liquidator is appointed.

Finally the *London Gazette* is an official publication used to satisfy the requirement of providing public notice of certain legal events, in the case of a liquidation for example, notice of a creditors meeting.

The Basic Aspects of a Company Liquidation

We have already seen that when the process of winding-up has been completed the company will be struck off the register of companies and will cease to exist. Of course no further claims can then be made against it. Consequently for anyone who is connected with the company, whether as an investor, creditor or employee, winding-up is of great significance.

Although statutory winding up provisions are detailed, and sometimes complex, there are basically three aspects to a liquidation:

(a) who has the ability to institute and control the winding up, and on what grounds;

(b) what are the legal provisions to be fulfilled during the procedure; and

(c) in what order are claims made against the company for payment met?

Methods of Winding Up

Under s.73 Insolvency Act 1986 two methods of winding up are recognised. These are:

(a) a voluntary winding up, which according to s.90 may be either:

(i) a members voluntary winding up, or

(ii) a creditors voluntary winding up, and

(b) a winding up by the court, usually referred to as a compulsory winding up.

Voluntary winding up is more common than compulsory liquidation. It is a less formal procedure, and is therefore quicker and cheaper.

Voluntary winding up

Shareholders can at any time resolve to end the company. They initiate the procedure by passing a resolution to wind up, either a special resolution if the company is solvent, or, in the case of insolvency, an extraordinary resolution that it cannot continue in business by reason of its liabilities. An ordinary resolution is sufficient where the time period fixed in the articles for the life of the company has passed, or an event stipulated in the articles as giving rise to dissolution has taken place.

Under s.86 when the resolution is passed the liquidation procedure begins. The consequences are that:

(i) the company ceases to carry on business, other than to enable it to wind up;

(ii) the company's corporate status remains intact until dissolution;

(iii) transfers of shares, and changes in member's rights are void unless sanctioned by the liquidator;

(iv) the director's powers cease when the liquidator is appointed, although he, or in a creditor's voluntary winding up they themselves, may permit the directors to continue; and

(v) if the liquidation is due to insolvency, company employees, who may include directors, will be dismissed. The liquidator may however employ them under a new contract.

Notice of the resolution must be advertised in the London Gazette within 14 days of it being passed. If a majority of the directors within five weeks of the passing of the resolution make a statutory declaration that the company is solvent, then the company members manage the winding up. This includes the appointment of their own liquidator. This is a valuable power for the person appointed will be under their control, rather than the control of the creditors or the court. The court can nevertheless remove a liquidator on the basis of unfitness for office. The declaration of solvency states that the directors have examined the company's affairs and formed the opinion that within a stated period (up to a maximum of twelve months) the company will be able to pay its debts in full. If a declaration of solvency is not made the winding up is creditors winding up. A creditors meeting must be summoned by the company. Details of this meeting must be posted to creditors and members giving them at least seven days notice, and be advertised in the London Gazette and two local newspapers.

The business of the creditors' meeting is to receive from the directors a full statement of the company's affairs, to draw up a list of creditors with estimates of their claims, to appoint a liquidator who will insert a notice in the London Gazette notifying other creditors to send in claims and if considered necessary appoint a liquidation committee.

The liquidation committee cannot consist of more than five people. It is designed to work in conjunction with the liquidator.

The liquidator's powers in a voluntary winding up

The liquidator has wide powers to act for and in the name of the company, without the need to consult anyone or obtain the sanction of the court. The liquidator can:

(i) bring or defend legal proceedings on behalf of the company;

(ii) continue to operate the company's business to the extent necessary to wind it up beneficially;

(iii) issue company documents and use the company seal;

(iv) claim in insolvency proceedings brought by the company against an insolvent estate in which the company has an interest;

(v) deal with any negotiable instrument issued by or received by the company;

(vi) raise money needed by the company on security of its assets;

(vii) collect in monies due from contributories;

(viii) appoint an agent to carry out work on behalf of the liquidator.

In addition to these powers the liquidator may, in a members voluntary winding up with the sanction of an extraordinary resolution of the company, or in a creditors' voluntary winding up with the sanction of the Court, the liquidation committee or the creditors:

(i) pay off in full any class of creditors;

(ii) enter into any compromise or arrangement with creditors.

It is possible for a voluntary winding up to be converted into a compulsory winding up, on a petition to the Court by a creditor or contributory. This will only be successful if the Court is satisfied that it is inappropriate for the winding up to proceed as a voluntary one, for instance where the liquidator is found to have some personal interest in the company he is winding up.

Compulsory winding up

A compulsory winding up is carried out by the Court. This is either the High Court or, if the company's paid up share capital does not exceed £120,000 the County Court in whose district the company has its registered office. Not all County Courts however, possess the necessary insolvency jurisdiction.

Proceedings are commenced by a person presenting a petition to the appropriate court. The petitioner may be the company itself, by resolution, the Secretary of State following an investigation or, in most cases, a creditor.

In Re: *Othery Construction Ltd.* 1966 Lord Buckley stated that if a fully paid up shareholder is to successfully petition to wind up:

"... he must show either that there will be a surplus available for distribution amongst the shareholders or that the affairs of the company require investigation in respects which are likely to produce such a surplus".

Under s.122 a company may be wound up by the court if:

(a) the company has passed a special resolution requesting it; or

(b) in the case of a company registered as a public company, the company has been registered for more than a year, but as yet no certificate of ability to commence business has been issued. This certificate, which is issued by the Registrar, can only be obtained when certain financial details have been given to him. The company cannot commence business until the certificate, which is required under s.117 Companies Act 1985, has been issued. Private companies do not require such a certificate and can commence business immediately on incorporation; or

(c) the company does not commence business in the first year of its incorporation, or suspends business at any time for a whole year. An order will only be granted on this ground if the company has no intention of carrying on business again.

In Re: *Middlesbrough Assembly Rooms Co.* 1880 a shareholder petitioned for winding up where the company had suspended trading for over three years, because of a trade depression. The majority shareholders opposed the petition on the basis that the company intended to recommence trading when the economic situation improved. It was held that in the circumstances the petition should be dismissed;

(d) if the membership has fallen below two; or

(e) if the company is unable to pay its debts. This is the ground most commonly relied upon. The company is deemed to be unable to pay its debts if a creditor who is owed a sum exceeding £750 by the company has left a written demand for it at the company's registered office, and the demand has remained unpaid for a period of three clear weeks. The company is not however regarded as neglecting the debt if it bona fide disputes the payment of it. Alternatively the company is deemed unable to pay its debts if:

(i) execution has been issued on a judgment in favour of a creditor which is returned either wholly or partially unsatisfied; or

(ii) it is proved to the satisfaction of the court that the company is unable to pay its debts as they fall due.

In Re: *A Company* 1986 it was held that a company can be regarded as unable to pay its debts under this ground, where it has funds but persistently fails or neglects to pay its debts unless it is forced to do so. Many companies have a deliberate policy of holding back payment for as long as possible, and for some this may be their means of survival; or

(iii) where the court is satisfied that taking into account the company's present and future liabilities, the value of its assets is less than the amount of its liabilities; or

(e) the court is of the opinion that it is just and equitable that the company should be wound up. This ground covers a number of situations. For instance it covers cases where the substratum of the company has been destroyed.

In Re: *German Date Coffee Co.* 1882 the company was wound up on the basis that it had become impossible to carry out the main object in the memorandum of association, namely the acquisition and working of a German patent to make coffee from dates, because the patent could not be obtained.

It also extends to circumstances in which the company has been formed for a fraudulent purpose; where the company is a sham, having no business or property; or where the rights of members are being flouted.

In *Loch v. John Blackwood Ltd.* 1924 a director with voting control refused to hold meetings, produce accounts or pay dividends. The court held that the company could be wound up.

In *Ebrahami v. Westbourne Galleries* 1972 two individuals E and N had operated successfully in partnership together for many years. Later they converted the business to a company, with themselves as sole shareholders and directors, and after a time N's son was allowed into the business. This was granted as a favour by the plaintiff, who transferred some of his shares to the son. Unfortunately his generosity was met by N and his son combining their interests to force the plaintiff out of the business. The court granted the plaintiff's application to wind up. commenting on the expression "just and equitable" Lord Wilberforce said:

"The words are a recognition of the fact that a limited company is more than a mere legal entity, with a personality in law of its own; that there is room in company law for the recognition of the fact that behind it, or amongst it, there are individuals, with rights, expectations and obligations ... which are not necessarily submerged in the company structure".

The petition to wind up is presented to the district judge of the court who fixes a time and place for the hearing. The petition must be advertised in the London Gazette at least seven clear days (excluding Saturday and Sunday) before the hearing. Rules of Court set out the form in which this advertised information must be provided; if they are not complied with the petitioner may have to meet all the court costs. The aim of the advertisement is to invite interested parties, the company's creditors and contributories, to oppose or support the petition. A person intending to appear at the hearing must give notice of this to the petitioner. After presentation of the petition a provisional liquidator may be appointed who is generally the Official Receiver. In any event when the hearing takes place, and the court makes a winding-up order, the Official Receiver becomes provisional liquidator by statute, and continues as liquidator unless the meeting of the creditors and contributories agree to the appointment of some other liquidator. This person must be an insolvency practitioner. The 1986 Act sets out the liquidator's powers. Essentially his task is to collect and realise the company's assets, including unpaid sums due to the company from contributories for their shares, to settle the lists of creditors and contributories, pay the company's debts in a fixed order, and finally to adjust the rights of the contributories distributing any surplus assets among them. At meetings of creditors and contributories it may be decided to apply to the court to form a committee of inspection. Having fulfilled these responsibilities the liquidator applies to the court for an order that the company be dissolved, and is then released from his or her role. The court, it should be noted, has a complete and unfettered discretion as to whether to make an order for winding up. It may as an alternative conditionally or unconditionally adjourn the hearing, make an interim order, or dismiss the petition altogether.

The order of priorities

On dissolution there are likely to be many claims against the assets of the company. Provided the company is solvent this does not create any problems, but if it is insolvent the question which arises is how the shortfall is dealt with. Do all the companies creditors absorb the loss according to the proportion of credit they have provided, or do some creditors rank before others, so that whilst those at the top of the list may be repaid in full, those at the bottom could find themselves with nothing?

The answer is that the Insolvency Act 1986 lays down an order of priorities for the distribution of assets. The relevant provisions are contained in ss.175 and 176, which lays down the following order:

(a) the costs of winding up (for example the liquidator's fees);

(b) preferential debts. These include: income tax deducted from the pay of company employees under the PAYE system over the past year; VAT payments owed by the company that have accrued over the past six months; wages and salaries of employees outstanding for the previous four months, up to a present maximum figure of £800 per employee. A director may be a salaried employee, and thus qualify under this head, however a director's fee rather than a salary will not rank as a preferential debt. If assets are sufficient, preferential debts are paid in full. If not, the available assets are distributed rateably between the preferential creditors, and in these circumstances property subject to a floating charge must be applied first in the payment of preferential debts, the holder being entitled only to the balance. Creditors who have the security of a fixed charge over assets of the company are, of course, able to realise the assets charged to meet the company's liability towards them;

(c) ordinary unsecured debts, such as sums owing to trade creditors. If these cannot be paid in full they are paid rateably amongst the creditors;

(d) the members according to their rights under the memorandum and articles. It may be that one class of shareholders is entitled to repayment of a certain amount of the surplus before the others, thus preference shareholders may receive repayment of their paid up capital in priority to ordinary shareholders.

Advantages and disadvantages of compulsory winding up

The main advantages of a compulsory winding up over a voluntary winding up are:

(a) Under s.129 Insolvency Act 1986 a compulsory winding up is deemed to commence when the petition is presented, whilst in a voluntary winding up it commences when the resolution is passed (s.86). The effect is that a compulsory winding up will commence earlier. This can be important since as part of the task of collecting in assets the liquidator can apply to the court to recover assets disposed of by the company within a fixed period before the insolvency, and can seek to have certain transactions set aside where these transactions occurred within a certain date of the insolvency. Going back further into the recent past of the company may mean the recovery of a larger quantity of assets. Examples include:

(i) the setting aside of a transaction made by the company at undervalue within the two years before the winding up has commenced. A transaction at undervalue would cover a gift made by the company at a time it was unable to pay its debts;

(ii) the setting aside of a preference made by the company to a connected person (e.g. a director) within two years of the winding up commencing, or to any other person (e.g. a trade creditor) within six months of the winding up commencing. Again this must have occurred at a time when the company was unable to pay its debts. A preference would occur where the directors, in the knowledge that the company is completely insolvent, settle the debts of just one of the company's creditors, in the expectation that if they subsequently set up a new company the trade creditor will continue to supply them;

(iii) the avoidance of floating charges created by the company within the two years prior to the insolvency if the chargee is a connected person, and one year if the chargee is anyone else.

(b) Wider powers of investigation into the management of the company's affairs, for example where the directors have been acting wrongfully.

The main disadvantages are that a compulsory liquidation will be slower and more expensive. The company will always be the respondent under a compulsory winding up order, and as the 'loser' in the action it will meet both sides costs, thus reducing the money available for the creditors when the realised assets are finally distributed.

Alternatives to Winding Up

Whilst as we have seen, a company may be dissolved for reasons other than financial difficulty, many dissolutions are the result of a financial crisis. Directors faced with this situation may have the future affairs of the company taken out of their hands in a compulsory or creditors liquidation, the result of which will be that the life of the company will come to an end, and some creditors at least will be left with their debts unsatisfied. One of the aims of the Insolvency Act 1986 was to provide alternatives to this drastic outcome, which would act as financial rescue packages for companies in difficulty.

(a) Corporate voluntary arrangements - compositions with creditors

These are provided for by ss1-7 Insolvency Act 1986. They enable a company which is insolvent or partially insolvent to follow a procedure which will result in a legally binding arrangement with its creditors. In outline the following stages have to be followed. The directors, or the liquidator if a winding up is in progress, choose an insolvency practitioner to act as a 'nominee', and help them produce proposals to put to the creditors. These may be a composition (see Chapter 6) or a scheme of arrangement for the company i.e. the revision of its financial affairs in some way, such as alterations to class rights, or the extension of time for payment given by debenture notices.

The proposals are reported to the court and a meeting of creditors and shareholders is called both of which must approve them. The outcome is reported to the court. If approved, the proposals bind all the creditors and shareholders having notice of them, under s.5.

(b) Administration orders

One of the problems with a voluntary arrangement is of course the difficulty of obtaining the agreement of large creditors, such as banks. They will want greater control over the organisation of the company's affairs. In such circumstances an administration order may be a useful device. Such an order can be made by the court once it is satisfied that the company is, or is likely to become, unable to pay its debts, and that an administration order would be likely to achieve:

(i) the survival of the company, and the whole or any part of its undertaking as a going concern; or

(ii) the approval of a voluntary arrangement (i.e. because of the appointment of an administrator); or

(iii) a more advantageous realisation of the company's assets than in a winding up.

The company itself, its directors, a creditor or creditors may petition the court for such an order, and if granted the court will appoint the receiver who will be responsible for the management of the affairs, business and property of the company for the duration of the order. This can include the calling of meetings and the appointment and removal of directors. Any winding up petition previously presented must be dismissed on the grant of an administration order. The administrator is empowered to carry on the business of the company generally, including dealing with and disposing of its assets, borrowing, employing agents and so on. He can establish subsidiary companies and transfer the whole or some part of the existing business to them. He can remove directors, and appoint new directors, and call meetings of the members and the creditors. His duties are to control and manage the company's assets and business operations, initially in accordance with directions from the court given in the order, and subsequently in accordance with the proposals he has put forward as to how the purposes stated in the order are to be achieved. The administrator's proposals must be sent to the Registrar of Companies and all the creditors within three months of the administration order being made. A creditors meeting must then be held to approve the proposals before they can be implemented.

> It remains to be seen how much use will be made of the administration order as an alternative to liquidation, however a useful illustration of an order in operation occurred in Re: *Consumer & Industrial Press* 1987. The company involved, a small printing and publishing organisation, had only one major asset when it became insolvent, a magazine which it published. An application was made for the appointment of an administrator, so that he could exercise the statutory power to borrow in the company's name in order to continue publishing the magazine. In this way it could be sold as a going concern, rather than it going out of publication and having far less value. The Court held that in the interests of the creditors the order should be granted.

Individual Insolvency

Personal insolvency occurs when an individual finds himself in serious financial difficulties and is unable to pay his creditors when debts fall due. If the creditors are unwilling or unable to wait for payment, the debtor may face bankruptcy proceedings under the Insolvency Act 1986. Broadly the purpose of bankruptcy is to ensure a fair distribution of assets to creditors and to allow the debtor to make a fresh start after his discharge.

The law relating to individual insolvency has undergone substantial change in recent years. The procedures under the Bankruptcy Act 1914 have been abolished and replaced with simpler procedures first introduced by the Insolvency Act 1985 and now contained in the Insolvency Act 1986. The new legislation was introduced with two main aims:

(a) to encourage voluntary arrangements between debtors and creditors; and

(b) to simplify and update bankruptcy procedures and bring them into line with the procedures applicable to company liquidations.

Under the 1986 Act there are two possible outcomes of individual insolvency: a *voluntary arrangement* or a *bankruptcy order*.

Voluntary arrangements

Where an individual is facing insolvency, he may try to avoid a bankruptcy order by proposing a voluntary arrangement with his creditors. The advantages from the debtor's point of view of such an arrangement are that he avoids the stigma, loss of status and adverse publicity associated with a bankruptcy order, and avoids the disabilities to which an undischarged bankrupt is subject. The benefit of a voluntary arrangement for the creditor is that it should be less expensive, leaving more assets available for payment to him; and it will usually be quicker than bankruptcy procedure, which means that he will be paid sooner. The disadvantage from the creditors point of view is that the supervisor of a voluntary arrangement will not have as many powers as a trustee in bankruptcy, for example to set aside transactions at an undervalue or preferences.

The option of making a voluntary arrangement existed under the old bankruptcy law. Such an arrangement could be made under the Deeds of Arrangement Act 1914. In practice, however, deeds of arrangement are not used to any great extent, mainly because any one creditor, no matter how small the sum owed to him, could petition for bankruptcy if he did not accept the debtor's proposals. He could do this even though all of the other creditors were prepared to accept them. Under the 1986 Act, as we shall see, a dissenting creditor must accept a voluntary arrangement if more than 75% by value of creditors agree to it.

Procedure for making a voluntary arrangement under Part VIII of the Insolvency Act 1986

If a debtor wishes to make a voluntary arrangement he must choose an insolvency practitioner to help him draw up a proposal which can be presented to his creditors. An insolvency practitioner, usually an accountant or a solicitor, must be qualified in relation to insolvency and must be authorised by the Department of Trade to act in that capacity. The insolvency practitioner will have an important role to play in the voluntary arrangement, first as a "nominee" preparing and presenting the proposal; and later as supervisor, implementing the proposal if it is accepted by the creditors.

When the proposal is prepared, and an insolvency practitioner has agreed to act nominee, the debtor must apply to the court for an interim order. Once this application is made, the court has power to suspend any legal proceedings against the debtor or his property.

The court will make an interim order if it is satisfied that it would be appropriate to do so, in order to allow the debtor to go ahead and make his proposal. If the court believes that the debtor is not acting in good faith or that the proposal is wholly unrealistic it may refuse to make the order. If an interim order is made, it will last for 14 days unless it is extended by the court. The effect of the order is that no bankruptcy petition can be presented against the debtor and

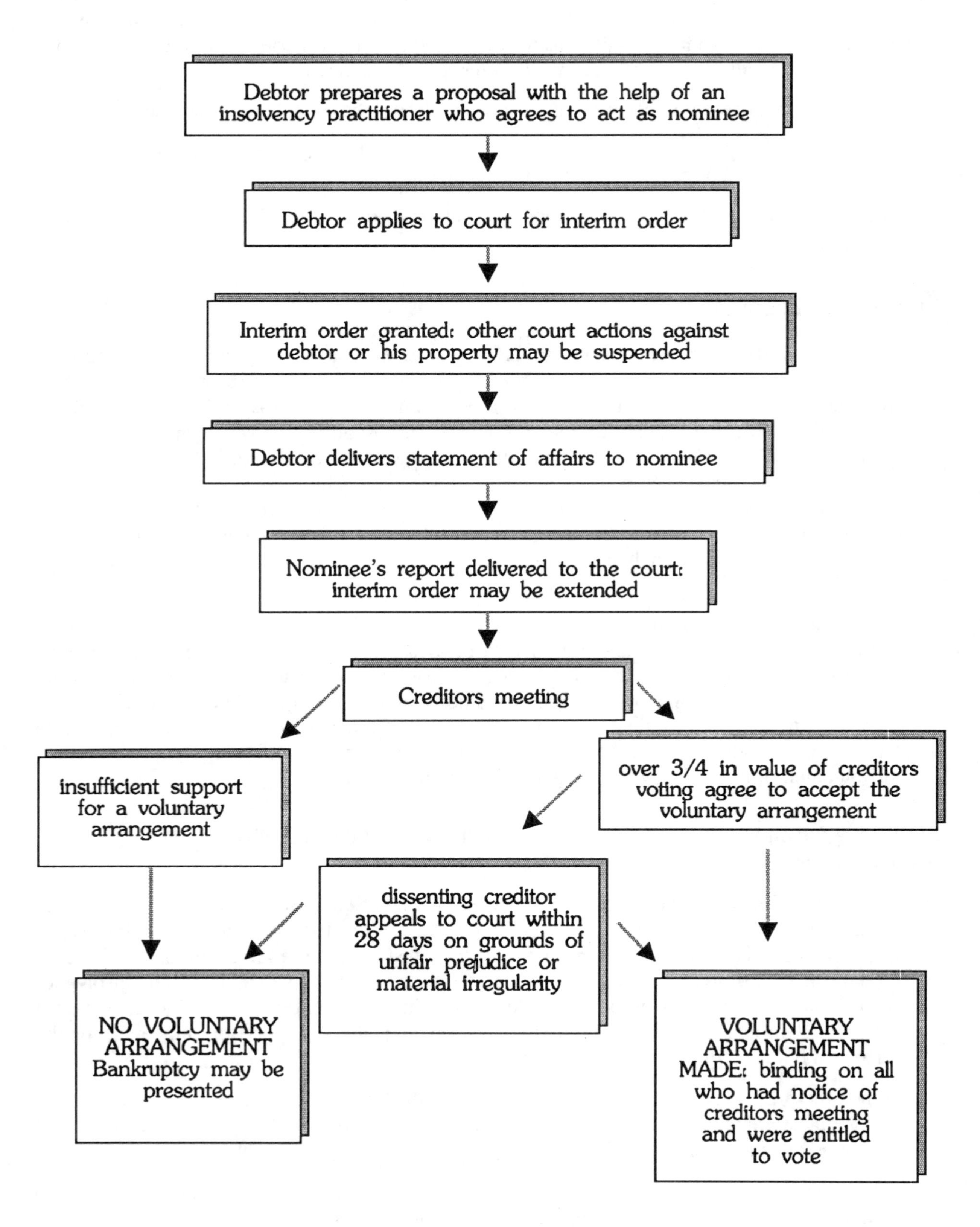

Fig 4.1 Procedure for Making a Voluntary Arrangement

no other legal proceedings may be commenced or continued against him without the court's permission.

Before the interim order expires, the nominee must report to the court stating whether he thinks that a meeting of creditors ought to be summoned to consider the debtor's proposal. To enable the nominee to make his report, the debtor has a duty to deliver a statement of affairs to him, together with the details of his proposal.

After receiving the nominee's report, the court will extend the interim order to allow the creditors to consider the debtor's proposal. The nominee must call a meeting of creditors. He must inform every creditor of whom he is aware about the meeting.

The purpose of the creditors meeting is to decide whether or not to accept the debtor's proposals for a voluntary arrangement, either in the form put forward by the debtor or in a modified form.

If the creditors are unable to agree to the proposal, the court can discharge the interim order and normal bankruptcy proceedings will probably follow. If a scheme is approved by over 75% in value of creditors voting at the meeting, the voluntary arrangement will be binding upon all creditors who had notice of the meeting and were entitled to vote.

The voluntary arrangement may be challenged by a dissatisfied creditor who must apply to the court to set it aside within 28 days. His application can be made on the grounds that there was a material irregularity in the calling or conduct of the creditors meeting; or that the voluntary arrangements unfairly prejudice his interests as a creditor.

If the proposal is approved at the creditors meeting, the nominee becomes its supervisor. The debtor must hand over his property to the supervisor, who will then carry out the arrangements. During the implementation of the voluntary arrangement by the supervisor, any of the parties, including the debtor, any creditors or the supervisor himself may apply to the court for directions to resolve any problems that may arise. When the task of supervision has been completed, the supervisor must notify all creditors and the debtor.

Bankruptcy Orders

A petition for a bankruptcy order may be presented by a creditor, the debtor himself, or by the supervisor or a creditor bound by a voluntary arrangement where the debtor has defaulted under the arrangement.

Petition by a creditor

A petition by a creditor must be based on an unpaid debt or debts owed to him by the debtor. The amount owing must be at least £750. In order to commence bankruptcy proceedings, a creditor either must obtain a judgment debt for at least £750 and be unable to enforce it; or he must serve on the debtor a *"statutory demand"* for payment of the debt (see Figure 4.2). Where a statutory demand is served and the debtor fails to pay within three weeks, the creditor can petition the court for a bankruptcy order. The court can dismiss the creditor's petition if it is satisfied that the debtor is able to pay all of his debts or that he has made an offer to provide security for the payment of the debt or to enter into a voluntary arrangement and the creditor has unreasonably refused to accept his offer.

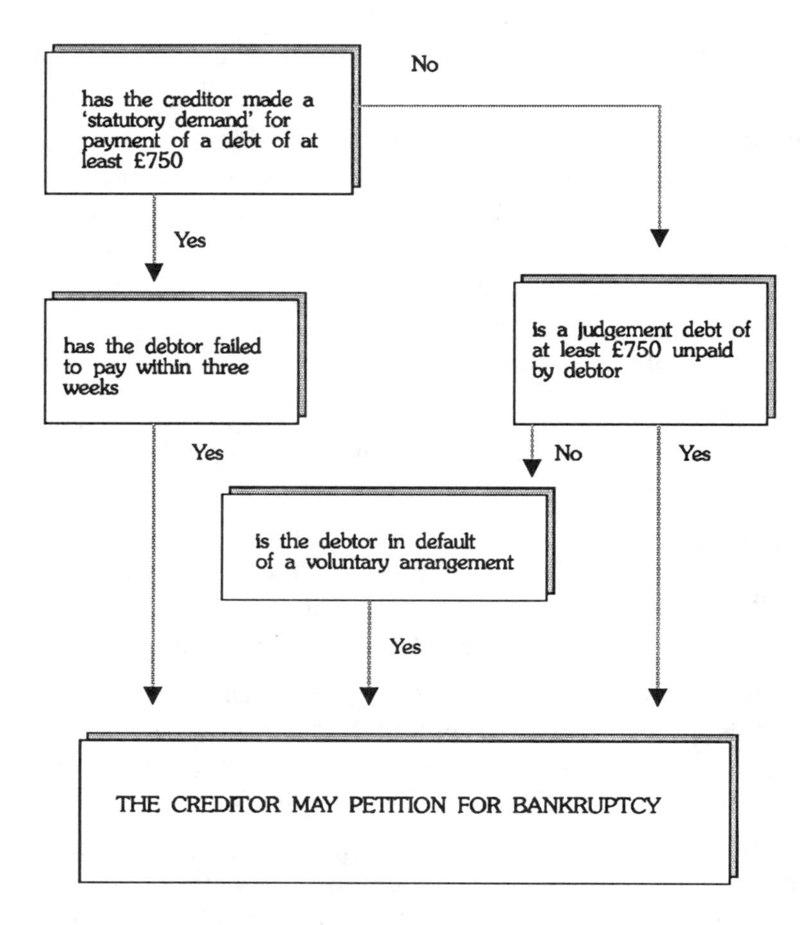

Fig. 4.2 Bankruptcy Petition by a Creditor

Petition by the debtor

The sole ground on which a debtor may petition for his own bankruptcy is that he is unable to pay his debts. His petition must be accompanied by a *"statement of affairs"* setting out details of his assets and liabilities.

Where the debtor's unsecured debts are less than £20,000, his assets are £2,000 or more and he has not been bankrupt or made a voluntary arrangement within the last 5 years, the court will appoint an insolvency practitioner to investigate the possibility of a voluntary arrangement and prepare a report. If the report is favourable the court will make an interim order with a view to a creditors meeting and a voluntary arrangement. If the report of the insolvency practitioner indicates that a voluntary arrangement would be unlikely to succeed, the court, if it agrees, will make a bankruptcy order. In these circumstances the order will be by way of a summary administration of the bankrupt's estate.

The advantages of a summary administration are that the procedures are simple and, from the debtor's point of view, he will be discharged from the bankruptcy after two years.

The trustee in bankruptcy

The function of the trustee in bankruptcy is to collect in the assets of the bankrupt and distribute them in accordance with the rules in the Insolvency Act. The order of priority for repayment of debts is similar to that described for the winding-up of companies. All of the bankrupts property vests in the trustee in bankruptcy, with the exception of tools, vehicles and equipment for use by the bankrupt in his employment or business; and such clothing, bedding, furniture and household equipment as are necessary to satisfy the basic domestic needs of the bankrupt and his family.

Any property which is acquired by the bankrupt before he is discharged can be claimed by the trustee. The trustee may also apply to the court for an *"income payments order"*. Under the terms of such an order part of any income to which the bankrupt is entitled whilst undischarged will be transferred to the trustee for the benefit of the creditors.

Creditors must submit proof of any debts to the trustee in bankruptcy. When the trustee has collected in all the bankrupts property he can declare and distribute a final dividend to creditors. After this has been done he will call a final general meeting of creditors and report on the administration of the estate.

Two further powers of the trustee enable him to apply to the court for an order to overcome certain types of transaction entered into by the bankrupt prior to the presentation of the bankruptcy petition. These are transaction at *"an undervalue"*, meaning a transaction in which the consideration received by the bankrupt is significantly less than that he has given (or is non existent), and *"preferences"*, which involves the bankrupt putting a creditor in a better financial position than he would have been in for the purpose of distributing the assets of the bankrupt's estate; in other words advancing the interests of one or more creditors to the disadvantage of others.

Almost identical powers are available to a liquidator in the event of a company winding-up, in cases where prior to the winding up, the company, through its directors, has entered into individual transactions or has given preference to certain of its creditors. Although such activities may be fraudulent, fraud does not need to be established for the court to consider the issue of an order to set aside such transactions.

Duration of bankruptcy

The bankruptcy continues until an individual is discharged from it. If a person is bankrupt for the first time, he will be discharged automatically after three years from the date of the Bankruptcy Order. In a summary administration, as we have seen, discharge will occur after two years. In either case, the period can be extended by the court if the bankrupt has failed to comply with any of his obligations under the Insolvency Act 1986. If the bankrupt has previously been an undischarged bankrupt during the previous fifteen years, he will not automatically be discharged. He must apply to the court for discharge after five years from the making of the Bankruptcy Order. Where such an application is made, the court may refuse to discharge the bankrupt. It may grant a discharge, either unconditionally or upon condition that he, for example, makes further payments to his creditors.

An undischarged bankrupt is subject to certain legal disabilities. He cannot obtain credit; or become a member of Parliament, a justice of the peace or a councillor.

Discharge from bankruptcy releases the bankrupt from the debts which existed at the commencement of his bankruptcy. A discharge from bankruptcy, however, does not affect his liability for fines imposed by a court for any criminal offence, or the enforcement of any security by a secured creditor.

Insolvency statistics

The insolvency statistics given below show the level at which insolvencies, both corporate and personal, have been occurring over the past three years

Insolvencies for England and Wales - Companies

	Total	Company Liquidations	Creditors Voluntary Liquidations
1988	9 427	3 667	5 760
1989	10 456	4 020	6 436
1990	15 051	5 977	9 074

Insolvencies for England and Wales - Individuals

	Total	Bankruptcy orders	Individual Voluntary Arrangements	Deeds of Arrangement
1988	8 507	7 717	779	11
1989	9 365	8 138	1 224	3
1990	13 987	12 058	1 927	2

Administrator appointments and Company Voluntary Arrangements: England and Wales

	Administrator Appointments	Company Voluntary Arrangements
1988	198	47
1989	135	43
1990	211	58

The level of corporate insolvencies for England and Wales in 1990 represents a ratio of 1.35 to the total number of companies on the register for that period, and a ratio of 1.15 of all active companies for that period.

Source: *Department of Trade and Industry*

Assignment *Trouble at Mills*

In 1985 Mark Mills, together with his cousin Bryan and a business associate of Bryan's, an accountant called Peter Marshall, decided to form a company to deal in personal insurance services. The company received its certificate of incorporation at the end of 1980. It was called Mills & Co. (Insurance Services) Ltd. and its premises were in Leeds. Mark and Bryan took up 35% of the shares each, Peter took the remainder. The company objects stated that it could carry on the business of providing "personal insurance of any kind".

In 1988 Peter was anxious that his wife should join the company, and each of the existing shareholders agreed to transfer some of their shares to her. As a result she obtained a 25% stake, Mark, Bryan and Peter's shareholding being reduced to 25% each.

Mark was happy with the company structure, since Peter's wife brought to the business considerable commercial expertise, and he received a large sum for the shares he transferred to her. Within a year however, the relationship between the shareholders had deteriorated. In particular Mark felt increasingly isolated. He was anxious that the company expand its insurance business to provide insurance facilities for commercial as well as personal computers. The other shareholders however were of the view that the company, which was suffering a reduced level of profit, should diversify, and move into the lucrative field of marketing, the area in which Peter's wife had previously worked.

By 1991 Mark had decided to form a separate business to offer a complete range of insurance facilities. He formed a partnership with James Blake-Smith, an old schoolfriend, to carry on the additional business. He did not reveal the existence of this business to his fellow shareholders in Mills & Co. Ltd., assuming that since it was based in Barnsley, a town twenty miles away from the company's place of business in Leeds, it had nothing to do with them. No partnership articles were drawn up.

The other members of Mills & Co. Ltd. recently discovered the existence of Mark's new firm. They responded by calling a company meeting, at which, during very stormy business they resolved to alter the company articles to enable it to pursue marketing work, to sell off the company's present business undertaking at a figure well below what Mark believes to be its true value, and to remove him as a director. In addition they are threatening to take away his voting rights. Marks problems have been compounded by problems in the partnership. He has discovered that James Blake-Smith has been in financial difficulties, and that bankruptcy proceedings have been commenced against him this week. He has also purchased, in a firm's name, an expensive computer system, despite a recent partnership meeting at which it was agreed to defer the expenditure until the next financial year.

In an effort to clarify the legal position in relation to these business difficulties Mark has sought your help, as someone with a business of your own and a knowledge of the legal principles applicable to business organisations. Prior to meeting Mark in a couple of days time, you have decided to analyse the legal position he has found himself in, in order to fully advise him as to the extent of his rights and liabilities.

Task

Draft an outline report which you can give to Mark at your meeting with him, that expresses your considered legal opinion on his present business problems.

Chapter 5

The Nature and Formation of Contracts

Introduction

Economic activity, which we may regard as the acquisition, use and disposal of resources, is one of the most fundamental characteristics of human patterns of behaviour. Organisations and individuals all participate to a greater or lesser extent in this activity, and a nation's material well-being is usually judged in terms of its economic fitness, in other words how economically active it is. There are many factors contributing towards a fit and flourishing economy. They include the presence of natural physical resources, the skills and mobility of the labour force, and the devices used by government to manage the economy. These factors are not matters for consideration in a book of this kind. What however, we are concerned with is a less obvious but nonetheless indispensable component of the economic process, namely the rules and principles which govern the conduct of the participants engaged in negotiating and carrying out the millions of transactions by which economic objectives are achieved. This body of rules and principles is referred to collectively as the law of contract.

Without an effective legal framework to regulate the enormous number of transactions which an industrialised economy demands each day to function effectively, economic activity would go into decline. The reason for this is that most industrial and commercial organisations would be unwilling to take the financial risks inherent in trading, if it were not for the existence of well established, formalised rules of trading, supported by legal sanctions if they are broken. Although it is not possible to prevent a fellow trader from breaking promises, if those promises are included in a contract, then at least one has the reassurance of knowing that since a legal obligation has been broken, court action can if necessary be taken to obtain redress. The remedy which is sought in such cases is usually that of damages, the legal expression used to describe any form of monetary compensation. Thus if a bank is to grant a mortgage, a civil engineering company to construct a motorway, a landowner to grant a lease of land or an employer to take on staff, there needs to be a measure of confidence underlying such agreements so that if they are not carried out a legal remedy is available to the injured party. Without the security of a binding contract there would be little confidence in forming trading bonds. In the absence of any legal sanction the only security likely to exist would depend upon whether the other party either;

(a) felt a moral obligation to meet the promises given, or

(b) believed it could be damaging to his business reputation and standing if it became known that he did not honour his agreements.

It is not only in the economic sphere that contractual ground rules are important. There can also be social implications associated with contractual activities. Some examples may help to illustrate this point. If a manufacturer of children's toys produces items which are dangerous to their users, or an employer dismisses an employee out of spite, or a tour operator sells holidays which it knows do not meet the claims made in the brochure, most people will view this as socially unacceptable conduct in terms of the consequences likely to result from it. As a society it concerns us if children are hurt when playing with dangerous toys whose design faults could not have been discovered at the time their parents purchased them. We would conclude, no doubt, that whatever the manufacturer's legal responsibilities may be, he has been grossly socially irresponsible. Similarly it concerns us that the employee has lost his job without good cause, and the family on holiday with young children find the beach is not 100 metres away from the hotel as they were promised, but 2 kilometres away. In each case there is a social cost, not merely a financial one. The redundant employee cannot find alternative employment nearby, and has to move with the family to another part of the country, disturbing the children's education, incurring debts and creating conditions of stress, whilst the family on holiday suffer considerable disappointment and inconvenience.

Sometimes particular forms of contractual activity may be both economically and socially undesirable. Suppose for example that a major UK employer were to insist on all employees signing an undertaking not to seek further employment with any rival organisation anywhere in the UK, for a period of ten years after leaving the present employer. The effect is likely to be:

(i) to create an unfair trading advantage to the present employer, gained by excluding similar employers who may operate their business more efficiently drawing from the full pool of skilled labour potentially available;

(ii) to prevent employees from exercising the freedom of opportunity to obtain the best salaries that their skills can command; and

(iii) in general economic terms to distort the mobility of labour.

Arguably in circumstances of this kind the desirability of giving the employer the freedom to set employment terms which grant him business protection is offset by the undesirability of allowing him to interfere in the free operation of this particular market.

The need to regulate agreements

It is clear then that rules are necessary to regulate the agreements used in transacting. These rules are needed in order to:

(a) provide a legal framework that offers security and enables commercial activity to expand and prosper;

(b) restrict activities which are economically harmful;

(c) pursue the aims of social justice where appropriate, and

(d) identify the technical means by which parties who wish to do so can make agreements which the law will enforce. An agreement which is legally enforceable is known as a contract.

Before examining the concept of the contract in more depth it is helpful to say a little about the thinking which has guided the lawmakers in creating and developing the principles and rules which make up this vital body of law. As we shall see the law of contract is founded upon common law principles, having been developed by the courts rather than by Parliament.

The Concept of Freedom of Contract

Contracting parties have never enjoyed unlimited freedom to make whatever bargain they choose. Throughout the long development of the English law of contract, which has taken place over many centuries, certain restrictions have always existed. No court, for example has ever been prepared to enforce a contract whose purpose is unlawful, such as an agreement to commit a criminal offence. However the extent of contractual regulation has varied over time, reflecting the thinking current during different periods.

Under the capitalist philosophy of the nineteenth century a laissez-faire approach to the development of the economy was advocated. This involved leaving the markets for goods and services, as far as reasonably practicable, to regulate themselves. The idea of a free market, which should be left to control itself unhindered by the interventions of the courts or Parliament, helped to reinforce the view that had been influential since the eighteenth century of *freedom of contract*. The advocates of freedom of contract considered that as few restrictions as possible should be placed upon the liberty of individuals to make agreements. The Master of the Rolls, Sir George Jessel, expressed it in the following way in 1875: *"If there is one thing which more than any other public policy requires it is that men of full age and understanding shall have the utmost liberty of contracting and their contracts when entered into freely and voluntarily shall be held sacred and shall be enforced by the courts of justice."*

There appear to be some compelling reasons for supporting this view. Firstly the law of contract is a part of private law, which means that the creation and performance of contracts is the responsibility of parties themselves. As we shall see later, contractual rights and obligations only attach to the actual parties entering the contract, although this principle is subject to certain exceptions. Consequently contractual rights and obligations are purely personal. If a contract is broken the only person with the right to a remedy is the injured party, no one else can sue the contract breaker. Secondly it is the parties themselves who are best able to judge their own contractual needs. If their negotiations are not concluded to their mutual satisfaction then they will not go ahead and complete the contract. If on the other hand they are both in agreement they will be happy to bind themselves formally, and incur contractual obligations. They should be left alone to make the contract that suits them, free from external interference.

The objectives of freedom of contract

The underlying reasons for allowing a wide measure of contractual freedom include:

(a) *market needs:*
in the interests of healthy markets the participants in market activity should be allowed to trade unhindered. The able will survive and the weak will flounder. External intervention in this process will tend to weaken rather than strengthen economic performance by the artificial distortion of the bargaining process ;

(b) *personal liberty:*
interference in contract making is an infringement of individual liberty. In the same way that a person chooses when to marry, or for whom to vote, they should be allowed the freedom to make the contracts of their choosing. If subsequently the choice turns out to be a bad one it is of concern to nobody but the contract maker. The contract is a private, not a public event.

(c) *knowledge:*
contracting parties can be assumed to know what they are doing. They act in a

rational manner and will therefore ensure that the contract they make is the contract they want. Nobody else is better placed to identify contractual wants and needs than the parties who are making the contract.

On closer analysis however, it is possible to identify major weaknesses which are inherent in the factors referred to above. In simple terms the underlying flaw in all of them is that they do not reflect the reality of modern contract making. It is important to an understanding of the law of contract to appreciate why the ideas upon which the notion of freedom of contract are based, are in reality largely myths.

The Reality of Business Contracting

The role of consent

In one sense there is complete contractual freedom. Individuals and organisations alike are free to choose whether to enter into a contractual relationship. It cannot be forced on them for consent is a precondition of the relationship. But what precisely does consent mean? To answer this question we need to examine how the courts discriminate between situations where there is a genuine consent, and those in which the consent is in reality artificial. Where the consent is unreal there is no *'consensus ad idem'*, or meeting of the minds of the parties, even though on a mechanical level they have gone through the motions of reaching an agreement. Circumstances in which the courts will be prepared to consider a claim that the consent is unreal are in cases of misrepresentation, mistake, fraud, duress or undue influence. They are referred to technically as vitiating (invalidating) elements. Once established they have the effect of either invalidating the contract in its entirety in which case the contract is said to be *void*, or of entitling the injured party to escape from the contract if he or she wishes to do so. In such circumstances the contract is said to be *voidable* in their favour. To vitiate literally means to make invalid or ineffectual. We will return to void and voidable contracts later.

Vitiating elements are dealt with in the next chapter, but we may note here that by granting relief where consent is a sham because a person has been misled, tricked, coerced or mistaken, the courts are demonstrating that they will look at what the parties believed they were agreeing to when the contract was made. Equally of course, the notion of freedom carries with it responsibility, and it is certainly not the role of the courts to repair bad bargains made through lack of prudence. The balance between intervening in an attempt to right legitimate wrongs, leaving the parties to learn from their trading mistakes is not easily achieved. The point is that the courts are prepared in the right circumstances to untie the bond that has been made, thereby protecting parties in a limited way from the consequences that complete freedom of contract would otherwise produce.

Bargaining inequality

A further important element in examining the concept of freedom of contract is the matter of bargaining power. True consensus is only possible where the parties meet as bargaining equals, but it is commonplace to find that there is an inequality of bargaining power so that one party is able to dominate the other. The result is that far from arriving at agreement through a process of negotiation, the contract is a one sided arrangement in which the dominant party presents terms to the weaker party on a take-it-or-leave it basis. Commonly the dominant party will only be prepared to do business on the basis of standard terms designed to provide him with a high level of commercial protection (see figure 5.2). If the dominant party is a monopoly supplier, like British Gas or British Rail, the consumer is unable to shop around for a better deal. Even in a reasonably competitive market situation, however, it is often the case that suppliers of goods or services trade on the same or very similar terms, for instance by using a contract designed by the trade association of which they are a member. Contracts arising in this way are sometimes referred to as contracts of *adhesion*, for the weaker party is required to adhere all the terms imposed by the stronger party.

Legal Intervention in the Market Place

To help redress such imbalance Parliament has used legislation to bolster the rights of consumers, whether they be businesses or individuals. This legislation is considered elsewhere in the book, but the most notable examples are the Consumer Credit Act 1974, the Unfair Contract Terms Act 1977, and Sale of Goods Act 1979, the Supply of Goods and Services Act 1982 and the Consumer Protection Act 1987.

Even the courts have been prepared to intervene in circumstances of exceptional exploitation. To do so they have applied an equitable principle known as *undue influence*.

> A good illustration is provided by the decision of the Court of Appeal in *Lloyds Bank Ltd. v. Bundy* 1975. Here an elderly farmer, who was ill and had little business knowledge, agreed with the bank to guarantee the account of his son's company. The company was in difficulties, and over a period of time the father increased the size of the guarantee, which was secured by a mortgage on his house, so that eventually the mortgage on the property was for more than the property was worth. This arrangement had been made by the father in consultation with the bank manager, upon whom he implicitly relied. The company's debts remained outstanding, and the bank sought to sell the father's house in order to realise the guarantee. The Court of Appeal unanimously set aside the agreement between the father and the bank. In the course of his judgment Lord Denning M R made the following important observations: *"no bargain will be upset which is the result of the ordinary interplay of forces. There are many hard cases which are caught by this rule . . . yet there are exceptions to this general rule . . . in which the courts will set aside a contract, or a transfer of property, when the parties have not met on equal terms, when the one is so strong in bargaining power and the other so weak that, as a matter of common fairness, it is not right that the strong should be allowed to push the weak to the wall . . . . English law gives relief to one who, without independent advice, enters into a contract on terms which are very unfair or transfers property for a consideration which is grossly inadequate . . . "*

Anti-competitive practices

Finally both Parliament and the courts have been prepared to intervene in cases where the effect of a contract is to act as a restraint of trade. In the words of Lord McNaghten in *Nordenfelt v. Maxim Nordenfelt Gun & Ammunition Co. Ltd.* 1894 *"The public have an interest in every person's carrying on his trade freely; so has the individual. All interference with individual liberty of action in trading, and all restraints of trade themselves, if there is nothing more, are contrary to public policy, and are therefore void."*

Of the many types of restraint of trade recognised, the following are the most common:

(a) restraints on employment. These usually appear as terms inserted in the contract of employment by the employer, designed to prevent employees from setting up in competition when they leave the employment;

(b) agreements between suppliers and retailers under which the retailer agrees to sell only the supplier's goods. The best example of such arrangements can be seen in the practices of the petrol industry. Petrol companies impose *'solus'* agreements upon petrol stations, requiring them to sell only the petrol and other products of that particular petrol company;

(c) price fixing agreements and agreements which seek to restrict or limit supplies of goods.

The essence of a contract in restraint of trade is that it contains an undertaking by one of the parties to restrict that person's freedom of trading action with others in the future. The grounds for legal interference in such arrangements are those of public policy: what the courts and Parliament are seeking to prevent are practices which restrict competition to the detriment of the public.

Summary

It can be seen that despite a general desire to allow parties freedom to make the bargains of their choosing, intervention is exercised in a variety of situations which appear to demand it. In summary these are

(a) where consent is not a true consent;

(b) in circumstances of significant bargaining inequality; and

(c) where the best interests of trade are not being achieved by specific market practices, through the use of anti-competitive devices.

Having examined some of the ideas underlying the concept of what a contract is, we now turn to consider whether any formalities are prescribed by law for creating a contract, and how classifications of contracts are made according to their form and nature.

Classifying Contracts

Introduction - defining the contract

It is a commonly held view that a contract is not valid unless it is written. This is simply not the case, as can be illustrated by the number of times we make purchases of goods or pay for services without even contemplating the need for a written contract. Indeed contracts are invariably carried out by parties who are not even aware that they have been involved in a legal relationship at all. If written contracts were necessary to effect all transactions, a moment's reflection will demonstrate how time consuming, wasteful of paper and largely irrelevant to our needs such a requirement would be. There are, however, some sound reasons in support of the view that a written contract may be worthwhile;

(a) because the writing would stand as evidence of the transaction should anyone challenge its existence, and

(b) because the task of reducing an agreement into writing would presumably prompt the parties into expressing themselves clearly, and thinking about the nature of the transaction they are involved in. It would indicate the rights and obligations of the people making it.

But what exactly is a contract? A contract may be simply defined as a legally enforceable agreement. We need therefore to ascertain what it is that makes certain agreements legally enforceable, and since most of these agreements come into being as simple contracts, the logical starting point is to examine the nature of the simple contract.

Simple Contracts

At common law, parties are free to express a contract in any way, hence the term *'simple'* meaning non-technical. These contracts may be oral, written, or even be inferred from the conduct of the parties. Most simple contracts are oral agreements; buying food, petrol, a record or tape, clothes and so on. Those that are commonly expressed in writing include taking a package holiday, arranging for credit facilities, having building work carried out, joining a bookclub, employing staff, and opening a bank account. There are of course many more. Sometimes the contract may be part written and part oral. Two companies may for instance enter into an agreement where some of the terms such as price are in writing, but others such as delivery arrangements are left to be orally negotiated. Even contracts arising out of conduct are not uncommon. An example will help to illustrate how such a situation can occur. Let us suppose a fuel supplier provides a customer with a fixed quantity of oil each month, under an agreement to run for a year. In the event that the supplier delivers the same quantity of oil in the first month of the following year, and the oil is used by the customer, a new contract would be inferred from the conduct of the parties, even though they have not met face to face. The terms of the new contract will be those of the original.

> In *Brogden v. Metropolitan Railway Co.* 1877 the railway company had been supplied with coal from Brogden for many years. The company was keen to have a formal agreement. It drew up a draft agreement, which was sent to Brogden, and was returned by him to the company marked 'approved', although he had inserted a new term to the draft. For the next two years coal was supplied and paid for between the parties in accordance with the draft agreement, although the company never gave notification that they had accepted it. In fact over the two years it lay in a desk drawer. Then a dispute arose between the parties. Brogden alleged there was no contract binding them. The House of Lords disagreed, taking the view that there was a contract, based upon conduct. This occurred when the order was placed for the coal on the terms of the draft agreement, although it had never been formally accepted. The Lord Chancellor, Lord Cairns, remarked, *"there may be a consensus between the parties far short of a mode of expressing it, and that consensus may be discovered from letters or from other documents of an imperfect and incomplete description"*.

Whilst the law adopts a flexible attitude towards the means by which a contract can be formed, it is most particular about the components which must be present if the transaction is to be legally enforceable. At common law a simple contract must include:

(a) an agreement between the contracting parties;

(b) the provision of consideration to support the contract;

(c) an intention to become legally bound; and

(d) legal capacity held by the parties.

These four vital components are essential. The absence of any one of them will prevent the creation of a contract.

A simple contract which meets these requirements may however still fail for some other reason. Chapter 6 explores in detail how such a failure may occur. Whatever the reason for the failure, it is of the greatest importance to be certain of the effect it has on the contract. The specific nature of the failure determines whether, and if so how, the contract survives, and this in turn tells us about the liabilities of the parties. For the moment, though, we need to concentrate on the classifications applied to contracts generally, and then go on to examine how a contract is formed.

Speciality Contracts, or Deeds

Speciality contracts, which are commonly referred to as deeds, are formal contracts. Up until 1989 a deed had to meet the requirements of being in writing, and signed, sealed and delivered by the person or persons making it. The Law of Property (Miscellaneous Provisions) Act 1989 has abolished the need for a seal when an individual executes a deed, and also the need for a deed to be written on parchment or paper. The only formalities which now must be met are that the signature of the person making the deed be witnessed and attested. The deed must of course be in writing however this writing may be expressed in any form provided it is clear on the face of the document that it is intended to be a deed.

There are relatively few circumstances in which the law demands the use of a deed to give the effect to a contract. A deed is required under the Law of Property Act 1925 to transfer legal ownership in freehold land, and to create a lease of more than three years duration. Although most deeds will arise out of agreements between parties who have exchanged promises of value, a deed is valid without the need for consideration to support it. Validity is achieved by the technical form of the document. Although it was originally necessary for corporate bodies to contract using the corporate seal, the Corporate Bodies Contracts Act 1960 specifies that a corporation can make contracts as though it were an individual, thus there are no longer any special formal requirements attached to corporations and their contract making. It is not uncommon however to find that under their internal rules corporations are obliged to use the corporate seal for contracts above a certain financial amount, for security reasons.

Void, voidable and unenforceable contracts

Sometimes a contract will fail in such a fundamental way as to render it *void*. A void contract carries no contractual rights or obligations, so if goods have been transferred under such a contract, ownership in them will not pass and they can be recovered from the person in possession of them. Where services are rendered under a void contract, a reasonable sum is recoverable for the work done, under the quantum meruit rule, discussed later on page 221.

> This occurred in *Craven-Ellis v. Canons Ltd.* 1936 where it was found that the plaintiff, who had worked for some time as the managing director of the defendant company, had in fact been employed under a deed which was void because he had failed to take up shares in the company as required by the company's articles. Nevertheless, he was entitled to remuneration for the work he had done.

The term 'void contract' is really a contradiction in terms, since if the contract is void there is no legally enforceable agreement amounting to a contract. An example of a void contract is one whose purpose is illegal, such as an agreement to commit a criminal act, or trade with an enemy alien during time of war. Sometimes the contract will not be void but merely *voidable*. Where this is so, one of the parties has the option of avoiding the contract, but until this is done the contract still stands. An example is provided in the case of contracts induced by fraud, where the deceived party can avoid the contract.

Finally, a contract may be *unenforceable*. Where this is so the court is unable to enforce it, if called upon to do so by one of the parties. In other respects however it may possess some effect. For instance if a collateral contract such as a guarantee is built upon it the unenforceability will not invalidate the collateral contract. Unenforceability can occur because of a failure to satisfy some technical requirement, such as the need for written evidence to support certain types of contract.

There is a significant difference between merely requiring written evidence of an agreement, and requiring the entire contract to be in writing. In particular the burden of satisfying the former requirement is less onerous than it is to satisfy the latter.

Contracts where writing is necessary

Statute requires that certain contracts be made in writing. The reason for demanding this is, in some cases, to provide the consumer with a measure of protection, but more usually it is required in an effort to oblige parties involved in technical transactions to record their respective obligations. Examples include:

(a) Hire purchase and conditional sale agreements. Under s.65(1) of the Consumer Credit Act 1974 such an agreement cannot be enforced unless it is properly executed. It is properly executed when a legible document containing all the express terms of the agreement and in the prescribed form is signed by the parties.

(b) The transfer of shares in a registered company. This is required under s.183 Companies Act 1985, which states that a *"proper instrument of transfer"* must be delivered to the company. The company cannot register the transfer until this is done.

(c) An acknowledgement of a debt which has become statute-barred, under the Limitation Act 1980.

(d) An assignment of copyright, under s.90 Copyright Designs and Patents Act 1988.

(e) Cheques, bills of exchange and promissory notes, under the Bills of Exchange Act 1882.

(f) Contracts for the sale or other disposition of land under the Law of Property (Miscellaneous Provisions) Act 1989. The writing required under the Act must incorporate all the terms expressly agreed by the parties and appear in a single document, or where contracts are exchanged, in both. The 1989 Act abolishes the rule previously contained in s.40(1) Law of Property Act 1925, which simply required that in transactions involving land there be written evidence of the transaction to make it enforceable. Now the contract itself has to be in writing.

Failure to comply with these statutory requirements renders the contract invalid.

There remains one type of contract which still only requires written evidence of its existence, rather than a written contract containing it, the contract of guarantee. Such contracts are covered by the Statute of Frauds 1677 (as amended). A contract of guarantee is a *"promise to answer for the debt, default or miscarriage of another person"* and the guarantor's liability arises only upon the failure of the debtor to pay.

Which law applies?

When contracts are made between parties who are residents or nationals of different countries one question which arises is which body of laws will apply to their agreement. Generally this question does not become important unless a dispute occurs. It may then become apparent that by applying the contractual rules of their respective states different outcomes are obtained. A further issue will be which courts have the jurisdiction to deal with the dispute if it is taken to law. These are important issues, involving consideration not only as to what the law of the different jurisdictions is, but also how effective their different systems of civil justice are. The costs involved in bringing proceedings, the likely duration of those proceedings, and factors of convenience associated with the location of the relevant courts all need to be borne in mind.

As part of the process of legal harmonisation between the member states of the EC, the United Kingdom has incorporated a number of European conventions dealing with contractual conflict of laws in the Contracts (Applicable Law) Act 1990. The Act is likely to come into operation in 1991. The major convention which the Act introduces is the Rome convention. Article 3 provides that the parties to a contract are free to choose which country's law shall govern it. If they have not chosen Article 4 provides that the contract shall be governed by the law of the country with which it is most closely connected, and the presumption is that this will be the country, *"where the party who is to effect the performance which is characteristic of the contract"* has habitual residence or in the case of a business organisation has its central administration. In a contract for the sale of goods between a buyer in France and a seller in England it would be English law which would apply. If however it is clear that in all the circumstances the contract is more closely associated with another country, then the presumption will not apply. Under Article 5, if the contract involves the supply of goods or services to a consumer for a purpose outside his or her trade or profession, the applicable law is that of the country where the consumer habitually resides if, inter alia, *"the supplier received the order from the consumer in that country."*

Although as we have seen the parties can choose which law shall apply to them, even if they do so the Rome convention indicates that in certain circumstances this will be overridden. One circumstance where this will occur is in the case of a consumer transaction coming within Article 5 above. So if a private consumer in the UK agrees to purchase a motor vehicle from a German motor dealer by placing the order with the German company's agent in London, then even though the contract specifies that German law shall apply to it, the applicable law will be UK law, or at least that part of UK law which, in the words of the convention is *"mandatory"*. Mandatory rules of law are defined as those rules which cannot be ousted under the contract, such as implied conditions under the Sale of Goods Act 1979.

It would seem that with the introduction of the single market the application of these rules under the 1990 Act will become of increasing importance to businesses and consumers alike.

Having considered the formalities that are attached to contracting, we now need to look in some depth at the elements involved in forming a valid contract.

Formation of Contracts

Agreement

A contract cannot be created without the parties reaching an agreement. The idea of agreement is therefore central to an understanding of the law of contract. In the business context there are two basic legal questions which arise in respect of all transactions. These are firstly whether a legally enforceable agreement has been made, and secondly what are the terms upon which it is based.

The answer to the second question will reveal the specific obligations each party has towards the other, a matter of considerable importance to them both. It is only by identifying the content and extent of their mutual undertakings that the parties are able to know when they have discharged their responsibilities under the contract, and freed themselves from their legal bond. The two questions are, of course, very closely connected, because it is through the process of reaching their agreement that the parties will expressly fix the terms that are to regulate their contract. In other words, agreements are arrangements to do, or sometimes refrain from doing, specific things, and these specific things are the terms of the contract.

It may be true that most people can instinctively tell whether they have an agreement or not, however for legal purposes it is not sufficient to rely upon subjective judgments to decide such significant events. If a disputed agreement comes before a court, obviously the court cannot get inside the minds of the parties to discover their actual intentions. At best all that can be achieved is to look at the way they have conducted themselves, examining what they have said and done, in order to decide the issue on the basis of what a reasonable person would assume.

What the courts do is objectively to assess the evidence and to apply established criteria to help resolve contractual disputes. These criteria take the form of fixed and certain rules, which over a long period have been developed and refined by the judiciary and which are used by all courts to determine what constitutes an enforceable agreement. It follows that a person may find himself legally bound by an agreement, which, in his own mind, he does not consider he has made. How important then, for organisations and individuals alike, to know and understand these rules. Certainly no business can effectively conduct its affairs without the application of such knowledge.

For the sake of convenience agreements can be divided into two separate components:

(i) an offer, made by one party to the other; and

(ii) an acceptance by the other of the terms contained in the offer.

If a court cannot identify the presence of these two components in a transaction, a simple contract will not have materialised, although as we have seen a person can become bound contractually by expressing a promise in the form of a deed. This is not a common practice, and all we need to note here is that the validity of a deed lies in the specialised form in which the promise is made, rather than in the need for agreement.

The process of negotiation

The person making an offer is referred to as the *offeror*, and the person to whom it is addressed is the *offeree*. In business it is usual to find the parties reaching agreement following a period of negotiation. Such negotiations will be concerned with the details of the proposed transaction, and are likely to include matters such as price, specifications regarding the subject matter of the agreement, and the time and place for performing it. Often during these negotiations offers will be made by one party to the other which are rejected, or met by a fresh offer. Thus either of the parties to the transaction is able to make an offer, not just the one who wishes to sell the goods or services in question or who is the owner or supplier of them.

Examining the negotiating process is important for four reasons:

(i) because it enables us to identify which party made the final offer;

(ii) because it enables us to identify the time at which the contract is made;

(iii) because having established who made the offer we can identify the terms upon which the offer was based, and hence on which the contract is founded;

(iv) because during negotiations false statements are sometimes made by one of the parties which induce the other to enter into the contract. These are referred to as misrepresentations.

Characteristics of a Valid Offer

To be legally effective an offer must satisfy the following requirements:

(a) the offer must be firmly made;

(b) the offer must be communicated;

(c) the terms of the offer must be certain; and

(d) the offer must not have terminated.

Firm offer or invitation to treat

The offeror must intend his offer to be unequivocal, so that when acceptance occurs he will be bound. The difficulty that can arise here lies in distinguishing firm offers from statements which do not carry the full legal status of offers. Sometimes what appears to be a firm offer is merely an incentive or encouragement designed by the person making it to encourage the making of offers to him and is certainly not intended to be legally binding. A statement of this kind is known as an invitation to treat. It is an indication that the person is willing to do business with anyone who is interested.

> In *Pharmaceutical Society of Great Britain v. Boots Cash Chemists (Southern) Ltd.* 1953 one of the shops in the company's chain had been converted into a self-service supermarket. Some of the shelves carried poisons which by statute were required to be sold in the presence of a qualified chemist. The chemist was in attendance at the checkout. The Pharmaceutical Society which had a duty to enforce the statutory provisions claimed that the company was in breach of them. The Society argued that the contract was made at the shelves where there was no pharmacist in attendance. The court however held that the goods displayed on the shelves were merely invitations to treat. The contract was made at the checkout. The customers made the offer when presenting the goods for payment and the offer was accepted by the cashier.
>
> Clearly there can be no real distinction between goods displayed on shelves inside a shop and goods displayed in the window. Thus in *Fisher v. Bell* 1961 a shop keeper was prosecuted for displaying a flick-knife inside his shop win-

dow with a price ticket attached. He was found by the court not to have committed the offence of offering for sale an offensive weapon contrary to the Restriction of Offensive Weapons Act 1959. The display was simply an invitation to treat.

Advertisements are also generally regarded as constituting invitations to treat. In *Partridge v. Crittenden* 1968 the Divisional Court of the Queens Bench Division was asked to determine whether an advertisement in a magazine which read, *"Bramblefinch cocks, bramblefinch hens 25/- each"*, constituted the offence of offering to sell wild birds contrary to the Protection of Birds Act 1954. The court quashed the conviction against the defendant which had been issued in the Magistrates Court. The advertisement was simply an encouragement to stimulate the market into making offers. Members of the public responding to the advert made the offers, but of course they could not commit an offence since they were offering to buy, not to sell. The defendant should have been charged with the separate offence contained in the Act of selling wild birds.

The legal inference that advertisements will not normally amount to firm offers to sell is of some value to businesses that trade on a mail-order basis. For instance a company that takes out advertising in a newspaper or colour supplement cannot be sure of the demand for its goods that will result. If the advertisement were to constitute an offer, then the response of a member of the public in sending a cheque or postal order to buy the advertised goods would amount to an acceptance. The company could find itself overwhelmed by the demand, and under a legal obligation to supply goods it simply does not have if its stocks are exhausted.

Perhaps the clearest example of an invitation to treat can be seen in an auction sale. This occurs when the auctioneer presents items in the auction, and asks for bids from those who are present, using expressions such as *"how much am I bid for . . . ?"* and *"do I see £20?"* The auctioneer is testing demand, and having assessed it will try to increase it and push the price up. The auctioneer is certainly not offering to sell. The bids themselves constitute offers which the auctioneer is able to accept or reject.

As can be seen in the cases above, it is usually in connection with criminal offences that the question of what constitutes an offer will arise. In relation to auction sales an illustration of this position is provided by *British Car Auctions Ltd. v. Wright* 1972. An unroadworthy car had been sold at auction. The auctioneers were convicted in the Magistrates court of offering to sell an unroadworthy vehicle, contrary to the Road Traffic Act 1972. In quashing the conviction Widgery LCJ stated: *"The auctioneer when he stands on his rostrum does not make an offer to sell the goods on behalf of the vendor; he stands there making an invitation to those present at the auction themselves to make offers to buy".*

Further examples of the invitation to treat are advertisements inviting suppliers of goods and services to submit tenders, and prospectuses issued by limited companies inviting members of the public to subscribe for shares.

Tenders

The use of tenders is a common commercial practice. Indeed local authorities are required by the Local Government Act 1972 to contract in this way. Under s.135 a contract made by an authority must comply with its standing orders and these standing orders must include provisions for securing competition and for regulating the manner in which tenders are invited in the case of contracts for the supply of goods or materials or for the execution of works. This is usually satisfied by inviting tenders from contractors on an approved list maintained by the authority. The Local Government Act 1988 imposes particular restrictions on local authorities by requiring that certain activities cannot be carried out by the council's own workforce without first going to competitive tender, which will involve the authority itself in making a written bid for the work. The activities covered by the Act include contracts for the collection of refuse, school and other catering arrangements, ground maintenance and the repair and maintenance of motor vehicles. Under the tendering process a tender is an offer and an invitation to tender is an invitation to treat. It is merely an invitation by an individual or organisation wishing to purchase goods or services to request suppliers to submit a contractual offer in the form of a tender.

In appropriate circumstances however it is possible to treat an invitation to tender as giving rise to a binding contractual obligation. If there is clear evidence from what the parties have said and done that a contractual obligation to consider a particular tender in conjunction with all other tenders meeting the tendering requirements was intended, then the Court will enforce it.

> In *Blackpool and Fylde Aero Club v. Blackpool Borough Council* 1990 the local authority owned and managed an airport. The plaintiff flying club had for some years operated pleasure flights from the airport. When the grant of the club's concession came up for renewal the council prepared invitations to tender. These were then sent to the club and six other parties. The forms sent out stated that the council did not bind itself, *"to accept all or any part of any tender"*. The form added, *"No tender which is received after the last date and time specified shall be admitted for consideration."*
>
> The plaintiffs delivered their tender to the council offices before the deadline, however because council staff failed to empty the council letter box when they should have done the council received the tender too late to be considered, and accepted a tender from another tenderer lower in value than the plaintiff's tender. The club sued for damages alleging breach of contract and negligence. The Court held that although contracts in such circumstances should not be freely implied, the evidence here was of a clear intention that the council was contractually obliged to consider the plaintiff's tender with the other tenders, or at least that it would be considered if all the others were. The claim for breach of contract was successful. The question of whether the council would have owed the plaintiffs a duty to take reasonable care to consider a tender submitted within the stated time limit, in the absence of an implied contractual obligation to do so, was not decided.

If the invitation to tender stipulates expressly or impliedly that the goods or services will be required, then an acceptance of the tender will create a binding contract. Alternatively, the invitation may stipulate that the goods or services *may* be required, in which case an acceptance of the tender results in a standing offer to supply as and when required. A failure to order by the buyer in such circumstances will not result in a breach of contract.

> In *Harvela Investments Ltd. v. Royal Trust Co. of Canada Ltd.* 1985 the House of Lords was required to examine the nature of an invitation to tender in the context of the sale of shares. Royal Trust of Canada was prepared to sell some of its shares, and invited two companies, Harvela and Outerbridge to tender for them. The invitation to do so stipulated that the tender should contain a single offer price, and be sealed i.e. be made privately. It

also stated that the highest bid would be accepted. Harvela's bid was $2,175,000. Outerbridge offered $2,100,000 or $101,000 in excess of any other higher bid, whichever was the higher. A bid of this kind is known as a referential bid. The seller informed both parties that the shares had been purchased by Outerbridge, at a price of $2,276,000. Harvela challenged this claim. The court held that on the facts the referential bid by Outerbridge was invalid. It took the view that the presumed intention of the sellers should be deduced from the terms of the invitation read as a whole, and this was then intended to create a fixed bidding scale. In support of this presumed intention were the facts that they had undertaken to accept the highest offer which they had extended to both bidders thus giving them an equal opportunity to purchase the shares. The fact that the sellers insisted on confidentiality in the submission of bids to provoke the best price that each party was prepared to pay was consistent with the presumed intention to create a fixed bidding scale. Accordingly Outerbridge had not been entitled to submit a referential bid and the sellers had not been entitled to accept it. The court ordered the transfer of the shares to Harvela at the price of $2,175,000.

It should be noted however that the invitation to treat is not devoid of legal effect. It can give rise to legal liability in the following ways:

(a) As a statement it can amount to an actionable misrepresentation (see later).

(b) It may also give rise to criminal liability under the Trade Descriptions Act 1968, if it constitutes a false trade description, or under the Consumer Protection Act 1987 if it gives a false or misleading indication as to the price of goods or services.

(c) Under specific legislation it may give rise to legal liability. For instance in the case of a company prospectus, s.166 Companies Act 1985 provides that the person responsible for a prospectus is liable to compensate anyone acquiring shares to which the prospectus relates, if they suffer loss as a result of an untrue or misleading statement in it.

An offer must be communicated

The party to whom an offer is directed must be aware of it. An offer will normally be made to a single individual or organisation, however there is nothing to prevent an offer being directed to a specific group of individuals, anyone or more of whom may choose to accept it. For instance a private limited company that is going public may offer some of its shares at favourable rates to the members of its workforce.

It is possible to make an offer to the public generally, where the offeror is not able at the time the offer is made to identify who the possible recipients are. This principle has been in existence for a long time, and seems to be derived from the willingness of the courts to recognise a contractual obligation on the part of someone offering to pay any member of the public a reward, for example in return for information or the return of property. It is not uncommon to find banks offering financial rewards for information leading to the conviction of bank robbers by displaying notices inside the banks. In such circumstances anyone who satisfies the terms of the offer will be entitled to the reward, as long as they were aware of the offer beforehand. One of the most celebrated instances of an offer made to the public at large, occurred in *Carlill v. Carbolic Smokeball Co.* 1893 which is considered below.

What constitutes communication is a question of fact for the court.

The terms of an offer must be certain

In the event of a dispute between the parties as to the meaning of a term it will ultimately fall to the court to decide the question. The courts will always endeavour to find certainty so that the contract is able to survive wherever possible but if a term is obscure or meaningless then it will fail. This may not prove fatal to the contract if the term constitutes only a minor part of the overall obligations, but where the term is central to the functioning of the contract, uncertainty as to its meaning will defeat the contract as a whole. The following cases illustrate the position.

> In *Loftus v. Roberts* 1902 an agreement provided for the appointment of an actress by another person at a *"West End salary to be mutually agreed between us."* Subsequently the parties were unable to arrive at a salary which satisfied them both. The court held that the contract must fail. Even if it were possible to assess a suitable salary by reference to West End rates of pay, the court could not impose such a figure since the parties had already stated that it had to be mutually agreed, something they had been unable to achieve. What they had was an agreement to agree at a further date. The contract failed.

> In *Scammel v. Ouston* 1941 an agreement for the sale of a van where the balance of the price was to be met *"on hire purchase terms over a period of two years"* also failed. Since there was no previous course of dealing between the parties to enable the court to identify what these "hire purchase" terms might be, the only alternative would have been to treat the terms as standard hire purchase terms. Unfortunately, as the court observed, hire purchase terms are not standardised and identical, but vary from agreement to agreement so that for example rates of interest will vary from company to company.

A meaningless term can however often be ignored.

> In *Nicolene Ltd. v. Simmonds* 1953 a contract was made for the sale of 3000 tons of steel bars. The seller then broke the contract, and when the buyer sued for damages the seller argued there was no contract between them, relying on a statement in one of the contractual documents that, *"we are in agreement that the usual conditions of acceptance apply"*. The court, whilst recognising that there were no "usual conditions of acceptance", between the parties, found that the contract was in every other respect clear as to the obligations of the parties. The meaningless term could be cut out from the rest of the contract. In the course of his judgment Lord Denning MR commented that, *"A clause which is meaningless can often be ignored . . . ; whereas a clause which has yet to be agreed may mean there is no contract at all."*

A common example of a clause or term which the parties have yet to agree is price, and price is obviously a vital term in any contract. In the unlikely event that the parties have reached agreement whilst overlooking the question of price altogether how will this affect their agreement? In such circumstances it may still be possible to enforce the agreement. In the case of sales of goods, the Sale of Goods Act 1979 provides under s.8 that if the parties have not agreed price, or arranged a method for fixing price, or previously dealt with each other so that there is a price level in existence, then the buyer is bound to pay a reasonable price. This will usually be the market price. A similar rule applies in relation to those contracts which are covered by the Supply of Goods and Services Act 1982. As we saw in *Loftus v. Roberts* the most difficult situation to overcome is one in which an agreement has been made to settle price at a later date.

> In *May and Butcher v. R.* 1929 Lord Buckmaster said of this situation, *"It has long been a well-recognised principle of contract law that an agreement between two parties to enter into an agreement in which some critical part of the contract is left undetermined is no contract at all."*

It is an entirely different matter however, if machinery has been agreed which can be used to fix the price, or indeed resolve any other aspect of uncertainty.

> In *Sykes (F & G) Wessex v. Fine Fare* 1967 a supplier of chickens undertook to supply a supermarket chain with between 30,000 and 80,000 birds each week over a period of one year. The agreement also provided that for a further four years the supplier would provide chickens in quantities *"as might be agreed"*. The court held that since the contract provided for arbitration to settle disagreements, the contract was not void on the basis of the uncertainty of the term as to quantity.
>
> In the context of arbitration arrangements of this kind the decision in *Sudbrook Trading Estate Ltd. v. Eggleton* 1982 is worth noting. Here the tenant of some land had the right to buy the freehold before the lease ran out. The purchase price was to be determined by two arbitrators, one appointed by the tenant and the other by the landlord. The tenant exercised his option, but later the landlord refused to appoint an arbitrator. The House of Lords held that in these circumstances the court itself would order the transfer and make separate arrangements to fix the price.

When the sale of land is being negotiated it is usual practice for parties initially to reach an agreement *"subject to contract."* Transactions involving land are considered in detail later in the book and here all we are concerned with are general observations regarding issues of offer and acceptance in the sale of land. Agreement on a subject to contract basis usually achieves no more than to demonstrate a willingness on the part of the prospective purchaser to proceed towards a formal agreement if his professional advisors make no adverse discoveries concerning the property in question. The technical nature of land transactions makes it extremely unwise for a purchaser to enter into a binding agreement without first making inquiries regarding the property. Thus a purchaser will seek to show the vendor that it is his intention to purchase provided the inquiries that are made prove satisfactory. To achieve this he will make a 'conditional offer,' or a 'conditional acceptance' by using an expression like 'subject to contract'. It is well settled that this creates no binding obligation on the parties.

Prior to the Law of Property (Miscellaneous Provisions) Act 1989 the use of the words subject to contract on all letters and other documents signed by either party or his agent or representative before exchange of contracts was essential, as such documents could otherwise amount to written evidence of the contract under s.40 Law of Property Act 1925. This would enable the other party to sue on the agreement even where no contracts were formally signed or exchanged.

With the coming into effect of the 1989 Act, however, the rule in s.40 has been repealed and it is no longer possible to enforce an oral contract for the sale of land which is merely evidenced in writing. Rather, under s.2 of the 1989 Act, the contract must be made in writing, signed by the parties and contain all of the express terms in order to be valid.

The offer must not have terminated

If the offer has come to an end in some way before the offeree accepts it, the acceptance is of no legal effect for there is no longer an offer to accept. However we need to look closely at how offers once made can legally be regarded as at an end. This can occur in the following ways:

(a) where the offeror has revoked the offer;
or

(b) where the offer has lapsed;
or

(c) where the offer has been accepted or met with a counter offer.

Where the offeror has revoked the offer

Revocation is permissible at any time before the offeree has accepted it, and the revocation can be effective even if it is not communicated directly by the offeror, provided it is communicated through some reliable channel. However, like an offer, a revocation will only be effective when it is actually communicated by being brought to the attention of the offeree. The following cases illustrate these points.

> In *Dickinson v. Dodds* 1876 an offer to sell some houses was expressed to remain open until 9 a.m. on Friday. The offeree however learnt from a reliable third party on Thursday that the offeror had negotiated a sale to another purchaser. This was held to be sufficient to amount to a revocation .

> In *Byrne & Co. v. Leon Van Tienhoven & Co.* 1880 an offer to sell tin plate was received by the offeree on 11 October, and immediately accepted by telegram. The offeror however had posted a revocation which the offeree received on 20 October. It was held the revocation was only effective when actually received, and was therefore too late.

Does actual receipt mean physical delivery to the business premises of the offeree or must it in addition be opened and read? The House of Lords has suggested that it will be effective even if it has not been opened, provided that it would have been opened, *"if the ordinary course of business was followed"*. This comment, which was made in *Eagleshill Ltd. v. J Needham (Builders) Ltd.* 1972 makes clear that a business which for whatever reason fails to promptly deal with its mail may nonetheless find itself bound by the contents of any letters of revocation it has received. The *Blackpool and Fylde Aero Club* case referred to previously, provides a further illustration of the possible consequences of failing to deal with mail promptly.

If the offeror seeks to revoke an offer made to the world at large, although there is no decided case on the point, it is likely that the revocation can be effected by using the same publicity as that afforded to the original offer. For instance if a new supermarket which is to open next week advertised in the local paper that the first twenty customers taking goods to the checkout on opening day would receive a free bottle of champagne, then a further advertisement in the same paper informing the public that no champagne will be available should be a sufficient act of revocation. It may however do little for business goodwill.

Sometimes an offeror may seek to revoke the offer after the offeree has started to perform the act required by the offeror, but has not yet completed it. Suppose for example that in an attempt to increase the sales, a national newspaper offers £100,000 to the first person to produce a pollution free petrol engine by a certain date. Before this date the newspaper, which is in financial difficulties announces that it is withdrawing its offer. In the meantime an engineer has made considerable progress on a pollution free engine design. It seems that the revocation will not be effective as regards the engineer, on the grounds that the offer carried with it an implied undertaking that it would remain open until the specified date, and that in any event once the engineer starts to carry out the work he has accepted the offer which cannot thereafter be revoked.

Where the offer has lapsed

An offer will lapse automatically in the following circumstances:

(a) after a stated time limit for which it was to be held open has passed;

(b) if there is no such time limit, after a reasonable time;

In *Ramsgate Victoria Hotel Co. Ltd. v. Montefiore* 1866 the defendant offered by letter on 8 June to buy shares in the company, and was allotted the shares on 23 November. It was held that the defendant was entitle to refuse the shares, since his offer had lapsed before the company had made the allotment. Clearly the market value of shares can fluctuate widely over a period of six months;

(c) if the situation on which it was based has fundamentally changed, as for example where the property which has been offered for sale has been destroyed by fire, or has been stolen before acceptance occurs;

(d) where the offeror has died, if this is known to the offeree before acceptance. If the offeree is unaware of the offeror's death the latter's estate will be bound by the contract.

There is no legal obligation on an offeror to keep the offer open for any particular length of time, unless some separate contract has been entered into between the offeror and the offeree to this effect.

Characteristics of a Valid Acceptance

Acceptance is defined as the unconditional assent to all the terms of the offer. It must therefore be unequivocal. As we have already seen a conditional acceptance will occur when a potential purchaser of land agrees to buy it subject to contract. This is acceptance subject to happening of a future event which may or may not occur, and is not therefore binding.

The following points provide an indication of how to determine whether an acceptance is valid:

It must be unconditional

It is surprisingly common to find people believing that they have accepted the offer, when in fact they have made a fresh offer themselves by accepting on conditions. The general position regarding the need for unconditional assent is as follows:

(a) a conditional acceptance will constitute a counter offer. Thus a conditional acceptance does not complete the transaction but rather continues the negotiations;

(b) a counter offer both rejects and extinguishes an original offer.

In *Hyde v. Wrench* 1840 the defendant offered his farm to the plaintiff for £1,000. The plaintiff replied offering £950. The defendant subsequently rejected this, so the plaintiff purported to accept the original £1,000 offer. It was held that there was no contract since the original offer had been extinguished by the counter offer. Although expressed as an acceptance, it was in fact a fresh offer;

(c) any alteration to the terms of the offer will render the acceptance invalid.

For instance in *Northland Airlines Ltd. v. Dennis Ferranti Meters Ltd.* 1970 which involved negotiations for the purchase of an aircraft by Northland from Ferranti, a telegram from Ferranti stated, *"confirming sale to you - aircraft - £27,000. Winnipeg. Please remit £5,000 for account of . . . "* to which Northland replied by telegram, *"This is to confirm your cable and my purchase - aircraft on terms set out in your cable. Price £27,000 delivered Winnipeg. £5,000 forwarded to your bank in trust for your account pending delivery. Balance payable on delivery. Please confirm delivery to be made 30 days within this date."* This was held by the Court of Appeal to be a counter offer, for it contained new terms provisions regarding delivery, and payment of the deposit in trust rather than outright, so that it did not transfer to the seller until physical delivery had occurred;

(d) in commercial dealings between parties each trading on their standard terms, the terms which apply to the contract will often be those belonging to the party who fired the last shot. This situation has become known as the 'battle of the forms'.

In *Butler Machine Tool Co. v. Ex-Cell-O Corporation (England) Ltd.* 1979 the plaintiffs offered to sell a machine tool to the defendants in a quotation. This contained a price variation clause, which by means of a specific formula enabled the plaintiffs to raise the quoted price between contract and delivery if their own costs rose. The defendants ordered the goods but on their own standard terms which did not include a price variation clause. The plaintiffs, on receipt of the order form, signed and returned an acknowledgement slip which it contained. The plaintiff's costs rose considerably between contract and delivery. The Court of Appeal regarded the defendant's order as a counter offer, and the return of the acknowledgement slip as the plaintiff's acceptance. The contract between them did not therefore contain a price variation clause.

The acceptance must be communicated

It is open to the offeror to stipulate the method by which acceptance may be made. If no stipulation is made, anything that achieves communication will suffice; words, writing or conduct. If it is clear that the offeror demands a particular method of acceptance only, then no other method will be effective. In most cases however, the offeror is likely to do little more than to give a general indication of the form of acceptance to be used. Where this occurs but the offeree adopts a different method of acceptance which is as quick or quicker than the specified method, the acceptance will be effective, since no disadvantage will have been caused to the offeror.

> Consequently the Court of Appeal in *Yates Building Co. v. R J Pulleyn & Son (York)* 1976 held that an acceptance by means of ordinary post was effective, despite the offeror directing that registered post or recorded delivery should be used.

Given the need for positive action in communicating, it follows that silence can never amount to an effective acceptance of the offer. This holds true even if the parties have, in advance, agreed upon such procedure. For instance, if following an interview, an employer says to the interviewee that the job is his or hers if they hear nothing from the employer in the next five days, the interviewee agrees this arrangement, and the five days elapse without word from the employer, a binding contract will not have come into existence. What the law requires is some positive act.

> In *Felthouse v. Bindley* 1862 an uncle wrote to his nephew offering to buy the nephew's horse for £30.15s. and stating *"If I hear no more about him I shall consider the horse mine at that price".* The nephew gave instructions to the defendant, an auctioneer, not to sell the horse as he intended it for his uncle. The defendant inadvertently sold the horse, and the uncle sued him in the tort of conversion. The court held that action must fail. The horse had not become the uncle's for there was not a contract.

The existence of this common law principle did not in the past act as a disincentive to curb the practice of inertia selling, and it was not until the passing of the Unsolicited Goods and Services Act 1971 (as amended) that the practice was effectively controlled. Inertia selling involves sending goods by post to recipients who have not requested them. Usually an accompanying letter will indicate that if the goods are not wanted they should be returned, but that if the recipient retains possession of them beyond a stated period (usually between seven and twenty one days) this will be treated as acceptance, and payment should then be made. Prior to 1971 this type of 'hard sell' was widespread: it is an example of the way in which the less scrupulous try to take advantage of the public's absence of legal knowledge and awareness. The 1971 Act provides that the recipient of unsolicited goods can treat them as an unconditional gift after six months have elapsed. The period is reduced to thirty days if the recipient serves notice on the sender asking that that goods be collected and the sender fails to do this .

There are two circumstances in which acceptance can operate without communication occurring at the same time, firstly in cases where the post is used to create the contract and secondly where the nature of the offer makes formal notification of acceptance unrealistic.

Transactions using the post

Transactions effected by means of correspondence in the form of letters, fax's, invoices, quotations and share applications are obviously very common in commercial life. From a practical standpoint a business organisation will wish to keep records of its business activities, and the use of written correspondence is an effective way of achieving this.

Where the post is used there will always be a period during which the letter is in transit when the person to whom it is addressed is unaware of its contents. In the case of an offer or revocation of an offer made by post the communication is effective only when it is received by the party to whom it is sent. However, in the case of an acceptance by post the courts have laid down a rule that the letter is effective at the time and place of posting, provided it was correctly addressed and pre-paid. This rule applies even if the letter of acceptance is lost or destroyed in the post.

The case of *Henthorn v. Fraser* 1882 illustrates the practical application of the post rules. Fraser offered to sell some houses to Henthorn and gave him fourteen days to consider. The following day Fraser decided the price he had quoted was too low and wrote to Henthorn revoking the offer. After the letter of revocation had been posted but before he had received it, Henthorn decided to buy the houses, and posted his letter of acceptance at 3.50 p.m. It was held that a binding contract had come into existence at 3.50 p.m. The letter of revocation was ineffective, for it had arrived too late.

This position was confirmed in the case of *Brinkibon Ltd. v. Stahag Stahl und Stahlwarenghandel* 1983. The parties had contracted using telex facilities. The plaintiffs were in London and the defendants in Vienna. The acceptance was telexed from London to Vienna. The defendants were alleged by the plaintiffs to be in breach of contract and the plaintiffs sought leave to serve a writ on the defendants. Since the defendants were outside the jurisdiction of the English Courts, having their business in Austria, the only way the writ could be served under the rules of the Supreme Court was if the contract had been made in England. The House of Lords held that the contract had been made in Vienna.

It is, of course, open to the parties to vary these rules if they wish to do so, and it may be prudent for an offeror to stipulate that an acceptance in writing which is posted to him shall not be effective until it is actually received. It is common to find terms in standard form business contracts to this effect, and the courts seem willing to infer a variation of the post rules whenever possible.

In *Holwell Securities Ltd. v. Hughes* 1974 an option (offer) provided that it should be exercisable *"by notice in writing"*. The court held that this requirement effectively excluded the postal rule and that actual receipt of the letter of acceptance was necessary to conclude a contract.

The consequences of the post rules can be remarkable. In *Household Fire Insurance Co. v. Grant* 1879 the defendant applied for 100 shares in the plaintiff company. The company received his application form, and the company secretary in consequence completed and posted a letter of allotment to the defendant, and entered his name on the register of shareholders. The letter never arrived. Some time later the company went into liquidation, and the liquidator claimed the payment outstanding on the shares from the defendant. By a majority the Court of Appeal held that the defendant was liable for this sum. The shares became his when the letter of allotment was posted, even though he never received it and was therefore unaware that he had become a shareholder.

Formal acceptance unrealistic

Sometimes the circumstances of the offer are such that the courts will regard conduct which occurs without the knowledge of the offeror as a sufficient method of acceptance. Although in a sense this is not the same as silence, from the offeror's point of view it amounts to the same thing, since if the offeree does not have to make contact with the offeror, the offeror remains in the dark. Where an offer has been made to the public at large the courts may take the view that the offeror could not possibly have expected to receive an acceptance from every person who has decided to take up the offer. This would be a commercial nonsense.

> In *Carlill v. Carbolic Smokeball Co.* 1893 the defendant company advertised a medical preparation which they manufactured, and claimed in the advertisement that they would pay £100 reward to anybody who contracted *"the increasing epidemic of influenza"* after purchasing and using the product as directed. The advertisement added that £1000 was deposited with the Alliance Bank *"showing our sincerity in the matter"* The plaintiff purchased a smokeball, used it as directed, then caught influenza. She sued for her £100 reward. The court held that the advertisement constituted a firm offer intended to be legally binding, since the bank deposit indicated an intention to meet claims, the offer could be made to the public at large, and acceptance of the offer in such circumstances could be implied by the conduct of those like the plaintiff, who performed the stated conditions. In consequence the company were held liable.

It is only when the parties have reached an agreement which satisfies the common law requirements relating to offer and acceptance that a contract can be said to have been made. One of the traditional views of contracting sees the contract in terms of a meeting of minds or *consensus ad idem*, however an examination of the law relating to agreement reveals that sometimes a binding agreement can occur where the minds of the parties are not entirely at one. This situation can be seen most clearly in the next chapter, which considers the effect of circumstances where consent to the agreement is not a true consent. Sometimes, however, even the presence of a consensus between the parties will not be enough for an agreement to be treated as legally valid if the fundamental principles of offer and acceptance have not been met.

> In *Gibson v. Manchester City Council* 1979 the parties were engaged in negotiations for the sale of a council house to the plaintiff, a council tenant. The plaintiff, having completed a request for information received a letter from the council saying it might be prepared to sell the house to him for £2,180 freehold and that if he wished to make a formal application to purchase he should return the application form. This the tenant did. Unfortunately he left the purchase price blank requesting that the price should take into account defects in the path of the property. A further letter from the council stated that defects in the path had been taken into account in fixing the price. In interpreting the above correspondence a majority of the Court of Appeal held that a contract of sale had indeed been entered into. Lord Denning M R put forward the view that in such circumstances there was no need to look for a strict offer and acceptance rather, *"you should look at the correspondence as a whole and at the conduct of the parties and see therefrom whether the parties have come to an agreement on everything that was material".* This decision was later reversed following a further appeal to the House of Lords in 1979. The Law Lords adopted the more traditional approach by analysing each piece of correspondence ,and held that no firm offer had been made or accepted by the council. The words that the council *"may be prepared to sell"* only amounted to an invitation to treat and thus no contract of sale had resulted.

It is clear in Gibson that whilst no contract actually resulted from their negotiations, both sides were, at least initially, willing to contract over the sale of the property. There are other authorities by way of contrast which suggest that under suitable conditions a contract may arise where there is clearly no consensus between the parties, but where logic or common-sense seems to demand that the court read one into the situation.

> In *Clarke v. Dunraven* 1897 the parties were yacht owners who entered their vessels for a yacht club regatta. Each owner who took part in the regatta undertook in a letter sent to the yacht club to obey its rules. These included an obligation to pay *"all damages"* caused by fouling another vessel. Whilst preparing for a race Clarke's yacht, the Satanita, fouled Dunraven's vessel, which sank. Under statute Clarke was liable to pay only limited damages of £8 per ton of the registered tonnage of the vessel, however Dunraven claimed the existence of a contract between the parties, on the terms of the club rules, and sought to recover full damages. The House of Lords accepted his argument that a contract existed, even though the parties had not dealt contractually with each other. Lord Herschell stated *"The effect of their entering for the race, and undertaking to be bound by the rules to the knowledge of each other ... is to indicate a liability on the part of the one to the other ... to create a contractual obligation to discharge that liability."*

> In *Rayfield v. Hands* 1960, a case involving the transfer of shares in a registered company, Vaisey J applied the principle laid down by *Clarke v. Dunraven*. He took the view that the taking up of shares not only creates a contract between the shareholder and the company, but also, at least in the case of a private limited company, gives rise to a contract between the shareholder and all the other members of the company. The terms of this contract are the provisions contained in the articles.

Consideration

Under English law the simple contract has always been seen in terms of a bargain struck between the parties. The bargain is arrived at by negotiations and concluded when a definite and certain offer has been made which has been met with an unequivocal acceptance. Millions of transactions of this kind are made each day.

Making an agreement, as we have already seen, involves giving undertakings or promises. The offeror makes his promise, and indicates what the offeree must do in return. For instance the seller of goods undertakes to transfer ownership in the goods, and specifies the price to be paid by the buyers for acquiring ownership. The employer indicates the type of work the employee will be required to perform, and promises a certain wage rate or salary for doing it. The idea of a contract as an exchange of promises is fundamental to an understanding of the simple contract. We have already encountered a basic definition of a contract as being a legally enforceable agreement. There are others however. A definition provided by Sir Frederick Pollock, a leading legal writer, described the contract as *"a promise or a set of promises which the law will enforce"*. Pollock was seeing the 'agreement' of our first definition as something always made up of promises.

Bilateral and unilateral contracts

If promises are exchanged the contract is said to be *bilateral*. This is the most common type of arrangement. For instance, if a partnership offers a person a place in the business if they are prepared to contribute £5,000 to the capital of the business, and the prospective partner undertakes to do so the contract is a bilateral one. If however the offeror, rather than requiring a promise in return requires of the offeree some other act, then the contract is said to be *unilateral.* An example of a unilateral contract occurs where a company promises to make payment or provide goods to any of its customers who collect a certain number of tokens from buying the company's products. Petrol companies frequently use this type of device to compete with their rivals, so that by the time a customer has purchased a specific quantity of petrol they become entitled to items such as glasses or cutlery. The customer has made no promise to the garage, but is certainly entitled to the advertised items if he satisfies the requirements stipulated by the petrol company to qualify for the 'gifts'.

Executory and executed consideration

Consideration, and hence the contract itself, is said to be *executory* where the promises that have been made are to be performed in the future. An example is an agreement whereby the seller promises to deliver goods next week, and the buyer agrees to pay for them on delivery. Consideration is said to be *executed* where in return for a promise the offeree provides the required consideration which also acts as acceptance of the offer. This would occur, for instance, in the case of a member of the public who provides the Post Office with information that leads to the conviction of those responsible for an armed robbery at a sub-post office, where the Post Office has offered a reward for such information.

An agreement in which the consideration exchanged is entirely executory is fully enforceable, although legal action for breach of contract can only be commenced after the date for performance has passed, or if before this time one of the parties has made clear that they will not perform their obligations when they fall due. This referred to as anticipatory breach of contract. Where a contract is entirely executory, legal action on it may prove difficult to sustain if there is no written evidence and the other party disputes the existence of the alleged agreement.

There are a number of important principles which apply to consideration and we now need to examine them.

Consideration is needed to support all simple contracts

In the absence of valid consideration passing between the parties the general rule is the agreement they have made will be of no legal effect. If however their agreement is expressed in the form of a deed, the absence of a valuable promise made by the promisee to the promisor does not invalidate the contract. If a person executes a deed under which he promises to make a payment or transfer property to someone else a future date, the promise will bind him, and be enforceable by the promisee, despite the absence of any consideration provided by that person.

Consideration need not be adequate but must have some value

The word *adequate* in this context means equal to the promise given. The principle of adequacy of consideration has developed to cope with contractual disputes in which one of the parties is arguing that the contract is bad because the value of the consideration provided by the other party is not the economic equivalent of the value of the promise given in return.

The courts are not prepared to defeat an agreement merely on the grounds that one of the parties has, in effect, made a bad bargain. Bad bargains are a fact of commercial life. A deal that is struck where one of the parties has entered it in haste, or without proper enquiry, or has been swayed by convincing salesmanship, may be bitterly regretted subsequently, but it is certainly not possible in such circumstances to escape liability on the grounds that "I gave more than I got". Consequently there is no relief for the business or the individual who is at the receiving end of a hard bargain. For instance, suppose a company is in need of a specific item of machinery without which the manufacturing process cannot function. It eventually locates suitable machinery owned by the seller, with whom the company negotiates to make a purchase. The seller is aware of the company's pressing need, and responds by raising the price to a figure well beyond the usual selling price. The company agrees to buy at this price, but before receiving delivery discovers another machine of the same type which is available from an alternative supplier at the usual selling price. Can the company escape from its original contract on the grounds that the cost of the machinery was well in excess of the usual market price, and therefore that the consideration it will receive (the machinery) is not adequate to sustain the promise of payment it has made? The answer is clearly no. The parties fixed their price by agreement. The company received what it wanted, and the price level merely reflected the sellers bargaining strength and the buyers urgent need.

> The case of *Haigh v. Brooks* 1839 provides a useful illustration of the idea of the bargain taken to its most extreme position. The plaintiffs were owed large sums of money by a third party, and the defendant agreed to guarantee these debts. He later asked the plaintiffs if they would cancel the guarantee. This they agreed to, provided that in return the defendant would pay off certain debts they owed. He agreed, and the guarantee was returned to him. On examination the defendant discovered that because the written guarantee failed to meet certain statutory requirements it was unenforceable, and indeed always had been. He refused to pay the debts on the grounds that all he had received in return was a worthless piece of paper. The court held that the agreement was binding. Even though the guarantee was legally invalid the defendant had received what the bargained for - his release from the supposed liability. Lord Chief Justice Denman remarked, *"The plaintiffs were induced by the defendant's promise to part with something they might have kept, and the defendant obtained what he desired by means of that promise"*.

> Similarly in *Mountford v. Scott* 1975 the defendant made an agreement with the plaintiff, granting the plaintiff an option to purchase the defendant's house for £10,000 within six months. The plaintiff paid £1 for the option, and later sought to exercise it. The value of the defendant's property had risen by this time and he refused to sell. The court was prepared to grant an order for specific performance (see Chapter 7), compelling the defendant to transfer the property for the agreed price. It was for the defendant to fix the value of the option. Some consideration was provided and this was enough. The trial judge commented: *"It is only necessary, as I see it, that the option should have been validly created"*.

However apparently insignificant the consideration may be, as long as it has some discernible value it will be valid.

> In *Chappell and Co. Ltd. v. Nestlé Co. Ltd.* 1960 the defendants, as part of a sales promotion, offered a record at a reduced price if their chocolate bar wrappers accompanied the payment. The plaintiffs held the copyright in the record, and argued that the royalties they were entitled to should be assessed on the price of the record plus the value of the wrappers, which the defendants in fact simply threw away when they had been received. The House of Lords agreed with the plaintiffs, seeing the subsequent disposal of the wrappers as irrelevant, since each wrapper in reality represented the

profit on the sale of a bar of chocolate, and was therefore part of the consideration.

Adequacy is not determined solely by economic criteria. It is enough, for instance, that the promise is a promise to refrain from doing something which the promisor is legally entitled to do. It may be a promise not to take legal proceedings, or not to exercise a legal right such as a right of way. Even where the promise is related to a positive act the act may have little to do with anything capable of economic valuation, yet still be good consideration in the eyes of the law. A parent may undertake to pay a sum of money to a son or daughter in the event of them marrying, or graduating, and the marriage or graduation will be valid consideration in these circumstances.

Moreover it is not necessary that the promisor should obtain direct personal benefit from the consideration provided by the promisee. Thus a parent's promise to a son or daughter to pay them £10,000 to help them set up in business is enforceable if the business is established, whether or not the parent has a financial stake in it.

The case of *Shadwell v. Shadwell* 1860 illustrates how the courts will accept as valuable consideration promises which cannot be valued purely economically. Here an uncle promised to pay his nephew a yearly sum in consideration of the nephew getting married. The nephew married, but the annuity fell into arrears. On his uncle's death the nephew brought action against the executors of the estate. They were held bound since, *inter alia,* the nephew's marriage was something of interest to the uncle.

The question of whether a forbearance will operate as adequate consideration may in particular cases be of some concern to those engaged in business and commercial activity. Suppose for example that the owner of the only retail travel agency in a small town is approached by a larger company, with a number of agencies in the area. The owner is told that in consideration of the payment of £30,000 by him to the company, it will not set up a competing business in the town. Would this be a valid agreement? In *Thorne v. Motor Trade Association* 1937 Lord Atkin, commented, *"it appears to me that if a man may lawfully, in the furtherance of business interests, do acts which will seriously injure another in his business he may also lawfully, if he is still acting in the furtherance of his business interests, invite that other to pay him a sum of money as an alternative to doing the injurious acts".*

Consideration must be sufficient

Consideration is treated as insufficient, and therefore incapable of supporting a contract, when it involves the promisor undertaking to do something he is already obliged to do legally. The rationale here is that since the promisor is bound to carry out the promise anyway, there can be no true bargain in using performance of this promise to support another contract. Consideration is insufficient therefore in the following circumstances:

(a) **Where the promisor has an existing contractual obligation to carry out the promise offered as consideration.**

In *Stilk v. Myrick* 1809 a promise by a ships captain to pay sailors an additional sum for working the ship on the return voyage was unenforceable, even though they had to work harder due to the desertion of two crew members. The court found that their existing contracts bound them to work the ship home in such circumstances, thus they had provided no new consideration to support the promise of extra wages.

In dramatically changed circumstances it may be possible to show that a fresh contract has been negotiated.

> In *Hartley v. Ponsonby* 1857, a ships crew was so depleted that the ship was dangerous to work. In these circumstances the promise of the captain to pay extra wages was held to be enforceable.
>
> In *Williams v. Roffey Bros. & Nicholls (Contractors) Ltd.* 1990 the defendants had a contract with a housing association for the refurbishment of a number of flats. They subcontracted the joinery work to the plaintiff. After performing most of his obligations under the contract the plaintiff found himself in financial difficulties, for the agreed price of £20,000 was too low. The defendants were anxious for their contract with the housing association to be completed by the agreed date, since under a penalty clause they would suffer financially for late completion. The defendants met the plaintiff and agreed to pay him an additional £10,300 for completion of the joinery work. He then carried out most of the remaining work, but refused to complete it when the defendants indicated that they would not pay him the additional agreed sum. They argued that he was under a contractual obligation to carry out the work arising from the original contract. He had given no new consideration for the promise of extra payment.
>
> The Court of Appeal held that the new agreement was binding on the defendants. By promising the extra money they had received a benefit, namely the avoidance of a penalty payment, or alternatively the need to employ another sub-contractor. This benefit was consideration to support the new agreement even though the plaintiff was not required to any more work than he had originally undertaken. The court approved the decision in *Stilk v. Myrick*, however on its facts the Williams case seems to suggest that the courts are now prepared to take a more liberal approach in their willingness to recognise a fresh contract and what can be properly regarded as good consideration.

Of further relevance to the question of how to assess sufficiency is the old common law principle that payment of a lesser amount to a creditor than the full debt cannot discharge the debtor from liability for the full amount even though the creditor agrees it, and accepts the lesser amount. This is known as the rule in *Pinnel's Case* 1602. It is based upon the view that there can be no real bargain in a person agreeing to accept a lesser sum than they are legally entitled to. But if the varied agreement contains an additional element, such a promise to pay the reduced sum earlier than the date on which the full debt is due, then provided the creditor agrees it, this will be binding. It may be of considerable commercial advantage to receive a smaller amount immediately than have to wait for the full sum, where, for example, the creditor is experiencing cash flow problems.

In addition to early payment of a reduced amount if agreed by the creditor, there are certain other exceptions to the rule in Pinnel's case. They include:

(i) Substituted performance. This arises where the creditor accepts some other form of consideration instead of money, such as the delivery of goods. Alternatively payment of a lesser sum together with an additional element, such as a promise to repair the creditor's car, would suffice.

(ii) Payment of a lesser sum by a third party. Such an arrangement operates to discharge the full debt.

(iii) A creditor's composition. This occurs where two or more creditors whose full debts cannot be met by the debtor agree between themselves to accept a reduced payment, and the debtor pays this to each of them. Such an arrangement is an alternative to bankruptcy proceedings, or a winding up, and usually it will involve the debtor paying off the debts according to a fixed percentage, for instance, 50p in the £. Where a composition is made, creditors are precluded from subsequently pursuing the debtor for the outstanding amount.

(iv) Payment of a lesser sum where the debtor is disputing the value of the work that has been performed, and the creditor accepts the reduced amount. The reason why the creditor is bound by such an arrangement is that if the dispute were to be resolved by court action, the court might determine the value of the work performed as worth even less than the debtor has offered to pay, hence accepting the reduced sum may be seen as a new bargain.

(v) When the equitable doctrine of promissory estoppel applies.

Points (iv) and (v) are examined in more detail in the discussion of discharge of contract in Chapter 7.

(b) **Where the promisor has a public obligation to carry out the act.**

Performance of a public duty as a means of furnishing consideration is insufficient to support the contract.

> This is demonstrated in the case of *Collins v. Godefroy* 1831. The plaintiff had received a *subpoena* (a court order) to give evidence in court. He then agreed with the defendant to give the evidence in return for his expenses. The court held that there was no contract for the payment of expenses, as the promise of payment was not support by sufficient consideration. The plaintiff was under an existing duty to give evidence.

However if the promisor performs some act beyond the public duty, this will operate as valid consideration.

> In *Harris v. Sheffield United F C* 1987 the football club challenged its contractual liability to pay for the policing of its football ground during home matches. It was held that the contract between itself and the police authority was valid. The number of officers provided was in excess of those who would have been provided had the police simply been fulfilling their public obligation to keep the peace and prevent disorder.

Consideration must be legal

If it is illegal the whole contract will be invalidated.

There are two classes of illegal contract, those existing under the common law and those made illegal by Parliament. Illegality at common law arises in cases where the contract is regarded as being contrary to public policy, for example contracts involving sexual immorality, contracts involving the commission of crime and contracts associated with corruption in public life. In these cases it is the moral wrongdoing associated with them that has lead the judiciary to regard the nature of the promises being exchanged between the parties as unlawful and thus unenforceable. Amongst those contracts rendered illegal by parliament are agreements made between the suppliers of goods to refuse to sell to retailers who are not prepared to comply with minimum resale price arrangements (s.1 Resale Prices Act 1976). Such arrangements, by means of which retailers are effectively blacklisted, are regarded by Parliament as morally reprehensible, and thus illegal. It is however the case that both Parliament and the judiciary also recognise further classes of contracts which whilst not unlawful, are nonetheless void and unenforceable because their effects are regarded as undesirable for social or economic reasons. Contracts falling within this category are not therefore tainted by being regarded as morally reprehensible. They include contracts in restraint of trade. The question of illegality and public policy is considered further in the next chapter. It should be noted that attempting to enter into an illegal contract may itself give rise to criminal liability.

Consideration must not be past

A party to contract cannot use a past act as a basis for consideration. Therefore, if one party performs an act for another, and only receives a promise of reward after the act is complete, the past act would be past consideration. What is required is that the promise of one of the parties to the alleged contract is given in response to the promise of the other. If an act is carried out with no promise of reward having been made, it will be treated as purely gratuitous.

> In *Roscorla v. Thomas* 1842 the seller of a horse, after the buyer had purchased it, promised the buyer that it was sound and free from vice. It was not, and the buyer sued the seller on the promise. The action failed. The promise was supported by no new consideration.

The principle of past consideration has relevance in business dealings for it is common to find statements that amount to promises being given after the contract is concluded, for instance car salesmen giving undertakings after the customer has bought the vehicle and builders making claims about their properties to purchasers moving into the new house. In these circumstances the buyer may have protection under the Sale of Goods Act 1979 (see later).

There are three exceptions to the rule:

(a) where the work has been performed in circumstances which carry an implication of a promise to pay.

> In *Re Casey's Patents, Stewart v. Casey* 1892 the joint owners of a patent agreed with Casey that he should manage and publicise their invention. Two years later they promised him a third share in the patent, *"consideration of your services as manager"*. The court rejected the view that this promise was supported by past consideration from Casey. The request to him to render his services carried an implied promise to pay for them. The promise of a third share was simply the fixing of the price.

> By way of contrast in *Re: Magrath* 1934 Durham County Council agreed with its treasurer in 1931 to pay him an additional £700, representing extra work he had carried out between 1920 and 1925, but which had not been recognised in his salary. The payment was successfully challenged as being unlawful, for it was not supported by consideration, thus making the payment a gratuity to the treasurer. The payment of gratuities to council officers is illegal. Council members who had voted for the payment were surcharged. Lord Maugham stated: *"It is, I think, clear that the local authority cannot out of public money's give gratuities to their officers and servants over and above their fixed salaries and wages... Different considerations might well apply to a case where the officer or servant was asked to perform extra services in respect of a specified job or undertaking, on the understanding that as soon as the work was complete the authority would determine the amount of his special remuneration";*

(b) where a debt, which has become unrecoverable by operation of the limitation period (i.e. statute barred) is revived by a subsequent acknowledgement of it by the debtor, which is made in writing. In such circumstances the Limitation Act 1980 states that no consideration of any kind need be sought to enforce the debt;

(c) under s.27 Bills of Exchange Act 1882, which provides that an antecedent debt or liability will support a bill of exchange.

Only the parties to the agreement who have provided each other with consideration can sue on the contract. A person who has provided no consideration does not have the right to sue on the contract, for that person is not a party to it. This principle is known as privity of contract, and it is examined in the next Chapter.

Intention to Create Legal Relations

Having established the existence of a valid agreement supported by consideration, a contract may still fail unless it is able to satisfy a further legal test. The additional requirement is that the parties intended their agreement to have legal consequences. Many agreements are made in which it is abundantly obvious from the context of the event that it was never in the contemplation of the parties to bind themselves legally. How then can a court discriminate between those arrangements when the parties did intend their agreement to be legally enforceable, and those where this was not the intention? To answer this question the court will look at all the available evidence, and in particular whether the parties have expressly indicated their intention. For instance committing an agreement into written form may suggest a more formal type of relationship.

Common law presumptions regarding intention

At common law certain presumptions regarding intention are applied by the courts. If the subject matter of the agreement is of a social or domestic kind, where the context of the agreement or the relationship between the parties is such as to suggest an absence of full legal commitment, then the courts will presume there was no intention to create a contract. This does not mean, for example, that it is impossible for members of the same family to contract each with the other, and certainly many families are participants in joint business ventures such as partnerships which are founded on a contractual relationship. Rather it is simply a requirement of the common law that there is clear evidence of such an intention. This must be sufficient to rebut the presumption that the parties did not intend to contract.

> Thus in *Snelling v. John G. Snelling Ltd.* 1972 the court had to identify the nature of an agreement between the plaintiff and his two brothers, who together were all directors of the defendant company. Each of them had provided loans to the company, and when they took a further loan from a finance company the brothers agreed not to reduce their own loan until the amount borrowed from the finance company had been repaid. By a separate agreement made between the three of them they undertook that if any of them resigned voluntarily as a director before repayment to the finance company had been made, repayment of the loan to the defendant company would be forfeited. The plaintiff voluntarily resigned and sued the company for the return of his money. The court held that the agreement between the brothers was intended to create legal rights, not least because it had emerged out of strong disagreements between the brothers.

Commercial transactions - honour clauses and letters of comfort

In relation to commercial contracts the courts will presume an intention that they are intended to be legally binding. So whenever there is a business dimension to the agreement the only way in which it is possible to prevent the judicial presumption from operating is to indicate clearly that the agreement is not intended to be a contract. The inclusion of the phrase *"binding in honour"* on a football coupon was held by the court in *Jones v. Vernons Pools Ltd.* 1938 to amount to clear evidence that there was no intention to create a contract.

> In *Rose and Frank Co. v. Crompton Bros* 1923 a written agreement entered into by two commercial organisations included the following clause *"This arrangement is not entered into, nor is this memorandum written, as a formal or legal agreement... but... is only a definite expression and record of the purpose and intention of the ... parties concerned, to which they each honourably pledge themselves"*. This clause, the court held, was sufficient evidence to overturn the presumption that the commercial agreement was intended to be legally binding.

Since 'honour clauses' have the effect of making an otherwise legally enforceable agreement unenforceable by means of court action, they need to be treated with some care. There may appear to be sound reasons for their use in the right circumstances, but the inability to bring a claim for breach of the terms of the agreement before the courts does have the effect of leaving the parties commercially vulnerable. Suppose such a term is included in an agreement between the sole supplier of a particular type of goods and a customer who makes his profits form reselling these goods. The customer has no legal protection against the supplier unilaterally determining the agreement, leaving the customer with orders that cannot be met and the task of finding a new type of business. Of course the supplier may be left with a large quantity of goods he will have to find new outlets for. This may be difficult or even impossible at short notice, however he will be unable to recover his losses by legal action.

A particular commercial practice which can sometimes give rise to questions of contractual intention is the use of the so called 'letter of comfort'. These are letters which are designed to provide commercial reassurance, and their use is illustrated in the following case.

> In *Kleinwort Benson Ltd. v. Malaysia Mining Corporation Bhd* 1989 the plaintiff bank agreed to make loan facilities of up to £10M available to a subsidiary company owned by the defendants. The defendants were not prepared to give the bank a formal guarantee to cover the loan facility to the subsidiary, MMC Metals Ltd., however they wrote to the bank stating, *"It is our policy to ensure that the business (of MMC Metals) is at all times in a position to meet its liabilities to you...,"* and, *"We confirm that we will not reduce our current financial interest in MMC Metals Ltd."*.
>
> Subsequently MMC Metals, a tin dealer, went into liquidation following the collapse of the world tin market. The bank looked to the defendants to make good the loss suffered by it on the loans it had made to MMC. The Court of Appeal held that on the facts the defendants letter did not give rise to a binding contract, for on a proper construction of it, it showed no intention to create a legal relationship. In particular the use of the expression "policy" indicated that the defendants were making it clear they were not to be legally bound. Companies are free to change their policies, and often do. The parties were trading equals, and the bank ought to have been aware of the implications of being offered a letter of comfort rather than a letter of guarantee.

Clauses ousting the court's jurisdiction and arbitration clauses

It is important to bear in mind that a term which attempts entirely to exclude the court's jurisdiction will be void on the grounds that its effect would be to prevent a court from even determining the preliminary issue of the nature of the agreement itself. It is quite legitimate however to insert an arbitration clause into the contract. Arbitration clauses are a common feature of business agreements, for they provide a dispute solving mechanism which is generally cheaper, quicker and more private than court proceedings. The rights of consumers as regards agreements they have entered into which contain arbitration clauses are now protected under the Consumer Arbitration Agreements Act 1988. The Act provides that where a consumer has entered into a contract which provides for future differences between the parties to be referred to arbitration, the arbitration arrangements cannot be enforced against him unless, under s.1:

(a) he has consented in writing after the difference has occurred to the use of the arbitration; or

(b) he has submitted to the arbitration; or

(c) the court has made an order under s.4. This enables the court to determine that the consumer will not suffer a detriment to his interests by having the difference determined by the arbitration arrangements rather than by court proceedings.

The court must consider all relevant matters, including the availability of legal aid (i.e. financial support provided by the State for meeting the costs of court proceedings).

A *consumer* is someone who enters into the contract without making the contract in the course of a business or holding himself out as doing so, the other party does make the contract in the course of a business, and if the contract is a sale of goods transaction the goods are of a type ordinarily supplied for private use or consumption.

The Act is designed to deal with contracts where an arbitration clause is being used by a business as a mechanism for preventing a dispute from being heard before the courts, so that the consumer is bound to follow arbitration arrangements which may well be weighted against him.

Collective agreements

Contractual intention is also of significance in relation to collective agreements, A *collective agreement* is one between trade unions and employers' organisations by which an agreement or arrangement is made about matters such as terms and conditions of employment. It is estimated that as many as 14 million employees within the United Kingdom are employed under contracts which are regulated in part by collective agreements. Section 18 of the Trade Union and Labour Relations Act 1974 provides that a collective agreement is presumed not to have been intended by the parties to be a legally enforceable contract unless the agreement is in writing and contains a statement that the parties intend it to be legally enforceable. Often the statutory statement of the particulars of the employment which the employer is legally obliged to give the employee will make express reference to a collective agreement in operation within the particular employment sector involved, and this will have the effect of incorporating it into the individual contract of employment. Once this has occurred changes in the contract of employment created by re-negotiation of the collective agreement will automatically vary the individual employee's contractual relationship with the employer.

Capacity to Contract

Capacity is an expression that describes a person's ability to do something. In legal terms this covers the ability to make contracts, commit torts and commit crimes.

The general rule under English law is that anyone can bind himself by a contract, as long as it is not illegal, or void for public policy. There are however exceptions to the rule, of which the most significant are contracts made by corporations and contracts made by minors.

Corporations

The nature of corporate bodies is dealt with in Chapter 3, and it will be recalled that they are regarded as legal persons in their own right, thus enabling then to make contracts, commit torts (and some crimes), and hold land. Since they enjoy legal rights and are subject to legal obligations they can sue, and be sued, in respect of these rights and obligations.

Whilst corporations are created in different ways, for example by registration in the case of limited companies and by specific statute in the case of state corporations, they share certain common characteristics, and as far as their capacity is concerned they are all subject to the principle of ultra vires, although in the case of registered companies the Companies Act 1989 has severely limited its scope.

The doctrine of ultra vires

A corporation must be formed with stated objectives. These are located in the documents which create the organisation: its charter, the statute which establishes it or its memorandum and articles of association. If the corporation acts outside these objectives it is said to be acting ultra vires - beyond its powers - and at common law it cannot be bound. It lacks the capacity to do anything that its stated objectives do not authorise. Equally all activities falling within these objectives can be validly achieved, for they are intra vires - within the powers. Other than in the case of a registered company, no action can be brought to enforce a contract which is ultra vires a corporation: if there is any liability it will rest with those who have authorised or carried out the ultra vires activity. The issue of ultra vires will emerge either where a corporation is using it as a defence in circumstances where it is refusing to perform its contractual obligations, or where a challenge is being brought against the corporation by someone with a legal interest in doing so, in an attempt at preventing the corporation from carrying out an alleged ultra vires act. These two possibilities are illustrated in the following cases.

> In *Ashbury Railway and Iron Co. v. Riche* 1875 the company's objectives as expressed in the memorandum of association included the power to manufacture or sell railway rolling stock and to carry on business as mechanical engineers and general contractors. The company bought a concession to fully construct a railway line in Belgium from Antwerp to Tournai, and entered into an agreement with contractors, Messrs Riche, to carry out the work. The work was begun and money was paid to the contractors but later as a result of shareholders action the directors of the company repudiated the contract, and contractors sued for breach. The company claimed its contract with the contractors was ultra vires, and the House of Lords agreed. The action by the contractors failed.

In *Attorney General v. Fulham Corporation* 1921 the corporation had power by statute to operate wash-houses where its inhabitants could wash their own clothes. The corporation established a municipal laundry, acting under these statutory powers, where the washing work could be carried out by employed staff. A ratepayer challenged the legality of this action, and through the Attorney General proceedings were brought against the corporation. The court held that the statutory powers did not extend to the running of a laundry, and therefore the activity was ultra vires. An injunction was granted restraining the corporation from running it.

A further possibility is the use of ultra vires as a defence raised not by the corporation itself but by the other party.

In *Bell Houses Ltd. v. City Wall Properties Ltd.* 1966 the objects clause in the memorandum of association of Bell Houses stated the principal object to be the developing of housing estates, but in addition it could *"carry on any other business whatsoever which can, in the opinion of the board of directors, be advantageously carried out by the company in connection with or as ancillary to the general business of the company"*. The company entered into a transaction with City Wall Properties to introduce it to a financier who would be able to provide financial help for property development. City Wall Properties refused to pay an agreed commission of £20,000 for the work done by the company on the grounds that the transaction was ultra vires the company. Bell Houses sued. The Court of Appeal held that the company was entitled to its fee, on the grounds that the agreement was within the company's powers provided the directors honestly believed it to be advantageous to the company, in relation to its principal business objects.

Limitations upon the ultra vires doctrine

Although the ultra vires doctrine is still of great importance in some spheres, notably the activities of central and local government, the impact on registered companies is no longer as significant as it used to be. This is because:

(i) the courts are prepared to recognise objects clauses which are broadly drafted. An example of such a clause is that by Bell Houses (above);

(ii) the courts interpret objects clauses less strictly than they did in the past;

In Re: *New Finance and Mortgage Co.* 1975 the company's objects allowed it to carry on business as *"financiers, capitalists, concessionaires, bankers, commercial agents, mortgage brokers, financial agents and advisers, exporters and importers of goods and merchandise of all kinds and merchants generally"*. The company ran a filling station business, which owed Total £24,000 for the petrol. The business went in to liquidation. The liquidator claimed the business was an ultra vires activity, and refused to meet the payment. The court held the words *"and merchants generally"* to cover the running of a petrol filling station business, and thus that Total's claim was good;

(iii) the courts imply powers necessary for a company to achieve its stated objects.

In *Deuchar v. Gas Light and Coke Co.* 1925 the defendant company's main object was making and selling gas and the conversion of residual products into a marketable state. One residual product was napthalene which the company converted into beta-napthol which it sold commercially. The conversion required caustic soda, which the company originally bought from another company, however it realised that it would be cost effective to manufacture the soda itself. This it started to do. Deuchar was the secretary of the company which had previously supplied the soda. It was aggrieved at the loss of its business with the defendant company, but had no means available to challenge the ending of the business relationship with the defendant company. Instead Deuchar bought shares in the company, and then sought an injunction, in his capacity as a member, to prevent the manufacture of the caustic soda which he claimed was ultra vires. The House of Lords held the activity to be intra vires on the grounds that the company had implied power manufacture the products which were reasonably incidental to its express powers of converting residual products into a marketable state;

(iv) the Companies Act 1989 has come close to completely removing the availability of an ultra vires defence for a company in the face of a claim brought by a creditor. The Act has introduced a new s.35 into the Companies Act 1985. This topic is thoroughly considered in Chapter 3. Since the common law position on ultra vires (points (i) to (iii) above) is now so liberal, very few commercial transactions made by companies are likely to be ultra vires, and thus the impact of 1989 Act is far less significant than it might seem.

Ultra vires and local authorities

We have already seen that the same basic principles apply to local authorities as to registered companies. Local authorities are statutory bodies under the Local Government Act 1972 and the objects which such corporations may legitimately pursue must be ascertained from the Act itself. Over the years however, the ultra vires doctrine has not been applied rigidly to local authorities and the courts have consistently held that local authorities may not only do things for which there is express or implied authority, but also whatever is reasonably incidental to the doing of those things.

Thus in *Attorney General v. Smethwick Corporation* 1932 a resolution was passed by the corporation for the establishment of a printing and stationery works which would meet all the printing requirements of the authority. An action was brought by the Attorney General on behalf of a ratepayer on the grounds that the proposal was ultra vires. The court held that the formation of this department was reasonably incidental or consequential upon the carrying out of the corporation's statutory duties and was not therefore ultra vires.

This common law rule was reflected in the general power to contract conferred on local authorities by virtue of s.111 Local Government Act 1972. This section provides that authorities are empowered to do anything (whether or not involving the expenditure, borrowing or lending of money or the acquisition or disposal of any property or rights) which is calculated to facilitate, or is conducive or incidental to, the discharge of any of their functions. Provided therefore that the activity carried on is related to the particular functions of the council in question it seems that it can be justified. This general power to contract conferred on local authorities is of course supplemented by a multiplicity of specific powers from various statutes. The Local Authority (Goods and Services) Act 1970 for instance, enables an authority to contract with other public bodies for the supply of goods and services.

In *Hazell v. Hammersmith and Fulham LBC* 1991 the local authority had during the period 1987 to 1989 engaged in speculative financial activities using a capital market fund set up by the Director of Finance for the authority. The activities involved an attempt at making gains through financial transactions on the London capital and money markets through taking advantage of favourable interest rate movements sums of over £100M were involved. If these transactions involved proper management of the Council's funds then under s.111 they would be lawful, but if they constituted the carrying on of a business they would be ultra vires and unlawful. The Court of Appeal held that interest rate risk management could be regarded as coming within the Council's implied powers, although it would be unlawful to engage in purely speculative trading transactions. The House of Lords however reversed this decision. It held that a local authority has no specific statutory power to enter into interest rate swap transactions of the kind made by Hammersmith, and said that these transactions were not saved by s.111 as they were not incidental or conducive to, nor did they facilitate the discharge of the council's borrowing functions. In addition although the council in question was incorporated by royal charter granting it the powers of a natural person this did not enable it to exercise any greater powers than any other local authority since it was still essentially a statutory corporation established under the London Government Act 1963.

Minors

The law has always sought to protect minors from the consequences of entering into transactions which are detrimental to them. The aim has been to provide minors with some protection from their lack of commercial experience, whilst at the same time recognising circumstances where it is appropriate that they should be fully accountable for the agreements they make. The result is a mixture of common law and statutory rules which seek to achieve a balance between these conflicting objectives. The expression *minor* refers to anyone under the age of eighteen, this being the age of majority under the Family Law Reform Act 1969. There are three categories of contracts which may be entered into by a minor. They are:

(a) Valid contracts, which include beneficial contracts of employment, and contracts for necessaries. A beneficial contract of employment is one which is substantially for the minor's benefit. Benefit is invariably taken to mean that the contract must include some element of training or education,although this will probably be easily established. The court will set aside a contract of employment which viewed overall is not beneficial.

In *De Francesco v. Barnum* 1890 a minor's contract of apprenticeship provided that she was to be totally at the disposal of her principal, who had no obligation to pay her. The court held the contract to be invalid, since its terms were harsh and onerous.

In *Roberts v. Gray* 1913 the defendant, a minor, with a view to becoming a professional billiards player, had entered an agreement with the plaintiff, himself a leading professional, to accompany the plaintiff on a world tour. The plaintiff spent time and money organising the tour, but following a dispute the defendant refused to go. The plaintiff sought damages of £6000 for breach of contract. The Court of Appeal held that the contract was for the defendant's benefit, being in the nature of a course of instruction in the game of billiards. The plaintiff was awarded £1500 damages.

Necessaries are defined in s.3 Sale of Goods Act 1979 as *"goods suitable to the condition in life of the minor ... and to his actual requirements at the time of sale and delivery."* This is a subjective test of the minors needs, found by reference to his economic and social status.

(b) Voidable contracts, which bind the minor until he repudiates them. This may be done before reaching majority or within a reasonable time thereafter. If a repudiation has not taken place after this time the contract becomes valid. Contracts falling within this category are those of a long term nature, such as non-beneficial contracts of employment, contracts for a lease, contracts to take shares in a company, and partnership agreements.

(c) Contracts of what have been described as a *negatively voidable* kind, that is contracts which the minor can enforce to a certain extent, but which cannot be enforced against him. As a general principle contracts that do not come within the previous two categories fall within this one. In particular it includes contracts for non-necessary goods, and contracts in which the minor has set up in business as a trader. Originally the common law regulated the position regarding these contracts. Then the Infants Relief Act 1874 altered the common law position by providing that contracts for the repayment of money lent or to be lent, contracts for non-necessary goods, and accounts stated were, in the words of the Act *"absolutely void"*. If such a contract was ratified by the minor on reaching the age of majority a new contract was required, involving fresh consideration.

Following recommendations made by the Law Commission in 1984 concerning reform of the law in this area, the Minor's Contracts Act 1987 was enacted. The effects of the Minor's Contracts Act can be summarised as follows:

(i) the provisions of the Infants Relief Act 1874 no longer apply (except in Northern Ireland), thus restoring the original common law position. This means that in the case of those contracts coming under the old 1874 Act, the 'absolutely void' category mentioned above, if a minor makes such a contract it (a) is binding on the other party, (b) is not binding on the *minor* unless ratified on reaching the age of majority, in which case it becomes binding without the need for a fresh contract, Ratification may be express or implied;

(ii) a guarantee entered into by an adult to support a loan to a minor is enforceable against the adult guarantor. It is common to find contractual documents which require a parent or guardian to sign them if the other party to the agreement is a minor, the adult being obliged either to act as the other party in place of the minor, or act in the capacity of guarantor;

(iii) if the minor performs the contract, that is carries it out, then he is in exactly the same position as an adult would be, so the only circumstances in which he can recover money or property he has transferred is when there has been a total failure of consideration;

(iv) property acquired by the minor under a contract which does not bind him and in which he defaults may be recovered by the other party if the court considers this to be *"just and equitable"*. Alternatively if the original property has been exchanged for other property by the minor, or he has obtained cash by selling it and the cash can be identified, the exchanged goods or cash can be recovered. This is provided for by s.3 of the 1987 Act, which allows an adult to recover money or property acquired as a result of fraud under the equitable doctrine of restitution.

Consequently the circumstances in which a claim against the minor will clearly not succeed are those in which the court would not regard it as just and equitable to exercise the powers under s.3, or where the minor has consumed the goods or otherwise dealt with them so that recovery has been frustrated. For instance, a minor who buys on credit bottles of vintage wine which are drunk at a party he holds for his friends will not be liable to compensate the unpaid seller.

The lowering of the age of majority in 1969, together with the reluctance of many organisations such as mail order companies to deal with minors has meant that the law as it affects negatively voidable contracts is no longer probably of great significance.

Assignment *Are we Agreed?*

You work as a legal assistant in the legal department of Anglo-Amalgamated Metal Industries plc. On returning from your summer holiday you find two files in your in-tray. They are accompanied by a memorandum from your superior, one of the company's lawyers, which states, "Please respond to the letters contained in the attached files. See me if you have any difficulties."

The first file contains the following letter from a solicitor:

I represent Miss Sally Goldwell. I understand from my client that she was interviewed for a clerical post with your company. Following the interview she was asked if she would be willing to accept the post, and she indicated that she would. Two days later, on 10th September 199X, she received a formal offer of the post from your company's Personnel Officer. She was asked to reply in writing within five days. She was ill at the time and arranged for a friend to notify you of her acceptance by phone. Her friend telephoned sometime after 7 pm on 13th September 199X. This was a Friday, and her friend had to leave a message on the Personnel Department's answerphone. I gather that the Personnel Department closes from 4.30pm on Friday, until 8.30 the following Monday, and that the message only reached the Personnel Officer at Midday on Monday 16th September. He had that morning telephoned another interviewee to offer her the job, which she accepted. My client subsequently heard from you that the post was no longer available for her.

I am of the opinion that a contract exists between my client and yourselves, in respect of which you are in breach. I look forward to your prompt response.

Yours faithfully,

Roger Major

Roger Major

The second file contained the following letter from one of the company's suppliers, Humberside Steels Ltd.:

We refer to our offer to supply you with 40 tonnes reinforced steel bars, to which you responded with an order (68747/5/NX) for the goods to be delivered to you on 1st May. We replied immediately informing you that due to circumstances beyond our control delivery would be on the 24th May. We heard nothing from you, and delivered the goods on 24th May, only to find that you rejected them on the basis that they had not been ordered. We are at a loss to understand your action, particularly as we have often varied the delivery date with you in this way in the past, without complaint by you.

We should be grateful therefore to receive your remittance in due course.

Yours faithfully

James Leach

James Leach pp
Humberside Steels Ltd.

Tasks

1. Draft replies to each of these letters, in which you state the legal basis upon which the company challenges the contractual claims they make.
2. In the form of a memorandum to your superior, Jane West, state the action you have taken, and indicate any weakness you feel may exist in the company's legal position in respect of the two claims.

Development Task

The local citizens advice bureau has approached you to give a short talk to its voluntary workers concerning the way in which contractual agreements are made. Produce a short information sheet outlining the nature of a contract which you can give to the workers at the end of a meeting.

Assignment *The Brothers*

Tim and Anthony O'Brien are brothers who set up together in business as builders a few years ago. The business was based in Dagenham where they both lived. In 1985 Tim married and moved some miles away to Colchester. As as a result the business was dissolved, each brother re-establishing a business in his own right. Tim was more successful than Anthony, who was not such as good businessman. Anthony acquired a reputation as a bad credit risk, and found it increasingly difficult to find suppliers who were prepared to deliver building materials without payment in advance. He told Tim about the problem.

Tim's main supplier was a company called Anglian Associated Materials Ltd. Tim knew the managing director well, since they both belonged to the local golf club and were District Councillors together. Tim mentioned his brother's problem to Charlie, the managing director, and Charlie agreed to supply Anthony. "Obviously I'll see you all right Charlie, if anything goes wrong", responded Tim.

Earlier this year Anthony placed an order with Charlie's company for £2,000 worth of timber, and £4,000 of scaffolding. Due to acute cashflow problems he subsequently found himself unable to pay the full debt when it was demanded, and contacted Charlie direct to discuss the matter. Charlie reluctantly agreed to accept £1,000 for the timber, but insisted the scaffolding had to be paid for in full. Charlie then approached Tim, reminding him of his earlier promise, and requesting him to meet the outstanding £1,000 debt. Tim subsequently replied by letter as follows:

> Dear Charlie,
>
> I have been advised that I have nor legal liability towards payment of the outstanding amount of my brothers indebtedness to your company. However, in recognition of our friendship and all the help you have given me in the past I am prepared to make a payment of £250 towards the bill.
>
> Yours sincerely,
>
> Tim O'Brien
>
> Tim O'Brien

later that week Tim wrote again:

> Dear Charlie,
>
> In understand that my brother's business is in credit again. In the circumstances I feel I must withdraw my offer to you, and suggest that you pursue him for the outstanding amount.
>
> Yours sincerely,
>
> Tim O'Brien
>
> Tim O'Brien

Task

As an administrative assistant to the Company Secretary of Anglian Associated Materials Ltd. you often deal with legal problems facing the company, and Charlie has asked you to consider whether the company has a legitimate claim for payment against either of the brothers.

Draft an informal report for the managing director in which you indicate the company's legal position in the matter.

Chapter 6

Validity and Content of Contracts

Introduction

In the previous chapter the fundamental issues we considered were how and when a contract is made. It would be encouraging to discover that no further contractual issues are ever likely to arise. The parties to the agreement, having met the basic legal requirements and formed their contract will simply carry out their respective responsibilities to their mutual satisfaction and performance will have been completed. This is indeed what usually happens. The contract is made and performed. Each side is satisfied. The transaction is completed.

But contracts do not always run so smoothly. They can go wrong, sometimes for technical reasons and sometimes for practical reasons. Among the more common claims that arise are the following:

(a) that the contract is not binding because there was not true consent given to it. Such a possibility was mentioned in the discussion of freedom of contract. It may be alleged that the contract was induced by the making of false statements, or that one or even both parties were mistaken in reaching their agreement. A further possibility is an allegation that one side exerted unfair influence over the other, or perhaps even made threats against the other;

(b) that the contract is invalid because its purpose is something contrary to the public interest, for instance because it imposes an unreasonable restraint upon trading freedom;

(c) that the obligations arising under the contract have not been performed either partially or in total, so that there has been a breach of contract;

(d) that some event has occurred which has brought the contract to an end, without performance having been completed.

Of these various possibilities the most frequent are claims of breach of contract. Whatever the nature of the claim may be, however, it will always involve the innocent party seeking some remedy; perhaps financial compensation, or a court order enforcing the performance of the contract, or a restoration of the parties to the position they were in before the contract was carried out.

In this chapter these further issues, concerning contractual rights and liabilities are examined under two sections. The first section considers the factors which can effect the validity of a contract. The second examines the contents of a contract.

Validity

Sometimes what appears superficially to be a properly constituted contract, proves on closer examination to contain some defect which was present when the agreement was made. Certain defects of this kind the law recognises as sufficiently serious to either partially or wholly invalidate the contract. Such defects are referred to as *vitiating* (invalidating) factors, and they occur in circumstances of misrepresentation, mistake, duress and undue influence.

Misrepresentation

Before arriving at a contractual agreement the parties will often be involved in a process of negotiation. Negotiations can range over any issues which the parties think are relevant to the protection of their interests, but they are certainly likely to cover questions of payment, when and how the contract is to be performed, and what terms will be attached to it. The aim of negotiating is both to obtain information and to drive a good bargain, and negotiating skill is a valuable commodity in most areas of commercial and industrial life. Not all contracts are preceded by negotiations however, and as a general rule the more marked the imbalance in trading strength is between the parties the less likely serious negotiation of terms and conditions will be. Thus transactions between large organisations on one side, and small organisations or private consumers on the other tend to be characterised by the dominant party presenting the weaker party with a set of terms which are not open to discussion but have to be accepted in their entirety if a contract is to be made.

The nature of representations

Statements made during the bargaining process may become a part of the contract itself, that is, they may become terms of the contract and rise to an action for breach of contract if they prove untrue. But in many cases there will be no intention by the maker of the statement that the statement should be absorbed into the contract at all. It will be made merely to induce the other party to make the contract. Statements of this sort are known as *representations*. If a representation is untrue for any reason it is referred to as a *misrepresentation*, and it will be actionable. The injured party (the misrepresentee) will base a claim not on breach of contract, but on the law applicable to misrepresentation. The reason is that the misrepresentation, whilst influential in the creation of the contract, has not been incorporated as a part of it. The contract itself has not been broken, but rather an assertion that was made in advance of it. It may however be possible to satisfy the court that in the particular circumstances a representation has become a contractual term, and in that event the action brought will be a contractual one. The important distinction between representations and terms is considered in more detail later.

A representation is a statement or assertion of fact made by one party to the other before or at a time of the contract, which induces the other to enter into a contract. The statement can be in any form. Thus it can be in writing, such as a company prospectus containing details of the company's trading activities, or it can be spoken, or be implied from conduct. The definition enables us to distinguish a number of statements whose form or content excludes them from being treated as representations.

Statements of opinion

It frequently occurs that during the negotiation process statements are given which are based upon the opinion of the maker. Since the representation must be one of fact, a statement expressed as an opinion cannot become a representation. It can be a difficult task to clearly discriminate between what is, or can be fairly regarded as an issue of fact rather than opinion. The following cases illustrate the judicial approach to this question.

> In *Bisset v. Wilkinson* 1927 the vendor of some land in New Zealand told the purchaser that the land would carry his 1,000 sheep. The purchaser was aware that the vendor had no experience of sheep farming, and also that the land had never carried sheep, but he went ahead and bought the land, only to find that it was too poor to support that number of animals. He brought an action against the vendor for rescission, i.e. cancellation of the contract. His action failed. The court considered that the purchaser was not justified in treating the vendor's statement about the carrying capacity of the land as anything more than an expression of opinion. It would have been different if the vendor had been a sheep farmer himself, for then he would have been in a position to give accurate information.

> In *Esso Petroleum Co. Ltd. v. Mardon*. 1976 Mardon took a tenancy of a filling station owned by Esso, having been given a forecast by an experienced Esso sales representative of the quantity of petrol the station could be expected to sell annually. This quantity was never reached during the four years Mardon remained as tenant, and the business ran at a loss. The Court of Appeal decided that the company had made a misrepresentation, since the sales representative's knowledge of such matters made the forecast a statement of fact rather than opinion, and the sales representative was acting in the capacity of an agent of the company. Mardon's claim for damages was successful. The misrepresentation was regarded as a negligent one, and the court also took the view that the representation amounted to a contractual warranty, that is a contractual promise. In his leading judgement Lord Denning MR commented: *"it was a forecast made by a party, Esso who had special knowledge and skill. It was the yardstick by which they measured the worth of a filling station. They knew the facts. They knew the traffic in the town. They knew the throughput of a comparable station. They had much experience and expertise at their disposal. They were in a much better position than Mr. Mardon to make a forecast. It seems to me that if such a person makes a forecast - intending that the other should act on it and he does act on it - it can well be interpreted as a warranty that the forecast is sound and reliable in this sense that they made it with reasonable care and skill. That warranty was broken. Most negligently Esso made a 'fatal error' in the forecast they stated to Mr. Mardon, and on which he took the tenancy. For this they are made liable in damages"*.

Clearly it is not possible to avoid liability for a statement which is expressed as, or is subsequently claimed to be an opinion, when the knowledge and experience of the representor in the matter is far greater than that of the representee.

Advertising and sales boasts

Although there is no rule of law which prevents such statements from amounting to representations they will be seen as no more than sales boasts, provided they are not capable of substantial verification. They do not attract any legal consequences. They are regarded simply as the over inflated belief the seller has in the product in his efforts at sales promotion. Examples include the estate agents, *'most desirable residence'*, and the carpet company's *'We cannot be equalled for price and quality'*. However to advertise that *'interest free credit is available on all items bought this month'*, or that a motor vehicle has returned *'31 mpg at a constant 75 mph'* are clearly statements of fact. If untrue they give rise to a criminal offence under the Trade Descriptions Act 1968 as well as amounting to misrepresentations.

Statements of law

A false statement of law cannot constitute a misrepresentation. This is based upon the general legal proposition that ignorance of the law does not excuse an otherwise unlawful act. The assumption is that the representee knows the law, and cannot therefore rely upon a plea that he relied upon inaccurate statements of law. Of course it would be quite different if these statements were being made by his legal adviser, upon whom he is placing reliance.

Distinguishing statements of law from statements of fact can in some cases be a difficult task. A single statement may be one of mixed law and fact. For example, to make a statement that a person is a *tenant* is both a statement of law, since the expression tenant carries a technical meaning which may or may not be accurate in this instance, and a statement of fact; either the individual is or is not a tenant. If a point of law is arrived at from a statement of the facts, then it seems the statement can be treated as one of law. An example would be a comment that, *"since this contract was made by post it became binding when the acceptance was sent"*. Sometimes a statement may involve distinguishing between law, opinion and fact.

> In *Smith v. Land and House Property Corporation* 1884 in a contract for the sale of an hotel the seller stated that it was leased to *"a most desirable tenant"*. In fact the tenant was far from desirable and the purchaser attempted to terminate the contract on the grounds of misrepresentation. The court held that the statement was not one of law, for its principal observation was not the evidence of the person being a tenant, but rather that the tenant was a person who had qualities of value to the purchaser.

Statements of future intention

A statement of future intention is not a statement of fact and is therefore not actionable. This is not so however where the statement of future intention conceals the present state of mind of the misrepresentor, which may constitute a fact.

> In *Edgington v. Fitzmaurice* 1885 the directors of a company invited a loan from the public to finance expansion. However their real intention was to use the money raised to pay off debts. This statement of intention was held to be a statement of fact which was false and actionable. Bowen LJ in the course of his judgment, remarked *"The state of a man's mind is as much a state of fact as the state of his digestion. It is true that it is difficult to prove what the state of man's mind at a particular time is, but if it can be ascertained it is as much a fact as anything else. A misrepresentation as to the state of a man's mind is, therefore, a misstatement of fact"*.

Silence

It might be thought that a representation could not arise in a situation where no statements of fact are made. However, although generally a non-disclosure cannot amount to a representation, there are some important exceptions to this rule. In contracts *uberrimae fidei* (of the utmost good faith) duties of full disclosure are imposed.

The obligation of disclosure under such contracts is based on the nature of this particular class of agreement. They are in general contracts where one party alone has full knowledge of all material facts. Insurance contracts and contracts for the sale of shares through the issue of a prospectus are examples of contracts uberrimae fidei. If full disclosure is not made in such cases the injured party can rescind the contract. Thus before entering into an insurance agreement the party seeking cover must disclose all facts which are material to the nature of the risk which is to be insured. In the case of a company issuing a prospectus, the Financial Services Act 1986 s.162 requires that the document must contain information prescribed under rules made by the Secretary for Trade and Industry (for instance the financial record of the company and details of contracts it has entered into.) A general duty of disclosure is laid down in s.163 which covers any information potential investors, or their professional advisers, would reasonably require in order to make an informed assessment of (a) the company's financial position and (b) the rights attaching to the shares to be issued. In determining what information comes within the general duty to disclose, the following matters are required by statute to be considered.:

(i) the nature of the shares and who issued them;

(ii) the nature of those who are likely to acquire them;

(iii) the fact that certain matters (i.e. of an investment nature) may reasonably be expected to be known by the professional advisers likely to be consulted by the acquirers of shares; and

(iv) information available to investors or their professional advisers under statute.

In contracts for the sale of land the vendor is under an obligation to disclose any defects in his title, that is in his ownership of the property, although the obligation does not apply to defects in the property itself, for instance dry rot or damp.

If a statement is true when made but becomes untrue before the contract is concluded, the representor will be under a duty to disclose this alteration to the representor.

> In *With v. O'Flanagan* 1936 the purchaser of a doctor's practice was able to rescind the contract because, despite being told accurately during negotiations that the annual income of the practice was £2,000, he was not informed prior to the sale, which took place some months later, that the income of the practice had fallen sharply because of an illness which prevented the doctor from working.

The Financial Services Act 1986, also deals with this possibility in relation to the issue of a prospectus. It requires the issue of a supplementary prospectus if a *"significant change"* occurs or a *"significant new matter"* arises after the issue of the original prospectus, whilst the offer for shares is still open.

Inducement

The representation must induce the person to enter into the contract. There can be no inducement in cases where the other party is unaware of the representation or does not believe the statement, or has relied on his own skill and judgement. In such cases no action will lie in misrepresentation.

> In *Attwood v. Small* 1838 during the course of negotiations for the sale of a mine, the vendor made exaggerated statements of its capacity. The buyers subsequently appointed their own experts to investigate the mine, and the agents reported back to the buyers that the vendor's statements were true. As a result the buyers purchased the mine, only to discover that the statements were inaccurate. It was held that the buyers had no remedy in

misrepresentation. They placed reliance upon their own independent investigation.

The representation need not be the sole or major inducement. It will be enough that it had a material affect upon the person's mind, in their decision to reach an agreement.

Types of misrepresentation

Actions for breach of contract and misrepresentation differ in an important respect. If a term of a contract is broken it is irrelevant to consider the state of mind of the contract breaker in establishing the existence and extent of liability. If however a mere representation has proved to be untrue i.e. it has become a misrepresentation, the effect this has on the liability of the misrepresentor depends on the state of mind accompanying it.

A misrepresentation may be made innocently, negligently or fraudulently.

A misrepresentation is innocent if the person making it had reasonable grounds for believing it to be true, and negligent where there was a lack of reasonable care taken to determine the accuracy of the statement. In contrast, a fraudulent misrepresentation is a representation which a person makes knowing it to be untrue, or believing it to be false, or which is made recklessly where the person making it does not care whether it is true or false. Thus it is a representation which is not honestly believed by the person making it, or where there has been complete disregard for the truth.

> Fraudulent misrepresentation was considered in the leading case of *Derry v. Peek* 1889. Under a private Act of Parliament a company was granted power to operate horse-drawn trams, and could run steam powered trams with the Board of Trades' consent. This the directors applied for, and in the belief that the consent would be granted, they went ahead and offered shares to the public through a prospectus that stated the company had power to run trams by steam. Shares were taken up. The consent was not given, and in consequence the company was wound up, many investors losing their money. Action was brought against the directors in the tort of deceit. The House of Lords defined a fraudulent misrepresentation as stated above, and having found that the directors believed the consent was simply a formality, held that the tort had not been committed. The directors were inaccurate but not dishonest, and inaccuracy without more is not fraud. They were not liable to pay damages.

At common law it has been possible since 1964 to claim damages in the tort of negligence for a negligent misrepresentation under the principle laid down in *Hedley Byrne v. Heller* 1964. This important case is considered extensively in Chapter 10 and all we need do here is simply to note the main aspects of the decision. Hedley Byrne provides that where there is a *special relationship* between the persons making a statement and the recipient of it, a duty of reasonable care is owed in making it. If a duty is broken damages will be available, representing the loss suffered. The 'special relationship' concept is central to the decision. The quality of this relationship was referred to by Lord Morris when he stated:

> *"Where in a sphere in which a person is so placed that others could reasonably rely on his judgment or his skill or on his ability to make careful inquiry, a person takes it on himself to give information or advice to, or allows his information or advice to be passed on to another, who, as he knows or should know, will place reliance on it then a duty of care will arise".*

The reliance placed on the statement by the recipient of it must be reasonable. In Hedley Byrne itself, a disclaimer of liability was enough to prevent reliance on a financial reference that had been given by a bank to a third party being reasonable. Following the decision in *Esso Petroleum v. Mardon* 1976 the Hedley Byrne principle has been extended to apply to a pre-contractual relationship, in addition to a non contractual relationship of the kind that appeared in Hedley Byrne.

Remedies available for misrepresentation

A variety of remedies are available to the misrepresentee. They include common law and equitable remedies, and the remedies available under the Misrepresentation Act 1967. At common law, as we have seen, damages are available in the tort of deceit for fraudulent misrepresentation, and in the tort of negligence for negligent misrepresentation. In equity *rescission* is available in any case of misrepresentation. This is a remedy which seeks to put the parties back to their pre-contractual position. If this cannot be achieved, for instance where the subject matter of the contract has been altered, lost or sold to a third party, rescission is not available. Nor can it be claimed if it would be inequitable to grant it. Thus if a person in full knowledge of the misrepresentation affirms the contract, i.e. expressly or by implication indicates that he intends to continue, the right to rescind will be lost. Affirmation can occur through delay in bringing an action.

> In *Leaf v. International Galleries* 1959 the plaintiff bought from the defendants a picture described as a Constable, and was held unable to rescind the contract some five years later when he discovered on trying to re-sell it that it was not a Constable after all. The plaintiff also argued, unsuccessfully, that the contract was affected by mistake (see later). It can be of advantage to a plaintiff to plead alternative legal arguments in this way, for if one proposition fails the other might succeed, and clearly a plaintiff would not choose to bring two separate actions, or even more, if the matter can be dealt with in one trial.

Unlike the common law remedy of damages, which are available as of right once liability has been established, rescission, being an equitable remedy, is discretionary. The court exercises this discretion in accordance with certain principles, referred to as *equitable maxims*. Essentially these principles are concerned with ensuring that in awarding equitable relief the court should be satisfied not only that the plaintiff has acted fairly, but also that the defendant will not be unfairly treated if the remedy sought by the plaintiff is granted. This is the justification for the restrictions on the granting of rescission, which have previously been referred to.

Under statute, damages are available under the Misrepresentation Act 1967 in respect of negligent and innocent misrepresentation. Under s.2(1) damages are available for negligent misrepresentation. It is a defence for the maker of the statement to show that up to the time of the contract he believed that the statement was true and that there was reasonable cause to believe this. Obviously such a belief will depend upon the steps taken by representor to verify the statement. There is an important difference between a claim brought for negligent misrepresentation under s.2(1) and a claim founded in the tort of negligence, which is that the burden of proof lies with the misrepresentor under s.2(1), but with the misrepresentee in negligence.

Under s.2(2), where a misrepresentation is a purely innocent one, damages may be awarded; however, the section requires that the party seeking relief must ask the court to rescind the contract. If the court is satisfied that grounds for rescission exist it may award damages instead, if it is of the opinion that it would be equitable to do so. The aim of this provision is apparently to cover cases where the misrepresentation is of a minor nature and give the court the discretion to award damages, whilst leaving the contract intact.

The diagram below illustrates the remedies available for the different types of misrepresentation.

	Fraudulent misrepresentation	**Negligent misrepresentation**	**Innocent misrepresentation**
At Common Law	Damages in the tort of deceit	Damages in the tort of negligence under the rule in *Hedley Byrne v. Heller (1964),* if a 'special relationship' exists	
In Equity	Rescission (and damages) If the contract is executory the fraud is a defence if the misrepresentor brings action for specific performance	Rescission	Rescission
Under the Misrepresent ation Act 1967		In addition to rescission, or, at the court's discretion instead of rescission, damages under s.2(1) if as a result of the misrepresentation the innocent party has suffered loss. If the defendant can prove that up to the time of the contract he believed, with reasonable cause, that his statements were true, this will be a defence.	If the grounds for rescission exist, the court, in its discretion, may award damages instead under s.2(2).

Figure 6.1 *Remedies for Misrepresentation*

Under s.2 of the Act a person may not avoid liability in respect of claims brought under ss.2(1) and (2), unless the court, in its discretion, considers that reliance on a provision seeking to avoid such liability is fair and reasonable in the circumstances of the case. The case of *Howard Marine v. Ogden* 1978 provides an illustration of a claim brought under s.2(1), and the use of an exemption clause coming within s.3.

The facts of *Howard Marine & Dredging Co. Ltd. v. Ogden & Sons (Excavations) Ltd.* 1978 were as follows. Ogdens agreed to hire two sea going barges from Howards, for the purpose of dumping earth at sea. Howards quoted a price in a letter to Ogdens, stating the cubic capacity of each vessel. At a later meeting Ogdens enquired of Howards representative what the carrying capacity of the vessels was in tonnes. The representative stated this to be about 1,600 tonnes. He made the statement honestly, based upon his recollection of the tonnage specified in Lloyds Register in London, which he had previously examined. He had also seen the shipping documents for the two vessels, which indicated the tonnage as 1,195 tonnes per vessel. This was in fact the correct figure, but all the representative remembered at the time of his statement was the Lloyds entry, which unusually was incorrect. The lack of carrying capacity held up Ogden's work, and they refused to pay the hire charges. Howards withdrew the barges, and sued for damages. Ogdens counterclaimed, seeking damages under s.2(1) Misrepresentation Act 1967. The agreement between the parties, referred to technically where a vessel is being hired as a charterparty, contained the following exemption clause: *"Charterers acceptance of handing over the vessel shall be conclusive that (it is) in all respects fit for the intended and contemplated use by the Charterers and in every other way satisfactory to them."*

By a majority the Court of Appeal held that Howards were in breach of s.2(1), and they could not rely on the exemption clause. Accordingly Ogdens could recover damages representing their losses. Bridge LJ stated: *"In the course of negotiations leading to a contract the 1967 Act imposes an absolute obligation not to state facts which the representor cannot prove he had reasonable grounds to believe."* On the facts the representative was found by the court not to have established this 'reasonable ground', for he had overlooked the disparity in tonnage between the shipping documents and the Register, recalling only the latter document with its inaccurate information.

On the issue of the exemption clause the court held that since its effect was to seek to exempt for negligent misrepresentation it was not a reasonable clause, and thus reliance on it was not fair and reasonable.

In cases of this kind, whilst the courts task is to apply the law to the facts, this will often involve issues of legal discretion. The courts are guided in their exercise of such discretion by recognising the commercial reality of the situation. In his dissenting judgment Lord Denning MR commented of the exemption, *"The parties here were commercial concerns and were of equal bargaining power. The clause was not foisted by one on the other in a standard printed form. It was contained in all the drafts which passed between them, and it was no doubt given close consideration by both sides . . . It is a clause common in charterparty's of this kind . . . it is specially applicable in cases where the contractor has the opportunity of checking the position for himself. It tells him that he should do so; and that he should not rely on any information given beforehand, for it may be inaccurate. Thus it provides a valuable safeguard against the consequences of innocent misrepresentation."*

The general legal position regarding liability for false statements is summarised in Figure 6.2 below

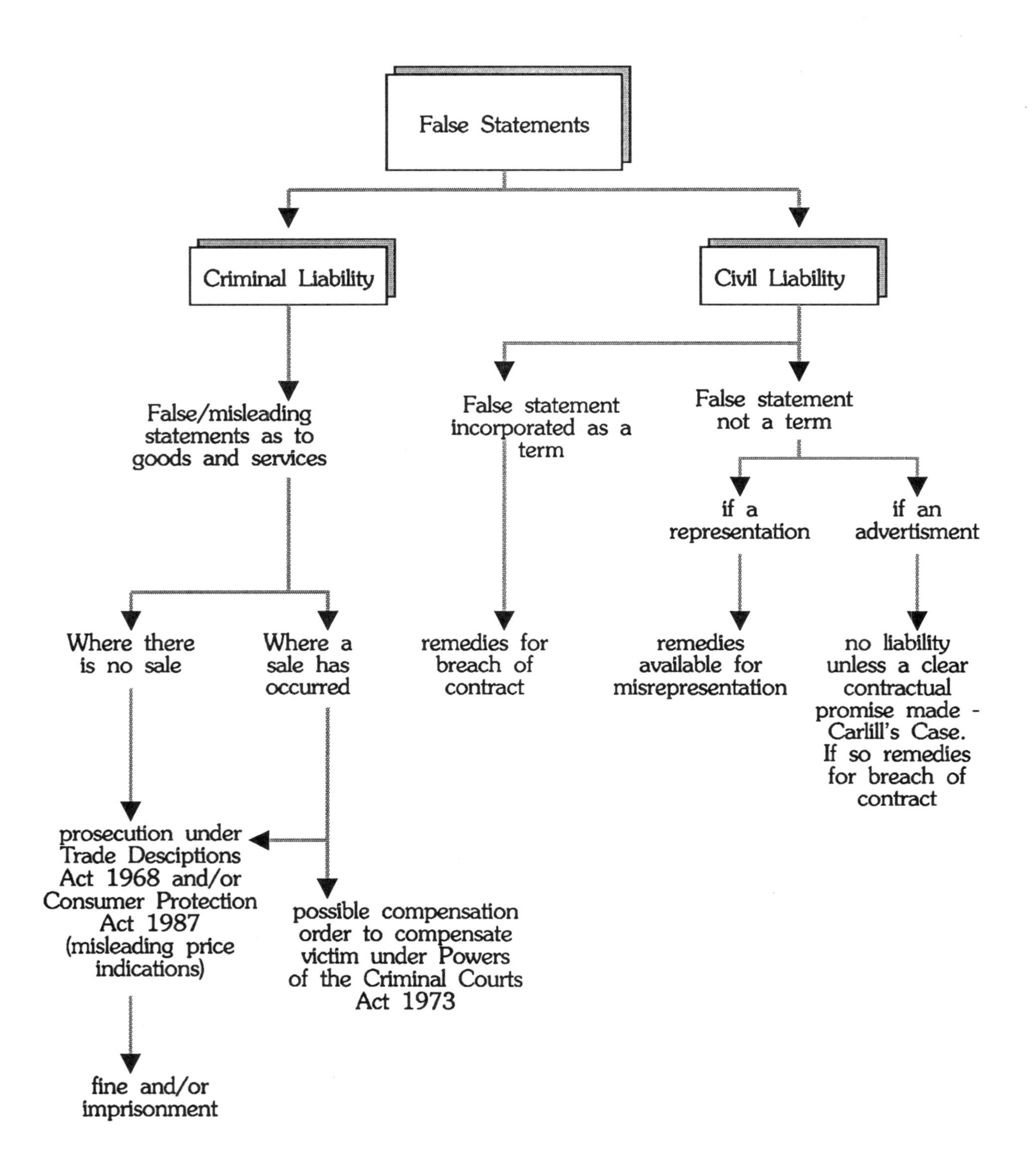

Fig. 6.2 Liability for False Statement

Mistake

Traditionally the courts have shown reticence in treating mistake as a ground for the avoidance of contractual liabilities. We have already seen that a contract will remain valid despite its proving to be economically disadvantageous to one of the parties because of what is, in effect, a mistake as to the value or quality of the subject matter. *Haigh v. Brooks* 1839 provides a very useful illustration (see Chapter 5). It is not the responsibility of the courts to interfere with such agreements where the parties openly and voluntarily make their bargain. Where goods are the subject matter of the contract the common law rule was expressed as *caveat emptor* (let the buyer beware) and despite considerable erosion of this rule, principally through the passing of legislation such as the Sale of Goods Act 1979, certain aspects of it still remain. The purchaser of an item he believes is a valuable antique has no remedy when the mistake is discovered, finding he has paid far more than the item is worth. It may of course be different if the seller made false representation before the sale. The converse is also true where an item such as a painting, which is sold by its owner for next to nothing, subsequently realises many thousands of pounds at auction for its new owner. The original owner can only lament the error of judgment made in selling it in the first place. The caveat emptor rule remains of considerable importance in private sales. It is of less significance where the seller is a business, for Parliament has sought to provide protection for consumers who buy from businesses, and will not generally permit business sellers to hide behind the caveat emptor rule.

The following types of mistake will not effect the validity of a contract:

(a) A mistake of law.

(b) An error of judgment about the value of the subject matter of the contract, unless a misrepresentation was made.

(c) A mistake about the meaning of a trade term. In *Harrison & Jones Ltd. v. Bunten & Lancaster Ltd.* 1953 a buyer purchased 100 bales of 'Sree brand' kapok from the seller. Both parties believed that this type of kapok was pure, but when the buyer discovered that Sree brand was a mixture of different types of kapok he claimed that the contract was void for mistake. The court, however, held that the contract was valid, being unaffected by the mistake.

(d) A mistake about ability to perform the contract within a certain time, e.g. in a building contract.

Despite this wide range of mistake situations which are ignored in law, there are nevertheless circumstances where the mistake is regarded as of so fundamental a nature that the courts will treat it as affecting the contract. Such mistakes are known as *operative* mistakes, and they render the contract void. The following is an outline of the types of operative mistakes which are recognised.

Mistake about the nature of a signed document

We are brought up on words of warning about care in signing documents, for good reason, since it will be no defence for the signatory to say he failed to read, or did not understand, the document. A defence known as *non est factum* (not my deed) is available, however, if the following conditions are satisfied:

(i) that the document signed is fundamentally or radically different from the one the signatory believed it to be; and

(ii) that the signatory exercised reasonable care in signing the document; and

(iii) that fraud was used to induce the signature.

> In *Saunders v. Anglia Building Society* 1974 the House of Lords indicated the narrow limits of the defence of non est factum. The facts were that a 78 year old widow signed a document which a Mr. Lee had told her was a deed of gift of her house to her nephew. She did not read the document since, *"at the time of signing her glasses were broken."* The document in fact transferred her property to Lee, who subsequently mortgaged the property to a building society. The widow now sought to recover the deeds, pleading non est factum. The action failed. The document had been signed with carelessness, and furthermore it was not substantially different from the one she believed she was signing: they were both assignments of property.

There will sometimes be grounds other than mistake on which a person who has signed a contractual document can rely to avoid the contract. For example, in the case of consumer credit agreements such as hire-purchase agreements, the Consumer Credit Act 1974 grants a five-day period after the agreement is made within which the debtor can cancel the agreement, provided it was signed somewhere other than on the creditor's premises. Putting a signature to a contract which is void at law, such as an illegal contract, will incur no contractual liability.

Mistake as to the identity of the other party

Mistake of this kind is usually unilateral, where only one of the parties is mistaken about the identity of the other party to the contract. When this occurs the contract will be void if the mistaken party can show that the question of identity was material to the making of the contract, and that the other part knew or ought to have known of the mistake. The majority of cases in which this type of mistake has occurred involve fraud, so the requirement of knowledge of the mistake will have been satisfied, and the mistaken party will be left with the difficult task of trying to show that he would not have made the contract if the true identity of the other party had been known.

> In *Cundy v. Lindsay & Co.* 1878 the respondents, a firm of linen manufacturers in Belfast, received an order for 250 dozen handkerchiefs from a rogue called Blenkarn whose address was 38 Wood Street, Cheapside. He signed the order to make it appear that it had come from a firm called Blenkiron and Company who traded at 123 Wood Street, Cheapside. The respondents knew Blenkiron and Company to be a reputable firm, and therefore sent the goods, together with an invoice headed Blenkiron and Company, to 37 Wood Street. Blenkarn then sold the goods to the appellant, who was unaware of the fraud. Lindsay & Company were held to be entitled to the goods since their contract with Blenkarn was void. His existence was entirely unknown to them; they intended to deal only with Blenkiron and Company.

If the parties deal face to face, mistake about identity will be far more difficult to establish. In a shop, for instance, the shopkeeper presumably intends a contract with the person on the other side of the counter, irrespective of what the person calls himself.

> In *Phillips v. Brooks* 1919 a rogue called North entered a jeweller's shop where he represented himself to be a gentleman called Sir George Bullough. He purchased a ring for £450, for which he gave the jeweller a worthless cheque. The following day North sold the ring to a firm of pawn brokers. On discovering his loss later, the jeweller traced the ring to the pawnbrokers and sought to recover it from them, alleging that his original

contract with North was void for mistake. The court disagreed, since the parties had dealt face to face. The contract was, however, voidable on the grounds of fraud. Unfortunately, this did not help the jeweller, as he had not taken steps to avoid the contract until after the ring had been purchased by the pawnbroker, who now has a good title (i.e. legal ownership) to it.

The expression voidable contract was considered in the last chapter. A voidable contract, such as one induced by fraud, gives the fraudulent party ownership of the goods until the innocent party takes action to avoid the contract, for example by informing the police of the loss. If before the contract has been avoided the rogue has sold the goods to a third party who buys in good faith and is unaware of the fraud, that third party becomes the owner of the goods, and the original owner cannot reclaim them. This was the position that Phillips the jeweller found himself in.

An example of the limited extent to which a unilateral mistake may affect the validity of a contract is provided by *Centrovincial Estates plc v. Merchant Investors Assurance Co. Ltd.* 1983 a case involving a business tenancy between the plaintiffs, the landlords, and the defendants who were the tenants. The issue concerned the fixing of a new rent, under a rent review clause in the lease. The mistake in question was made by solicitors acting for the plaintiffs who wrote to the defendants on June 22 1982 asking them to agree to a new rent of £65,000 per annum to operate from the rent review date. The defendants were happy to agree to the new rent by letter the following day, for the figure suggested was a reduction of over £3,000 per annum on the current rent. The plaintiff's solicitors, when they discovered the error a few days later attempted to persuade the defendants to accept the true figure of £126,000 per annum. The plaintiffs claimed the mistake had prevented any consensus ad idem between the parties. The Court of Appeal, applying strict contract law, held that acceptance of an unambiguous offer resulted in a contract. The mere assertion of a mistake, of which the offeree was unaware, did not affect the contract's validity.

Bilateral mistakes

The instances of mistake considered so far concern mistakes made by just one of the parties. These are consequently known as unilateral mistakes. In cases of bilateral mistakes both the parties are mistaken, either about the same thing, *common* mistake, or about something different, *mutual* mistake.

Mutual mistake

Where a mutual mistake occurs the parties are at cross purposes, and in cases of fundamental error arguably there can be no contract in existence anyway, on grounds of the uncertainty of their agreement. For example if one company agrees to sell a machine to another, and the description of it is so vague that the seller believes he is selling an entirely different machine to the one the buyer believes he is buying, there is no effective agreement within the process of offer and acceptance. The approach applied by the courts in these circumstances is an objective one.

In *Raffles v. Wichelhaus* 1864 the buyer purchased a cargo of cotton from the seller, to arrive *"ex Peerless from Bombay"*. Remarkably there were two ships named Peerless sailing from Bombay, one in October which the buyer had in mind and one in December which the seller had in mind. The court held that no contract had been entered into. Viewed objectively the facts denied the existence of an offer and an acceptance for there was no consensus ad idem.

Common mistake

An example of a common mistake occurred in *Couturier v. Hastie* 1856. A contract was made for the sale of some wheat which at the time was being carried on board a ship. Unknown to both parties, when they made the agreement the wheat had already been sold by the ship's captain because during the voyage it had started to overheat. The court held the contract to be void, since it was a contract of impossibility.

There are some significant exceptions to this type of claim. At common law relief from a contract affected by a common mistake will not be available where the mistake:

(a) Occurs after the contract is made. In *Amalgamated Investment & Property Co. Ltd. v. John Walker & Sons Ltd.* 1976 the defendants sold the plaintiffs a warehouse for £1.7m. The defendants knew the plaintiffs intended to redevelop the site, and both knew planning permission would be necessary. Contracts were exchanged on 25 September. On 26 September the defendants were informed by the Department of the Environment that the building had become 'listed'. This made development consent most unlikely, and without it the property was worth £200,000. The plaintiffs sought to rescind the contract. The Court of Appeal rejected the claim. There was no mistake in the minds of the parties when the contracts were exchanged sufficient to set the contracts aside;

(b) is as to quality. An example of a mistake about quality is seen in *Leaf v. International Galleries* 1950 where the purchaser believed he was buying a Constable painting only to discover later that Constable was not the artist. The mistake was not operative, since the purchaser had received under the contract what he had bargained for, namely the painting.

A further illustration occurred in *Bell v. Lever Bros. Ltd.* 1932. Bell, who was the managing director of a company controlled by Lever Bros. Ltd., became redundant as a result of company amalgamations, and Lever Bros. Ltd. paid him, £30,000 as compensation for his loss of office. It was subsequently discovered that as managing director he had committed serious breaches of duty by secret trading and could have been summarily dismissed without compensation. Although Bell had not revealed his misconduct to the company before he received the compensation, he was not acting fraudulently because he was unaware that what he had done rendered him liable to dismissal without compensation. The company sought to recover the compensation it had paid to Bell on the grounds of mistake. The House of Lords decided that it could not do so, since the company had paid the compensation in the belief that Bell was an employee who had carried out his duties in a proper way. They were therefore mistaken about the quality of their employee, which was insufficient to give rise to an operative mistake.

The doctrine of common mistake was reviewed by the court in *Associated Japanese Bank (International) Ltd. v. Credit Du Nord SA* 1988. The facts of the case were that an individual, Bennett, purported to sell specified items of machinery to the plaintiff bank, which the bank then leased back to him. Under the transaction Bennett received approximately £1 million. The plaintiff bank required Bennett to provide a guarantee from another bank, and this he obtained from the defendants. The machinery was non-existent. Bennett disappeared with the money, and the plaintiffs claimed under the guarantee against the defendants. The defendants argued that (i) the guarantee was subject to an express or implied condition that the machinery existed, or alternatively (ii) that the guarantee was void from the outset on the grounds of the mistaken belief of both parties that the machinery existed. The plaintiff's claim failed. On the facts the judge, Steyn J took the view that the guarantee agreement included an express condition that the machinery existed. Even if it had not, he was of the view that it would contain an implied term to this effect for a reasonable man would regard this as so obvious as to hardly required saying. The guarantee was also void from the outset for the mistake, at common law. Steyn J summarised the common law approach to mistake as follows:

(i) the courts should seek to uphold rather than defeat apparent contracts;

(ii) the rules regarding mistake are designed to deal with the effect of exceptional circumstances upon apparent contracts;

(iii) the mistake must concern existing facts at the time of the contract, and both sides must substantially share the mistake;

(iv) the mistake must render the subject matter of the contract essentially and radically different from what was in the minds of the parties; and

(v) there must be reasonable grounds for the belief of both parties.

Remedies

At common law

The effect of an operative mistake at common law is to render the contract void *ab initio* - from the outset. The true owner is thus entitled to the return of goods, or damages from whoever is in wrongful possession.

In equity

The position in equity is different however, for equity recognises certain types of operative mistake, which the common law does not grant relief for, in particular in cases involving mistake as to quality. The following cases illustrate the position.

In *Solle v. Butcher* 1950 the parties entered into a lease in the mistaken belief that, due to substantial improvements carried out to it, the flat being let was not subject to rent control legislation. The tenant had been paying rent at the agreed rate of £250 p.a. when it was discovered that the flat was subject to rent control. The maximum rent recoverable was £140 p.a., although if the landlord had served a statutory notice on the tenant before the lease had been executed, he would have been entitled legitimately to charge £250 p.a., the extra amount representing the value to the tenant of the improvements. The tenant claimed to the overpayment of rent. The landlord counterclaimed for possession. The Court of Appeal found itself unable to grant relief at common law for the mistake was one of quality. However exercising its equitable jurisdiction the court allowed the lease to be rescinded on condition that a new lease on the same terms at the higher rent be offered to the tenant, the new lease enabling the landlord to serve the relevant notice on the tenant.

In *Magee v. Pennine Insurance Co. Ltd.* 1969 a proposal for insurance for a motor car had been incorrectly completed without the insured's knowledge. Following a crash, a claim was made and the insurance company agreed to pay £385 which the insured was willing to accept. On discovery of the material inaccuracy in the policy however, the company withdrew their offer of payment for which they were then sued. The Court of Appeal held that under the common law the common mistaken belief that the policy was valid was inoperative and the contract of the insurance was valid. In equity however the agreement to pay £385 would be set aside as there had been a fundamental misapprehension, and the party seeking to rescind was not at fault.

Rectification

In the context of considering equitable relief where parties to a contract have been in error, the equitable remedy of rectification is worth noting. Where it applies the court will rectify a written document so that it accords with the true agreement of the parties. For rectification to operate there must be:

(i) agreement on the particular aspect in question,

(ii) which is certain and unchanged at the time of writing, and

(iii) the writing must fail to express the agreement.

In *Craddock Bros. v. Hunt* 1923 an oral agreement for the sale of a house expressly excluded an adjoining yard and yet the later written agreement and conveyance included the yard. The court ordered a rectification of the documents in order to express the parties true original intention.

The equitable remedy of rectification will not be available however simply because one party has made a miscalculation and the agreement entered into does not express his intention.

In *Riverplate Properties v. Paul* 1975 the plaintiff granted a long lease of a maisonette to the defendant and had intended that the lessee should pay half the cost of exterior and structural repairs that were required. The lease however put the entire burden on the plaintiff. The defendant believed that she was not responsible for those repairs and the plaintiff claimed for rectification or rescission of the lease. The court held that a unilateral mistake of this kind could have no impact on the terms of the lease agreed by the parties. There was no justification for equity to disrupt the transaction actually entered into and the mistake was inoperative. The error in failing to include a suitable term in the lease was the plaintiffs.

Duress and Undue Influence

The term duress at common law involves coercion of a person into making a contract by means of actual or threatened violence to them. The threat must be illegal. The plea of duress is an extremely unusual one, although it was raised in a case that was heard by the Privy Council in 1976.

> *Barton v. Armstong* 1976 involved death threats made by Armstrong against Barton, designed to force Barton to purchase Armstrong's shares in a company of which they were both major shareholders. There was evidence that Barton regarded the acquisition as a satisfactory business arrangement in any event. He subsequently sought to have the deed by which he purchased Armstrong's share declared void. By a majority the court held the agreement to be void, although the minority view was that the claim should fail. This was because it seemed that although Barton took the threats seriously, the real reason for making the purchase was commercial.

A more subtle form of improper pressure is undue influence, which equity recognises as giving the innocent party the right to rescind the contract. In some relationships a presumption of undue influence arises. This is the case where there is a fiduciary relationship, or where one person is in a position of dominance over the other e.g. parent and child, solicitor and client, doctor and patient, trustee and beneficiary. The dominant party who attempts to uphold a transaction entered into in such a relationship must rebut the presumption of undue influence by showing that he has not abused his position in any way. Evidence that the innocent party has taken independent advice will go a long way to rebutting the presumption and saving the contract.

> In *Lancashire Loans v. Black* 1934 the Court of Appeal recognised that the presumption of undue influence between a parent and a child can transcend the child marrying and leaving home. Here a married daughter, without independent advice, had contracted to pay off part of her mother's debts. The court held that the transaction could be set aside as the daughter had not exercised her free will but acted under the influence of her mother.

The courts are still prepared to recognise new relationships where the doctrine applies, for example an influential secretary companion and his elderly employee in Re *Craig* 1971, and a banker who seeks to obtain a benefit from his customer in *Lloyds Bank v. Bundy* 1975.

> In *National Westminster Bank plc v. Morgan* 1985 a wife, as joint owner of the matrimonial home, had been advised to execute a second mortgage to refinance the old mortgage of the property. The advice had been given by the manager of the bank mortgagee who has assured the wife that the mortgage did not cover business debts. Although made in good faith this statement was untrue and the wife subsequently applied to have the mortgage set aside when the husband died, on the grounds of undue influence. The court held that the relationship had raised the presumption of undue influence as the manager's advice was relied on and the bank mortgagee had gained an advantage. Also the failure to suggest independent advice on these facts meant that the mortgage could be set aside on the ground of undue influence.

In modern times the courts have demonstrated an increased willingness to see the principles underlying duress and undue influence as elements in a broader principle of law which Lord Denning referred to in *Lloyds Bank v. Bundy* 1975 as *"inequality of bargaining power."* It may be useful to refer to his judgment, which is contained in Chapter 5.

The idea of economic duress falls under this broad terminology. The following cases provide a clear illustration of situations in which the courts have been prepared to recognise economic duress.

> In *Clifford Davies Management Ltd. v. WEA Records Ltd.* two composer members of a pop group entered into an agreement with their manager to assign the copyright in all their work to him for a period of ten years, for a

very small financial consideration and his promise to use his best endeavours to publish the work they composed. The Court of Appeal found that on the basis of bargaining inequality the contract could be set aside at the option of the composers. The factors cited by the court that pointed to the inequality were:

(i) the overall unfairness of a ten year tie, supported by vague consideration offered in return by the manager;

(ii) the conflict of interest arising from the manager acting as the business adviser to the composers, whilst at the same time representing his own company's interests in negotiating with them; and

(iii) the absence of any independent advice available to the composers, and their reliance upon the manger who exerted undue influence over them.

In *Universe Tankships Inc. of Monrovia v. International Transport Workers' Federation* 1982 a ship, the Universe Sentinal, owned by Universe Tankships, was blacked by a union, the ITWF, which refused to make tugs available to assist in docking at Milford Haven. The blacking was based upon the ship sailing under a flag of convenience. Following negotiations between the parties, the ITWF agreed to lift the restriction in return for an undertaking from Universe Tankships to improve crew pay and conditions on the vessel and make a contribution to an ITWF fund - The Seafarers' International Welfare Protection and Assistance Fund. The company later sought to recover their $6480 contribution, and the House of Lords held they were entitled to its return, since it had been paid under economic duress. The agreement was voidable.

In *Atlas Express v. Kafco (Importers and Distributors)* 1989 the defendants were a small company involved in the import and distribution of basketware. They sold a quantity of their goods to Woolworths, and agreed with the plaintiffs, a national road carrier, for deliveries to be made by the plaintiffs. The plaintiffs depot manager quoted a price for deliveries based upon his guess as to how many cartons of goods would be carried on each load. In the event he overestimated how many cartons would be required to be carried on each load, and now refused to proceed with the contract unless the defendants agreed to a minimum payment for each load of £440, in substitution for the original arrangement of £1.10 per carton. Anxious to ensure the goods were delivered on time, and unable in the circumstances to find an alternative carrier, the defendants agreed to the new arrangement, but later refused to pay. The plaintiff's claim failed. The court took the view that the plaintiff's threat to break the contract together with their knowledge of the defendants dependency on them represented a clear example of economic duress.

The Effect of Public Policy on Contracts

We have already seen that whilst contracts are part of the private law, this does not mean contract making is the exclusive domain of the parties themselves, allowing them complete freedom to make whatever type of contract they choose. At common law certain types of contract are regarded as illegal on the basis that they are contrary to public policy. The list of illegal contracts has been added to by statute.

Public policy is a vague term which has never been clearly defined. The legal writer Pollock saw it as *"a principle of judicial legislation or interpretation founded on the current needs of the community."* This appears to mean that it is concerned with the public good, rather than with what is politically appropriate; and in practice public policy involves the court in applying economic, moral and other criteria to the contract in question to decide whether it is desirable in the general public interest. By these means the courts have held many types of contract to be illegal including contracts to commit criminal and tortious acts, contracts for trading with the enemy in times of war, and contracts which oust the jurisdiction of the courts.

The effects of declaring a contract illegal will vary. Sometimes a party who is unaware of the illegality will be allowed to sue on the contract, but where the parties are fully aware of the illegal nature of the transaction the court will deny them any remedy.

> In *Foster v. Driscoll* 1927 a group of people entered into a partnership agreement in England, the object of which was to smuggle a ship-load of whisky into the USA. This was a violation of the prohibition laws then in force in the USA, so the partnership was illegal on the grounds of public policy, and it was held that no action could be brought in respect of any matter arising out of the agreement.

Contracts in Restraint of Trade

One aspect of common law illegality which is of particular application within the sphere of business and commerce involves contracts that are regarded as being in restraint of trade. This area of law is of sufficient importance that some types of restraints contained in a contract are regulated by statute. The essence of such a contract is that it contains an agreement by one of the parties to it to restrict that party's freedom of trade with others outside the contract in the future. What constitutes such a contract can be discovered only by applying the principles set out by the courts, and in more recent times by Parliament. These are considered below. It should be borne in mind that because the doctrine of restraint of trade is guided by considerations of public policy, the categories of contract to which it applies alter as economic and social conditions change. Examination of the law regarding restraints tends to show that what the courts and Parliament are largely seeking to prevent are practices which restrict competition to the detriment of the public.

For convenience restraints are considered below under two headings:

(a) restraints controlled at common law; and

(b) restraints controlled by statute.

Restraints at common law

The leading authority here is the decision of the House of Lords in the Nordenfelt case.

> In *Nordenfelt v. Maxim Nordenfelt Guns and Ammunition Co. Ltd.* 1894 the seller of a gun and ammunition manufacturing business agreed with the buyer not to manufacture guns or ammunition anywhere in the world, or compete in any way, for a period of twenty five years. Although the undertaking not to compete in any way was considered unreasonable by the court as being too wide, it was severed from the rest of the restraint, which was considered to be a reasonable protection for the buyer. The seller, who was an inventor, had a worldwide reputation in the field of munitions, and this

helped to explain the length and geographical location of the restraint clause. In the course of his judgment Lord MacNaghten laid down the following principle:

"The public have an interest in every person's carrying out his trade freely; so has the individual. All interference with individual liberty of action in trading, and all restraints of trade themselves, if there is nothing more, are contrary to public policy, and therefore void".

This is a *prima facie* presumption i.e. one made on first sight. It can be rebutted where the restraint can be shown to be reasonable.

Restraints take many forms, but among the more important are the following:

(a) Restraints on employment. These are imposed by employers as a device to prevent employees from setting up in competition when they leave the employment. (see Chapter 12)

(b) Agreements between suppliers and retailers under which the retailer agrees to sell only the supplier's goods. Most cases have involved *solus* agreements under which petrol stations have agreed to sell only the petrol and other products of a particular petrol company.

(c) Price fixing agreements and agreements which seek to regulate or limit supplies of goods. Such agreements are governed by statute (see later).

As noted above, whilst there is an assumption that a contract in restraint of trade is void, if the restraint can be shown to be reasonable both in the interests of the parties to it and in the interests of the public generally, then it will be treated as valid and will survive.

When an employer asks employees to covenant not to compete if they leave the employment, the restraint will usually specify the nature of the work that employees are prevented from carrying out, the geographical area over which the restraint is to operate and the length of time that it is to run. Each of these elements must be reasonable. Generally if any part of the restraint is unreasonable this will render void the whole contract, but sometimes the court will be able to sever, i.e. cut out, the invalid part enabling the reasonable part to survive.

In *Scorer v. Seymour-Jones* 1966 an employee of an estate agent who had offices in Kingsbridge and Dartmouth had entered into a contract not to carry on a business similar to that of his employer for a period of three years after leaving the employment, within a five mile radius of the Kingsbridge office. When he left his employer he set up in business as an estate agent within five miles of the Kingsbridge office, and his employer sought an injunction to restrain him from doing so. The injunction was granted by the court. The geographical area of the restraint was reasonable in the case of the Kingsbridge office, although there was no justification for the restraint regarding the Dartmouth office, since the employee had not worked there; however, it could be severed from the valid part of the contract.

Restraint clauses in contracts of employment are considered in some depth in Chapter 12.

As we have seen in the Nordenfelt case where a person sells a business the buyer will usually seek some form of protection to prevent the seller from setting up in competition. Restraints that are imposed in such cases are more likely to survive than those imposed on employees, since the buyer and seller of a business will be negotiating on an equal footing. Nevertheless, if the clause is too wide it will fail.

In *British Reinforced Concrete Engineering Co. Ltd. v. Schelff* 1921 the defendant who operated a business selling road reinforcements in the UK, sold his business to the plaintiff. In the contract of sale the seller agreed not to compete for a specified period in the *"sale or manufacture of road reinforcements"* in the UK. The defendant took employment in the same type of business working for a competitor, and the plaintiff sued to enforce the restraint clause. The court held that had the clause been confined to 'sales' it would have been valid, but to include 'the manufacture of reinforcements' made the restraint wider than was necessary, and therefore void.

In the case of solus and similar agreements there is no rule of law which prevents a supplier and a dealer from entering into an agreement under which the supplier is to be the retailer's sole supplier, but the duration of such an agreement must not be for an unreasonable length of time, or the restraint will be void as being against the public interest.

In *Esso Petroleum Co. Ltd. v. Harpers Garage (Stourport) Ltd.* 1968 Harpers Garage entered into a solus agreement with Esso for the supply of Esso petroleum to two garages owned by Harpers. They received a discount from Esso for agreeing for take only Esso petroleum and for undertaking to keep the two garages open at all reasonable hours. The House of Lords held that the restraint which tied one garage to the agreement for four years and five months was valid, but the restraint which tied the other garage to take only Esso petroleum for twenty one years, in return for a £7000 loan to assist in the purchase and improvement of the garage, was too long and therefore invalid.

Restraints controlled by statute

Successive governments have used legislation to curb market practices which are considered to be anti-competitive and therefore contrary to the public interest. In a sense this gives rise to a curious situation in which the government attempts to limit trading freedom to make agreements which reduce competition, whilst at the same time encouraging a free market in which the stronger organisations inevitably seek to eliminate their competitors. Legislation in this field seeks to find a balance between these conflicting forces.

Legal control of monopolies and mergers

The first piece of modern legislation was the Monopolies and Trade Practices Act 1948, which created the body now known as the Monopolies and Mergers Commission. legislative powers were strengthened by the Monopolies and Mergers Act 1965. The Commission's main responsibility is to act as a watchdog enquiring into possible monopoly or oligopoly situations, reporting its findings to the government for possible further action. The Fair Trading Act 1973 repealed and re-enacted the 1948 and 1965 Acts and established the Office of the Director-General of Fair Trading. The Director-General was given authority to refer to the Commission possible areas where market concentration could be detrimental to the public interest, and was also given authority to assist the Commission in its investigation of such situations.

The 1973 Act:

(a) defines both a monopoly situation and a merger situation,

(b) grants investigatory powers to the Secretary of State for Trade and Industry to issue orders to deal with monopolies and mergers.

Under the 1973 Act a monopoly/merger situation exists if the following circumstances arise:

(i) either a single enterprise has (or through a merger, is likely to have) control of 25% of an individual market (a monopoly share)

(ii) or if the total assets of the organisation exceed £30M.

The Monopolies and Mergers Commission is technically independent of the government. It has the duty to *"investigate and report on any question...with respect to the existence of a monopoly situation...or with respect to the creation of a merger situation.."* Both the Secretary of State and the Director-General of Fair Trading can report matters to the Commission for investigation.

In its report the Commission will decide if either of the above circumstances exist and, if so, whether or not there are any factors which could justify the government in allowing them to continue. There are many instances of industries in which there is one company with more than twenty five percent of the market and the fact that they have not been referred to the Commission reflects the belief of successive governments that competition is nonetheless adequate in these industries. If a referral is made, the Commission will consider whether or not the merger or the level of concentration operates in the public interest. To decide this, the Commission must bear in mind factors such as:

(i) the need to promote effective competition within the UK:

(ii) the need to protect consumers' interests regarding the price and variety of goods:

(iii) the need to minimise the costs of production;

(iv) the need to develop new techniques and products;

(v) the need to ensure unrestricted entry for new competitors into existing markets; and

(vi) the need to ensure a balanced distribution of industry and employment within the UK.

If the Commission's report indicates areas of concern, the Secretary of State for Trade and Industry on behalf of the government has the following options open to him. He may by order:

(a) require the transfer of property from one organisation to another;

(b) require the adjustment of contracts;

(c) require the reallocation of shares in an organisation;

(d) prohibit a merger taking place.

The above orders are enforceable by court action through an injunction, that is a court order prohibiting or requiring specified action. Injunctions are examined later in the next chapter.

The process described above is illustrated diagrammatically in Figure 6.3

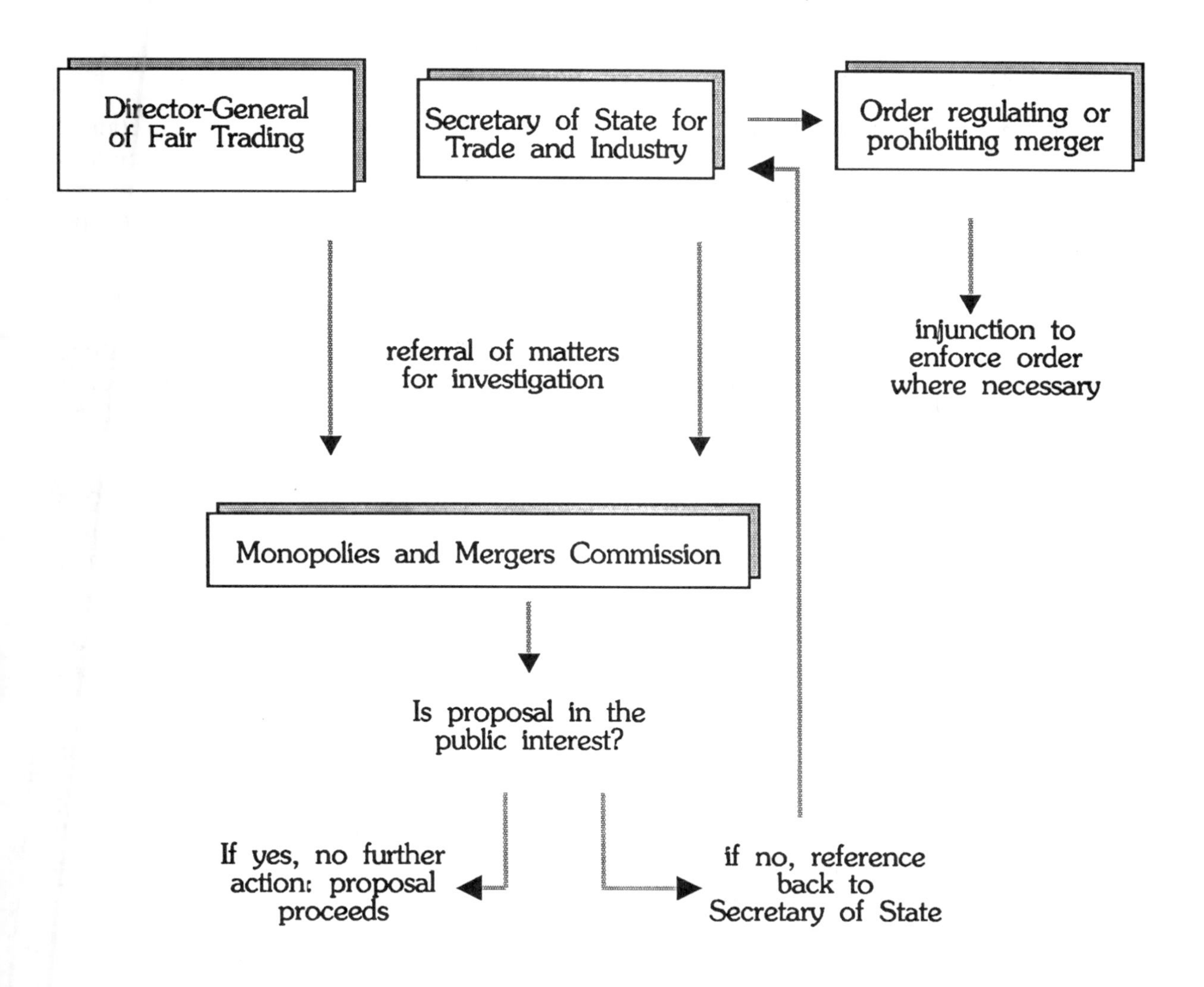

Fig. 6.3 Referral to the Monopolies and Mergers Commission

Legal control of anti-competitive practices

In order to make sense of the legislation designed to control trading practices regarded as anti-competitive, it is useful both to identify the parties involved in operating them, and the nature of the restraints imposed.

Restraints in the form of restrictive trade practices are commonly operated within agreements made between suppliers, and in agreements between suppliers and their distributors and retailers.

(a) Agreements between suppliers

Suppliers often from agreements or associations with other suppliers in the same industry with the aim of either:

(i) limiting the supply of goods or services;

(ii) fixing a standard price;

(iii) standardising contractual terms of sale;

(iv) purchasing raw materials through a 'common pool' at an agreed price.

(b) Agreements between suppliers and distributors or retailers

Suppliers who are dominant in a market may enter into agreements with distributors or retailers under which a minimum price is set for the resale of the supplier's products. These agreements may also restrict the distributor who may be required to exclusively stock the supplier's products. In return the retailer may be granted sole dealership over the product in a particular area and substantial discounts on the supplier's standard price.

Examples of other restrictive practices include:

Full line Forcing. This involves a supplier requiring a distributor or retailer who wishes to stock the supplier's major product, to carry the full range of his products. For example, a shopkeeper wishing to sell a major brand of baked beans may be required to carry the full range of the supplier's tinned products.

Tie-in sales. This is a less extreme form of the same arrangement, whereby the sale of one product is tied to the sale of others. Thus, a purchaser of a certain type of photocopier may also have to enter into a service agreement with the supplier to purchase all photocopying paper from him.

Reciprocal trading. This involves organisations agreeing to purchase each other's products exclusively. Thus other competitor's products cannot be purchased where such an agreement is in force.

Long term contracts. Here a distributor agrees to carry the supplier's products exclusively for a long period and therefore effectively restricts competitors from entering the market.

The individual practices mentioned above are all examples of the means by which dominant suppliers may exert pressure on distributors or retailers. The ultimate sanction which may be used against distributors or retailers who fail to agree to such practices is a withdrawal of supplies.

The use of anti-competitive trading practices is not confined to the United Kingdom, such practices operate within the other member states of the European Community. In consequence legislative control of such practices is found in domestic legislation and under Community law.

EC competition law

The main competition provisions are found in Articles 85 and 86 of the Treaty of Rome. They prohibit trade agreements that endanger freedom of trade between member states by preventing, restricting or distorting competition within the Common Market. Examples of such agreements are those which:

(a) fix prices or trading conditions;

(b) limit production, markets, technical developments or investment;

(c) share markets or sources of supply;

(d) apply dissimilar conditions to equivalent transactions with other trading parties;

(e) make the conclusion of a contract subject to the acceptance of unconnected supplementary obligations.

Fines can be imposed by the EC Commission on the parties to such an agreement. However, an agreement that otherwise infringes the Articles may be allowed to continue in certain circumstances, for example where the agreement exists in order to promote technical or economic progress which will also benefit consumers.

UK competition legislation

The Competition Act 1980 echoes the language of EC competition legislation. Under the Act trade practices, other than those registrable under the Restrictive Trade Practices Act 1976, (see below) which *"involve a course of conduct which has, and is intended to have the effects of restricting, distorting or preventing competition in connection with the production, supply and acquisition of goods and the securing of services in the UK"* are treated as *"anti-competitive practices"*. Whereas EC legislation deals with competition within the broad geographical area of the Community, the 1980 Act is obviously restricted to UK markets.

A detailed investigation procedure is set out under the 1980 Act and is shown in the figure below (figure 6.4). Essentially all the alleged anti-competitive practices are subject to preliminary investigation by the Director General of Fair Trading. If the practice is proven to be anti-competitive, action can be taken by the Secretary for Trade and Industry.

Fig 6.4 Investigation procedure under the Competition Act 1980

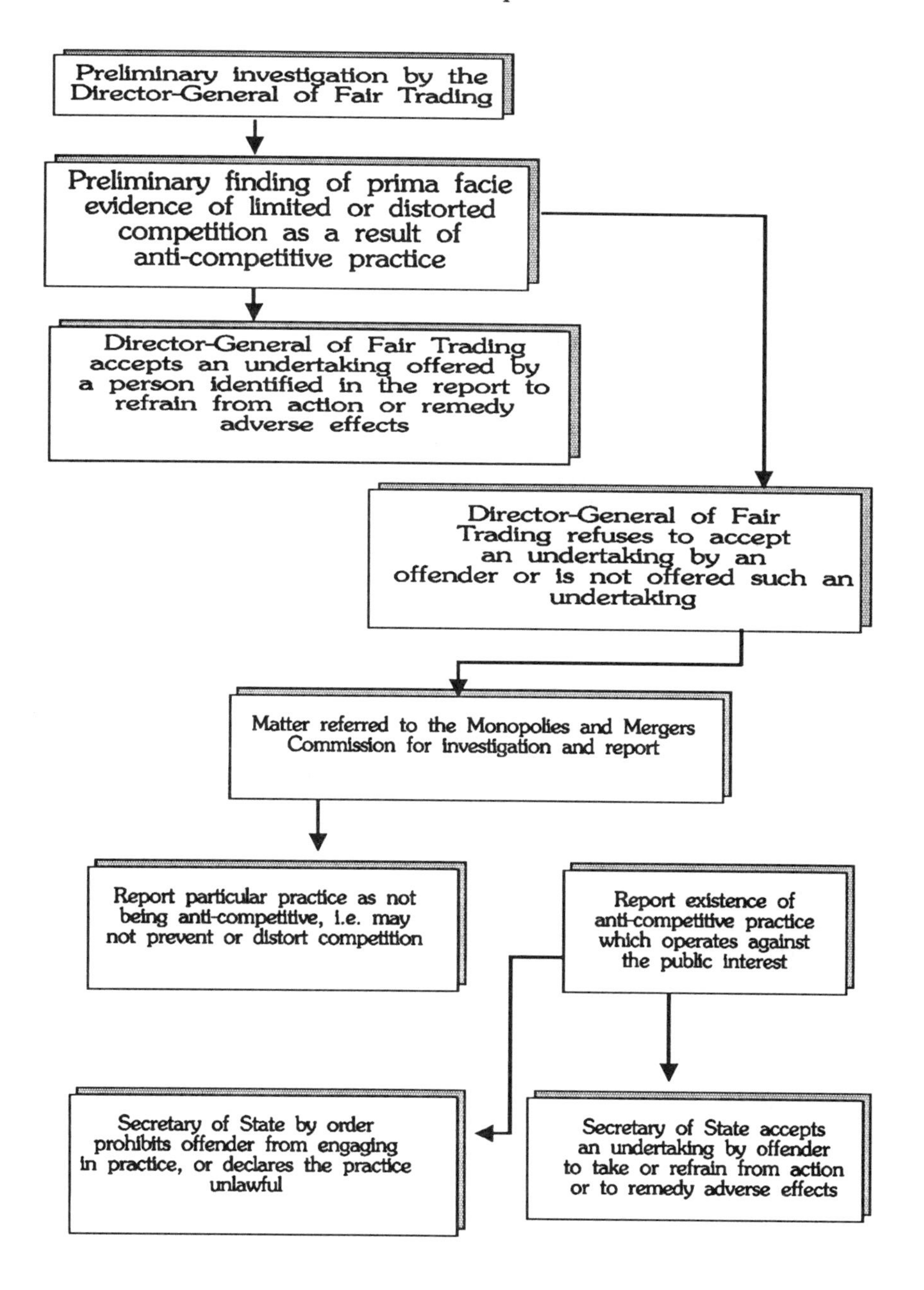

Particular practices by individual organisations may now be investigated and if necessary prevented without the need to investigate the industry as a whole. However, only large organisations are brought under scrutiny, that is companies with a turnover of more than £5m or more than a 25 percent share of their particular market.

Unlike the Restrictive Trade Practices Act 1976 (see below) there is no presumption under the 1980 Act that an agreement referred to the Commission operates against the public interest. In determining this question of public interest, the Commission simply takes into account all matters which appear to it to be relevant in the particular circumstances. For example, a manufacturer may offer his product to a supermarket at much bigger discounts than he offers to corner shops. The practice of offering such discounts could be referred to the Commission as being 'anti-competitive' in that the number of corner shops is likely to be reduced because of his practice. The Commission in deciding the question of public interest, would have to balance the advantage to the consumer of obtaining lower-priced products against the convenience of the consumer of local shopping.

Having reached a conclusion on a reference, the Commission must then report to the Secretary of State for Trade who has the power, by order, to declare an anti-competitive practice unlawful if the offender refuses to refrain from that type of conduct. The Act expressly excludes restrictive practices already registrable under the Restrictive Trade Practices Act 1976 to prevent an overlap of proceedings.

The types of practice which may be investigated by the Director-General of Fair Trading under the 1980 Act include the giving of specific discounts, rebates and allowances, full-line forcing, tie-in sales, reciprocal trading and long-term contracts.

The Restrictive Trade Practices Act 1976

It was mentioned above that the Competition Act 1980 does not apply to agreements registered under the Restrictive Trade Practices Act 1976. Under this Act, duties are imposed on the Director-General of Fair Trading. He is required to compile and maintain a register of restrictive agreements, and also to bring such agreements before the Restrictive Practices Court, which has the function of deciding whether they are contrary to the public interest. The types of agreement registrable under the Act are those made by suppliers of goods which leas to a restriction relating to:

(a) the price charged for goods;

(b) the terms and conditions of supply of goods;

(c) the quantities or description of goods to be supplied;

(d) the process of manufacture to be applied to any goods;

(e) those who may obtain the goods;

(f) the area in which the goods may be obtained.

A registrable agreement is presumed to be contrary to public policy and it is for this reason the Director-General of Fair Trading must bring such agreements before the Restrictive Practices Court. If the parties can satisfy the court that the agreement does not harm the public interest then it may be declared valid. To assist the parties there are eight grounds, called the *eight gateways*, set out in the Act. If they can establish any one of the gateways then the agreement will be treated as a valid one.

The gateways seek to:

(i) protect the public against injury;

(ii) counteract restrictive measures taken by anyone not a party to the agreement;

(iii) enable the parties to negotiate fair terms with a monopolistic supplier or customer.

In fact, relatively few agreements have been approved by the court, indicating the tough line that it has taken with regard to restrictive practices.

> In *Re Net Book Agreement* 1957 the court considered an agreement by book publishers not to permit the retailing of books below published prices. The agreement was justified on the grounds that its removal could lead to unfair competition from large supermarkets and department stores only carrying a limited number of best-sellers, which could mean that the specialist book sellers were forced out of business.

> In *Chemist Federation Agreement* 1958 an agreement by the Federation to limit the sale of patent medicines to the public, only by qualified pharmacists, was declared void. The court was unimpressed by the argument that the restriction was necessary to protect the public against injury in view of the potentially dangerous nature of the goods being sold.

> The agreement itself does not need to be legally enforceable. In one case an arrangement between a group of contractors to delay submitting their individual tenders until they had met to discuss each others tenders was held to constitute a restrictive trading agreement (Re: *Installations at Exeter Hospital Agreement* 1970).

The Resale Prices Act 1976

One of the most fundamental aspects of competition between retailers is that they should have the ability to charge whatever price they wish. Yet one of the most widely used restrictive agreements was the practice by dominant suppliers of imposing standard prices for their goods on all their retail outlets. These *resale price maintenance* agreements were forced on distributors and retailers by suppliers, who could always threaten to withhold supplies to ensure compliance. Such agreements were originally controlled by legislation in 1964, their regulation now being contained in the Resale Prices Act 1976. Under this Act it is unlawful for suppliers to make agreements to withhold supplies from, or supply on less favourable terms to, distributors who do not observe resale price conditions. As with other restrictive practices, the Restrictive Practices Court has power to grant exemption on one or other of the grounds specified in the Act upon an application made by the Director-General of Fair Trading.

So far, only three exemptions have been made, relating to books, drugs and maps. Apart from these exemptions it is *prima facie* unlawful for a manufacturer to withhold supplies in an attempt to enforce a minimum resale price. Such a refusal to supply goods could, however, be justified if the producer shows that the dealer in question has, within the preceding 12 months, been selling the same or similar goods as a *loss leader*, that is selling at a retail price below wholesale cost in order to attract custom for that and other products.

> In *Oxford Printing Ltd. v. Letraset Ltd.* 1970 the defendants withheld supplies from the plaintiffs, who had cut the price of the defendant's products and also used them to promote the sales of a competitor's product. Such withholding of supplies was held to be lawful in the circumstances.

At common law the difficulty of directly enforcing a resale price maintenance agreement can be seen in *Dunlop Pneumatic Tyre Co. Ltd. v. Selfridge and Co. Ltd.* 1915.

> In *Dunlop v. Selfridge* 1915 Dunlops sold tyres to a wholesaler on terms that he should resell them only at list price. The terms of the sale read as follows:
>
> *"Price Maintenance agreement is to be entered into by trade purchasers of Dunlop Motor Tyres*
>
> 1. *We will not alter or remove or in any way tamper with any of the manufacture marks or numbers on Dunlop covers or tubes.*
> 2. *We will not sell or offer any Dunlop motor tyres, covers or tubes to any private customers or to any co-operative society at prices below those mentioned in the said price list current at the time of sale, nor give to any such customer or society any cash or other discounts, or advantages reducing the same. We will not sell or offer any Dunlop motor tyres, covers or tubes to any other person, firm or company at prices less than those mentioned in the said price list.*
> 3. *We will not supply any such goods to any person who supplies the Dunlop Company may decide to suspend nor to exhibit goods of Dunlop manufacture at any exhibition in the United Kingdom without the written consent of the Dunlop Company first had and obtained.*
> 4. *We will not export any tyres, covers or tubes supplied hereunder to any country outside the United Kingdom without the written consent of the Dunlop Company first had and obtained.*
> 5. *We agree to pay to the Dunlop Pneumatic Tyre Co. Ltd., the sum of £5 for each and every tyre, cover or tube sold or offered in breach of this agreement, as and by way of liquidated damages and not as a penalty, but without prejudice to any other rights or remedies you or the Dunlop Pneumatic Tyre Co. Ltd., may have hereunder."*
>
> The wholesaler sold some of the tyres to Selfridges, who also agreed not to sell at below Dunlop's list price. However they subsequently did so and Dunlop sought an injunction against them and damages. The House of Lords held that the action must fail, since there was no privity of contract between Selfridges and themselves.

What, though, is *privity of contract*?. We now need to examine this important concept.

Privity of Contract

The doctrine of privity of contract has already been referred to, in the context of the principles applying to contractual consideration. The effect of the doctrine can be significant as the Dunlop case shows. The doctrine arises out of the contractual principle that consideration must move from the promisee, so that as a general rule the legal effects of a contract apply only to the contracting parties. The shareholder in a company is unable to take the benefit of a contract made by the company in the sense of obtaining personal rights under it, for the company and the shareholder are separate persons. When a purchaser of a new vehicle discovered faults in it he has contractual rights against the garage which sold it, but not against the manufacturer. The manufacturer was not privy or party to the contract. The position would be different if the manufacturer issued a guarantee which the customer had completed and returned when the vehicle was purchased. If the faults were the cause of physical injury to the purchaser a remedy could be pursued in the tort of negligence.

There are a number of exceptions to the doctrine of privity of contract, where a person who has not provided consideration under a contract and is therefore a *stranger* to it may nevertheless possess legal rights and obligations. They include the following:

(a) Contracts made by an agent acting within his authority, but contracting on his principals behalf without indicating to the other party that he is an agent. In such circumstances the doctrine of undisclosed principal allows the principal to step in and sue, or be sued, on the contract.

(b) Where there has been an assignment of contractual rights, such as the right to a debt, the assignee can sue the original debtor under s.136 Law of Property Act 1925 if the creditor fails to notify the debtor that the assignment has been made, the debtor can validly discharge the debt by payment to the creditor rather than the assignee.

(c) The holder for value of a bill of exchange can sue the acceptor and prior parties.

(d) s.11 Married Womens' Property Act 1882 enables the parties who benefit under a life policy if they are a surviving spouse and/or children of the insured to sue the insurance company on the policy.

(e) A further example of other parties than the insured being able to claim under an insurance policy that is not their own arises under the Road Traffic Act 1988, which enables a person driving a vehicle with the owners consent to cover under the owners insurance policy in certain circumstances. It also permits recovery of compensation to a third party injured by a driver in respect of his compulsory third party risks cover.

(f) In respect of restrictive covenants imposed upon land subsequent purchasers will be bound to observe the covenant.

(g) Under the Resale Prices Act 1976 what the Restrictive Practices Court has exempted a resale price maintenance agreement, resale price maintenance conditions imposed by a seller will bind anyone obtaining the goods with a view to resale, if they have notice of the restriction.

Beyond these exceptions it seems that common law development to reduce the impact of the privity principle are unlikely.

> Lord Denning attempted to do so in *Jackson v. Horizon Holidays* 1975. The plaintiff had booked a months holiday in Ceylon staying in an hotel. The defendant's brochure described the hotel facilities. These included a swimming pool, a mini-golf course and a hairdressing salon. The hotel in fact had none of these facilities and its food was poor. The Court of Appeal granted the plaintiff damages of £1,100. This represented not only his loss, but also that of his family who accompanied him, even though they were not parties to the contract. The court said that the plaintiff had made the contract partly for their benefit. The House of Lords in *Woodar v. Wimpey* 1980 criticised the Jackson decision. They rejected the view put forward in Jackson that there is any rule of English law enabling a contract made with A for the benefit of B, to entitle A to sue for damages suffered by B which B could have recovered if the contract had been made with him. Mr. Jackson's damages, said their Lordships, were increased because he not only suffered

discomfort and disappointment personally, but witnessed his family similarly distressed.

In *Foster v. Silvermere Golf and Equestrian Centre* 1981 Dillon J referred to this restriction on the parties to the contract only being able to recover for their personal loss as *"a blot on our law and most unjust."*

Contract Terms

The terms of a contract are the obligations owed by the parties to each other under it. All contracts contain terms. In transactions involving large sums of money, or where the agreement is of a complex or technical nature, the terms are likely to be numerous and detailed. By inserting terms into the contract the parties will be trying to clarify their mutual obligations. They will be attempting to define the nature and scope of the contract, and will try to anticipate eventualities which may possibly emerge after the contract as been made but before it has been carried out. Thus they may make provision for such contingencies as shortages of labour or materials. Different types of contract obviously reflect different sets of terms appropriate to the nature and purpose of the agreement. For example if the contract involves the construction of a building or a ship its terms will seek to clearly identify the specifications involved. On the other hand the granting of a lease or tenancy will concentrate on matters such as who has responsibility for carrying out repairs, and how the property should be used. It is not only large organisations which are involved in detailed and technical contracts; even small organisations will encounter documents such as leases when they set up in a business and seek accommodation. Clearly not all contracts contain detailed terms. In the simplest contracts terms will be single promises made by each party to the other. In more complete agreements the contract may run into many pages. A set of contract terms is given below. You might also find it useful to look at the contract of sale set out in Chapter 8.

Standard form contracts

Clearly it makes commercial sense to set out precisely and exhaustively the terms which are to apply to the contract, and the means used by the majority of organisations to achieve this in the standard form contract. A standard form contract is a printed document consisting of a uniform set of terms for use by an organisation as the basis upon which it trades. A standard form agreement is of advantage in business in two ways:

(a) it helps to save time by removing the need for the regular negotiations of terms; and

(b) it will seek to provide the organisation with the maximum amount of commercial protection possible, by relying on terms which are favourable to it, for instance, by enabling it to cancel the agreement in specified circumstances, raise its price in line with increases in manufacturing costs, and so on.

We have already referred to the imbalance in trading strength that frequently occurs in contract making with the dominant party dictating terms to the weaker party. We have seen that contracts, usually of a standard form kind, in which this dominance is asserted are often referred to as contracts of adhesion, for the weaker party is unable to negotiate but must simply adhere to the stronger party's terms.

The use of standard form agreements does not always indicate a situation of dominance by one party over the other. The standard agreement may be the basis upon which negotiations are conducted, or it may be that both sides have equal bargaining strength and both will try to insist on the use of their own form of agreement. In some areas of commercial and industrial activity standard terms are devised by organisations to represent the interests of the sector generally. For example local authorities may together produce sets of terms which they can all use in their dealings with suppliers of goods or services. In the building industry there are such arrangements. The present standard contract in use is the Joint Contracts Tribunal (JCT) form. Various versions of it are available to cover different types of building work. In transactions for the carrying out of construction work in the building trade the contract will usually commence with the Articles of Agreement in which the contractor expressly agrees to carry out the specified works as described and the employer agrees to furnish the 'contract sum' for the completion of the works. Here it is usual to identify the architect and surveyor and the procedure by which their replacements could be appointed. The Articles will also contain an arbitration clause for the settling of disputes and describing the circumstances and machinery for the appointment of an arbitrator. Usually a speciality contract is executed, for it gives the parties the added protection of a twelve year limitation period to take legal action following a breach. For a simple contract the limitation period is only six years, which in terms of building work is a relatively short period to discover defects.

A contract based upon the JCT form is likely to include the following terms, which are contained in it, and set out as contractual conditions:

(a) the contractor's obligations to carry out the work and use the materials of the specified standard;

(b) the payment of the contract sum and VAT;

(c) the duty of the contractor to comply with the architect's instructions and give him reasonable access to the site;

(d) the specified materials and payment for them;

(e) the statutory obligations in relation to such matters as the payment of fees and serving of notice that local authority inspection is required;

(f) the payment of royalties for use of patented materials;

(g) the power to vary the specified works and require defects to be remedied;

(h) the power to appoint a clerk of the works;

(i) the restriction on the parties' right to assign;

(j) the rights of the employer to take possession of completed parts;

(k) the provision of insurance cover for injury to persons or property and the contractor's agreement to indemnify the employer;

(l) the date of completion, possession, liquidated damages, time extensions, rights to determine on the happening of specified events;

(m) the system of certified payments by instalments as the work is completed in stages;

(n) the definition of who is to be treated as nominated subcontractor or supplier.

The classification of terms

The terms of a contract vary in importance. Sometimes the contract itself will say how much importance is attached to a certain term, while in other cases it may be left to the court to decide the question because the parties to the contract have not made it clear. The value that is attached to each term is of great significance because it determines what the consequences will be if the particular term is broken.

Major terms are called *conditions*. A condition is a term which is said to go to the root of the contract, and where performance is essential to the contract. If it is broken the innocent party has the right to treat the contract as repudiated and to refuse to perform his or her obligations under it. In addition the injured party may sue for damages.

Minor terms are called *warranties*. They are terms which are said to be collateral to the main purpose of the contract. In consequence, if a warranty is broken the contract still stands, and the innocent party does not have the right to treat the contract as being at an end, merely the right to damages.

Where breach of a condition occurs the injured party is not bound to repudiate the contract. As an alternative the injured party can elect to treat the contract as subsisting, treating the breach of condition as if it were a warranty. The obligation that had been broken is then referred to as an *ex post facto* warranty, and only damages will be available. There may be sound commercial reasons for treating a breach of condition as one of warranty, and letting the contract stand. The innocent party may realise that if the contract is repudiated it will be difficult to obtain an alternative supplier of the goods and services in question, or undue delay and inconvenience will be caused if the goods have to be disassembled, removed from the premises and returned to the supplier.

> Two similar cases illustrate the distinction between conditions and warranties. In *Bettini v. Gye* 1876 the plaintiff, an opera singer agreed in writing to sing in various concerts and operas over a period of three and a half months, and to be present at rehearsals for at least six days before the engagements were due to begin. Due to illness he arrived with only two days of rehearsals left, and as a result the defendant terminated the agreement. Looking at the contract as a whole, the court decided that the rehearsal clause was not a condition, but merely a warranty, for which damages alone was the remedy. The contract had been wrongfully terminated and the plaintiff could counter-claim for damages.
>
> In *Poussard v. Spiers and Pond* 1876 an opera singer was unable to take part in the first week of performances due to illness. In the meantime the management had engaged a substitute and refused the original singer the part when she arrived. They were held to be entitled to do so, for her non-attendance at the performances was a breach of a vital term of the contract.

Sometimes it is impossible to say whether a term is a condition or a warranty when it is first created because it will be so broadly framed that it could be broken in a major respect or a minor respect, and therefore it is only possible to say after the event what effect the particular breach should have on the contract. Such terms are referred to as *innominate*, meaning intermediate terms.

> The position is illustrated in *Hong Kong Fir Shipping Co. Ltd. v. Kawasaki Kaisen Kaisha Ltd.* 1962. Here a ship was chartered on terms that stated what it would be *"in every way fitted for ordinary cargo service"*. Inefficient engine-room staff and old engines contributed to a number of breakdowns so that during the first seven months of the charter the ship was only able to be at sea for eight and a half weeks. The charterers repudiated the contract. The Court of Appeal decided that this particular breach did not entitle the charterers to repudiate. Diplock J stated that the terms in the contract were

not really either a condition or a warranty but rather *"an undertaking, one breach of which may give rise to an event which relieves the charterer of further performance ... if he so elects and another breach of which may not give rise to such an event but entitle him only ... to damages."*

A further illustration is provided by the case of *Cehave NV v. Bremer Handelsgesellschaft, mbh, The Hansa Nord* 1975. A term in a contract under which the defendants agreed to sell citrus pulp pellets to the plaintiffs stipulated *"shipment to be made in good condition"*. Delivery was by consignments. When delivery of one of the consignments was made, out of the 3293 tons supplied 1260 tons were found to be damaged. The market price for such goods had fallen at this time, and the buyers used the damaged goods as an opportunity for repudiating the whole contract on grounds of breach of condition. In fact they later bought exactly the same cargo at well below half the original contract price from a third party who had obtained it from the original sellers. They then used it to make cattle food which was exactly what they had bought it for in the first place. The Court of Appeal held the term to be an intermediate one, and damages rather than repudiation was an appropriate remedy. Lord Denning commented *"if a small portion of the whole cargo was not in good condition and arrived a little unsound, it should be met by a price allowance. The buyer should not have the right to reject the whole cargo unless it was serious or substantial."* In the later case of *Bunge Corporation, New York v. Tradax Export SA Panama* 1981 the House of Lords emphasised that parties cannot artificially create intermediate terms. Whether a term is to be regarded as intermediate is a matter of construction.

How terms originate

So far the examples of terms that have been considered are those which have been expressly agreed between the parties. There are however two additional sources of contract terms, the courts and Parliament. Both these law making institutions are responsible for inserting terms into contracts, independent of the wishes of the parties involved, and the broad justification for doing so appears to be desire to enable the contract to 'work' and to achieve a level of protection for the consumer of goods and services. How contractual terms arise, is considered below.

Express terms

These are the terms which have been specifically detailed and agreed upon by the parties. The parties are free to classify them in advance as being conditions or warranties if they so wish. If they fail to do so it will be left to the court to decide how significant a particular breach is by looking at the term in relation to the contract as a whole. Even where the contract does classify a term or terms, the court still reserves the right to construe the meaning of the term looking at the contract as a whole.

In *L Schuler AG v. Wickham Machine Tool Sales* 1973 the appellant company, a German organisation, by an agreement, granted sole selling rights over their panel presses in England, to the respondents Wickham. The agreement provided that Wickham's representatives should visit six named firms every week for the purpose of seeking orders. Clause 7(6) indicated the status of this particular obligation stating that *"it shall be a condition of this agreement".* On certain occasions Wickham's employees failed to satisfy the requirement, and Schulers responded to this by claiming that they could repudiate, arguing that a single failure would be sufficient to constitute a breach. The House of Lords rejected this argument. Such a construction was so unreasonable that the parties could not have intended it.

As we have seen some statements made prior to contract will constitute representations. Sometimes a representation will actually become a term of the contract. This being so, if the term is broken the innocent party will be able to bring an action for breach of contract, rather than for misrepresentation. It is often difficult to determine whether a representation has in fact become a term where there has been no express incorporation of it, and the courts will take into consideration a number of factors. For instance, a representation will be presumed not to have become a term if a formal written contract is executed after the representation and does not contain it. There is, however, one main test to be applied: whether the person making the statement was promising its accuracy. If so, the statement will become a contractual term.

How difficult it can be to draw a distinction between representations and terms is illustrated by *Oscar Chess Ltd. v. Williams* 1975. The defendant wished to take a new car on hire-purchase terms from the from the plaintiffs, who were car dealers. In part exchange he offered them his own car, which was described in the log book as a 1948 Morris. He confirmed the vehicle to be a 1948 model, honestly believing this to be so, and received £290 part-exchange allowance. Eight months later the plaintiffs discovered that the car was a 1939 model, for which only £175 should have been allowed. They sued the defendant for the difference, i.e. £115. The Court of Appeal decided by a majority that the defendant's statement about the age of the car was not a term of the contract. Lord Denning made the point that, *"as motor dealers, the plaintiffs could without difficulty have checked the true age of the car with the manufacturers by giving them the engine chassis numbers."*

Terms implied by the courts

It is not the task of the courts to insert new terms into contracts, but rather to interpret those that already exist. But they will sometimes imply a term to give a contract 'business efficacy'. The rationale underlying such an approach is that since the parties clearly intended to create a binding agreement, they must have intended to include terms to make the contract 'work'.

Thus in *The Moorcock* 1889 a term was implied by the court in a contract between a ship owner and a firm of wharfingers. The contract was to use their wharf on the Thames for the discharging and loading of his vessel, the Moorcock. He was going to pay a charge for the use of the cranes alongside the wharf. While the vessel was moored there she was damaged when the tide ebbed and she came to rest on a ridge of hard ground. The Court of Appeal held that the wharfingers were liable for breach of an implied term that the mooring was safe for the vessel. *"In business transactions such as this,"* said Bowen LJ,*"what the law desires to effect by implication is to give such business efficacy to the transaction as must have been intended at all events by both parties who are businessmen."*

In *Irwin v. Liverpool City Council* 1977 the defendant council let a flat in an upper floor of a block of flats to the plaintiff tenant. A term was implied by the Court into a tenancy agreement between the plaintiff and the defendant Council to the effect that the defendants had an obligation to keep in repair the stairs and the lift in the block of flats which they owned, thus ensuring that the plaintiff could gain access to his property.

In *Baylis v. Barnett* 1988 the plaintiff lent the defendant a sum of money. The defendant knew this involved the plaintiff in borrowing the money from a bank. Although the parties did not discuss the question of interest the Court held there was an implied term that the defendant would indemnify the plaintiff for any interest he owed to the bank.

Two fields in which the courts have been active in implying terms are in the employment relationship, and in the landlord and tenant relationship. Thus at common law there are certain fundamental obligations owed by the employer to the employee and vice versa, which are implied by the courts. For instance the employee owes a duty of good faith to the employer at common law, whilst the employer has an obligation to provide for the employee's safety. In the landlord and tenant relationship the common law imposes an obligation upon the tenant not to commit waste, i.e. physical harm, to the premises being occupied, and upon the landlord to provide the tenant with quiet enjoyment, i.e. not to interfere with the tenant's occupation of the premises. Significantly, in both these fields, Parliament has also legislated to insert terms, primarily with the view to protecting the weaker party from exploitation by the stronger.

Statutory implied terms

Parliament has been particularly active during the post-war period in its use of legislation to introduce specific terms into particular types of contractual agreement. As a result statutory implied terms are now many and varied and, because they are statutory, the obligations they impose tend to be detailed. In many cases statutory terms are implied as a legislative attempt to counter-balance the inequalities that exist in a particular bargaining situation, for example by restricting the ability of organisations which trade on the basis of their own standard form contracts to exclude liability for breaches of contract which they have caused. In other cases statutory terms can be seen as a vehicle for effecting profound social and economic change, such as the insertion of the equality clause in contracts of employment. Yet again, there are those statutory terms which simply represent a codification of judicially recognised mercantile custom, for example under the Sale of Goods Act 1979.

Statutory terms implied under the 1979 Act are considered in Chapter 8, in conjunction with an examination of other implied statutory terms which grant rights to consumers.

The exclusion and restriction of liability

We have seen how a contract creates obligations which the parties making it are obliged to meet, and that failure to do so constitutes a breach of contract which can possibly lead to a claim for damages. It follows that a prudent person, recognising the potential liabilities involved in entering into a contract, will try to reduce or perhaps entirely remove any such risk. How far this is possible depends upon whether the clause in the contract excluding or restricting liability is successfully incorporated into the contract, and if it has been whether it satisfies certain tests of validity laid down by both Parliament and the courts. This legal issue is thoroughly examined in Chapter 8, and the account below provides a summary of its main features. The diagram on the next page (Figure 6.5) indicates the questions which have to be answered in order to determine whether a clause excluding or restricting liability will work.

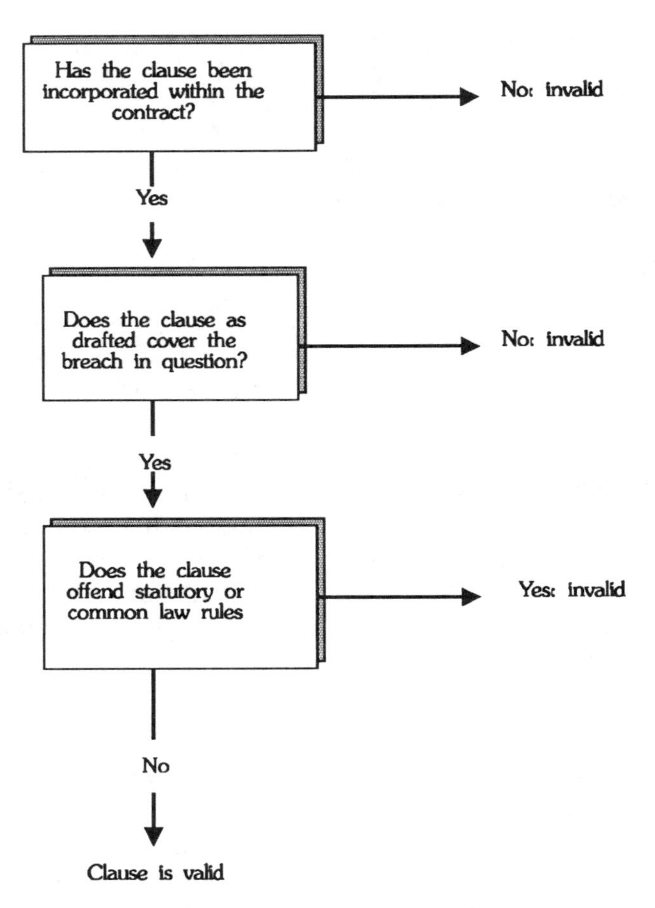

Figure 6.5 *The Exclusion/Restriction of Contractual Liabilities*

Incorporation and drafting of the terms

To become a part of a contract a term must be included in the contractual offer. We saw in Chapter 5 that a term is only valid if it is certain. In other words it must have a clear meaning which a court can, if needs be, specifically identify. So if a term does not form a part of the contractual offer, or is in some way unclear, it will be ineffective.

A good example of terms failing to become part of the contract occurs where the terms in question are introduced after the contract has been made.

> This happened in *Thornton v. Shoe Lane Parking* 1971 where the terms of the contract were contained on the back of a parking ticket. They could only be read therefore after the customer had inserted the money into the machine, and thus subsequent to the making of the contract.

Where the term is contained in an unsigned document, or on a notice, it will be effective only if the person relying on it took reasonable steps to bring it to the attention of the other party, and where the document or notice containing it might reasonably be regarded as contractual and likely to contain contractual terms. If a document containing contractual terms has been signed then in general the signatory will be bound by its terms whether or not they have been read.

The need to express contractual terms clearly is very important. This is especially so when the term is an attempt by one of the parties to exclude liability. As Scrutton LJ pointed out in *Alison (J Gordon) Ltd. v. Wallsend Shipway and Engineering Co. Ltd.* 1927 *"if a person is under a legal liability and wishes to get rid of it, he can only do so by using clear words."*

The courts use the following tests for determining whether the exclusion clause is valid:

(a) does it clearly and unequivocally cover the breach of contract in question. This is a rule of strict interpretation;

(b) is it ambiguous or doubtful?

Statutory control of exclusion clauses

One of the features of exclusion clauses is that they are a standard component in contracts of adhesion, the 'take it or leave it' contracts mentioned earlier in the chapter. A person who is in a weak bargaining position may have no effective control over the power of the stronger party to insert such exclusion clauses.

Under the Unfair Contract Terms Act 1977, Parliament has come to the aid of the weaker party. The Act applies not only to contractual exclusions but also tortious ones, for example a notice at the entrance of a public park that attempts to exonerate the council from liability for any harm suffered to the members of the public whilst in the park. Its provisions are considered in detail in Chapter 8, and here just an outline of the main provisions of the Act is provided.

Under s.2 a person cannot either by a contractual term or by notice, exclude or restrict his of her liability in contract or tort for death or personal injury arising from negligence. Liability for other loss or damage arising from negligence can still be excluded, provided the exclusion can be shown to be reasonable.

The kind of term that will be caught under the first limb of the section would be one which attempted a blanket exclusion such as *"any liability in respect of any personal injury howsoever arising is hereby excluded"*.

> An example of the second limb of the section being applied by the court is found in *Philips Products v. Hamstead Plant Hire* 1983. The hire company hired out a JCB to the plaintiffs under a standard term agreement. A driver was included, but the company excluded any liability in negligence for the driver's acts. In the event whilst he was working under the plaintiff's directions the driver damaged their factory through his own negligence. The court held the exclusion clause to be unreasonable and therefore invalid. It was unreasonable because the hire was for a short period giving the plaintiffs little opportunity to insure. They did not select, nor effectively control the driver, and moreover their experience of such hiring arrangements was very limited.

Under s.3 , where a person inserts in their own written standard terms of business any term purporting to exclude or restrict liability for breach of contract, the term must satisfy the test of reasonableness. If the other contractual party is a consumer the rule applies, even if the contract is not based upon the other's written terms. An example of the application of this section would be where a time limit is placed upon the period for making claims.

Section 5 of the Act deals with guarantees. It provides that where goods are of a type ordinarily supplied for private use or consumption, a term contained in a guarantee of the goods cannot exclude or restrict liability for loss or damage caused by the negligent manufacture or distribution of the goods, where the defect occurs when the goods are in consumer use.

Finally section 6 deals with exclusions of the implied conditions of the Sale of Goods Act 1979. Originally it was quite permissible for a seller to exclude the statutory implied conditions from a contract of sale, but under the 1977 Act the position is very different. S6 provides that if there is a sale to a consumer any clause excluding the terms implied by sections 12 to 15 of the Sale of Goods Act is ineffective. A person buys as a consumer if the goods are of a type ordinarily sold for private use or consumption by a seller in the course of business to a person who does not buy them in the course of business. In a non-consumer sale, for instance between two businesses, any attempt to exclude s.12 of the Sale of Goods Act is absolutely void, although sections 13, 14 and 15 can be excluded if the seller can show that this is reasonable. Whether it is reasonable to do so is determined by a number of guidelines laid down by the Act. These are:

(a) The respective bargaining strengths of the parties relative to each other. This involves considering possible alternative sources of supply. For instance a monopolist seller may have difficulty in establishing the reasonableness of a widely drafted exclusion clause.

(b) Whether the customer received an inducement to agree the term, or in accepting it had the opportunity of entering into a similar contract with other persons but without having to accept a similar term. The reference to other persons involves account being taken of the suppliers within the market and their terms of trading. Sometimes suppliers combine to produce standardised terms of trading, giving buyers no opportunity of finding improved terms. An example of an inducement would be a reduction in price.

(c) Whether the customer knew or ought reasonably to have known of the existence of the term. This involves the customer's knowledge of the trade in general, its terms and customs, and knowledge of the seller, with whom the customer may have previously traded on the same terms.

(d) Where the term excludes or restricts any relevant liability if some condition is not complied with, where it is reasonable at the time of the contract to expect that it would be practicable to comply with the condition. It might not be practicable, for example, to require the buyer to notify the seller of defects occurring in a large consignment of goods within a limited time period with a proviso that failure to notify in time will relieve the seller of any liability.

Assignment *The Premises*

Midlands & Northern Property Holdings plc is a company whose business involves the development of industrial and commercial sites for sale and for letting. R & C Enterprises Ltd., a small company based in Northampton, had been seeking commercial premises for some time when one of its directors became aware of an industrial unit that Midlands & Northern had available on a small development just outside town. Following a site visit and a meeting between the director and the representative of the property company, the director, Tom Armstrong raised with the rest of his board the possibility of taking a ten year lease of the premises, which Midlands & Northern were offering.

The company's main business is in coachworks, which involves it building and fitting different types of bodywork to lorry bases. Whilst the existing site was adequate for this work, the company had decided to diversify and use its skills and expertise in the construction of mobile buildings for schools and building sites. It was for this purpose that the new premises were required. Following a further meeting with the representative from Midlands & Northern, a number of questions were raised by Tom Armstrong. In particular he wanted to know if planning permission would be granted to use the premises in the way anticipated by the company; whether the large hard surfaced area to the rear of the site was included in the lease; and whether the premises were suitable for the anticipated use. The representative wrote in reply; "I can assure you that planning content for the change of use of the premises will be forthcoming, following a conversation I have had with the Chief Planning Officer of the local authority. I can confirm that the premises include the hard area referred to by you. I would add that the premises are entirely suited to the business operations planned by you, and that I see no reason why the business should not operate profitably."

R & C Enterprises Ltd. leased the premises. A month after doing so planning consent for their proposed change was refused. The lease granted to them makes no reference to the hard area to the rear of the premises, which is now being used by an adjoining owner, and the vehicular access to the premises is about to be cut off for a month for major works of repair and improvement to be carried out by sub-contractors acting for Midlands & Northern. You work for R & C Enterprises, and Tom Armstrong has asked you to produce a report for him, which he is anxious to establish whether it is possible to terminate the lease. He has also given you a letter received from Midlands & Northern which states that due to an error by the company surveyor in correctly measuring the internal dimensions of the premises, the quarterly rental being charged is 1,000 less than it should be. The letter adds, "you were aware that the rental of the premises was based upon the number of square meters of floor space in the factory site, since this was discussed by us during negotiations". Tom is wondering how to respond to the letter.

Task

Produce a report requested by Tom Armstrong, and draft a reply to the letter from Midlands & Northern, for Mr. Armstrong's approval, which rejects their claim, and contains a statement of the legal grounds for doing so.

Chapter 7

Discharge and Remedies

Introduction

This chapter considers the various ways in which a contract comes to an end, and goes on to explore the alternative remedies which are available to an injured party as a result of a breach of contract.

Discharge of Contract

Since a contract gives rise to legally enforceable obligations, contracting parties need to know how and when these obligations have been discharged and cease to be binding on them. Only then have their duties been discharged. Discharge may occur in any of the following ways:

(a) Discharge by performance

The general rule is that complete performance, complying precisely to the contractual terms, is necessary to discharge the contract.

> An illustration of this common law rule in the case of *Sumpter v. Hedges* 1898. Here the plaintiff builder agreed to erect some houses for a lump sum of £565. Having carried out half the work to the value of £333 the builder was unable to complete the work because of financial difficulties. In an action by the builder to recover compensation for the value of the work done, the Court of Appeal confirmed that he was not entitled to payment. The legal position was expressed by Smith, LJ who stated *"The law is that where there is a contract to do work for a lump sum, until the work is completed, the price of it cannot be recovered".*

On the face of it this decision appears harsh in its effect upon the builder. In fact the difficulty for the court is that a single sum has been arranged in consideration for the completion of specified works. If these works are not completed in their entirety the court would be varying the clearly expressed intentions of the parties if it was to award the builder payment of a proportionate part of the lump sum. In other words, by agreeing a lump sum the parties have impliedly excluded that possibility of part payment for partially fulfilled building work. Such a contract is said to be an *entire* contract.

The obligation on a contracting party to provide precise, complete performance of the contract before the contractual obligations can be treated as discharged can obviously produce injustice.

There are however two exceptions that grant limited relief to the party obliged to perform, where the contract is divisible, and where there has been substantial performance.

(i) A divisible contract. In some circumstances the courts are prepared to accept that a contract is a divisible one where part of the performance of the contract can be set off against part of the consideration to be given in return. Had the parties in *Sumpter v. Hedges* agreed a specified sum to be paid on completion of certain stages of the house building, then the builder could have recovered compensation for part of the work done. In practice it is usual in a building contract to provide for payment of parts of the total cost at various stages of completion.

It is not necessary for the parties to formally specify that the contract is a divisible one, although in contracts involving substantial work, such as civil engineering operations, or shipbuilding, it would be most unusual not to find that the contract has been split into stages, with payment due on completion of each stage. The courts seem willing to recognise a divisible contract wherever possible, and will, for example, regard a contract based upon an estimate or quotation given in advance, which itemises the work to be performed and with a breakdown of the costs as a divisible contract.

(ii) Substantial performance. If a party to a contract has substantially performed his contractual obligations subject only to minor defects, the courts have recognised that it would be unjust to prevent him recovering any of the contractual price. Therefore under this exception the contractual price would be recoverable, less of course a sum representing the value of the defects. It must be stressed that the exception will only operate where the defects are of a trifling nature. This question is determined by considering not only the nature of the defects but also the cost of rectifying them in relation to the total contract price.

> A claim of substantial performance of the contract was made in *Bolton v. Mahadeva* 1972. Here the plaintiff, a heating contractor, had agreed to install a central heating system in the defendant's house for £560. On completion of the work the system proved to be so defective that it would cost £174 to repair. The defendant refused to pay the plaintiff any of the cost of the work and the plaintiff sued. The County Court accepted the plaintiff's claim of substantial performance and awarded him the cost of the work less the cost of the repair. On appeal however, the Court of Appeal held that in the circumstances the plaintiff had not substantially performed the contract and he was not therefore entitled to recover any of the cost of the work. The exception would not operate where there were numerous defects requiring a relatively high cost of repair.

From the consumer's point of view it can be difficult to ascertain whether incomplete performance of the contract is nevertheless sufficient on the facts to amount to substantial performance. A refusal of payment may well be met with a legal action by the contractor to recover the debt owed. Further complications may be caused where the contractor offered to remedy the customer's complaint free of charge and the customer has refused to accept the offer. As we saw in Chapter 5 in the event of a dispute concerning the value of work performed, an offer of reduced payment by the debtor to the creditor will be binding on the creditor, an example of one of the exemptions to Pinnel's case.

> In *Lawson v. Supasink Ltd.* 1982 the plaintiff's employed the defendants to design, supply and install a fitted kitchen. The total cost was £1,200, and the plaintiffs had to pay a deposit. After the kitchen units had been fitted, but before work on the kitchen was completed, the plaintiffs informed the defendants of their dissatisfaction with the standard of workmanship. In response the defendants undertook to remedy the faults free of charge, but

the plaintiffs later rejected this, asked for the units to be removed and for the return of their deposit. The defendants refused. The Court of Appeal, having accepted that the shoddy work did not amount to substantial performance, then considered the offer to remedy made by the defendants. The question was whether they had failed to mitigate their loss, that is minimise the damage they had suffered. In *Fayzu Ltd. v. Saunders* 1919 Scrutton LJ commented, *"... in commercial contracts it is generally reasonable to accept an offer from the party in default."* In *Lawson* the Court held that the plaintiffs had not acted unreasonably for, in the words of Shaw LJ *"I do not see how the plaintiffs could be required ... to afford the defendants a second opportunity of doing properly what they singularly failed to do adequately in the first instance."*

The acceptance of partial performance

If a party to a contract partially performs his obligations and the other party accepts the benefit, then he is obliged to pay a reasonable price for it. In such circumstances the courts would allow an action on a quantum meruit basis (as much as he deserves). This exception however will only operate where the party receiving the benefit has the option of whether or not to accept or reject it. In *Sumpter v. Hedges* the owner had no choice but to accept the work done on the half completed houses and was therefore not obliged to pay for it. In a situation like that in *Lawson v. Supasink* the units were capable of being removed and returned.

Where performance is prevented

Obviously if a party to a contract is prevented from fulfilling his contractual obligations by the other party then he will not be in default. If in a building contract the owner prevents the builder from completing, in these circumstances the builder can recover a reasonable price for the work done on a quantum meruit.

As well as the above exceptions to the general rule that the performance of contractual obligations must be precise, it is important to note that if a party to a contract makes a valid tender (offer) of performance this may be regarded as equivalent to performance. The refusal of the other party to allow performance to take place will discharge any further obligations on the part of the tenderer. Thus if a seller of goods attempts to deliver them at the agreed time and place and the goods meet contract description, the refusal of the buyer to accept them will,

(i) amount to a valid tender of performance;
and

(ii) entitle the seller to sue the buyer under s.50 Sale of Goods Act 1979 for damages for non-acceptance of the goods.

Despite the problems that can occur in performance, most contracts are satisfactorily discharged in this way.

(b) Discharge by agreement

This method of discharge occurs where the parties to a contract agree to waive their rights and obligations under it. It is called bilateral discharge. To be an effective *waiver* the second agreement must be a contract, the consideration for which is the exchange of promises not to enforce the original contract. The situation however is more complex where one party to a contract has already executed or partly executed his consideration under it. Here for a waiver to be effective it must be embodied within a speciality contract or be supported by fresh consideration. This is called unilateral discharge and can only be achieved by *accord* and *satisfaction*. The accord is simply the agreement to discharge and the satisfaction is the consideration required to support it, e.g. X contracts to sell goods to Y for £50. X delivers the goods to Y and then hearing of Y's financial difficulties agrees to waive payment. Here the agreement of X to waive payment (the accord) is not enforceable unless supported by fresh consideration furnished by Y (the satisfaction). The fresh consideration of course must be of value but need not be adequate. As we saw in our examination of the principles of consideration, at common law the rule in *Pinnel's case* provides that there is no value in a creditor taking as satisfaction payment of a lesser sum than he was due under the original agreement.

> A creditor's promise to accept a reduced amount may however be binding on him, through the operation of the equitable doctrine of *promissory estoppel*, established in *Hughes v. Metropolitan Railway Co.* 1877 by the House of Lords, and by Denning J as he then was in *Central London Property Trust Ltd. v. High Trees House Ltd.* 1947. Here the defendant company took a 99-year lease on a block of flats from the plaintiff company at an annual rent of £2,500. The lease was granted in 1937. By 1940 the evacuation of large numbers of people out of London because of war meant that the defendant company was unable to let all the flats and could not meet the annual rent out of the profits it was making. As a result, the plaintiff company agreed to accept a reduced annual rent of £1,250. By the beginning of 1945 the flats were fully let again. An action was brought by the plaintiff company to recover the difference between the reduced rent and the full rent for the last two quarters of 1945. The action succeeded, for the court considered that the agreement of 1940 would continue only as long as wartime conditions prevailed. The Court also considered whether the plaintiffs could recover the remaining arrears from the defendants, relying on *Pinnel's case*. It took the view that such action would be inequitable, even though permissible at common law. In equity the creditor would be estopped, or denied the right of disowning his promise to accept the reduced amount, where the debtor had to the creditor's knowledge relied on the promise, and acted on it to his detriment. This rule is consequently referred to as promissory estoppel. It was said in the later case of *Combe v. Combe* 1951 that the doctrine is a shield rather than a sword, meaning that the person receiving the promise cannot sue on it, the 'sword', but can raise it as defence, 'the shield', if action is brought to recover the outstanding payment. The doctrine only arises within the context of a pre-existing contractual relationship, and does not remove consideration as a requirement of the simple contract.

It is worth pointing out that the High Trees decision is an authority which also supports the view that a deed can be varied by a simple contract. Prior to 1947 it has always been considered that because a simple contract is inferior to the more formal deed, that only a deed could vary a deed.

Being a form of equitable relief, it is only possible for a person to raise promissory estoppel as defence if he has acted in an equitable manner himself.

> In *D & C Builders v. Rees* 1965 Mr. & Mrs Rees exacted a promise from D & C Builders to accept a reduced amount than that originally agreed, for building work carried out to the Rees's home. They claimed the building work was substandard, but in fact they were simply attempting to escape the full payment due, using their knowledge that the builders were in financial

difficulties and desperate for cash. Sometime after the reduced payment had been made the company sued for the outstanding balance, and the defendants pleaded promissory estoppel. The Court refused to allow Mr. & Mrs Rees the equitable defence, on the grounds of their own lack of equity.

(c) Discharge by breach

If a party to a contract fails to perform his obligations under it or performs his obligations in a defective manner then he may be regarded as being in breach of contract. Generally, the remedy of an innocent party to a contract who has suffered as a result of a breach is to sue for damages. For some breaches of contract however, the innocent party is given the additional remedy of treating the contract as repudiated, in other words terminated, and thus discharging himself from the obligations under it. As previously mentioned terms in a contract are classified into different categories and it is only when a condition has been broken that repudiatory breach has occurred. If a breach of contract occurs before the time set for performance of the contract it is called an *anticipatory breach*. This will occur where a party to a contract expressly declares that he will not perform his part of the bargain. Once an anticipatory breach has occurred the innocent party does not have to wait for the date set for performance but has the option of immediately suing for breach of contract.

In *Hochester v. De La Tour* 1853 the defendant agreed in April to engage the plaintiff for work to commence in June. The defendant told the plaintiff in May that he would not require his services. The court held that a cause of action for breach of contract arose on the anticipatory breach in May.

Thus in such circumstances the injured party can commence legal action at the time of the anticipatory breach. Alternatively he can wait until performance is due to see if it is in fact carried out, and if it is not, commence action thereafter.

(d) Discharge by frustration or subsequent impossibility

A contract may be discharged by frustration where as a result of an event subsequent to making the contract, performance of the contract can no longer be carried out. The event must be subsequent to the contract for if the contract is impossible to perform at the time it is made there is no contract. Originally the common law did not take such a lenient view of changes in circumstances and required that the parties to a contract should provide for all eventualities. If because of a subsequent event performance of an obligation became impossible, the party required to perform the impossible obligation would be liable to pay damages for non performance.

In *Paradine v. Jane* 1647 the King's Bench Court held a tenant liable to pay three years' arrears of rent to a landlord despite the fact that the tenant had been dispossessed of his house by soldiers during the Civil War.

Today however the courts recognise that certain supervening events may frustrate a contract and thus release the parties from their obligation under it. Were the facts of *Paradine v. Jane* to come before a modern court, the outcome would probably be quite different.

In *National Carriers Ltd. v. Panalpina (Northern) Ltd.* 1981 the plaintiffs leased a warehouse in Hull to the defendants. The lease was for ten years, however for a period of twenty months the only access road to the premises was closed by the local authority due to the poor state of a listed building nearby. The defendants refused to pay any further rent to the plaintiffs. The House of Lords accepted the defendant's argument that a lease could, in law, become frustrated, but felt that twenty months out of a ten year period, was not sufficiently substantial to frustrate the contract.

There are a number of grounds upon which a contract may become frustrated. They include:

(i) Changes in the law. If because of new legislation performance of the contract would become illegal this would be a supervening event to frustrate the contract.

In *Denny, Mott and Dickson Ltd. v. James B. Fraser Ltd.* 1944 the House of Lords held that a contract for the sale of timber was frustrated because of the subsequent passage of various Control of Timber Orders rendering performance of the contract illegal.

(ii) Destruction of subject matter. If the subject matter or means of performance of the contract is destroyed this is an event which frustrates a contract.

In *Taylor v. Caldwell* 1863 the plaintiff agreed to hire the defendant's music hall to give some concerts. Prior to performance the hall was destroyed by fire and this event, the court held, released the parties from their obligations under the contract.

(iii) Inability to achieve main object. If as a result of change in circumstances performance of the contract would be radically different from the performance envisaged by the parties then the contract is frustrated. It must be shown that the parties are no longer able to achieve their main object under the contract.

In *Krell v. Henry* 1903 the defendant hired a flat for two days to enable him to watch Edward VII's Coronation procession. Due to the King's illness the Coronation was cancelled and the defendant naturally refused to pay. The Court of Appeal held that as the main object of the contract was to view the procession, and this could no longer be achieved, the foundation of the contract had collapsed. The contract was thus frustrated and the parties released from their obligations under it.

A further claim of frustration as a consequence of the cancellation of the Coronation was brought in *Herne Bay Steamboat Co. v. Hutton* 1903. Here a steamboat had been chartered to watch the naval review as part of the Coronation celebrations and also for a day's cruise round the fleet. The Court of Appeal had to determine whether the cancellation of the naval review released the defendant from his obligation to pay the hire charge. The Court held that there has not been a sufficient change in circumstances to constitute a frustration of the contract. Here the defendant could have derived some benefit from the contract and was therefore liable to pay the hire charges. A further distinction between *Henry* and *Hutton* is that in *Henry* the claim was brought by a private individual whereas in *Hutton* the hirer was engaged in a commercial enterprise, using the hired boat to take trips of sightseers to Spithead. Frustration is not available in a commercial transaction merely because the contract turns out to be less profitable than one of the parties expected.

(iv) Death or illness. In a contract for personal services the death or illness of the person required to perform will frustrate the contract. Temporary illness or incapacity will generally not release a party from his obligations. The illness must be such that it goes to the root of the contract.

Non frustrating events

The common law doctrine of frustration will not apply in the following circumstances:

(a) If performance of the contract has become more onerous on one party or financially less rewarding.

In *Davis Contractors Ltd. v. Fareham UDC* 1956 the plaintiff building company claimed that a building contract should be regarded as discharged by frustration due to the shortage of available labour and resultant increased costs. The House of Lords rejected the arguments that frustration had discharged the contract. Performance of the contract had simply been made more onerous than originally envisaged by the plaintiffs.

(b) If the parties to a contract have made express provision for the event which has occurred then the common law doctrine of frustration is inapplicable. The courts will simply give effect to the intention of the parties expressed in the contract.

(c) A distinction must be drawn between a frustrating event over which the parties have no control and a *self-induced* frustration. If it can be shown that a party to the contract caused the supposed frustrating event by his own conduct then there will be no frustration but there may be a contractual breach.

In *Maritime National Fish Ltd. v. Ocean Trawlers Ltd.* 1935 the appellants had chartered a trawler from the respondents. The vessel was fitted with an otter trawl, which it was unlawful to use without a government licence from the Minister. The appellants used five vessels for fishing and applied for five licences, but were granted three and were allowed to nominate which vessel the licence would cover. They did not nominate the vessel chartered from the respondents, and refused to pay the charter fee. The Court held that they were liable to pay it. They could not claim frustration since it was a self-induced situation which prevented them from using the vessel.

Consequences of frustration of contract

To determine the rights and duties of the parties following frustration it is necessary to consider the position at common law and under statute. Frustration of course will terminate a contract. However under common law it does not discharge the contract *ab initio* (from the outset) but only from the time of the frustrating event. Therefore, if before that date work had been done or money transferred, the common law rule is simply that losses lie where they fall. It is thus not possible to recover money due or paid prior to frustrating events, except if there is a total failure or consideration, for example if there has been performance of consideration by one party and non performance of consideration by the other.

The common law position has been altered to some extent by the Law Reform (Frustrated Contracts) Act 1943. The Act however does not apply to certain contracts such as insurance, charter-parties (shipping contracts) and contracts for the sale of specific goods, so the common law position is still relevant. Under the Act the following conditions apply:

(i) Money transferred prior to the frustrating event may be recovered.

(ii) Money due prior to the frustrating event is no longer due.

(iii) Expenses incurred prior to the frustrating event may be deducted from money to be returned.

(iv) Compensation may be recovered on a quantum meruit basis where one of the parties has carried out an act of part performance prior to the frustrating event and thus conferred a benefit on the other party.

Remedies for Breach of Contract

No account of the principles of the contract is complete without some mention of the various remedies available to an innocent party in the event of a breach. The options available are to claim damages and/or treat the contract as discharged under the common law, or pursue an equitable discretionary remedy.

Damages

The usual remedy is to sue for *unliquidated* damages under the common law. Unliquidated damages are damages whose level is determined by the court, exercising its own discretion. It is sometimes possible for a plaintiff to quantify the measure of damages being sought concisely, in which event the plaintiff will claim a *liquidated* amount e.g.: three weeks loss of salary where the salary is of a fixed amount.

The aim of awarding damages

Damages awarded under an unliquidated claim, should amount to a sum of money which will put the innocent party in the position he would have been in had the contract been performed properly, that is the loss resulting from the breach directly and naturally. Consequently a plaintiff should not be awarded damages when the result would be to put him in a better position financially than would have been the case if the contract had not been broken.

> In *C & B Haulage v. Middleton* 1983 the Court of Appeal refused to grant damages to an engineer, who was evicted from the business premises he occupied before the contractual licence he held had expired. The reason for the refusal was that he was working from home, and thus relieved from paying any further charges under the licence. Damages would make him better off.
>
> In *Paula Lee Ltd. v. Robert Zehil & Co. Ltd.* 1983, under an agreement made between the parties the defendants had undertaken to take 16,000 dresses from the plaintiff manufacturers each season, which they would sell in the Middle East. The dresses in question covered a range of prices. The defendants terminated the agreement with two seasons left, and were only willing to pay compensation representing loss of profit to the plaintiffs on the sale of 32,000 of their cheapest dresses. The Court took the view that for the purposes of determining the measure of damages a term could be implied into the original agreement that the 32,000 garments involved would have been selected in a reasonable manner from the various price ranges involved, thus increasing the damages beyond the minimum level suggested by the defendants.

Damages may be refused where the court is of the view that they are too speculative.

> On this basis the court awarded only nominal damages to the plaintiffs in *Entertainments Ltd. v. Great Yarmouth Borough Council* 1983. The council had repudiated an agreement under which the plaintiffs were to put on summer

shows in the town. The judge, Cantley J took the view that as it had not been established as probable that the shows would have made the plaintiffs a profit, to award anything other than nominal damages would be speculative.

Remoteness of damage

The consequences of a contractual breach can often extend well beyond the immediate, obvious losses. A failure to deliver goods may for example result in the buyer being unable to complete the work on a particular job, which will in turn put him in breach with the party who had contracted him to carry out the job. That party may in turn suffer further consequences, thus the original breach leads to a chain of events which become increasingly remote from it. Damages will only be awarded for losses which are proximate. The courts take the view that it is unfair to make a contract-breaker responsible for damage caused as a result of circumstances of which he was unaware.

In *Hadley v. Baxendale* 1854 the plaintiff mill owner contracted with a defendant carrier who agreed to take a broken millshaft to a repairer and then return it. The carrier delayed in delivery of the shaft and as a result the plaintiff sought to recover the loss of profit he would have made during the period of delay. The court held that this loss was not recoverable as it was too remote. The possible loss of profit was a circumstance of which the carrier was unaware at the time of the contract. The result would have been different however had the plaintiff expressly made the defendant aware that this loss of profit was the probable result of a breach of contract.

The decision in *Hadley v. Baxendale* has been approved by the House of Lords on many occasions and knowledge of the circumstances which could produce the damage it still a crucial factor in determining the extent of the liability for the breach.

In *Czarnikow v. Koufos (The Heron II)* 1969 a shipowner delayed in delivering a cargo of sugar to Basrah. The sugar was to be sold by the cargo owners at Basrah, where there was an established sugar market. During the nine days the ship was delayed the market price fell. The cargo owners successfully sued for their loss. The House of Lords considered that the loss ought to have been within the reasonable contemplation of the shipowners as a consequence of the delay. It was felt that the shipowners should have appreciated that a market for goods is something which by its nature fluctuates over time.

In *Diamond v. Campbell-Jones* 1961 the defendant seller of premises wrongfully repudiated the contract of sale to a dealer and was held liable for the loss of profit that the dealer would have made on a resale. The fact that the seller was unaware that the purchaser intended to convert the premises before resale, in order to command a higher price, meant that the seller was not liable for the larger profit that the dealer would have made.

Other principles applicable to a claim for damages

Where a breach has occurred the innocent party, if he accepts that the breach discharges the contract, must take all reasonable steps to mitigate the loss resulting from the breach. There is no requirement for the injured party to act immediately to take on a risky venture but rather act reasonably in order to minimise the loss rather than 'sitting on the breach'. For instance an hotel would be expected to try and relet a room that a customer, in breach of contract, had failed to use.

> In *Moore v. DER Ltd.* 1971 the plaintiff, a dentist, ordered a new Rover 2000 as a replacement for the one he had which was a total loss following an accident. He could have purchased a second-hand car. The Court of Appeal took the view that he had acted reasonably, for his practice was a busy one and he needed a car that was completely reliable. Nor did this arrangement prevent him from recovering the costs of hiring another vehicle during the period he was waiting for the new car, even though he could have bought a second-hand car much sooner.

> By way of contrast in *Luker v. Chapman* 1970 the plaintiff lost his right leg below the knee following a motor accident partly caused by the negligence of the defendant. This injury prevented him from continuing his work as a telephone engineer, but he was offered clerical work as an alternative. He refused it, choosing instead to go into teacher training. It was held that he could not recover as damages the loss of income suffered whilst he underwent the teacher training.

Damages are not limited to the pure economic cost of the loss of the bargain but may also be recovered for inconvenience, discomfort, distress or anxiety caused by the breach.

> In *Jarvis v. Swans Tours Ltd.* 1973 the Court of Appeal held that the plaintiff was entitled to damages for mental distress and disappointment due to loss of enjoyment caused by breach of a holiday contract.

> In *Perry v. Sidney Phillips & Son* 1982 a surveyor negligently failed to notify his client of defects in a house which the client subsequently bought. The defects included problems with a septic tank which caused offensive smells and violated health legislation. Damages for the client's distress and upset were granted.

In substantial contracts involving large sums, such as building contracts, it is usual to attempt to liquidate damages payable in the event of a breach. This is achieved by the parties expressly inserting a clause into the contract providing for a sum of compensation to be payable on a breach. Generally, provided such clauses represent a genuine pre-estimate of the future possible loss rather than amounting to a penalty to ensure performance of contract, they are enforceable by the courts.

A term will generally be regarded as a penalty clause if

(i) the amount involved is regarded as extravagant. In *Dunlop Pneumatic Tyre Co. Ltd. v. New Garage & Motor Co. Ltd.* 1915 the appellants supplied tyres to the respondents at a trade discount on terms that if the respondents sold the tyres below list price they would pay the appellants £5 per tyre. The House of Lords treated this as a genuine estimate of the harm which Dunlop would suffer by undercutting, and thus enforceable. However in *Ford Motor Co. v. Armstrong* 1915 Armstrong, a motor retailer, agreed to pay £250 to Fords for every car he sold below their list price. The Court of Appeal regarded this as an extravagant sum which was thus void as a penalty.

(ii) A fixed sum is payable on the occurrence of any one of several events, some of which may be minor breaches and some of which may be more serious.

(iii) The amount payable is greater than the maximum amount of loss that is likely to be sustained.

Once the court decides however that the sum stipulated represents a liquidated damages clause, rather than a penalty, it will be enforced, even though the actual loss sustained may be larger, or smaller, than damages specified.

> Thus in *Cellulose Acetate Silk Co. Ltd. v. Widnes Foundry Ltd.* 1933 the foundry had agreed to pay £20 for every week of delay in completing the construction of premises for Cellulose Acetate. Delays amounted in total to 30 weeks, and Cellulose Acetate sought £6,000 compensation for the actual losses they had suffered. The Court held that Widnes Foundry were only liable for damages of £600 (£20 x 30 weeks) as agreed.

Liquidated damage clauses are a common commercial device. If you have ever looked at a holiday booking form you will have seen the graduated cancellation charges inserted by the holiday company, which increase in amount the closer to the holiday the cancellation occurs. This reflects the anticipated difficulty the operator is likely to experience in reselling the holiday at short notice.

The right to treat a contract as discharged will depend upon the nature of the breach. For breaches of condition the innocent party may sue for damages and/or treat the contract as repudiated, whereas for less important terms the innocent party is limited to an action for damages.

Quantification of damages in relation to goods or land is essentially a question of assessing the market price and then determining the actual loss. The Sale of Goods Act 1979 provides for a number of remedies, including damages, available to an injured party to a sale of goods transaction. These are examined in outline below.

Remedies Available to Buyers and Sellers

In the event of a breach of the obligation owed by one party to the other under a sale of goods contract the injured party may seek redress against the other. The principal obligations that arise may be summarised as follows:

(a) the seller must transfer ownership in the goods to the buyer; physically deliver them to the buyer unless the contract provides otherwise; fulfil the implied conditions and warranties contained in ss. 12-15 of the 1979 Act;

(b) the buyer must accept the goods and pay for them. Note that payment and delivery are concurrent obligations, unless the parties agree otherwise. This means they occur at the same time, for instance in the case of cash sales in shops.

The remedies of a seller

If the seller is owed money by the buyer the Act gives the seller the following rights, even if the buyer has become the owner of the goods:

(i) a *lien* over the goods, i.e. a right to retain possession until he is paid;

(ii) if the goods are in transit and in possession of a carrier, a right to regain possession of them during the transit if the buyer has become insolvent;

(iii) a right of resale in certain circumstances, for instance when the goods are of a perishable nature, or where the seller gives the buyer notice of the intention to resell and the buyer does not within a reasonable time pay for the goods. In the event of a resale the seller can claim damages representing any loss suffered. Such a loss could be the reduced profit on a resale because of a drop in the market price of the goods, including the cost of advertising them;

(iv) an action for the price of the goods;

(v) an action for damages where the goods are still owned by the seller and the buyer refuses or simply fails to accept them. Damages awarded will represent the loss directly and naturally resulting from the non acceptance. *Prima facie*, this will be the difference between the contract price, and the market or current price at the time when the goods should have been accepted, assuming of course there is an available market. So if supply exceeds demand and there is a fixed retail price for the goods damages will then represent the loss of profit that would have been made on the sale, but if demand exceeds supply then damages will only be nominal as the goods can be readily resold.

The remedies of a buyer

(i) An action to recover damages when the seller wrongfully fails or refuses to deliver the goods. Again damages are measured in the same way was outlined above in a seller's action for non-acceptance. It should be stressed that in the case of a non-delivery by the seller, or a non-acceptance by a buyer it is the market price when the breach occurs that is used to determine the measure for damages;

> In *Pagnan v. Corbisa* 1970 Lord Justice Salmon made it quite clear that other market fluctuations are not relevant,"... *the innocent party is not bound to go on the market and buy or sell at the date of the breach. Nor is he bound to gamble on the market changing in his favour. He may wait if he chooses; and if the market turns against him this cannot increase the liability of the party in default. Similarly, if the market turns in his favour, the liability of the party in default is not diminished".*

(ii) recovery of the price paid if the goods are not delivered;

(iii) rejection of the goods where there has been a breach of condition, and damages for breach of warranty - the amount being the difference between the value of the goods as delivered, and their value if the warranty has been complied with. A buyer may elect treat a breach of condition as a breach of warranty.

Discretionary Remedies

These remedies are available because of the intervention of the Court of Chancery. They include the injunction, specific performance and the remedy of quantum meruit.

Injunctions

An injunction is an order of the court which directs a person not to break his contract, and is an appropriate remedy where the contract contains a negative stipulation.

This can be seen in *Warner Bros. Pictures v. Nelson* 1937. The defendant, the actress Bette Davis, had agreed to work for the plaintiff company for twelve months, and not to act or sing for anyone else or be otherwise employed for a period of two years, without the plaintiff's written consent. It was held that she could be restrained by injunction from breaking the negative aspects of her undertaking, thus preventing her from working under a new acting contract in England where she was earning more money. The injunction was however confined to her work as an actress, for it was recognised that if the negative terms in her contract were fully enforced it would have the effect of either forcing her to work for Warner Bros. or starve, and this would mean the injunction acting as a device for specific performance of the contract. Equity will not order specific performance of contracts of a personal kind which would involve constant supervision, and which, by their nature, depend upon the good faith of the parties. Similarly in *Page One Records Ltd. v. Britton* 1968 an injunction was applied for to prevent the Troggs pop group from engaging anyone as their manager other than the plaintiff. An injunction on these terms was refused, for to grant it would indirectly compel the pop group to continue to employ the plaintiff.

Types of injunction

There are three types of injunction which may be applied for:

(a) an interlocutory injunction. This is designed to regulate the position of the parties pending trial, the plaintiff undertaking to be responsible for any damage caused to the defendant through the use of the injunction if in the subsequent action the plaintiff is unsuccessful. In *American Cyanamid v. Ethicon* 1975 the House of Lords said that an interlocutory injunction should only be granted where the plaintiff can show that the matter to be tried is a serious one and that the balance of convenience is in his favour. In certain circumstances a specialised kind of interlocutory injunction, known as a *Mareva injunction*, may be sought. The Mareva injunction takes its name from the case in which it was first successfully applied for, *Mareva Compania Naviera v. International Bulk Carriers* 1980, and it is used when the subject matter of a contract is in danger of being removed from the area of the courts jurisdiction. If the action which is to be heard involves a claim for damages and the sale of the subject matter is likely to be used to pay them, a Mareva injunction can be used to restrict the removal of these assets from the courts' jurisdiction. This is a valuable protection in cases where the defendant is a foreign organisation. s.37 Supreme Court Act 1981 grants the High Court the power to issue such injunctions.

(b) a prohibitory injunction. This orders a defendant not to do a particular thing. The injunction sought in the *Nelson* case (above) was of this kind. Much of the case law concerning prohibitory injunctions is concerned with employment contracts, and as we have seen such an injunction can only be used to enforce a negative stipulation. In addition the remedy of a prohibitory injunction will not be given where a court is of the opinion that damages would be an adequate remedy, although in the words of Sachs LJ in *Evans Marshall v. Bertola SA* 1973 *"The standard question in relation to the grant of an injunction, are damages an adequate remedy? might perhaps, in the light of the authorities of recent years, be rewritten: is it just, in all the circumstances, that a plaintiff should be confined to his remedy in damages."*

A prohibitory injunction was used in *Decro-Wall International v. Practitioners in Marketing* 1971 where a manufacturer was restrained from breaking a sole distributorship agreement by an order preventing him from disposing of the goods to which the agreement related in any other way. The Court was not however prepared to order him to fulfil the positive part of the agreement which was to maintain supplies of the goods to the distributor, for this would have amounted to specific performance of the contract (see below).

In cases involving land an injunction may be used where for example, the purchaser has undertaken contractually with the vendor not to build on the land, but after the contract has been made seeks to break the promise.

(c) a mandatory injunction. This is used to order that a positive act be done, for example that a fence blocking a right of way be taken down.

In *Sky Petroleum Ltd. v. VIP Petroleum Ltd.* 1974 the parties entered into a ten year agreement in 1970 under which VIP undertook to supply all Sky's petrol requirements. Following a dispute in 1973 VIP refused to continue its supplies to Sky, and because of an oil crisis at the time Sky found itself unable to secure any other source of supply. The Court granted a temporary injunction against VIP restraining it from withholding a reasonable level of supplies.

Specific performance

The decree of specific performance is an order of the court requiring a party who is in breach of contract to carry out his promises. Failure to comply amounts to a contempt of court. As an equitable remedy it will only be granted if certain conditions apply. These are:

(a) Where damages would not provide an adequate remedy. Usually in commercial transactions damages will be adequate, and will enable the injured party to purchase the property or obtain the services from some alternative source. However where the subject matter of the contract is unique, for example a painting, specific performance will lie. The item must however be unique, and in *Cohen v. Roche* 1927 specific performance was not ordered of a contract to sell some rare Hepplewhite chairs since it was difficult, but not impossible, to buy similar chairs on the open market.

Land is always regarded as unique, and it is in the enforcement of contracts for the sale of land that specific performance is most commonly used.

A contract for the purchase of shares or debentures can also be specifically enforced.

(b) Where the court can properly supervise the performance.

In *Ryan v. Mutual Tontine Association* 1893 the Court of Appeal held that despite the fact that a lessor of a service flat was in clear breach of his obligation to provide a porter who was to be *"constantly in attendance"*, an application for specific performance of the lease was refused. This was on the ground that to ensure compliance constant supervision by the Court would be required. Damages only therefore should be awarded.

(c) Where it is not just and equitable.

> In *Malins v. Freeman* 1837 the Court refused the remedy where a bidder at an auction erroneously and carelessly bought property believing he had put in a bid for an entirely different lot. Damages was felt to be an adequate remedy against the bidder, who refused to complete the contract.

Further the plaintiff must satisfy the various equitable maxims which demand high standards of behaviour if relief is to be granted. Thus for example it is said that *"he who comes to equity must come with clean hands"*, meaning that the plaintiff's behaviour must be beyond reproach.

Quantum meruit

A quantum meruit claim (i.e. for as much as is deserved) is available where:

(a) damages is not an appropriate remedy. This could occur where performance of a contract has begun, but the plaintiff is unable to complete the contract because the defendant has repudiated it, thus preventing the plaintiff from obtaining payment.

(b) where work has been carried out under a void contract.

> In *British Steel Corporation v. Cleveland Bridge and Engineering Co. Ltd.* 1984 steel had been supplied to the defendants by the plaintiffs whilst the parties were still negotiating terms. The negotiations subsequently failed, and no contract was concluded between them. The court held that the plaintiffs were entitled to claim on a quantum meruit for the price of the steel supplied to the defendants and used by them.

A further illustration of the use of a quantum meruit claim can be seen in the case of *Craven-Ellis v. Canons Ltd.* 1936, which is considered in Chapter 5.

Assignment *A Bad Week at Britech*

The Managing Director of Britech Systems Ltd., an electronics company for which you work, has asked you to look into two problems facing the company which have blown up over the last week and are causing him considerable anxiety. The company is based to the west of London. One of these problems concerns a major contract negotiated between the company and an international telecommunications organisation ITTB. The contract involves the construction, installation and maintenance by the company of a highly sophisticated computer monitoring system to control signals beamed to and from the United Kingdom and North America using ITTB's own satellite. The system was due to be installed and be fully operational by the beginning of December, eight months away, but work has been halted due to the commercial collapse of Modem plc, which is only UK supplier of certain vital microelectronic components used by Britech in the construction of the monitoring system. Modem went into liquidation two weeks ago, and it is unclear whether there is any chance of receiving the components ordered by Britech from Modem. ITTB, aware of the problem, is arguing that its contract with Britech has been frustrated, and has indicated that it is seeking another company to supply the system as a matter of urgency.

Additionally one of Britech's senior employees, who left the company six months ago, has just set up his own business as a Microelectronics Consultant. In common with other senior staff the employee, Gerry McBain, had agreed to a clause in his contract of employment which stipulated, "The employee agrees and undertakes that in the event of the termination of his/her employment with the company, he/she will not compete in any way with the business of the company or so act as to cause damage to the interests of the company, for a period of five years, to run from the date of termination such undertaking to extend to the whole of England and Wales."

The managing director of Britech has arranged to meet you tomorrow to discuss the legal position in relation both to ITTB and to Mr McBain.

Tasks

Analyse the two situations described, and produce notes on them in which you seek to clarify the company's position, in order to advise the managing director (a) whether the company has a contractual claim against ITTB, and if it has what the measure of damages is likely to be, and (b) what the likelihood is of the company being able to successfully obtain an injunction to prevent the business operations of Mr. McBain.

Chapter 8

Sale of Goods and Related Transactions

This chapter aims to examine the contractual relationships arising between businesses and all those whom they supply. It is an area of critical importance in developing an understanding of business law, for it lies at the heart of commercial activity.

The primary objective of business activity is the provision of goods and services for consumers. Consumption of goods and services meets the private needs of individuals. All of us act as private consumers in this way. We make regular purchases of goods and services to satisfy our demand for a wide range of necessaries and luxuries, from food and clothing to motor cars, video recorders and holidays. Goods and services are also demanded by business organisations, who acquire them to meet their own internal requirements, as well as for the purpose of resale to other businesses in the chain of production or to consumers. The legal rules relating to interbusiness contracting are, in many cases, identical to those which apply where a business deals with a private consumer. However the law has increasingly sought to compensate for the relative economic weakness of individual consumers, by developing a framework of consumer protection.

The protection of the consumer has been sought by a combination of legal devices. These include:

(i) conferring remedies which are available by legal action in the civil courts, for example under the Sale of Goods Act 1979;

(ii) regulating certain types of trading activities, for instance through the licensing requirements under the Consumer Credit Act 1974; and,

(iii) imposing criminal liability in respect of certain types of unacceptable trading practices, for example under the Trade Descriptions Act 1968.

Figure 8.1 on the next page is designed to provide an overview of the major features of consumer protection under the civil and criminal law.

Types and Nature of Business Agreements

In the previous two chapters we examined the legal rules relating to the formation of business contracts and the discharge of obligations arising under them. The remedies available in the event of non compliance by one of the contracting parties were also considered. We shall now examine in more detail the various types of contract which are encountered in the business world and identify the features which distinguish them. Some types of contract involving the supply of goods, for example, which appear very similar, are nevertheless governed by different rules. The distinction between them may depend upon the provisions in the contract relating to the transfer of ownership or the time for payment. It is particularly important to be able to

	Civil Law	**Criminal Law**
Enforcement	Rescission of contract Sue for damages (or defence to an action for damages) in the County Court or High Court Arbitration	Local Authority: Trading Standards Department Prosecution in the Magistrates and Crown Courts Compensation orders under the Power of Criminal Courts Act 1973 Director General of Fair Trading
Defective Products	Sale of Goods Act 1979 Supply of Goods and Services Act 1982 Tort of Negligence Consumer Protection Act 1987 Codes of Practice	Consumer Protection Act 1987 Food Safety Act 1990 Road Traffic Act 1988 and other specific leglislation Health and Safety at Work Act 1974
Defective Services	Supply of Goods and Services Act 1982 Professional Negligence Regulation by trade or professional associations Codes of Practice	Trade Descriptions Act 1968 Consumer Credit Act 1974 Health and Safety at Work Act 1974
False Statements	Misrepresentation Breach of Contract Negligent mis-statement Tort of Deceit	Trade Descriptions Act 1968 Consumer Protection Act 1987 Weights and Measures Act 1985 Fair Trading Act 1973
Exclusion of Liability	Common Law rules of incorporation and interpretation Unfair Contract Terms Act 1977	Consumer Transactions (Restrictions on Statements)Order 1976 and (Amendment) Order 1978

Figure 8.1 *Consumer Protection under the Civil Law and the Criminal Law*

distinguish between the various types of contract otherwise there is a danger of applying the wrong legal rules.

1. Contracts for the sale of goods

Contracts for the sale of goods are perhaps the most significant category of business agreement because they are the type which are most commonly encountered in the commercial world. A sale of goods contract is basically one in which goods are exchanged for money. Examples of this type of contract range from the sale of a loaf of bread for seventy pence to the purchase of an aircraft for tens of millions of pounds.

The law relating to contracts for the sale of goods is contained in the Sale of Goods Act 1979. As a general rule the principle of freedom of contract applies to them. Essentially therefore the buyer and seller are free to negotiate the terms of the contract and make whatever bargain suits their own purposes. Many of the rules contained in the 1979 Act apply only where the parties have not expressly made their intentions clear on the matter in the contract. Some of the provisions in the Act, however, cannot be overridden by agreement between the parties.

A contract for the sale of goods is defined in s.2(1) which states:

> *"A contract for the sale of goods is a contract by which the seller transfers or agrees to transfer the property in goods to the buyer for a money consideration, called the price".*

A closer consideration of the definition reveals the following:

(a) There must be **'a contract'**. The formation of the contract is governed by the ordinary principles of the law of contract. No special formalities are required. The 1979 Act in s.4 states:

> *"a contract of sale may be made in writing (either with or without seal), or by word of mouth, or partly in writing and partly by word of mouth, or may be implied from the conduct of the parties".*

(b) **'the seller transfers or agrees to transfer'**. The Act distinguishes between *a sale* in which property is transferred to the buyer on the making of the contract and thus the seller's consideration is executed, and *an agreement to sell* in which property is transferred to the buyer at some future time and thus the seller's consideration is executory.

(c) **'property'**. This means full legal ownership and is also sometimes referred to as title. This must be distinguished from mere physical possession of goods which does not necessarily signify ownership.

(d) **'goods'**. This includes any form of personal property which is tangible and moveable for example a motor vehicle, a computer or a ship. The definition does not extend to land or to intangible property rights such as intellectual property, shares or debts.

(e) **'money consideration'**. In order for a contract to come within the definition in s.2(1) the price for the goods must include an element of money consideration. For this reason contracts of exchange or barter are not covered by the 1979 Act. However where goods are exchanged for a combination of money and other goods, a part exchange, the contract will come within the definition.

In *Aldridge v. Johnson* 1857 a contract for the exchange of 52 bullocks for a quantity of barley and a sum of money was held to be a contract for the sale of goods.

The importance of the definition in s.2(1) is that wherever there is a contract involving the exchange of ownership of goods for money the provisions of the Sale of Goods Act 1979 will apply to it.

2. Auction sales

Where goods are sold at auction the contract of sale will be governed by the Sale of Goods Act 1979. In relation to the formation of the contract of sale the auctioneer makes an invitation to treat when asking for bids. Each bid is a separate offer and no contract is concluded until a bid is accepted by the auctioneer. The 1979 Act provides in s.57 that:

> *"a sale by auction is complete when the auctioneer announces its completion by the fall of the hammer, or in other customary manner; and until the announcement is made any bidder may retract his bid".*

This section also allows the seller to place a reserve price on the goods and instruct the auctioneer not to sell below that price. The seller may bid himself up to the reserve price against any buyer. In each situation the seller must expressly reserve his right before the auction sale and bidders must be notified.

In an auction sale there are in fact three separate contracts: between the seller and the buyer; the seller and the auctioneer; and the buyer and the auctioneer.

(a) The contract between the seller and the buyer

This is a contract for the sale of goods and the provisions of the Sale of Goods Act 1979 apply to it except to the extent that they may have been varied by the express terms of the contract. When we examine the law relating to exclusion clauses in contracts below it will be seen that the buyer of goods at an auction sale can never 'deal as a consumer' for the purposes of the Unfair Contract Terms Act 1977. This means that the stronger legal protection afforded to consumers will not be available to the buyer at an auction, even if he is in fact buying consumer type goods for his personal use.

Under the Auctions (Bidding Agreements) Acts 1927 and 1969 where the person to whom goods have been sold at an auction sale is a party to a bidding ring the contract is voidable at the option of the seller. A bidding ring is an agreement between a person who attends auctions in the course of business for the purpose of buying goods to resell (a dealer) and any other person, in which it is agreed that the parties within the bidding ring will not try to outbid each other. The objective of the agreement is that the price of particular items are not forced up by competitive bidding. Its effect is that the seller loses money. Usually those involved in the bidding ring will meet after the auction to divide their spoils. Under these Acts it is also a criminal offence for a dealer to offer or agree to give an inducement or reward to another person in return for their abstaining from bidding at an auction.

(b) The contract between the auctioneer and the buyer

This contract is governed by the common law rather then the Sale of Goods Act 1979. The rights and obligations of the parties are a matter for agreement between the auctioneer and the buyer. In practice this usually means that the terms of the contract are laid down in the auctioneer's printed auction conditions. The common law implies the following terms into this contract unless the parties have expressly agreed on contrary terms:

(i) the auctioneer has the seller's authority to sell the goods;

(ii) the auctioneer will give possession of the goods to the purchaser once the price is paid;

(iii) the auctioneer may retain possession of the goods until the full price is paid or tendered;

(iv) neither the auctioneer nor the seller will interrupt the buyer's quiet possession of the goods; and

(v) the auctioneer knows of no reason by which the seller is legally unable to sell the goods.

(c) The contract between the auctioneer and the seller

This contract is also governed by the common law and its terms will be those which have been agreed between the auctioneer and the seller. Again these will usually be laid down in the auctioneer's printed conditions of contract. In the absence of agreed terms to the contrary, the common law implies a promise on the part of the auctioneer that he will not give the buyer possession of the goods without receiving payment. He will be personally liable to the seller for the price if the buyer takes the possession without making payment. The auctioneer has a common law lien on the proceeds of sale of the goods. This means that he is entitled to deduct his agreed fees from any sums which are due to the seller before making payment to him.

3. Contracts of barter

Barter is the method of trading used in the most primitive societies before the invention of money as a generally accepted medium of exchange. A contract of barter is one involving the exchange of goods or services for other goods or services in which no money actually changes hands. Such contracts are not governed by the Sale of Goods Act 1979 because of the absence of a money consideration.

A contract of barter or exchange is a *contract for the transfer of goods* as defined in Part I of the Supply of Goods and Services Act 1982.

4. Contracts of hire

The essence of a contract of hire is that the hirer, in return for some consideration, usually an agreed fee or the periodical payment of a sum of money, enjoys the possession and the use of goods belonging to someone else, the owner. It is never intended that the hirer shall become the owner of the goods himself under the terms of the contract. Contracts of hire are fairly common in the business world and the period of use by the hirer may range from hours to years. Examples of such contracts include the hire of a mobile crane for a specific task lasting two days; the rental of a household television set over a number of years; the hire of a car for a week whilst on holiday; and the hire of sports equipment at a sports centre. In recent times there has been a growth in the commercial leasing of plant and equipment, particularly motor vehicles, to businesses. Commercial leasing, which is a form of hiring, can be a tax efficient method of acquiring plant and equipment for use in a business.

Contracts of hire are governed partly by the Supply of Goods and Services Act 1982 and may also be regulated partly by the Consumer Credit Act 1974. In order to come within the 1974

Act the contract must be a 'consumer hire agreement'. This is defined in s.15(1) of the 1974 Act as:

> *"an agreement made by a person (the owner) with an individual (the hirer) for the bailment of goods, which:*
>
> *(a) is not a hire purchase agreement,*
>
> *(b) is capable of subsisting for more than three months, and*
>
> *(c) does not require the hirer to make payments exceeding £15,000".*

Some of the language of s.15(1) requires explanation:

(a) An agreement made **'by a person with an individual'**. The Act distinguishes between a person and an individual. Whilst the owner may be a person, the hirer must be an individual before the agreement will be regulated by the Act. An individual is a flesh and blood person or an unincorporated association, such as a partnership. Persons, on the other hand, include, as well as individuals, legally created corporate entities such as limited companies or local authorities.

(b) **'for the bailment of goods'**. The expression bailment describes a situation in which one person has possession of goods belonging to another. A contract of hire is one of several possible types of contract of bailment. Another example would be a contract under which goods are stored in a warehouse on behalf of a business.

(c) **'not a hire purchase agreement'**. The nature of a hire purchase agreement is examined below. At this stage it is sufficient to note that an agreement will not be a consumer hire agreement if its real purpose is the eventual acquisition of ownership of the goods by the hirer. The basic idea of any contract of pure hire is that the hirer never becomes the owner of the goods. The goods revert to the possession of the true owner once the period of hire has expired.

Consumer hire agreements are regulated by the Consumer Credit Act 1974 which lays down strict rules as to their form and content. The agreement must be in writing and signed personally by the hirer. If either of these conditions are not fulfilled the owner has no right to sue the hirer under the agreement. The hirer must be given a copy of the agreement containing full information about his rights and duties and about the protection given to him by the 1974 Act. If any of these formalities are not complied with then no legal action can be taken against the hirer without the permission of the court.

5. Contracts for the supply of services

A contract for the supply of services (or contract for services) usually involves the exchange of an individual's time skill or effort in return for money. A person providing a service could do so by engaging in such diverse activities as surveying a house, tuning a car engine, transporting commodities, or providing legal advice. The contract for services is distinct from the contract of employment (or contract of service) which we consider in a later chapter. The basic obligations owned by those who provide services in the course of a business are outlined in Part II of the Supply of Goods Act 1982.

6. Contracts for work done and materials supplied

Where services are provided and goods are supplied under the same contract, for example a contract to paint a portrait, to prepare and supply food or to service a motor vehicle, there may be some difficulty in classifying the contract. It could be a contract for the provision of services or a contract for the sale of goods. The court will decide into which category the contract falls by trying to identify the main purpose of the contract.

> In *Young and Marten v. McMannus Childs* 1968 the House of Lords held that a contract for the laying of tiles on the roof of a house was not a sale of goods contract even though the tiler supplied the tiles. The main purpose of the contract was the supply of services and so the contract was not within the Sale of Goods Act 1979.

> In *Robinson v. Graves* 1935 the Court of Appeal held that a contract under which an artist agreed to paint a client's portrait was not a contract for the sale of goods. The transfer of ownership of the canvas to the client was incidental to the main substance of the contract which was the provision by the artist of his skill, expertise and labour.

It may have been different if the client has selected a finished picture from the artist's studio and agreed to pay for it. Such an agreement is a contract for the sale of goods because the substance of the agreement is the transfer of ownership of a completed picture, not the provision of skill and labour by the artist. Parts I and II of the Supply of Goods and Services Act 1982 apply to contracts for work done and materials supplied.

7. Contracts for the sale or supply of goods on credit terms

There are various forms of credit transaction which provide ways of getting goods on tick, ranging from contracts of hire purchase, credit sale and conditional sale agreements, to the use of 'plastic money'. Credit transactions were aptly characterised by one County Court Judge who complained that most of his time was taken up by:

> *"people who are persuaded by persons whom they do not know to enter into contracts that they do not understand to purchase goods that they do not want with money that they have not got".*

Although this statement is somewhat exaggerated, it helps to highlight some of the problems with which the law has had to deal arising from such agreements, and we shall examine the ways in which the courts and parliament have sought to provide solutions to those problems in Chapter 9.

(a) Contracts of hire purchase

A contract of hire purchase, as its name suggests, combines elements of two types of contract. It is in effect a contract of hire which gives one party (the hirer or debtor) an option to purchase goods from the other (the owner or creditor) at the end of a period of hire. During the period of the agreement the debtor pays the creditor by instalments (usually monthly) and the ownership of the goods remains with the creditor. The agreement will contain a term giving the debtor an optional right to purchase the goods at a nominal price once all the instalments have been paid. Ownership of the goods will be transferred to the debtor if and when he exercises the option to purchase. He will invariably do this as soon as he has paid all of the instalments because the real point of the agreement, in practice, it to enable him to acquire ownership.

A hire purchase agreement is not a contract of sale falling within the Sale of Goods Act 1979. Many hire purchase agreements come within the definition of consumer credit agreements and these are regulated by the Consumer Credit Act 1974.

At first sight a hire purchase transaction appears to involve only two parties. In practice, however, the vast majority of hire purchase transactions involve a third party, a finance company. The person who supplies the goods may not be able to wait for his money and may require instant payment, while his customer wishes to have time for payment. The supplier will therefore sell the goods to a finance company, which will supply them to the customer on hire purchase terms under a separate contract.

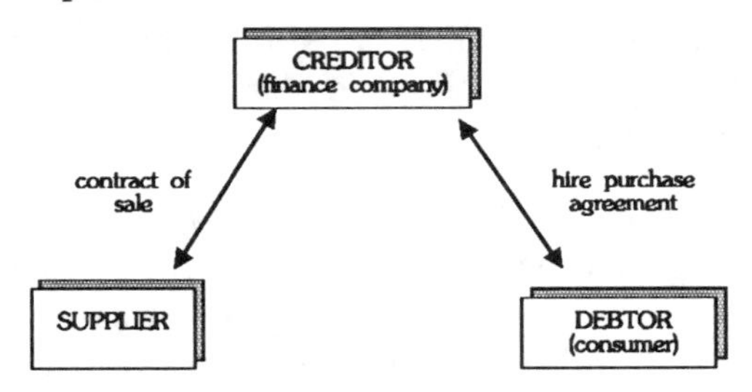

Figure 8.2a *Hire purchase transactions*

The supplier will have in his possession a stock of hire purchase forms belonging to the finance company with whom he usually deals. A customer wishing to take goods on credit will be asked to complete one of these forms and thus make a contractual offer to the finance company to take the goods on hire purchase. The supplier will complete a different form which will constitute a contractual offer to sell the goods to the finance company for cash. The supplier will forward both these offers to the finance company which will either accept or reject them both. If accepted, the supplier will be paid immediately by the finance company. The finance company becomes the owner of the goods and the customer will be bound by a contract of hire purchase with the finance company. Usually the customer will take possession of the goods from the supplier at this stage.

It would appear at first sight that there is no contract between the customer and the supplier where the finance company is involved in a credit transaction. If this were so, difficulties could arise for the customer, if, for example, he wished to sue the supplier for making false statements about the goods. The customer cannot at common law (though the position is different under the 1974 Act) rescind the contract with the finance company on the grounds that the supplier made a misrepresentation to him. However, the common law has recognised the existence of a contract between the customer and the supplier in these circumstances. The customer may sue the supplier for breach of this secondary or collateral contract.

> In *Andrews v. Hopkinson* 1956 the defendant car dealer showed a second hand car to the plaintiff and told him *"it's a good little bus. I would stake my life on it"*. As a result the plaintiff entered into a hire purchase contract with a finance company. Soon afterwards he was injured in a collision caused by a failure of the car steering mechanism. It was held that the defendant was liable in damages to the plaintiff for breach of a collateral contract between them. The court was satisfied that each of the parties had given consider-ation to support the contract. On the part of the defendant, this was his statement, which amounted to a promise that the car was in good condition and reasonably fit for use. On the part of the plaintiff, his entry into the con-

tract with the finance company was the consideration. It had been of direct benefit to the defendant as he was able to sell the car to the finance company as a result.

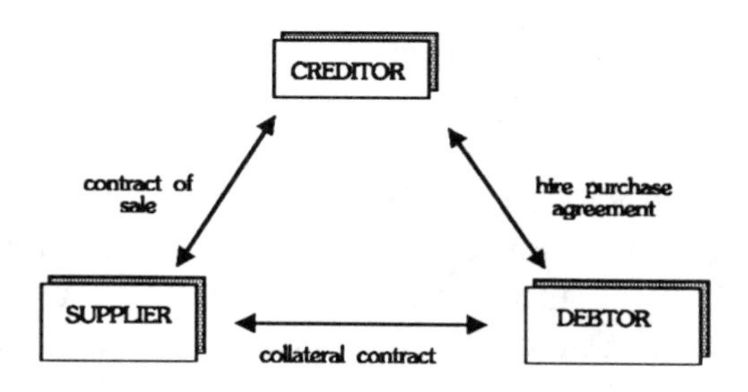

Figure 8.2b *Collateral contract*

As we shall see later, where the supplier and creditor have a business connection, the debtor will be able to sue the creditor as well as the supplier in these circumstances.

(b) Credit sale and conditional sale agreements

Credit sale and conditional sale agreements are credit transactions under which the price of goods is payable by instalments. They will often be financed by a finance company in exactly the same way as hire purchase agreements.

At common law the credit sale agreement is broadly similar to the conditional sale agreement. Each is a contract for the sale of goods under which the buyer commits himself at the outset to the purchase. Theoretically, this is not the case with a hire purchase agreement. Here the customer has an option to buy but is not legally bound to exercise that option.

The main difference at common law between credit sale and conditional sale agreements is that:

(i) in a credit sale agreement ownership of the goods in transferred to the buyer as soon as the contract is made, whereas

(ii) in a conditional sale agreement ownership of the goods is not transferred to the buyer until some condition (usually the payment of the final instalment) is met.

While the instalments are being paid, the buyer is the owner of goods under a credit sale agreement; but the seller is the owner of goods under a conditional sale agreement. In this important respect a conditional sale agreement is similar to a hire purchase agreement. This is why many of the statutory rights of a consumer under a hire purchase agreement such as the right of termination and the protected goods provisions, examined later, also apply to a conditional sale agreement. These rights do not arise in relation to a credit sale agreement.

Inter-Business Contracting and Consumer Contracting

The rights of the business customer and the degree of consumer protection available to him will vary considerably depending upon whether one or both of the parties are entering into the contract in the course of their business. Generally a greater degree of legal protection is available to a private individual than to a business. It is possible to envisage a number of different situations:

(a) private seller and private buyer or business buyer

(b) business seller and business buyer

(c) business seller and private buyer

Take as an example a contract for the sale of goods containing a clause excluding the seller's liability, where the buyer suffers loss because the goods are defective. On these facts the legal rules applicable in each of the above cases would be different, and the outcomes would vary accordingly. It is important then to be able to distinguish between a situation where someone is acting in the course of a trade or business on one hand, or dealing as a consumer on the other.

Dealing as a consumer

In a broad sense anyone to whom goods or services are supplied can be regarded as a consumer and, as we shall see later, the law gives protection to all consumers. However, the protection available is greater in the case of the private consumer. The Fair Trading Act 1973 defines a private consumer in s.137 as:

> *"the person to or for whom goods or services are, or are sought to be, supplied in the course of a business carried on by the supplier, and who does not receive or seek to receive the goods or services in the course of a business carried on by him".*

The Unfair Contract Terms Act 1977 also provides a statutory definition of a private consumer. The Act states in s.12 that:

> *"a party to a contract deals as a consumer in relation to another party if:*
>
> *(a) he neither makes the contract in the course of a business nor holds himself out as doing so; and*
>
> *(b) the other party does make the contract in the course of a business; and*
>
> *(c) where the contract involves the supply of goods, the goods are of a type ordinarily supplied for private use or consumption".*

Three aspects of the transaction must be examined in order to see whether the buyer deals as a consumer: the buyer, the seller and the goods themselves. If the buyer buys for his business or from a private seller or if the goods are of a type which would not usually be purchased for private use then the buyer cannot deal as a consumer. The courts have been prepared to give a fairly wide interpretation of s.12:

> In *Peter Symmonds & Co. v. Cook* 1981 the plaintiffs were partners in a firm of surveyors and they bought a second-hand Rolls Royce in the partnership name with partnership money. The car was intended for use by one of the partners only. The High Court held that the plaintiffs were dealing as consumers in the purchase of the car even though it was to be used partly for business purposes.
>
> A similar approach has been adopted more recently by the Court of Appeal in *R & B Customs Brokers Co. v. United Dominions Trust* 1988 which is considered more fully later in the context of the Unfair Contract Terms Act. In this case it was held that, in order for a purchase to be made *in the course of*

a business for the purposes of s.12, it must be established that such purchases are made with a degree of regularity. Where this is shown it can be said that the purchase is an integral part of the business (and therefore made in the course of the business) as opposed merely to being incidental to the carrying on of the business.

Where the contract is made at auction or by competitive tender, the customer can never be regarded as dealing as a consumer for the purposes of the Unfair Contract Terms Act.

Supplying in the course of a trade or business

Many of the legal rules which govern consumer protection apply only where goods or services are supplied in the course of a trade or business. There is no generally applicable precise definition of the expression 'business', although there are a number of decided cases which give some guidance.

In *Havering London Borough v. Stevenson* 1970 a car hire firm regularly sold its cars after a period of use in the business. A sale in these circumstances was held to be in the course of its trade or business as a car hire firm.

On the other hand, in *Davies v. Sumner* 1984 the defendant was a self employed courier, who had a contract with a T.V. company to transport films and video tapes. He purchased a new car in June 1980, and travelled 118,000 miles in it before trading it in for another in July 1981. The mileometer had gone around the clock, and showed only 18,000 miles. The defendant did not disclose the true milage, and was later charged with having applied a false trade description "in the course of a trade or business". The House of Lords held that he was not guilty, as this was a one-off sale which could not be regarded as an integral part of his business.

In *Blakemore v. Bellamy* 1983 the defendant's spare time activity of buying, refurbishing and selling cars was held to be a hobby rather than a business. This was so even though he had sold eight different cars over a period of fifteen months and he had not driven them all himself or had them insured.

Business sellers may sometimes masquerade as private sellers for example by advertising in the small ad's in a newspaper. The purchaser may be mislead by this and think that his legal remedies are limited because he has purchased from a private seller. In order to prevent such disguised business sales the Business Advertisements (Disclosure) Order 1977 was made under s.22 of The Fair Trading Act 1973. Under this regulation it is a criminal offence for a trader or a businessman to advertise goods for sale without making it reasonably clear that the goods are being sold in the course of a business.

Where goods are sold by an agent in the course of his business for a private seller, the sale will be treated, for the purposes of the implied terms in s.14 of the Sale of Goods Act 1979, as a sale by a seller acting in the course of a business unless:

(a) the buyer knows that he is purchasing from a private seller, or

(b) reasonable steps are taken to bring it to his attention before the contract is made.

This could apply, for example, where goods are sold by a private seller at a public auction.

Inter-business contracting

Where a contract is made between a business seller and a business buyer, the parties are allowed greater freedom of contract to agree their respective obligations by negotiation. The courts will be reluctant to interfere with the terms of a bargain made between contracting parties of equal bargaining power. Business consumers should be better placed in terms of their experience knowledge and bargaining power to look after their own interests than the private consumer would be. If there is unequal bargaining power, however, the courts may be prepared to step in and protect the weaker party to the transaction by invalidating part of the agreement under the Unfair Contract Terms Act 1977.

Standard form contracts

Standard form contracts covering many different types of transaction are in common use in the business world today. Standard form contracts are so called because the express terms of the contract are set out in a standard form or document which is used whenever an organisation enters into a contract with a customer. They are sometimes referred to as 'contracts of adhesion' because in practice one of the parties is obliged to adhere to terms dictated by the other.

The advantages for a business organisation of using standard form contracts are that they are administratively convenient as each customer is contracting on the same terms, and more importantly that the terms are fixed in advance by the organisation. The terms will be drafted in such a way as to weight the commercial advantage in favour of the organisation and maximise any legal protection available to it.

The danger of this type of economic oppression was pointed out by Lord Diplock in *Schroeder Music Publishing Co. Ltd. v. Macauley* 1974 when he stated:

> *"The terms of this kind of standard form of contract have not been the subject of negotiation between the parties to it, or approved by any organisation representing the interests of the weaker party. They have been dictated by that party whose bargaining power, either exercised alone, or in conjunction with others providing similar goods or services, enables him to say: "If you want these goods or services at all, these are the only terms on which they are available. Take it or leave it"."*

As we shall see, some of the more obvious abuses which were present at one time in this type of contract are now controlled by legislation; for example extortionate credit bargains by the Consumer Credit Act 1974, and exclusion or limitation of liability by the Unfair Contract Terms Act 1977.

Where parties of relatively equal bargaining strength deal with each other over a long period of time, standard form agreements may evolve by negotiation. Far from being oppressive, this type of standard form contract provides a framework of certainty for business transactions and an appropriate division of rights and responsibilities between the parties. It may take into account possible occurrences and contingencies. The apportionment of risks under it can be linked with the insurance arrangements of the parties. Such an agreement will be designed to avoid the risk of litigation between the parties, for example by use of arbitration and liquidated damages clauses.

A standard form contract for the sale of goods is set out below.

1. (a) THIS AGREEMENT is made the day of 19
BETWEEN of
(referred to in this agreement as "the seller") and

of
(referred to in this agreement as "the buyer")

WHEREBY IT IS AGREED that the seller shall sell and the buyer shall purchase the goods described in condition 2 in accordance with the terms of this contract.

(b) No amendments or modifications to these conditions and, in particular, no terms or conditions of purchase of the buyer shall form part of the contract or be binding upon the seller unless expressly agreed to in writing and signed by the seller.

2. (a) Description of goods:

(b) The description of the goods in condition 2(a) above is believed to be correct as to weights, dimensions, capacity, composition, performance and otherwise. Any error, omission or mis-statement therein (whether or not it materially affects the description of the goods) shall not annul the sale nor entitle the buyer to be discharged from the contract or to claim any compensation in consequence thereof. Provided that nothing in this condition shall oblige the buyer to accept any goods which differ substantially in any of the above-mentioned respects from the goods agreed to be sold if the buyer would be prejudiced by reason of such difference. In that event the buyer shall be entitled to rescind the contract and to claim repayment of the price, but the seller shall incur no further liability in respect thereof.

3. (a) In addition to the price of the goods, the buyer shall pay

(i) Vat or other taxes payable in respect of the goods;

(ii) the cost of insurance under condition 8; and

(iii) the cost of delivery under condition 4.

(b) The price of the goods is :
add V.A.T :
insurance :
delivery :
total amount due :

(c) Where the date of delivery specified in condition 4 is more than six months from the date of this agreement, the seller reserves the right to increase the price of the goods in proportion to any increase in costs to the seller of materials labour and other inputs between the date of this contract and the date of delivery.

(d) The buyer will pay the price of the goods and any other sums due to the seller under this contract within 30 days of the date of delivery. In the event of a failure to make payment by the due date interest at the rate of 10% per annum shall be payable on any sums outstanding.

4. (a) The delivery date is . This date is given as way of an estimate only and the seller shall not be liable for failure to deliver on time.

(b) Unless the seller is notified otherwise in writing at least seven days before the delivery date, the seller shall deliver the goods to the buyer's place of business. The cost of transportation and insurance up to the time of actual delivery will be paid by the buyer in accordance with condition 3.

(c) The seller shall be entitled at its sole discretion to make partial deliveries or deliveries by instalments.

(d) Deviations in quantity of the goods delivered (representing no more then 10% by value) from that stated in condition 2 shall not give the buyer any right to reject the goods or to claim damages. The buyer shall be obliged to accept and pay at the contract rate for the quantity of goods delivered.

5. (a) The seller reserves the right to modify the specification or design of the goods in whole or in part without prior notification to the buyer. The buyer shall accept such modified goods in performance of the contract.

   (b) The buyer shall be deemed to have accepted the goods unless within 14 days of delivery written notice is received by the seller to the contrary.

6. (a) The property in the goods shall remain with the seller until the seller has received payment in full for the goods and all other sums owing to the seller on whatever grounds.

   (b) If the buyer sells the goods prior to making payment in full for them, the rights of the seller under this condition shall attach to the proceeds of sale or to the claim for such proceeds. The buyer shall, if required to do so by the seller, formally assign any such rights.

   (c) For so long as the property in goods remains with the seller, the buyer shall store the goods separately so that they may readily be identified as the property of the seller. The seller shall during this time have the right to retake possession of the goods. For this purpose the buyer hereby irrevocably authorises the seller of his agents to enter upon any premises occupied by the buyer.

   (d) The seller may maintain an action for the price notwithstanding that property in the goods may not have passed to the buyer.

7. The goods shall be at risk of the buyer in all respects from the date of this contract or, if later, the date of manufacture by the seller.

8. Unless the buyer notifies the seller in writing to the contrary, the seller shall at the expense of the buyer insure the goods to the full replacement value thereof until the time of delivery.

9. (a) In the event that the goods supplied to the buyer fail to comply with the terms of this contract, or prove to be defective, the liability of the seller is limited to the replacement of the goods or, at the seller's option, the refund of all payments made by the buyer in respect of the goods.

   (b) Except as otherwise provided in condition 9(a), the seller shall be under no liability of whatsoever kind whether or not due to the negligence or wilful default of the seller or its servants or agents arising out of or in connection with any breach of the seller's obligations under this contract. All conditions, warranties or other terms, express or implied, statutory or otherwise, are hereby expressly excluded.

   (c) Nothing in this condition shall exclude or restrict any liability of the seller for death or personal injury resulting from the negligence of the seller or its servants or agents.

   (d) If it should be held in relation to any claim that the preceding provisions of this paragraph are ineffective, the buyer shall not be entitled to reject the goods and any damages recovered by the buyer shall be limited to the reasonable cost of remedying the breach of contract provided that the seller shall first be afforded the opportunity of itself carrying out such remedial work.

   (e) Nothing in this condition or in conditions 2(b) or 4(d) shall exclude or restrict any liability of the seller for breach of its implied undertakings as to title; and, where the buyer deals as a consumer, any liability of the seller for breach of its implied undertakings as to description, quality, fitness for purpose, or correspondence with sample.

(f) In the case of transactions covered by paragraphs (4) and (5) of the Consumer Transactions (Restrictions on Statements) Order 1976 the provisions of this contract shall not affect the statutory rights of the consumer.

10. The seller shall not be liable for non-performance in whole or in part of its obligations under this contract due to causes beyond the control either of the seller or of the seller's suppliers including any Act of God, fire, flood, tempest, act of state, war, civil commotion, embargo, accident, plant breakdown, hindrance in or prevention from obtaining any raw materials or other supplies, interference by labour disputes, inability to obtain adequate labour, manufacturing facilities or energy, or any other like cause. If any such event continues for a period of more than 6 weeks, the seller may cancel this contract or vary condition 4(a) hereof by notice in writing to the buyer without liability on the part of the seller.

11. (a) The seller shall have the right to terminate this contract by notice in writing in the event of the buyer's insolvency and the buyer shall indemnify the seller against all losses and damage suffered by reason of such termination.

    (b) Termination of the contract under this condition shall not affect the accrued rights of the parties arising in any way out of the contract as at the date of termination.

    (c) In the event of termination under this condition the seller shall have the right to enter any business premises occupied by the buyer and recover any goods which are the seller's property.

12. In the event of cancellation of this contract by the buyer for whatever reason, the buyer agrees to pay 20% of the purchase price to the seller by way of liquidated damages.

13. The benefit of this contract shall not be assigned or transferred by the buyer without the prior written consent of the seller. The seller shall have the right to assign to any of its associated companies all of the rights, powers, duties and obligations under this contract without the consent of the buyer. In the event of any such assignment by the seller references in this contract to the seller shall be deemed to be references to any company taking under the assignment.

14. If any difference shall arise between the seller and the buyer upon the meaning of any part of this contract or the rights and liabilities of the parties hereto, the same shall be referred the arbitration of two persons (one named by each party) or their umpire in accordance with the provisions of the Arbitration Act 1950 or any amending or substituted legislation for the time being in force.

SIGNED for and on behalf)

of the SELLER:)

SIGNED for and on behalf)

of the BUYER:)

Standard Form Contract for the Sale of Goods

The terms of the standard form contract above were drawn up by the seller, and it is clear that most of its contents are weighted in his favour. We shall now examine selected clauses of the agreement in order to see what they are attempting to achieve, and comment on any legal rules which may affect their validity.

Clause 1(b) attempts to exclude any conflicting terms of business on which the buyer usually trades, or any other variation of the terms set out in the seller's standard form. As we noted in Chapter 5, where there is a battle of forms like the one which occurred in *Butler Machine Tool Co. Ltd. v. Ex-Cell-O Corporation Ltd.* 1979, the rules of offer and acceptance will determine whether clause 1(b) is actually effective.

Clause 2(b) is an attempt to deal with the problem posed by s.13 of the Sale of Goods Act 1979, which provides that compliance with description is a condition of the contract. Under s.13 anything less than strict compliance with the contract description gives the buyer the right to reject the goods and rescind the contract, even if he suffers no loss as a result. This happened for example, in *Re Moore & Landauer* 1921 and *Arcos v. Ronnaasen* 1933. Clause 2(b) is a limitation of liability and will be subject to the controls in s.6 of the Unfair Contract Terms Act 1977.

Clause 3(c) is a price variation clause. This type of clause is particularly significant when the rate of inflation is high. It allows the seller to pass onto the buyer any increase in costs between the date of the contract and the date of delivery. Increases cannot be passed on under clause 3(c) if delivery takes place within six months of the making of the contract. Obviously the longer the period of time between contract and delivery, the more the price will increase. A buyer faced with this type of term will usually try to negotiate an upper limit on any price increase if he cannot persuade the seller to withdraw it altogether.

Clause 3(d) provides for the payment of interest in the event of late payment of sums due to the seller from the buyer. This is an attempt by the seller to ensure a steady cash flow in his business. In the absence of a contractual right to interest:

(i) no interest will be payable by the buyer in respect of late payments, unless the seller actually issues legal proceedings against him to recover the debt; and

(ii) the buyer can avoid having to pay interest by paying the money at any time before legal proceedings are issued.

Clause 4(a) makes provision for the date of delivery. Under a commercial contract, the agreed delivery date is usually a condition rather than a warranty, unless the parties agree otherwise. This was established in the case *Hartley v. Hymans* 1920. Under clause 4 (a) the delivery date in any contract made by reference to these standard terms is a warranty only. The clause goes even further, however, and excludes the liability of the seller for failure to deliver on time. This exclusion of liability will be covered by s.3 of the Unfair Contract Terms Act 1977.

Clause 4(b) fixes the place of delivery. Where no provision is made for this in a contract, s.29 of the Sale of Goods Act 1979 provides that the place of delivery is the seller's place of business if he has one, and if not, his residence; except that, if the contract is for the sale of specific goods, which to the knowledge of the parties when the contract is made are in some other place, then that place is the place of delivery.

Clause 4(d) excludes the seller's liability for delivery of the wrong quantity if the amount delivered is within 10% of the amount ordered, and obliges the buyer to take and pay for the quantity actually delivered. Without this clause, and clause 2(b) with which it overlaps, the buyer would be entitled, under s.30 of the Sale of Goods Act 1979, to choose, in the event of delivery of the wrong quantity, between:

(i) rejecting all of the goods delivered; or

(ii) rejecting any excess over the contractual quantity; or

(iii) accepting all of the goods delivered and paying for them at the contract rate in the event of short delivery.

Clause 5(b) limits the time during which the buyer can repudiate the contract by rejecting the goods for breach of condition. Once a buyer has accepted goods, as we shall see in Chapter 9, he is entitled to sue for damages only in the event of a breach of condition by the seller. Acceptance denies him the right of repudiation.

Clause 6 is a retention of title clause. This type of clause is examined in Chapter 9.

Clause 7 transfers risk to the buyer on the making of the contract. The transfer of risk is examined in Chapter 9, and at this stage we need only comment that the buyer should insure the goods once risk is transferred to him: a matter which is provided for in clause 8.

Clause 9 is an elaborate limitation of liability clause designed to minimise the seller's liability for breach of contract. As such it is covered by s.3 and s.6 of the Unfair Contract Terms Act 1977. The purpose of each subclause should become clear when you have studied the text on exclusion clauses and the Unfair Contract Terms Act 1977 later in this chapter.

Clause 10 is a force majeure clause which aims to make provision for events which otherwise could frustrate the contract.

Clause 12 is a liquidated damages clause. This type of clause aims to quantify the amount recoverable by one of the contracting parties where the other is in breach of contract. At common law a liquidated damages clause is valid if it represents a genuine pre-estimate of the amount of money which would be lost in the event of a breach of contract. If, however, it provides for a payment which is out of proportion to the actual losses which are likely, the clause will be void as a penalty. In *Dunlop Pneumatic Tyre Co. v. New Garage Motor Co.* 1915, Lord Dunedin stated that a liquidated damages clause:

> *"will be held to be a penalty if the sum stipulated for is extravagant and unconscionable in amount in comparison with the greatest loss that could conceivably be proved to have followed from the breach."*

Where the clause is held to be a penalty it is void and the innocent party can sue only for the loss actually sustained. On the other hand if the clause is valid and not a penalty, he can sue for the stipulated sum only, whether his actual loss is greater or smaller.

Clause 13 restricts the rights of the buyer to transfer the benefit of the contract. As we shall see in Chapter 18 the buyer's rights under the contract are a form of intangible business property (a chose in action) which can be sold or transferred to another person. Such a transfer would have to comply with the rules in s.136 of the Law of Property Act 1925, examined in Chapter 18.

Clause 14 is an arbitration clause. It enables either party to refer any dispute arising from the contract to arbitration. The process of arbitration is examined in Chapter 2 , which also gives an assessment of the advantages and disadvantages of arbitration as compared to legal action in the courts. It will be recalled that under the Consumer Arbitration Agreements Act 1988, this type of clause can only be enforced as against a consumer in limited circumstances.

Terms Implied by Statute

In Chapter 6 we noted that obligations may arise under a contract in two different ways. First because the law imposes them, for example by Act of Parliament, and second because the parties expressly agree to them. In a contract for the sale or supply of goods the law imposes obligations on the supplier by the legal mechanism of implied terms in the contract of supply. These statutory implied terms operate as if the seller had said to the buyer "I promise you that...". Most of these terms are conditions, which, if broken, will give rise to the right to repudiate the contract, reject the goods and sue for damages. There are a small number of implied warranties also. The buyer's remedy in the event of a breach of warranty is damages. In the case of a breach of condition, as we shall see later in the text the buyer may lose the right to reject the goods in certain circumstances.

The implied terms contained in Sections 12 to 15 of the Sale of Goods Act 1979 automatically become part of any contract for the sale of goods. These terms have been used as a model for incorporation by statute into all other contracts involving the supply of goods. Sections 8 to 11 of the Supply of Goods (Implied Terms) Act 1973 imply virtually identical terms in contracts of hire purchase. Sections 2 to 5 of the Supply of Goods and Services Act 1982 imply equivalent provisions into contracts for the transfer of goods, a term which includes contracts of barter and the supply of goods element of contracts for work done and materials supplied. Sections 7 to 10 of the 1982 Act also imply equivalent provisions into contracts for the hire of goods.

For convenience we shall refer to the 1979 Act for the purpose of examining the detailed content of the implied terms below.

Implied terms relating to title (s12 of the 1979 Act; s8, 1973 Act; s2 and s7, 1982 Act)

There is an implied condition that the seller has the right to sell the goods. If this is broken, for example because the goods belong to someone else, the buyer will be able to repudiate the contract and recover in full the price he paid.

> In *Rowland v. Divall* 1923 three months after buying a motor car the purchaser discovered that it had been stolen before it came into the seller's possession. The seller therefore had no right to sell it. The purchaser returned the car to its original owner and sued the seller under s.12. It was held that he was entitled to the return of the price because he had suffered a 'total failure of consideration'. The fact that the buyer had used the car for over three months did not affect his right to recover the full purchase price.

Where the seller is the true owner of the goods he may nevertheless have no right to sell them if for example they infringe intellectual property rights held by another person.

> In *Niblett v. Confectioners Materials Co.* 1921 the purchaser of a quantity of tins of preserved milk could not resell them without infringing the Nestle Company Trade Mark. This infringement arose because the labels placed on tins by the manufacturer bore the name 'Nissly Brand'. The seller was held to be in breach of s.12.

Under s.12 there is also an implied warranty that the goods are free from any potential claims by any third parties which had not been disclosed to the buyer. There is also an implied warranty that the buyer will enjoy quiet possession of the goods.

> In *Microbeads v. Vinhurst Road Markings* 1975 the seller sold road marking machines to the buyer. After the sale a third party obtained a patent on the machine. The continued use of the machine by the buyer was then in breach of the third party's patent rights. The buyer sued the seller under s.12 claiming that he was in breach of the implied condition that he had the right to sell, and of the implied warranty that the buyer would enjoy quiet possession. The Court of Appeal held that there was no breach of condition. At the time of the sale there was no infringement of the patent and therefore the seller had the right to sell. However, the seller was liable in damages for breach of the warranty that the buyer would enjoy quiet possession of the goods.

Implied terms relating to description (s13 of the 1979 Act; s9, 1973 Act; s3 and s8, 1982 Act)

Where there is a contract for the sale of goods by description there is an implied condition that the goods will correspond with the description. Whenever the buyer has not seen the goods before the contract is made the sale is obviously a sale by description. Also, if goods are packaged, for example food inside a tin or cardboard box, there is a sale by description. The buyer will only be able to see the goods after he has purchased them and opened the package. The vast majority of sales will be made by description. The 1979 Act provides in s.13(3) that a sale of goods is not prevented from being a sale by description by reason only that the goods are selected by the buyer after being exposed for sale, for example in a self-service store. The description can extend to such things as weight, size, quantity, composition and age.

> In *Dick Bentley Productions Ltd. v. Harold Smith Motors Ltd.* 1965 a car dealer sold a second-hand car with a recorded mileage of 30,000. In fact the true mileage was nearer 100,000. The seller was held liable for a breach of s.13.

Similar conduct today could make the seller criminally liable under the Trade Descriptions Act 1968 (considered in Chapter 9). One significant difference between the Sale of Goods Act and the Trade Descriptions Act is that the latter only applies where the sale is made in the course of a trade or business. Section 13 applies both to private and business sales.

> In *Beale v. Taylor* 1967 the buyer purchased a car advertised as a 1961 Herald Convertible having had a trial run in it as a passenger. The buyer soon found the car to be unsatisfactory. On an examination by a garage it was discovered that the car had been made up of halves of two different cars. The rear portion was part of a 1961 Triumph Herald 1200 model while the front was part of a earlier 948 model. The two portions had been welded together unsatisfactorily into one structure, and the vehicle was unroadworthy and unsafe. The Court of Appeal held that the seller had broken the promise implied into the contract by s.13 and was liable in damages to the buyer.

The seller will be in breach of s.13 if he does not comply strictly with the contract description.

> In *Arcos Ltd. v. E.A. Ronaasen & Son* 1933 the buyer agreed to purchase a quantity of wooden staves, half an inch thick, for making cement barrels. When they were delivered only 5% of them were exactly half an inch and the vast majority were nine sixteenths of an inch in thickness. An arbitrator found that the staves were still reasonably fit for making cement barrels. The House of Lords held that the buyers were entitled to reject the goods because the seller had not strictly complied with the contract description. Lord Atkin observed:
>
> *"a ton does not mean about a ton, or a yard about a yard. Still less when you descend to minute measurements does half an inch mean about half an inch. If the seller wants a margin he must and in my experience does stipulate for it".*

Very small deviations from the contractual specification can however be disregarded for example where a delivery of 250 gallons of oil is 2 pints short.

Where the seller does not comply with the contract description the buyer is entitled to reject the goods even though he suffers no damage.

> In Re: *Moore & Co. Ltd. and Landauer & Co.* 1921 the buyer purchased a quantity of canned fruit. The contract stipulated that each case should con-

tain thirty tins but on delivery about half the total quantity of tins were packed into cases of twenty four. The court held that the buyer was entitled to reject the goods, even though there was no evidence that the buyer would suffer any loss.

Buyers should beware when using specialised trade terms to purchase goods.

The buyer in *Grenfell v. E.D. Meyrovitz* 1931 was held to have no remedy under s.13 when a quantity of glass he had purchased under the description 'safety glass' proved unsuitable for use in goggles because it splintered under certain circumstances. The glass conformed with the technical meaning of safety glass.

In *Peter Darlington Partners Ltd. v. Gosho Ltd.* 1964 the seller supplied canary seed to the buyer. The seed was sold on a 'pure basis'. In fact it was only 98% pure. This was the highest quality of purity possible, and the Court rejected the buyer's claim that the seller was in breach of s.13.

Although it was noted above that the vast majority of sales will be made by description, it is possible even where the seller has applied a description to goods in the course of negotiations or in the contract itself, that the court may find that the sale is not made 'by' description. This can occur where the buyer places no reliance on the description and the court imputes no common intention that the description is an essential part of the contract.

In *Harlingdon & Leinster Enterprises Ltd. v. Christopher Hull Fine Art Ltd.* 1990 the plaintiffs were art dealers at a London gallery specialising in the German expressionist school. The defendants, who were dealers specialising in contemporary British artists, were asked to sell an oil painting described in an earlier auction catalogue as the work of Gabriele Munter, an artist of the German expressionist school. During the course of negotiations for the sale of the painting, it was made clear to the plaintiffs that the defendants did not know much about the painting and had no expertise in relation to it. It was described during negotiations and on the sales invoice as a Munter. Subsequent to the sale it was discovered to be a forgery and the plaintiffs sued to recover the purchase price under s.13. The Court of Appeal held that the plaintiffs claim failed because the sale was not made 'by' description. The plaintiffs had not relied on the description but had bought the painting purely on their own assessment of it.

It should be appreciated that whilst this conclusion may be justified in the particular circumstances of the Harlingdon case, the decision is not likely to have a much wider application beyond those narrow circumstances.

Implied terms relating to quality and fitness for purpose (s14 of the 1979 Act; s10, 1973 Act; s4 And s9, 1982 Act)

Merchantable quality

Section 14(2) of the 1979 Act provides:

"Where the seller sells goods in the course of a business there is an implied condition that the goods supplied under the contract are of merchantable quality, except that there is no such condition:

> (a) *as regards defects specifically drawn to the buyer's attention before the contract is made; or*
>
> (b) *if the buyer examines the goods before the contract is made, as regards defects which that examination ought to reveal".*

There are a number of important features of s.14(2) which should be noted:

(a) the seller must be a business seller. The implied condition does not apply to private sales;

(b) the seller may be anyone in the chain of distribution, such as a manufacturer, wholesaler or retailer;

(c) the condition does not apply where a defect has been drawn to the buyer's attention prior to the sale, or where the buyer has examined the goods before buying them and ought to have discovered the defect: (see *R & B Customs Brokers v. United Dominions Trust* 1988 and *Crow v. Barford and Holttum* 1963 discussed later in the text);

(d) in order to comply with this section, some system of quality control will need to be introduced. This is particularly so where the seller is also the manufacturer;

(e) liability under the section is strict:

> In *Frost v. Aylesbury Dairies Ltd.* 1905 the dairy supplied milk contaminated with typhoid germs and was held liable despite establishing that it had used all reasonable care to prevent such contamination.

The expression merchantable quality is defined in s.14(6) which provides:

> *"Goods of any kind are of merchantable quality if they are as fit for the purpose or purposes for which goods of that kind are commonly bought as it is reasonable to expect having regard to any description applied to them, the price (if relevant) and all other relevant circumstances".*

Under this definition the standard of quality will vary according to the circumstances of the case. Goods must be reasonably fit for their ordinary uses, although account may be taken of any description applied to them and, where relevant, the price. Clearly if goods are described as 'seconds' or 'manufacturer's rejects' they will not be expected to be of perfect quality. Similarly, the standard of quality and durability expected of shoes priced at £18 will be lower than that expected of those priced £58. However if the £58 shoes had been reduced in a sale to a price of £18, the sale price would probably not be relevant in determining the standard of quality expected.

> In *Bartlett v. Sydney Marcus Ltd.* 1965 the seller, who was a car dealer, warned the buyer that a second-hand car had a defective clutch. The buyer was given a choice of purchasing it for £550 as it was, or £575 after the seller had repaired it. The buyer opted to take the car as it was. The repairs cost more than the buyer expected. He sued the seller alleging that, for this reason, the car was not of merchantable quality. The Court of Appeal held that the seller was not liable as there was no breach of the implied term.
>
> In *Crowther v. Shannon Motor Company* 1975 it was held that a second-hand car which needed a replacement engine after three weeks was not of merchantable quality. The car had been described as being in excellent condition.

The requirement of merchantable quality extends not only to the goods themselves but also to their packaging and any instructions supplied with them.

> In *Wormell v. RHM Agriculture (East) Ltd.* 1987 the plaintiff was a farmer who purchased a chemical spray from the defendant in order to kill wild oats. The instructions provided with the spray indicated that its use outside a certain period carried the risk of injury to the crop. The plaintiff was aware of the warning and decided to take that risk. In fact, because of the late application, the spray was totally ineffective. The plaintiff claimed damages for the costs of the spray and the wasted labour in applying it. The Court of Appeal accepted that, as a matter of principle, any instructions supplied with goods would be treated as part of the goods themselves in assessing merchantability or fitness for purpose. On the facts, however, it was held that the seller was not liable as the instructions had clearly stated that spraying after a certain period of growth was not recommended. The seller was not bound to give full and exhaustive reasons for the instructions given.

The wording of s.14(2) makes it clear that the obligation applies to all goods which are supplied under the contract.

> In *Geddling v. Marsh* 1920 mineral water was sold in bottles which were to remain the property of the manufacturer. The buyer was injured when a defective bottle burst. It was held that he was entitled to damages under s.14 even though the bottles were loaned rather than sold to him under the terms of the contract.

This rule applies even if the item which causes the harm was mistakenly supplied with the contract goods:

> In *Wilson v. Rickett, Cockerell and Co. Ltd.* 1954 a delivery of 'Coalite' included a detonator from the mine, which exploded when it was put onto a household fire. The Court of Appeal held that the sellers were liable for a breach of s.14(2).

Goods may be unmerchantable even if they can easily be put right:

> In *Grant v. Austrailian Knitting Mills Ltd.* 1936 the buyer purchased underpants which contained a chemical. This caused dermatitis, a skin disease, when the buyer wore them. The chemical would have been removed if the buyer had washed them before he wore them. It was held that the goods were not of merchantable quality, and the seller was liable.

The seller will not be liable, however, if the defect in the goods is caused by the way in which the buyer treats them.

> In *Heil v. Hedges* 1951 the buyer was infected with tapeworms after eating a pork chop which had been undercooked. It was held that the seller was not liable because the meat would have been quite safe if it had been properly cooked.

It appears that a seller will not be liable under this section solely because there are no spare parts available to service the goods which he has supplied.

> In *L. Gent v. Eastman Machine Co. Ltd.* 1985 the plaintiff purchased a knitting machine from the defendant. Not long afterwards spare parts were required and it took four months for the spares to be supplied. It was held

that the knitting machine was not rendered unmerchantable by the seller's failure to be able to supply spare parts within a reasonable time.

In 1983 the Law Commission published a working paper, no. 85, entitled The Sale and Supply of Goods, followed by a report (Cm 137) in 1987. This recommended a clarification of the seller's obligations in relation to the quality of goods supplied. The phrase merchantable quality should be replaced with *'acceptable quality'*. Goods would be of acceptable quality if they were of a standard that a reasonable person would regard as acceptable, taking account of any description applied to them, the price, and all other relevant circumstances. Relevant circumstances would extend beyond the question of fitness of the goods for their common purposes, and include matters such as the appearance of the goods, their finish, suitability for immediate use, freedom from minor defects, safety, and durability. It is likely that legislation will incorporate the recommendations of the Law Commission eventually but, in the meantime, the Court of Appeal appears to have taken a lead in the same direction.

In *Rogers v. Parish (Scarbrough) Ltd.* 1987 the plaintiff bought a new Range Rover from the defendant's garage. Although it was driveable and roadworthy the car had a number of defects in its engine, gearbox, oil seals and bodywork. The defendant argued that the car was of merchantable quality within the definition in s.14(6) as it could be driven in safety on a road and therefore was "fit for the purpose for which goods of that kind are commonly bought". The Court of Appeal rejected the defendant's argument on the grounds that it was based upon too narrow an interpretation of s.14(6). Mustill LJ, declared that:

"the purpose for which goods of that kind are commonly bought would include not merely the purpose of driving the vehicle from one place to another but of doing so with the appropriate degree of comfort, ease of handling, reliability and pride in the vehicle's outward and interior appearance".

In two further cases, the Court of Appeal has made it clear that the principles laid down in *Rogers v. Parish* are equally applicable to sales of second hand cars.

In *Business Applications Specialists v. Nationwide Credit Corporation Ltd.* 1988 the plaintiff purchased a second-hand Mercedes motor car for £14,850. It was two years old and had a recorded mileage of 37,000. The plaintiff drove the car for 800 miles when it broke down due to burnt out valves and worn valve guides and guide seals. The cost of repairs was £635. The County Court judge dismissed the action on the grounds that the car was roadworthy despite the defects. The plaintiffs appeal was dismissed by the Court of Appeal which held that although judge had applied the wrong test he had reached the correct conclusion. He ought to have applied the test laid down in *Rogers v. Parish.*

In *Shine v. General Guarantee Corporation Ltd.* 1988 a second-hand Bertoni-bodied Fiat X19 had been advertised as 'superb' and described verbally as 'nice car, good runner, no problems'. In fact the car had been written off after having been submerged in water for 24 hours. The Court of Appeal held that, comparing the purchaser's reasonable expectations at the time of sale with the actual condition of the car, it was not of merchantable quality. In the words of Bush J:

"He was buying potentially a 'rogue car' and irrespective of its condition it was in fact one which no member of the public, knowing the facts, would touch with a barge pole unless they could get it at a substantially reduced price to reflect the

risk they were taking.... A car is not just a means of transport, it is a form also of investment (though a deteriorating one) and every purchaser of a car must have in mind the eventual saleability of the car as well as, in this particular case, his pride in it as a specialist car for the enthusiast".

Fitness for notified purpose

Where the buyer requires the goods for a special or unusual purpose, the seller may be liable for a breach of s.14(3) if the goods are not fit for that purpose. Under s.14(3):

> *"Where the seller sells goods in the course of a business and the buyer, expressly or by implication, makes known...to the seller...any particular purpose for which the goods are being bought, there is an implied condition that the goods supplied under the contract are reasonably for that purpose, whether or not that is a purpose for which such goods are commonly supplied, except where the circumstances show that the buyer does not rely, or that it is unreasonable for him to rely, on the skill or judgment of the seller".*

Consumers sometimes place reliance on the expertise of the seller. For example when a customer goes into a shop and asks whether the shop has something that will perform a particular task, say fixing a broken ornament or removing stains from a carpet. A business may describe its accounting procedures to a supplier of office equipment, relying on the supplier to provide a suitable system to cope with these procedures. In these cases the seller will be liable under s.14(3) if the goods, even though of merchantable quality, do not fulfil the purpose for which the buyer requires them.

> In *Cammell Laird & Co. Ltd. v. Manganese Bronze & Brass Co. Ltd.* 1934 the buyers supplied the sellers with a specification for ships' propellers which they were to manufacture for the buyers. Reliance was placed upon the sellers regarding matters outside the specification, including the thickness of metal to be used. The propellers were found on delivery to be too thin. The buyer's action was successful on the ground that the unfitness concerned a matter on which the buyers had relied upon the seller's skill.

There will be no liability under s.14(3) where the circumstances show that the buyer does not rely on the skill or judgment of the seller.

> In *Teheran-Europe Co. Ltd. v. ST Belton Tractors Ltd.* 1968 industrial equipment was sold to the plaintiff buyer for the purpose of exporting and resale in Persia. The seller knew this but was not familiar with the Persian market, unlike the buyer who carried on a business there. The equipment infringed Persian regulations and the plaintiff sued the seller for breach of s.14(3). The Court of Appeal held that the seller was not liable as the buyer had relied on his own skill and judgment as to whether the equipment was suitable for resale in Persia. There was no reliance on the skill or judgment of the seller.

When the product only has one purpose the buyer will be held to have impliedly made known to the seller the purpose for which he wants the goods.

> In *Priest v. Last* 1903 the buyer was held to have made known impliedly to the seller the purpose for which he required a hot water bottle. The seller was liable under s.14(3) when the bottle burst after a few days injuring the buyer.

The seller will not be liable however, where the buyer does not tell him of any particular requirements.

> In *Griffiths v. Peter Conway Ltd.* 1939 the buyer, who had particularly sensitive skin, developed dermatitis as a result of wearing a coat which she bought from the defendant. The coat would not have had this effect on a normal person and the buyer had not told the seller about her sensitivity. It was held that the seller was not liable under s.14(3).

Implied terms where goods are sold by sample (s15 of the 1979 Act; s11, 1973 Act; s5 and s10, 1982 Act)

Under s.15, where goods are sold according to a sample, there are implied conditions that:

(a) the bulk of the consignment will correspond with the sample in terms of quality;

(b) the buyer shall have a reasonable opportunity of comparing the bulk with the sample; and

(c) the goods shall be free from any defect rendering them unmerchantable which would not be apparent on a reasonable examination of the sample.

The function of a sample was described by Lord MacNaghten in *Drummond v. Van Ingen* 1887 when he stated:

> *"The office of a sample is to present to the eye the real meaning and intention of the parties with regard to the subject matter of the contract which, owing to the imperfections of language, it may be difficult or impossible to express in words. The sample speaks for itself".*

Many commercial and non-commercial transactions are made on the basis of samples, for example the purchase of a carpet or a made-to-measure suit by a consumer, or the purchase of raw materials by an industrial company.

Claims based on more than one ground

Where a person is injured by defective goods there may be a number of alternative grounds upon which he could sue. There is a considerable degree of overlap between s.14(2) and s.14(3), so that, for example the sellers in *Frost v. Aylesbury Dairies* 1905 and *Priest v. Last* 1903 were in breach of both implied conditions. The seller in *Beale v. Taylor* 1967 was found to be in breach of s.13, and would probably have been in breach of s.14 if he had sold the car in the course of a business. There is also a considerable overlap between the law of contract and the tort of negligence in this area. In *Grant v. Australian Knitting Mills* 1935 the retailer was liable because the goods were not of merchantable quality, and the manufacturer was liable in negligence.

In Chapter 10 a number of cases are examined in the field of product liability, for example *Lambert v. Lewis* 1981, in which the injured party's claim is based both in negligence and in contract. Part 1 of the Consumer Protection Act 1987 gives additional remedies to persons who are injured by defective products. It is quite conceivable that an injured party would have a claim in contract, in negligence and under the 1987 Act. Figure 10.2 at the end of Chapter 10 provides a comparison between these three alternatives. Of course the injured party can only recover damages once, but he may bring his claim under all of these headings by 'pleading in the alternative'. If he fails in one aspect of his claim, he can still recover damages if another succeeds.

The rule of privity of contract discussed in Chapter 5 means that only the buyer can claim for breach of the implied terms. If this claim against the seller succeeds then liability can be passed down the line through the chain of distribution. The seller can sue his supplier for an indemnity based upon the supplier's breach of contract. He is in effect trying to drop out of the picture by saying "if I am liable then as my supplier you are liable on the same basis". This process, known as third party proceedings, continues until the manufacturer is sued. Only an effective exclusion of liability clause can break the chain of indemnity.

> In *Godley v. Perry (Burton & Sons Ltd., Third Party; Graham, Fourth Party)* 1960 a boy of six lost the sight of one eye when firing a catapult which he had bought for 6d from the defendant's shop. The catapult fractured below the point where the handle joined the fork. The evidence showed that is was made of cheap brittle polystyrene, indifferently moulded and containing internal voids. The retailer had purchased the catapult from a wholesaler who had purchased it from an importer. The importer had bought the goods from a manufacturer in Hong Kong. The plaintiff sued the defendant shopkeeper who issued third party proceedings against the wholesaler. The wholesaler in turn claimed against the importer. The court decided that the catapult was not of merchantable quality, and that the retailer was liable to the purchaser. Liability passed up the line so at the end of the day the importer (or his insurers) were left either to bear the loss or pursue the manufacturer in the Hong Kong courts.

Implied terms in contracts for the supply of services

The Supply of Goods and Services Act 1982 sets out terms which will be implied both into contracts for the supply of services and into contracts for work done and materials supplied. These terms will apply, for example, to contracts for dry cleaning, entertainment and professional services, home improvements and motor vehicle maintenance. The major areas of concern in relation to this type of contract were identified in a report of the National Consumer Council in 1981 entitled 'Services Please'. These concerns were quality, delay in performance and cost. They are all dealt with by the 1982 Act. The aim of this part of the 1982 Act is simply to codify the common law without changing it. The NCC believed that this was necessary for three reasons: certainty and clarity; ease of reference, and in order to focus attention on the existence of the obligations owed by those who supply services.

Implied duty to use reasonable care and skill

The 1982 Act in s.13 provides:

> *"In a contract for the supply of a service where the supplier is acting in the course of a business, there is an implied term that the supplier will carry out the service with reasonable care and skill".*

The nature of the duty was explained by Lord Denning in *Greaves & Co. (Contractors) Ltd. v. Baynham Meikle and Partners* 1975 in the following terms:

> *"The law does not usually imply a warranty that the professional man will achieve the desired result, but only a term that he will use reasonable care and skill. The surgeon does not warrant that he will cure the patient. Nor does the solicitor warrant that he will win the case....whether it is a medical man, a lawyer, or an*

accountant, an architect or an engineer, his duty is to use reasonable care and skill".

The section has wide ranging application embracing most situations where a client or customer is paying for services. In addition to those professions mentioned by Lord Denning, it applied to builders, hairdressers, dry cleaners, surveyors, auctioneers, tour operators, bankers, car repairers and many others who provide services in the course of their business. The following cases illustrate the scope of the duty:

In *Curtis v. Chemical Cleaning and Dyeing Company* 1951 the plaintiff took a wedding dress to the defendant dry cleaners for cleaning. When she came to collect the dress she found that it had been stained. It was held that the company were liable for the damage to the dress which had been caused by their failure to take care of it.

In *Luxmoore-May v. Messenger May Baverstock* 1989 the defendant auctioneers accepted instructions to research, value and sell a number of paintings for the plaintiff. These included two painting of foxhounds, which the defendants valued at between £30 and £50. At auction they were given a reserve price of £40, but in fact sold for £840. Later they were attributed to George Stubbs by Sotheby's and sold for £88,000 the pair. The plaintiff sued the auctioneers arguing that they were in breach of the implied duty to use reasonable skill and care in providing the research and valuation services. It was held that the defendants were liable for their failure to carry out reasonably careful and skilful research, and the plaintiff was awarded damages of £76,222 representing the difference between the price which the plaintiff actually received and the market value of the paintings less the expenses that would have been incurred in a sale at market price.

In *Davey v. Cosmos Air Holidays* 1989 the plaintiff booked a two week package holiday in the Algarve for himself and his family. During the holiday the whole family suffered diarrhoea and the plaintiff's wife and son both contracted dysentery. The evidence showed that the illness was caused by a general lack of hygiene at the resort, and the fact that raw sewage was being pumped into the sea just fifty yards from the beach. The defendant tour operators had resident representatives at the resort who knew of the dangers. It was held that the defendants were liable for breach of the implied duty in the contract to take reasonable care to avoid exposing their clients to a significant risk of injury to their health.

In *Lawson and Lawson v. Supasink Ltd.* 1984 the plaintiffs employed the company to design, supply and install a fitted kitchen at a price of £1,200. Plans were drawn up and agreed but the company did not follow them when installing the units. The plaintiffs complained about the standard of work before the installation was complete. After taking independent expert advice the plaintiffs demanded the return of their deposit and asked the defendants to remove the kitchen units. The defendants refused and the plaintiffs sued. The judge found that the kitchen was installed in 'a shocking and shoddy manner' and that the work was 'beyond redemption'. He awarded damages of £500 for inconvenience and loss of the use of the kitchen; damages of the difference between the cost of equivalent units and the contract price; and the return of the deposit. On appeal the defendants argued that they had substantially performed the contract and were therefore entitled to the contract price less the cost of remedying any defects. This was rejected by the

Court of Appeal on the grounds that the standard of workmanship and design was so poor that the doctrine of substantial performance could not be applied, having regard to the large sums which would have to be spent to remedy the defects.

The contract in the *Supasink* case was a contract for work and materials. Section 13 of the 1982 Act applies to the work element in such a contract. In some cases it may be important to know whether the defect complained of is due to fault in the materials themselves or the supplier's failure to take care in doing the work. This is because the nature of the liability for each of the two elements of the contract is different. In relation to the supply of materials, the supplier will be strictly liable, even if he is not at fault (like the defendant in *Frost v. Aylesbury Dairies* 1905 above). If the work is defective the supplier will only be liable if he has failed to take reasonable care. Another reason why the distinction may be important is that different controls on the use of exclusion clauses are applied by the Unfair Contract Terms Act 1977 to each element of contracts of this type (see below).

Where services, or goods and services, are supplied by any person taking on work in connection with the provision of a dwelling house, s.1(1) of the Defective Premises Act 1972 imposes a duty of care on that person. He has a duty to see that the work is done in a workmanlike or professional manner with proper materials so that, in relation to the work he has taken on, the dwelling will be fit for habitation when it is completed.

Exemptions from the operation of section 13 of the 1982 Act have been made for company directors, who, as we have seen, have a duty to use such care as they would use in relation to their own personal affairs in performance of their duties as directors. A solicitor acting as an advocate before a court is also exempted from the section because of the rule that advocates cannot be made liable for professional negligence (see *Rondel v. Worsley* 1969 discussed in Chapter 10). The section has no application where services are provided for a client by a barrister, because the barrister does not have a contract with his client. A number of the cases discussed in relation to professional negligence in Chapter 10 provide further illustrations of the application of s.13.

Implied terms relating to time for performance

Section 14 of the 1982 Act provides:

> *"Where, under a contract for the supply of a service by a supplier acting in the course of a business, the time for the service to be carried out is not fixed by the contract,...there is an implied term that the supplier will carry out the service within a reasonable time. What is a reasonable time is a question of fact".*

In *Charnock v. Liverpool Corporation* 1968 the plaintiff recovered damages for the defendant's unreasonable delay in performing a contract. The defendant took eight weeks to repair the plaintiff's car when a reasonably competent repairer would have completed the repair within five weeks.

If a reasonable time has elapsed within which the contract should have been performed, the customer is entitled unilaterally to serve a notice fixing a time for the performance of the contract. The new time limit must be reasonable. If the supplier fails to meet it, the Court of Appeal held in *Charles Rickards Ltd. v. Oppenheim* 1950 that the customer is entitled to withdraw from the contract without penalty.

If the time for performance of the contract has been agreed then s.14 does not add an additional requirement that the services should be provided within a reasonable time.

Implied terms relating to the cost of the service

Section 15 of the 1982 Act deals with the cost of services supplied. It provides:

> *"Where under a contract for the supply of a service, the consideration for the service is not determined by the contract,...there is an implied term that the party contracting with the supplier will pay a reasonable charge. What is a reasonable charge is a question of fact".*

Section 15 does not enable a customer to reopen an agreement on the grounds that the charge for the service is unreasonably high, if the customer originally agreed to pay that charge. It applies only where there is no mechanism in the contract for determining the price and limits the amount recoverable to a reasonable sum.

Exclusion Clauses

Legal liability can arise in a variety of different ways, for example through misrepresentation, breach of contract or negligence. One way of trying to reduce or extinguish this liability is by the use of exclusion or limitation clauses. An exclusion clause in a contract is an express term which attempts to exempt one party from all liability for failure to perform some part of the contract.

An example of an exclusion clause in a contract for the supply of goods is: "the seller hereby excludes all liability for breach of any express or implied condition, term or warranty". A limitation clause on the other hand is slightly different for it aims to reduce rather than extinguish the liability. It could be drafted so as to place an overall financial limit on the liability of one party for breach of contract, to limit liability to the replacement of goods supplied, or to deprive the other of a particular remedy for the breach. In this text we will be dealing with the legal principles which apply both to the exclusion and limitation of liability, but, for convenience, we will refer to exclusion only and this can be taken to mean total or partial exclusion of liability.

The principle of freedom of contract permits the use of exclusion clauses, although the courts developed a number of common law principles which were designed to rob them of effect in certain circumstances. These principles were developed because the courts recognised that the use of exclusion clauses could result in unfairness to one of the contracting parties. Judicial controls were developed largely by the application of pe-existing principles of contract law and are therefore limited in scope. It was not until the 1970's that legislation was introduced. The Unfair Contract terms Act 1977 now provides a comprehensive set of rules which regulate both the use of exclusion clauses in contracts and the use of non-contractual notices.

In determining the validity of an exclusion clause, several legal principles have to be applied. The first step is to make sure that legal liability of one type or another would arise if the exclusion were not present. Next the common law rules of incorporation and interpretation (discussed below) must be applied. If the exclusion survives the application of the common law rules, we must then apply the provisions of the Unfair Contract Terms Act 1977. Figure 8.3 summarises these steps in diagrammatic form.

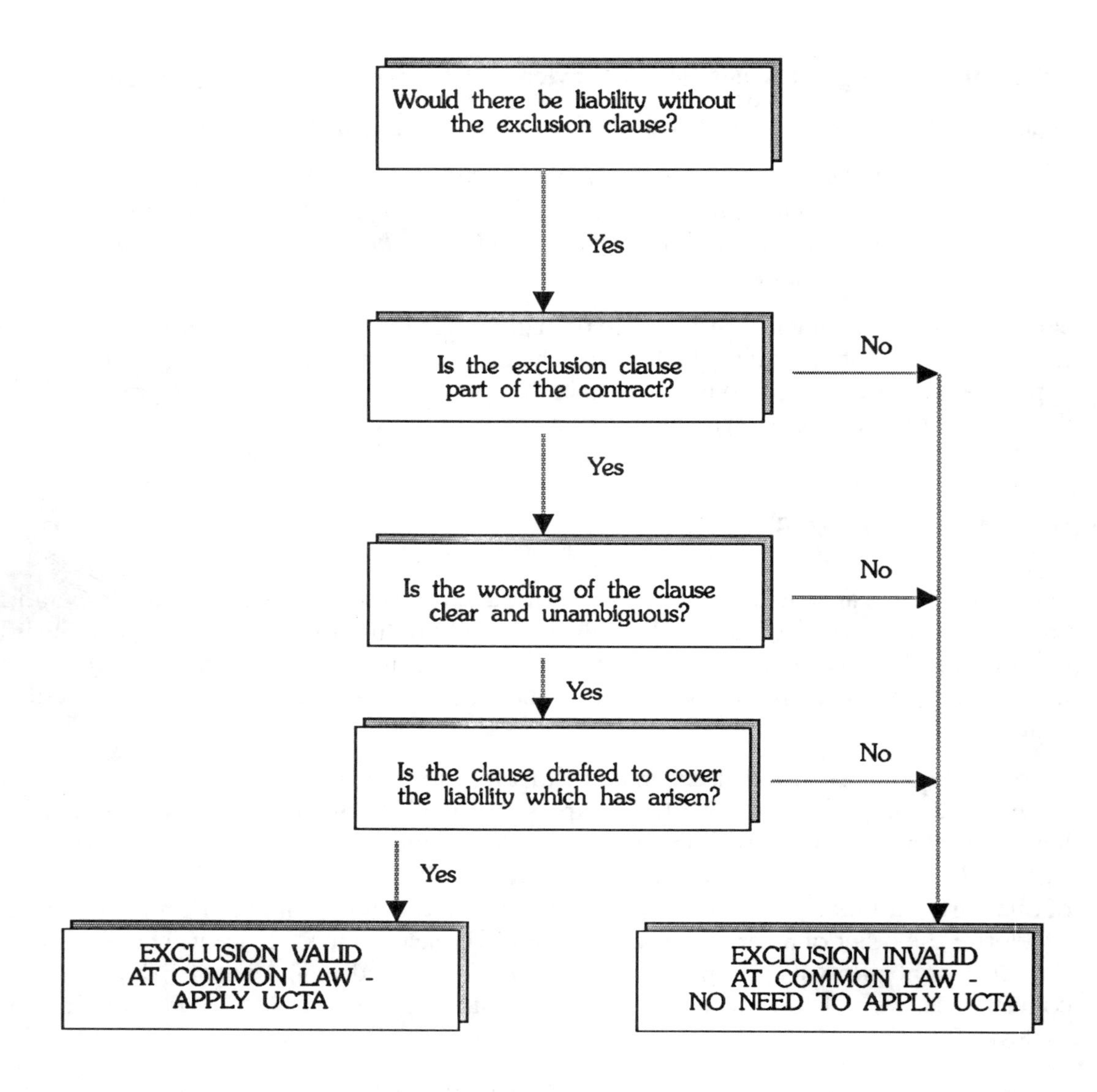

Fig. 8.3. Common Law Control over Exclusion and Restriction of Contractual Liability

Incorporation – is the term part of the contract?

Signed documents

Where a person has signed a document containing an exclusion clause he will be bound by the terms contained in the document whether or not he has read or understood them. The only exceptions to this rule are where the signature is induced by fraud or misrepresentation. Otherwise the exclusion clause will automatically be part of the contract.

> In *L'Estrange v. Graucob* 1934 the plaintiff, who was the proprietress of a cafe, bought a vending machine under the terms of a sales agreement which she signed without reading. The contract contained a clause excluding the seller's liability, among other things, for breach of the implied terms under the Sale of Goods Act. The vending machine was defective. The Court of Appeal held that the plaintiff had no remedy against the seller because she

was bound by the terms of the exclusion clause in the document which she had signed.

In *Spriggs v. Sotheby Parke Bernet and Co. Ltd.* 1984 the plaintiff deposited a diamond with Sotheby's to be auctioned. He signed a document, without reading it, and put it straight into his wallet. The document contained details of the agreement and a declaration in bold type immediately above the space for the plaintiff's signature. The declaration stated "I have read and agree to the instructions for sale as detailed on the reverse of this form". On the reverse of the form there was an exclusion clause. It was held that the clause had been validly incorporated into the contract.

Where the contents of the document have been misrepresented before it is signed, an exclusion clause in the document will not be effective to the extent that the effect of the clause was misrepresented.

In *Curtis v. Chemical Cleaning and Dyeing Co.* 1951 the plaintiff took a wedding dress to the defendant company for cleaning. An assistant asked her to sign a receipt, and before she signed she was told that the effect of her signature was to exclude the cleaner's liability for damage to any beads or sequins on the dress. In the process of cleaning the dress was stained, although no damage was done to the beads and sequins. In fact the signed receipt had excluded the defendants' liability for any damage to the dress 'howsoever caused'. The Court of Appeal held that the defendants were liable for the damage to the dress and could not rely on the full exclusion clause because they had misrepresented its effect to the plaintiff.

Unsigned documents

Where the term is contained in an unsigned document, or displayed on a notice, it will be effective only if the person relying on it took reasonable steps to bring it to the attention of the other party, and where the document or notice might reasonably be regarded as likely to contain contractual terms.

In *Chapelton v. Barry U.D.C.* 1940 the plaintiff hired a deck chair from the defendant for use on a beach. He paid an attendant and was given a ticket in return. He was injured when the chair collapsed as he sat down on it. There was an exclusion clause printed on the back of the ticket which the plaintiff had not read. The Court of Appeal held that the ticket was merely a receipt and not the sort of contractual document which a reasonable person might have expected to contain contractual terms. The exclusion clause was therefore ineffective and the defendants were liable.

Where a term is particularly onerous or unusual, then even if it contained in such a contractual document, the party seeking to enforce it must show that it has fairly and adequately been drawn to the other party's attention.

In *Interfoto Picture Library Ltd. v. Stiletto Visual Programmes Ltd.* 1988 the defendants, who were advertising agents, required photographs for a 1950's presentation. The plaintiffs, in response to their request, sent 47 transparencies with a delivery note which clearly stated that they were to be returned in 14 days. In the small print on the back of the delivery note, condition 2 stated *"a holding fee of £5 plus VAT per day will be charged for each transparency which is retained by you for longer than the said period of 14 days"*.

The defendants did not use the transparencies, put them to one side, and forgot about them for a further two weeks. The plaintiffs sent an invoice for £3,783.50 for the holding fee. The Court of Appeal held that, although the contract was made upon the terms in the delivery note, condition 2 was not part of the contract. The term was highly onerous, extortionate and unreasonable and could not be relied upon as it had not been sufficiently brought to the defendants' attention.

Before leaving this case it should be noted that condition 2 was not in fact on exclusion clause, and that whilst the principle laid down by the Court of Appeal applies to such clauses, it may be interpreted as having a wider application covering any onerous or unusual terms in an unsigned contract.

Terms introduced after the contract is made

An exclusion clause will not be effective unless it is adequately brought to the attention of the other party before the contract is made. It must be part of the contractual offer, and the rules of offer and acceptance can be used to determine whether the clause is actually part of the contract.

In *Olley v. Marlborough Court Hotel Ltd.* 1949 the plaintiff booked into an hotel and paid for the room in advance. She went up to her hotel room where there was a notice which stated *"The proprietors will not hold themselves responsible for articles lost or stolen unless handed to the Manageress for safe custody"*. The plaintiff left her fur coat in the room and it was stolen. The Court of Appeal held that the defendant was not entitled to rely on the exclusion clause as it was not a term of the contract. The contract was concluded at the reception desk and the plaintiff had no notice of the clause at that stage.

In *Thornton v. Shoe Lane Parking* 1971 the plaintiff drove into a car park which he had not used before. At the entrance there was a machine which issued a ticket to him before raising a barrier to allow entry. On the back of the ticket there was a statement that it was issued subject to terms and conditions displayed within the car park. One of these conditions purported to exclude the defendant's liability for injury to customers howsoever caused. The plaintiff was injured by the defendant's negligence when he came to collect his car. The Court of Appeal held that the exclusion clause was ineffective because it had been introduced after the contract was concluded. Lord Denning analysed the process of contract formation in the following way:

"The customer pays his money and gets a ticket. He cannot refuse it. He cannot get his money back. He may protest to the machine, even swear at it; but it will remain unmoved. He is committed beyond recall. He was committed at the very moment when he put his money into the machine: the contract was concluded at that time. It can be translated into offer and acceptance in this way. The offer is made when the proprietor of the machine holds it out as being ready to receive the money. The acceptance takes place when the customer puts his money into the slot. The terms of the offer are contained in the notice placed on or near the machine stating what is offered for the money. The customer is bound by these terms as long as they are sufficiently brought to his notice beforehand, but not otherwise. He is not bound by the terms printed on the ticket, if they differ from

the notice, because the ticket comes too late. The contract has already been made".

Where there is a previous course of dealing between the parties the court may be prepared to recognise the incorporation of an exclusion clause into a contract even though it was not specifically referred to at the time the contract was made. This will occur where the past dealings between the parties have consistently been made on the same terms and with the exclusion clause.

In *Spurling v. Bradshaw* 1956 the plaintiffs were warehousemen who had dealt with the defendant for many years and always on the plaintiff's standard contractual terms. These terms excluded the plaintiff's liability for 'negligence, wrongful act of default'. The defendant delivered eight barrels of orange juice to the plaintiff for storage and a few days later received an acknowledgement which referred to the standard terms of contract. When the defendant came to collect the barrels they were found to be empty. He refused to pay the storage charges and the plaintiff sued. It was held that the exclusion clause, although on this occasion introduced after the contract was made, was part of the contract. This was because the parties had regularly dealt with each other in the past and had done so consistently on the same contractual terms. The defendant was therefore well aware of these terms when he deposited the goods. The exclusion of liability was valid and the plaintiff's claim for storage charges succeeded.

overriding oral promise

An exclusion clause may be overridden by a later statement by the seller to the buyer.

In *Harling v. Eddy* 1951 the plaintiff bought a heifer at a cattle auction. One of the auctioneer's printed conditions of sale stated that no warranty was given in respect of any animal sold. When the heifer was put up for sale little interest was shown and no bids were made until the auctioneer said *"there is nothing wrong with her. I will guarantee her in every respect and I will take her back if she is not what I say she is".* The plaintiff bought the animal which died of tuberculosis four months later. It was held by the Court of Appeal that the verbal statement overrode the exclusion clause in the printed conditions, and the plaintiff's claim succeeded.

Interpretation and drafting of exclusion clauses

An exclusion clause must be drafted carefully. It must be clear and unambiguous, and it must cover the liability which has arisen. The clause will be interpreted narrowly against the party seeking to rely on it. This is known as the 'contra proferentem' rule.

In *Andrews Ltd. v. Singer and Co. Ltd.* 1934 the plaintiff agreed in writing to buy a 'new Singer car'. The contract contained a clause which excluded the defendant's liability for breach of *'all conditions, warranties and liabilities implied by statute, common law or otherwise'.* The car delivered to the plaintiff had in fact done a considerable number of miles. It was held that the seller was in breach of an express condition that the car would be new. He could not therefore rely on an exclusion of implied terms, and was liable to the plaintiff.

In *Baldry v. Marshall* 1925 the plaintiff told the defendant that he required a car suitable for touring. The defendant was a car dealer and, on his recommendation, the plaintiff bought a Bugatti from him. The written contract of sale excluded the seller's liability for breach of any *'guarantee or warranty, statutory or otherwise'*. The car proved unsuitable for touring. It was held that the seller was in breach of the implied condition under s.14 of the Sale of Goods Act that the car would be suitable for a purpose made known to the seller. The exclusion clause was ineffective because it excluded only guarantees or warranties and did not exclude liability for breach of a condition of the contract.

Exclusion clauses are sometimes introduced by words which indicate that the party imposing them will take all reasonable care or will make every effort to perform his obligations. This type of wording may be interpreted by the courts as imposing a pre-condition for the operation of the exclusion clause. If the party relying on the clause does not fulfil the pre-condition he cannot take the benefit of the exclusion.

In *B & S Contracts Ltd. v. Victor Green Publications Ltd.* 1984 the plaintiffs were contractors who traded on standard terms which excluded their liability for non-performance which resulted from industrial action by their workforce. The exclusion clause began with the words *"Every effort will be made to carry out the contract, but..."* The Court of Appeal held that the contractors were obliged to take reasonable steps to perform the contract before they could rely on the exclusion clause. They failed to prove that they had done this and were therefore unable to rely on the exclusion clause.

The approach of the courts to the interpretation of exclusion clauses has changed with the introduction of the statutory controls contained in the Unfair Contract Terms Act 1977. Before the 1977 Act the courts had few means of invalidating exclusion clauses in contracts and, because of the potential injustice which they caused, were prepared to interpret such clauses in a hostile manner. Judges would sometimes place a strained meaning on the words of the clause in order to deprive it of effect. However since the introduction of the 1977 Act, the potential unfairness of such clauses has been reduced greatly and the courts are now able to adopt a less hostile approach in interpreting their wording.

In *Photo Productions Ltd. v. Securicor Transport Ltd.* 1980 the defendant contracted to provide security services, including night patrols, at the plaintiff's factory. While on patrol one of the defendant's employees deliberately lit a small fire which got out of control and destroyed the factory and its contents. The contract, which was on Securicor's standard terms, contained the following condition:

"Under no circumstances shall the company (Securicor) be responsible for any injurious act or default by any employee of the company unless such act or default could have been foreseen and avoided by the exercise of due diligence on the part of the company as his employer; nor, in any event, shall the company be held responsible for; (a) any loss suffered by the customer through burglary, theft, fire or any other cause, except insofar as such loss is solely attributable to the negligence of the company's employees acting within the course of their employment..."

The House of Lords held that the exclusion clause was ineffective. It was clear and unambiguous and it covered the breach of contract complained of. Lord Diplock stated:

"in commercial contracts negotiated between businessmen capable of looking after their own interests and of deciding how risks inherent in the performance of various kinds of contract can be most economically borne (generally by insur-

ance) it is, in my view, wrong to place a strained interpretation on words in an exclusion clause..."

Control of exclusion clauses by legislation

The **Unfair Contract Terms Act 1977**, which is examined in detail below, is the major legislation which controls the use of exclusion clauses across a wide spectrum of business liability. There are, however, a number of specific provisions in other Acts which apply in particular situations to restrict or prevent the use of such clauses.

The **Defective Premises Act 1972**, in s.6(3) renders invalid any term of an agreement which tries to exclude or restrict the duty arising under the Act or attempts to limit any liability for breach of the duty.

The **Consumer Protection Act 1987**, in s.7, invalidates any attempt to exclude liability arising under Part I of the Act for injuries caused by defective products. Additionally, under s.41 of the 1987 Act there can be no exclusion of liability for breach of statutory duties in relation to consumer safety.

The **Consumer Credit Act 1974**, in s.173, forbids the inclusion in any agreement regulated by the Act of any term which attempts to diminish the protection which the Act affords to the consumer.

Under the **Misrepresentation Act 1967**, s.3, any contract term excluding or restricting liability for misrepresentation will be invalid unless it is shown to be reasonable, applying the reasonableness test in s.11 of the Unfair Contract Terms Act 1977.

The Unfair Contract Terms Act 1977

The Unfair Contract Terms Act 1977 is the first attempt by Parliament to deal with exclusion and limitation of liability in a comprehensive way. There are provisions in the Act which control attempts to exclude or limit liability in relation to negligence, contractual obligations, indemnities, guarantees, implied terms in contract to supply goods and misrepresentation. For the purposes of the 1977 Act, exclusion or restriction of liability is widely defined so as to include:

(a) making enforcement of a remedy subject to restrictive conditions, for example a requirement that notice of loss or damage must be given within a specified time or in a specified manner,

(b) excluding or restricting any right or remedy, for example taking away the right to reject goods for breach of condition and confining the buyer's remedy to damages only,

(c) restricting the liability, for example to a maximum amount recoverable,

(d) restricting the time within which the remedy may be claimed, for example by specifying that no claim may be made more than 28 days after the date of the contract,

(e) preventing liability arising in the first place, for example by including a term which provides that the seller does not give any warranty or undertaking that the goods are fit for any purpose.

The Act only applies to *business liability*. This is defined as liability for breach of obligations arising from things done in the course of a business or from the occupation of premises used for business purposes. The meaning of the term business was discussed earlier, and for the purposes of this Act it includes a profession, and the activities of any government department or local or public authority. The Act provides varying degrees of protection against exclusion clauses and notices. Some are totally invalidated, others are subjected to a test of reasonableness, and there are others to which the Act does not apply at all.

Exclusion clauses to which the Act does not apply

The Act does not apply in the following situations. In these cases the exclusion will be subject only to the common law rules discussed above:

(a) where the liability in question is not a business liability, for example liability arising from the defective state of a private house;

(b) where the situation falls outside the wording of a particular section of the Act. A verbal contract in which neither party deals as a consumer is, for example, outside the scope of s.3;

(c) where the Act specifically states that it does not apply. Schedule 1 tells us that the Act, in whole or in part, does not extend to the following types of contract:

- (i) insurance contracts
- (ii) contracts involving land
- (iii) contracts dealing with intellectual property
- (iv) contracts relating to the formation or dissolution of business organisations
- (v) contracts involving the creation or transfer of securities
- (vi) in relation to contracts of employment, s.2 does not apply except in favour of the employee.

The reasonableness test

Where the Act subjects an exclusion clause to the reasonableness test, the burden of proving that the contract term or notice is reasonable lies with the party seeking to rely on the exclusion. The test in relation to a contract term is that the term shall have been a fair and reasonable one to be included in the contract, having regard to the circumstances which were or should have been known to the parties at the time when the contract was made. In relation to a non-contractual notice the test is whether it would be fair and reasonable to allow reliance on it, having regard to all the circumstances at the time when the liability arose. An example of a non-contractual notice would be a notice displayed at the entrance to a public park.

Schedule 2 of the Act lays down guidelines which the court can take into account in determining whether a contract term satisfies the requirement of reasonableness. The guidelines are discussed below in connection with s.6 and s.7.

Exclusion of liability for negligence

In dealing with exclusion of liability for negligence, the Act defines the term 'negligence' to cover the following:

(a) contractual negligence, or the breach of any duty to use reasonable skill and care in the performance of a contract,

(b) common law negligence, for example under the rule in *Donoghue v. Stevenson* 1932 discussed in Chapter 10, and

(c) liability for breach of the common duty of care, owed to visitors by an occupier of premises, under the Occupier's Liability Act 1957.

Section 2 of the 1977 Act provides:

> "(1) *A person cannot by reference to any contract term or to a notice given to persons generally or to particular persons exclude or restrict his liability for death or personal injury resulting from negligence.*
>
> (2) *In the case of other loss or damage, a person cannot so exclude or restrict his liability for negligence except insofar as the term or notice satisfies the requirement of reasonableness".*

This gives us two important basic rules. First that it is not possible to exclude liability for death or personal injury resulting from negligence. The case of *White v. Blackmore* 1972, considered in Chapter 10, gives an example of a notice which, before the Act, effectively excluded negligence liability for death or personal injury. Such a notice is now invalid. The plaintiff in that case would have succeeded had the Act been in force at the time of the negligent act. Furthermore in *Thornton v. Shoe Lane Parking* 1971 discussed above, the exclusion of liability for personal injury would have been wholly ineffective under the 1977 Act, if it had actually been part of the contract.

The second rule is that liability for loss or damage other than death or personal injury cannot be excluded unless the exclusion is reasonable. This would apply, for example, to clauses which excluded liability for damage to property or financial loss caused by negligence. Under this provision the exclusion clauses in cases like *Spurling v. Bradshaw* 1956 and *Olley v. Marlborough Court Hotel* 1949 would be subject to the reasonableness test. In the next chapter there are a number of examples of cases in which the reasonableness test has been applied, for example *Smith v. Eric S. Bush* 1989, *Stevenson v. Nationwide Building Society* 1984 and *Harris v. Wyre Forest District Council* 1989.

> In *Spriggs v. Sotheby Parke Bernet and Co. Ltd.* 1984, considered earlier in the chapter, the plaintiff, who was a businessman, deposited a diamond with Sotheby's to be auctioned. He signed a document which, among other things, excluded Sotheby's liability for negligence. He was given the opportunity to insure the diamond but did not do so. Whilst the diamond was on view prior to the auction, it was stolen despite the defendant's fairly comprehensive security system. The plaintiff sued for negligence and the defendants relied on the exclusion clause. Under s.2(2) the clause is only valid if the defendant can show that it is reasonable. The court held that the clause in this case was reasonable and valid. The plaintiff was a successful and experienced businessman and no doubt was used to contracts containing exclusion clauses. He could not be regarded as having unequal bargaining power. The risk was one which could have been covered by insurance but the plaintiff turned down the opportunity to take this precaution.
>
> In *Phillips Products v. Hampstead Plant Hire* 1983 the defendant hired out a JCB to the plaintiffs under a standard term agreement. They supplied the driver but excluded any liability in negligence for his acts. Whilst he was working under the plaintiffs' direction, the driver damaged their factory through his own negligence. It was held that the exclusion clause was unreasonable and invalid. This was because the hire was for a short period and the plaintiffs and little opportunity to insure. They did not select, nor effectively

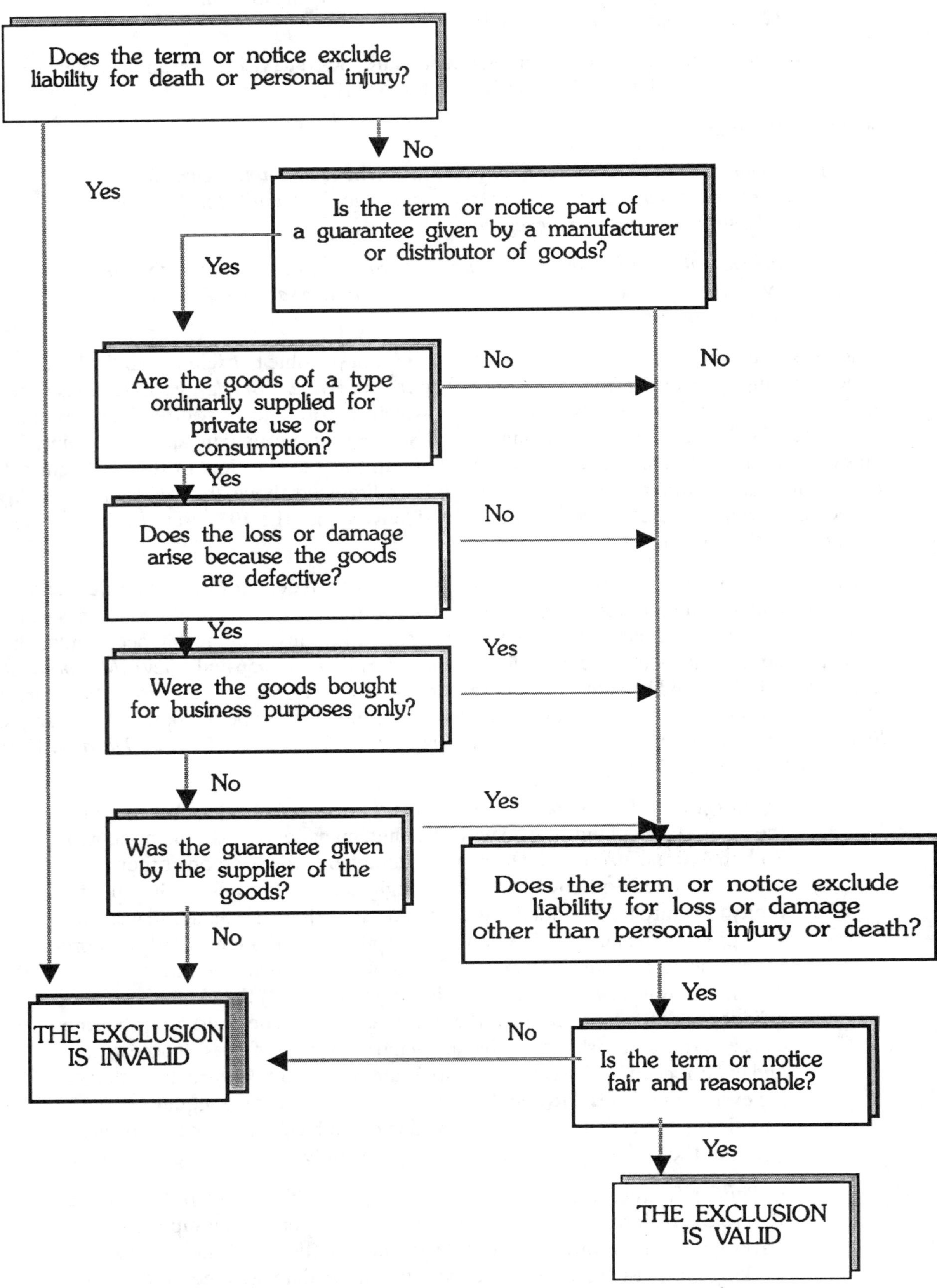

Fig. 8.4. Exclusion of Liability for Negligence Section 2 and Section 5 Unfair Contract Terms Act 1977

> control the driver. Their experience of such hiring arrangements was very limited.

An exclusion of liability for negligence is sometimes contained in a guarantee given by a manufacturer or distributor of goods. Such a guarantee will usually offer to repair or replace faulty goods such as televisions, washing machines and other electrical goods, free of charge within a specified time period commencing with the date of purchase; and will often be subject to stated exceptions, for example that the defect is not due to misuse, accidental damage or attempted repair by an unqualified person. In some cases, however, a guarantee may attempt to do more than qualify the benefit which it gives. It may purport to take away other rights of the consumer which are independent of the guarantee, such as the right to sue the manufacturer in the tort of negligence. This could be done by supplying a postcard with the goods which the consumer is asked to fill in and send to the manufacturer within a specified time in order to 'preserve his rights under the guarantee'. The postcard would then refer to the rights under the guarantee and contain an exclusion clause limiting the consumer's other rights.

In relation to exclusion clauses in guarantees, s.5(1) provides:

> *"In the case of goods of a type ordinarily supplied for private use or consumption, where loss or damage:*
>
> *(a) arises from the goods proving defective while in consumer use; and*
>
> *(b) results from the negligence of a person concerned in the manufacture or distribution of the goods, liability for the loss or damage cannot be excluded or restricted by reference to any contract term or notice contained in or operating by reference to a guarantee of the goods".*

For these purposes the goods are *'in consumer use'* when a person is using them or has them in his possession for use, otherwise than exclusively for the purposes of a business; and a *'guarantee'* includes anything in writing which contains some promise or assurance (however worded or presented) that defects will be made good by repair, replacement, financial compensation or otherwise. This section does not apply where the guarantee is given by the seller as part of the contract of sale with the buyer. In such a case other provisions of the Act would apply. Figure 8.4 illustrates the combined effect of s.2 and s.5 of the Act.

Exclusion of liability for breach of contract

Section 3 of the Act applies where one of the parties to a contract deals as a consumer, or where the contract is made on written standard terms of business. In either of these situations, the section subjects to the test of reasonableness any term in which the other party:

> *"(a) when himself in breach of contract, excludes or restricts any liability of his in respect of the breach; or*
>
> *(b) claims to be entitled -*
>
> *(i) to render a contractual performance substantially different from that which was reasonably expected from him, or*
>
> *(ii) in respect of the whole or any part of his contractual obligation, to render no performance at all".*

This section is extremely wide in its application covering all types of business contract, and all manner of exclusion or limitation of liability clauses. In the case of contracts for the supply of goods, even tighter controls are applied under the provisions of s.6 and s.7, examined below. Many of the exclusion clauses considered in previous cases, such as *Curtis v. Chemical Cleaning*

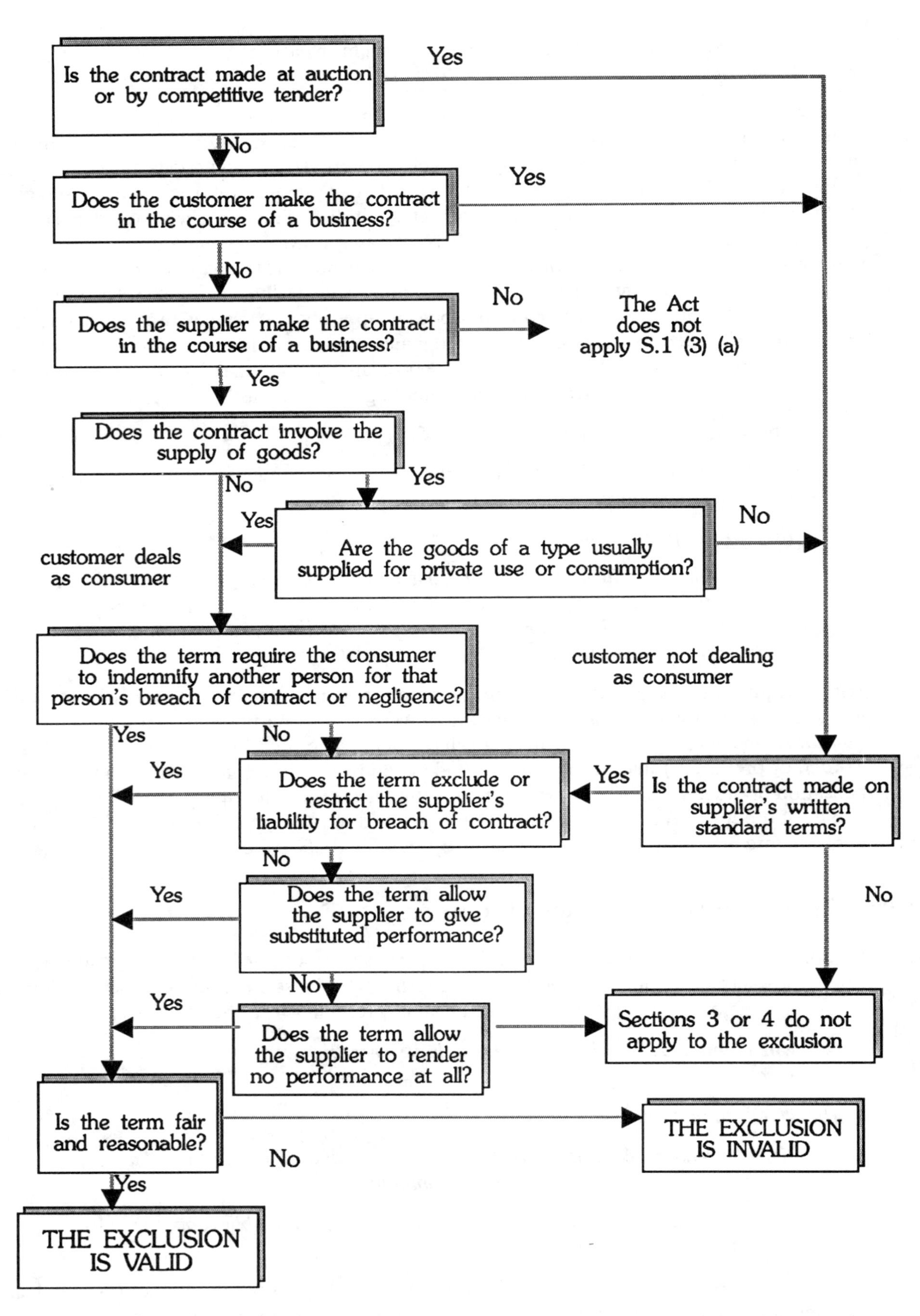

Fig. 8.5. Exclusion of Liability in Contract Section 3 and Section 4 Unfair Contract Terms Act 1977

and Dyeing Company 1951, *Olley v. Marlborough Court Hotel* 1949 and *Photo Productions Ltd. v. Securicor Transport Ltd.* 1980 would be caught by s.3.

In addition to straightforward exclusion clauses, the section applies to contract terms in which one party claims to be entitled to give substituted performance, for example in a holiday contract where the travel operator reserves the right to change the destination. It also applies to contract terms in which one party claims to be entitled to render no performance at all.

The application of s.3 can be seen in the following cases involving contracts for the development and printing of photographs.

> In *Woodman v. Photo Trade Processing Ltd.* 1981 the plaintiff sent a reel of film of wedding photographs to the defendant for processing. The film was lost by the defendant. The contract contained the following clause *"all photographic materials are accepted on the basis that their value does not exceed the cost of the material itself. Responsibility is limited to the replacement of the films. No liability will be accepted consequential or otherwise, however caused"*. In considering the reasonableness of this clause, the Judge referred to the Code of Practice for the Photographic Industry, which had been approved by the Office of Fair Trading. This code recognised the possibility of a two tier system of trade, the lowest tier of which would be a cheaper service with full exclusion of liability; and the other would be a more expensive service with the processors accepting a greater degree of liability. The Judge concluded that this approach, which had not been adopted by the defendant, would be both reasonable and practicable. On that basis the Court held that the defendants had not proved that their arrangements were reasonable and they were held liable.

> In *Warren v. Truprint Ltd.* 1986 photographs of the plaintiff's silver wedding were sent to the defendant for processing. They also were lost and the defendant sought to rely on an exclusion clause printed on their envelope. This limited their liability to the cost of unexposed films plus a refund of the processing charge and postage. The clause went on to say that *"we will undertake further liability at a supplementary charge. Written details on request"*. The Court held that this was not sufficient to make the clause reasonable under the 1977 Act. A reasonable clause would, plainly and clearly, set out the alternative with details of the cost to the consumer. The plaintiff's claim succeeded and he was awarded £50 damages.

Section 4 provides that a person dealing as a consumer cannot by reference to any contract term be made to indemnify another person for liability for breach of contract or negligence unless the indemnity term satisfies the reasonableness test. This is a further restriction on the effective transfer of liability by the use of an indirect exclusion clause.

The combined effect of s.3 and s.4 of the Act are summarised in figure 8.5.

Exclusion of liability for breach of statutory implied terms in contracts for the supply of goods

Section 6 of the 1977 Act applies to contracts for the sale of goods and hire purchase agreements, while s.7 applies to all other contracts under which the possession or ownership of goods passes to the customer. The rules contained in each section are very similar, although there are some minor differences between them. The extent of the protection given to a customer under these rules depends on whether or not he deals as a consumer.

Where the customer deals as a consumer, there can be no exclusion of the terms implied under Sections 12 to 15 of the Sale of Goods Act 1979 and the equivalent provisions in the Supply of Goods (Implied Terms) Act 1973 and the Supply of Goods and Services Act 1982. The expression 'dealing as a consumer' is defined in s.12 of the 1977 Act, and its meaning is examined earlier in the text. Clearly a purchaser who deals as a consumer obtains a high level of protection under s.6 and s.7 of the Act. The courts have been prepared to interpret the expression widely and extend this protection accordingly.

> In *R & B Customs Brokers Co. Ltd. v. United Dominions Trust Ltd.* 1988 the plaintiff company bought a second hand Colt Shogun car for the use of one of its directors, and signed a conditional sale agreement which excluded liability in relation to quality and fitness unless the buyer was dealing as a consumer. The director discovered that the roof of the car leaked before the defendant finance company signed its part of the agreement thereby concluding the contract. The plaintiff rejected the car for breach of the implied terms relating to merchantable quality and fitness for purpose. At first instance the judge held that the plaintiff could not rely on the implied condition as to merchantable quality as he had notice of the defect before the contract was made, but that the defendant was in breach of the implied condition as to fitness for purpose. The judge took the view that the plaintiff had been dealing as a consumer and accordingly that the exclusion of liability was invalid under s.6 of the 1977 Act. On appeal, the decision of the judge was upheld. The principal issue was whether the company was dealing a consumer. Neil, LJ stated:
>
> *"In the present case the director gave evidence on behalf of the company that the car was only the second or third vehicle acquired on credit terms. It follows, therefore, that no pattern of regular purchases had been established for this business, nor can it be suggested that this transaction was an adventure in the nature of trade. I am therefore satisfied that in relation to the purchase of this car the company was dealing as consumer within the meaning of s.12 of the 1977 Act."*

Where the customer deals otherwise than as a consumer, for example because the supplier is not in business or because the goods are of a type which are not normally bought for private use, there can be no exclusion of liability for breach of the implied terms relating to title. The other implied terms can however be excluded as against such a customer, but only if the clause satisfies the test of reasonableness.

In the case of a contract of hire, where there is an exclusion of the implied terms relating to the supplier's right to transfer possession of the goods, this exclusion will be subject to the test of reasonableness and will not automatically be rendered void under s.7(4). This applies whether or not the hirer is dealing as a consumer. Figure 8.6 summarises the application of s.6 and s.7, except as regards the exclusion of the implied terms relating to the transfer of possession in hire contracts.

For the purpose of s.6 and s.7, the Act lays down guidelines which the court may take into account in determining whether an exclusion clause is reasonable. Strictly speaking, the Act does not apply these guidelines to determine reasonableness in relation to the other sections which apply the reasonableness test, but in practice the courts take them into account in those cases also. The factors to be taken into account under the guidelines are:

(a) the relative bargaining strength of the parties;

(b) whether there was an opportunity to purchase the product elsewhere without submitting to the clause;

(c) whether any inducement was given to the buyer in return for accepting the clause, for example the differential pricing arrangements suggested in the photo processing cases;

(d) whether the goods were made to the buyer's design or specification;

(e) whether the customer knew or ought reasonably to have known of the existence of the clause;

(f) the extent to which it was open for the parties to cover themselves by insurance; and

(g) the particular circumstances of the case.

In *George Mitchell Ltd. v. Finney Lock Seeds Ltd.* 1983 the plaintiff was a farmer who purchased cabbage seed from the defendant. The seeds were described as those of a solid heading late winter cabbage. In fact they were of a different type, of inferior quality and unfit for human consumption. The plaintiff planted 63 acres of these cabbages. They proved to be of no value and had to be ploughed in. The seed had cost £192 but the plaintiff's loss was in excess of £61,000. The plaintiff was not insured for this loss and sued the seller for breach of the term implied by s.13 of the Sale of Goods Act 1979 that the goods would correspond with their description. The defence put forward by the sellers was an exclusion clause limiting liability to either the cost of the seed or its replacement value. The clause read:

"in the event of any seeds or plants sold or agreed to be sold by us not complying with the express terms of the contract of sale or with a representation made by us or by any duly authorised agent or representative on our behalf prior to, at the time of, or in any such contract, or any seeds or plants proving defective in varietal purity we will, at our option, replace the defective seeds or plants, free of charge to the buyer or will refund all payments made to us by the buyer in respect of the defective seeds or plants and this shall be the limit of our obligation. We hereby exclude all liability for any loss or damage arising from the use of any seeds or plants supplied by us and for any consequential loss or damage arising out of such use or any failure in the performance of or any defect in any seeds or plants supplied by us or for any other loss or damage whatsoever save for, at our option, liability for any such replacement or refund as aforesaid".

The House of Lords affirmed the decision of the Court of Appeal that the clause was ineffective. Lord Denning, in his last judgment before retiring, considered a number of questions relevant to the validity of the clause. The first was whether the clause was part of the agreement. He found that it was since such conditions were usual in the trade, and therefore well known, and in any event the clause was included on the back of the invoice. The second was the wording of the clause, and whether as drafted it covered and effectively limited the supplier's liability. He found that the clause clearly did so. Finally the question arose as to whether the clause was a reasonable one. It had been imposed by the defendant without negotiation. The seedsmen could insure against the risk of crop failure without materially affecting the price of the seeds. The defendants could have tested the seeds but the plaintiffs had no opportunity of discovering the defectiveness of the seed until it was too late. In addition there was evidence that the defendants would

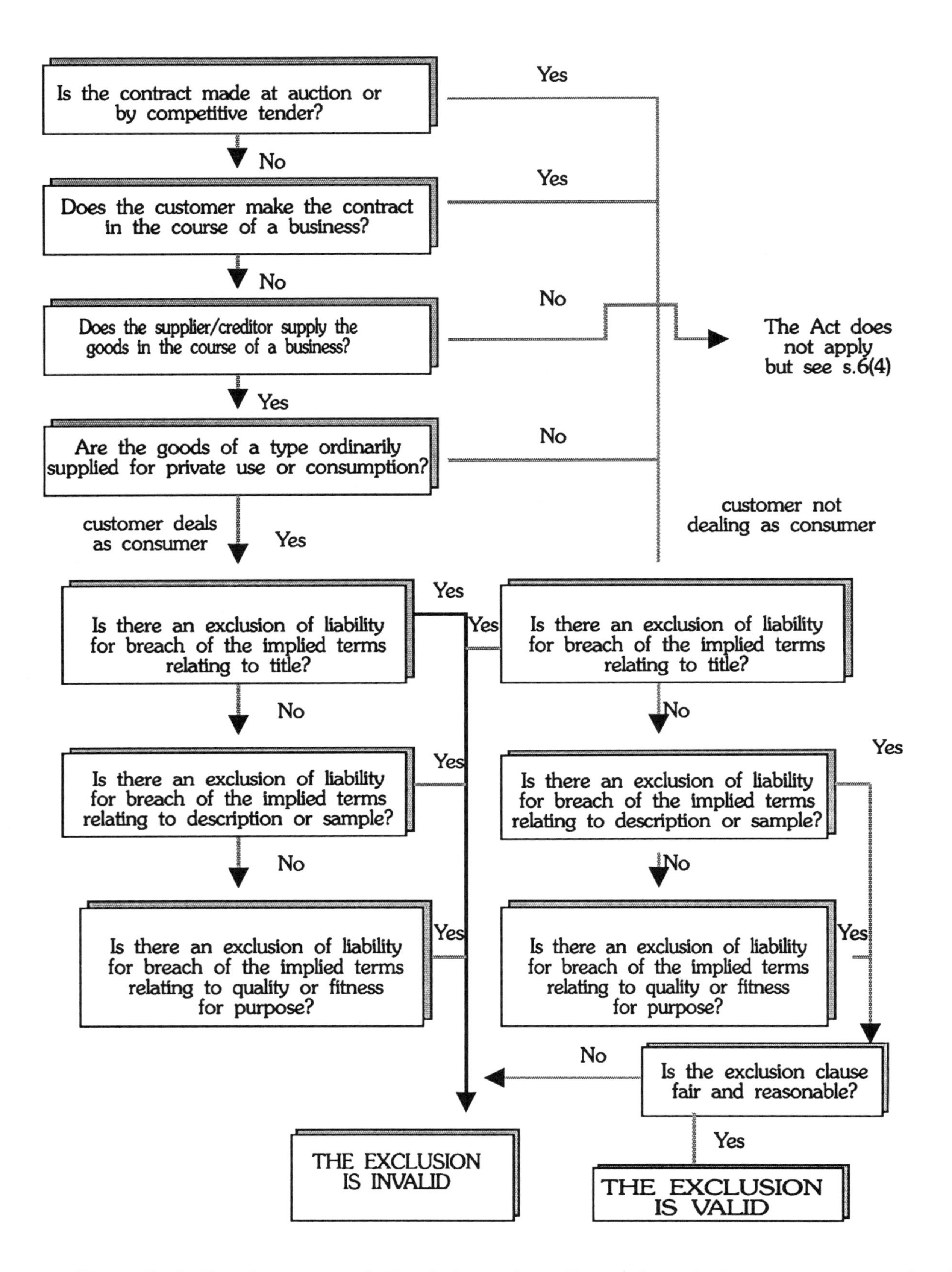

Fig. 8.6 Exclusion of Liability for Breach of Statutory Implied Terms in Contract for Sale and Supply of Goods Section 6 and Section 7 Unfair Contract Terms Act 1977

usually negotiate a realistic settlement where a claim was justified in similar circumstances. Taking these factors into account the clause was held to be unreasonable and invalid.

In *R.W. Green Ltd. v. Cade Brothers Farms* 1978 the plaintiffs purchased a quantity of seed potatoes from the defendants under the terms of a written standard form contract which included a clause limiting liability of the defendants to a refund of the price. The potatoes were infected with a virus which could only be detected at harvest time. The crop failed and the plaintiffs sued the defendants for breach of the terms implied into the contract by s.14 of the Sale of Goods Act. It was held that the defendants were in breach of the implied terms, but were not liable because the exclusion clause was reasonable in the circumstances of the case. The seed had been sold cheaply because it was uncertified and the plaintiffs could have paid more and bought certified seed potato. The terms of the contract had not been imposed by the seller, rather they were the product of many years negotiation by trade associations and unions representing both sides of the industry.

Criminal liability for the use of invalid exclusion clauses

The Unfair Contract Terms Act 1977 invalidates many exclusion clauses so that they cannot be relied upon as a defence to an action for damages. The Act does not, however, prevent the trader from using invalid clauses. The clause may have no legal validity, but the consumer may be misled because of his lack of legal knowledge. The Consumer Transactions (Restrictions on Statements) Order 1976 (as amended in 1978) was made under the Fair Trading Act 1973 to prevent this unfair trading practice in a limited range of situations. The order applies to any clause in a consumer transaction which purports to exclude liability for breach of Sections 13, 14 or 15 of the Sale of Goods Act 1979. Under the order it is a criminal offence for a person, in the course of a business, to do any of the following:

(a) display a notice of such a clause at a place where consumer deals are likely to be made,

(b) publish any advertisement to supply goods which includes such a clause,

(c) provide the consumer with a written contract or other document containing such a clause, or

(d) supply goods bearing any statement about the seller's liability in relation to description quality or fitness for purpose, unless the statement makes it clear that it does not affect the statutory rights of the consumer.

Assignment *An Incident at Ashburne Pool*

Ashburne District Council owns and operates a sports complex in Ashburne town centre. A notice at the main entrance to the centre states:

> *"The Council can accept no responsibility for loss or damage to visitors personal possessions within this complex, howsoever arising."*

A notice at the bottom of the steps in the main pool leading to the high diving board states:

> *"Divers: you are using the diving board at your own risk."*

Peter and his sister Mary visited the leisure complex in order to swim. They paid ten pence each for keys to the cubicles in the changing rooms and locked the doors when they left. Whilst Mary swam in the pool Peter climbed the ladder to the diving board. The non-slip coating on the board had worn. Peter lost his footing and plunged into the pool injuring himself. He was rushed to hospital.

When Mary subsequently returned to collect their clothes from the cubicles she found the doors open and the clothes gone. She angrily complained to the changing room attendant who explained that he had left his desk to see what was happening when Peter had his accident, and could only assume that during this time someone had used the master keys from behind the desk to gain access to the cubicles. Changing room attendants are under strict instructions from the council never to leave the desk unattended.

The theft was reported to the police who a week later during a routine inspection of market stalls in Ashburne market, identified Mary's jewellery being worn by Phyllis, one of the stall-holders. During an interview with the police Phyllis revealed that she had purchased the items earlier in the day from Joe, another stall-holder. Peter's watch had not yet turned up.

Tasks

1. You work as a clerical assistant in Ashburne Leisure Services Department. The Director of Leisure Services is seeking your advice concerning the potential legal liability faced by his department for the injury suffered by Peter and the losses sustained by Peter and his sister. He has asked you to prepare a report which analyses the situation. Produce the report requested by the Director, and in it identify (a) the validity of the notices; and (b) the legal effect of the council's instructions to the changing room attendant.

2. Phyllis, who belongs to the same squash club as you, has mentioned the problem concerning the jewellery. Provide her with advice on the matter, indicating whether she has a good title to the jewellery.

Assignment *A Good Little Runner*

You are a voluntary worker at your local citizens advice bureau. You work at the bureau on a part-time basis. Each month the organiser of the bureau arranges a case study meeting for all workers, in which one of them is asked to present a case study based upon an actual problem he or she has actually encountered in the bureau, and this month your turn has arrived to give the presentation. You have decided to tell the story of the sale of a motor vehicle, which you had to deal with earlier in the year. The case centred upon a Mr. Tony Livingstone. The facts were as follows:

Tony Livingstone is in full time employment as a clerk in a firm of turf accountants. His spare time activity is the acquisition of motor cars which he fixes up, runs around in for a while, and resells at a profit. He usually has two or three cars at any given time, and at the time in question had sold twelve vehicles through the classified columns of his local newspaper during the previous eighteen months, in each case giving the impression that he was selling the family car.

Livingstone bought a 1984 Ford Escort for £800 in February. The bodywork of the car was thin and rusty in places, and he repaired it using plaster filler and fibreglass patches. He repainted the car completely after smoothing down the repairs. He advertised the car for sale at £1,600, describing it as "a good little runner, in excellent condition for its age."

The advertisement was replied to by Mary Walsh. After a test drive and some negotiation she agreed to buy the escort for £1,450.

Mary became extremely dissatisfied with the car. Within a month of purchase the plaster filler and fibre glass patches started showing through the paintwork. More seriously, she discovered that the car was in fact two halves of different cars welded together, the front being part of a 1984 Escort and the rear part of a slightly older model. The mechanic in her local garage, whose examination of the car revealed this, told her that the car was unroadworthy because of it.

Mary responded by writing the following letter:

Dear Mr. Livingstone,

About the car you sold me five weeks ago. You said it was a good little runner. Well I took it to the garage the other day and the mechanic told me it's total rubbish - made up from bits of other cars! The rust is coming through and its quite obvious you just bodged it up. You said it was your family car for years. You must have known it had been in an accident or something. Anyway, I've been round to the trading standards people at the council. They say you'll have to give me my money back. And they're looking into it further. They've heard of you before and you could get prosecuted. I'll be coming round to your house on Saturday morning to bring the car back so you better have my money ready.

Mary Walsh

Mary Walsh.

Chapter 9

Sale of Goods and Consumer Protection

Sale of Goods: Ownership and Risk

Transfer of ownership

The transfer of ownership, or passing of property, or title, must be distinguished from the transfer of physical possession of goods. As a general rule, s.28 of the Sale of Goods Act 1979 provides that, unless otherwise agreed, the buyer is entitled to delivery only upon payment for the goods. Ownership, on the other hand, can be transferred at any time depending upon the terms of the contract. It may be at the time of making the contract, or after the buyer has paid the price, or at some other time.

It is important to know exactly when ownership of goods is transferred under a contract of sale for a number of reasons:

(a) under s.20, the risk of accidental loss or damage is transferred to the buyer when property passes to him, unless otherwise agreed. The party which bears the risk of accidental loss or damage will probably wish to insure the goods;

(b) under s.49 the seller can normally only sue for the price after property has passed to the buyer;

(c) in considering whether the contract has been frustrated due to perishing of the goods. The contract cannot be frustrated if property has passed to the buyer before the goods perish;

(d) in the event of the insolvency of the buyer, the seller may be able to retake possession of the goods if property has not passed to the buyer; and

(e) if the buyer resells the goods immediately, as a general rule, the sub-buyer will get a good title only if property has previously passed to the buyer.

In order to determine when property passes in a contract for the sale of goods, it is of crucial importance to decide whether the goods are specific, unascertained, or ascertained.

Specific goods are defined in s.61 of the Act as:

> *"goods which are identified and agreed upon at the time the contract for sale is made".*

Goods which are not singled out in this way at the time of contracting are unascertained goods. Ascertained goods are those which were unascertained and are subsequently set aside for the performance of the contract. Goods which were not identified and agreed upon at the time of the contract can never become specific goods.

In *Kursell v. Timber Operators Limited* 1927 under a contract for the sale of uncut timber standing in a forest, the buyers were entitled to cut and remove, within 15 years, all timber above a certain minimum size. The forest was subsequently nationalised and the Court had to determine whether the ownership of trees fitting the contract specification had passed to the buyer. It was held that property had not passed because the trees were unascertained goods. They could not be specific goods because trees fitting the contract description were merely identifiable. They had not actually been identified.

At the time the contract is made, the goods can only be one of two types, specific or unascertained. If the particular goods to be used in performance of the contract are identified and agreed upon at that time, the goods are specific. If not the goods are unascertained. Unascertained goods cannot subsequently become specific goods. They will become ascertained goods after they have been identified.

Passing of property in specific goods

The general rule is contained in s.17 of the Act which provides:

"(1) *Where there is a contract for the sale of specific or ascertained goods the property in them is transferred to the buyer at such time as the parties to the contract intend it to be transferred.*

(2) *For the purpose of ascertaining the intention of the parties regard shall be had to the terms of the contract, the conduct of the parties and the circumstances of the case.*"

This allows the parties to make whatever agreement they think fit in relation to the passing of property in the goods. Many standard form contracts include a retention of title clause under which property does not pass to the buyer until the purchase price has been paid. Such clauses, examined later, are permitted by s.17.

Where no provision is made in the contract and it is not clear from the circumstances what the parties' intentions are, s.18 provides a number of rules which can be applied in order to determine when property passes.

Rule 1:

"Where there is an unconditional contract for the sale of specific goods in a deliverable state, the property in the goods passes to the buyer when the contract is made and it is immaterial whether the time of payment or the time of delivery, or both, be postponed".

Under this rule the ownership of goods may be transferred to the buyer even though they are still in the seller's possession.

In *Tarling v. Baxter* 1927 the seller sold a quantity of hay to the buyer, but the hay remained on the seller's land pending collection. Before it was collected it was destroyed by fire. It was held that property passed to the buyer when the contract was made. The loss was therefore his as he carried the risk of accidental destruction.

In *Dennant v. Skinner and Collom Ltd.* 1948 a rogue successfully bid for a car at auction and was allowed to take it away after paying by cheque. After the sale was complete, he signed a form agreeing that ownership of the vehicle would not pass to him until the cheque was cleared. He quickly resold the car to the defendant. When the cheque was dishonoured the original seller sued the defendant for the return of the car. It was held that the terms in the document signed by the rogue were introduced after the contract had been made at the auction. That contract was complete on the fall of the hammer. As no reference had been made to the retention of title clause prior to that moment, the clause was not part of the contract. Property therefore passed to the rogue on the making of the contract under s.18 r.1. He passed a good title to the defendant when he resold the vehicle. The plaintiff's claim therefore failed.

The goods must be in a *deliverable state* before r.1 will apply. Under s.61(5):

> *"goods are in a deliverable state ... when they are in such a state that the buyer would under the contract be bound to take delivery of them".*

In *Underwood v. Burgh Castle Brick and Cement Syndicate* 1922 the plaintiff sold a condensing engine to the defendants. The engine weighed over 30 tons and was cemented to the floor of the plaintiff's premises. It had to be dismantled and detached from the floor and the seller agreed to do this. The engine was damaged in the process. It was held that property had not passed to the buyer at the time it was damaged as the goods were not then in a deliverable state. The risk was therefore with the seller who had to bear the loss.

Goods are not in a deliverable state merely because they are transportable. Whether goods are in a deliverable state will depend in each case on the terms of the contract. Where specific goods are not in a deliverable state at the time the contract is made, r.2 may apply.

Rule 2:

> *"Where there is a contract for the sale of specific goods and the seller is bound to do something to the goods for the purpose of putting them into a deliverable state, the property does not pass until the thing is done and the buyer has notice that it has been done".*

This rule will apply if, for example, a contract for the sale of a motor vehicle contained a term that the seller would replace the exhaust system before delivery to the buyer. The ownership of the car would not be transferred until the work had been done and the buyer had been notified.

Rule 3:

> *"Where there is a contract for the sale of specific goods in a deliverable state but the seller is bound to weigh, measure, test or do some other act or thing with reference to the goods for the purpose of ascertaining the price, the property does not pass until the act or thing is done and the buyer has notice that it has been done".*

This rule, like r.2, only applies where it is the seller who must do something to the goods. If something must be done by the buyer rather than the seller, property will pass under s.18 r.1 on the making of the contract.

In *Turley v. Bates* 1863 a contract for the sale of clay provided that the buyer had to weigh it in order to determine the price. It was held that property passed to the buyer when the contract was made.

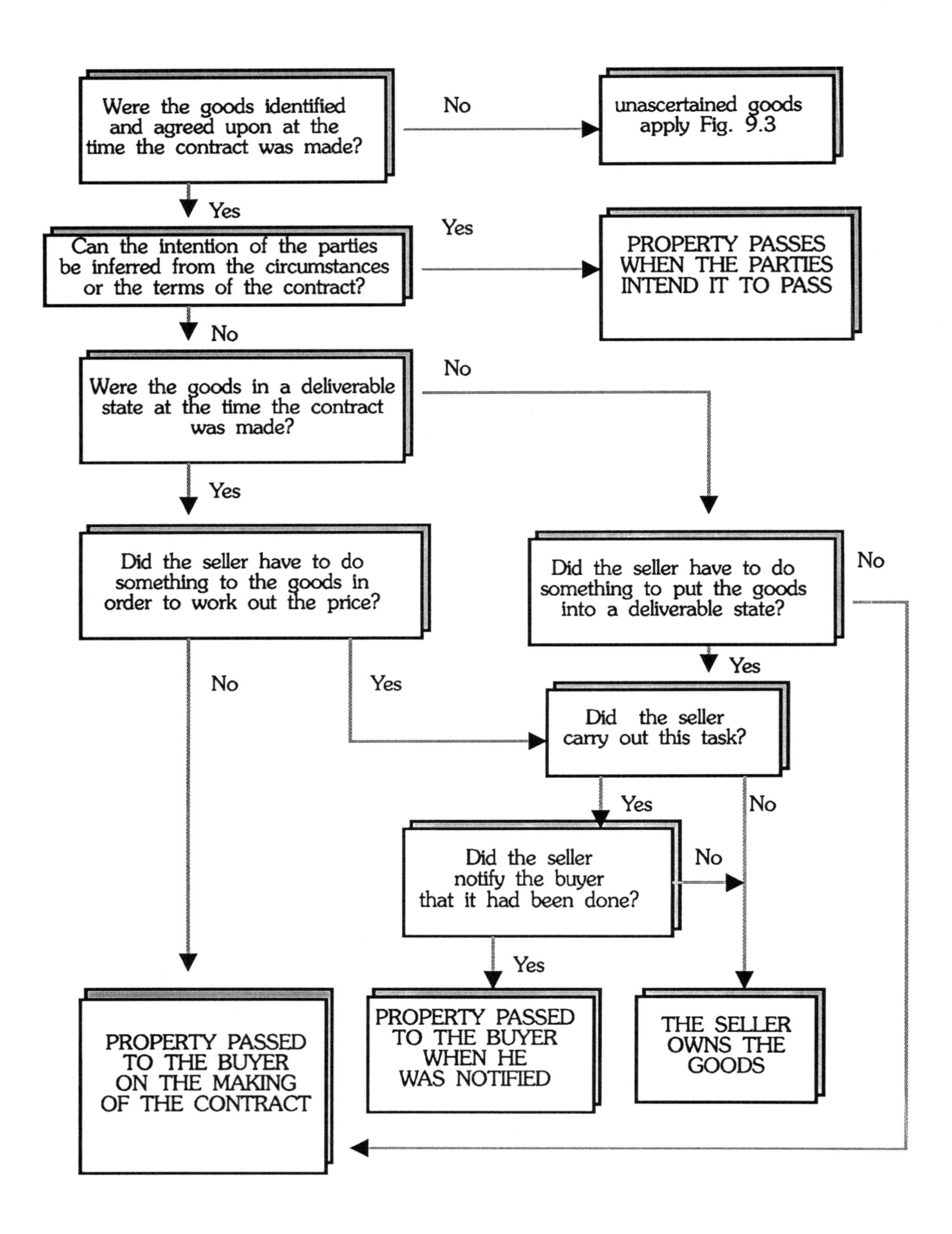

Fig. 9.1. Passing of Property in Specific Goods

Passing of property where goods are delivered on sale or return

Section 18 rule 4 applies where goods are delivered to the buyer on approval or on sale or return terms. It is unnecessary for the purposes of r.4 to decide whether the goods are specific or unascertained.

Rule 4:

> *"When goods are delivered to the buyer on approval or on sale or return or other similar terms, the property in the goods passes to the buyer:*
>
> *(a) when he signifies his approval or acceptance to the seller or does any other act adopting the transaction;*
>
> *(b) if he does not signify his approval or acceptance to the seller but retains the goods without giving notice of rejection, then, if a time has been fixed for the return of the goods, on the expiration of that time, and, if no time has been fixed, on the expiration of a reasonable time".*

Any act of the buyer, such as using or selling the goods, which is inconsistent with the ownership of the original seller, will be *an act adopting the transaction* for the purposes of r.4(a).

> In *Kirkham v. Attenborough* 1897 the plaintiff gave goods to a customer on sale or return terms. He pawned the goods. The plaintiff was never paid and claimed the goods from the pawnbroker. It was held that he could not recover them because the pawning of the goods was 'an act adopting the transaction'. Ownership passed to the customer as a result and he transferred it on to the pawnbroker.
>
> In *Weiner v. Gill* 1906 the plaintiff delivered goods to his customer on sale or return under a standing contract which provided that "goods had on approbation or on sale or return remain the property of Samuel Weiner until such goods are settled for or charged". The goods were pawned with the defendant, from whom the plaintiff sought to recover them. It was held that s.18 r.4 did not apply. It was overridden by the express term in the contract, which, under s.17, governed the transfer of ownership. The rules in s.18 apply only where no intention has been made clear by the parties. Under the express terms of the contract the goods remained the property of the plaintiff. (Despite this, however, the defendant actually did get a good title under s.2 of the Factors Act 1889, discussed later in this chapter).

If the customer is unable to return goods within the approval period for a reason outside his control, for example because they have been stolen or accidentally destroyed without any fault on his part, he will not be deemed to have adopted the transaction and property will not pass to him.

If goods have been sent to the customer without his asking for them, the Unsolicited Goods and Services Act 1971 may apply. Under this Act the goods will become the property of the customer as an unconditional gift after the expiration of the time limit specified in the Act.

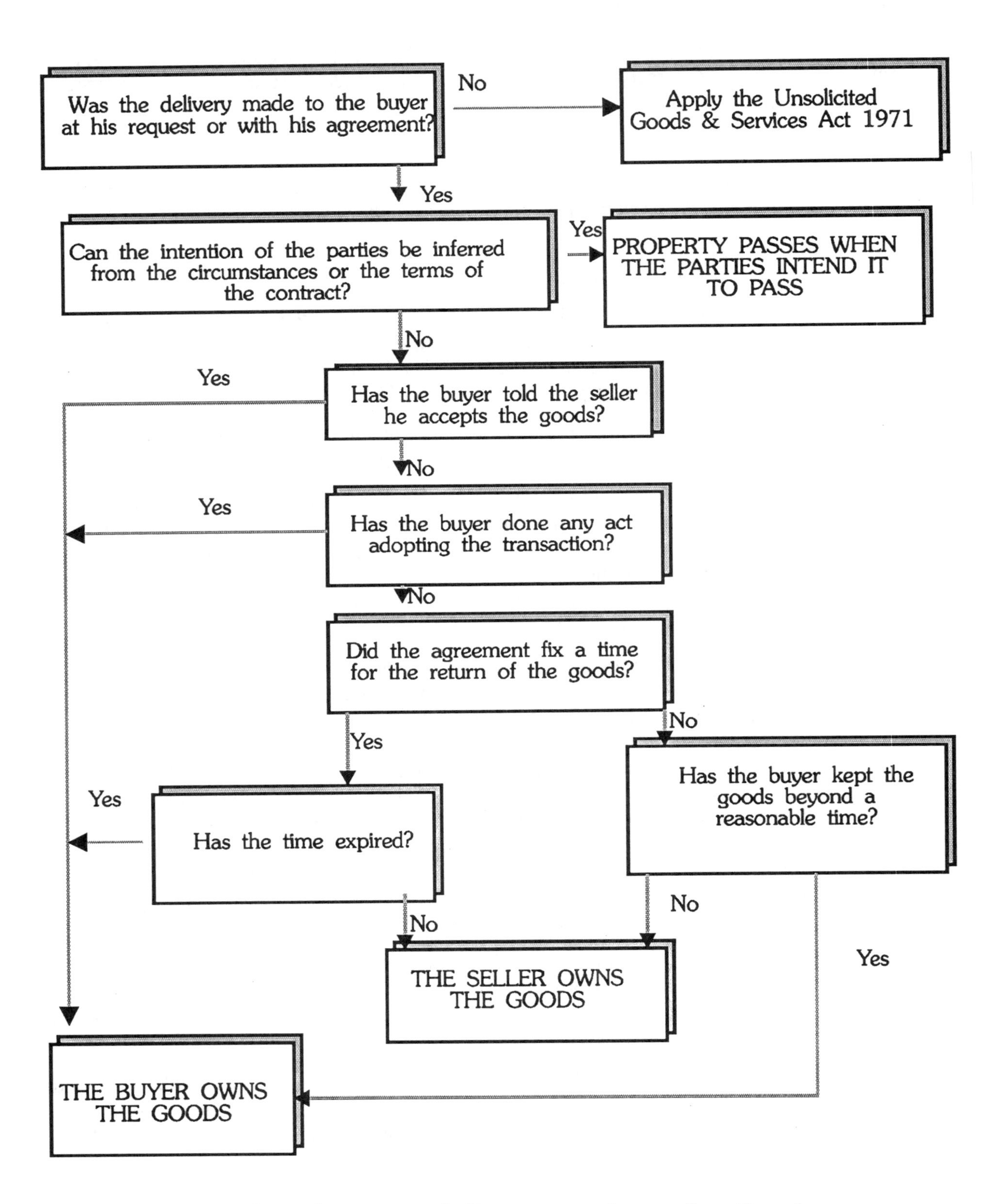

Fig. 9.2. Passing of Property where the Goods are delivered on approval or on sale or return

Passing of property in unascertained goods

Until the parties have identified which goods are the subject of the contract, property cannot pass from the seller to the buyer.

Section 16 provides:

> *"Where there is a contract for the sale of unascertained goods no property in the goods is transferred to the buyer unless and until the goods are ascertained".*

This section cannot be used to determine when property passes to the buyer, it only tells us that property cannot pass until the goods have been ascertained. Once this has occurred s.17 will apply if there is evidence of the parties' contractual intention, otherwise rule 5 of s.18 must be applied. The following case provides an example of the application of s.16:

> In *Healey v. Howlett & Sons* 1917 the defendant ordered twenty boxes of mackerel from the plaintiff, who was a fish merchant. One hundred and ninety boxes were dispatched by rail, and railway officials were instructed to set aside twenty boxes for the defendant. The train was delayed and, before twenty boxes were set aside, the fish deteriorated. It was held that property in the goods remained with the plaintiff at least until they were set apart. They were therefore at the seller's risk when they deteriorated.

Once goods are ascertained, it is a question of contractual intention under s.17 as to when ownership is transferred. If, for example, the contract contains a retention of title clause, this will govern the passing of property. Where no contractual intention appears, however, s.18 r.5 provides:

> *"Where there is a contract for the sale of unascertained or future goods by description, and goods of that description and in a deliverable state are unconditionally appropriated to the contract, either by the seller with the assent of the buyer or by the buyer with the assent of the seller, the property in the goods then passes to the buyer; and the assent may be expressed or implied, and may be given either before or after the appropriation is made".*

Property cannot pass under s.18 r.5 unless the goods are in a deliverable state. It was noted earlier that goods are in a deliverable state when they are in such condition that the buyer would be bound to accept them under the terms of the contract.

> In *Philip Head and Sons Ltd. v. Showfronts Ltd.* 1970 the plaintiff sold carpeting under a contract which required them to lay it in the defendants' premises. Carpeting which was delivered for this purpose was stolen before it could be laid. The plaintiff sued for the price. It was held that the carpet was not in a deliverable state, as the seller was bound to lay it under the terms of the contract. The seller owned the carpet at the time it was stolen and had to bear the loss.

The expression *unconditional appropriation* is not defined in the Act. For an appropriation to be unconditional, the seller or the buyer must set goods aside irrevocably for the performance of the contract.

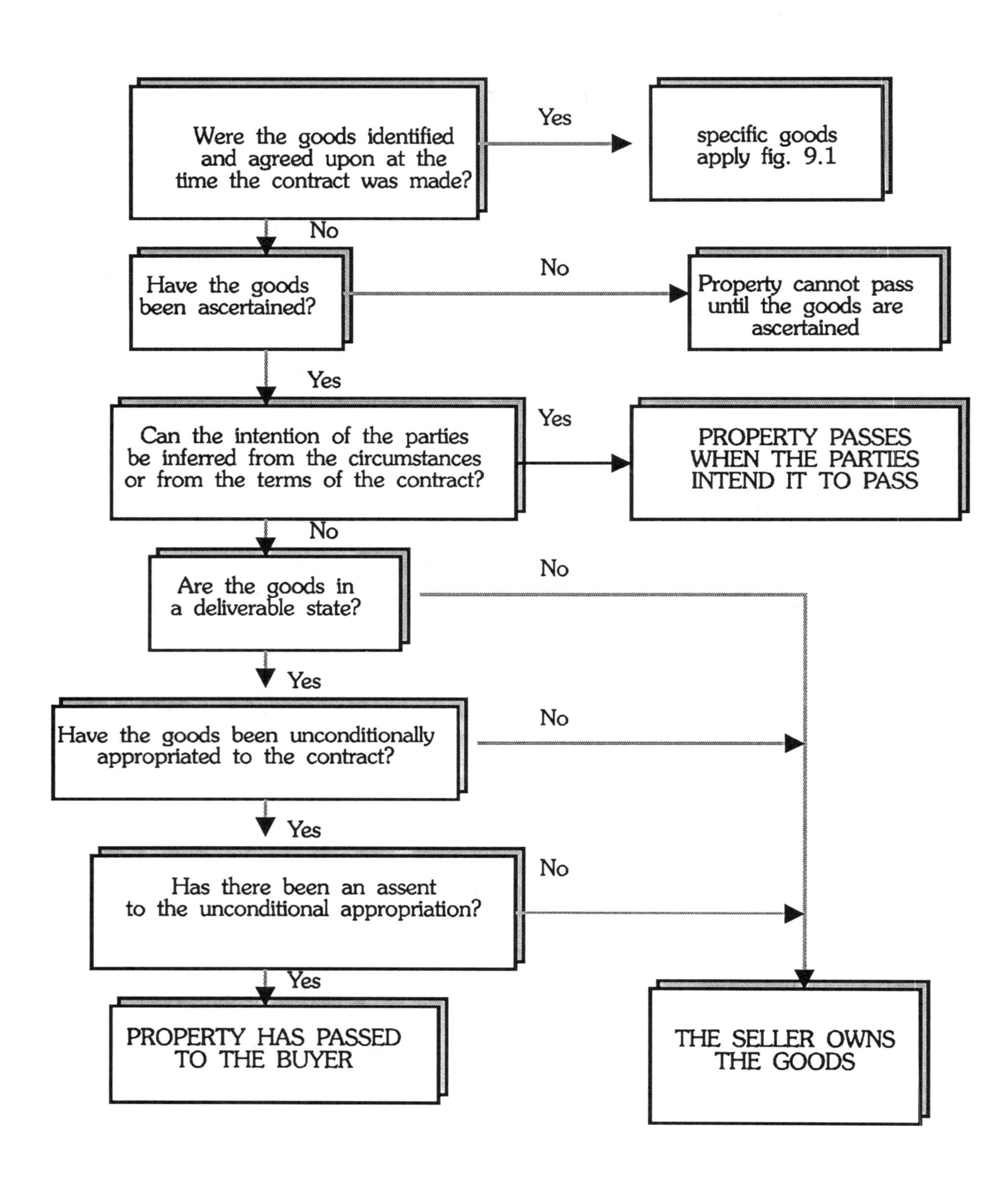

Fig. 9.3. Passing of Property in Unascertained Goods

In *Carlos Federspiel & Co. v. Charles Twigg and Co. Ltd.* 1957 the seller manufactured goods for the buyers. The goods were packed in containers with the buyers' name and address on them. The seller became insolvent. The buyers claimed that the ownership of a number of containers, still in the seller's possession, had passed to them under rule 5. It was held that there had not been an unconditional appropriation of the goods and therefore they were still in the seller's ownership. Pearson, J., stated that:

"a mere setting apart or selection by the seller of the goods which he expects to use in performance of the contract is not enough. If that is all, he can change his mind and use those goods in performance of some other contract and use some other goods in performance of this contact. To constitute an appropriation of the goods to the contract the parties must have had, or be reasonable supposed to have had, an intention to attach the contract irrevocably to those goods, so that those goods and no others are the subject of the sale and become the property of the buyer".

Rule 5(2) provides:

"where in pursuance of the contract, the seller delivers the goods to the buyer or to a carrier for the purpose of transmission to the buyer, he is deemed to have unconditionally appropriated the goods to the contract".

There must be an assent to the appropriation before property will pass to the buyer. Rule 5 provides that an assent may be express or implied and may be given either before or after the appropriation is made.

In *Pignatoro v. Gilroy and Son* 1919 there was a contract for the sale of rice, which the buyer had agreed to collect. The seller packaged the rice and informed the buyer that it was ready for collection. The buyer delayed for over three weeks before coming to collect. By this time the rice had been stolen. It was held that property had passed to the buyer under r.5 and he must bear the loss. His delay and the failure to object to the appropriation within a reasonable time was evidence of an implied assent.

Retention of title

The 1979 Act in s.17 envisages that the parties may make express provision in the contract for the transfer of ownership. A retention (or reservation) of title clause is an express term which provides that ownership of goods will not be transferred to the buyer until payment has been made. The major advantage of retention of title, from the seller's point of view, is that the goods belong to him until he receives payment for them.

If the buyer becomes insolvent after delivery but before payment, the seller will be able to reclaim the goods because they belong to him. Without a retention of title clause the goods belong to the buyer. They will be available for distribution to the buyer's creditors on insolvency. The seller will be in the position of an unsecured trade creditor and therefore low down in the order of priority for repayment of debts. A retention of title clause effectively places the seller first in the order of priority in relation to goods which are still in the buyer's possession.

In *Aluminium Industrie Vaassen BV v. Romalpa Aluminium Ltd.* 1976 the seller sold aluminium foil to Romalpa, an English company, for use in its manufacturing processes. At the time of manufacture the foil became mixed with other materials. The written contract contained a retention of title clause, under which ownership of the aluminium foil would be transferred to Romalpa when it had paid all sums owing to the seller. The clause went on to reserve ownership over any goods which were mixed with the aluminium foil. Romalpa became insolvent and a receiver was appointed. The seller claimed the ownership of aluminium foil still held by the company; and the proceeds of resale of unmixed foil sold by the receiver to third parties. No claim was made in respect of mixed goods or the proceeds of sale of mixed goods. The Court of Appeal held that the retention of title was valid and the seller's claim succeeded in full.

Transfer of risk

The party who carries risk must bear the loss where goods deteriorate or are stolen, damaged or destroyed in circumstances where no-on else can be made liable for the loss. The party who carries risk will usually protect himself by insurance.

Under a contract for the sale of goods risk can be transferred from the seller to the buyer at any time. If the parties make no express provision for the transfer of risk, it will take place at the same time as the transfer of ownership. The 1979 Act in s.20(1) provides:

> *"Unless otherwise agreed, the goods remain at the seller's risk until the property in them is transferred to the buyer but when the property in them is transferred to the buyer the goods are at the buyer's risk whether delivery has been made or not".*

Many standard form contracts transfer risk to the buyer on the making of the contract, or at the time of delivery.

It is possible that goods may be exposed to additional risks if one of the contracting parties does not comply with his obligations. To cover this possibility, the 1979 Act in s.20(2) provides:

> *"where delivery has been delayed through the fault of either the buyer or seller the goods are at the risk of the party at fault as regards any loss which might not have occurred but for such fault".*

In *Demby Hamilton v. Barden* 1949 there was a contract for the sale of thirty tons of apple juice by sample. The buyer agreed to take delivery in weekly loads. The seller crushed all thirty tons of juice at once in order to ensure correspondence with the sample. The buyer took delivery of the first few instalments and then took no further deliveries for a period of time, during which the juice went off. It was held that the buyer must bear the loss. Risk transferred to him under s.20(2) even though property remained with the seller.

Transfer of Title by a Non-Owner

Under a contract of sale, the principal obligation of the seller is to transfer the ownership of goods to the buyer. Clearly this presents no difficulty where the seller actually owns the goods or has the authority of the owner to sell them. However where the goods are stolen or where the seller holds them under the terms of a hire purchase agreement, in an attempted sale the seller does not have the legal right to transfer ownership. A person who buys such goods will not acquire a good title to them because the seller cannot pass on to the buyer that which he does not have. This rule is expressed in the latin maxim *'nemo dat quod non habet'*. This means no-one can give what he has not got.

The rule is embodied in s.21 of the Sale of Goods Act 1979, which provides:

> *"Where goods are sold by a person who is not their owner, the buyer acquires no better title to the goods than the seller had".*

A thief has no legal title to goods and a purchaser from a thief acquires no better title. The thief could be prosecuted under s.1 of the Theft Act 1968 for the offence of theft. He could also be sued by the owner for damages, under the Torts (Interference with Goods) Act 1977.

If the purchaser knew that the goods were stolen at the time he bought them, he could be prosecuted under the Theft Act 1968 for the offence of handling stolen goods. He could also be sued by the owner for damages, or for an order of specific delivery, under the Torts (Interference with Goods) Act 1977. In turn, he could sue the thief for breach of the implied terms relating to title, under s.12 of the Sale of Goods Act 1979 provided he purchased the goods innocently.

Where the purchaser acts in complete innocence and the thief disappears with the purchase money, the owner and the purchaser are left in dispute about the ownership of the goods. Each has some justification for his claim. In these circumstances the law has recognised that some balance must be struck between the protection of the property rights of the original owner, and the protection of the legitimate claim of a purchaser acting in good faith.

In *Pearson v. Rose and Young Ltd.* 1951 Lord Denning summed up the difficulty of striking a fair balance between two innocent victims:

> *"In the early days of the common law the governing principle of our law of property was that no person could give a better title than he himself had got, but the needs of commerce have led to a progressive modification of this principle so as to protect innocent purchasers...the cases show how difficult it is to strike the right balance between the claims of true owners and the claims of innocent purchasers".*

In an attempt to strike this balance, a number of exceptions to the general rule have been evolved. The principal exceptions are:

(a) estoppel;

(b) sale under common law or statutory powers, or by court order;

(c) sale in market overt;

(d) sale under a voidable title;

(e) sale by a seller in possession;

(f) sale by a mercantile agent;

(g) sale by a buyer in possession; and

(h) sale of a motor vehicle subject to a hire purchase agreement.

Estoppel

This exception is contained in s.21 of the 1979 Act which, after stating the general rule that a buyer can acquire no better title to goods than the seller had, continues with the words:

> *"... unless the owner of the goods is by his conduct precluded from denying the seller's authority to sell".*

An estoppel arises where the owner of goods, by his conduct, has allowed the purchaser to believe that the seller has a right to sell them. The true owner is prevented or estopped from denying to the purchaser that the seller had authority to sell.

An example of conduct amounting to an estoppel can be seen in *Eastern Distributors Ltd. v. Goldring* 1967 where the owner of a van wished to raise a loan. He got together with a car dealer in order to deceive a finance company by making it appear that the dealer owned the van and the original owner wished to acquire it from him on hire purchase. The standard forms were forwarded to the plaintiff finance company who received them in good faith believing that the van belonged to the trader. The plaintiff bought the van and let it to the original owner on hire purchase. The original owner did not pay his instalments and subsequently sold the van to the defendant, an innocent purchaser. The finance company sued the ultimate purchaser of the van claiming ownership. It was held that the conduct of the original owner in making it appear that the car dealer owned the vehicle, acted as an estoppel. Thus he was prevented from denying that the finance company had the ownership of the van. This meant that the original owner could not transfer a good title to the ultimate purchaser. The van therefore belonged to the finance company.

Sale under common law or statutory powers, or under the order of a court

Such a sale will vest a good title in the purchaser, regardless of whether or not the original owner authorised or approved of it, so long as the power of sale exists and is properly exercised.

Sale in market overt

Market overt is the term used to describe any open, public and legally constituted market in England. There are no markets overt in Wales or Scotland. In the City of London all shops are market overt.

The 1979 Act, in s.22 provides:

"Where goods are sold in market overt, according to the usage of the market, the buyer acquires a good title to the goods, provided he buys them in good faith and without notice of any defect or want of title on the part of the seller".

Goods must be sold according to the usage or usual customs of the market, otherwise the buyer will not get a good title. Generally goods must be on display and sold in a public part of the market or shop, and the sale must take place during normal business hours between sunrise and sunset.

In *Bishopsgate Motor Finance Co. v. Transport Brakes Ltd.* 1949 a customer acquired a motor car on hire purchase from the plaintiff. Before completing the repayments under the agreement, he took it to Maidstone Market where he instructed an auctioneer to sell it. The car did not reach its reserve price and he sold it privately to the defendant who bought it in good faith and had no knowledge of the hire purchase agreement. The Court held that a private sale was within the usage of the market and therefore the defendant obtained a good title to the car. In the course of his judgment, Lord Denning summed up the problem of conflicting legal principle which a court has to deal with where there is a sale by a non-owner:

> *"In the development of our law, two principles have striven for mastery. The first is for the protection of property: no-one can give a better title than he himself possesses. The second is for the protection of commercial transactions: the person who takes in good faith and for value without notice should get a good title. The first principle has held sway for a long time, but it has been modified by the common law itself and by statute".*

Sale under a voidable title

A contract may be voidable at the option of one of the contracting parties, for example where the buyer is induced by misrepresentation to make the agreement. The contract is binding until the buyer chooses to avoid it or set it aside. Similarly, where the buyer fraudulently persuades the seller to accept a cheque which is subsequently dishonoured, the contract is valid until the seller does some overt act evidencing an intention to avoid it.

Property may pass to a buyer under a voidable contract. His title to the goods is also voidable and will be lost if the seller avoids the contract. If the buyer resells the goods before the seller avoids the contract, the new buyer will obtain title. If the resale takes place after the seller avoids the first contract, the new buyer does not have title and the original seller can recover the goods from him.

This is provided for in s.23 of the 1979 Act, which states:

> *"When the seller of goods has a voidable title to them, but his title has not been avoided at the time of the sale, the buyer acquires a good title to the goods, provided he buys them in good faith and without notice of the seller's defect of title."*

> In *Phillips v. Brooks* 1919 a rogue obtained a ring worth £450 from a jeweller. The rogue had a voidable title to the ring and subsequently pawned it with the defendant pawnbroker. In an action by the jeweller to recover the ring from the pawnbroker, it was held that the pawnbroker had a good title to it. The jeweller had not avoided his contract with the rogue at the time the ring was pawned.

A contract can be avoided by informing the other party that the contract is at an end. This may not be possible however where the other party has made off with the goods dishonestly. In such a case the seller must do some other act evidencing his intention to avoid the contract, for example informing the police of the fraud.

> In *Car and Universal Finance Co. v. Caldwell* 1963 the plaintiff sold a car to a buyer, who fraudulently induced him to accept a cheque in payment. The cheque was dishonoured. The plaintiff contacted the police and the A.A. and asked them to recover the car for him. Subsequently the buyer resold the car to the defendant, from whom the plaintiff reclaimed it. It was held that the contract between the plaintiff and the buyer was voidable. The plaintiff's act of informing the police and the A.A. was sufficient to evidence an intention to avoid it. This had occurred before the buyer's resale to the defendant and therefore the car belonged to the plaintiff.

Where the original owner seeks to recover goods in the possession of someone who was not a party to the voidable transaction, and it is not clear whether the transaction was avoided before or after a resale by the purchaser from the original owner, the onus will be upon the person in possession of the goods to prove that he has a good title.

In *Thomas v. Heelas* 1988 the defendant advertised his car for sale. After the banks had closed on Maundy Thursday a man came, inspected the car and agreed to buy it for £2,200. He gave the defendant a bankers draft in the sum of £2,200 and drove the car away. On Tuesday morning, when the banks re-opened after Easter weekend, the defendant discovered that the bankers draft was a forgery. He immediately reported the theft of the car to the police. Six months later the car was found in the possession of the plaintiff, having been bought and sold a number of times in between. There was no evidence to indicate whether the first resale by the thief had taken place before or after the defendant avoided the contract on Easter Tuesday. The Court of Appeal held that the defendant was entitled to the return of his car, as the onus was on the plaintiff to demonstrate that the first resale had taken place before the contract was avoided and the plaintiff had been unable to do so.

Sale by a seller in possession

This exception, contained in s.24 of the 1979 Act, applies where a seller has sold goods to a buyer (B1) to whom property has passed. The seller, still in possession of the goods, resells them to a second buyer (B2). Applying the general principle, B2 would not obtain ownership because the seller has already transferred it to B1. However, if the conditions laid down in s.24 are satisfied, B2 will obtain a good title.

The 1979 Act, in s.24 provides:

> *"Where a person having sold goods continues or is in possession of the goods, or of the documents of title to the goods, the delivery or transfer by that person, or by a mercantile agent acting for him, of the goods or documents of title under any sale, pledge, or other disposition thereof, to any person receiving the same in good faith and without notice of the previous sale, has the same effect as if the person making the delivery or transfer were expressly authorised by the owner of the goods to make the same".*

B2 will get a good title if he is acting honestly and does not know of the previous sale to B1. There must be an actual delivery of the goods or documents of title to him. B1 will be left with the right to sue the seller for damages for breach of contract. He will have no rights against B2 or against the goods.

In *Pacific Motor Auctions Ltd. v. Motor Credits (Hire Finance) Ltd.* 1965 the seller, a car dealer, sold a number of cars to the plaintiffs (B1) under a 'display agreement' whereby the seller remained in possession of the cars for display in his showroom. He was paid 90% of the purchase price and was authorised to sell the cars as the plaintiff's agent. The seller got into financial difficulties and the plaintiffs cancelled his authority to sell the cars. Disregarding their instructions, he sold a car to the defendant (B2) who took it in good faith and without notice of the previous sale. The Court held that the defendant, who had taken delivery of the car, obtained a good title to it by virtue of s.24.

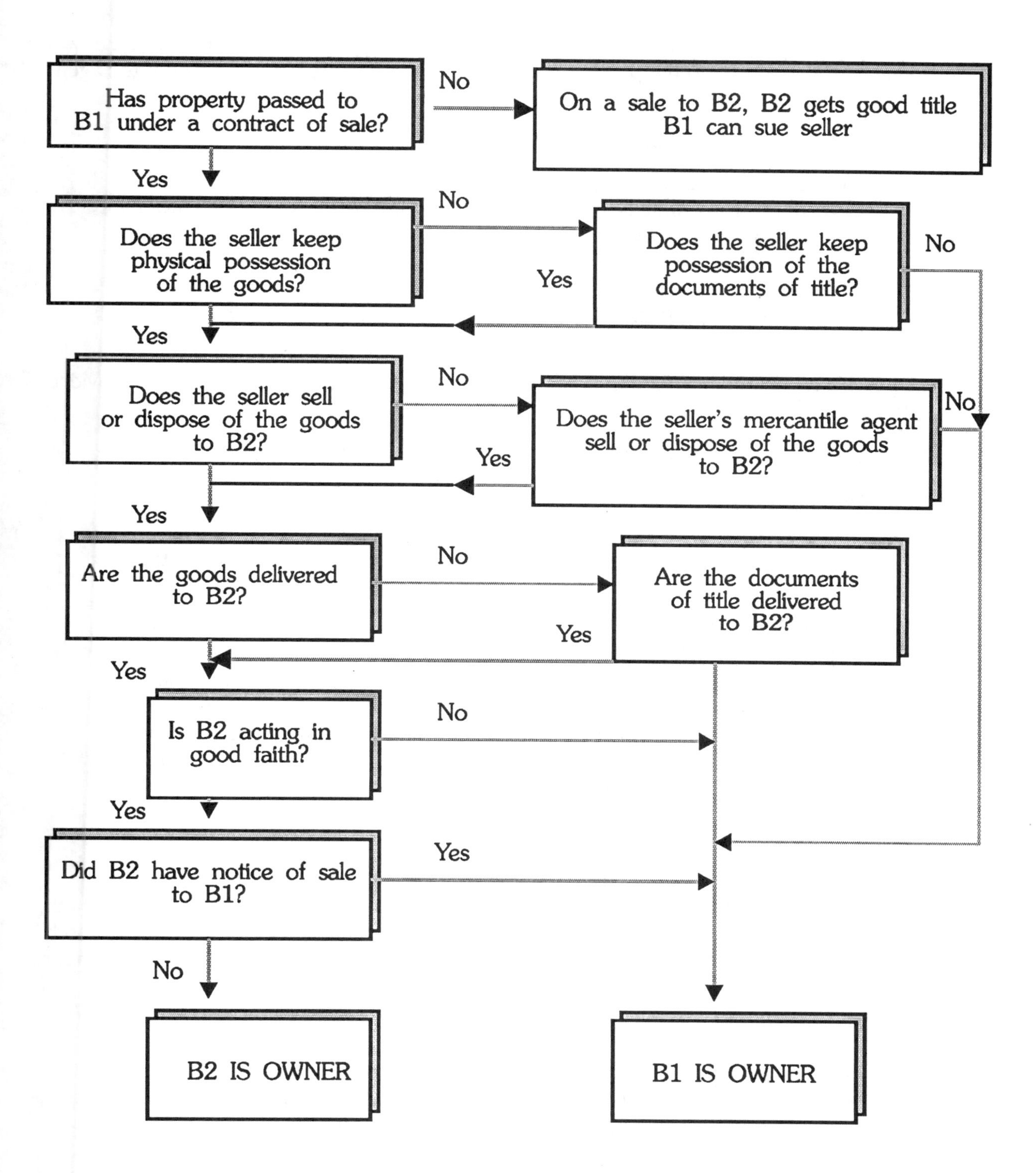

Fig. 9.4 Sale by a Seller in Possession: Section 24 Sale of Goods Act 1979

Sale by a mercantile agent

A mercantile agent, or factor, is a person who, in the ordinary course of his business, buys, sells or otherwise deals with goods on behalf of others. A sale of goods by a mercantile agent will usually pass a good title to the purchaser under s.2 of the Factors Act 1889 even if the agent has no express authority to sell the goods.

The 1889 Act in s.2 (1) provides:

> *"Where a mercantile agent is, with the consent of the owner, in possession of goods or of the documents of title to goods, any sale, pledge, or other disposition of the goods, made by him when acting in the ordinary course of business of a mercantile agent, shall ... be valid as if he were expressly authorised by the owner of the goods to make the same; provided that the person taking under the disposition acts in good faith, and has not at the time of the disposition notice that the person making the disposition has not the authority to make the same".*

The purchaser will obtain a good title, even though the agent had no authority to sell, provided that:

- (i) the agent is in possession of the goods with the owner's consent;
- (ii) the sale is made within the ordinary course of business of a mercantile agent; and
- (iii) the purchaser did not know of the agent's lack of authority to sell the goods.

In *Folkes v. King* 1923 the plaintiff delivered his car to a car dealer with instructions to sell it for not less than £575. The car dealer sold it to the defendant for £340 and absconded with the proceeds. The plaintiff sued for the return of the car from the defendant. The Court held that the car dealer was a mercantile agent as he bought and sold goods in the ordinary course of his business. The defendant bought the car from him in good faith and therefore obtained a good title to it under s.2(1) of the Factors Act 1889.

Sale by a buyer in possession

This exception to the general rule applies where a buyer obtains possession of goods, but property has not passed to him under the terms of the contract. If the buyer resells the goods before the property passes to him, the sub-buyer may obtain a good title to the goods under s.25 of the 1979 Act.

Section 25 provides:

> *"Where a person having bought or agreed to buy goods obtains, with the consent of the seller, possession of the goods or the documents of title to the goods, the delivery or transfer by that person, or by a mercantile agent acting for him, of the goods or documents of title, under any sale, pledge or other disposition thereof, to any person receiving the same in good faith and without notice of any lien or other right of the original seller in respect of the goods, has the same effect as if the person making the delivery or transfer were a mercantile agent in possession of the goods or documents of title with the consent of the owner".*

Figure 9.6 sets out in diagrammatic form the conditions which must be fulfilled in order for the sub-purchaser to obtain title under s.25.

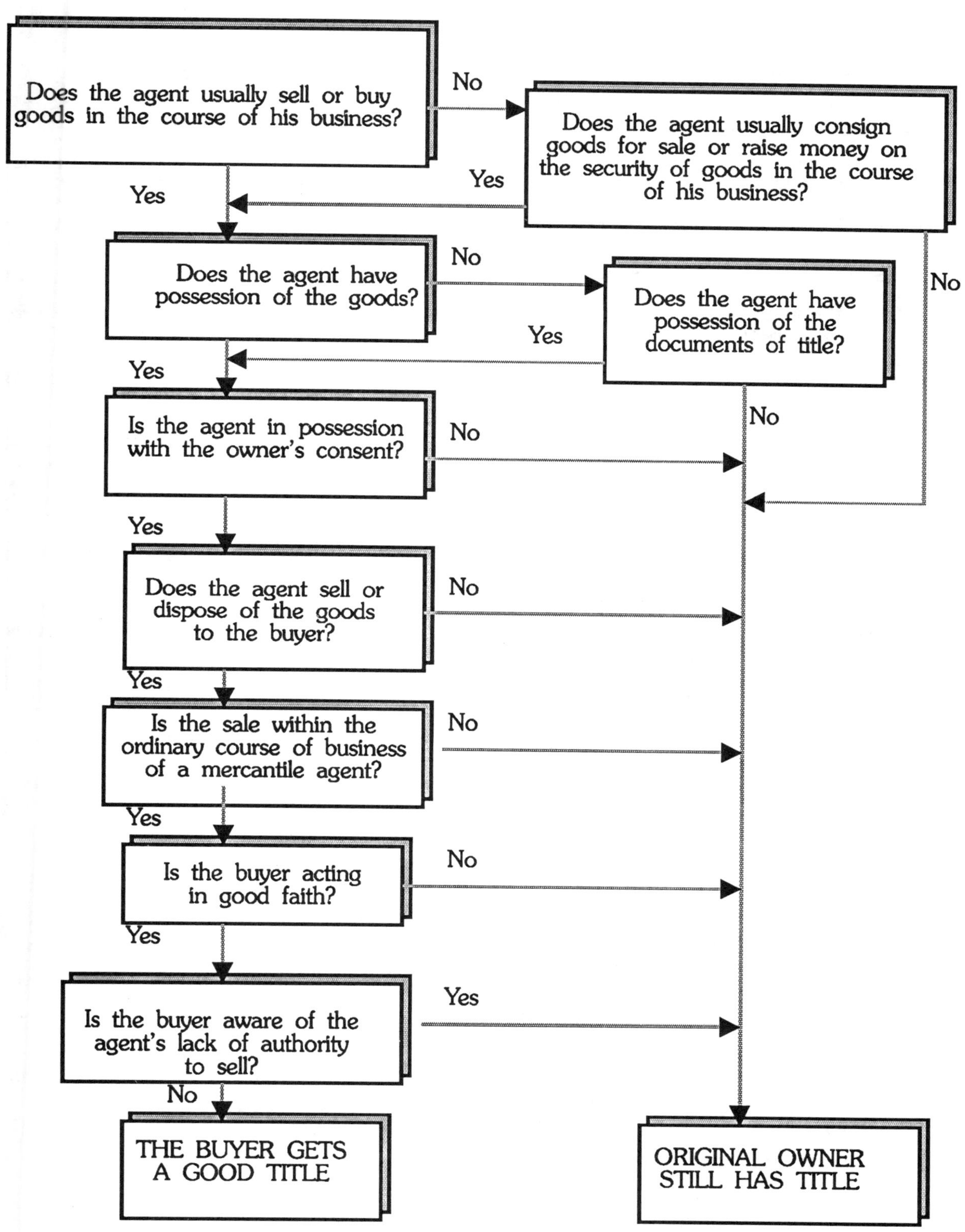

Fig. 9.5 Sale by a Mercantile Agent in Possession S2 (1) Factors Act 1889

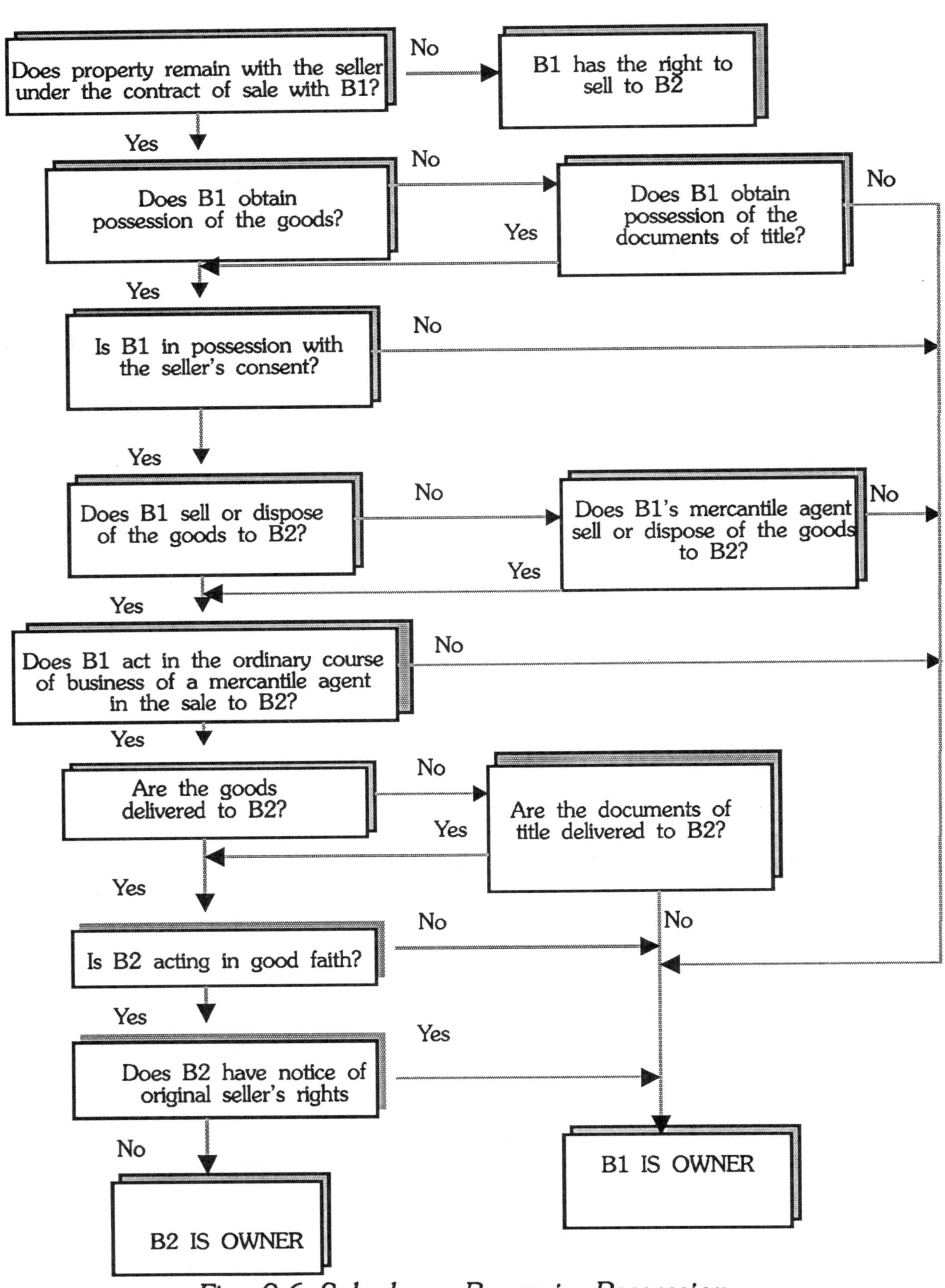

Fig. 9.6 Sale by a Buyer in Possession: Section 25 Sale of Goods Act 1979

The rule in s.25 will only apply where the seller retains ownership of goods which are in the buyer's possession after a contract of sale. This situation could occur under s.18 r.2 or r.3, although more usually it would be one in which there is a retention of title clause in the contract.

> In *Newtons of Wembley Ltd. v. Williams* 1964 the plaintiff sold a car to a rogue and was paid by cheque. The parties expressly agreed that ownership of the car would remain with the plaintiff until the cheque was cleared. The rogue took the car, with its registration book, and resold it to the defendant in Warren Street, London, a recognised second hand car market where dealers regularly operated. The defendant purchased the car in good faith and without notice. The rogue's cheque was dishonoured and the plaintiff claimed the car from the defendant. The Court of Appeal held that the rogue was a buyer in possession under s.25. The requirements of the section were satisfied and the defendant obtained a good title to the car.

> In *Four Point Garage Ltd. v. Carter* 1985 the seller sold a car to B1, who resold it to B2, the defendant. Each contract contained a retention of title clause. The defendant paid B1 for the car. B1, who became insolvent, had not paid the plaintiff. It was held that, although property had not passed to B1, he was a buyer in possession and the defendant obtained good title to the car under s.25.

Where the original seller has a defective title to goods, it appears that B2, the sub-buyer from the buyer in possession, will not obtain title under s.25. The House of Lords has recently held that the section does not have the effect of perfecting the defective title.

> In *National Employers Mutual Insurance Association Ltd. v. Jones* 1988 a car was stolen, and eventually, after passing through the hands of a number of dealers, it was bought in good faith by the defendant. The original owner sued for the return of the car, but the defendant claimed to have acquired a good title to it by virtue of s.25(1), because the previous purchaser, Mid Glamorgan Motors, had bought the car from an earlier purchaser, Autochoice, and obtained possession with the consent of Autochoice. The effect of this, the defendant argued, was as if Mid Glamorgan Motors were a mercantile agent in possession of the goods with the consent of the owner (ie the plaintiff). The defendants argument was consistent with a literal interpretation of s.25(1). The House of Lords, however, decided that the plaintiff was entitled to the return of the car, declining to give a literal interpretation to the word 'owner' at the end of s.25(1), and preferring to interpret it as meaning the earlier non owning seller (ie Autochoice on the facts). A bona fide purchaser was not able to override the true owner's title when the true owner had ceased to have possession of the goods because they were stolen.

Sale of a motor vehicle subject to a hire purchase agreement

This exception is contained in Part III of the Hire Purchase Act 1964. It applies where the debtor under a hire purchase or conditional sale agreement disposes of a motor vehicle before property passes to him under the terms of the credit agreement. The exception applies to motor vehicles only and not to goods of any other type.

The Hire Purchase Act 1964, in s.27 provides:

> *"Where a motor vehicle has been let under a hire purchase agreement, or has been agreed to be sold under a conditional sale agreement, and, at a time before*

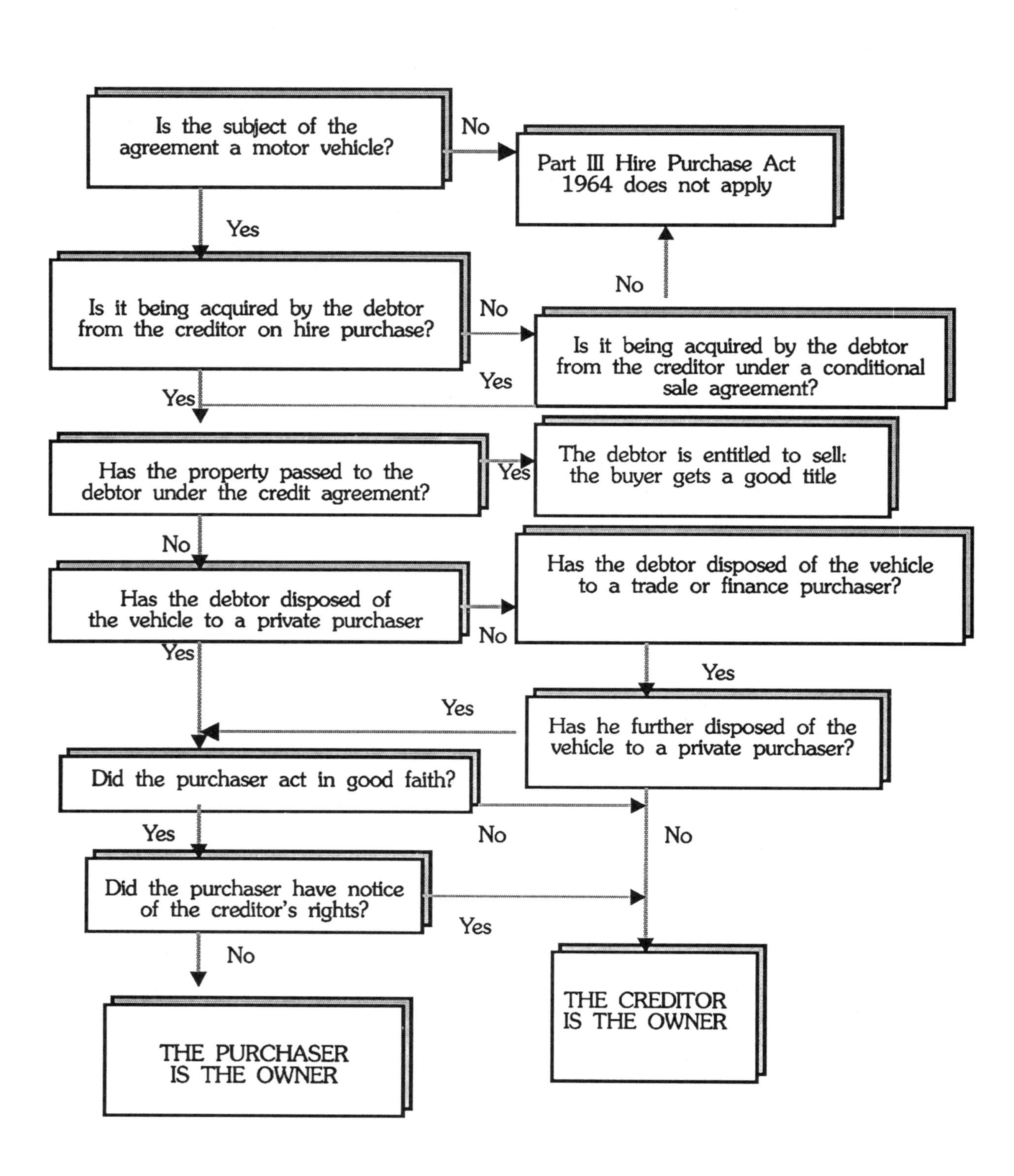

Fig. 9.7 Sale of Motor Vehicle while on Hire Purchase: Part III Hire Purchase Act 1964

the property in the vehicle has become vested in the hirer or buyer, he disposes of the vehicle ... to a private purchaser ... in good faith and without notice of the hire purchase agreement or conditional sale agreement, that disposition shall have effect as if the title of the owner or seller to the vehicle had been vested in the hirer or buyer immediately before that disposition."

Only a private purchaser of a motor vehicle is protected by s.27 A 'trade or finance purchaser', for example a garage or finance company, is not protected by the section because there are facilities, within these trades, to check up on the existence of an outstanding credit agreement relating to any motor vehicle. However, where a trade or finance purchaser buys a motor vehicle and then resells it, the first private purchaser to buy it will obtain the original creditor's title under s.27.

A private purchaser will be protected by s.27 so long as he acts in good faith and has no notice of the rights of the original creditor.

> In *Barker v. Bell* 1971 the debtor had a car on hire purchase from a finance company. Before he paid off the sums due under the hire purchase agreement, he sold the car to an innocent private purchaser. He told the purchaser that the car had been subject to a hire purchase agreement which was paid off, and showed him a receipt marked with the words 'final payment'. The Court of Appeal held that property passed to the purchaser by virtue of s.27 of the 1964 Act. The finance company's argument that the purchaser had notice of the hire purchase agreement was rejected. In his judgment, Lord Denning stated that:
>
> *"A purchaser is only affected by notice if he has actual notice that the car is on hire purchase. He is not affected merely by being told that it was previously on hire purchase which has now been paid off".*

Delivery Acceptance and Payment

Delivery

Section 27 of the 1979 Act sets out the basic obligations of the buyer and seller under the contract for the sale of goods:

"It is the duty of the seller to deliver the goods, and of the buyer to accept and pay for them in accordance with the contract of sale".

The rules relating to delivery and payment which are contained in the Act can be displaced by agreement between the parties, but where there is no such agreement the provisions of the Act apply. Section 28 provides:

"Unless otherwise agreed, delivery of the goods and payment of the price are concurrent conditions, that is to say, the seller must be ready and willing to give possession of the goods to the buyer in exchange for the price and the buyer must be ready and willing to pay the price in exchange for possession of the goods".

The sellers duty to deliver the goods does not necessarily mean that he has to take them physically to the buyer, as delivery is defined in s.61 as *'the voluntary transfer of possession from one person to another'*. Where there is no agreement to the contrary, the place of delivery, by s.29(2), is the seller's place of business, if he has one, and if not his residence. However, where the contract is for the sale of specific goods, which to the knowledge of the parties when the contract is made are in some other place, then that place is the place of delivery. Where the seller has agreed to convey the goods to the buyer, he must do so within a reasonable time, to arrive at a reasonable hour.

In any event, as we have previously seen, time for delivery is normally a condition rather than a warranty in a commercial contract under the rule in *Hartley v. Hyams* 1920. Thus if a delivery date is agreed and the seller fails to deliver on that date the buyer will be entitled to repudiate the contract and sue for damages.

Delivery by the seller of the wrong quantity of goods is dealt with by s.30 which states:

> *"(1) where the seller delivers to the buyer a quantity of goods less than he contracted to sell, the buyer may reject them, but if the buyer accepts the goods so delivered he must pay for them at the contract rate.*
>
> *(2) where the seller delivers to the buyer a quantity of goods larger than he contracted to sell, the buyer may accept the goods included in the contract and reject the rest, or he may reject the whole.*
>
> *(3) where the seller delivers to the buyer a quantity of goods larger than he contracted to sell and the buyer accepts the whole of the goods so delivered he must pay for them at the contract rate.*
>
> *(4) where the seller delivers to the buyer the goods he contracted to sell mixed with goods of a different description not included in the contract, the buyer may accept the goods which are in accordance with the contract and reject the rest or he may reject the whole".*

Damages for non delivery

Where the seller wrongfully neglects or refuses to deliver the goods to the buyer, the buyer can sue him for damages for non delivery under s.51. The measure of damages is the estimated loss directly and naturally resulting in the ordinary course of events from the seller's breach of contract. Under s.51(3) the measure of damages, where there is an available market for the goods in question, is prima facie the difference between the contract price and the market price at the time that the goods ought to have been delivered, or if no time for delivery was fixed, at the time of the refusal to deliver. It may be noted that under s.51 the amount of damages to which the buyer is entitled may be different to the actual losses which he has suffered.

Payment

It is the duty of the buyer to accept and pay for the goods, under s.28, and in the absence of contrary agreement the buyer is not bound to make payment until delivery is made. However, it is possible where the goods have been accidentally destroyed or stolen, and risk has been transferred to the buyer under the terms of the contract, that he will be liable to make payment even if delivery never takes place.

In the event of non payment by the buyer, the seller can sue him for the price under s.49 provided the buyer has wrongfully refused or neglected to pay according to the terms of the contract, and either property has passed to the buyer or the price is payable on a fixed date irrespective of delivery. In addition to an action for the price, the seller may be able to obtain damages under s.37(1), which provides:

> *"When the seller is ready and willing to deliver the goods, and requests the buyer to take delivery, and the buyer does not within a reasonable time after such request take delivery of the goods, he is liable to the seller for any loss occasioned by his neglect or refusal to take delivery, and also for a reasonable charge for the care and custody of the goods".*

Damages for non acceptance

If the conditions of s.49 are not fulfilled, and the seller is unable to sue for the price, he may nonetheless be able to sue for damages for non-acceptance under s.50 where the buyer refuses to accept and pay for the goods. The measure of damages where the seller can resell the goods is the difference between the contract price and the market price at the time the goods ought to have been accepted.

The sellers rights in regard to non acceptance have been curtailed in a limited way by regulations made under the European Communities Act 1972. These are the Consumer Protection (Cancellation of Contracts) Regulations 1987 which apply where a consumer has purchased goods from a doorstep trader who has called on an unsolicited visit. Where the total payment for the goods exceeds £35, the consumer can cancel the contract within seven days. The regulations bring this type of sale into line with the provisions for cancellation of credit transactions under the Consumer Credit Act 1974, discussed below.

Rights of the unpaid seller

Where the seller is unpaid, either because the whole of the price has not been paid to him or because he has received a form of conditional payment, such as a cheque, which has been dishonoured, he may be able to exercise 'real' remedies over the goods themselves. The first of these remedies is a lien, or a right to withhold delivery until payment is made. This arises under s.41 where either no credit was agreed, or an agreed credit period has expired, or the buyer has become insolvent; and the goods are still in the seller's possession. He may keep the goods until payment is made, and may ultimately be able to resell them under s.48.

The second is a right of stoppage in transit which arises under s.44 where the buyer becomes insolvent and the unpaid seller has parted with goods to a carrier. The seller may stop the goods at any time before they reach the buyer or his agent, and retain them pending payment of the price.

The unpaid seller may have a right of resale under s.48(3) which provides:

> *"Where the goods are of a perishable nature, or where the unpaid seller gives notice to the buyer of his intention to resell and the buyer does not within a reasonable time pay or tender the price, the unpaid seller may resell the goods and recover from the original buyer damages for any loss occasioned by his breach of contract."*

In addition to the unpaid seller's rights of lien, stoppage and resale, the seller may benefit from further valuable protection in the event of non payment, or the insolvency of the buyer, where there is a retention of title clause in the contract. As we have seen, this may enable the unpaid seller to reclaim goods, or the proceeds of sale of goods, in the hands of the buyer.

Rejection of the goods by the buyer

It was noted earlier that the remedy available to a buyer in the event of a breach of any term of a contract by the seller depends upon whether the term is classified as a condition or a warranty. Most of the implied terms by statute into contracts for the supply of goods are conditions, and the buyer's remedy for breach, in addition to damages, will be to reject the goods and recover the price. It is of course open to the buyer to choose to affirm the contract, thereby waiving his right to reject but retaining the right to sue for damages.

The right to reject may also be lost, in the case of a sale of goods contract, where there has been an acceptance of the goods by the buyer. This is provided for in s.11(4) of the Sale of Goods Act 1979, which states:

> *"Where a contract of sale is not severable, and the buyer has accepted the goods, or part of them, the breach of a condition to be fulfilled by the seller can only be treated as a breach of warranty, and not as a ground for rejecting the goods and treating the contract as repudiated, unless there is an express or implied term of the contract to that effect".*

Where the buyer has accepted the goods, then, he loses the right of rejection but still has a claim for damages, which is the normal remedy for breach of warranty. The situations in which the buyer will be deemed to have accepted the goods are set out in s.34 and s.35. Section 34 deals with the buyer's right to examine the goods, and provides:

> *"(1) where the goods are delivered to the buyer, and he has not previously examined them, he is not deemed to have accepted them until he has had a reasonable opportunity of examining them for the purpose of ascertaining whether they are in conformity with the contract.*
>
> *(2) Unless otherwise agreed, when the seller tenders delivery of the goods to the buyer, he is bound, on request, to afford the buyer a reasonable opportunity of examining the goods for the purpose of ascertaining whether they are in conformity with the contract".*

Section 35(1) states:

> *"The buyer is deemed to have accepted the goods when he intimates to the seller that he has accepted them, or (except where s.34 otherwise provides) when the goods have been delivered to him, and he does any act in relation to them which is inconsistent with the ownership of the seller, or when after the lapse of a reasonable time, he retains the goods without intimating to the seller that he has rejected them".*

Where a buyer resells goods without examining them - an act clearly inconsistent with the seller's ownership - the question of acceptance will depend upon whether he has had a reasonable opportunity of examination. This in turn will depend on the place of examination under the contract. In *Perkins v. Bell* 1893 it was held that there is a presumption that the place of delivery under the contract is the place where inspection ought to take place. If the buyer fails to examine them there and forwards them to a sub-buyer, he will lose the right to reject if it transpires that the seller is in breach of a condition of the contract. However, the rule in *Perkins v. Bell* is only a presumption, and not an absolute rule. It will be displaced if, for example, it would not be reasonable to inspect at the place of delivery, or where a different place of examination is within the contemplation of the parties.

> In *Molling & Co. v. Dean & Son* 1901 the buyer ordered a large quantity of books to be produced by the plaintiffs intending, to the plaintiffs knowledge,

to resell them directly to a sub-buyer abroad. The plaintiffs packed them for shipment to the sub-buyer and the buyer took delivery. Without inspection the buyer forwarded the goods to the sub-buyer, who rejected them for breach of condition. The buyer in turn rejected the goods and the plaintiffs sued for the price, arguing that the buyer had accepted the goods by shipping them to the sub-buyer. It was held that the buyer had not accepted the goods. As the goods had been packed for the sub-buyer by the plaintiffs, it was within the contemplation of the parties that the place of inspection was on delivery to the sub-buyer. The buyer had not therefore had a reasonable opportunity to examine the goods previously and were entitled to reject them.

A purchaser who retains goods for longer than a reasonable time without giving notice of rejection will be deemed to have accepted them under s.35(1)

In *Lee v. York Coach and Marine* 1977 a buyer purchased a second hand car which had defective brakes. The seller was therefore in breach of the implied condition that the car would be of merchantable quality. The buyer purported to reject the car some five months after taking delivery. It was held that she had accepted the car by retaining it beyond a reasonable time. Her only remedy was damages as she had lost the right of rejection.

Whilst it would be difficult to argue with the conclusion in the *Lee* case that retention of goods for five months was beyond a reasonable time, the decision in a more recent case that a period of three weeks is to be regarded in the same way is perhaps more surprising.

In *Bernstein v. Pamson Motors (Golders Green) Ltd.* 1987 the plaintiff purchased a new Nissan car from the defendant for £8,000. The plaintiff was ill at the time of the purchase and consequently did not use the car a great deal. Three weeks after delivery, when the car had done only 140 miles, the engine seized up. The plaintiff rejected the car on the grounds that it was not of merchantable quality, and demanded the return of the purchase price. The defendant repaired the car so that it was as good as new, but the plaintiff refused to take it back. Rougier J., in the High Court, held that the car was not of merchantable quality and that the plaintiff was entitled to damages, assessed at £250. He was not, however, entitled to reject the car because, by driving it for 140 miles, and retaining it for three weeks, he had accepted the car within the meaning of s.35(1).

Specific performance

Section 52 provides:

"In any action for breach of contract to deliver specific or ascertained goods the court may, if it thinks fit, by its judgment or decree direct that the contract shall be performed specifically, without giving the defendant the option of retaining the goods on payment of damages".

The court will refuse to make an order of specific performance where damages would be an adequate remedy.

In *Societe des Industries Metallurgiques SA v. Bronx Engineering Co. Ltd.* 1975 for example, the Court refused to make an order in relation to a machine manufactured by the defendants even though another such machine was not available on the market immediately. The plaintiff was awarded damages for the defendant's breach of contract, including a sum for losses sustained while waiting for up to a year a new machine to be built.

Consumer Credit

The Consumer Credit Act 1974 was introduced with the aim of ensuring 'truth in lending'. The Act applies to a wide range of types of credit agreement and places strict controls upon persons who provide credit facilities in the course of their business. Overall responsibility for administering the Act lies with the Director General of Fair Trading. The Act creates many criminal offences and enforcement in relation to these is by local authority Trading Standards Officers.

Agreements regulated by the Act fall within two broad categories, consumer hire agreements (defined above), and consumer credit agreements. Under s.8:

> *"A consumer credit agreement is an agreement between an individual (the debtor) and any other person (the creditor) by which the creditor provides the debtor with credit not exceeding £15,000".*

The agreement must be for the provision of 'credit'. This is defined in wide terms by s.9(1) to include 'cash loans and any other form of financial accommodation'. Hire purchase, conditional sale and credit sale agreements will all be consumer credit agreements if they satisfy the other elements of the definition. Certain types of credit agreement, particularly those concerned with the purchase and development of land and buildings, are excluded from the operation of the Act and are not consumer credit agreements.

An agreement will not be a consumer credit agreement where:

(a) the debtor is a limited company, and therefore not 'an individual' (a flesh and blood person), or

(b) the amount of credit provided is in excess of £15,000.

In these cases most of the provisions of the Act will not apply and the agreement will be governed by common law principles.

Licensing of creditors

Any person who intends to carry on the business of providing credit cannot do so unless he first obtains a licence from the Director General of Fair Trading. The Director General must grant a licence to any person who makes an application, provided he is satisfied that:

(a) the name under which the business is operating is neither misleading nor undesirable, and

(b) the applicant is a fit person to engage in the activities covered by licence.

A consumer credit agreement made with an unlicensed creditor is not enforceable against the debtor without the consent of the Director General of Fair Trading.

Equal liability of the creditor and the supplier

Earlier in this chapter it was noted that many credit transactions involved three parties: debtor, creditor, and supplier. The policy of the 1974 Act is to make the creditor, in addition to the supplier, answerable to the debtor if anything goes wrong. This applies only where a business connection exists between the creditor and the supplier, for example where the supplier has an arrangement with a particular finance company under which the company provides credit for all suitable customers of the supplier. Because the creditor is responsible for the acts of the supplier, he will be careful to deal only with suppliers who are reputable. The long term aim of this policy is to raise general standards of trading and squeeze 'cowboy' suppliers out of business. The policy is reflected in s.56 and s.75 of the Act.

Where there is a business connection between the supplier and the creditor, the supplier is deemed, by s. 56, to be the agent of the creditor when he negotiates with the debtor before a consumer credit agreement is made. If the debtor is induced to enter an agreement by the supplier's misrepresentation, he is entitled under s.56 to exercise a right of rescission against the creditor.

Under s.75 the debtor can claim against the creditor, as well as the supplier, for any breach of contract or misrepresentation by the supplier. Again this applies only where there is a business connection between the creditor and the supplier. At common law the debtor could claim, under the rule in *Andrews v. Hopkinson* 1956, against the supplier only and had no claim against the creditor. The effect of s.75 can be far reaching, for example if goods are purchased with a credit card (such as Access or Barclaycard), the finance company behind the card can be sued for the retailer's breach of contract or misrepresentation.

Where the debtor sues the creditor under s.56 or s.75, the creditor in turn has a right of indemnity from the supplier.

Annual percentage rate (APR)

The Act introduces a uniform system which all lenders must use in quoting the cost of credit. This is the annual percentage rate or APR. It enables the consumer to make a true comparison between interest rates and other costs charged by one lender as against those charged by another.

Prior to the introduction of APR there was no standard method of calculating the percentage rate. At that time loans on identical terms in relation to interest and other costs could be advertised at widely varying rates, depending upon the statistical method used to calculate the rate. Consumers therefore had no reliable yardstick against which the different deals on offer could be measured.

All traders must now calculate the cost of credit using the statistical method laid down by the Act. The APR, arrived at in this way, must be shown on certain types of credit advertisement, for example in newspapers, catalogues or shop windows. In addition, the consumer has the right to ask for a written quotation of credit terms, which must specify the APR, where a trader advertises that credit is available.

Form and content of consumer credit agreements

The Consumer Credit Act lays down strict rules governing the form and content of agreements. The object of the rules is to protect the debtor by giving him the fullest possible information about his rights and obligations.

The agreement must be in a form which complies with regulations made under the Act. It must contain details of such things as:

(a) the names and addresses of the parties

(b) the APR

(c) the cash price

(d) any deposit

(e) the amount of credit

(f) the total amount payable

(g) the amount of each payment

(h) repayment dates

(i) sums payable on default

(j) certain rights and protections under that Act.

The agreement must be in writing and signed personally by the debtor. If either of these requirements is not met, the creditor will be unable to sue the debtor if he defaults, for example by stopping his payments.

The debtor must receive a copy of the agreement when he signs it, and a further copy as soon as it has been signed by the creditor. If this requirement is not complied with, the creditor cannot sue the debtor, or enforce the agreement in any other way, for example by repossession, unless he previously obtains the permission of the court.

Credit reference agencies

A credit reference agency is an organisation which collects financial information about individuals. This includes a person's record in paying off debts and previous credit agreements, and outstanding judgments recorded against them in the county court. Creditors will usually consult credit reference agencies before entering into agreements with new customers. There are two national credit reference agencies.

These are:
CCM Systems limited,
Talbot House,
Talbot Street,
Nottingham NG1 5HF.

and
Credit Data Limited,
Regency House,
38 Whitworth Street,
Manchester M60 1QH.

In addition there are a number of local agencies. Where an individual applies for credit he may require the trader to provide him with the name and address of any credit reference agency which has been consulted about him.

An individual has the right, under s.158 of the 1974 Act, to know what information is being held about him by a credit reference agency. He also has the right to correct any false information in the file kept by the agency. To exercise this right he must make a written request, containing sufficient particulars to enable the agency to identify the file, and accompanied by a fee of £1.

The agency must supply the individual with a copy of any file which it keeps relating to him. The copy must be in plain English and accompanied by a notice of the individual's right to correct false information. If the agency does not keep a file relating to the individual, it must write informing him of that fact.

If any of the information in the file is incorrect, the individual can ask the agency to correct it. If the agency refuses to alter the file to the satisfaction of the individual, or if it does not reply within 28 days of a request, the individual can write a note of correction of up to 200 words.

The agency must add the note of correction to the file. It also has a duty to send details of the correction to anyone who obtained information from the file within the previous 6 months.

An agency will be guilty of a criminal offence if it fails to comply with a duty imposed on it by the 1974 Act.

Cooling off and cancellation

It is a well established principle of the law of contract that once an agreement has been entered into, cancellation by one of the parties is a breach of contract which entitles the other to sue for damages. The Consumer Credit Act 1974 provides an important exception to this principle.

An agreement will be cancellable under the Act where:

(a) statements are made by the trader in the presence of the debtor prior to making the agreement, and

(b) the debtor signs the agreement at a place other than the trader's place of business, for example at home.

The right of cancellation typically applies to credit transactions entered into with doorstep salesmen, although the right exists whenever the above conditions are fulfilled. Where an agreement is cancellable, it must contain a notice informing the debtor of his right to cancel. The agreement can be cancelled at any time up to the end of the fifth full day after it has been signed by both parties.

Notice of cancellation must be given in writing. It can be expressed in any manner, so long as it indicates an intention to withdraw from the agreement. Where a debtor exercises the right to cancel, he ceases to be liable under the agreement and is entitled to the return of all sums paid by him.

Default by the debtor

default notice

Where a debtor is in breach of a consumer credit agreement, the creditor cannot terminate the agreement or demand early payment or recover possession of goods until a "default notice" has been served on the debtor. The notice must in the form prescribed by the Act. It must specify the nature of the breach, the action required to remedy it, and the date (giving at least 7 days) by which remedial action must be taken.

The creditor cannot take any steps to enforce an agreement until the date specified in the notice has passed. If the debtor complies with a default notice within the required period, the breach of agreement by him is treated as not having occurred.

protected goods

Where the debtor under a hire purchase or conditional sale agreement has paid at least one third of the total price, the goods are 'protected goods'. If the debtor is in default of the agreement, the creditor at common law has an unrestricted right to repossess the goods because at this stage he still owns them. However, under s.90 of the 1974 Act, the creditor cannot retake possession of protected goods without either a court order or the debtor's permission. If he does so the agreement terminates. The debtor is released from all liability under it. In addition he is entitled to recover from the creditor all sums previously paid by him under the agreement.

In *Capital Finance v. Bray* 1964 a finance company repossessed a car without a court order. As the debtor had repaid more than one third of the total price, the car was covered by the protected goods rules. The company, realising its mistake, returned the car to the debtor by leaving it outside his house. The debtor used the car for several months but refused to make any further payments. The finance company sued for payment. The debtor counterclaimed for the return of all money paid by him under the agreement. It was held that the finance company had wrongfully repossessed the car and could not correct the mistake by returning it to the debtor. The debtor was entitled to repayment of all sums which he had paid under the agreement.

Extortionate credit bargains

Under s.137 of the 1974 Act, the courts have power to re-open any credit agreement, whether or not it is a consumer credit agreement, which is part of an extortionate credit bargain, and relieve a debtor from payment of any sum in excess of that which is fair and reasonable. The courts have wide powers under this section and can order a creditor to repay all or part of any sum already paid; or set aside any obligation imposed on the debtor, or alter the agreement in any other way in order to do justice between the parties.

A credit bargain is extortionate under the Act if it requires the debtor to make payments which are *'grossly exorbitant'* or which otherwise *'grossly contravene the ordinary principles of fair dealing'*. In order to determine whether a credit bargain is extortionate a number of factors will be taken into account, including:

(a) interest rates prevailing at the time it was made;

(b) the age, experience, business capacity and state of health of the debtor;

(c) the degree and nature of any financial pressure on the debtor when the bargain was made;

(d) the degree of risk accepted by the creditor and his relationship to the debtor;

(e) whether or not a cash price was quoted;

(f) how far any linked transaction was reasonably required for the protection of the creditor, or was in the interest of the debtor.

In *A. Ketley v. Scott* 1981 the defendant borrowed £20,500 in order to enable him to complete the purchase of a house. The money was released by the plaintiff on the same day that he was approached for the loan. The defendant did not tell him that his bank account was £2,000 overdrawn, the bank had a first mortgage on the house, and he was also liable under a £5,000 guarantee. Nor did he disclose that the house had been valued at £24,000. The loan was for three months at an annual rate of interest of 48%. At the expiry of its term the plaintiff sued for repayment of capital and interest. The defendant counterclaimed for the re-opening of the agreement as an extortionate credit bargain. It was held that the plaintiff was entitled to enforce the agreement. This was not an extortionate credit bargain because the lender had taken a considerable risk; obtained little security; had been deceived by the defendant; had no time to check the defendant's financial position, and advanced the money with extraordinary speed.

Termination by the debtor

A debtor under a hire purchase or conditional sale agreement may terminate the agreement under s.99 at any time before the final payment falls due. He must give notice in writing to the creditor, or to any person authorised to receive payment on the creditor's behalf. The debtor must return the goods to the creditor.

Under s.100 the debtor's liability on termination is limited to:

(a) any sums already due for payment before the date on which he exercises the right of termination; and

(b) a further sum to bring his total payments up to one half of the total price (or less if the agreement so provides) or any lesser sum which in the opinion of the court represents the creditor's loss on termination; and

(c) if he has broken an obligation to take reasonable care of the goods, compensation for this.

Contracting out

Under s.173 of the 1974 Act it is not possible to insert a term into a consumer credit agreement which takes away any of the protection given to the debtor by the Act. Contracting out is absolutely prohibited.

Administrative Machinery of Consumer Protection

Both central and local government have important roles to play in the field of consumer protection. The major role of central government is the promotion and implementation of legislation, whilst the enforcement of this legislation is mainly the responsibility of local government.

The role of central government in consumer protection

The consumer protection responsibilities of central government are spread across a number of departments, many of which have a junior minister with responsibility for consumer affairs.

The Home Office has responsibility for liquor licensing, dangerous drugs and poisons; as well as explosives and firearms.

The Department of Trade's responsibilities in the field of consumer protection include weights and measures, consumer credit, fair trading, consumer safety, trading standards, and monopolies, mergers and restrictive practices. The Department is also responsible for a number of national consumer protection bodies, including:

(a) the Office of Fair Trading

(b) the Monopolies and Mergers Commission

(c) the British Hallmarking Council

(d) the National Consumer Council

(e) the Consumer Protection Advisory Committee

(f) the Nationalised Industry Consumer Councils

and

(g) the British Standards Institution.

The Ministry of Agriculture Fisheries and Food looks after food and drugs, food additives, pesticides, and public health standards in slaughterhouses. The Food Safety Directorate created in 1989, has specific responsibility for food safety matters.

The Office of Fair Trading

The Office of Fair Trading, created by the Fair Trading Act 1973, has a significant national role in relation to the broad task of protecting the interests of the consumer. The 1973 Act created the post of Director General of Fair Trading. The Director has wide powers under the 1973 Act and other legislation, notably the Consumer Credit Act 1974 and the Estate Agents Act 1979.

The duties of the Director are:

(a) to review commercial activities and report to the Secretary of State;

(b) to refer adverse trade practices to the Consumer Protection Advisory Committee;

(c) to take action against traders who are persistently unfair to consumers;

(d) to supervise the enforcement of the Consumer Credit Act 1974 and the administration of the licensing system under that Act;

(e) to arrange for information and advice to be published for the benefit of consumers in relation to the supply of goods and services and consumer credit;

(f) to encourage trade associations to produce voluntary Codes of Practice; and

(g) to superintend the working and enforcement of the Estate Agents Act 1979.

Review of commercial practices

Under this general heading the Director has three functions:

(i) to keep under review commercial activities in the U.K. relating to the supply of goods and services to consumers; and to collect information about these activities in order to become aware of practices which may adversely affect the *economic interests* of consumers;

(ii) to receive and collect evidence of commercial activities which he thinks are adversely affecting the *general interests* of consumers, for example on economic, health or safety grounds;

(iii) to supply information relating to adverse trade practices to the Secretary of State and make recommendations as to any action which the Director considers necessary to combat them.

Referral of adverse trade practices to the Consumer Protection Advisory Committee

The Director has power to refer to the Consumer Protection Advisory Committee any consumer trade practice which in his opinion adversely affects the economic interests of consumers. The type of activity which can give rise to such a reference include trade practices relating to:

(i) the terms or conditions on which goods or services are supplied,

(ii) the manner in which those terms or conditions are communicated to the consumer,

(iii) promotion of goods or services by advertising, labelling or marking of goods, or canvassing,

(iv) methods of salesmanship employed in dealing with consumers,

(v) the way in which goods are packed, or

(vi) methods of demanding or securing payments for goods or services supplied.

A reference by the Director may include proposals for the creation of delegated legislation by the Secretary of State. The Director has power to make such proposals where he considers that a consumer trade practice is likely to have any one of the following effects:

(i) misleading consumers as to their rights and obligations under the transactions; or

(ii) withholding adequate information on the rights and obligations of consumers; or

(iii) subjecting consumers to undue pressure to enter into transactions; or

(iv) causing the terms of the consumer transactions in question to be so adverse as to be oppressive.

The Consumer Protection Advisory Committee must report to the Secretary of State, usually within three months, indicating whether it agrees with the Director's proposals as they stand, or in a modified form. If so the Secretary of State may make regulations giving effect to the proposals. Under s.22 of the 1973 Act it is a criminal offence to contravene any such regulations.

Examples of regulations made under this procedure include the Consumer Transactions (Restrictions on Statements) Order 1976 and (Amendment) Order 1978, and the Business Advertisements (Disclosure) Order 1977, which were examined in the last chapter. Another example is the Mail Order Transactions (Information) Order 1976, which applies to goods sold by mail order which have to be paid for in advance. Under the regulations, any advertisement for such goods must state the true name or company name of the person carrying on the mail order business, as well as the true address of the business. Thus, for example, an advertiser giving only a P.O. Box number would be committing an offence if he required payment in advance.

Taking action against persistently unfair traders

The Director has power to bring proceedings in the Restrictive Practices Court against any person who persistently maintains a course of conduct which is unfair to consumers. Before making a reference to the Court, the Director must first attempt to obtain a written assurance from the trader that he will refrain from the unfair trade practice. If the trader refuses to give an assurance, or breaks an assurance once it has been given, the Director must apply for an order restraining the continuance of the unfair conduct. If the trader does not comply with the order, he will be in contempt of court and liable to imprisonment.

A course of conduct will be regarded as being unfair to consumers if it involves a breach of any legal obligations, either criminal or civil, by the trader. Examples of unfair conduct include persistently giving short measure or applying false trade descriptions, or repeatedly delivering unmerchantable goods.

Encouraging voluntary Codes of Practice

The Director has a duty to encourage trade associations and other organisations to prepare Codes of Practice and circulate them to their members. The codes should be designed to give guidance to traders relating to the safeguarding and protection of the interests of consumers.

A code of practice is a statement by a trade association which aims to establish and define the standards of trading which it expects from its members. Voluntary codes of this type have been introduced, following consultation with the Office of Fair Trading, to cover many areas of business. Such codes often provide a mechanism for the arbitration of consumer complaints as an alternative to legal proceedings in the courts.

Codes of practice provide a means whereby, in effect, a sector of industry or commerce can regulate itself. There are a number of costs and benefits to this. The main advantages are:

(a) a code can encourage positive approach to trading standards and set high standards in excess of the legal minimum;

(b) a code can be changed fairly quickly in order to meet changing circumstances;

(c) a code can be expressed in non-technical language and interpreted positively according to its spirit;

(d) a code normally deals only with one type of business or product. It can be drawn up to meet particular problems which are likely to arise in the limited area which it covers. Legislation, on the other hand, usually applies to all sectors of business;

(e) a code can clarify the rights and obligations of the trader and the customer in simple language;

(f) a code can often provide procedures and remedies which are appropriate to its subject matter in a more flexible way than legislation.

There are, however, a number of drawbacks associated with self regulation by Codes of Practice. The main disadvantages are:

(a) limited sanctions are available in the event that a trader does not comply with the provisions of a code. The ultimate penalty is usually expulsion from the trade association. In some sectors at least, this is not a very real punishment;

(b) the trade association may be in a position of conflict of interests when drawing up a code. Its principal function is the protection of the interests of its members;

(c) the consumer may not be aware of the existence of a code or the remedies which it offers;

(d) a code will not apply to a trader who is not a member of the trade association. In some sectors, particularly where the trade association has a high profile, for example A.B.T.A. in the travel trade, most traders are members. In other sectors, however, only a minority of traders belong to a trade association.

The final point is perhaps the most significant disadvantage of the system of self regulation by codes of practice. In a discussion paper issued by the Office of Fair Trading in 1986, entitled 'A general duty to trade fairly', this problem was recognised. It was proposed that new legislation should be introduced to impose a duty on all traders, regardless of their membership of trade associations, to trade fairly. Compliance with a relevant code of practice would be enforced by the criminal law. As we shall see later, this model has been adopted by the Consumer Protection Act 1987 in relation to misleading price indications.

The role of local authorities in consumer protection

Responsibility for the enforcement of most consumer protection legislation, other than that which gives the consumer a right to sue for damages, rests with local authorities. It is carried out by trading standards or consumer protection departments. In practice, these departments see their major role as one of giving guidance to traders. This is done by a combination of education and persuasion. Prosecution for criminal offences is seen as a last resort when other measures fail.

Another important aspect of the work of these departments is the verification of weights and measuring apparatus, and the analysis of samples. They also act as a channel of information from members of the public to the Office of Fair Trading about unfair trade practices.

Trading standards officers have wide investigatory powers to enable them to carry out their enforcement functions effectively. They can make sample purchases of goods or services; enter premises; require suppliers to produce documents; carry out tests on equipment; and seize and detain property. A person who obstructs a trading standards officer, or makes a false statements to him commits a criminal offence.

Many Acts of Parliament and regulations made under them are enforced by trading standards officers. A number of these are examined below, including the Consumer Credit Act 1974, the Food Safety Act 1990, parts of the Road Traffic Act 1988, the Trade Descriptions Act 1968, the Weights and Measures Act 1985, the Unsolicited Goods and Services Act 1971, and the Consumer Protection Act 1987. Before we consider this legislation in detail we shall examine the power of the criminal courts to award compensation to the consumer following the conviction of a trader for a criminal offence.

Consumer Protection by Means of the Criminal Law

Most, but not all, of the criminal offences designed to protect the consumer apply only to persons supplying goods or services in the course of a trade or business. Enforcement of the criminal law in this area is, as we have seen, primarily the function of trading standards departments. Traders who are charged with criminal offences will be prosecuted in the Magistrates or the Crown Court. If convicted, they will be liable to a fine or, in some cases, imprisonment. Following a conviction the criminal courts also have power to make a 'compensation order' to the victim of the crime. In this context the victim will be the consumer who has suffered loss as a result of the offence.

The power to make a compensation order is contained in s.35 of the Powers of Criminal Courts Act 1973. This provides that any court convicting a person of an offence may, in addition to its sentencing power, make an order requiring the offender to pay compensation for any personal injury, loss or damage resulting from the offence or any other offence taken into consideration.

In deciding whether to make an order the court must take account of the ability of the defendant to pay. There is a limit of £1,000 compensation for each offence of which the accused is convicted. Under s.67 of the Criminal Justice Act 1982 the power to make compensation orders was extended. They may now be made "instead of or in addition to" a fine.

The power to make compensation orders is particularly useful from the point of view of the consumer. It saves him the trouble and expense of bringing proceedings in the civil courts. It will be used only in relatively straightforward cases, however. It is not designed to deal for example with complicated claims involving issues of causation or remoteness of damage.

The Food Safety Act 1990

The Food Safety Act 1990 is designed to strengthen consumer protection in relation to food safety, an area of increasing concern in recent years. The Act consolidates existing provision in this areas, adds a number of new regulatory powers and substantially increases the penalties for offences relating to the quality and safety of foods.

It is an offence, under s. 7, to process or treat food intended for sale for human consumption in any way which makes it injurious to health. Food is injurious to health if it causes any permanent or temporary impairment of health. The offence can be committed by food manufacturers, food handlers, retailers or restaurants. The offence may be committed, for example, by adding a harmful ingredient, or subjecting food to harmful treatment such as storing it at an incorrect temperature or storing cooked meat alongside uncooked meat.

Under s.8 of the Act, food intended for human consumption must satisfy the *food safety requirement*. It is an offence to sell, offer or have in one's possession for sale, prepare or deposit with another for sale any food which fails to meet this requirement. Food which is injurious to health, unfit for human consumption, or so contaminated that it is not reasonable to expect it to be eaten, will fail to satisfy the food safety requirement.

> In *David Greig Ltd. v. Goldfinch* 1961 a trader was convicted of selling food which was unfit for human consumption (under an equivalent provision in the Food and Drugs Act 1955). He sold a pork pie which had small patches of mould under the crust. The fact that the mould was of a type which was not harmful to human beings was held to be no defence to the charge.

It is an offence, under s.14 of the Food Safety Act, for a supplier to sell, to the prejudice of the consumer, any food which is not of the nature, substance or quality demanded. This provision is a restatement of previous law and again can be illustrated by reference to earlier caselaw. It may be noted that the gist of s.14 is the supply of something which is different from that which the consumer has requested, and that an offence may be committed where no illness or injury results, although often it may.

> In *Meah v. Roberts* 1978 an employee of a brewery cleaned the beer pumps and taps in a restaurant with caustic soda. He placed the remaining fluid in an empty lemonade bottle labelled 'cleaner' which he left for use by the restaurant. The caustic soda was mistakenly served to a customer who order lemonade. The customer became seriously ill as a result. It was held that the restaurant proprietor was guilty of the offence because the food was not of the nature demanded.

Liability under s.14 is strict and the trader may be guilty even though he has taken reasonable care.

> In *Smedleys Ltd. v. Breed* 1974 a customer was supplied with a tin of peas which contained a small green caterpillar. The caterpillar had been sterilised in the defendants' processes and did not constitute a danger to health. The defendants had an extremely efficient system for eliminating foreign bodies from their products. They were found to have taken all reasonable care to avoid the presence of the caterpillar in the tin. Nevertheless, their convic-

tion for supplying food which was not of the substance demanded was upheld by the House of Lords.

Section 15 of the Act creates a number of offences relating to the false description of food; including the publication of misleading advertisements, selling food which is falsely described, presenting food in a misleading way or selling food with a label which is likely to mislead the consumer as to its nature, substance or quality.

As with many other statutes creating criminal offences of strict liability, a number of defences are available, for example under s.20 it is a defence to a show that the commission of the offence was due to the act or default of another or, under s.21, that it was committed as a result of reliance on information supplied by another. Similarly, if the defendant can show that he exercised all due diligence and all reasonable precautions to avoid the commission of the offence, he will escape liability by virtue of s.21. These defences apply to charges for any offences brought under s.7, s.8, s.14 and s.15 of the Act.

The Ministry of Agriculture, Fisheries and Food has overall responsibility for food, and the Food Safety Directorate has particular responsibility for food safety matters. Under the Act the Minister has to make regulations in relation to food safety, governing such matters as the regulation of processes or treatments, the content and composition of food, presentation, labelling and packaging. The Minister also has powers to make 'emergency control orders' where it appears that an imminent risk of injury to health arises from commercial activities concerned with food; and power to require minimum standards of training for food handlers.

Responsibility for enforcing the Act lies mainly with local authority trading standards officers and environmental health officers. They have wide powers of inspection, entry to premises, taking samples and preventing the sale or movement of food. The Act makes provision for the registration of all food premises with the local authority, which will assist in enforcement by giving the authority more information about food premises in its area, and the power to prohibit their use as such if they are not registered.

The Weights and Measures Act 1985

The 1985 Act provides for the inspection and testing of weighing and measuring equipment for use in trade. Under s.17 of the Act it is an offence to use for trade, or to have in one's possession for use in trade, any weighing or measuring equipment which is false or unjust. It is also an offence under s.28 to give short weight or short measure.

The Act restricts the units of measurement which can lawfully be used by a trader. It lays down detailed requirements as to the packing, marking and making up of certain types of goods; and provides that, in relation to pre-packed or containerised goods, a written statement must be marked on the container giving information about the net quantity of its contents.

Consumer Credit Act 1974

Schedule 1 of the Consumer Credit Act 1974 contains a list of over 35 criminal offences associated with contravention of the Act. These include, for example, trading without a licence; failure to supply copies of consumer credit agreements; refusal of a trader to give the name of a credit reference agency which he has consulted; failure by a credit reference agency to correct information on its files; and obstruction of enforcement authority officers.

Road Traffic Act 1988

The Road Traffic Acts, and regulations made under them, contain a large number of criminal offences relating to the construction and use of motor vehicles and the safe loading of vehicles. Under s.75 of the 1988 Act it is an offence for any person, whether or not he is a trader, to sell or supply a motor vehicle which is unroadworthy. This offence will be committed where, for example, a vehicle is sold with defects in its braking or steering system or in its tyres. It is also an offence under s.75 to fit defective or unsuitable parts to a motor vehicle; and under s.17(2) to sell a motor cycle crash helmet which does not comply with safety regulations.

The Unsolicited Goods and Services Act 1971

This Act was passed to impose criminal and civil liability on traders carrying on the practice of *inertia selling*. This involves sending goods or providing services which have not been ordered and demanding payment or threatening legal action if payment is not made. The Act provides that unsolicited goods or services need not to be paid for, and unordered goods may be retained by the recipient if they are not collected by the sender within six months of delivery. It is an offence for the sender to demand payment for unsolicited goods or services.

Trade Descriptions Legislation

We have previously examined the circumstances in which a person would be regarded as transacting in the course of a trade or business. An important application of this question arises in relation to criminal liability under the Trade Descriptions Act 1968 for false statements made in business transactions. There can be no liability under the 1968 Act unless the person applying the false description does so within the course of a trade or business rather than a private sale. This is one reason why the Business Advertisements (Disclosure) Order 1977 requires a trader to identify himself as such when he advertises in the classified advertisements in newspapers. The fact that a business organisation is the vendor or purchaser does not automatically mean that a sale is in the course of a trade. The transaction must be of a type that is a regular occurrence in that particular business, so that a sale of business assets would not normally qualify as a sale in the course of a trade or business.

Where there is a genuine private sale and, for example, the seller falsely describes the goods, the buyer's remedy will be rescission. He may also claim damages in a civil law action for misrepresentation or breach of the term implied into the contract by s.13 of the Sale of Goods Act 1979. A buyer from a business seller can also exercise these remedies, but in addition may report the trader to the trading standards department with a view to a prosecution for a breach of the criminal law under the 1968 Act. In all trade descriptions cases there is potentially liability under the civil law which illustrates the fact that here consumer protection law is founded upon the interrelationship between civil and criminal activities. Prosecutions for trade description offences are brought in the Magistrates Court and exceptionally in the Crown Court with the possibility of an appeal to the Divisional Court of the Queen's Bench Division of the High Court by way of case-stated on a point of law. There is no requirement for a re-hearing of the evidence, rather the appeal court is concerned with determining the validity of the legal reasoning upon which the decision to convict or acquit is based.

Two principal offences under the Trade Descriptions Act 1968 relate to false description of goods, and making misleading statements about services. A number of defences are also provided for. Further offences of giving misleading price indications were originally contained in s.11 of the Act, and the Price Marking (Bargain Offers) Order 1979 made under the Prices

Act 1974. These offences have been replaced by others under Part III of the Consumer Protection Act 1987, and are considered separately below.

False Description of Goods

The 1968 Act provides, in s.1(1) that: *"Any person who, in the course of a trade or business:*

(a) applies a false trade description to any goods; or

(b) supplies or offers to supply any goods to which a false trade description is applied;

shall, subject to the provisions of this Act, be guilty of an offence".

Two different types of conduct will amount to offences under this section. The first is where the trader himself applies the false trade description contrary to s.1(1)(a). This offence could be committed, for example, by a trader who turns back the mileometer of a car to make it appear that the car has not travelled as many miles as it actually has. The second, under s.1(1)(b), involves supplying or offering to supply goods to which a false trade description has been applied by another person, for example where a retailer sells a garment to which the label "pure new wool" has been attached by the manufacturer, where the garment is partly composed of manmade fibres. There is a strict duty therefore not to pass on false trade descriptions applied by another subject to a defence which we will consider later.

In relation to the s.1(1)(b) offence, the trader will not be able to rely on a Fisher v. Bell type defence where he displays goods for sale.

> In *Fisher v. Bell* 1961, a shopkeeper who displayed flick knives for sale was acquitted of an offence of *"offering to supply"* them on the grounds that the display was an invitation to treat rather than a contractual offer.

The 1968 Act, in s.6, closes this loophole by providing that

> *"a person exposing goods for supply or having goods in his possession for supply shall be deemed to offer to supply them".*

A false trade description may be applied verbally or in writing, for example in a label on goods or in an advertisement, communicated by pictorial representation or even by conduct.

> In *Yugotours Ltd. v. Wadsley* 1988 a photograph of a three-masted schooner and the words "the excitement of being under full sail on board this majestic schooner" in a tour operator's brochure was held to constitute a statement for the purpose of the Act. By providing customers who had booked a holiday relying on the brochure with only a two masted schooner without sails the tour operator was guilty of recklessly making a false statement contrary to the Trade Descriptions Act.

The meaning of the term "trade description" extends, by s.2, to statements relating to quantity, size, composition, method of manufacture, fitness for purpose, place or date of manufacture, approval by any person or other history including previous ownership of goods.

> In *Sherratt v. Geralds The American Jewellers Ltd.* 1970 the defendant sold a watch described by the maker as a diver's watch and inscribed with the word "waterproof". The watch filled with water and stopped after it had been immersed in water. It was held that the defendant was guilty of an offence under s.1(1)(b).

To constitute an offence under the Act the trade description must be false or misleading to a material degree.

In *Robertson v. Dicicco* 1972 a secondhand motor vehicle was advertised for sale by a dealer and described as "a beautiful car". The car, although having a visually pleasing exterior was unroadworthy and not fit for use. The defendant was charged with an offence under s.1(1)(a). He argued that his statement was true as he had intended it to refer only to the visual appearance of the vehicle. It was held that he was guilty because the description was false to a material degree. A reasonable person would have taken the statement to refer to the mechanics of the car as well as its external appearance.

A similar approach was taken in *Kensington and Chelsea Borough Council v. Riley* 1973 where the trader was convicted of an offence under s.1(1)(a). It was held that the description "in immaculate condition" was false when applied to a car which required repairs costing £250 to make it roadworthy.

A trade description applied to goods for sale can be false for the purpose of s.1(1)(b) even when it is scientifically correct if it is likely to mislead a customer without specialist knowledge.

In *Dixon Ltd. v. Barnett* 1989 a customer was supplied with an Astral 500 telescope which was described as being capable of up to "455 x magnification". The evidence showed that the maximum useful magnification was only 120 times, although scientifically 455 times magnification could be achieved. The Divisional Court held that the store was nevertheless guilty of an offence despite the fact that the statement was scientifically sound. An ordinary customer would have been misled by the statement because he would be interested in the maximum useful magnification rather than a blurred image produced at 455 times magnification.

A half truth is false for the purpose of the Act, so that while it was technically true to describe a vehicle as only having one previous owner in *R v. Inner London Justices and another* 1983 the fact that the owner was a leasing company and the car had had five different keepers meant that the statement was grossly misleading and false.

In *Routledge v. Ansa Motors (Chester-le-Street) Limited* 1980 a Ford Escort motor car which was manufactured in 1972 was first registered in 1975. Subsequently it was advertised by the defendant as "a used 1975 Ford Escort". It was held that the defendant had applied a false trade description to the car, contrary to s. 1(1)(a).

Recently the Divisional Court in *Denard v. Smith and another* 1990 considered whether it is a false trade description to advertise goods in a shop at the point of sale as items offered for sale when they are temporarily out of stock and are not immediately available. The court held that unless customers are informed of the non-availability of the goods at the time of purchase the advertisement constituted a false trade description of offering to supply goods.

In order to be guilty of an offence under s.1, the trader must make the statement in connection with a sale or supply of goods.

In *Wickens Motors (Gloucester) Ltd. v. Hall* 1972 the purchaser of a car from the defendant complained about its performance. The complaint was made

40 days after the car had been supplied to him. The defendant told him that there was nothing wrong with the car, although this was untrue. It was held that the defendant was not guilty of an offence under s.1(1)(a) because there was insufficient connection between the false description and the sale.

An offence under s.1 may be committed by *"any person"*. This is not limited to the seller, but may include the buyer, particularly where he is an expert in relation to the subject matter of the contract.

In *Fletcher v. Budgen* 1974 a car dealer bought an old car from a customer for £2 saying that it was only fit to be scrapped. In fact the dealer repaired the car and advertised it for a resale for £135. It was held that he was guilty of an offence under s.1(1)(a) because he applied a false trade description to the car when he bought it in the course of his business.

Where defects in goods are disguised and the trader has no reason to realise or suspect that they are present, he will not be guilty of an offence under s.1(1)(b).

In *Cottee v. Douglas Seaton Ltd.* 1972 the bodywork of a car which had been in very poor condition was repaired using plastic body filler. This was smoothed down and the car repainted before it was sold to the defendant. The defendant was unaware of the fact that the bodywork was defective. He resold the car to a purchaser who subsequently discovered the defect. It was held that the disguised defects amounted to a false trade description as the goods, in effect, told a lie about themselves. The defendant was not guilty of an offence, however, because he was unaware that the description had been applied to the goods.

A person may be guilty of an offence under s.1(1)(b), even though he does not know the description is false, provided he knows that the description has been applied to the goods by another person. This situation may arise for example where a car dealer sells a car which records an incorrectly low mileage on its mileometer. If a dealer is uncertain as to the accuracy of the recorded mileage, he may try to ensure that a false trade description is not applied by displaying a notice disclaiming the accuracy of the mileage reading.

In *Norman v. Bennett* 1974 a customer bought a secondhand car with a recorded mileage of 23,000 miles. In fact the true mileage was about 68,000 miles. He signed an agreement containing a clause which said that the reading was not guaranteed. It was held that this was not an effective disclaimer. Lord Widgery, the Lord Chief Justice, stated that, in order to be effective, a disclaimer:

"must be as bold, precise and compelling as the trade desciption itself and must be as effectively brought to the notice of any person to whom the goods may be supplied. In other words, the disclaimer must equal the trade description in the extent to which it is likely to get home to anyone interested in receiving the goods".

The use of a disclaimer will be an effective defence providced it complies with the test laid down in *Norman v. Bennett.* The Motor Trade Code of Practice, approved by Director General of Fair Trading in 1976, recommends the use of the following form of wording in these circumstances:

"We do not guarantee the accuracy of the recorded mileage. To the best of our knowledge and belief, however the recording is correct/incorrect".

Clearly a disclaimer will only be an effective defence to a charge under s.1(1)(b). If the trader himself has turned back the mileage he will be unable to rely on this defence.

A disclaimer cannot exclude liability once it has arisen and is only effective to the extent that it prevents the commission of a criminal offence. The disclaimer could:

(a) prevent an indication being regarded as a trade description; or

(b) qualify a description so that it does not mislead; or

(c) qualify a description so that it is not false to a material degree.

Certainly it would be pointless to attempt to disclaim liability after an offence has already been committed.

> In *Doble v. David Greig Ltd.* 1972 the defendants displayed bottles of Ribena for sale in their self service store at a particular price with an indication that a deposit on each bottle was refundable on its return. At the cash till however, a different notice stated that in fact no deposit would be charged because in the interest of hygiene the store would not accept the return of empty bottles. The retailer was convicted of the offence of offering to supply goods with a false price indication. The court held that the offence of offering to supply was committed when the goods were displayed and the subsequent notice at the cash till was ineffective in disclaiming liability.

While a disclaimer may prevent the commission of an offence of offering to supply goods, it will not apply to an offence of applying a false trade description.

> In *Newham LBC v. Singh* 1988 as the defendant car dealer had not been aware that a car mileometer had been altered and had not been the person applying the false trade description to the car, he could successfully rely on a disclaimer when charged under s.1.

Finally, an important feature of disclaimers is that it is for the prosecution to establish the offence and prove that the disclaimer is ineffective whereas later we will see that the defences under the Act must be established by the defendant.

False statements relating to the provision of services, accommodation or facilities

Suppliers of services, such as holiday tour operators, hairdressers and drycleaners will be liable to prosecution under s.14 of the Trade Descriptions Act 1968 if they make false statements knowingly or recklessly in the course of their business. Under s.14(1):

"It shall be an offence for any person in the course of any trade or business:

(a) to make a statements which he knows to be false; or

(b) recklessly to make a statement which is false;as to any of the following matters:

(i) the provision ... of any services, accommodation or facilities;

(ii) the nature of any services, accommodation or facilities ...

(iii) the time at which, the manner in which or persons by whom any services, accommodation or facilities are provided;

(iv) the examination, approval or evaluation by any person of any services, accommodation or facilities;or

(v) the location or amenities of any accommodation ..."

In order to obtain a conviction under s.14, the prosecution must show mens rea, (guilty mind) either that the trader knew that the statment was false, or that he was reckless as to its truth or falsity. A statement is made recklessly if it is made regardless of whether it is true or false. It need not necessarily be dishonest. The knowledge or recklessness must be present at the time the statement is made.

> In *Sunair Holidays Ltd. v. Dodd* 1970 the defendant's travel brochure described a package holiday in a hotel with "all twin bedded rooms with bath, shower and terrace". The defendant had a contract with the hotel owners under which they were obliged to provide accommodation of that description. A customer who booked the package was given a room without a terrace. The defendant had not checked with the hotel to make sure that its customers were given the correct accommodation of that description. It was held that the statement was not false when it was made, and therefore the defendant was not guilty of an offence under s.14.

It must be shown that the trader, at the time the statement is made, either knows that it is false or is reckless as to its truth or falsity; and that the statement actually *is* false. Subsequent developments are irrelevant if these elements are present at the time the statement is made.

> In *Cowburn v. Focus Television Rentals Ltd.* 1983 the defendant's advertisement stated: "Hire 20 feature films absolutely free when you rent a video recorder". In response to the advertisement a customer rented a video recorder. The documentation supplied with it indicated that he was entitled only to 6 films, and that they were not absolutely free because he had to pay postage and packing. When he complained, the defendant refunded his postage and packing and supplied 20 free films to him. It was held that the defendant was guilty of an offence under s.14 because the statement in his advertisement was false and recklessly made. The fact that he subsequently honoured the advertisement provided no defence, as this was done after the offence had been committed.

Conduct of the defendant subsequent to the false statement is relevant however to determine whether an inference of recklessness can be maintained.

> In *Yugotours Ltd. v. Wadsley* 1988 (mentioned previously) the fact that statements in a holiday brochure and accompanying letter were clearly false and known to be so by the company meant that when the company failed to correct the statement. The court stated that there was sufficient material before the court to infer recklessness on the part of the maker of the statement. *"If a statement is false and known to be false, and nothing whatever is done to correct it, then the company making the statement can properly be found guilty of recklessness notwithstanding the absence of specific evidence of recklessness".*

> In *Wings Ltd. v. Ellis* 1984 the false nature of a statement in their travel brochure was not known by a tour operator when its brochure was published. Some 250,000 copies of the brochure contained an inacurate statement that rooms in a hotel in Sri Lanka were air conditioned. The brochure also contained a photograph purporting to be a room in the same hotel which was of a room in a different hotel. When the mistake was discovered, reasonable steps were taken to remedy it by informing agents and customers who had already booked by letter. Despite this, a holiday was booked by a customer on the basis of the false information. It was held by the House of Lords that the tour operator was guilty of an offence under s.14 because the statement was made when the brochure was read by the customer, and at the time the defendant knew that it was false. The fact that the tour operator was unaware

that the uncorrected statement was being made to the customer did not prevent the offence being committed. As a result of this judgment the offence under s.1(1)(a) has been described rather crudely as a *"half mens rea offence"*. Knowledge that a statement is false is necessary but there is no need to show mens rea as to the making of the statement.

For corporate liability under s.14 the prosecution must establish that a high ranking official of the company had the necessary mens rea. The Chairman of a company would certainly suffice but not the "Contracts Manager" in *Wings Ltd. v. Ellis* who had approved the photograph of the hotel which gave a wrong impression.

Defences under the Trade Descriptions Act 1968

It is a defence to any charge under the 1968 Act that the defendant innocently published a misleading advertisement received by him for publication in the ordinary course of his business. This defence, available for example to newspapers, is provided by s.25.

A number of separate defences are contained in s.24. These are available to a defendant who can prove

"(a) That the commission of the offence was due to a mistake or to reliance on information supplied to him or to the act or default of another person, an accident, or some other cause beyond his control; and

(b) that he took all reasonable precautions and exercised all due diligence to avoid the commission of such an offence by himself or any person under his control".

In order to have an effective defence under s.24, the onus is on the defendant to prove any one of the reasons listed in paragraph (a) above and all of the elements in (b). He must also supply to the prosecution, at least 7 days before the hearing, a written notice giving such information as he has to enable the other person to be identified.

In *Baxters (Butchers) v. Manley* 1985 the defendant was accused of offences under the 1968 Act in relation to the pricing and weight of meat exposed for sale in his butcher's shop. He claimed that the offences were due to the act or default of the shop manager. This claim was accepted by the court, but the defence under s.24 failed because he was unable to prove that he had taken reasonable precautions to avoid the commission of the offence by his manager. In particular he had failed to give the manager any detailed instructions or guidelines on the requirements of the Act; there was no staff training; and the standard of supervision by a district manager was inadequate.

In *Lewin v. Rothersthorpe Road Garage* 1984 the s.24 defence was raised in response to a prosecution for selling a motor car to which a false trade description had been applied. The defendant was a member of the Motor Agents Association, and had adopted the code of practice drawn up by the Association in consultation with the Office of Fair Trading. Staff had been instructed in the contents of the code of practice. The court held that he had taken reasonable precautions to avoid the commission of an offence by his employee.

To establish that he took all reasonable precautions and exercised all due diligence the defendant needs to show that he has an effective system of operation. A court should also bear in mind the size and resources of the organisation in determining the steps you would expect a reasonable business to take.

In *Denard v. Smith* 1990 (mentioned previously) the defendant attempted to establish a s.24 defence when charged with falsely advertising at the point of sale that particular goods were offered for sale when in fact they were out of stock and not available. The court found that an elementary requirement of *"due diligence"* would have been to issue some instructions that some amendment should be made to the point of sale literature. A simple notice hung over or beside the advertising placard would have been sufficient to show reasonable precautions and due diligence for the purposes of s.24.

Where an offence has been committed under the 1968 Act due to the act or default of another person, the other person may be proseucted under s.23. This is the only situation under the Act where a person can be guilty of an offence even though he is not acting in the course of a trade of business.

> In *Olgeirsson v. Kitching* 1986 the defendant was a private individual who had owned a Ford Granada car. It had previously belonged to Humberside police and whilst in their ownership required a new mileometer. At that stage the car had travelled 64,000 miles. When the police sold it to the defendant the recorded mileage was 10,500 miles, although the true mileage was disclosed. The defendant later sold the car to a garage, telling them that it had only travelled 38,000 miles. The car was resold on that basis. Later the truth was discovered and the defendant was charged under s.23. It was held that he was guilty and the fact that he was not a trader did not bring him outside the scope of the offence.

In relation to enforcement of the 1968 Act, as we have seen, wide investigatory powers are conferred on local authority trading standards officers. Before a prosecution is brought, however, the local authority is required to inform the Department of Trade. This is to prevent numerous unnecessary prosecutions for the same false trade description.

> The legality of bringing a second prosecution where there are a number of complaints in relation to the same false statement was at issue in *R. v. Thomson Holidays Limited* 1973. In this case a misleading statement in a travel brochure constituted an offence under s.14. The Court of Appeal held that a separate offence was committed every time someone read the brochure, and that it was not necessarily improper to bring more than one prosecution in these circumstances.

Misleading price indications: Part III of the Consumer Protection Act 1987

The provisions of the Consumer Protection Act 1987, s.20 to s.26, replace both s.11 of the Trade Descriptions Act 1968 and the Price Marking (Bargain Offers) Order 1979. The previous provisions had proved to be badly drafted and difficult to enforce.

The offence of giving a misleading price indication is contained in s.20 of the 1987 Act, which provides:

> *"A person shall be guilty of an offence if, in the course of any business of his, he gives (by any means whatever) to any consumers an indication which is misleading as to the price at which any goods, services, accommodation or facilities are available".*

The types of statements which would be caught by s.20 include:

(a) false comparisons with recommended prices, for example a false claim that goods are £20 less than the recommended price; or

(b) indications that the price is less than the real price, for example where hidden extras are added to an advertised price; or

(c) false comparisons with a previous price, for example a false statement that goods were £50 and are now £30; or

(d) where the stated method of determining the price is different to the method actually used.

Failure to correct a price indication which initially was true, but has become untrue, is also an offence under s.20.

The Secretary of State, after consulting the Director General of Fair Trading, has issued a code of practice designed to give practical guidance on the requirements of s.20. It aims to promote good practice in relation to giving price indications. Breach of the code will not, of itself, give rise to criminal or civil liability, but may be used as evidence to establish either that an offence had been committed under s.20, or that a trader has a defence to such a charge.

The following cases, decided under previous legislation, illustrate the type of behaviour which will be contrary to s.20.

> In *Richards v. Westminster Motors Ltd.* 1975 the defendant advertised a commercial vehicle for sale at a price of £1,350. When the buyer purchased the vehicle he was required to pay the asking price plus VAT, which made a total price of £1,534. It was held that the defendant was guilty of giving a misleading indication as to the price at which he was prepared to sell goods.

> In *Read Bros. Cycles (Leyton) v. Waltham Forest London Borough* 1978 the defendant advertised a motor cycle for sale at a reduced price of £540, £40 below the list price. A customer agreed to purchase the motor cycle and negotiated a £90 part exchange allowance on his old vehicle. The defendant charged him the full list price for the new cycle, and stated that the reduced price did not apply where goods were given in part exchange. It was held that the defendant was guilty of giving a misleading price indication.

In one significant respect the offence under s.20 is narrower than the offences which it replaced. This is that s.20 only applies to consumer transactions. For the purpose of s.20, the expression 'consumer' means:

(a) in relation to any goods, any person who might wish to be supplied with the goods for his own private use or consumption;

(b) in relation to any services or facilities, any person who might wish to be provided with the services or facilities otherwise than for the purposes of any business of his; and

(c) in relation to any accommodation, any person who might wish to occupy the accommodation otherwise than for the purposes of any business of his.

A consequence of the narrowing down of the offence is that misleading price indications to business customers will not be caught by it. On the facts of *Richards v. Westminster Motors*, for example, the defendant would not now be guilty of an offence under s.20 because the customer was not a consumer.

Consumer Safety

Part II Consumer Protection Act 1987

Part II of the Consumer Protection Act 1987 consolidates, with amendments, previous legislation on consumer safety including the Consumer Safety Act 1978 and the Consumer Safety (Amendment) Act 1986.

The 1987 Act creates a new offence, in s.10, of supplying consumer goods which are not reasonably safe. An offence is also committed by offering or agreeing to supply unsafe goods or exposing or possessing them for supply.

In deciding whether goods are reasonably safe, the court must examine all the circumstances, including:

(a) the way in which the goods are marketed;

(b) the use of any mark, for example indicating compliance with safety standards;

(c) instructions or warnings as to the use of the goods;

(d) whether the goods comply with relevant published safety standards;

(e) whether there is a way in which the goods could reasonably have been made safer.

The offence in s.10 can be committed only in relation to consumer goods. Consumer goods are goods which are ordinarily intended for private use or consumption, with the exception of food, water, gas, motor vehicles, medical products and tobacco.

The Secretary of State has power, under s.11, to make regulations for the purpose of ensuring that goods of any particular type are safe. Safety regulations can cover the design, composition or finish of goods; and ensure that appropriate information is given in relation to them. They may also restrict the distribution of particular types of goods or prohibit their supply or exposure for supply.

A considerable number of regulations, made under previous legislation, are still in force. These relate for example to aerosols, babies' dummies, balloons, cosmetics, electrical goods, night-dresses, toys and many other types of product. Breach of safety regulations is an offence under s.12 of the 1987 Act.

Under s.41 of the 1987 Act any person who suffers injury or loss as a result of a breach of safety regulations has the right to sue the trader for damages for breach of statutory duty. This right cannot be restricted or excluded by any term or notice in any contract.

The Secretary of State also has a number of other powers under the 1987 Act. He may, for example, serve a 'prohibition notice' on a trader requiring him to stop trading in unsafe goods of a particular description. Alternatively, where a trader has distributed goods which are unsafe, the Secretary of State may serve on him a 'notice to warn'. This requires the trader, at his own expense, to publish warnings about the unsafe goods to persons to whom they have been supplied.

Power is also given to local authorities under the Act, to serve a 'suspension notice' on any trader. This in effect freezes the goods in the hands of the trader for up to six months. The power to serve a suspension notice arises if the authority has reasonable grounds for suspecting that goods are not reasonably safe under s.10, or are in breach of safety regulations. A trader who fails to comply with a suspension notice is guilty of a criminal offence.

A Magistrates Court has power to order the forfeiture of goods where there has been a contravention of the safety provisions of the 1987 Act. Where goods are forfeit they must, under s.16, either be destroyed, or released for the purposes of being repaired, reconditioned or scrapped.

Assignment *David and Christine Geary*

Ian Trodd, who runs a smallholding, placed the following advertisement in the local newspaper:

> *FOR SALE: six Aberdeen Angus bull calves, four Hereford calves, up to five weeks old; quantity of hay and straw.*

David Geary, a local farmer, responded to the advertisement and agreed to buy the six Aberdeen Angus bull calves and two of the Hereford heifers at an inclusive price of £850. David noticed that none of the calves had ear tags and Ian subsequently agreed to tag them ready for collection by David the following morning.

David also agreed to buy 500 of the 2,000 bales of hay in Ian's barn for £750 and all of the straw bales in the same barn at a price of £40 per ton. The straw was to be loaded onto David's wagon the next day and weighed by him at a nearby public weighbridge. When David arrived the following morning he found that Ian's barn and all of its contents had been destroyed by a fire in which all of the Aberdeen Angus and Hereford calves have perished.

Tasks

1. David Geary is a member of the National Farmers Union (NFU), and has sought the Union's advice concerning his agreement with Mr. Trodd. You are an officer employed by the NFU, and have been asked to telephone Mr. Geary to explain to him his position in this matter. Prepare notes prior to making the telephone call, which identify clearly and precisely the legal issues raised by it. Bear in mind that Mr. Geary will wish to know exactly how he should proceed.

2. Following your telephone conversation with David Geary he raises a further issue with you, on which he seeks your help. His wife Christine runs a pottery business, supplying her products to sales outlets, usually craft shops, on a sale or return basis. Last month she supplied pottery to The Craft Corner, a shop in Bury St Edmunds, and to Flair, a specialist china and pottery shop in Exeter. She now learns that The Craft Corner has now closed down and sold all its stock to Suffolk Art Supplies, and that her pottery has been stolen from the shop in Exeter. David asks if you will write informing Christine of any rights she has to payment from Suffolk Arts Supplies, and from Flair, since she believes she will have to personally bear the loss. Write a suitable letter to Christine.

Developmental Task

Draw up a set of standard trading terms for use by anyone operating a business which involves the supply of goods on sale or return. The terms should reflect the commercial protection necessary in such a trading activity, taking into account in particular (i) transfer of ownership, (ii) risk, (iii) insurance, and (iv) time limits for the return of goods.

Assignment *Les Trois Vallés*

Calder Travel plc is a large tour operator specialising in Winter Ski-ing holidays which are sold by retail travel agents throughout the United Kingdom. The company resolves to attempt to increase its share of the market for ski-ing holidays in France, in particular the Trois Vallés. To enable the company to achieve this, a decision is taken to make an offer of a financial inducement to prospective clients. Accordingly in their Winter Holiday 1991 brochure, of which 200,000 are distributed, Calder Travel make the following offer:

Throughout the 1991 winter season for every individual package ski-ing holiday booked at a resort in the Trois Vallés at a cost of £400 or more:

(a) ski equipment and ski passes and ski lessons will be provided absolutely free for the duration of the holiday; and

(b) a voucher will be issued which will entitle the holder to a 20% discount on any ski clothing purchased at "Sherrats Ski Wear", a retailer with outlets all over the UK.

Three weeks after the brochure containing this offer has been circulated to travel agents, Geoffery Swift, the company secretary of Calder Travel, despite having given prior approval for the offer, decided that after a closer consideration the offer should be amended on the grounds that the first part of it could be regarded as ambiguous. All company staff and sales agents are therefore instructed to inform travel agents that the offer of free ski equipment hire relates to down-hill skis and sticks only and does not extend to ski boots or cross country equipment. The offer of free ski lessons applies to beginners only and not to intermediate or advanced skiers. Furthermore the free ski pass only relates to the resort at which the client books his holiday rather than all the resorts of the Trois Vallés. Travel agents are told to give the information to clients at the time of booking and inform those who had already booked by letter. Unfortunately some travel agents are never informed of the new instructions and a small proportion who are informed fail to pass it on to the clients. Consequently a large number of complaints are made both to Calder Travel, Travel Agents and local authorities by disappointed clients throughout the 1991 season. The main grievances relate to:

(a) the fact that ski boots are not provided on free hire to clients who had booked relevant holidays and that lessons are only free for beginners;

(b) the fact that free ski passes issued relate only to the resort booked rather than the other resorts in the Trois Valles where ski-ing is available;

(c) that despite the fact that Sherrats Ski Wear shops display notices stating that they accept Calder discount vouchers, the available discount does not extend to clothing which is advertised as 'on sale'.

Task

You are employed as a trading standards officer in the South East of England. Numerous complaints have been made to your office regarding the various 'free offers' made by Calder Travel plc. You are required to present an informal report to your senior officer in which you advise whether any trade descriptions offences have been committed and assess the chances of bringing a successful prosecution.

Chapter 10

Negligence

The Nature of Liability in Negligence

Liability in the tort of negligence arises where foreseeable damage to the plaintiff is caused by the defendant's breach of a legal duty to take care. The tort has wide application and includes liability for losses or injuries suffered at work, on the roads, in dangerous premises, or as a result of medical accidents, professional malpractice or defective products.

A central feature of liability in negligence is that liability is fault-based. A defendant will be liable only if the court is satisfied that he failed to take reasonable care. Negligence provides a mechanism for loss distribution and the apportionment of the risks inherent in activities likely to result in loss or injury. It can be argued that a fault-based system is far from ideal as a means of ensuring fair treatment and proper financial assistance to those who are injured or disabled through no fault of their own. Indeed it has often been said that the law of negligence is like a lottery in which a few successful litigants are handsomely rewarded. Many other claimants are unable to obtain compensation due to lack of evidence of fault, lack of a substantial defendant to pursue or the refusal of the court to impose liability in the circumstances of the case.

One alternative to a system of fault-based liability is the introduction of strict liability for injuries sustained either generally or in particular categories of situation. Under a system of strict liability the injured party should find it much easier to obtain compensation because he will not need to prove a failure to take care on the part of the defendant. Such a system could be financed centrally through taxation, for example an additional tax on petrol to finance a scheme for road accidents. Alternatively it could be funded by compulsory insurance for those who would be exposed to liability, for example medical practitioners in respect of medical accidents. A further alternative is to have a combination of both methods of funding. However the likelihood of the widespread introduction of strict liability for these and other categories of personal injuries in the foreseeable future is remote.

A notable exception is the introduction of strict liability for injuries caused by defective products to the customer in the Consumer Protection Act 1987. This is examined in a later part of this chapter. The effect of the 1987 Act will be to increase substantially the number of successful claims against manufacturers of defective products. The Act, however, does not impose an obligation on those affect to insure against the liability it creates, nor does it provide an independent source of funds to compensate claimants. It falls upon the individual business-man to make sure that his own insurance arrangements are adequate to cover the additional liability which he is likely to face.

The significance of negligence liability for the businessman

The businessman is exposed to potential claims in negligence from a number of diverse sources. He is especially vulnerable because, under the rules of vicarious liability examined in Chapter 13 he is liable as an employer for wrongful acts committed by his employees in the course of their work. The prudent businessman will wish to take steps to minimise the liabilities to which he would otherwise be exposed. There are two things which he can do. First he can try to ensure that his business practices and the systems under which his employees operate are tightly structured and controlled so as to reduce the risk of injury and thereby prevent claims arising. Second he would be well advised to maintain an appropriate range of insurance policies to cover those risks which are most likely to affect his particular type of business.

Types of insurance cover available

Insurance companies usually offer a wide range of policies and will arrange cover to meet the requirements of the individual business. Some types of cover are compulsory and therefore all businesses affected must have them; whilst others, although not compulsory, are such that no prudent businessman would consider it worthwhile to operate without them. Most businesses would be covered by all or most of the following types of policy:

(a) **employers liability** - in Chapter 13 we consider the duty of care owned by the employer at common law to provide a safe system of work, safe equipment and premises and safe fellow employees; and examine the employer's liability in negligence for injury to an employee caused by a breach of any of these duties. Under the Employers Liability (Compulsory Insurance) Act 1969 all employers other than Local Authorities and nationalised industries are required to insure against the risk of personal injury to their employees. The insurance must be contained in an approved policy which has prescribed contents. The policy must be issued by an authorised insurer.

(b) **motor vehicles** - under the Road Traffic Act 1988 the driver of a motor vehicle is required to be insured against third party personal injury and property risks. Most businesses running motor vehicles, and indeed most other motorists, obtain insurance cover well beyond the minimum laid down by the Act. Additional cover beyond the statutory minimum could include the risks of fire, theft of the vehicle, or full comprehensive cover which would include losses of the insured person's vehicle or property caused by his own fault.

(c) **product liability** - a policy of this type is designed to cover liability for injury or losses caused by defective products manufactured or supplied by the insured in the course of his business. It should cover liabilities arising in contract, negligence or under the Consumer Protection Act 1987.

(d) **public liability** - product liability cover is often included in this type of policy. The policy generally includes loss or injury sustained by a member of the public as a result of the activities of the business, for example liability under the Occupiers Liability Act 1957 for injury to a customer caused by the unsafe state of the business premises, or the organisation's liability in negligence resulting from an accident caused by an employee in failing safely to carry out his duties.

(e) **premises and stock** - this provides insurance against loss of or damage to business property caused by fire, theft or negligence.

(f) **professional indemnity** - a policy of this type covers the insured for claims made against him in respect of professional negligence, for example a claim against an architect for miscalculating the depth of the foundations of a multi-storey building or specifying inadequate reinforcements for the structure. In some professions, for example, solicitors, professional indemnity insurance is in effect compulsory because the professional body will refuse to issue a Practising Certificate without evidence of premium payment on an appropriate policy.

(g) **legal expenses insurance** - this is a relative newcomer to the UK insurance market and provides the insured with a full indemnity for legal costs incurred in engaging in legal action in the civil or criminal courts.

Having identified some of the major types of insurance cover available to protect the businessman from losses which could otherwise be incurred by the business, it is worth pointing out that the levels of cover, in terms of the financial limits on the claims that the insurer would satisfy, are a matter of commercial judgement which will depend on the nature of the business concerned.

Additionally, the businessman entering into a contract of insurance must disclose all material facts which could affect the insurer's assessment of the risk. He would also be well advised to examine carefully the detailed wording of the policy in order to be certain that he is actually getting the cover which he wants.

It is interesting to notice that, because of the universal use of insurance by businesses, many of the commercial cases litigated before the courts are in reality disputes between insurance companies standing in the shoes of the named plaintiffs and defendants who have often already been paid out by the insurance companies.

Essential Elements of Liability in Negligence

In order to succeed in a claim in negligence the plaintiff will have to prove three things:

(a) that the defendant owed him a legal duty of care,

(b) that the duty was broken, and

(c) that the defendant's breach of duty resulted in foreseeable loss or damage to the plaintiff.

Once the plaintiff has established these elements there are a number of defences available to the defendant. He may try to establish:

(a) that the plaintiff contributed to his injury by his own negligence - the defence of contributory negligence.

(b) that the plaintiff had voluntarily assumed the risk of injury - a defence based on consent known technically as a volenti non fit injuria, or

(c) that the plaintiff's claim is out of time and therefore statute-barred under the Limitation Act 1980 (as amended).

We shall now examine in more detail the elements of liability and the defences available in a negligence claim.

The Development of the Duty of Care in Negligence

The tort of negligence is an area of legal liability which has been developed by the common law through the decisions of judges in individual cases over the centuries. The process is a continuing one and significant developments have taken place in recent years particularly in relation to the question of when a duty of care is owed by a defendant to the plaintiff.

The major milestone in the evolution of the law of negligence is the decision of the House of Lords in *Donoghue v. Stevenson* 1932 in which Lord Atkin laid down general principles which could be applied to any situation in order to determine whether a duty of care is owed. Prior to 1932 there were no legal principles of general application which defined the circumstances in which a person could be liable for loss or injury caused by his carelessness to another.

> The facts of *Donoghue v. Stevenson* 1932 are that the plaintiff's friend bought her a bottle of ginger beer in a cafe. The ginger beer was in an opaque bottle and, after pouring some of it and drinking from her glass, the remainder was poured from the bottle into the glass. This was found to contain the remains of a decomposed snail, the sight of which caused the plaintiff to suffer shock and become ill. As the drink was a gift from her friend, the plaintiff had no contract with the seller. She therefore sued the manufacturer claiming that he owed a duty of care to her to ensure that his product was not contaminated during the process of manufacture. The defendant argued that he owed no legal duty to the plaintiff because there was no contract between them and the case fell outside the existing recognised categories of duty. The House of Lords rejected the defendant's arguments and, by a slim majority of three judges to two, found for the plaintiff.

This case is important for two reasons. First, in the field of product liability, examined later in this chapter, because Lord Atkin's judgement defines the duty of a manufacturer of a product towards a person injured by a defect in the product.

Second, in the context of the development of the law of negligence as a whole, because Lord Atkin in formulating the neighbour principle, laid down a unifying principle of liability for harm caused unintentionally by the defendant. For this reason the decision in *Donoghue* is often regarded as marking the birth of negligence as a tort. In the celebrated passage from his judgement Lord Atkin said:

> *"The rule that you are to love your neighbour becomes in law, you must not injure your neighbour; and the lawyers question, Who is my neighbour? receives a restricted reply. You must take reasonable care to avoid acts or omissions which you can reasonably foresee would be likely to injure your neighbour. Who, then, in law is my neighbour? The answer seems to be - persons who are so closely and directly affected by my act that I ought reasonably to have them in contemplation as being so affected when I am directing my mind to the acts or omissions which are called in question."*

The defendant's duty is a duty to take reasonable care to avoid causing foreseeable harm and it is owed to anyone closely and directly affected by the defendant's conduct. The close relationship necessary between the defendant and plaintiff in order for a duty to exist is often referred to as a relationship of proximity between the parties.

> The status of the neighbour principle as a rule of general applicability was underlined by the House of Lords in *Home Office v. Dorset Yacht Co.* 1970. Here the plaintiff's yacht was damaged by borstal trainees who had escaped while on a training exercise on an island. They had been carelessly left un-

supervised by their guards. Applying the neighbour principle, it was held that the defendant owed a duty of care to the plaintiff whose yacht had been moored between the island and the mainland, as it was reasonably foreseeable that the trainees might use the yacht as a means of escape. The defendant was vicariously liable for the failure of its employees to supervise the trainees. This breach of duty caused the plaintiff's loss for which the Home Office was liable.

In a leading judgement, Lord Reid stated:

> *"Donoghue v. Stevenson may be regarded as a milestone, and the well known passage in Lord Atkin's speech should I think be regarded as a statement of principle. It is not to be treated as if it were a statutory definition. It will require qualification in new circumstances. But I think that the time has come when we can and should say that it ought to apply unless there is some justification or valid explanation for its exclusion."*

Restrictions on the application of the neighbour principle

Lord Reid's statement implies that there may be cases in which a straight application of the neighbour principle will suggest the existence of a duty of care, but nevertheless the court would refuse to recognise a duty because there are valid justifications for failing to impose liability. The justifications which are used in these circumstances are often referred to as considerations of public policy. We can interpret this expression as meaning reasons based on judicial perceptions of what may or may not be in the best interests of the community at large. It is inevitable that policy issues arise in the course of deciding cases in negligence. This is because Parliament has rarely intervened to influence the direction of legal developments in this field by passing legislation. The judges have, therefore, found it necessary to make decisions on policy issues as part of the process of deciding cases and developing an acceptable coherent and workable body of legal rules.

It should be appreciated that in the majority of claims for personal injuries or damage to property, for example in the field of product liability, there will not be any policy considerations restricting the application of the neighbour principle in order to establish that a duty of care exists. It is in relation to claims for financial loss, for example in the area of professional negligence, that policy considerations - such as the fear of creating open-ended liability - may be taken in to account.

In *McLoughlin v. O'Brien* 1982 Lord Scarman expressed the view that the judges should not concern themselves with issues of public policy. He argued that their function and expertise concerned the logical development of legal principles and the application of these principles to factual situations. The question of whether the application of the neighbour principle should be restricted or denied on grounds of policy is one which, in Lord Scarman's view, should be answered by Parliament. The reason for this is that the judicial process is not well equipped to make decisions involving political, social or economic issues:

> *"I am persuaded that in this branch of the law it is not for the court but for the legislature to set limits, if any be needed, to the law's development. This case raises directly a question as to the balance in our law between the functions of judge and legislature. The common law covers everything which is not covered by statute. It knows no gaps. The function of the court is to decide the case before it, even though the decision may require the extension or adaptation of a principle or in some cases the creation of new law to meet the justice of the case. But, whatever the court decides to do, it starts from a baseline of existing principle and*

> *seeks a solution consistent with or analogous to a principle or principles already recognised.*
>
> *By concentrating on principle the judges can keep the common law alive, flexible and consistent, and can keep the legal system clear of policy problems which neither they, nor the process which it is their duty to operate, are equipped to resolve. If principle leads to results which are thought to be socially unacceptable, Parliament can legislate to draw a line or map out a new path.*
>
> *The problem in this case is one of social, economic, and financial policy. The considerations relevant to a decision are not such as to be capable of being handled within the limits of the judicial process."*

Lord Scarman's view, however, has not found favour with the majority of senior judges. They are prepared to accept that policy issues are constantly being resolved by the courts and that this is inevitable, given that Parliament is not likely to produce legislation on a subject in which there is little immediate political impact. In any event Parliament would be able to step in and legislate if there was major dissatisfaction with the decisions which the courts were making.

The views expressed by Lord Reid in *Home Office v. Dorset Yacht Co.* 1970 about the significance of the neighbour principle were supported by the House of Lords in *Anns v. London Borough of Merton* 1977. Lord Wilberforce explained the approach which a court should take in determining whether a duty of care exists in any given case:

> *"... the position has now been reached that in order to establish that a duty of care arises in a particular situation, it is not necessary to bring the facts of that situation within those of previous situations in which a duty of care has been held to exist. Rather the question has to be approached in two stages.*
>
> *First, one has to ask whether, as between the alleged wrongdoer and the person who has suffered damage there is a sufficient relationship of proximity or neighbourhood such that, in the reasonable contemplation of the former carelessness on his part may be likely to cause damage to the latter, in which case a prima facie duty of care arises. Secondly, if the first question is answered affirmatively, it is necessary to consider whether there are any considerations which ought to negative, or to reduce or limit the scope of the duty or the class of person to whom it is owed or the damages to which a breach of it may give rise."*

The introduction of Lord Wilberforce's two-stage test led to a reassessment of the existence and scope of the duty of care in some situations. Some judges believed that it relieved them of the obligation to follow restrictive pre-1977 precedents and allowed them re-assess those situations having regard only to the two-stage test.

It was seen as providing a relatively straightforward unified general principle which could be applied to every situation to determine whether a duty of care was owed, and, if so, the scope of the duty. Its effect was to expand, considerably in some areas, the boundaries of the tort of negligence and as this became increasingly apparent, the House of Lords sought to curtail its effects and retreated from it.

The retreat from *Anns* can be traced through a significant number of decisions of the House of Lords and the Privy Council in recent years. One of the first was the decision in *Leigh & Sillavan Ltd. v. Aliakmon Shipping Co. Ltd, The Aliakmon* 1986 where Lord Brandon, delivering a judgement with which the other presiding Law Lords were in complete agreement, expressed the view that the test applied only to novel types of factual situation and that the test was not to be applied where the situation was already covered by pre-1977 precedents. Referring to the two-stage test, Lord Brandon stated that it:

> *"... does not provide, and cannot in my view have been intended by Lord Wilberforce to provide, a universally applicable test of the existence and scope of a duty of care in the law of negligence. In this connection I would draw attention to a passage in the speech of Lord Keith in Governors of the Peabody Donation Fund v. Sir Lindsay Parkinson & Co. Ltd. 1984. After citing a passage from Lord Wilberforce's speech in the Anns case now under discussion, he said:*
>
> *'There has been a tendency in some recent cases to treat these passages as being of themselves of a definitive character. This is a temptation which should be resisted.'"*

The process was taken further in *Curran v. Northern Ireland Co-ownership Housing Association Ltd.* 1987 when Lord Bridge, delivering the single judgement of the House of Lords, stated that the approach adopted in *Anns*:

> *"may be said to represent the high water mark of a trend in the development of the law of negligence by your Lordship's House towards the elevation of the 'neighbourhood' principle ... into one of general application from which a duty of care may always be derived unless there are clear counterveiling considerations to exclude it."*

The movement away from *Anns* was further signalled by Lord Bridge's approval, in *Curran*, of the judgement of Brennan J in the Australian case *Sutherland Shire Council v. Heyman* 1985 where he said:

> *"It is preferable in my view that the law should develop novel categories of negligence incrementally and by analogy with existing categories, rather than by a massive extension of prima facie duty of care restrained only by indefinable 'considerations which ought to negative, or to reduce or limit the scope of the duty or the class of persons to whom it is owed'."*

It is clear that the tide of judicial creativity which rose on the strength of the two-stage test in *Anns*, reached, for a relatively brief period, a high water mark from which it has steadily retreated as a result of a number of decisions both of the House of Lords and the Privy Council over recent years. The present position can perhaps best be summed up by quoting from the judgment of Lord Bridge in *Caparo Industries plc v. Dickman* 1990:

> *"What emerges is that, in addition to the foreseeability of damage, necessary ingredients in any situation giving rise to a duty of care are that there should exist between the party owing the duty and the party to whom it is owed a relationship characterised by the law as one of 'proximity' or 'neighbourhood' and that the situation should be one in which the court considers it fair, just and reasonable that the law should impose a duty of a given scope on the one party for the benefit of the other. But it is implicit in the passages referred to that the concepts of proximity and fairness embodied in these additional ingredients are not susceptible of any such precise definition as would be necessary to give them utility as practical tests, but amount in effect to little more than convenient labels to attach to the features of different specific situations which, on a detailed examination of all the circumstances, the law recognises pragmatically as giving rise to a duty of care of a given scope. Whilst recognising, of course, the importance of the underlying general principles common to the whole field of negligence, I think the law has now moved in the direction of attaching greater significance to the more traditional categorisation of distinct and recognisable situations as guides to the existence, the scope and the limits of the varied duties of care which the law imposes."*

Breach of Duty

Once it has been established that the defendant in a given situation owes a duty of care to avoid injury to the plaintiff, the next question which falls to be decided is whether the defendant was in breach of that duty. It should be stressed that these are two separate issues and only after the court is satisfied that a duty exists will it go on to consider the question of breach. A breach of duty is a failure to take reasonable care. This involves a finding of fault on the part of the defendant.

In the words of Alderson B. in *Blyth v. Birmingham Waterworks Co.* 1856:

> *"Negligence (in the sense of a breach of duty) is the omission to do something which a reasonable man, guided upon those considerations which ordinarily regulate the conduct of human affairs, would do, or something which a reasonable and prudent man would not do."*

The duty of care is broken when a person fails to do what a reasonable man would do in the same circumstances. The standard of care required of the defendant in a particular case will vary according to the circumstances of the case and the skills which the defendant holds himself out as possessing. Thus a surgeon carrying out out an operation is required to demonstrate the skills and knowledge of a reasonably competent surgeon. On the other hand the degree of care expected of a hospital porter is not so exacting. Whilst the standard of care required of a skilled defendant such as a professional person will be high, the reverse cannot be said to be true. An inexperienced or unskilled defendant will not be able to argue that the standard of care which he is required to demonstrate is correspondingly low.

> Thus in *Nettleship v. Weston* 1971 the Court of Appeal held that a learner driver was in breach of her duty of care to the plaintiff, a passenger, for failing to demonstrate the driving skills of a reasonably competent qualified driver, and was liable for the injuries sustained by the plaintiff as a result.
>
> The same principle was applied by the Court of Appeal in *Wilsher v. Essex Area Health Authority* 1986 when it held, by a majority of two judges to one, that inexperience was no defence to an action in negligence against a junior doctor, who would be in breach of his duty of care if he failed to demonstrate the skill of a reasonably competent qualified doctor. On the facts of the case, however, the junior doctor had discharged his duty by asking a more senior colleague to check his work.

In determining whether a duty of care has been broken the court must assess the conduct of the defendant and decide whether he acted reasonably or unreasonably. This assessment allows the judge a large measure of discretion in an individual case, although it could be argued that it also produces some uncertainty in the law. The main factors which the court will take into account in deciding whether there has been a breach of the duty of care are:

(a) the extent of the risk created by the defendant's conduct - whether the risk was serious or obvious;

(b) the nature of the harm which is likely to be caused to the plaintiff;

(c) the practicability and expense of taking steps to minimise the risk;

(d) the particular circumstances of the case.

A good example of the way in which the courts attempt to balance these factors is provided by the case of *Bolton v. Stone* 1951.

In *Bolton v. Stone* the plaintiff was standing on the highway outside her home and was struck by a cricket ball hit by a visiting batsman off the pitch of the local cricket club. She sued the members and committee of the cricket club. The ground had been used for cricket since 1864, well before the surrounding houses were built. Balls were rarely hit out of the ground and onto the highway, perhaps only six times in the previous thirty years, and there was no record of any previous accident. The ball in question had travelled seventy-eight yards before passing over the fence and about twenty-five yards further before hitting the plaintiff. The top of the fence was seven feet about the highway and seventeen feet above the pitch. The House of Lords held that the defendants were not liable because they had taken reasonable care. The chances of such an accident were so slim that the reasonable man would have done no more than the defendants had done to prevent it from happening. In the course of his judgement, Lord Ratcliffe stated:

"A breach of duty has taken place if the defendants are guilty of a failure to take reasonable care to prevent the accident. One may phrase it as 'reasonable care' or 'ordinary care' or 'proper care' - all these phrases are to be found in decisions of authority - but the fact remains that, unless there has been something which a reasonable man would blame as falling beneath the standard of conduct that he would set for himself and require of his neighbour, there has been no breach of legal duty. It seems to me in this case that a reasonable man, taking account of the chances against an accident happening, would not have felt himself called upon either to abandon the use of the ground for cricket or to increase the height of his surrounding fences."

In a later chapter we examine a number of cases involving a breach of the employer's duty of care for the safety of his employees - see for instance *Latimer v. AEC* 1953 and *Paris v. Stepney Borough Council* 1951. Consideration of those cases will further demonstrate the approach of the courts in balancing the factors which are relevant to the question of breach of duty.

Proof of the defendant's breach of duty

The normal rule in a civil case is that the plaintiff must adduce evidence to prove his case on balance of probabilities. It will therefore be the plaintiff's job, in a negligence case, to show that the defendant did not act in a reasonable way. If he is unable to do this his claim will fail.

In *Wakelin v. London and South Western Railway Co.* 1886 the body of the plaintiff's husband was found near a level crossing on a railway. He had been hit by a train but there was no evidence to suggest what had happened. The accident could have been his own fault or it could have been attributable to the fault of the defendant. As the plaintiff was unable to prove that the defendant acted in an unreasonable manner, her claim failed.

The difficulty involved in proving that a defendant is in breach of the duty of care is illustrated by the legal claims arising from the injuries caused to unborn children by the drug Thalidomide. Although legal proceedings were issued in the UK, none of the claims were ever brought before the courts. There were two main legal reasons for this. Firstly because it was not certain that a duty of care could be owed to an unborn child (this has since been established by legislation under the Congenital Disabilities (Civil Liability) Act 1976). Secondly because the plaintiffs would probably have been unable to prove that the defendants had failed to take reasonable care. The drug had undergone extensive testing before it was released onto the market. Although it had not been tested on pregnant women, it is not clear that a reasonable drug manufacturer would have tested a drug of that type - a tranquilliser - for its effect upon the developing child within the womb of the pregnant woman, given the state of scientific knowledge within the pharmaceutical industry at that time. After protracted negotiations an out of court settlement was reached between the parties on terms dictated by the defendants. The levels of agreed compensation were widely regarded as being well below those which might have been awarded at the conclusion of a successful trial. Some observers believe that the defendants would not even have agreed to settle the claims on those terms had it not been for the considerable pressure of public opinion and the efforts of a well organised group of the defendant company 's own shareholders on the plaintiffs' behalf.

Res ipsa loquitur

In some cases the plaintiff may be relieved of the burden of proving negligence if the court accepts a plea of res ipsa loquitur (the thing speaks for itself). This is a rule of evidence which applies where the plaintiff's injury is one that would not in the ordinary course of events have happened without negligence and there is no satisfactory alternative explanation for the injury other than negligence by the defendant.

The effect of the rule is that the court will infer negligence on the part of the defendant without the need for the plaintiff to pinpoint the cause of the injury or explain how the defendant failed to take reasonable care. The defendant will be liable unless he furnishes evidence to show that his negligence did not cause the plaintiff's loss.

The rule will be of great assistance to the plaintiff where it seems to be obvious that the defendant was negligent but the plaintiff is unable to pinpoint the exact nature of the defendant's breach of duty.

In *Scott v. London and St. Catherine Docks Co.* 1865 a customs officer was injured when six sacks of sugar fell on him as he was passing the defendant's warehouse. The court held that the res ipsa loquitur rule applied and inferred negligence on the part of the defendant which it was unable to disprove. During the course of his judgement, Erle, C.J. stated:

"Where the thing is shown to be under the management of the defendant, or his servants, and the accident is such as, in the ordinary course of things, does not happen if those who have the management use proper care, it affords reasonable evidence, in the absence of explanation by the defendant, that the accident arose from want of care."

In *Cassidy v. Ministry of Health* 1951, the plaintiff was injured in a surgical operation on his hand. Denning, L.J. asserted that the res ipsa loquitur rule enabled the plaintiff to say, in effect:

"... I went into hospital to be cured of two stiff fingers. I have come out with four stiff fingers, and my hand is useless. That should not have happened if due care had been used. Explain it, if you can."

The defendant was held liable as he was unable to explain how such a result was consistent with the use of reasonable care.

In *Ward v. Tesco Stores* 1976 the plaintiff was injured when she slipped on a pool of yoghurt which had previously been spilled onto the floor of the defendant's supermarket and had not been cleaned up. The Court of Appeal applied the res ipsa loquitur rule and the defendant was held liable as it was unable to show that it had taken reasonable care.

Fatal accidents

Where the defendant's breach of duty has resulted in death, legal action may be brought on behalf of the estate of the deceased person under the Law Reform (Miscellaneous Provisions) Acts 1934 and 1970. The dependants of the deceased will have a separate claim under the Fatal Accidents Act 1976 as amended by the Administration of Justice Act 1982.

We shall consider each type of claim in turn:

(a) The personal representatives may pursue any claim which the deceased person would have had if he had survived. Here damages are restricted to items of loss which arose between the injury and the death. The claim could include pain and suffering, loss of earnings and medical expenses, in each case up to the time of death. Funeral expenses are also recoverable but losses or notional losses in respect of the years after the death cannot be claimed in an action by the deceased's personal representatives.

(b) Certain relatives who were financially dependent on the deceased person are entitled to claim against the defendant. These are his spouse, parents, grandparents, children, grandchildren, sisters, brothers, aunts and uncles, and their issue. In addition, any co-habitee who lived with him as husband or wife for at least two years immediately before the death may claim. The aim of the court will be to provide maintenance for those relatives who have lost the financial support which he provided before his death. In order to succeed, the plaintiff must show:

    (i) that he is a relative,

    (ii) that there is actionable negligence, and

    (iii) that he was a dependant and has suffered financially as a result of the death.

In addition, a claim for a bereavement award for suffering and grief, which is for a fixed sum of £3,500, may be made by the spouse of the deceased or the parents of a child under 18 who is killed.

Resulting Damage

The third essential element of liability in negligence is that the defendant's breach of duty resulted in foreseeable loss or damage to the plaintiff. In reality this involves two separate issues - the issues of causation and remoteness of damage.

Causation of damage

The causation issue is concerned with the question of cause and effect: was the defendant's breach of duty the operative cause of the plaintiff's loss. The plaintiff's claim will fail if he is unable to prove this link. He must show that but for the defendant's negligence his loss would not have occurred.

In *Barnett v. Chelsea and Kensington Hospital Management Committee* 1969 the plaintiff's husband was a night watchman, who called at the defendant's hospital in the early hours of the morning complaining of vomiting. He was sent home without being examined and was told to contact his own doctor later that day. He was suffering from arsenic poisoning and died a few hours later. The court held that the defendants were in breach of their duty of care, but the claim failed because the negligence of the hospital had not caused the death. The court accepted on the evidence that even if he had been examined immediately, the plaintiff's husband would still have died from arsenic poisoning.

Remoteness of damage

Where the plaintiff proves that his injuries were caused by the defendant's breach of duty, he can recover damages provided that his injuries were not too remote a consequence of the breach. The law does not necessarily impose liability for all of the consequences of a negligent act. Some damage may be too remote. Only damage which was reasonably foreseeable at the time of the negligent act can be recovered by the plaintiff.

In *The Wagon Mound* 1961 a large quantity of fuel oil was carelessly spilled by the defendant's employees while a ship was taking on fuel in Sydney Harbour. Some of the oil spread to the plaintiff's wharf where welding operations were taking place. The plaintiff stopped welding temporarily, but recommenced after receiving expert opinion that fuel oil would not ignite when spread on water. Two days later the oil ignited when a drop of molten metal fell onto a piece of waste floating in the oil, causing extensive damage to the plaintiff's wharf. The court found as a fact that it was not reasonably foreseeable that the oil would ignite in these circumstances. It was held that the damage to the wharf was too remote, and the plaintiff's claim failed.

The plaintiff's damage may be held to be too remote where an unforeseen new independent act, outside the defendant's control, intervenes to break the chain of causation. If the plaintiff's damage is caused by such a *'novus actus interveniens'* the defendant will not be liable for it. For example an employer's liability for injury suffered by an employee at work will not extend to further injuries received in the course of negligent medical treatment in hospital.

In *Cobb v. Great Western Railway* 1894 the defendant allowed a railway carriage to become overcrowded. As a result the plaintiff's pocket was picked and he lost nearly £100. It was held that the act of the thief was a novus actus interveniens and therefore that the plaintiff's loss was too remote.

Defences to a Negligence Action

Contributory negligence

Where the plaintiff has successfully established all of the elements of a negligence action, but has in some way contributed to his injuries by his own negligence, the defendant may raise the defence of contributory negligence.

Section 1(1) of the Law Reform (Contributory Negligence) Act 1945 provides:

"Where any person suffers damage as the result partly of his own fault and partly of the fault of any other person or persons, a claim in respect of that damage shall not be defeated by reason of the fault of the person suffering the damage, but the damages recoverable in respect thereof shall be reduced to such extent as

the court thinks just and equitable having regard to the claimant's share in the responsibility for the damage."

The effect of this provision is simply that the plaintiff's damages will be reduced in direct proportion to the extent to which he is to blame for his injuries.

In *Davies v. Swan Motor Co. (Swansea) Ltd. (third party James)* 1949 the plaintiff's damages were reduced by 20% when he was held to be contributorily negligent. He was riding on the back of a dust lorry contrary to his employer's instructions and was injured when the dust lorry was in collision with a bus.

In *Stapley v. Gypsum Mines* 1953 the plaintiffs were miners who, contrary to specific instructions by their employer, worked under a dangerous roof. They were injured when the roof collapsed and fell in on them. Their damages were reduced by 80% for contributory negligence.

In *Froom v. Butcher* 1976 it was held that the failure to wear a seat belt was contributory negligence and that the appropriate reduction in damages was 25% if the seat belt would have prevented the injury altogether, or 15% if it would merely have reduced the extent of the injury.

In *Sayers v. Harlow UDC* 1958 the plaintiff became locked inside a public lavatory because of the defendant's negligence in failing to maintain the door lock. After failing to attract attention or assistance, she attempted to climb out over the top of the door. In doing so she fell and was injured. It was held that the defendant was liable in negligence, but the plaintiff's damages were reduced by 25% for contributory negligence.

Voluntary assumption of risk (volenti non fit injuria)

This defence, which is universally referred to by its latin name *volenti non fit injuria*, is available to the defendant where the plaintiff freely and voluntarily accepts a risk of which he has full knowledge. In modern times the courts have been reluctant to apply the defence, which has the effect of completely defeating the plaintiff's claim, other than in exceptional circumstances. The reason for this is that the type of behaviour which would come within the defence would also usually amount to contributory negligence. The courts probably take the view that a more just outcome can be achieved by applying the rules of contributory negligence.

In *Smith v. Charles Baker & Sons* 1891 the plaintiff was employed in the excavation of a railway cutting. He was injured by a stone which fell from an overhead crane. He had known that there was an element of risk in working beneath the crane but had not objected to his employer. As a defence to his action for compensation, the employer argued that the plaintiff had voluntarily undertaken the risk of injury. The House of Lords held that the employer was liable. The defence failed because mere knowledge of the risk was not the same as consent to the danger. Lord Herschell stated the volenti rule in the following terms:

"One who has invited or assented to an act being done towards him cannot, when he suffers from it, complain of it as a wrong ... if then, the employer thus fails in his duty towards the employed, I do not think that because (the employee) does not straightaway refuse to continue his service, it is true to say that he is willing that his employer should act thus towards him. I believe it would be contrary to the facts to assert that the plaintiff in this case either invited or assented to the employer's negligence."

In *Bowater v. Rowley Regis Corporation* 1944 the plaintiff was employed as a carter, and was ordered to take out a particular horse to pull his cart. He protested because the horse was known to be vicious but his protests were in vain. He was injured by the horse and in an action for damages the defendant raised the defence of volenti non fit injuria. It was held that the defence was inapplicable because the plaintiff had not genuinely consented to run the risk. In reality he had little choice but to take out the horse.

The defence of *volenti non fit injuria* will not usually be available where the plaintiff has been injured while attempting to rescue someone from a peril created by the defendant's negligence. In these circumstances the rescuer cannot normally be regarded as having freely consented to the risk of injury.

In *Haynes v. Harwood* 1935 for example, a policeman was injured while stopping a runaway horse and cart which endangered the safety of members of the public, including children, in a busy street. It was held that, in the circumstances, he had at least a moral duty to intervene, and his claim for damages succeeded.

By way of contrast in *Cutler v. United Dairies Ltd.* 1933 the plaintiff intervened to stop a runaway horse within a field. It posed no risk of injury to anyone. The plaintiff was unable to recover damages for the injuries which he sustained as the court held that he had voluntarily assumed the risk of injury.

Exclusion of liability for negligence

Under the rules of common law it used to be possible for a defendant to exclude his liability for negligence, either by including an appropriately worded term in a contract, or by displaying a notice to that effect.

In *White v. Blakemore* 1972, for example, the plaintiff's husband, a member of a racing club, stood next to the ropes near a stake watching a race. The wheel of a racing car caught on the rope pulling the stake out of the ground. The stake killed the plaintiff's husband. Notices had been displayed by the defendant in prominent positions excluding all liability for accidents howsoever caused. It was held that the notices were effective to protect the defendant from liability.

Since the introduction of the Unfair Contract Terms Act 1977, however, the scope of the common rules have been considerably cut down. You will recall that under s.2 of the 1977 Act liability for death or personal injury caused by negligence cannot be excluded, but that it may be possible to exclude liability for other types of damage or loss. Such an exclusion will only be effective however if the defendant can prove that it is fair and reasonable to allow reliance on it in the circumstances of the case.

Time limits for claims in negligence

The Limitation Act 1980, as amended by the Latent Damage Act 1986, provides that no legal action may be taken in respect of certain types of claim unless proceedings are issued within the limitation period. After this time the claim is said to be statute barred and the court will refuse to entertain it. The limitation period varies according to the legal basis of the claim and the type of injury or damage suffered by the plaintiff.

(a) Personal injuries or death

Personal injury claims in negligence and in contract are subject to a limitation period of three years. Time starts to run either on the date on which the right to sue first arises, or, if later, on the date on which the plaintiff is aware:

(i) that he has suffered significant injury,

(ii) that this is attributable to the defendant's negligence or breach of contract, and

(iii) of the identity of the defendant.

Where this formula applies there is no final long term cut off date after which the plaintiff's claim cannot be brought. The plaintiff will usually use this formula when he is suing for injuries which did not manifest themselves at the time of the negligent act. This could apply if, for example, the plaintiff contracted a lung disease through exposure to industrial dust from asbestos or coal, and the disease did not become apparent for a number of years.

(b) Claims other than personal injury

In the case of a claim which does not involve personal injury, for example for property damage or financial loss, the limitation period both in negligence and in contract is six years from the date on which the right to sue first arises. In the case of a negligence claim for this type of loss the Latent Damage Act 1986 enables the plaintiff to commence legal proceedings outside the six year period (NB the 1986 Act does not apply to a contract claim). Under the Act the claim must be made within three years of the date on which the plaintiff became aware:

(i) that the damage was significant,

(ii) that it was attributable to the negligence of the defendant, and

(iii) of the identity of the defendant.

Under the 1986 Act, however, the limitation period cannot be extended beyond 15 years of the date of the event which constituted the defendant's breach of duty. As we noted above there is no such 'long stop' date beyond which the period for bringing a personal injuries claim cannot be extended.

One of the principal reasons for the introduction of the Latent Damages Act 1986 was to provide an effective remedy for a person in the situation of the plaintiff in the case of *Pirelli v. Oscar Faber.*

> In *Pirelli General Cable Works Ltd. v. Oscar Faber & Partners* 1983 the defendants were consulting engineers who advised the plaintiffs on the design and erection of a large chimney for the boiler at their factory. The design was defective and expert evidence showed that internal cracks had occurred within the chimney before April 1970. The damage was not discovered, however, until 1977 and the plaintiff did not commence legal proceedings until 1978. The House of Lords held that the six year limitation period began to run as soon as the damage occurred and therefore the claim was statute barred. The limitation period had expired even before the plaintiffs knew that they had suffered any damage.

Under the provisions of the 1986 Act the issue of limitation would have been decided in the plaintiff's favour on the facts of the Pirelli case. The Act is designed to eliminate this type of injustice.

Professional Negligence

The field of professional negligence is a growth area within the law of negligence. It operates in a situation where a client or a third party suffers loss or damage as a result of the failure by a person to exercise care in carrying out his profession. Where this occurs, the injured party may have a number of avenues of redress open to him, in addition to legal action in the courts.

Alternatives to court action

Most professionals, for example, lawyers, doctors, architects, surveyors and accountants, are regulated by professional associations. These bodies are almost invariably authorised, through contractual conditions of membership or by Act of Parliament, to exercise disciplinary powers over members of the profession. These disciplinary powers are usually exercised, in the more serious cases, by a domestic tribunal. The tribunal will act rather like a court and will hear formal complaints against members of the profession. If a complaint is proven, the tribunal will have power to impose punishments ranging from a simple reprimand to the imposition of a fine or the suspension or withdrawal of the right to practise as a member of the profession.

In addition to disciplinary tribunals, many professional bodies sponsor arbitration schemes which provide a means by which compensation claims can be adjudicated without reference to the courts. One example is the Solicitors Arbitration Scheme set up by the Law Society in 1986. The scheme is run by the Chartered Institute of Arbitrators. In order to use the scheme both the solicitor and the claimant must agree. They will be bound by the decision of the arbitrator and neither party can subsequently take the matter to court. The arbitrator will look at written submissions by the parties and other supporting documents. He will decide whether the claim is valid and fix the amount of compensation to be awarded. In exceptional cases, where it appears that a decision cannot be made on the examination of documents alone, there is provision for a verbal hearing with the agreement of both parties. Each party must pay a registration fee in advance but the fee will be refunded to the successful party. The remaining costs of the scheme are paid by the Law Society itself. The process of arbitration is examined further in Chapter 2.

The legal basis of a professional negligence claim

The vast majority of professional negligence claims are made by clients of the professional, rather than by third parties who have no contractual relationship with him. Most claims will therefore be based upon an allegation of a breach of contract. The professional has a contractual duty to his client to take reasonable care in providing professional services. This is recognised in s.13 of the Supply of Goods and Services Act 1982 which provides:

> *"In a contract for the supply of a service where the supplier is acting in the course of a business, there is an implied term that the supplier will carry out the service using reasonable skill and care."*

We have already examined a number of cases coming within the scope of this contractual duty in the context of consumer protection in the previous chapter. The duty is also significant in relation to professional negligence. We may use the term contractual negligence to refer to liability for breach of this duty. A small number of exceptions to the duty are provided for by s.12(4) of the 1982 Act. These include the duties owed by company directors and barristers and are examined more closely elsewhere in this text.

Where the plaintiff has no contractual relationship with the professional, he will have to establish that a duty of care is owed to him under general principles of the tort of negligence. Without a contract he will obviously be unable to rely on s.13 of the 1982 Act. The term 'third party negligence' may be used for the sake of convenience to distinguish this situation from one of contractual negligence.

There are a number of important differences between contractual negligence and third party negligence, and these are summarised in figure 10.1.

Figure 10.1 *Professional negligence: main differences between claims in contract and tort.*

	CONTRACT	**TORT**
who can sue	client only	client or third party
type of loss recoverable if not too remote	all types of loss	all types except that pure financial loss is recoverable only in very limited circumstances
test for remoteness of damage	Hadley v. Baxendale (i) damage arising in the ordinary course of events (ii) unusual losses if known to be likely at time of contract	The Wagon Mound damage of a type which was reasonably foreseeable at the time of the breach of duty
time limits for claims	(i) time runs from breach (ii) Latent Damage Act 1986 does not apply (iii) see Fig. 10.2 for time limits	(i) time runs from damage (ii) Latent Damage Act 1986 does apply (iii) see Fig. 10.2 for time limits
exclusion of liability	s.2 and s.3 Unfair Contract Terms Act 1977	s.2 Unfair Contract Terms Act 1977

Financial loss caused by professional negligence

Where the plaintiff is suing for contractual negligence there will be little difficulty in establishing liability for financial loss caused by the defendant's breach of contract, provided that the loss is not too remote. The rules of remoteness of damage in contract were laid down in *Hadley v. Baxendale* 1854 and are examined in Chapter 7.

Where the claim is based upon tortious or third party negligence, the plaintiff may have more difficulty in establishing that the defendant owed a duty of care to avoid causing his financial loss. A claim for financial loss (sometimes referred to as economic loss) usually takes the form of a claim for the loss of profits which the plaintiff would have made but for the defendant's negligence or the loss of money invested as a result of advice or information given by the defendant. As we previously noted when examining the development of the duty of care, the duty can readily be established by applying the neighbour principle where the claim relates to personal injury or property damage. Where the plaintiff's loss is financial, however, considerations of public policy may come into play in determining the existence and scope of the duty of care.

Across the spectrum of professional activities it is possible to distinguish two broad categories of claim for financial loss:

(1) financial loss caused by negligent statements

(2) financial loss caused by negligent acts.

The basis and scope of the duty of care will vary according to which of these categories the plaintiff's claim comes within. We shall examine the basic ground rules for each category, returning to the

m later when we consider the liability of members of some particular professions for negligence.

1. Financial loss caused by negligent statements

Prior to the decision of the House of Lords in *Hedley Byrne v. Heller* 1964 it was well settled law that there could be no liability in tort for financial loss caused by negligently made statements. In *Candler v. Crane, Christmas & Co.* 1951, for example, the Court of Appeal by a majority held that a false statement, carelessly made, was not actionable in the tort of negligence. Lord Denning dissented and was prepared to recognise the existence of a duty of care where the defendant had some special knowledge or skill upon which the plaintiff relied. He stated:

> *"From early times it has been held that persons who engage in a calling which requires special knowledge and skill owe a duty of care to those who are closely and directly affected by their work, apart altogether from any contract or undertaking in that behalf."*

The judgement of Lord Denning was approved by the house of Lords in *Hedley Byrne v. Heller*, and the decision of the majority in the *Candler* case was overruled.

> In *Hedley Byrne & Co. v. Heller and Partners Ltd.* 1964 the plaintiffs were advertising agents whose clients, Easipower Ltd, were customers of the defendant merchant bank. The plaintiffs had been instructed to buy advertising space for Easipower's products on television and in the newspapers. This involved them in the expenditure of large sums of money. Never having dealt with Easipower before, the plaintiffs sought a reference as to their creditworthiness to the extent of £100,000 from the defendant. The reference

was given 'without responsibility on the part of the bank' and stated with reference to Easipower: "Respectably constituted company, considered good for its ordinary business engagements. Your figures are larger than we are accustomed to see". In fact Easipower had an overdraft with the bank, which ought to have known that the company would have difficulty meeting payments to the plaintiff. Within one week of giving the reference the bank was pressing Easipower to reduce its overdraft. Relying on the reference the plaintiffs incurred personal liability by placing advertising contracts. Easipower then went into liquidation due to insolvency and as a result the plaintiffs lost over £17,500. The actual decision in the case was that the defendant was not liable as the disclaimer of responsibility was effective to prevent the bank from assuming a duty of care.

The principal importance of the decision, however, is that the House of Lords recognised the existence, in certain circumstances, of a duty of care in relation to financial loss caused by negligently made statements. Lord Morris stated:

"if someone possessed of a special skill undertakes, quite irrespective of contract, to apply that skill for the assistance of another person who relies upon such skill, a duty of care will arise."

Lord Pearce expressed the view that the duty would only arise in relation to a statement about *"a business or professional transaction whose nature makes clear the gravity of the inquiry and the importance and influence attached to the answer".*

For reasons of public policy, the scope of the duty and the class of persons to whom it is owed was restricted by the House of Lords. The main policy reason for this was a reluctance to create open ended liability by exposing a defendant to claims by numerous plaintiffs for a single instance of negligence. In Lord Reid's view the danger of 'opening the floodgates' in this way was particularly acute for a number of reasons:

"I would think that the law must treat negligent words differently from negligent acts... Quite careful people often express definite opinions on social or informal occasions even when they see that others are likely to be influenced by them; and they often do so without taking that care which they would take if asked for their opinion professionally or in a business connection... But it is at least unusual casually to put into circulation negligently made articles which are dangerous... Another obvious difference is that a negligently made article will only cause one accident and so it is not very difficult to find the necessary degree of proximity or neighbourhood between the negligent manufacturer and the person injured. But words can be broadcast with or without the consent or the foresight of the speaker or writer. It would be one thing to say that the speaker owes a duty to a limited class, but it would be going very far to say that he owes a duty to every ultimate 'consumer' who acts on those words to his detriment."

For these reasons the House of Lords held that in order for a duty to arise there must be a *special relationship of reliance* between the parties. It was characterised by Lord Devlin as *'a relationship equivalent to a contract'* (albeit lacking the essential ingredient of consideration). The most authoritative definition of the special relationship of reliance was given by Lord Reid who said that it included:

"... all those relationships where it is plain that the party seeking information or advice was trusting the other to exercise such a degree of care as the circumstances required, where it is reasonable for him to do that, and where the other gave the

information or advice when he knew or ought to have known that the inquirer was relying on him."

Clearly there would be no special relationship of reliance in respect of casual remarks in the course of conversation on a social or informal occasion. In any event the person who is asked for information or an opinion could refuse to give it; make clear that it was given without careful consideration, or, as happened in the *Hedley Byrne* case, disclaim responsibility for it. In Lord Reid's opinion:

> *"A reasonable man, knowing that he was being trusted or that his skill and judgement were being relied on, would, I think, have three courses open to him. He could keep silent or decline to give the information or advice sought: or he could give an answer with a clear qualification that he accepted no responsibility for it or that it was given without that reflection or inquiry which a careful answer would require: or he could simply answer without any such qualification. If he chooses to adopt the last course he must, I think, be held to have accepted some responsibility for his answer being given carefully, or to have accepted a relationship with the inquirer which requires him to exercise such care as the circumstances require."*

Where the person making the statement excludes liability for it or states that it is given without responsibility, the Unfair Contract Terms Act 1977 applies with the result that the disclaimer will be invalid unless the person who made the statement proves that it is fair and reasonable in the circumstances to allow reliance on the disclaimer. It may be then that a case with similar facts to those of *Hedley Byrne v. Heller* would be decided differently if it came before the courts today.

The test for determining whether a duty of care exists outside a contract in relation to careless statements causing financial loss is whether a special relationship of reliance exists between the parties. This is narrower in its scope than the neighbour principle and under it the duty will be established if the plaintiff can prove:

(i) that the defendant possessed special skill or knowledge,

(ii) that the plaintiff relied on the defendant to exercise care,

(iii) that the defendant knew or ought to have know that the plaintiff was relying on him, and

(iv) that reliance by the plaintiff was reasonable in the circumstances.

We have already seen in Chapter 7 that damages for loss caused by a careless statement may be recovered under the Misrepresentation Act 1967 where the statement is a negligent misrepresentation which induces a person to enter a contract. When we considered liability for negligent misrepresentation many of the cases which we examined were argued on the basis both of the Misrepresentation Act and of the *Hedley Byrne* principle. It may be useful to refer in particular to *Esso Petroleum Co. Ltd. v. Mardon* 1976 and *Howard Marine and Dredging Co. v. Ogden (A.) & Sons (Excavations)* 1978.

2. Financial loss caused by negligent acts

It has been a long-standing principle of law of negligence that pure financial (or economic) loss caused by a negligent act rather than a statement is not recoverable.

> Thus for example in *Weller Co. v. Foot & Mouth Disease Research Institute* 1965 the defendants carried out research into foot and mouth disease, a

highly infectious disease affecting cattle. The virus escaped from their premises and affected cattle in the surrounding area. As a result restrictions on the movement of cattle were introduced and two cattle markets belonging to the plaintiff auctioneers had to be closed. The plaintiffs sued for loss caused to their business. It was held that, because the loss was purely financial and not connected with any physical harm caused to the plaintiffs or their property, no duty of care was owed by the defendants to the plaintiffs, and the claim failed.

The major policy reason for refusing to recognise a duty of care for pure financial loss is that it could lead to open ended liability. In the *Weller* case, for example, the closure of the markets would have affected the businesses of all those who transported cattle to and from the markets; of the shops, cafes and public houses in the vicinity of the markets; of the banks which would have handled the money in the sale and purchase of cattle; and the destruction of cattle caused by the escape of the virus could have adversely affected the economic interests of cattle feed suppliers, agricultural workers and milkmen, with substantial knock-on effects throughout the local economy. If the defendants were not to be liable for all of these consequences, the line of legal liability has to be drawn restrictively. Thus claims can be brought for injury to the person and damage to property, and for financial losses which are closely associated with such injury or damage. However, with one exception discussed below, claims for pure financial loss caused by the defendant's negligent act are not allowed. The extent of a plaintiff's financial loss may not readily be foreseen by the defendant before the negligent act occurs and the plaintiff will be in the best position to assess the extent and insure against the risk of financial loss.

Financial loss directly associated with physical injury may be referred to as 'consequential' rather than 'pure' financial loss. Here the defendant may owe a duty to the plaintiff under the neighbour principle. An example of the distinction between these types of financial loss can be seen in *Spartan Steel v. Martin.*

In *Spartan Steel & Alloys Ltd. v. Martin & Co. (Contractors) Ltd.* 1972 the defendant's employee, while digging up a road with a mechanical excavator, carelessly damaged an electricity supply cable and cut off the power to the plaintiff's factory. In order to prevent damage to a furnace, the molten metal in it had to be poured off before it solidified. The melt was damaged to the value of £368, and the plaintiffs lost the profit of £400 which they would have made had the process been completed. The electricity supply was cut off for 14 hours during which four additional melts could have been processed. The profit on the additional melts would have been £1,767. The Court of Appeal held that the first two items claimed were recoverable - these were damage to property and consequential financial loss. The loss of profits on additional melts, however, was a pure financial loss not sufficiently connected with the physical damage and therefore not recoverable.

A 1982 decision of the House of Lords has created an exception to the rule that no duty can be owed in respect of pure financial loss unassociated with physical damage.

In *Junior Books Ltd. v. Veitchi Co. Ltd.* 1982 the plaintiff engaged a main contractor to build a new factory. The main contractor, at the request of the plaintiff, engaged the defendant to lay the floor of the building. The defendant was therefore a nominated sub-contractor and had no contractual relationship with the plaintiff. Due to the defendant's failure to mix and lay the floor with reasonable care, the floor began to crack up leaving the plaintiff with an unserviceable building bearing high maintenance costs. The plaintiff ceased production, had the floor relaid and sued the defendant for all the costs and losses incurred by him. The defendant denied that he owed a duty to the plaintiff in respect of that part of the claim which represented pure financial loss. The House of Lords, by a majority, held the defendant liable for the full claim, including the element of pure financial loss. The duty of care was thus extended beyond one of preventing physical harm being done by faulty work to a duty to avoid the presence of defects in the work itself and to avoid the resultant financial losses. Lord Fraser, in his judgement, stressed that he was deciding the case *"strictly on its own facts. I rely particularly on the very close proximity between the parties."* After discussing the floodgates argument Lord Fraser continued: *"The proximity between the parties is extremely close, falling only just short of a direct contractual relationship. The injury to the plaintiff was a direct and foreseeable result of negligence by the defendants. The plaintiffs nominated the defendants as specialist sub-contractors and they must therefore have relied on their skill and knowledge."*

The *Junior Books* case has been treated in subsequent cases as laying down a narrow exception to a general principle, rather than as a springboard for the extension of liability. Thus in *Muirhead v. Industrial Tank Specialities* 1985, discussed below in the context of product liability, the Court of Appeal refused to extend the duty to a manufacturer of defective electric motors which caused financial loss to the ultimate consumer. The decision was made on the grounds that there was not a sufficient degree of close proximity between the plaintiff and the defendant to give rise to a duty of care to avoid causing financial loss.

In *D & F Estates Ltd. v. Church Commissioners for England* 1988 the third defendants, who were builders, had been employed to erect flats on land owned by the Church Commissioners. The plaintiff, a tenant of one of the flats, found that the plaster on the wall of its flat was loose, and sued the builders for the cost of replastering the flat. The basis of the claim was that the plastering was defective in quality. There was no allegation that it had caused damage to other property of the plaintiff or that it had caused personal injury. The claim was therefore to recover damages for pure economic loss in the tort of negligence. The House of Lords held that the builders were not liable as such losses are irrecoverable. The decision in *Junior Books v. Veitchi* was treated as *"not laying down any principle of general application"*, and as being dependent upon the finding of a *"unique, albeit non-contractual relationship"* and the ratio of *Junior Books* was effectively confined to its own particular facts.

In any case in which a plaintiff claims damages for economic loss resulting from damage to property caused by a negligent act, it should be noted that the plaintiff cannot succeed unless he has a proprietary or possessory interest in the property at the time the damage occurs.

In *Leigh & Sillavan Ltd. v. Aliakmon Shipping Co. Ltd. The Aliakmon* 1986 the House of Lords held that the buyer under an export contract, to whom the ownership of the goods had not passed, but to whom the risk of accidental destruction had been transferred by the terms of the contract, could not sue the shipowner in negligence for pure financial loss caused to him by the fact that the goods were damaged whilst in transit on board ship, as he had no proprietary or possessory interest in the goods at the time they were damaged.

Professional Negligence Liability and Specific Professions

We shall now consider the way in which the courts have applied the principles outlined above in a variety of circumstances involving allegations of negligence against members of a number of specific professions. In doing so we should bear in mind that the rules laid down in relation to one profession can often be applied to other professions. You may find it useful, in relation to each case, to attempt to identify the essential elements of each negligence action as they arise, and to analyse each decision so as to pinpoint the element which is at the centre of the dispute.

Medical practitioners

Most claims against members of the medical profession arise as a result of personal injuries suffered by patients in their care. Establishing the existence of a duty of care will usually present few difficulties for the plaintiff. However his task of proving a breach of duty may be more problematic.

> In *Bolam v. Friern Hospital Management Committee* 1957 the plaintiff broke his pelvis during electro-convulsive therapy treatment at the defendant's hospital. He claimed that the doctor was negligent principally because he failed to exercise any manual control over the plaintiff during treatment beyond merely arranging for his shoulders to be held, his chin supported, a gag used, and a pillow put under his back. Informed medical opinion consisted of two schools of thought regarding the use of restraint in these circumstances, one view favouring restraint, the other against it. It was held that there had been no breach of duty by the defendants.

McNair J., discussing the standard of care required of a professional man, stated:

> " *where you get a situation which involves the use of some special skill or competence, then the test as to whether there has been negligence or not ... is the standard of the ordinary skilled man exercising and professing to have that special skill. A man need not possess the highest expert skill; it is well established law that it is sufficient if he exercises the ordinary skill of an ordinary competent man exercising that particular art ...*
>
> *A doctor is not guilty of negligence if he has acted in accordance with a practice accepted as proper by a responsible body of medical men skilled in that particular art. Putting it the other way round, a man is not negligent, if he is acting in accordance with such a practice, merely because there is a body of opinion who take a contrary view.*"

The statements of McNair J., were approved by the House of Lords in *Whitehouse v. Jordan.*

> In *Whitehouse v. Jordan* 1981 a senior hospital registrar in charge of a difficult birth used forceps to assist in the birth. The use of forceps was unsuccessful and the baby was eventually delivered by Caesarean section. The baby was born with brain damage. It was alleged that this resulted from the defendant's negligence in pulling too hard and too long with the forceps. The Court of Appeal held that the defendant was not liable in negligence even though he had made an error of judgement. Lord Denning, M.R., in a statement which was not accepted as valid by the House of Lords, stated:

"we must say, and say firmly, that, in a professional man an error of judgement is not negligent"

The House of Lords, whilst confirming the decision of the Court of Appeal, disagreed with the statement by Lord Denning. Lord Fraser stated:

" I think that Lord Denning M.R. must have meant to say that an error of judgement 'is not necessarily negligent'... Merely to describe something as an error of judgement tells us nothing about whether it is negligent or not. The true position is that an error of judgement may, or may not, be negligent; it depends on the nature of the error. If it is one that would not have been made by a reasonably competent professional man professing to have the standard and type of skill that the defendant held himself out as having, and acting with ordinary care, then it is negligent. If, on the other hand, it is an error that a man, acting with ordinary care, might have made, then it is not negligence."

In relation to the liability of medical practitioners for professional negligence reference can be made to the cases of *Cassidy v. Ministry of Health* 1951 and *Wilsher v. Essex Area Health Authority* 1986 examined earlier in this chapter.

Where a doctor writes a prescription which is illegible, and as a result a pharmacist dispenses the wrong drugs and the patient is injured, both the doctor and the pharmacist may be liable in negligence.

In *Prendergast v. Sam & Dee Ltd.* 1988 the plaintiff was prescribed a fairly common drug for a chest infection. The doctor's handwriting was not clear, and the pharmacist read it as being a drug for diabetes. It escaped his notice that if it had been the diabetes drug, the dosage, the number of tablets and the size of the tablets were wrong. In addition a prescription for diabetes would have been free whereas the plaintiff was asked to pay. As a result of taking the wrong drug the plaintiff suffered brain damage. It was held that the pharmacist fell below the standard of skill of a reasonably competent pharmacist, who would have been alerted by the inconsistencies, and was liable in negligence. The doctor too was negligent, and liability was apportioned 25% to the doctor and 75% to the pharmacist.

Accountants

In recent years there has been some uncertainty as to the precise extent of the accountant's liability in negligence. The uncertainty has centred around the situation in which the accountant, acting as auditor of a limited company, negligently paints too rosy a financial picture of the company in its accounts, and a third party loses money in a transaction entered into on the strength of that financial picture. A limited company's accounts are widely circulated. They are filed with the annual report at the Companies Registry and are available for public inspection. Consequently a wide range of people may use them for a variety of purposes. Many such people will have no contractual relationship with the auditor. After a period of uncertainty, the legal principles governing the auditor's liability to such people have now been settled by the House of Lords in *Caparo Industries plc v. Dickman* 1990. Before examining some of the relevant caselaw, it may be useful to remind ourselves of the position of auditors of a plc under the Companies Act 1985. This was summarised by Bingham L.J. in the *Caparo* case as follows:

"The members, or shareholders, of the company are its owners. But they are too numerous, and in most cases too unskilled, to undertake the day-to-day management of that which they own. So responsibility for day-to-day manage-

> *ment of the company is delegated to directors. The shareholders, despite their overall powers of control, are in most companies for most of the time investors and little more. But it would, of course, be unsatisfactory and open to abuse if the shareholders received no report on the financial stewardship of their investment save from those to whom the stewardship had been entrusted. So provision is made for the company in general meeting to appoint an auditor (Companies Act 1985, s.384) whose duty is to investigate and form an opinion on the adequacy of the company's accounting records and returns and the correspondence between the company's accounting records and returns and its accounts (s.237). The auditor has then to report to the company's members (among other things) whether in his opinion the company's accounts give a true and fair view of the company's financial position (s.236). In carrying out his investigation and in forming his opinion the auditor necessarily works very closely with the directors and officers of the company. He receives his remuneration from the company. He naturally, and rightly, regards the company as his client. But he is employed by the company to exercise his professional skill and judgement for the purpose of giving the shareholders an independent report on the reliability of the company's accounts and thus on their investment. Vaughan Williams J. said in Re Kingston Cotton Mill Co [1896] 1 Ch 6 at 11: "No doubt he is acting antagonistically to the directors in the sense that he is appointed by the shareholders to be a check upon them." The auditor's report must be read before the company in general meeting and must be open to inspection by any member of the company (s.241). It is attached to and forms part of the company's accounts (ss.238(3) and 239). A copy of the company's accounts (including the auditor's report) must be sent to every member (s.240)."*

There are a large number of outstanding claims for professional negligence against accountants in the UK. Such claims are invariably for financial loss and are governed by the rules of contractual negligence or by the principles laid down by the House of Lords in *Hedley Byrne v. Heller* 1964 and *Caparo Industries plc v. Dickman* 1990. In the discussion of the *Hedley Byrne* case earlier in this chapter, reference was made to the dissenting judgement of Lord Denning in *Candler v. Crane Christmas* 1951, which has been approved by the House of Lords on a number of occasions.

> In *Candler v. Crane Christmas & Co.* 1951 the plaintiff proposed to invest £2,000 in a company, but before making the investment he wished to examine the company's accounts. The defendant accountants were in the course of preparing the accounts. They were instructed by the managing director of the company to complete their work quickly and to show the accounts to the plaintiff. On the strength of the accounts the plaintiff invested his money in the company. The accounts were carelessly prepared and gave a wholly misleading picture of the state of the company, which was wound up within a year. The plaintiff lost his investment and sued the accountants for professional negligence. In a majority decision which has since been overruled by the House of Lords, the Court of Appeal held that the defendant owed no duty of care to the plaintiff. The dissenting judgement of Lord Denning was described in the *Caparo* case by Lord Bridge as a *"masterly analysis, requiring little, if any, amplification or modification in the light of later authority."* Lord Denning stated that a duty to use care in making statements is owed by:
>
> *"those persons such as accountants, surveyors, valuers and analysts, whose profession and occupation is to examine books, accounts, and other things,*

and to make reports on which other people - other than their clients - rely in the ordinary course of business. Their duty is not merely a duty to use care in their reports. They also have a duty to use care in their work which results in their reports." and he continued "to whom do these professional people owe this duty? I will take accountants, but the same reasoning applies to the others. They owe the duty, of course to their employer or client; and also I think to any third person to whom they themselves show the accounts, or to whom they know their employer is going to show the accounts, so as to induce him to invest money or take some other action on them. But I do not think the duty can be extended still further so as to include strangers of whom they have heard nothing and to whom their employer without their knowledge may choose to show their accounts. Once the accountants have handed their accounts to their employer they are not, as a rule, responsible for what he does with them without their knowledge or consent.

... It will be noticed that I have confined the duty to cases where the accountant prepares his accounts and makes his report for the guidance of the very person in the transaction in question. That is sufficient for the decision in this case. I can well understand that it would be going too far to make an accountant liable to any person in the land who chooses to rely on the accounts in matters of business, for that would expose him to "liability in an indeterminate amount for an indeterminate time to an indeterminate class".

One final word: I think that the law would fail to serve the best interests of the community if it should hold that accountants and auditors owe a duty to no one but their client. Its influence would be most marked in cases where their client is a company or firm controlled by one man. It would encourage accountants to accept the information which the one man gives them, without verifying it; and to prepare and present the accounts rather as a lawyer prepares and presents a case, putting the best appearance on the accounts they can, without expressing their personal opinion of them. This is, to my way of thinking, an entirely wrong approach. The lawyer is never called upon to express his personal belief in the truth of his client's case; whereas the accountant, who certifies the accounts of his client, is always called on to express his personal opinion as to whether the accounts exhibit a true and correct view of his client's affairs; and he is required to do this, not so much for the satisfaction of his own client, but more for the guidance of shareholders, investors, revenue authorities, and others who may have to rely on the accounts in serious matters of business."

Candler v. Crane Christmas was followed in 1964 by the decision of the House of Lords in *Hedley Byrne v. Heller* which, in addition to approving Lord Denning's judgement in *Candler*, established the *special relationship of reliance* as the test to be applied in determining whether a duty of care is owed by a person making a careless statement, including an accountant carelessly preparing misleading accounts, and causing financial loss.

Subsequently, however, the Court of Appeal in *JEB Fasteners Ltd. v. Marks Bloom & Co.* 1983 appeared to have abandoned the special relationship test preferring to follow the less restrictive approach outlined by Lord Wilberforce in *Anns v. Merton* 1977.

In *JEB Fasteners Ltd. v. Marks Bloom & Co.* 1983 the plaintiff proposed to take over another company called B.G. Fasteners Ltd. The principal reason for the takeover was that the plaintiff wished to acquire the services of the two directors of the target company. A copy of the audited accounts of the target company had been certified by the defendant accountants, without qualification, as giving atrue and fair view of the state of the company. The accounts were relied upon by the plaintiff, which acquired the entire share capital of B.G. Fasteners. The accounts had been carelessly prepared and gave a misleading picture as to the value of the company. At the time the accounts were audited the defendants had no knowledge of the plaintiff or its intentions, and were not aware that a takeover from any source was contemplated. The Court of Appeal held that the defendants owed a duty of care to the plaintiff even though it was a complete stranger to them at the time of the audit. The defendants ought to have foreseen that B.G. Fasteners would require funds from money lenders or investors in the short term and that such persons were likely to rely on the audited accounts; secondly that the defendants were in breach of the duty of care as the accounts did not provide a true and fair view of the company. In particular there was a gross overvaluation of stock which caused the profit and loss account to show a profit when in reality the company had made a loss in excess of £13,000; and thirdly that the plaintiff's claim failed on the issue of causation of loss. The evidence clearly indicated that, even if the plaintiff had known the true financial position of the target company, it would nonetheless have gone ahead with the takeover. This was because the plaintiff's overriding object was to acquire the services of the two directors of B.G. Fasteners. Therefore the defendant's negligence was not the operative cause of the plaintiff's loss.

This decision caused a good deal of uncertainty because the Court of Appeal approached the question of duty by applying the broad test of reasonable foresight of harm - the neighbour principle - rather than the more restrictive test of whether there was a special relationship of reliance between the parties. The Court of Appeal felt able to do this, despite the considerable authority of the *Hedley Byrne* decision, by applying the two-stage test laid down by Lord Wilberforce in *Anns v. Merton* 1977. This uncertainty persisted until the House of Lords in *Caparo Industries plc v. Dickman* 1990 disapproved the approach adopted in the *JEB Fastners* case, and reaffirmed *Hedley Byrne v. Heller* 1964.

In *Caparo Industries plc v. Dickman* 1990 the plaintiff owned shares in a public company, Fidelity plc, whose accounts for the year ending 31 March 1984 showed profits far short of the predicted figure. This resulted in a substantial drop in the quoted share price. After receiving the accounts for the year, which had been audited by the third defendant, Touche Ross & Co, the plaintiff purchased further shares in Fidelity plc and shortly afterward made a successful takeover bid. The plaintiff sued the auditors in negligence, claiming that the accounts were inaccurate and misleading in that they showed a profit of £1,200,000, when in fact there had been a loss of over £400,000. The plaintiff argued that the auditors owed it a duty of care either as a potential bidder for Fidelity plc because they ought to have foreseen that the 1984 results made Fidelity plc vulnerable to a takeover bid, or as an existing shareholder of Fidelity plc interested in buying more shares. The House of Lords held that a duty of care in making a statement arises only where there is a relationship of proximity between the maker of the statement (in this case the auditors) and the person relying on it (the plaintiff). A relationship of proximity is created where the maker of the statement knows that the statement will be communicated to the person relying on it specifically in connection with a particular transaction and that person would be very likely to rely on it for the purpose of deciding whether to enter into the transaction. Applying this principle to the case, the House of Lords held that no duty of care was owed by the auditors to the plaintiff as there was no relationship of proximity on the facts as the auditors were not aware of the plaintiff or its intentions at the time the statement was made. Although auditors owe a statutory duty to shareholders, this is owed to them as a class rather than as individuals. The nature of this duty was explained by Lord Jauncey who stated:

"the purpose of the annual accounts, so far as members are concerned, is to enable them to question the past management of the company, to exercise their voting rights, and to influence future policy and management. Advice to individual shareholders in relation to present or future investment in the company is no part of this purpose."

The principles laid down by the House of Lords in the *Caparo* case have been applied by the Court of Appeal in two further cases within a very short period of time. In the first of the two, *Caparo* was distinguished.

In *Morgan Crucible Co. Plc v. Hill Samuel Bank Ltd. and Others* 1991 the plaintiff announced a takeover bid for a company called First Castle Electronics plc. First Castle recommended it shareholders not to accept the bid, and issued a number of documents to its shareholders intended to encourage them to retain their shares in order to defend the company from the proposed takeover. One of the defence documents forecast an increase in profits of 38% for the financial year and included a letter from the accountants stating that the profit forecast had been properly compiled. Shortly afterwards the plaintiff increased its bid and succeeded in acquiring First Castle. Subsequently the plaintiff sued claiming that the accounting policies adopted in the profit forecast were negligently misleading and grossly overstated the profits. On an appeal relating to the preliminary issue of whether a duty of care could arise in these circumstances, the Court of Appeal held that it could on the basis that if during a contested takeover bid the directors and financial advisers of the target company made express representations after an identified bidder had emerged, intending that the bidder would rely on those representations, they owed the bidder a duty of care not to mislead him.

In the second of the two cases, the *Caparo* decision was applied.

In *James McNaughton Papers Group Ltd. v. Hicks Anderson & Co.* 1991 the plaintiff was negotiating an agreed takeover of a loss making rival company, MK Papers. The defendants were accountants for MK. At MK's request draft accounts were quickly prepared for use in the negotiations. During a meeting between the plaintiff and MK, a representative of the defendants stated, in answer to a question, that as a result of rationalisation MK was breaking even or doing marginally worse. After the takeover was completed the plaintiff discovered discrepancies in the draft accounts and sued the defendants in negligence. The Court of Appeal, applying principles laid down in *Caparo*, held that the defendants did not owe a duty of care to the plaintiff, in particular because the accounts were produced for use by MK and not the plaintiff, they were merely draft accounts and the defendants could not reasonably have foreseen that the plaintiff would treat them as final accounts. The defendants did not take part in the negotiations, and the plaintiff was aware that MK was in a poor state and could be expected to consult their own accountant. Further it could not reasonably be foreseen that the plaintiff would rely on the answer given to the question without further inquiry or advice, particularly because the answer was in very general terms.

Surveyors

In Chapter 16 we examine the process of conveyancing in relation to the acquisition of land and premises by a business, and look at the role of the surveyor within that process. A surveyor, in carrying out a valuation of a dwellinghouse which is being purchased with the aid of a Building Society mortgage, owes a duty of care to the purchaser of the property to carry out a reasonably careful visual inspection. This was established by the decision of the High Court in *Yianni v. Edwin Evans* 1981.

The *Yianni* case was approved by the House of Lords in *Smith v. Bush* and *Harris v. Wyre Forest DC,* two cases which were heard together in 1989.

> In *Smith v. Eric S. Bush (a firm)* the defendants were engaged by the Abbey National Building Society to carry out a survey and valuation of a house as required by s.13 Building Societies Act 1986. The plaintiff, who intended to purchase the house, paid for the inspection. She later purchased without the benefit of any structural survey. Eighteen months after the purchase, part of the house fell in because the flues in the attic were left unsupported when the chimney breast in the room below had been taken out, a defect which the defendants had overlooked when surveying the house.
>
> In *Harris v. Wyre Forest District Council,* the plaintiffs applied to the defendants for a 90% mortgage to assist in the purchase of their council house. The defendants also had a statutory duty to obtain a valuation before advancing the money and instructed their own valuation surveyor to carry it out. After receiving the report they granted the mortgage to the plaintiffs who assumed therefore that the surveyor had found no serious defects and purchased the property without their own independent survey. Three years later they discovered that the house was subject to settlement, was virtually unsaleable and could only be repaired at a cost greater than the purchase price.
>
> The House of Lords held that a valuer who carried out a mortgage valuation for a typical house purchase owed a duty of care both to the lender and to the borrower to carry out his valuation with reasonable skill and care. The valuer would know that the valuation fee had been paid by the borrower and that the valuation would probably be relied upon by him in deciding whether or not to enter into a contract to purchase the house. This knowledge could readily be implied in relation to a borrower within the lower or middle range of the housing market, although the position would be different in the case of very expensive residential property or commercial property. In each case the House of Lords held that the defendants were in breach of their duty to carry out reasonably careful visual inspections of the premises. The scope of the duty was described by Lord Templeman:
>
> *"The valuer will value the house after taking into consideration major defects which are, or ought to be, obvious to him in the course of a visual inspection of so much of the exterior and interior of the house as may be accessible to him without undue difficulty."*

In carrying out a mortgage valuation, a surveyor will be liable if he fails to notice defects, such as signs of structural movement, dry or wet rot, or dampness which are observable by a careful visual examination. He is not, however, expected to lift carpets, move furniture or carry out a detailed inspection of the roof space unless he observes something which would lead a reasonably competent surveyor to make further investigations. Lord Templeman expressly approved the view expressed by Ian Kennedy J in *Roberts v. J Hampson & Co.* 1989:

> *"If a surveyor misses a defect because its signs are hidden, that is a risk that his client must accept. But, if there is a specific ground for suspicion and the trail of suspicion leads behind furniture or under carpets, the surveyor must take reasonable steps to follow the trail until he has all the information which it is reasonable for him to have before making his valuation."*

In the *Bush* and *Harris* cases, the House of Lords had also to deal with disclaimers of liability which were contained in the valuation reports. It was held that such disclaimers were subject to the test of reasonableness under s.2(2) of the Unfair Contract Terms Act 1977. Having regard to the high cost of houses and the high rates of interest charged to borrowers, their Lordships decided that it would not be fair and reasonable for mortgagees and valuers to impose on purchasers the risk of loss arising as a result of incompetence or carelessness on the part of valuers, and that the disclaimers were therefore ineffective.

The reasonableness of a disclaimer of liability in similar circumstances to *Smith v. Bush* was considered in *Stevenson v. Nationwide Building Society* 1984. In this case, however, the purchaser was an estate agent who was well familiar with the difference between a valuation and a structural survey. It was held that the disclaimer was reasonable and effective to protect the defendant, when its staff surveyor failed to notice a substantial structural defect during the course of a visual inspection.

Where the elements of duty and breach are established by a plaintiff, the claim may still fail on the issue of causation.

> In *Shankie-Williams and others v. Heavey* 1986 the defendant was employed by Mr. & Mrs. Shankie-Williams (the first and second plaintiffs) to carry out a survey for dry rot on a flat which they intended to buy. The surveyor wrongly reported that there was no dry rot and the purchase went ahead. The third plaintiff saw the report and, believing that it referred to the whole building, bought the flat immediately above. In fact both flats were badly affected by dry rot. The Court of Appeal held that the defendant owed no duty of care to the third plaintiff. The claim of the first and second plaintiffs also failed on the issue of causation. A duty of care was owed to them but the court was satisfied that, on the evidence, they would have purchased the flat without a reduction of the purchase price had they known of the dry rot. The surveyor's negligence therefore was not the operative cause of their loss.

Where a surveyor carries out a mortgage valuation and negligently overvalues the premises, he may be liable to the mortgagee if he suffers loss on a forced sale following the borrower's default on the loan.

> In *Swingcastle Ltd. v. Alastair Gibson* 1991, the House of Lords held the defendant surveyors liable where they valued a house at £18,000 on a forced sale with vacant possession when the house was in fact sold for only £12,000 after the plaintiff finance company obtained a possession order.

The legal profession

In Chapter 1 we noted the fact that the legal profession in the UK is divided into two distinct branches and discussed the roles of solicitors and barristers in the legal process. In relation to that part of their work which involves the presentation of cases before a court, members of both branches of the legal profession enjoy an immunity from liability for professional negligence, for reasons which we will consider below. This immunity is of particular significance for the barrister, as most of his work will involve advocacy in the courts.

Barristers

In *Rondel v. Worsley* 1967 the plaintiff, who had been convicted of causing grievous bodily harm, sued his barrister for professional negligence. He claimed that the defendant barrister had failed to take reasonable care in the conduct of his criminal defence and that he would have been acquitted if the case had been properly handled. The House of Lords held that the plaintiff's claim failed. A barrister's conduct of a case in court could never give rise to a claim in negligence.

The decision was made on the grounds of public policy. It would be contrary to the public interest to allow such a claim for the following reasons:

(a) A barrister owes a duty not only to his client but also to the court, for example he has a duty not to mislead the court. These twin duties could, on occasion, conflict with each other. He should not be placed, under the pressure of a potential negligence claim, in a position in which he might be tempted to disregard his duty to the court.

(b) A finding of negligence would necessarily involve a finding that the case in question had been wrongly decided. Thus the negligence proceedings would amount to a retrial of the original case and cast uncertainty on the finality of the previous decision.

(c) The judge in the original case has a duty to ensure a fair trial and will intervene if necessary to ensure that all of the relevant issues are properly considered.

(d) Barristers operate under the so-called cab rank principle which means that they have no choice but to accept a client provided the proper fee is paid.

The immunity of the barrister in these circumstances was said by the majority of the Law Lords in *Rondel's* case to extend to solicitors engaged in litigation before the courts.

The scope of the barrister's immunity was further considered by the House of Lords in *Saif Ali v. Sydney Mitchell & Co.* 1978. A barrister failed to advise the plaintiff to bring proceedings against the correct defendant in a personal injuries claim within the three year limitation period. The House of Lords held that the barrister was not immune from proceedings in negligence in these circumstances because the immunity only extends to matters of pre-trial work which are intimately connected with the conduct of the case in court.

In relation to work carried out by a barrister which is not connected with litigation, for example giving opinions and drawing up wills, he may be liable for professional negligence under the principles laid down by the House of Lords in *Hedley Byrne v. Heller* 1964. However he cannot be sued for breach of contract as he has no contractual relationship with his client.

Solicitors

The extent of the solicitor's immunity under the principles laid down in *Saif Ali* was considered by the Court of Appeal in *Somasundaram v. Julius Melchior & Co.* 1989. The plaintiff claimed that the defendant solicitors had been negligent in overpersuading him to plead guilty to the malicious wounding of his wife whom he had stabbed during an argument. The defendant argued that advice as to plea of guilty or not guilty in a criminal case is so intimately connected with the conduct of the case in court as to be covered by immunity. The Court of Appeal accepted this argument and recognised that the immunity applied both to barristers and to solicitors when acting as advocates. However the court did not accept that the immunity applied to a solicitor when a barrister had also been engaged to advise. Despite this finding, the plaintiff did not succeed in his action, as the court also held, as a matter of causation, that the barrister's advice as to plea breaks the chain of causation between the solicitor's advice and the client's plea; and in any event an action for negligence against a barrister or a solicitor could not be brought where its effect would be to challenge the decision of a court of competent jurisdiction.

A solicitors may be liable in negligence to a third party with whom he has no contract:

In *Ross v. Caunters* 1979, for example, a solicitor drew up a will and sent it out for his client to sign. The solicitor gave instructions for the signing and witnessing of the will but forgot to warn his client that if the will was witnessed by a beneficiary or the spouse of a beneficiary then the gift would be invalidated. The will was witnessed by the husband of the plaintiff and the mistake was not discovered until after the client's death. The plaintiff, who was a beneficiary under the will, lost her gift and sued the solicitor for the financial loss caused by his negligence. It was held that the solicitor owed a duty of care to the plaintiff and was liable as his failure to take care had caused her loss.

Whether the courts will recognise the existence of a duty of care in tort where there is a contract between the parties is now an open point.

In *Midland Bank Trust Co. Ltd v. Hett, Stubbs and Kemp* 1979 the defendant solicitors carelessly failed to register as a land charge an option to purchase a farm granted to their client. The client's right to exercise the option to purchase was defeated, because of the failure to register, on the sale of the farm to a third party. The client sued in negligence and the court held that the solicitors were in breach of their duty of care to the client both in contract and in tort under the *Hedley Byrne* principle. It was essential to the success of the claim that the court recognised the existence of a duty in tort in addition to the contractual duty. This is because the plaintiff's claim in contract was statute-barred under the Limitation Act as more than six years had elapsed since the breach of contract by the solicitors. The limitation period in the tort of negligence, however, does not begin to run until the damage has occurred, in this case the date on which the farm was sold to the third party. As this was within six years of the commencement of proceedings in this case, the claim in negligence was not time-barred.

It appears that the approach taken by the High Court in the *Midland Bank Trust* case may no longer be sustainable. Although there has not been a further decision specifically on the point, a number of recent cases strongly suggest that the courts are unwilling to recognise the existence of liability in tort where the relationship between the parties is based on contract.

> In *Tai Hing Cotton Mills v. Liu Chong Hing Bank Ltd.* 1986, a decision of the Privy Council, Lord Scarman stated:
>
> *"Their Lordships do not believe that there is anything to the advantage of the law's development in searching for a liability in tort where the parties are in a contractual relationship."*
>
> A similar approach was adopted more recently by the Court of Appeal in *National Bank of Greece SA v. Pinios Shipping Co. The Maria* 1989 where the court took the view that, in the words of Lloyd, L.J *"if the plaintiff fails in contract, he must necessarily fail in tort".*

Product Liability in Negligence

It was seen in Chapter 8 that the right to make a product liability claim in contract is confined to an injured person who actually buys the goods himself. The contract claim can be brought against the supplier of the goods only. The supplier is strictly liable, even if he is not at fault. In negligence anyone injured by the product can sue anyone who has failed to take reasonable care in relation to it thereby causing the injury.

We shall now examine those elements of negligence liability which are particularly significant in defective product claims:

The duty of care

In relation to liability for manufactured products we have seen that it was not until as late as 1932 that it was recognised that a general duty of care was owed by manufacturers to consumers. This was established by the decision of the House of Lords in the case of *Donoghue v. Stevenson* the facts of which were described earlier. The importance of the decision in the field of product liability lies in the fact that, in his judgment, Lord Atkin described the duty of a manufacturer in the following terms:

> *"... a manufacturer of products, which he sells in such a form as to show that he intends them to reach the ultimate consumer in the form in which they left him with no reasonable possibility of intermediate examination, and with the knowledge that the absence of reasonable care in the preparation or putting up of the products will result in an injury to the consumer's life or property, owes a duty to the consumer to take that reasonable care."*

Although this statement has been developed by subsequent interpretation it can still be regarded as the framework within which a court will decide whether a duty of care exists. Four elements within the framework require closer examination:

(a) Who can be sued

Lord Atkin's reference to *a manufacturer of products* embraces everyone involved in the manufacturing enterprise from design to distribution. It also extends to others who have worked on the goods at any time.

> In *Stennet v. Hancock* 1939, for example, the plaintiff was a pedestrian who was injured when part of the wheel of a lorry broke away whilst the lorry was

being driven. The defect in the wheel was the result of a repair which had not been carried out properly. The court held that the repairers were liable under Lord Atkin's manufacturing principle.

(b) What type of defects will give rise to liability

Lord Atkin referred to products which the manufacturer sells *in such a form as to show that he intends them to reach the ultimate consumer in the form in which they left him with no reasonable possibility of intermediate examination.* This has been interpreted as limiting the application of the duty to products with latent defects. Latent defects are faults which are not apparent on an examination of the goods. Lord Wright in *Grant v. Australian Knitting Mills Ltd.* 1936 stated that:

> *"The principle of Donoghue's case can only be applied where the defect is hidden and unknown to the consumer ... the man who consumes or uses a thing which he knows to be noxious cannot complain in respect of whatever mischief follows, because it follows from his own conscious volition in choosing to incur the risk or certainty of mischance."*

This interpretation of Lord Atkin's principle was followed in the case of *Crow v. Barford (Agricultural) Ltd.* and *H.B. Holttum & Co. Ltd.* 1963. The plaintiff bought a rotary lawn mower known as a Barford Rotomo from Holttum after it was demonstrated to him at home. The machine was designed in such a way that the guard for the blades had an opening to allow the grass to be expelled as it was being cut. To start the lawn mower the user's foot had to be placed on the casing containing the blade. While starting the Rotomo the plaintiff's foot slipped into the opening and two of his toes were cut off.

The claim against the manufacturer was made on the basis of the principle in *Donoghue v. Stevenson* but the Court of Appeal decided that this did not apply because the danger was "perfectly obvious" and not hidden or unknown to the plaintiff. The claim in contract against the retailer was also unsuccessful because the plaintiff had inspected the lawn mower during the demonstration before he purchased it. This brought the case within the exception contained in s.14(2) of the Sale of Goods Act that the seller does not promise that the goods are of merchantable quality in relation to defects which ought to have been revealed by the buyer's prior examination of the goods.

(c) To whom is the duty owed

Lord Atkin tells us that the duty of care is owed to the *ultimate consumer* of the product. This expression has been interpreted widely so as to include the purchaser, any person injured while using or consuming the product and any other person, such as the plaintiff in *Stennet v. Hancock,* who is injured by the product in circumstances where injury to him ought reasonably to have been foreseen.

For example, in *Lambert v. Lewis (Lexmead Ltd., third party; Dixon Bate Ltd., fourth party)* 1982 the driver of a car and his son were killed and the plaintiffs, his wife and daughter, were injured when their car was hit by a trailer which had become detached from a farmer's Land Rover and careered across the road into the path of their car. The accident was caused by a design defect in the towing hitch, which was unable to cope with the stresses to which it was subjected in normal use. The evidence showed that part of

> the towing hitch had been missing for a number of months before the accident and that the farmer should have realised this.
>
> The trial judge decided that the manufacturer was 75% to blame for the accident and that the farmer was 25% to blame and apportioned liability accordingly. The farmer issued third party proceedings against the retailer from whom he had purchased the towing hitch. He was seeking indemnity for the damages for which he was liable and basing his claim in contract on the retailer's breach of the implied terms in s.14 Sale of Goods Act. The retailer in turn issued fourth party proceedings against the manufacturer in contract and in negligence. On appeal the House of Lords decided that the retailer was not liable to the farmer because the farmer's own negligence, rather than the retailer's breach of contract, was the operative cause of his loss. The fourth party proceedings were consequently dismissed because the retailer had no liability to pass on to the manufacturer.

(d) What type of damage is recoverable

In his statement of the duty of care owed by a manufacturer, Lord Atkin confines the scope of the duty to *injury to the consumer's life or property*. Within this damages are recoverable for death, personal injury or damage to property, excluding damage to the product itself.

One category of loss which cannot always be sued for in negligence, as we have seen, is pure financial loss. A 1985 case provides a good illustration of this rule in the context of product liability.

> In *Muirhead v. Industrial Tank Specialities (ITT Marlow, third party; Leroy Somer Electric Motors Ltd., fourth party)* 1985, the plaintiff was a wholesale fish merchant who installed in his premises a large seawater tank in which to store lobsters. The seawater had to be filtered, oxygenated and recirculated. This was done by a series of pumps working 24 hours per day. The tank and pumps were installed by I.T.S. Ltd. The pumps were manufactured by Leroy Somer Electric Motors Ltd and supplied to the plaintiff by I.T.S. Ltd. through other suppliers in the chain of distribution. The pumps constantly broke down and on one occasion the recirculation of water was affected so that the plaintiff lost his entire stock of lobsters. The plaintiff successfully sued I.T.S. Ltd. in contract but the company went into liquidation unable to satisfy the judgement against it. The plaintiff then proceeded with action against the manufacturers claiming damages for all of the losses incurred as a result of the defects in the pumps. The vast bulk of the claim was for the loss of profits on intended sales but the Court of Appeal decided that this was pure financial loss and therefore not recoverable in a negligence action. The rest of the plaintiff's claim succeeded.

Breach of duty

Once it has been established that the manufacturer in a given case owes a duty of care to avoid injury to the plaintiff, the second major element of negligence liability which the plaintiff must prove is that the manufacturer was in breach of that duty. A breach of duty is a failure to take reasonable care and involves a finding of fault on the part of the manufacturer. In many cases the task of proving this may be a difficult one for the plaintiff, involving a detailed investigation of the defendant's processes of manufacture design and testing and a comparison with procedures adopted by other producers in the same field. The plaintiff will need to employ expert witnesses who can analyse these processes and procedures and pinpoint any lack of care which may have caused the defect in the product and therefore caused the injury. If the plaintiff is unable to prove a breach of duty he may have to bear the loss himself without compensation, unless there is another available legal basis for his claim.

A breach of the duty of care may occur outside the process of development design and manufacture.

> In the case of *Vacwell Engineering v. BDH Chemicals Ltd.* 1971 for example, the manufacturer of a chemical produced for industrial use was held liable in negligence for a failure to give proper and adequate warnings that the chemical would explode when mixed with water. This should have been achieved by clear labelling of the product.
>
> In *Walton v. British Leyland (UK) Ltd.* 1978 the failure of British Leyland to recall the Austin Allegro car after a large number of 'wheel drift' faults had been reported to the company was held to be a breach of the duty of care. Leyland were held liable to the plaintiffs who were severely injured when the wheel of their Allegro came off as the vehicle was travelling at 60 mph on a motorway. The Judge, Willis J., in the High Court stated:
>
> *"The duty of care owed by Leyland to the public was to make a clean breast of the problem and recall all cars which they could in order that safety washers could be fitted ... The company seriously considered recall and made an estimate of the cost at a figure (£300,000 in 1974) which seems to me to be in no way out of proportion to the risks involved. It was decided not to follow this course for commercial reasons. I think this involved a failure to observe their duty of care for the safety of the many who were bound to remain at risk ..."*

Res ipsa loquitur

In the context of product liability the principle of res ipsa loquitur is of considerable significance. The tendency in recent times has been for the courts to allow the plaintiff to rely on the rule in many cases involving defective products. Res ipsa loquitur is considered in detail earlier in this chapter. Here we may note its application in product liability cases.

> In *Chaproniere v. Mason* 1905 the plaintiff broke a tooth when eating a bread bun which was found to contain a pebble. He pleaded res ipsa loquitur and the defendant baker was held to be liable because he was unable to prove that he had not been negligent.

Where the plaintiff pleads res ipsa loquitur, the manufacturer will need to produce strong evidence if he is to satisfy the court that the injuries were not caused by his negligence. It will not be sufficient for him to show that he has a good system of work and provides adequate supervision during the process of manufacture.

> In *Grant v. Australian Knitting Mills* 1936 the plaintiff contracted dermatitis because of the presence in his underwear of excess sulphite after the process of manufacture by the defendant. The defendant's evidence was that he had manufactured over four and a half million pairs of underpants and had received no other complaints. Nevertheless he was held liable because the probability was that someone in his employment for whose acts he was legally responsible had failed to take care.
>
> In *Hill v. James Crowe (Cases) Ltd.* 1978 the plaintiff, a lorry driver, was injured when he fell off a badly nailed wooden packing case on which he was

> standing in order to load his lorry. The manufacturer of the packing case gave evidence that the standards of workmanship and supervision in his factory were high and argued that he had not failed to fulfil his duty to the plaintiff to take reasonable care in producing the case. The Court held that the defendant was liable for the bad workmanship of one of his employees even though, in general terms, he had a good production system. He had not proved that the plaintiff's injuries were not due to the negligence of one of his employees.

This case provides an example of the manufacturer's liability for a foreseeable misuse of his product.

The extremely high standard of care which the courts are prepared to impose on a manufacturer can be seen in *Winward v. TVR.*

> In *Winward v. TVR Engineering* 1986 the defendants were in the business of producing specialist sports cars. They were responsible for the design and assembly of the vehicles using components bought in from other sources. The car in question incorporated a Ford engine which was supplied to the defendants fitted with a Weber carburettor. The carburettor had a basic design fault which ultimately caused petrol to leak from it. The plaintiff's wife was injured when leaking petrol came into contact with the hot engine. The defendants argued that it was reasonable for them to rely on the expertise of their supplier, particularly as the design fault had never previously manifested itself. The Court of Appeal held that the defendants were in breach of their duty through their failure to test the component and modify its design.

Part I of the Consumer Protection Act 1987

Part I of the Consumer Protection Act 1987, which introduces a framework of strict liability for defective products, was enacted in order to fulfil UK obligations under the EEC Directive on Product Liability (85/374/EEC).

The EEC Directive

We saw in Chapter 1 that a consequence of our membership of the EEC is that we are obliged to implement legal changes agreed within the Community. One method of achieving legal change is through the use of the directive. A directive is binding as to the result to be achieved but allows the member state to choose the precise method of implementation.

The preamble to this Directive tells us that it has a two-fold purpose:

(i) to establish a uniform system of product liability within the EEC in order to remove distortions of trade and competition which arise because of the differences between the laws of member states in this field; and

(ii) to solve the problem of a fair apportionment of the risks inherent in modern technological production.

There were lengthy negotiations between the EEC member states on the terms of the Directive. Final adoption in July 1985 was only possible because of an agreement to differ on some of the sticking points in the negotiations.

This gave rise to a number of optional provisions in final text of the Directive and means that full harmonisation of some aspects of product liability law throughout the EEC has not been achieved. A practical consequence of this may be *forum shopping* by the injured party. Where there are two possible defendants, each in a different EEC country, the forum shopper will bring his claim in the country in which he stands the best chance of success, having regard to the options adopted there.

The Directive provides for a review of the working of the optional provisions in 1995 in order to reconsider the question of full harmonisation after that review.

The UK response to the three options which were available under the Directive has been:

(i) to incorporate the development risks defence;

(ii) to exclude unprocessed agricultural produce and game, and

(iii) to reject an overall financial limit (£41m) for damage caused by identical products with the same defect.

The Consumer Protection Act 1987

Liability under s.2(1) of the Act arises *"where any damage is caused wholly or partly by a defect in a product"*. In order to succeed in a claim, the plaintiff must prove two things:

(a) that the product was defective, and

(b) that the defect caused the injury or damage.

If the plaintiff can prove these things, the defendant will be liable even though he took all possible care in relation to the product. This is the crucial difference between strict liability under the Act and liability based upon negligence which, as we have seen, depends upon proof of fault by the defendant.

Who is liable?

Liability falls upon all or any of the following persons:

(a) the **producer** - this term is defined in s.1(2) and includes the manufacturer of the product, the producer of any raw materials or the manufacturer of a component part.

(b) the **'own brander'** - any person who, by putting his name on the product or using a trade mark or other distinguishing marks in relation to it, has held himself out to be the producer of the product

(c) the **importer into the EEC** - a person importing the product into the Community from a non Community state for the purpose of supplying it in the course of his business.

(d) any **supplier** who cannot identify the person who produced the product, or supplied it to him. In such circumstances that person will be liable, regardless of whether he was a business supplier, provided he supplied the product to someone else, and the following conditions are met:

  (i) he is requested by a person suffering any damage to identify any producer, own brander or importer into the EEC;

(ii) the request is made within a reasonable time after the damage occurs;

(iii) at the time of the request it is not reasonably practicable for the injured party to identify all of the potential defendants; and

(iv) he fails, within a reasonable time, to comply with the request or to identify the person who supplied the product to him.

Thus it will be imperative, where litigation is threatened, for businesses to be able to identify the supplier of the products or component parts used in any goods sold by the business. It will be particularly important to differentiate, by product coding for example, between the products of two or more suppliers who are supplying identical components for incorporation into the same type of finished product. This will apply to all component parts ranging from electric motors to nuts and bolts.

Where two or more persons are liable for the injury each can be sued for the full amount of the damage. The party who is sued may be entitled to a contribution or indemnity from anyone else who is liable, under the Civil Liability (Contribution) Act 1978. Of course the injured person can only recover compensation once, regardless of the number of possible defendants or the legal basis of his claim. The injured person will usually choose to sue the defendant against whom liability can most easily be established and who is most likely to be able to afford to pay damages or to have insurance cover.

When is a product defective?

In order to succeed in a claim the plaintiff will have to prove that his injury was caused by a defect in the product. Section 3 tells us that a product will be regarded as defective when *"the safety of the product is not such as persons generally are entitled to expect"*. It is clear that the lawnmower in *Crow v. Barford and Holttum* above would be defective under this definition. The question of when a product is defective is likely to be central to much of the litigation under the Act. Section 3(2) gives us some guidance as to the factors which will be relevant in deciding whether a product is defective. It provides:

"In determining what persons generally are entitled to expect in relation to a product all the circumstances shall be taken into account, including -

(a) the manner in which, and purposes for which, the product has been marketed, its get-up, the use of any mark in relation to the product and any instructions for, or warnings with respect to, doing or refraining from doing anything with or in relation to the product;

(b) what might reasonably be expected to be done with or in relation to the product; and

(c) the time when the product was supplied by its producer to another person;

and nothing in this section shall require a defect to be inferred from the fact alone that the safety of a product which is supplied after that time is greater than the safety of the product in question."

Clearly it is very important for any business to ensure that the packaging of their products is such that it does not suggest or imply that the product can be used in a manner or for a purpose which is unsafe. Appropriate warnings of the dangers associated with the use or foreseeable misuse of the product must be amply displayed on the packaging and, where necessary, on the goods themselves. A further precaution which may be taken by the producer of goods is the date coding of products in order to take advantage of the defence suggested by the final part of s.3(2). Thus if a safer product is subsequently developed and put onto the market, the level of safety provided by the original product cannot be judged solely by reference to improved safety features in the new product.

Defences

A number of specific defences are provided for in s.4 of the Consumer Protection Act. These are in addition to the obvious defences that the product was not defective or that it was not the cause of the plaintiff's loss. Thus it is a defence to show:

(a) that the defect was attributable to the defendant's compliance with a legal requirement, or

(b) that the defendant did not supply the goods to anyone.

In this connection it is interesting to notice s.1(3) which says that where a finished product incorporates component products or raw materials, the supplier of the finished product will not be treated as a supplier of the component products or raw materials by reason only of his supply of the finished product. Thus, for example, a builder using high alumina cement could argue that he was not a supplier of that cement for the purposes of the Act. He could invoke this defence if the building subsequently deteriorated due to defects in the cement.

(c) Section 4 also enables the defendant to escape liability if he can show that he had not supplied the goods in the course of his business and that he had not own branded, imported into the EEC, or produced the goods with a view to profit.

This defence could be invoked, for example, in relation to the sale of home made jam at a coffee morning in aid of charity.

(d) The nature of the fourth defence under s.4 depends upon whether the defendant is a producer, own brander or importer into the EEC. If he is, he can escape liability by proving that the defect was not present in the product at the time he supplied it. If he is not, he must show that the defect was not present in the product at the time it was last supplied by any person of that description.

(e) Section 4 provides the *development risks* defence that, given the state of scientific and technical knowledge at the time the product was put into circulation, no producer of a product of that kind could have been expected to have discovered the defect if it had existed in his products while they were under his control.

The development risks defence has provoked much discussion. Its adoption was optional under the terms of the directive. It is argued that the defence reduces the strictness of liability by introducing considerations which are more relevant to negligence. Its main impact will be seen in those areas which are at the forefront of scientific and technical development. The pharmaceutical industry, for example, could benefit from it in relation to the development of new drugs. It may seem ironic that if an event like the Thalidomide tragedy were to re-occur the victims could be prevented from recovering compensation because of the operation of this defence. The tragedy was in fact a major cause of pressure for the introduction of strict product liability laws throughout Europe.

(f) Where the defendant is a producer of a component product, he will have a defence under s.4 if he can show that the defect in the finished product is wholly attributable to its design or to compliance with instructions given by the producer of the finished product.

Damage

Assuming the plaintiff succeeds in his claim, the question arises as to the types of loss he will be compensated for. Under s.5 damages are recoverable for death or for personal injury. This includes any disease or other impairment of a person's physical or mental condition. The plaintiff will also be able to claim compensation for damage to his property. However, exceptions to this provide significant limitations on liability under the Act. There is no liability for loss of or damage to:

(a) the product itself,

(b) any property in respect of which the amount of the claim would be below £275,

(c) any commercial property - property of a type which is not ordinarily intended for private use, occupation or consumption and which is not actually intended by the plaintiff for his own private use, occupation or consumption.

Any of these excluded losses could of course be the subject of a claim in contract or negligence.

Contracting out

Section 7 of the Consumer Protection Act provides for an absolute prohibition on the limitation or exclusion of liability arising under the Act.

Time limits for claims

The limitation period provided for in the Act, regardless of the type of damage, is three years from the date on which the right to take action arises, or, if later, three years from the date on which the plaintiff is aware:

(a) that he has suffered significant damage,

(b) that the damage is attributable to a defect in the product, and

(c) of the identity of the defendant.

There is an overall cut off point 10 years after the product is put into circulation. After the 10 year period has elapsed no new claims can be made although any proceedings which have already been started may continue.

Figure 10.2 *Comparison of Alternative Forms of Legal Liability Injuries Caused by Defective Products*

	Contract	Negligence	Consumer Protection Act
who is liable	seller; he may claim an indemnity from the previous seller in the chain of distribution	manufacturer; includes designer, repairer, processor and other persons working on goods	producer, own brander, importer into EEC, supplier who refuses to identify previous supplier or producer
who can claim	buyer only	ultimate consumer provided injury to him is foreseeable	any person injured by a defect in the product
basis of liability	strict; if goods not reasonably fit for usual or notified special purposes	fault; failure to take reasonable care in relation to the product	strict; where the product does not provide the safety which persons are entitled to expect
types of loss	personal injury death damage to property financial loss	personal injury death damage to property other than the product financial loss	personal injury death damage £275+ to consumer property other than product
exclusion of liability	prohibited if buyer dealing as consumer otherwise possible if exclusion is reasonable	prohibited if death or personal injury otherwise possible if exclusion is reasonable	prohibited in all cases
time limit for claims	personal injury; 3 years from the date on which the plaintiff had knowledge of the material facts giving rise to the claim other claims; 6 years from the date on which cause of action arose; or in negligence cases only, (if later) 3 years from the date of plaintiff's knowledge of the material facts if within 15 years of the negligent act		3 years from the date on which the plaintiff was aware of the damage the defect and the identity of the defendant if no more than 10 years since the product was put into circulation

Assignment *An Arabian Tale*

Thompsons Importers was owned and managed by Michael Thompson. Michael had decided to sell the business, having reached an age at which he felt he ought to be taking life more easily. The major activity carried on by Thompsons was the import into the United Kingdom of luxury goods from the Middle East and India.

The business was put on the market, and one of Michael's trading competitors, Arabian Exportex Ltd. expressed an interest in acquiring it. The managing director of the company, Alan Naseem, indicated to Michael that the company would require a report on the condition and future prospects of the business and Michael agreed to this.

The report was prepared by Rupert Gray, an accountant with Frayne and Company a reputable firm of accountants in Birmingham. Alan Naseem happened to know Rupert Gray, and encouraged him to make the report, "as pessimistic in assessing the future prospects of Thompsons as you feel truth will permit."

Rupert Gray's report contained a number of reasons for doubting the future viability of Thompsons. In particular it contained statements that: "the business is unlikely to withstand competition from foreign competitors whose profit margins and overheads are lower, and who are attracting and increasing share of the market"; and "import duties on luxury goods from outside the EEC are to be increased from next year."

Rupert Gray actually had no knowledge or information about foreign competition either for the present of the future, but had relied on observations made by Alan Naseem during a conversation with him. He had however read an article in Accountancy World in which it was stated that "import duties on some luxury items brought into the United Kingdom from outside the EEC are to be revised." Arabia Exportex Ltd. sent a copy of the report to Michael Thompson, who in consequence dropped his price by £100,000. Arabia Exportex Ltd. purchased at the lower price.

Two years after selling out to Arabia Exportex Ltd., Michael happened to meet a former business colleague who knows the import business well. Michael discovered that no changes had been made to import duties since he sold the business, and the foreign competition referred to in the report had not materialised. Following an angry phone call to Alan Naseem, Mr. Naseem has revealed the instruction he gave to Rupert Gray regarding the report, and says his company cannot be held responsible for a report produced by an independent professional.

Task

You are employed by a large firm of accountants who for many years have handled Michael Thompson's affairs. You are called upon to provide legal advice from time to time, and the senior partner has passed on to you the situations described above, as told to him by Michael Thompson. The senior partner suggests that probably a solicitor needs to be involved, but has asked you to arrange to meet Mr. Thompson to discuss the matter when he calls in to the office next week, or alternatively to write advising him.

Prepare notes on the issues involved as a preliminary to meeting and discussing the matter with Mr. Thompson.

Assignment *The New Complaints Department*

Spicer and Sharp plc is an expanding company based in the West Midlands. The company is engaged in the production of power tools, D.I.Y. equipment and accessories. Most of its products, or their components, are actually manufactured by subcontractors and supplied to Spicer and Sharp's main works in Kings Norton, where they are assembled and packaged in the distinctive style of the company under the Spicer and Sharp brand name. The company's expansion is based on an aggressive marketing strategy which aims to establish strong product identity and brand loyalty in order to capture a major share of the UK market.

With the introduction of the Consumer Protection Act 1987, the company is facing an increase in the number of customer complaints and product liability claims against it. This is imposing a considerable strain on the resources of the company's small legal department. The directors have decided to establish a new consumer complaints department to act as a filtering mechanism, dealing with less serious complaints and referring on to the legal department those which are likely to result in substantial claims against the company. In relation to the more serious complaints, the task of the consumer complaints department will be to obtain as much relevant information as possible from the complainant and from internal sources within the company; to make a preliminary assessment of the legal basis of the claim and any defences which may be available to the company; and to make broad recommendations as to any action which should be taken by the company, for example in relation to its quality control procedures, in order to prevent further similar claims. A report dealing with all of these matters must be prepared by the department, and copies given to the legal department and to Mr. Philip Sharp, the director to whom the department will be responsible.

Having been in post as a legal assistant in Spicer and Sharp's legal department for three years, you have been appointed to set up and run the new consumer complaints department. Your first task is to deal with a complaint which has recently been received relating to injuries sustained by Andrew Tucker while using a circular saw fitted with a Spicer and Sharp circular saw blade and belonging to his brother Alan. Alan Purchases the new blade for his Spicer and Sharp Circular saw from Sedgewick's Home Handyman Stores and loaned it to Andrew who was constructing built-in wardrobes in his daughter's bedroom.

While Andrew was using the saw, the blade shattered when it was applied to a piece of second hand timber which contained a number of old nails. Part of the blade flew up hitting Andrew who suffered facial injuries and may be disfigured permanently as a result. It appears likely that the steel used in the blade had been subjected to excessive hardening in the process of production with the result that it was unusually brittle and more likely to shatter in these circumstances.

Sedgewick's Home Handyman Stores purchased the saw blade from Spicer and Sharp as part of a larger consignment of the company's products. Unfortunately there is no certain means of establishing the identity of the supplier of the defective saw blade to Spicer and Sharp because three separate suppliers are under contract to supply identical blades to the company. However, detailed records of the initial testing and subsequent random testing of each of the three supplier's products are on file in the quality control department at Kings Norton. Examination of the records gives no indication that this type of defect had ever come to light in respect of any of the blades which had previously been tested.

Task

Prepare a report for circulation to the legal department and to Philip Sharp, in which you indicate:

1. whether Andrew would have a viable claim against the company in the tort of negligence or under part 1 of the Consumer Protection Act 1987;

2. the nature of any defences which may be available to the company in the event of any claim;

3. whether any steps should be taken in relation to circular saw blades still in the possession of the company or its retails customers, given that three further complaints have been received involving circular saw blades within a month of the complaint by Andrew Tucker.

Developmental Task

As part of the process of setting up the consumer complaint department, you are required to design an incident report form to send out as part of the company's initial response to a complaint. The form should be designed to enable you to obtain the material facts about the case from the complainant.

Chapter 11

Employment Relationships

An employment relationship exists where one person, an employer, who could be an individual, partnership, corporate body or unincorporate association, employs another person or persons under a contract of employment. In the Employment Protection (Consolidation) Act 1978 (EPCA 78) an employee is defined in s.153 as *an individual who has entered into or works under a contract of employment* and it is to employees that the bulk of individual employment rights apply. Some employees, for instance civil servants, the police, prison officers and health services employees, are regarded as special categories and their legal position tends to differ from employees generally. Also while an apprentice is not regarded strictly as an employee, in practice both the common law and statutory rights are very similar to any full-time worker under a contract of service. Expiration of the apprenticeship contract however does not carry with it a right to a redundancy payment or the right to claim unfair dismissal in the case where there is no offer of full time employment.

Where full time employment is offered, but only on a temporary basis, perhaps to cover for an employee on maternity leave or secondment, then the fact that there is an undertaking as to the temporary nature of the work is important in determining the rights of the parties when the contract is terminated. Certainly the dismissal of a temporary worker eligible to present a claim for unfair dismissal is not automatically 'fair' but could be regarded as such if the employer has acted reasonably in the circumstances in reaching his decision to dismiss. This would be the same for an employee who is required to serve out a probationary period and is dismissed having worked for the necessary period of continuous employment to qualify to present a claim for unfair dismissal.

While the presumption is that people on government training schemes are not employees, the Employment Appeal Tribunal has held that participants in a community programme to provide temporary work, worked under a contract of service.

A company director is regarded as an office holder rather than as having an employment relationship with the company. Increasingly, however, company directors have executive positions in their companies and in such circumstances a contract will specify their management role. It is then that an employment relationship will arise under which the director could be regarded as an employee of the company, or in some cases an independent contractor.

Employees and Contractors

There are an infinite variety of terms and conditions under which one person will do work for another. The requirements of employers will range from the need to engage full-time employees where a long standing relationship with their workers is envisaged, characterised by mutual trust and confidence between the parties, to the use of temporary workers engaged to complete a particular task. It may be that the temporary worker, such as the accountant or solicitor, provides a specialist skill which is required by the employer only on an intermittent basis. Alternatively temporary and casual employment only may be offered, because of economic necessity or the expansion or contraction of the size of the workforce in line with demand. Independent contractors (or self employed workers) are now well established as a substantial proportion of the workforce of some industries, for instance, the media, catering and construction. Of the million or so construction workers, well over half a million are self employed. The changing face of employment patterns in Britain is shown by official figures which reveal that while 62.3% of household income is earned from wages and salaries, over 10% is now derived from self-employment. This form of employment has many advantages for both sides. The employer 'gets the job done' and the contractor is normally well paid in return. A criticism of the system is that it provides no support for the older or infirm worker, no security of employment and may lead to a general reduction in health and safety standards. Because of the increasing use of the self employed in business to execute work and provide services both in the public and private sectors it is the basic division between the employed and self employed to which we must devote attention.

There are a large number of legal and economic consequences stemming from the distinction between employed and self employed status. For this reason it is necessary to be able to identify the status of the employment relationship that has been entered into. Employment legislation and the common law both recognise the distinction between employment under a contract of service and self employment under a contract for services. The distinction is a relatively straightforward one to make in the majority of cases. It is only in a small proportion of cases that difficulties arise, often where employers, or those they employ are seeking to achieve contractor status for economic advantage or in order to evade legal responsibilities. In the following table there is a summary of the major legal and economic consequences of the employment classification.

Legal and Economic Consequences of Employment Classification

Contract of Service (Employed Persons)	**Contract for Services** (Self-employed Persons)
Liability	
An employer may be made vicariously liable for the wrongful acts of employees committed during the course of their employment.	As a general principle an employer may not be made liable for the wrongful acts of contractors he employs other than in exceptional cases.
Common Law Employment Terms	
Numerous terms are implied into a contract of employment by the common law to regulate the relationship of employer and employee eg trust and confidence.	The common law is much less likely to intervene in the relationship of employer and contractor.
Health and Safety	
A high standard of care is owed by an employer both under statute and the common law with regard to the health and safety of his employees.	While both the common law and statute recognise the existence of a duty of care by an employer in relation to the contractors he employs at common law it is of a lesser standard than the duty owed to employees.

Contract of Service (Employed Persons)	**Contract for Services** (Self-employed Persons)
Statutory Employment Rights	
A large number of individual employment rights are conferred on employees by statute which generally arise after a period of service eg the right to unfair dismissal protection, redundancy payments, to belong to a trade union and take part in trade union activities, to protection in the event of the employer's insolvency, to guarantee payments, to security of employment after maternity leave, to statutory maternity pay, to a written statement of the main terms and conditions of employment and the right not to be discriminated against on the grounds of sex, race or marital status.	Contractors are effectively excluded from the mass of individual employment rights conferred by statute. One notable exception however is the legislation in relation to sex and race discrimination which protects the self-employed when they are providing personal services.
Income Tax	
The income tax payable by an employee is deducted at source by the employer under the pay as you earn scheme ie PAYE (Schedule E).	The income tax of a self employed person is payable by the taxpayer and not his employer on a lump sum preceding year basis (Schedule D). Apart from the obvious advantage of retaining the tax until it falls due at the end of the year it is also felt that such a taxpayer has more favourable treatment of reasonable expenses when assessed for tax. Furthermore an independent subcontractor may have to charge VAT on services.
Welfare Benefits	
Under the Social Security Act 1975 both employer and employee must contribute to the payment of Class 1 National Insurance contributions assessed on an earnings related basis which entitles the employee to claim all the available welfare benefits eg unemployment benefit, statutory sick pay, industrial disablement benefit, state retirement pension.	Under the Social Security Act 1975 a self-employed person is individually responsible for the payment of lower Class 2 National Insurance contributions and has only limited rights to claim welfare benefits eg statutory sick pay.

Distinguishing between the Employed and Self Employed

In the final analysis the determination of whether an individual is an employee or a contractor is a question of law for the courts rather than placing sole reliance on the description of the contract given by the parties to it. Over the years a number of tests have been formulated by the courts to attempt to determine any given worker's status. Originally the courts would only consider the level of control over a worker by an employer. In *Performing Rights Society Ltd. v. Mitchell and Booker* 1924, McCardie J. said that *"the final test, if there is to be a final test, and certainly the test to be generally applied, lies in the nature and degree of detailed control over the person alleged to be a servant"*. If an employer could tell his workers not only what to do, but also how and when to do it, then the workers would be regarded as employees, employed under a contract of service. Today the courts adopt a much wider approach and take account of all the circumstances to determine a worker's status. This is not to say that control is no longer a significant factor, for it would be difficult to imagine a contract of service where the employer did not have the authority to control the work performed by the employee.

Control is of course a less obvious feature the more specialised, skilled or trusted the workers become, for example a surgeon. This was why in the 1950s and 60s it was thought necessary to move away from a test based solely on control over the worker. The integration or organisational test favoured by the Court of Appeal was expressed by Denning L J in *Stevenson, Jordan and Harrison v. MacDonald and Evans* 1952. Here he said that *"under a contract of service a man is employed as part of the business and his work is done as an integral part of the business, whereas, under a contract for service, his work, although done for the business, is not integrated into it, but is only accessory to it"*. Adopting this approach the Court of Appeal was able to determine that medical staff in a hospital were employees and that a trapeze artist in a circus who also helped out with general duties was also an employee. In both cases their work was regarded as an integral part of the organisation.

The present approach of the courts in viewing all of the circumstances of the case to determine status has been described in various ways as the mixed, multiple or economic reality test. It has its origins in the following case.

> In *Ready Mixed Concrete Ltd. v. Ministry of Pensions* 1968 under a peculiar procedure laid down in National Insurance legislation MacKenna J, a single judge of the Queens Bench Division of the High Court, sat as the final appellate court to decide the employment status of a driver for the plaintiff company. This was in order to determine the employer's responsibility in relation to the National Insurance contributions of his drivers. The Ministry of Pensions had rejected the employer's contention that its drivers were self employed, despite the existence of written contracts of employment (30 pages long) which had attempted to create a contract for services rather than contracts of service. The declaration that the driver was self employed was not decisive and all aspects of his job were considered, for instance the fact that the driver purchased the lorry from the company; had to maintain it; pay was calculated on the basis of the driving. These factors pointed to the driver being a contractor, whilst others pointed to his status as an employee. He had to paint the lorry in the company colours, he had to use it exclusively for company business and he was required to obey reasonable orders. McKenna J stated that there is a contract of service if an individual agrees to provide his own work, submits to his employer's control and in addition the majority of the contractual provisions are consistent with a contract of service. This approach has since been referred to as the mixed or multiple test. On the facts the power to delegate work was regarded as a de-

cisive indication that the drivers were self employed under a contract for services.

The status of self employment cannot be achieved simply by including an express provision in a contract. The courts will look to the substance of an employment relationship rather than the label applied by the parties in order to decide a worker's status.

In *Ferguson v. John Dawson Ltd.* 1976 the plaintiff, a builder's labourer agreed to work as a 'self employed labour only sub contractor' an arrangement commonly known as 'the lump'. When working on a flat roof he fell and suffered injuries. No guard rail had been provided, in breach of the duty to employees owned under the Construction (Working Places) Regulations 1966. The High Court decided that the employer was in breach of this statutory duty towards the plaintiff and damages of over £30,000 were awarded. On appeal the employer argued that as the plaintiff was self employed the statutory duty was not owed to him. It was the plaintiff's responsibility to ensure that the guard rail was in place. The Court of Appeal held, by a majority, that the plaintiff was in reality an employee and so entitled to the compensation awarded. The 'lump' was no more than a device to attempt to gain tax advantages and whilst a declaration as to employment status may be relevant, it is not the conclusive factor to determine the true nature of the employment relationship.

A difficult case to reconcile with the decision in *Ferguson* 1976 is *Massey v. Crown Life Insurance Company* 1978. Here a branch manager of an insurance company, who also acted as a general agent, decided to become 'self employed' on his accountant's advice, despite the fact that his duties remained unchanged. The Court of Appeal concluded that a change of employment status had in fact taken place so that he was unable to bring a claim for unfair dismissal. Ld Denning M R stated that if there is ambiguity in the relationship then this can be resolved with a declaration one way or the other.

Whilst there was a degree of ambiguity in the above case in the branch manager's original position as manager/agent, it was significant that here was a 'professional' man, having considered independent advice, making a declaration which he believed would be to his benefit. This is in contrast to the labourer in *Ferguson* 1976 who was unadvised and could not be said to have consciously chosen to be a contractor with the legal consequences that this involved.

Despite the existence of a clear agreement between the employer and the worker that he should be treated as self employed this may nevertheless be regarded by the courts as a false designation and overturned.

In *Young & Wood Ltd. v. West* 1980 the complainant, a sheet metal worker, asked his employer if he could be treated as self employed. This was accepted and despite the fact that there was no difference between his working conditions and those of PAYE workers, he was paid without deductions of tax and was not given holiday entitlement or sick pay. Furthermore the Inland Revenue had accepted the change resulting in an estimated tax advantage of about £500 over five years because of assessment under schedule D rather than schedule E. Stephenson L J seemed to cast doubt on Lord Denning M R's approach in *Massey* 1978 by stating that *"It must be the court's duty to see whether the label correctly represents the true legal relationship between the parties"*. The Court of Appeal found that as it was impossible to regard the complainant as in 'business on his own account' he

> was not self employed but remained an employee. Consequently the tribunal had jurisdiction to hear his complaint of unfair dismissal.

By asking the question whether the worker is "in business on his own account" or under the control of an employer under a continuing business relationship, the courts have found it possible to conclude that a relationship that was traditionally regarded as self employment, that of a homeworker, was in reality a contract of service. Questions posed in applying this entrepreneurial test would include whether the individual was in business on his own, provides his own equipment, employs other workers and has a financial stake in the business.

> In *Airfix Footwear Ltd. v. Cope* 1978 the court held that homeworkers, employed to assemble shoe parts for a company using equipment supplied by them, were not contractors but employees. While the work was provided on a regular basis, the employer argued that there was no obligation to provide work and the worker could also refuse it. In the present case the employment relationship had continued over the seven year period. In reality the employer decided on the things to be done, the manner, means, and the time and place of performance. The homeworker should therefore be regarded as an employee.

> Reliance on a pool of casual workers has long been a tradition in some sectors of business including the catering industry and the legal status of so called 'regular casuals' was put to the test in *O'Kelly and Others v. Trusthouse Forte plc* 1983. Here a banqueting department run by the employer was staffed in part by full time employees but mainly by so called 'casuals'. Among the casuals were 'regulars' who were given preference when work was available, often expected to work very long hours and consequently had no other employment. The applicants, in this case were 'regulars' but when they became Trade Union shop stewards they were told by the employer that their services would no longer be required. In a claim for unfair dismissal brought by the applicants, the first issue the Industrial Tribunal had to deal with was whether they were employed under a contract of service and so protected by the law relating to unfair dismissal. In determining their employment status the Tribunal acknowledged that its role was to *"consider all aspects of the relationship, no feature being itself decisive, each of which may vary in weight and direction and, having given such a balance to the factors as seem appropriate determine whether the person was carrying on business on his own account"*. Applying this mixed or multiple test the Tribunal isolated factors consistent with a contract of service including the lack of mutual obligations on the part of the employer to provide work and on the part of the worker to offer services (referred to as mutuality of obligation). In addition there was the custom and practice of the catering industry to employ large numbers on a casual basis. By placing most emphasis on the inconsistent factors the Tribunal found that the applicants were not employees and therefore not entitled to statutory protection. The Court of Appeal later found it unable to interfere with the Tribunal's decision.

While there is no doubt that the decision in *O'Kelly* supports the custom and practice of the hotel and catering industry and confirms the fact that a fundamental feature of the contract of employment is the requirement to provide work and offer services, it is nevertheless difficult to reconcile with previous decisions, in particular *Ferguson* 1976. The reality of *O'Kelly* is that the regular casuals were subject to the same control as full time employees. They often worked longer hours than full time staff and a failure to work when required had the dramatic consequences of removal from the regular casual lists. Having no alternative employment, capital equipment or profit sharing, it would be difficult to describe them as business people working on their 'own account'.

> The significance of 'mutuality of obligations' for the purpose of identifying a contract of service re-emerged in *Hellyer Brothers Ltd. v. McLeod* 1987. The question faced by the Court of Appeal was whether trawlermen who had sailed exclusively for the same employer for a number of years were entitled to redundancy payments now that their services were no longer required. The difficulty for the crewman was that according to the custom and practice of the industry each voyage was covered by a separate crew agreement which was terminated by mutual consent on completion of each voyage. The crewmen invariably returned to the same employer for the next voyage despite being under no legal obligation to do so. To qualify for redundancy payments however they had to show that they were continuously employed under one overall contract of employment. Due to the lack of mutuality of obligation over the period of employment both the EAT and Court of Appeal held that there was no overall contract of service and so no entitlement to redundancy payments.
>
> Recently the Privy Council in *Lee v. 1.Chung and 2.Shun Shing Construction and Engineering Company Ltd.* 1990 was given an opportunity to express its opinion as to the legal process by which the legal status of a worker is to be determined. Here the appellant, a mason, claimed compensation when he suffered injury during the course of his work on a construction site in Hong Kong. The accident happened when he was working for a building sub contractor who had been delegated work by the main contractor on the site. Both the District Court and the Court of Appeal of Hong Kong had rejected the claim on the basis that the right to compensation arose in respect of injury caused to a person who worked under a contract of service, and in the circumstances the appellant was employed as an independent contractor. On final appeal, the Privy Council held that as the relevant Ordinance in Hong Kong which dealt with the legal position had been modelled on English Workman's Compensation Acts, then the status of a worker should be determined by applying English common law standards. Confirming that no single test is decisive, the court felt that the standard to be applied was best stated by Cooke J. in *Market Investigations v Ministry of Social Security* 1969 when he set out the fundamental test as being *"Is the person who has engaged himself to perform these services performing them as a person in business on his own account"*. Control is important but not the sole determining factor. *"Other matters which may be of importance are whether the worker provides his own equipment, whether he hires his own helpers, what degree of financial risk he takes, what degree of responsibility he has for investment and management and whether and how far he has an opportunity to profit from sound management in the performance of his task."* The decision will depend upon an evaluation of the facts... *"There will be many borderline cases in which similarly instructed minds may come to different conclusions"*. Such a decision should therefore be left to the trial court and changed only by an appellate court in exceptional cases where the trial court *"took a view of the facts which could not reasonably be entertained"*. In the present case, their Lordships were entitled to reverse the lower court's decision and find that the worker was in reality an employee. All the indicators pointed to the conclusion that the appellant was an employee. *"The picture that emerged from the facts was that of a skilled artisan earning his living by working for more*

than one employer as an employee, not as a small businessman venturing into business on his own account as a independent contractor, with all the attendant risks. The appellant ran no risk whatsoever save that of being unable to find employment which is a risk faced by all 'employees'".

The fact that there has been such litigation on the employed/self employed distinction suggests that in the borderline cases in particular, decisions are by no means clear cut. The courts are faced with the difficult task of maintaining a balance between the freedom of employers to offer employment on the terms that best suit their interest and the rights of workers, for the most part in an unequal bargaining position, to obtain the benefits of status as an employee. Certainly the fact that the question of employment status is one of mixed fact and law rather than pure law has meant that the appellate bodies have shown a marked reluctance to interfere with the decisions of Industrial Tribunals and this has further fuelled the inconsistency. Both the EAT and the Court of Appeal will only reverse a decision of the tribunal on employment status on the grounds of a misdirection of law or its perversity.

Formation of the Contract of Employment

Despite the unique nature of a contract of service, common law principles of the law of contract are still applicable to its formation, construction and discharge. The general contractual rules governing offer and acceptance are relevant to determine when a contract of employment has been entered into. A job advertisement is a mere invitation to treat. This could lead to a written application followed by an interview at which the employer will assess the merits of the various candidates. An express contractual offer of the job is then made to the successful candidate on specific terms which may differ from the initial advertisement. A counter offer by the applicant would extinguish the original offer. Usually, at this stage of course, the parties to the contract have reached consensus, and the contract is concluded on the communication of the applicant's acceptance.

Quite often an offer of employment is made conditional, for instance "subject to the receipt of satisfactory written references" or the " passing of a medical examination".

Recently the Court of Appeal in *Wishart v. National Association of Citizens Advice Bureaux Ltd.* 1990 considered a case where the plaintiff had been offered the post of information officer "subject to satisfactory references" and then when the employer discovered his past attendance record withdrew the job offer. The issue before the Court of Appeal was whether the employer's decision to treat the references as unsatisfactory could be viewed objectively and tested by the standard of the reasonable person in the position of the employer. In fact the court decided that unlike medical opinion as to the employee's fitness which could be tested objectively, there was no obligation in law on the employer other than to decide in good faith whether the references were satisfactory. *"The natural reading of a communication, the purpose of which is to tell the prospective employee that part of the decision on whether he is firmly offered the post has yet to be made, is that the employer is reserving the right to make up his own mind when the references have been received and studied. "*

As a general principle, employers are free to pick and choose to whom they offer employment. However if a reason for not engaging an individual is related to race, gender or marital status, this may be unlawful under the Race Relations Act 1976 and the Sex Discrimination Act 1975. A further limitation on the freedom to employ is embodied within the Disabled Persons (Employment) Act 1958 which provides that an employer with twenty or more employees must in the absence of an exemption certificate, have a minimum of three percent of the workforce registered disabled persons. Indeed in certain jobs disabled persons must be given priority.

Furthermore, rather than stigmatising an individual for life because of his past conduct, the Rehabilitation of Offenders Act 1974 allows past offenders who have criminal convictions to regard them as 'spent' in certain circumstances. This means that on a job application the past conviction need not be mentioned and the failure to disclose it is no ground for an employer to refuse to employ or dismiss a past offender. It is reasonable of course for an employer to expect full disclosure of information on a job application and this would most certainly include a prospective employee providing details of criminal convictions which were not spent.

Contrary to popular belief, apart from merchant seaman and apprentices, there is no legal requirement that a contract of employment be in writing. While there are problems associated with identifying the terms of an oral agreement, nevertheless, given the fluid nature of a contract of employment there is no guarantee that a requirement to reduce the original contract to writing would solve all the problems of interpreting its content.

Statutory Statement of the Main Terms of Employment

Following the Contract of Employment Act 1963, now s.1 Employment Protection (Consolidation) Act 1978 (EPCA 78), there is a statutory requirement on employers to provide their employees within thirteen weeks of the commencement of employment with a written statement of the main terms of employment. Certain classes of employees are excluded from s.1 including registered dock workers, Crown employees, employees who work wholly or mainly outside Great Britain and part time workers. The objective of s.1 is to ensure that employees have written confirmation and a source to scrutinise at least the main terms of their employment contracts. Particulars which must be included in the statutory statement include:

(a) reference to the parties and the dates on which the period of continuous employment began (stating whether a previous period of employment is included as part of continuous employment);

(b) the scale of remuneration and the method of calculation;

(c) the intervals at which remuneration is paid (whether weekly or monthly or some other period);

(d) the terms and conditions relating to hours of work;

(e) the terms and conditions relating to holidays and holiday pay (sufficient to enable the employee's entitlement to accrued holiday pay on the termination of employment to be precisely calculated);

(f) the terms and conditions relating to sickness or injury and sickness pay;

(g) the terms and conditions relating to pension and pension scheme;

(h) the length of notice which the employee is obliged to give and entitled to receive;

(i) the title of the job which the employee is employed to do;

(j) in addition every statement given shall include a note containing a specification of any disciplinary rules or reference to an accessible document containing such rules;

(k) the name of the person to whom the employee can apply if he is dissatisfied with any disciplinary decision relating to him;

(l) the name of the person to whom the employer can apply to seek the redress of any grievance;

(m) whether a contracting out certificate under the provisions of the Social Security Act 1975 is in force in relation to the employment.

A significant amendment to s.1 EPCA 78 was made by s.13 of the Employment Act 1989 (EA 89). This section exempts an employer from the requirement to include a note on disciplinary proceedings in the written statement where that employer (together with any associated employer) has less than twenty employees on the date when the employee's employment began.

Reference is made several times in s.1 to "terms and conditions" of employment and yet there has been no attempt in statute or common law to satisfactorily distinguish between these expressions. The prevalent view seems to be that "terms" are those parts of the contract that are mutually agreed, expressly or by implication and are found in the contract, collective agreements and occasionally in statutory provisions. "Conditions" on the other hand have a lower status and are unilateral instructions from the employer and will specify how and when employment duties are to be fulfilled. Conditions are usually found in work rules, disciplinary and grievance procedures and job descriptions.

To satisfy the requirements of s.1 it is not sufficient simply to be told or shown the above particulars of employment. The employer must present the employee with a document containing the information or at least make such a document available for inspection (e.g. a collective agreement and a rule book). It should be stressed that a statutory statement is not the contract of employment but rather strong prima facie evidence of its terms. Certainly the mere acknowledgement of its receipt does not turn the statement into a contract.

> In *System Floors (UK) Ltd. v. Daniel* 1982, Browne-Wilkinson J said in relation to the statement that *"It provides very strong prima facie evidence of what were the terms of the contract between the parties. Nor are the statements of the terms finally conclusive: at most, they place a heavy burden on the employer to show that the actual terms of the contract are different from those which he had set out in the statutory statement"*. This view of the status of the statutory statement was subsequently approved by the Court of Appeal in *Robertson v. British Gas Company* 1983 where it was held that if the written statement does not accurately reflect the agreed terms then the agreed terms prevail.

Contractual terms we shall discover, are often the subject of change, in which case an employer is obliged to notify the employee of changes in the statement within one month of the change. An employer who fails to comply with obligations in relation to the statutory statement could be the subject of a complaint to the Industrial Tribunal. The Tribunal has power to determine what particulars ought to have been included, in a case where no statement has been supplied, or the statement supplied is incomplete or inaccurate. With no effective sanction available for employers who fail to comply with s.1, complaints to Tribunals are rare, and only arise usually in connection with other complaints, for instance in relation to unfair dismissal. Finally it should be mentioned that those employers who provide their employees with a written contract of employment which covers all the matters which must be referred to in the statutory statement, do not have to supply their employees with a separate statutory statement.

Chapter 12

The Contract of Employment

Terms of Employment

A contract of employment is composed of its terms, the mutual promises and obligations of the parties to it. Contractual terms may be 'express' and become part of the contract through the express agreement of the parties. Usually of course, there is simply agreement by the prospective employee to the standard terms dictated by the prospective employer or terms previously agreed between the employer and a trade union. Alternatively, contractual terms may be implied into the contract of employment by an external source. The major sources for implication we shall discover, are the courts and Tribunals but occasionally terms are implied into contracts of employment by statutory provisions or through custom. Such mutual obligations have legal significance and a failure to comply with the requirement of a term of the contract could provide the innocent party with the option of securing legal redress. An action for breach of contract may be brought to secure damages against the party in breach of a contractual term. If damages would not suffice to provide a remedy, an injunction could be sought to restrain the breach of contract. In such circumstances an interlocutory (temporary) injunction is often sought as a remedy. One rarely used option for an employee who feels that his employer is unreasonably requiring him to do work which is not part of his contactual obligations is to seek an injunction to maintain the status quo at work.

> In *Hughs v. London Borough of Southwark* 1988 a number of social workers applied to the High Court for an injunction to stop their employers requiring them to staff community areas on a temporary basis and so terminate their normal hospital work. The High Court held that the employer's instruction was in breach of contract and the plaintiff social workers were entitled to an injunction to restrain the breach. The Court of Appeal in *Powell v. The London Borough of Brent* 1987 had previously held that the court has power to grant an injunction to restrain the breach of a contract of service provided that there was mutual confidence between the employer and employee. Here, despite the dispute, the employers retained confidence in the social workers. In this case the employers had *"failed to consult with the hospital or have sufficient steps in investigation properly to inform themselves as to the balance of work priorities. Although it is for managers to manage, that principle was flawed in the present case by their failure to inform themselves of the relevant considerations before deciding on priorities"*.

A further option for an employee in these circumstances is to apply to the High Court for a declaration as to the legal position.

> In *Creswell v. Board of Inland Revenue* 1984, employees sought a court declaration that their employers had broken the terms of their contract of

> employment by introducing new technology and expecting them to adapt to it. The High Court declared, however, that, provided they received adequate training, employees were expected to adapt to new methods and new techniques. There is a general contractual duty on employees to adapt to changing working methods. This is an example of the court implying a term into the contract of employment imposing an obligation on employees to be flexible and be willing to adopt to new methods and techniques. There was also a right for the employer to withhold pay for those employees who refused to conform to the new methods, for they are in breach of their contractual obligations.

Later in the Chapter we shall see that if a breach of contract is regarded as so serious as to be repudiatory, then the innocent party has the option of accepting the breach and terminating the contract. A repudiatory breach by an employer could, if accepted by the employee, entitle him to regard himself as constructively dismissed if he walks out as a result. Alternatively, a repudiatory breach by the employee could in some circumstances justify summary dismissal by the employer.

In the majority of cases of conflict or dispute between the employer and employee, the true legal position can only be assessed by identifying and analysing the express terms of employment and any implied terms which have become incorporated into the contract.

Express Terms

As previously stated, the express terms of the contract of employment may be reduced to writing or be purely oral, and the statutory statement of the main terms of employment will provide strong prima facie evidence as to their content. Matters such as salary, hours (including shift work, overtime, and overtime rates), job description, job title, holidays and holiday pay, sick pay, pensions, notice, confidentiality, restraints, disciplinary and grievance procedure, are covered by the express terms and in the vast majority of cases presented in a standard form to the employee with little room for negotiation. Of course what has been expressly agreed may still require interpretation in the courts and tribunals.

> In *Cole v. Midland Display Ltd.* 1973 the tribunal was faced with the problem of determining the meaning of the term, "employed on a staff basis" when it was applied to a manager. The Tribunal held that the phrase meant that the employee was entitled to wages during periods of sickness or no work but in return the employee could be required to work overtime without pay.

> Also in *McCaffrey v. A. E. Jeavons & Company Ltd.* 1967 an employee employed expressly as a "travelling man" in the building trade was held to be contractually obliged to move his place of employment anywhere in the country when required to by the employer.

> An employee whose job title was described as carrying out "general duties" in *Peter Carnie & Son Ltd. v. Paton* 1979 was held to be required to be very flexible in relation to the needs of his employer for the type of work to be carried out.

The task of identifying the express terms of the contract is more onerous when a number of documents purport to contain express statements of the terms of employment as well as verbal statements between the parties. The various sources of express terms could include a formal contract, a letter of appointment, a statutory statement of the main terms and conditions, oral statements made prior to the contracts and even the job advertisement. Express statements made prior to the contract may become part of it but post contractual statements will be ineffective unless they constitute a mutual agreement to vary the original terms. In the previous Chapter we considered the position where the statutory statement of the main terms and conditions of employment conflict with the terms and conditions originally agreed in the contract. In such circumstances the original terms prevail.

Variation of Terms

The express terms of a contract of employment may be varied by mutual agreement between the employer and employee or even the employer and a trade union by means of collective bargaining. If there is no agreement to a proposed change and the employer attempts to unilaterally impose a more onerous term on an employee, for example a wage cut, then the employee has a number of options. He could:

(a) accept the variation as a repudiatory breach of the contract, walk out and claim constructive dismissal;

(b) remain passive without protest and eventually be taken to have accepted the varied contract;

(c) continue to work under protest and sue for damages for breach of contract.

> In *Rigby v. Ferodo Ltd.* 1988 the employee, in response to a unilateral wage cut, took the final option and sued for damages representing the unpaid wages. Both the High Court and the Court of Appeal agreed that there had been no mutual variation of the contract of employment so that the unreduced wage was payable and, further, that the damages should not be limited to the twelve week notice period under which the employee could have been dismissed. The House of Lords agreed and held that a repudiatory breach does not automatically terminate a contract of employment unless the breach is accepted by the employee as a repudiation, *"an unaccepted breach is a thing writ in water and of no value to anybody"*. Damages were not limited therefore to the notice period of twelve weeks and the primary contractual obligation to pay the full wage survived. The alternative notion that a unilateral reduction of wages should be taken as notice to terminate a contract of employment was also rejected by the Law Lords.

While a consensual variation of the terms of employment requires a clear indication from the employee or a bargaining agent that the new terms are acceptable, a unilateral variation may achieve the objective of changing the contract if there is passive acceptance of it.

> In *Jones v. Associated Tunnelling Company Ltd.* 1981 however, the EAT stressed that continuing to work is not necessarily an implied assent to a unilateral variation by the employer, particularly where the variation has no immediate practical effect on the employee.

Certainly by continuing to work under protest the employee is demonstrating his unwillingness to accept a contractual change and is entitled to a period of grace during which he can assess his legal position.

> In *Marriott v. Oxford District Cooperative Society Ltd.* 1969 a foreman supervisor was told by his employer that the position of foreman was no longer

required and that his wages were to be reduced by £1 per week to reflect his loss of status. The employee continued to work under protest for three weeks before terminating his contract of employment by notice and claiming a redundancy payment. The Court of Appeal held, reversing the Divisional Court's judgment, that as there was no implied assent to the contractual change, it amounted to a repudiation of the contract of employment. The employee's reaction of continuing to work for a short period under protest was understandable and in no way constituted implied assent to the contractual change.

Industrial Action and Breach of Contract

By taking industrial action, other than a voluntary overtime ban, an employee will normally be in breach of his contract of employment whether on strike or as is more usual, on limited industrial action. The employer's obligation to pay wages is clearly suspended during strike action.

If, as part of limited industrial action on the instructions of a union, an employee performs only a proportion of his contractual obligations, an employer has the option of accepting the part performance, but withholding wages to reflect the work not performed.

This was the case in *Miles v. Wakefield Metropolitan District Council* 1987 where the plaintiff, a superintendent registrar acting in accordance with NALGO instructions, refused to perform marriages on a Saturday morning although he was willing to perform other duties. The Council made it clear that if he was not willing to perform the full range of his duties on a Saturday morning his wages would be reduced. Subsequently the employer withheld 3/37ths of his pay and so withheld the total wage for Saturday morning work. The plaintiff's claim to recover the wages withheld was eventually dismissed by the House of Lords. Their Lordships stressed the point that in a contract of employment *"wages and work go together and if the work declines the employer need not pay"*. Here the employer had made it clear that he was not willing to accept the plaintiff's partial performance so that his position was on Saturday mornings as if he was refusing to work at all. The employer was entitled to withhold the whole of remuneration due for the periods the employee had made it clear that he was not ready and willing to perform the full range of work he could properly be required to do. *"Since the plaintiff could not successfully claim that he was at the material time ready and willing to perform the work which he was properly required to do on Saturdays his action for the remuneration attributable to that work must fail."*

Certainly for an employer to be lawfully justified in making a deduction from the wages of an employee pursuing limited industrial action it is necessary to show that the work not performed falls squarely within an employee's contractual obligation.

In *Sim v. Rotherham Metropolitan Borough Council* 1986 the teachers' industrial action amounted to not providing cover for absent colleagues, a system which their union argued operated as a matter of goodwill rather than contractual obligation. The employer took a different view however, and deducted a sum from the teacher's wages which represented the teacher's failure to take a class for the period in question. In an action to recover the sums deducted, the High Court held that the teachers'

> requirement to provide cover was an implied contractual obligation and failure to do so for a thirty five minute period was a breach of contract. It was immaterial that their contracts were silent on the matter: *"school teachers are members of a profession and a professional's contract of employment would not normally be expected to detail the professional obligations expected of the employee under the contract"*. To determine the amount of a teacher's contractual obligations it is necessary *"to ask whether the obligation in question is part of the professional obligations owed by a teacher to pupils or to his or her school"*. As it is a professional obligation to cooperate in the running of the school in accordance with reasonable administrative arrangements and this must involve complying with cover arrangements, failure to do so was a breach of contract for which the employer was entitled to deduct an appropriate sum from the employee's salary.

Recently the Court of Appeal expressed the view that limited industrial action which involves non-performance of a part of an employee's contractual duties will prejudice an employee's claim for wages or even partial wages during the relevant period. This is certainly the case where the employer makes it clear that he does not condone part performance of the contract by the employee, so that he can regard any contractual duties performed as purely voluntary. By allowing the employee to come to work and carry out less than his full contractual duties the employer is not accepting a partial performance of the contract, and there is no requirement to prevent the employee working.

Work Rules

It is common practice in many spheres of employment for the employer to issue work rules by printing notices or handing out rule books. Such rule books often contain instructions as to time-keeping, meal breaks, disciplinary offences and grievance procedure, sickness and pension rights, job descriptions, and the employer's safety policy. Although there is still some doubt as to the legal status of work rules, the present view is that such documents are unlikely to contain contractual terms. One school of thought is that work rules should be regarded as 'conditions' rather than 'terms' of employment, hence the expression, "terms and conditions of employment" and as such they should be subject to unilateral change by the employer. For example, while the number of hours worked would normally be the subject of express agreement and constitute a contractual 'term', instructions as to when these hours should be worked will normally be contained in a rule book and as a 'condition' be liable to unilateral change.

> In *Cadoux v. Central Regional Council* 1986 the employee's contract of employment was to be subject to the Conditions of Service laid down by the National Joint Council for Local Authorities' Administrative, Technical and Clerical Services, as supplemented by the Authorities Rules, as amended from time to time. The issue in the case was whether, under the Authorities' rules, the employer was entitled to introduce a non-contributory life assurance scheme for staff and then subsequently unilaterally withdraw it. The Court of Session held that here the "Authorities' Rules" were clearly incorporated into contracts of employment. They were however, made unilaterally by the employer, and although introduced after consultation, they were the "Authorities' Rules" and not subject to mutual agreement. Consequently there was *"no limitation on the employer's right to vary, alter or cancel any of the provisions of the Rules. The reference to the Authorities Rules, "as amended from time to time", led to the clear inference that the employer could alter their rules at their own hand"*. In the present case therefore

the employer was entitled unilaterally to withdraw the provision of the non-contributory life assurance scheme.

In *Secretary of State for Employment v. ASLEF (No 2)* 1972 Lord Denning expressed the view that rule books issued to railwaymen by their employers did not contain contractual terms but rather instructions to an employee as to how he was to do his work.

Where, however, a rule book is given or referred to by the employer at the time the contract of employment is formed, the fact that the employee has agreed that it is to be part of the contract and acknowledges that fact by his signature would more than likely give the rule book contractual effect. Certainly there is case law authority which suggests that by posting a notice of the fact that the rule book has contractual effect, an employer would ensure that the rules become incorporated into individual contracts of employment.

Implied Terms

A contract of employment is composed of contractual terms which have been expressly agreed or incorporated into the contract by an extraneous source such as a collective agreement, the custom and practice of a particular trade or business, or the common law. To have a full appreciation of the content of a contract of employment you should be aware of the role of the common law in defining rights and duties of employers and employees. In addition to a large number of common law rights and duties relating to such matters as good faith, confidentiality, health and safety, and obedience, there is an increased willingness of the courts and tribunals to imply terms into employment contracts to deal with issues such as trust and confidence, mutual respect and sexual harassment. Later when we consider the termination of employment, you will discover that the need to point to a clear breach of the contract of employment to establish a constructive dismissal has encouraged judicial ingenuity in incorporating implied terms which the court then declares that the employer has broken.

Apart from one notable exception in relation to equal pay, statute is not a major source of implied terms of employment. On the creation of a contract of employment, however, a number of statutory rights arise immediately, most of which are non-excludable and further rights attach to the contract after a period of continuous employment.

The fact that common law implied terms confer rights and impose duties on both parties to the employment relationship, suggests that they can be more meaningfully examined by considering each of them in turn in relation to both the employer and the employee. Most of the implied terms can be categorised under broad headings such as the wage/work bargain, health and safety, good faith, confidentiality, fidelity, and trust and confidence.

While the courts have been careful to stress that terms are implied into a contract of employment by applying the 'business efficacy' test referred to in Chapter 6 to give effect to the presumed intention of the parties, more realistically it seems that terms are implied when the courts find it necessary.

In *Mears v. Safecar Security* 1983 the Court of Appeal held that if there is no express agreement on a matter, the courts are entitled to consider all the facts and circumstances of the relationship, including the parties' conduct, to determine whether a term should be implied into the contract of employment.

In *Courtaulds Northern Spinning Ltd. v. Sibson* 1988 the Court of Appeal was called on to determine the nature and extent of an implied term in a contract of employment in relation to the place of work. Slade L J said that *"in cases ... where it is essential to imply some term into the contract of employment as to place of work, the court does not have to be satisfied that the parties, if asked, would in fact have agreed the term before entering the contract. The court merely has to be satisfied that the implied term is one which the parties would probably have agreed if they were being reasonable."*

In *Prestwick Circuits Ltd. v. McAndrew* 1990 it was held that *"An implied right to order an employee to transfer from one place of employment to another must be subject to the implied qualification that reasonable notice must be given in all the circumstances of the case. Even where the proposed transfer involves a reasonable distance it is necessary to imply the qualification that the employee be given reasonable notice so as to preclude a contractual right of the employer to transfer the employee to some other place at a moment's notice. Whether the notice given in a particular case was reasonable is a question of fact and degree for the Industrial Tribunal to determine".*

The Wage/Work Bargain

In a contract of employment there is an implied duty on the employee to provide personal service for which the employer is obliged to provide a wage. At the appointed time therefore, an employee is required to present himself for work and be ready and willing to perform at the direction of the employer. Absence from work without good reason would clearly constitute a breach of contract which would entitle the employer to adjust the wage accordingly. If the absence is due to industrial action there is an increasing tendency for the courts and tribunals to deal with conflict over entitlement to a wage or a partial wage by applying strict contractual principles.

The principle of 'no work no pay' was reaffirmed by the House of Lords in *Miles v. Wakefield MBC* 1987. Here industrial action taken by Registrars involved them in refusing to carry out a proportion of their work, that of performing marriages, on Saturday mornings. While the Registrars attended for work on Saturdays and performed other duties the employer made it clear that wages would be deducted for Saturday morning hours if the employees were unwilling to perform the full range of their duties. The House of Lords upheld the employer's position that they were entitled to withhold the Saturday wage despite the fact that a substantial part of the work was performed. Lord Templeman said that *"in a contract of employment, wages and work go together, in an action by an employee to recover his pay he must allege and be ready to prove that he worked or was willing to work".*

If an employer makes it clear that he is not willing to accept partial performance of the employees' contractual duties, any work performed by the employee could be rejected as purely voluntary with no obligation on the employer to pay even a partial wage.

If the employer accepts partial performance of the contract then the employee is entitled to his wage, subject to a set-off deduction representing the damage suffered by the employer. Lord Templeman has suggested that in such circumstances wages should be paid on a quantum meruit basis.

A unilateral decision by the employer to withhold wages without just cause would put him in breach of his fundamental obligation under the contract and give the employee the right to repudiate. Such a breach does not however automatically terminate the contract.

In *Rigby v. Ferodo Ltd.* 1987 (mentioned previously in this chapter) the employer attempted to impose a lower wage on the employees. On their behalf, the trade union made it clear to the employer that the lower wage was unacceptable and while the employees continued to work they nevertheless regarded the employer as in repudiatory breach of the contract of employment. When an action was brought to recover the unpaid wages, the House of Lords held that the employees were entitled to the full contractual wage from the time that the reduction was unilaterally imposed.

While it seems that there is an obligation to pay the contractual wage, this does not carry with it a duty to provide the employees with work. The general proposition was illustrated by Asquith L J in *Collier v. Sunday Referee Publishing Company Ltd.* 1940 when he said, *"Provided I pay my cook her wages regularly she cannot complain if I choose to take any or all of my meals out."*.

If an employee's pay depends upon work being provided, for instance piece work, or commission, then the employer is under an implied obligation to provide sufficient work to enable a reasonable wage to be earned. The obligation to provide work would also apply where the employee's occupation is such that the opportunity to work is an essential feature of the contract because of the possibility of loss of reputation due to inactivity.

Health and Safety

At common law an employer is obliged to provide his workers with a safe system of work. This common law duty encompasses an obligation to ensure that workers are provided with safe plant and appliances, appropriate safety equipment, safe work methods and safe fellow workers.

In *British Aircraft Corporation v. Austin* 1978 the employer was held to be in breach of his implied duty of safety when he failed to investigate a complaint relating to the suitability of protective glasses for an employee. This conduct was held to be a repudiatory breach of the contract of employment sufficient to entitle the employee to terminate the contract and regard himself as constructively dismissed.

Employees themselves are under a duty to cooperate in relation to their own safety and that of their work colleagues. An employee who is unduly negligent in the performance of his work will be in breach of his employment contract and while he is unlikely to be sued by his employer, this could be used as a justifiable reason for dismissal.

In *Lister v. Romford Ice and Cold Storage Co. Ltd.* 1957 the House of Lords held that an employee who caused injury by negligently reversing his lorry, was in breach of an implied term of his contract of employment.

The law relating to health and safety at work is examined in more depth in Chapter 13

Good Faith (mutual trust and confidence)

Of all the implied duties, the duty of good faith and mutual respect is the most difficult to define precisely. This is because good faith is such a wide ranging concept and involves an obligation on the employee to respect confidences, obey reasonable instructions, take care of the employer's property, account for money received in the performance of duties and not disrupt the employer's business. An employer on the other hand must treat his workforce with respect, indemnify them for expenses incurred in the performance of their duties and when providing a reference, ensure that it is accurate and fair.

Employee's duty of good faith

Any attempt by an employee to use his position for undisclosed personal gain, for instance by accepting bribes or making a secret commission, will constitute a breach of the employment contract. The origins of this implied duty can be traced back to nineteenth century case-law.

> In *Boston Deep Sea Fishing and Ice Company v. Ansell* 1889 an employee who received secret commissions from other companies for placing orders with them was held to be in breach of this implied duty of his contract of employment.

Part of the obligation of good faith requires an employee to submit to his employer's control and this involves obeying reasonable orders. What would constitute a reasonable instruction depends upon an objective interpretation of the employee's contractual duties both express and implied.

> In *Pepper v. Webb* 1969 the head gardener who responded to the request to plant some flowers with the words, *"I couldn't care less about your bloody greenhouse or your sodding garden"* was held to be in breach of the implied duty to obey reasonable instructions.

Even if an instruction is within the scope of an employee's duties, it may not be reasonable if it involves a risk of serious injury or a breach of the criminal law. Certainly the duty of good faith would require an employee to be flexible and move with the times, so that an instruction to adopt work techniques involving new technology, after proper training has been given, would normally be regarded as reasonable.

> In *Creswell v. Board of Inland Revenue* 1984, a case mentioned earlier in this chapter, Walton J said that *"there can really be no doubt as to the fact that an employee is expected to adapt himself to new methods and techniques introduced in the course of employment"*.

It is important to distinguish however, between a change in work methods and change in the job itself which if not authorised or agreed to, could not be unilaterally imposed without a possible claim for a redundancy payment or compensation for unfair dismissal.

This is also true of the implied obligation to take care of the employer's property. An employee who negligently allows his employer's property to be stolen or causes it wilful damage will be in breach of his employment contract and liable to dismissal.

Given that the objective of industrial action is normally to cause disruption to the employer's business, an employee who takes part in a strike, go-slow, partial performance or even a 'work to rule' will be in breach of his contract of employment. Industrial action of itself involves a withdrawal of good faith so it is arguable that even an overtime ban, where there is no contractual obligation to work overtime, could be regarded as a breach of contract.

While there is no implied obligation on an employee to reveal to an employer his own misconduct or deficiencies, the relationship of trust and confidence may demand that an employee in a managerial capacity should report the misconduct of others in the organisation.

In *Sybron Corporation v. Rochem Ltd. and Others* 1983 the Court of Appeal held that an employee may be so placed in the hierarchy of an organisation so as to have a duty to report either his 'superior's' or 'inferior's' misconduct.

Good faith most certainly includes respecting confidences so there would be a clear breach of the contract of employment if the employee revealed confidential information relating to any aspect of his employer's business to a competitor, or made use of such information for his own purposes.

Business goodwill revealed in customer lists and accounts or trade secrets such as manufacturing processes or designs, are in the nature of rights in property which the employer is entitled to protect during the employment relationship and to some degree even after its termination. It is a question of fact in each case whether information could be classified or confidential but some guidance was provided in *Marshall Thomas (Exports) Ltd. v. Guinle* 1978 where relevant factors were identified:

(a) the owner of the information must reasonably believe that its release would benefit a competitor or cause detriment to himself;

(b) the owner must reasonably believe that the information is confidential and not already public knowledge;

(c) the information must be judged bearing in mind the practice of the particular trade or industry.

By relying on the duty of fidelity an employer could obtain an injunction to prevent an employee working for a competitor in his spare time or revealing confidential information to a competitor. Breach of confidence could also be a reason relied on by an employer to convince an Industrial Tribunal that in the circumstances the decision to dismiss an employee was fair.

It has been argued that the implied term not to reveal or make use of confidential information acquired during the course of employment can extend beyond the termination of employment.

Such a duty of confidentiality was alleged by the employer to bind his ex-employee in *Faccenda Chicken Ltd. v. Fowler* 1986. Here the defendant, having previously worked for the plaintiff as a salesman, set up business in competition. The defendant recruited a number of the plaintiff's staff and the majority of his customers were ex-customers of the plaintiff. The plaintiff then claimed damages from the defendant for using confidential sales information relating to prices and customer requirements in breach of his contract of employment. Both the High Court and the Court of Appeal dismissed the claim holding that the use of the information did not in this case involve a breach of contract. The Court of Appeal laid down a number of legal principles to be applied, where in the absence of an express term, an ex-employee makes use of information acquired during the course of employment. The duty of confidentiality in these circumstances is much more restricted in its scope than the general duty of good faith which covers a subsisting employment relationship. Also, such a duty will extend to information which is 'confidential' only in the sense that unauthorised use of it while the contract subsisted would be a breach of the duty of good faith. To determine whether information would fall within the implied term and be capable of protection beyond the termination of employment, it is necessary to consider the following:

(a) the nature of the employment;

(b) the nature of the information;

(c) whether the information can be easily isolated from other information which the employee is free to use; and

(d) whether the employer impressed upon the employee the need for confidentiality.

It seems then that only genuine trade secrets are capable of protection by an implied term relating to confidentiality following the termination of employment. To achieve a greater degree of protection therefore, a prudent employer should ensure that an express restraint clause is inserted into the employment contract. Such a clause is of course an example of an express term in a contract of employment. Restraint clauses are given special treatment under the common law and are dealt with later.

Employer's duty of good faith

It is only relatively recently that the courts and tribunals have recognised that an employee's duty to trust and respect his employer is in fact a mutual obligation in an employment relationship.

> In *Woods v. W H Car Services (Peterborough) Ltd.* 1982 the EAT recognised that in every employment contract there is an implied term of great importance, that of trust and confidence between the parties. Such a term requires that employers *"will not, without reasonable and proper cause, conduct themselves in a manner calculated or likely to destroy or damage the relationship of trust and confidence between employer and employee"*.

Employers who have been guilty of conduct such as verbal or physical abuse of their employees or unilateral attempts to impose unreasonable changes in employment terms have found themselves in breach of this implied term. Later in Chapter 14 when we consider the termination of employment, you will discover that the development of this particular implied term is tied to the doctrine of constructive dismissal, and the need for an employee to establish a repudiatory breach of the contract of employment by the employer.

> In *Lewis v. Motorworld Garages Ltd.* 1985 over a long period the employer was guilty of consistently repudiating his employee's contract of employment by insisting on unilateral variations of it. These changes were in fact accepted by the employee so that they could not be raised to support an allegation of constructive dismissal. The Court of Appeal held that such imposed variations did, however, establish a course of conduct so that if an employee did not waive a subsequent breach he could also raise this previous conduct to show that the employer was in breach of the implied term of trust and confidence.

The notion that an employee is under the control of his employer carries with it an obligation to indemnify the employee for expenses incurred in the performance of his duties. Furthermore we shall see in the chapter on health and safety that an employer may be made vicariously liable for the wrongs committed by an employee during the course of his employment.

Finally, while there is no duty to provide one, if an employee decides to supply his employee with a reference the employer should ensure that it is a fair and accurate assessment of the employee in question. If it is alleged that the reference supplied contains a defamatory statement, the employee is entitled to raise the defence of qualified privilege which is effective, provided that the employer can show that the statements were made without malicious intent. Also, developments in the tort of negligence would now enable an individual who has suffered loss after reliance on a negligently produced reference, to receive damages for the financial loss sustained. It may, however, be possible for an employer to disclaim any liability by ensuring that any reference given includes a well drafted exclusion clause.

Restraint of Trade

Previously we mentioned that an express term found in many contracts of employment is a clause which purports to restrict the freedom of the employees, on the termination of employment, from engaging in a competing business or working for a competitor for a specified period. Provided such a clause is inserted to protect a genuine proprietary interest of the employer and is reasonable in extent, the express restraint will be valid and enforceable. A restraint clause which purports to restrict the free choice of an ex-employee as to the employment options open is prima facie void as a contract in restraint of trade. Such a contract is nevertheless valid and enforceable if reasonable in the circumstances because:

(a) the employer has a genuine proprietary interest worthy of protection such as clientele, confidential information, or trade connection; and

(b) the restraint clause is drafted in such a way that it is no wider than is reasonably necessary to achieve the desired objective.

If the court is satisfied that the purpose of the restraint clause is no more than to prevent healthy competition then it will be declared void and of no legal effect.

> In *Strange v. Mann* 1965 the manager of a bookmakers agreed not to engage in a similar business to that of his employer within a twelve mile radius on the termination of his employment. In an action to enforce the clause, the court held that, as the bookmaker had little or no influence over the firm's clientele and in fact communicated with them mainly by telephone, the employer had no valid interest to protect. As the primary aim of the clause was simply to prevent competition it was declared void.

A distinction must be drawn between an attempt by an employer to prevent his ex-employee revealing trade secrets or lists of clients to competitors and simply preventing an ex-employee putting into practice the knowledge, skills and abilities that he acquired during his period of employment.

> In *Herbert Morris Ltd. v. Saxelby* 1916 a seven year restraint on the employee was held to be void as simply an attempt to prevent the employee making use of the technical skill and knowledge which he acquired with his employer if he took up employment with a rival firm.

> In *Forster and Sons v. Suggett* 1918, on the other hand, a covenant which was aimed at preventing the defendant divulging a secret glass making process to any rival organisation in the United Kingdom, was held to be valid and enforceable.

Having identified a proprietary interest worthy of protection, the next step is to analyse the restraint clause to discover whether it is reasonable in the circumstances. A number of factors are deserving of attention to assist in the analysis, such as the area of the restraint, the length of time it is to run and the nature of the work which the employer is attempting to restrain. The wording of the restraint clause is therefore crucial, for if it is too extensive in the geographical area of protection, or too long in time, it will be unenforceable. Each case turns on its own facts and all the circumstances are considered.

In *Fitch v. Dewes* 1921 a lifetime restraint on a solicitor's clerk from working for another solicitor within a radius of seven miles of Tamworth Town Hall was nevertheless held to be valid. The House of Lords felt that the modest area of the restraint which the employer relied on for his clientele justified even a lifetime restraint.

If a restraint clause is drafted in such a way that it purports to prevent the ex-employer from obtaining non-competitive employment then it will be declared void.

In *Fellows & Sons v. Fisher* 1976 a conveyancing clerk employed by a firm in Walthamstow agreed that for five years after the termination of employment he would not be employed or concerned in the legal profession anywhere within the postal district of Walthamstow and Chingford or solicit any person who had been a client of the firm when he had worked there. Not only was the five year restraint thought to be too long, bearing in mind the large population in the areas identified, but the attempt to exclude any work in the legal profession, which would include legal work in local government and the administration of justice, was also thought to be unreasonable and the restraint was declared void.

In *Mason v. Provident Clothing and Supply Company* 1913 the restraint clause purported to prevent the plaintiff canvasser from competing with the defendants within a twenty-five mile radius of the centre of London. The fact that the plaintiff had only come into contact with her employer's customers in a specified area of London meant that the restraint clause was too extensive in nature and declared by the House of Lords to be void.

In *Commercial Plastics v. Vincent* 1965 the defendant was employed as a plastics technologist to coordinate research and development in the production of thin PVC calendering. In that role he had access to secret information so that it was a condition of his contract of employment that he would not seek employment with any of the plaintiff's competitors in the calendering field for one year after leaving employment. The Court of Appeal held that in the circumstances the restraint clause was drafted in such a way that it purported to protect the employer on a world-wide basis when, in fact, the company did not require protection outside the United Kingdom. Accordingly the condition was unreasonable and consequently void and unenforceable.

A different attitude to restraint clauses is illustrated by the decision of the Court of Appeal in *Littlewoods Organisation v. Harris* 1978. Here the defendant was employed as a director by Littlewoods, a large company which competes with Great Universal Stores Ltd. for the major share of the mail order business in the United Kingdom. As a consequence, the defendant agreed in his contract of employment that he would not, for a period of twelve months after its termination, enter into a contract of employment with Great Universal Stores Ltd. or any subsidiary company. Littlewoods, by such a restraint clause was seeking to protect confidential information of which the defendant was aware, relating to the preparation of their mail order catalogue. As Great Universal Stores operated all over the world it was argued that the restraint clause was wider than reasonably necessary to protect Littlewoods' interest in the UK. A majority of the court held however that restraint clauses should be interpreted bearing in mind their object

> and intention. As a proper construction, the clause was intended to relate to the UK mail order business only and was therefore valid and enforceable.

It is crucial to the validity of a restraint clause that the employer limits its extent to protect the clientele and business locations which apply to the employee's term of employment. It would be unreasonable for an employer to attempt to prevent competition in geographical locations into which it has not yet operated.

> In *Greer v. Sketchley Ltd.* 1979 the restraint clause purported to prevent the employer competing nationwide when in fact the employer's business was limited to the Midlands and London. The argument that an employer is entitled to seek protection in geographical areas in which he intends to expand, was rejected.

> In *WAC Ltd. v. Whillock* 1990 the Scottish Court of Session emphasised that restrictive covenants must be construed fairly and it is *"the duty of the Court to give effect to them as they are expressed and not to correct their errors or to supply their omissions"*. Here the clause in question specifically prevented any ex-company-shareholders for two years carrying on business in competition with the company. The clause did not impose any restriction on the right of an employee to be a director or employee of another company which carried on business in competition and so could not prevent the employee/shareholder from becoming a director of a competing company.

If a restraint clause is drafted in such a way that it is reasonable in extent, then provided it does not offend the public interest it will be binding and can be enforced by means of an injunction. In practice such injunctions are rarely granted for the very presence of the clause acts as a sufficient deterrent.

> In *Lawrence David Ltd. v. Ashton* 1989 the Court of Appeal emphasised that the decision whether or not to grant an interlocutory (temporary) injunction to enforce a restraint of trade clause should be taken in accordance with the principles laid down in *American Cyanamid Company. v. Ethicon Ltd.* 1975. In restraint of trade cases, the most relevant criterion is whether or not an employer would have any real prospect of succeeding in a claim for a permanent injunction at the trial.

There have also been a few exceptional cases where the courts have determined that part of a restraint clause is unreasonable but other separate parts of the clause are reasonable and would be valid and enforceable. In such circumstances, rather than declare the whole clause to be void and unenforceable, the courts have severed the unreasonable part of the contract and, provided that what remains can stand alone, declared it to be valid and enforceable.

> In *Lucas T & Company v. Mitchell* 1974 the defendant salesman contracted that he should not for one year after the determination of his employment:
>
> (a) solicit orders within his trading area from present customers and those whom his employer supplied during the previous twelve months; and
>
> (b) deal in the same or similar goods to those that he sold.
>
> In an action for breach of contract, the court found that two obligations were severable so that the second clause against dealing was unreasonable and void but the first clause not to solicit orders was valid and enforceable.

> In *Rex Stewart Ltd. v. Parker* 1988 the defendant who was the joint managing director of the plaintiff's advertising agency, moved to an agency which he

set up himself. The move was alleged to be in breach of his covenant not to solicit the plaintiff's clients for eighteen months after his employment with them had terminated. The defendant claimed that the plaintiffs had forfeited their right to rely on the covenant by giving him six months salary in lieu of notice rather than the actual notice, and in any case the covenant was unreasonably wide and should be declared void. The Court of Appeal upheld the High Court decision that the payment was not in breach of covenant, and that the covenant was not unreasonably wide after irrelevant prohibitions had been severed.

The case of *Provident Financial Group v. Hayward* 1989 is an example of a practice known as 'garden leave' where an employer under notice is not working for his employer but paid in full provided he does not work for anyone else. The employer in question was the financial director of an estate agency business who was seeking to take up employment with a rival agency. The Court of Appeal upheld the High Court's decision to refuse an interlocutory injunction to restrain the employee from working for anyone else while on 'garden leave'. It was within the High Courts judge's legitimate discretion to refuse the injunction because of the level of prospective detriment to the plaintiffs if it were not granted. The director had not been working with sensitive information and the new employer was operating in a different part of the estate agency market.*" The defendant here is to have his full salary, together with his company car and all other benefit until 31 December after which he is free. No starvation. Even considering idleness, per se, as a separate matter, it can hardly arise in this case. The defendant's status as an accountant is one unlikely to atrophy in a period of three months. Nor is he likely to suffer severe withdrawal symptoms from lack of job satisfaction over the period."*

One final issue that may be addressed in relation to restraint clauses and contractual terms generally is the extent to which they remain enforceable when clearly expressed in an original contract of employment but not re-stated on various promotions within the organisation.

In *Marley Tile Co Ltd. v. Johnson* 1982 the defendant's original letter of appointment contained a number of restraint clauses designed to prevent him seeking employment from rivals or competing for a period of twelve months on the termination of his employment. On promotion to area manager years later, the defendant agreed similar restraint clauses but when made a unit manager, his letter of appointment made no reference to them. When the defendant resigned and took up employment with a rival his employer sought an injunction to enforce the clause. The Court of Appeal held that covenants which form part of the employee's original contract applied to his subsequent appointment , despite the failure to refer to them. Lord Denning MR said, *"All that had happened in the present case was that the defendant had been promoted in the same company. Both parties would assume that the original terms of employment, including the restrictive covenants, would continue unless something was said to the contrary"* . Eveleigh LJ said that, "*The defendant's appointment as a unit manager was varied. No reference was made in the memorandum and letter of appointment to the motor car which the defendant continued to have, or to telephone expenses, or to lunch and subsistence allowances, all of which were matters dealt with in the previous formal agreement". The covenants although part of the contract were held to be void because they were too wide.*

Statutory Employment Rights

Statutory right	Statutory source	Means of enforcement	Time limits	Redress
To be supplied with a written statement of particulars of terms of employment	EPCA 78 s.1	Complaint by an employee to an Industrial Tribunal	Within three months of cessation of employment (where appropriate)	A declaration and /or compensation
To be given an itemised pay statement in writing containing specified particulars	EPCA 78 s.8	Complaint by an employee to an Industrial Tribunal	.. ..	.. ..
To guarantee payment for an employee with continuous employment of one month	EPCA 78 s.12	.. ..	Within three months of the day to which the payment relates	An award of the payment
To be paid during suspension from work on medical grounds for an employee with continous employment of three months	EPCA 78 s.19	.. ..	.. ..	An award of remuneration
To a minimum period of notice on the termination of employment for an employee of one month	EPCA 78 s.49	Complaint by an employee to the Court	Within six years of the breach of contract	An award of damages
To a written statement of the reasons for dismissal for an employee with continuous employment of two years	EPCA 78 s.53(1)	Complaint by an employee to an Industrial Tribunal	Within three months of the effective date of termination	An award of two weeks pay
Not to be unfairly dismissed for an employee with continuous employ ment of two years	EPCA 78 s.54	.. ..	.. ..	An award of compensation , reinstatement or re-engagement
Not to be dismissed for trade union membership or activities	EPCA 78 s.58	.. .	.. ..	..
Not to have action short of dismissal taken because of trade union membership or activities	EPCA 78 s.23	.. ..	Within three months of the act complained of	An award of compensation
Not to be unreasonably excluded or expelled from membership of a trade union where a closed shop is in operation	Employ ment Act 1980 s.4	.. ..	Within six months of the act complained of	A declaration and /or compensation

Statutory right	**Statutory source**	**Means of enforcement**	**Time limits**	**Redress**
Not be unjustifiably disciplined by a trade union for refusing to participate in industrial action	Employ ment Act 1988 s.3	Complaint by a trade union member to an Industrial Tribunal	Within three months of the allegation that the right has been infringed	A declaration
Not to be called to participate in industrial action without the approval of a secret ballot	Employ ment Act 1988 s.1(1)	Complaint by a trade union to a Court	After the internal grievance procedure or six months of invoking the procedure and it is not complete	A court order that is appropriate
Not to be refused employment because of membership or non-membership of a trade union	Employ ment Act 1990	Complaint to an Industrial Tribunal	Within three months of the conduct complained of	A declaration/com pensation/recom mendation
To prevent a trade union indemnifying an individual in respect of penalties for relevant offences or contempts	Employ ment Act 1988 s.8	Complaint to the Court		A Court order that is appropriate
To be paid maternity pay and be entitled to return to work in the event of pregnancy or confinement for an employee with two years continuous employment	EPCA 78 s.33	Complaint to an Industrial Tribunal	Within three months of the last day of the payment period	An award of compensation
To be paid time off to carry out trade union duties for an official of a recognised union	EPCA 78 s.27	.. ..	Within three months of the failure	A declara tion/ compensation
To take time off to carry out public duties	EPCA 78 s.29	.. ..	.. ..	..
To take time off for trade union activities for a member of a recognised union	EPCA 78 s.28	.. ..	.. ..	..
To take reasonable time off to look for work or make arrangements for training following notice of redundancy	EPCA78 s.31	.. ..	.. ..	..
To a redundancy payment for an employee who has two years continuous employment	EPCA 78 s.81	.. ..	Within six months of the relevant date	..
Not to be discriminated against because of race, gender or marital status in securing work, at work, or in the case of dismissal	Sex Discrimin ation Act 1975 (as amended) Race Relations Act 1976	.. ..	Within three months of the act of discrimination	..
To equal pay when engaged on like work or equivalent work	Equal Pay Act 1970 (as amended)	.. ..	Within six months of termination of employment (where appropriate)	..

Assignment *New Technology*

Monks plc is a large retail chain with its headquarters in Manchester. At the head office there is a Personnel department which employs over thirty clerical staff the majority of whom are members of the NUCS, The National Union of Clerical Staff.

Nine months ago the clerical staff in Personnel were required to attend a six week intensive in service training course to equip them with the skills necessary to operate a new computerised system of storing staff records installed at head office. On behalf of the clerical staff, the NUCS have attempted to negotiate a 5 per cent pay rise to reflect the willingness of the clerical staff to acquire new skills and use the new technology. The management of Monks have rejected the claim for a wage rise out of hand, and argued forcefully that all staff they employ are required to adapt to new working methods in the interests of efficiency. The management also announces that when the new system is operating there will be a twenty per cent reduction in their clerical staff requirements in Personnel. In response and after consulting the members the NUCS inform the management of Monks that they are in dispute and instruct their members to boycott the new technology. For the last three months the gross wages of those staff boycotting the new system have been reduced by one third. Furthermore last week the management wrote to the staff in dispute stating that *"if they continued to boycott the new system their work would be regarded as purely voluntary and no wages would be paid. Failure to report for work will be regarded as an implied resignation".*

Task

You are employed as a regional officer by the NUCS and have been called to a meeting with local shop stewards at Monks to discuss the dispute and then address the union members at a union meeting. You will be required to give your opinion on the legal validity on the response of the management of Monks to the industrial action. For this purpose your task is to research the present law relating to industrial action and breach of contract and prepare some briefing notes which will assist you in the meetings with the stewards and the union members.

Chapter 13

Health and Safety at Work

All individuals engaged in business should be aware that the production of goods and services may involve some degree of risk and that the health and safety at the work place has since the mid nineteenth century been the subject of legal intervention. The law relating to health and safety at work could be said to have two major objectives. Firstly to minimise the risk of injury and to enhance the welfare of those at the work place by imposing legal duties on employers, employees, contractors, manufacturers and others, which may be enforced by means of criminal sanctions. Secondly to provide the means by which those who are injured at the workplace may secure some form of redress.

Health and Safety law is embodied within statute and numerous statutory instruments, imposing minimum standards enforced by criminal sanctions. It is also found in the common law, providing an avenue of redress for those who suffer injury. Furthermore, health and safety at the workplace is a priority objective for European Community Institutions who aim to ensure minimum standards throughout the European Community. Part of this chapter will be devoted therefore to a consideration of the process and extent to which Community law on health and safety at the workplace is being incorporated into British law.

The Criminal Code

The criminal code in relation to health and safety has its origins in early nineteenth century legislation and until 1974 progress had been made by means of piecemeal legislation applying to particular industries and different workplaces, e.g. mines, factories, offices, shops, railways and agriculture. The report of the Robens Committee on Safety and Health at Work in 1972 criticised the then fragmented state of the legislation and subsequently the Health and Safety at Work etc. Act 1974 was passed. The aims of the Act were to

(a) lay down general duties applicable across the industrial spectrum;

(b) provide a unified system of enforcement under the control of the Health and Safety Executive and local authorities.

The Act was designed to promote a constructive attitude to health and safety in the working environment by bringing all those who work or are affected by work activities within the scope of the legislation. Broad general duties (considered later in the chapter) are imposed upon employers, suppliers of equipment, manufacturers etc., by the Act with the aim of ensuring, in so far as it is reasonably practicable, a safe working environment.

The Health and Safety Commission was created to assist in the process of changing attitudes and given the task of producing detailed regulations, applicable to each industrial sector backed up by codes of practice designed to give guidance as to how general duties and specific regulations could be satisfied. It is the specific regulations, given legal force by statutory instruments made by order of the Secretary of State for Employment, that are the very heart of the Health and Safety at Work Act. While previous legislation relating to health and safety remains in force e.g. the Factories Act 1961, the aim is that eventually it will be replaced by regulations made under the Health and Safety at Work Act. Regulations are designed to impose specific obligations on particular industries, for instance, welders in the shipbuilding industry must, by regulation, be provided with certain safety equipment by their employers. Furthermore a code of practice, although not law, gives guidance to an employer as to how this regulation may be fulfilled. In relation to welders, the code will prescribe safety equipment to be worn such as goggles, boots, spats etc. It should be stressed that failure to comply strictly with a code of practice does not necessarily constitute a failure to comply with a statutory regulation. Consequently such a failure may not constitute a breach of the law. It could however be used as evidence in a criminal prosecution to support an allegation that a regulation has been broken.

The 1974 Act specifically provides that the breach of a general duty shall not give rise to civil liability but that a breach of any regulation made under the Act shall do so unless otherwise stated. This means that if an individual suffers injury at the workplace, due to the breach of a specific regulation, then he may be able to maintain a cause of action for damages for breach of statutory duty in addition to alleging possible liability under the criminal law. Regulations are designed to cover a wide range of matters including: the repeal and amendment of the existing statutory provisions; the imposition of requirements and prohibitions in relation to the design, construction, manufacture and use of articles and substances at work; those exempt and those responsible under the Act and the modification of general duties to particular industries. It should be stressed that unlike civil proceedings, there could be a breach of a specific regulation or a general duty leading to a successful prosecution where no injury has occurred.

Enforcement

Enforcement of the safety legislation is in the hands of the Health and Safety Executive and local authorities which have a number of powers at their disposal. The main power is to appoint inspectors who have authority to enter premises, take samples and require information to be given. The breach of a general duty or a specific regulation under the 1974 Act is a criminal offence. This can lead to a prosecution in the criminal courts. Less serious offences are dealt with summarily in the Magistrates Court and those of a more serious nature are tried on indictment in the Crown Court. Conviction in summary proceedings carries a fine of £400 or in some cases £1000, or for an indictable offence, an unlimited fine and/or up to two years imprisonment. The fundamental aim of those enforcing the 1974 Act is to encourage a positive attitude to health and safety at the workplace rather than to take numerous employers through the criminal courts. There is no doubt however that some employers resent the economic cost of health and safety and it may only be the threat of criminal prosecution, that will cause the more recalcitrant employers to respond.

One of the major innovations of the Act was the introduction of constructive sanctions. A Health and Safety Inspector who believes that an employer is contravening one of the statutory provisions may serve on that person an improvement notice requiring that the contravention be remedied within a specific period of not less than twenty one days. The notice will specify the provision which is contravened and state how it is being broken. In cases where the contravention involves an immediate risk of serious injury, the inspector may serve a prohibition notice which will direct that the particular activity is terminated until the contravention is rectified. Such a notice may take immediate effect or be deferred for a specified time. Failure to comply with a prohibition notice, for example by using a machine which has been identified as a serious source of danger, is an offence triable on indictment in the Crown Court.

General Duties

Most of the general duties contained in the 1974 Act impose on a number of different categories of person, a standard of care based on the idea of reasonable practicability. The most important general duty is that contained in s.2(1) and imposes on employers a duty to ensure, so far as is reasonably practicable, the health, safety and welfare of their workers. More specifically this duty involves under s.2(2) in so far as is reasonably practicable:

(a) *providing and maintaining safe plant and safe work systems*

(b) *making arrangements for the use, handling, storage and transport of articles and substances;*

(c) *providing any necessary information, instruction, training and supervision;*

(d) *maintaining a safe place of work and a safe access to and exit from it;*

(e) *maintaining a safe working environment.*

The scope of the general duty, contained in s.2, qualified by the words "reasonably practicable" is difficult to determine and little guidance has been provided by the courts. However the meaning of this phrase is obviously crucial in determining the scope of an employer's duty. It would be wrong to assume that it imposes a standard of care comparable with the duty to take reasonable care at common law. The statutory duty requires the employer to take action to ensure health and safety unless, on the facts, it is impracticable in the circumstances.

> In *Associated Dairies v. Hartley* 1979 the employer supplied his workers with safety shoes which they could pay for at £1 per week. An employee who had not purchased the shoes suffered a fractured toe when the wheel of a roller truck ran over it. There was an obvious risk to workers from roller trucks in the employer's warehouse. Accordingly an improvement notice was served on the employer requiring him to provide his employers with safety shoes free of charge (estimated cost £20,000 in the first year and £10,000 per annum thereafter). The Court of Appeal held that while such a requirement was practicable in all the circumstances of the case, it was not reasonably so, bearing in mind the cost in relation to the risk of injury. The improvement notice was therefore cancelled, the court confirming that in relation to the general duty, practicability alone is not the test, for it is qualified by the term "reasonable".

> The issue of 'practicability' under s.2 and its scope in relation to an employer with a large workforce working with contractors was raised in *R. v. Swan Hunter Shipbuilders Ltd., and Telemeter Installation Ltd.* 1981. Here eight men had been tragically killed by a fire which broke out on a ship under construction on the River Tyne. The fire had been fuelled by an oxygen enriched atmosphere caused by the failure of an employee of a sub-contractor (Telemeter) to turn off the oxygen supply over night. Both the employer and the sub-contractor were convicted of offences under the Act in the Crown Court and subsequently appealed to the Court of Appeal. The employer argued that the duty to provide a safe system of work to persons other than their own employees imposed an intolerable burden where there

was a large workforce with many different direct employers. The Court however having examined the wording of s.2(1) and s.2(2), decided that providing employees with a safe system of work may involve a duty to an employer to provide instruction and information to persons other than their own employees about potential dangers. Such instructions need not be given if the employer can show on the balance of probabilities that it was not reasonably practicable in the circumstances. Here the employer was aware of the dangers and by sub-contracting the work, they were under a duty to 'inform and instruct'. In the words of Dunn L J *"If the provision of a safe system of work for the benefit of his own employees involves information and instruction as to potential dangers being given to persons other than the employer's own employees, then the employer is under a duty to provide such information and instruction. His protection is contained in the words 'so far as is reasonably practicable' which appear in all the relevant provisions. The onus is on the defendants to prove on the balance of probabilities that it was not reasonably practicable in the particular circumstances of the case".*

The fact that a working practice adopted by employers is universal within the industry is not conclusive evidence that the general duty under s.2(1) has been discharged. The High Court in *Martin v. Boulton and Paul (Steel Construction) Ltd.* 1982 held that a universal practice whilst of great weight, is not conclusive evidence that it was not reasonably practicable to use some other and safer method.

Safety Representatives

A further requirement of s.2 for employers other than those with less than five employees is the obligation to prepare and revise a written statement of their general policy on health and safety and bring this statement to the notice of their employees. The statement should be more than a bland statement of responsibilities but rather a genuine attempt to identify specific health and safety problems of the employer in question and the arrangements that have been made to deal with them. Matters to be included would cover inspection procedures, emergency arrangements, safety precautions, consultative arrangements and training. Safety representatives may be appointed by recognised trade unions in which case s.2 further provides that it is the duty of an employer to consult with such representatives in order to promote health and safety at the workplace. In many cases this will involve consultations with safety committees which have the function of reviewing measures taken to ensure health and safety at work. Safety representatives have a number of powers, including the right to inspect the workplace and require the establishment of a safety committee. By regulation, a safety representative is entitled to paid time off work to undergo such training as is reasonable in the circumstances. It is worth noting that the general duties owed under s.2 apply to employees only and this would not include those training under a Youth Training Scheme as they are not treated as persons working under a contract of service. Following the Health and Safety (Youth Training Scheme) Regulations 1983 however, trainees on YTS are included under the umbrella of the Act.

Both employers and those who are self employed are required, in the words of s.3, to *"conduct their undertakings in such a way, in so far as is reasonably practicable", to protect persons other than their own employees from risks to their health and safety."* This would require an employer to give anyone who may be affected, information relating to health and safety risks arising from the way in which the business is run.

In *Carmichael v. Rosehall Engineering Works Ltd.* 1983 an employer was found to be in breach of his duty under s.3 when he failed to provide two youths on a work experience programme with suitable clothing for carrying out a cleaning operation using flammable liquid. The failure to give proper instruction and information, as to the possible risks to their health and safety, was a factor which led to the death of one of the boys when his paraffin soaked overalls burst into flames.

Further guidance as to the interpretation of s.3 was provided by the Court of Appeal in *R. v. Mara* 1987. Here the defendant, Mr. Mara, a director of a cleaning company called CMS Ltd., was convicted of an offence in that he had permitted a breach of his company's duty under s.3. The company had failed to conduct its undertaking in such a way as to ensure that persons not in its employment were exposed to health and safety risks. The facts were that the cleaning company had contracted to clean premises owned by International Stores plc on weekdays. This involved using electrical cleaning machines. As the loading bay could not be cleaned because it was in constant use, it was agreed that employees of International Stores should do the work using CMS equipment. One Saturday morning whilst using a CMS cleaning machine, a Store's employee was electrocuted due to the defective condition of the machine's cable. Mr. Mara was convicted and fined for an offence under s.3. On appeal however it was submitted that as the incident occurred on a Saturday morning, when the cleaning company did not work, it was not 'conducting its undertaking' at all, and so could not be in breach of its duty. The Court of Appeal rejected the submission however, holding that s.3 could not be limited to situations where a company's undertaking is in the process of actively being carried on. The way in which CMS Ltd. conducted its undertaking was to clean during weekdays and leave their equipment for use by their client's employees, at weekends. By failing to ensure that its equipment was safely wired the company was in breach of its s.3 duty to its client's employees. Consequently the director had rightly been convicted of an offence.

By virtue of s.4 a general duty is imposed on those who control work premises to ensure *so far as is reasonably practicable the safety of the premises, any means of access and exit from the place of work, and of any plant or substance provided for use on the premises.*

The duty extends to persons in control of non-domestic premises which are made available as a place of work and is owed to those who are not their employees. Under s.4(2) *"It shall be the duty of each person who has control of non-domestic premises or of the means of access thereto or therefrom or any plant or equipment in such premises, to take such measures as is reasonable for a person in his position to take to ensure, so far as is reasonably practicable, that the premises, all means of access available for use by persons using the premises and any plant or equipment in such premises is safe and without risk to health."*

In *H M Inspector of Factories v. Austin Rover Group Ltd.* 1989 the defendants were prosecuted for a breach of s.4(2) when the employee of a contractor working on the defendants' premises was killed following a sudden flash fire where he was working. A combination of breaches of safety instructions had contributed to the cause of the fire and at the original trial the defendants were convicted of a s.4(2) offence for failing to take precautions which would have constituted "reasonable measures" and been "reasonably practicable" for a person in the position of Austin Rover. On appeal and then further appeal to the House of Lords however, it was held that in determining the reasonableness of the measures to be taken under s.4(2) account must be taken of the extent of control and knowledge of the occupier in relation to the actual use to which the premises are put. *"If the premises are not a reasonably foreseeable cause of danger, to anyone acting in a way which a person reasonably may be expected to act, in circumstances which reasonably may be expected to occur during the carrying out of the work, or the use of the plant or substance for the purpose of which the premises were made available, it would not be reasonable to require an individual to take further measures against unknown and unexpected risks."*

A successful prosecution under s.4(2) requires the proof of:

(a) unsafe premises and a risk to health;

(b) the identity of the individual having control of the premises; and

(c) the fact that the person in control ought reasonably to have taken measures to ensure safety.

On proof of these three matters the onus then shifts to the accused to show that it was not reasonably practicable to take such measures. As in the present case, the defendant could not have reasonably forseen the unknown and unexpected events which made the premises unsafe, they would not be held to be in breach of s.4(2). Lord Jauncey made the important point that the *"safety of premises was not an abstract concept. It must be related to the purpose for which the premises were being used at any one time. Some premises might be unsafe for any normal use, for instance because of large unguarded holes in the floor or unstable walls. Other premises might be completely safe for the purposes for which they were designed but completely unsafe for other purposes, for example, an upper floor warehouse designed to a loading capacity of x lbs might become unsafe if loaded to a capacity of 2xlbs. If A made the warehouse available to B who used it within the designed loading capacity, it could not be said that the warehouse was unsafe and a risk to health under s.4(2) because B at some future date exceeds that capacity contrary to A's instructions".*

A further general duty imposed on those who control work premises is to *use the best practicable means to prevent the emission of offensive substances and to render harmless and inoffensive those substances emitted.* Again there is an overlap between this duty and obligations owed under the Control of Pollution Act 1974 and the Public Health Act 1936.

Those who design, manufacture, import or supply any article for use at work are required in so far as is reasonably practicable to ensure the article's safety, to carry out necessary testing and examining and provide sufficient information about the use of the article at work to render it safe and without risks to health.

Finally there is a general duty on every employee while at work to take reasonable care for the health and safety of himself and of other persons who may be affected by his acts or omissions at work and to cooperate with employers in the discharge of their health and safety duties. Those employees who act in disregard of health and safety should be counselled but in the end dismissed if they are a danger to themselves or others. Wilful breaches of a safety rule, for instance a no smoking policy was held to be a justifiable reason for dismissal in *Roger v. Wicks and Wilson* 1988.

At the end of the chapter the extent to which domestic legislation on health and safety is, and will be supplemented by Community law, is considered.

Civil Redress

A further major objective of the law relating to health and safety at the workplace is to provide a means by which those who have suffered injury may recover compensation. Since the mid 1960s, state benefit has been available for employees who suffer injury from accidents arising out of and in the course of employment or contract prescribed industrial diseases. If injury is caused through fault however, whether of the employer or a fellow worker, an injured person can bring a claim for damages through the courts. If it can be shown that injury has occurred as a result of a failure to comply with a regulation under the Health and Safety at Work Act 1974 or some other statutory obligation, for instance under the Factories Act 1961, then a claim could be brought for damages under a civil action for breach of statutory duty. This action has the status of a separate tort and can provide a means of redress for persons who suffer harm as a result of a breach of a duty imposed by statute.

The Tort of Breach of Statutory Duty

To succeed in an action based upon breach of statutory duty it is necessary to prove:

(a) that the statute in question imposes a statutory duty on the defendant which is owed to the plaintiff;

(b) that the defendant is in breach of the statutory duty; and

(c) that the plaintiff suffered injury as a result and the harm caused was of a kind contemplated by the statute.

In cases where the duty imposed by statute is a strict one, then the burden on the plaintiff is to prove that it has been broken without the need to show any fault on the part of the defendant. In applying s.14(1) of the Factories Act 1961 therefore, "*Every dangerous part of any machinery ... shall be securely fenced unless it is in such a position or of such construction as to be as safe to every person employed or working on the premises as it would be if securely fenced*" , it is necessary to show:

(a) that the Factories Act applies to the premises in question and that the s.14(1) duty is imposed on the employer and is owed to the employee;

(b) that the machine in question is a source of danger and that it was not securely fenced;

(c) that the employee suffered injury as a result of the failure to securely fence and the harm was a type contemplated by the section.

> In *H Wearing v. Pirelli Ltd.* 1977 the plaintiff suffered a broken wrist when his hand came into contact with a rubber coating around a revolving metal drum which had not been securely fenced. The House of Lords held that the employers were liable for breach of their statutory duty under s.14(1) to fence securely dangerous parts of machinery despite the fact that the employee's hand had come in contact with the rubber coating only, rather than the machinery itself.

Common Law Negligence

An alternative course of action for an employee who has suffered harm due to the fault of his employer or a fellow employee is to base a claim on common law negligence. Under the common law, an employer owes a legal duty of care to ensure the health and safety of his employees and this duty takes effect on an implied term of the contract of employment. An employer is required to take reasonable care with regard to the safety of his employees by providing a safe system of work. The provision of a safe system of work involves an obligation to provide safe fellow employees, safe plant and equipment, safe working premises and safe working methods. If an employer is in breach of his common law duty to take reasonable care, and damage in the form of injury is caused as a result, he will be liable.

It should be stressed that in civil proceedings it is often the case that a claim is based upon both the breach of a common law duty and for breach of statutory duty if relevant.

> In *Smith v. Vange Scaffolding & Engineering Company Ltd. and Another* 1970 the plaintiff scaffolder suffered injury when he fell over a welding cable when walking back from his place of work. The High Court held that the employee's immediate employers were liable for breach of their common law duty of care because they were aware of the dangerous state of the site where their employees worked. In addition the employers were in breach of their statutory duty imposed, by regulation 6 of the Construction (working places) Regulations 1966, to provide a suitable and sufficient access to an egress from the plaintiff's place of work.

Certainly there is no intention that statutory regulation is designed to supersede the common law so that even if an employer has complied with a regulation, for instance to supply his workers with safety equipment, an employee is still entitled to pursue a claim under the common law if he is injured due to a failure to wear it.

> In *Bux v. Slough Metals* 1973 the plaintiff lost the sight of one eye as a result of a splash from molten metal when he was pouring it into a die. While safety goggles had been supplied, the plaintiff refused to wear them because they misted up, and no attempt was made to persuade him otherwise. The Court of Appeal held that while the employer had provided suitable goggles for the purpose of safety regulations, they were nevertheless negligent under the common law. The evidence suggested that the plaintiff would have followed clear instructions to wear the goggles, and that the question whether or not an employer's common law duty of care extended to instructing, persuading or insisting on the use of protective equipment depended on the facts. By failing to make use of the goggles the plaintiff was guilty of contributory fault and damages were reduced by forty percent.

As far as safety equipment is concerned, the contemporary view seems to be that the common law duty to make it available and ensure that employees are aware of it does not necessarily carry with it any further obligation to inspect it or insist that it is worn. Obviously there is some obligation on the employee to take some responsibility for his own safety by ensuring that safety equipment is renewed when necessary.

> In *Smith v. Scott Bowyers Ltd.* 1986 the plaintiff, who was just twenty years of age, and employed by the company for nineteen months, suffered injury when he slipped on the greasy factory floor. To help minimise the risk the employer provided the workers with wellington boots with diamond ridge soles and they were renewed on request. Having already replaced one pair

of boots the accident was due to the plaintiff's failure to renew the replacement pair which had also worn out and were a danger. In an action for damages for breach of the employer's duty of care, the High Court found that the failure of the employers to emphasise the danger and carry out checks of the safety equipment made them in breach of the legal duty of care they owed to the plaintiff. Damages were to be reduced by one third however, due to the plaintiff's contributory fault. On appeal however, the Court of Appeal reversed the decision and held that there was no breach of the employer's duty to take reasonable care. The failure of the employee to renew the boots was due to his own lack of care and could not be taken as the fault of the employer. *"The employer's duty to provide employees with properly designed Wellington boots would not be filled out with any further obligation to instruct them to wear them or to inspect the condition of the soles from time to time."*

The common law duty encompasses an obligation to provide safe plant and appliances. If an employer was aware that machinery or tools are not reasonably safe, and an employee is injured as a result, the employer will be in breach of his duty under the common law.

In *Bradford v. Robinson Rentals* 1967 the employer provided an unheated van for the employee, a 57 year old, to make a 400 mile journey during the winter, which would involve him in at least 20 hours driving. The court held that the employer was liable for the employee's frost bite, which was the type of injury that was reasonably foreseeable from prolonged exposure to severe cold and fatigue. The court also confirmed that even if the plaintiff had been abnormally susceptible to frost bite he would still be entitled to succeed under the rule that the defendant must take his victim as he finds him.

In the past an employer could satisfy his duty to provide safe equipment by showing that he purchased the equipment from a reputable supplier and that he had no knowledge of any defect. Now however, following the Employers Liability (Defective Equipment) Act 1969, injury occurring to an employee under those circumstances may be attributed to the deemed negligence of the employer. If damages are awarded against the employer then it is up to him to seek a remedy from the supplier of the defective equipment.

The obligation to provide a safe system of work also encompasses a requirement to provide safe fellow employees. If there are untrained or unskilled people employed at the workplace then a higher standard of care is owed by the employer to ensure their safety and the safety of those who work with them.

In *Hawkins v. Ross Castings Ltd.* 1970 the plaintiff was injured following a spillage of molten metal, due partly to the employer's failure to comply with safety regulations in relation to the maintenance of a safe pouring systems. An additional contributing factor was the fact that the plaintiff was working closely with a seventeen year old untrained Indian who spoke little English and yet was required to carry and pour molten metal with the plaintiff. This factor contributed to the employer's liability.

The duty to provide safe fellow employees exits irrespective of any issue of the employer's vicarious liability for the actions of his employees. Vicarious or substituted liability is considered later in the chapter.

The employer's common law duty also imposes an obligation to provide safe working methods and safe working premises. To determine whether an employer is providing safe working methods, it is necessary to consider a number of factors including the layout of the work place, training and supervision, warnings and whether protective equipment is provided. It should be stressed that the common law duty on an employer is to take reasonable care, and if he gives proper instructions which the employee fails to observe then the employer will not be liable if the employee is then injured.

> In *Charlton v. Forrest Printing Ink Company Ltd.* 1980 the employer gave proper instructions to an employee who was given the job of collecting the firm's wages. The instructions required the employee to vary his collecting arrangements to prevent robbery. The employee failed to do this and suffered severe injury when he was robbed. The Court of Appeal held that the employer was not liable as he had taken reasonable steps to cut down the risk. The normal industrial practice of firms of that size in that area was to make their own payroll collection rather than employ a security firm. The employers *"did what was reasonable in the circumstances to eliminate the risk and no more could have been expected of them. They could not be held liable for the injuries incurred by the employee"*.

It should be stressed that the common law duty is not one of strict liability but rather a duty to take reasonable care in the circumstances.

> In *Latimer v. AEC* 1953 after a factory was flooded, the employer asked his workforce to return, warning them of the dangerous state of the factory floor. Sawdust had been used to cover most of the damp areas but not enough was available, and the plaintiff slipped, and was injured. To determine whether the employer had broken the common law duty of care he owed his employees the court weighed the cost of avoiding the injury against the risk of injury and held that the employer had acted reasonably in the circumstances.

In addition, the standard of care owed by an employer will vary with regard to each individual employee. A young apprentice should be provided with effective supervision while this may not be required for an experienced employee.

> In *Paris v. Stepney BC* 1951 the plaintiff, a one-eyed motor mechanic, lost the sight of his good eye while working at chipping rust from under a bus. Despite there being no usual practice to provide mechanics with safety goggles, the court decided that they should have been provided to the plaintiff. The defendants were liable as they could foresee serious consequences for the plaintiff if he suffered eye injury. *"The special risk of injury is a relevant consideration in determining the precautions which the employer should take in the fulfilment of the duty of care which he owes to the workman."*

Defences available to the Employer

Finally it should be mentioned that in very exceptional cases the plaintiff may be taken to have consented to the risk of injury and the defence of "volenti non fit injuria" (no wrong is done to one who consents) established.

> In *Imperial Chemical Industries v. Shatwell* 1965 two employees, both experienced shot firers, in contravention of specific safety instructions, fired a shot causing injury to both of them. The House of Lords held that the employer

could rely on volenti as an absolute defence to the action, due to the act of gross disobedience.

It is more likely that the employer will be able to rely on the Law Reform (Contributory Negligence) Act 1945 which provides a partial defence. If the employer can show that the injured employee contributed to his injury by his own fault then damages may be reduced to *"such extent as the court thinks just and equitable having regard to the claimants share in the responsibility for the damage"*. You will remember that in the case of *Bux v. Slough Metals* 1973 mentioned previously, the damages awarded were reduced by forty per cent to reflect the plaintiff employee's contributory fault.

As we mentioned earlier, part of the common law duty is that an employer must take reasonable care to ensure that he provides his workers with safe fellow workers. To engage an employee who has a past record of dangerous behaviour could put the employees at risk and constitute a negligent act on the part of the employer for which he could be made directly liable. Certainly if an employer is aware of an employee who by incompetence or practical jokes is creating a dangerous situation at work he should take steps to discipline him and if necessary dismiss him. Moreover the legal responsibility of an employer covers the situation when an employee under his control causes harm to a fellow employee or a third party by some wrongful act. This is by virtue of the doctrine of vicarious (substituted) liability.

Vicarious Liability

There are some situations where the law is prepared to impose vicarious (substituted) liability on an individual who is not at fault for the commission of the wrongful (tortious) act of another. The best known example of this situation is the common law rule which imposes vicarious liability on employers in respect of torts committed by their employees during the course of their employment. Accordingly, if one employee (Jones) by his negligent act causes harm to a fellow employee (Smith) then in addition to the possibility of (Smith) pursuing a legal action against (Jones) he may have the further option of suing his employer who will have become vicariously liable if the negligent act occurred during the course of Jones's employment. The same principle applies equally where the injuries are caused by an employee to some third party. However, while employers have a choice as to whether they insure against the risk of injury to third parties, under the Employer's Liability (Compulsory Insurance) Act 1969, an employer is required to insure himself in respect of injuries caused by his employees to their colleagues.

The imposition of vicarious liability does not require proof of any fault on the employer's part, or any express or implied authorisation to commit the wrongful act. All that must be proved for the purpose of vicarious liability is:

(1) an actionable wrong committed by the worker;

(2) that the worker is an employee;

(3) that the wrongful act occurred during the course of his employment.

What then is the theoretical basis for imposing liability in these circumstances? A number of reasons have emerged, such as he who creates and benefits from a situation should assume the risk of liability arising from it. There is also the idea that if an organisation embarks on an enterprise and as a result harm is caused by one member of the organisation, it should be the responsibility of the organisation to compensate for the harm. It is after all the employer who selects and controls the employees who work for him. The employer has the responsibility of training staff and can of course dismiss those whose work is performed incompetently. The practical reason for vicarious liability is of course that if the employee were solely liable he would have to insure himself, and the cost of this would be indirectly borne by the employer in the form of higher wages. Under the present system insurance costs are borne directly by the employer who, as a principle of sound business practice, will normally carry adequate insurance.

To determine an employer's liability it is first necessary to establish the employment status of the worker who is alleged to have committed the wrongful act. This is because the legal position differs dramatically depending on whether the worker is employed as an employee under a contract of service rather than as a self employed contractor under a contract for services. Usually this issue may be settled without argument but in the small proportion of cases where there is doubt the courts are left with the task of identifying the true contractual status of the worker by applying the law contained in Chapter 11. It is convenient to deal with the legal position of employees and independent contractors separately.

Employees

As a general principle an employer is vicariously liable for the tortious acts of his employees committed during the course of their employment. The phrase 'course of employment' has produced numerous interpretations in the courts, but essentially it concerns the question of whether the employee was doing his job at the time of the tortious act. It should be emphasised that an employee will have both express and implied authority to perform work for his employer and while he will normally have no authority to commit torts, he may nevertheless be guilty of a tortious act in the performance of his authorised duties.

> In *Century Insurance Ltd. v. Northern Ireland Road Transport Board* 1942 a tanker driver while delivering petrol at a garage, lit a cigarette and carelessly threw away the lighted match which caused an explosion and considerable damage. His employer was held to be vicariously liable for his negligence as the employee had acted within the course of his employment. By supervising the unloading, the employee was doing his job, but by smoking he was doing it in a grossly negligent manner.

Even if an employee is carrying out an act outside the basic obligation of his contract of employment, his employer may nevertheless be made vicariously liable if the act is carried out for the benefit of the employer.

> In *Kay v. ITW* 1968 the employee injured a colleague when he negligently drove a five ton diesel lorry which was blocking his way. Despite the fact that he was contractually authorised to drive only small vans and trucks, his employer was held to be vicariously liable for his action.

If an employee is doing something of purely personal benefit at the time of the negligent act then he may be regarded, to quote from the colourful language of the Victorian era as "off on a frolic of his own", and his employer will not be responsible.

> In *Hilton v. Thomas Burton (Rhodes) Ltd.* 1961 the plaintiff's husband was a demolition worker who was killed through the negligent driving of one of his colleagues. The defendant employer denied vicarious liability as, at the time of the accident, the van was being driven from a cafe on an unauthorised break. The court held that although the van had been driven with the permission of the employer, at the time of the incident the driver was not doing that which he was employed to do. Accordingly the employer was not liable for the negligent driving.

> Guidance in relation to the possiblity of vicarious liability being imposed when industrial action causes damage to property was recently provided by the Judicial Committee of the Privy Council in *General Engineering Services Ltd. v. Kingston and St. Andrews Corporation* 1989. The claim was based upon the notion that the corporation, having a statutory duty to extinguish fires, were vicariously liable for the negligence of the members of their fire brigade who had failed to respond promptly to an emergency call. The reason for the delay was that the fire brigade, in dispute with their employer, were operating a go slow. As a consequence of taking seventeen rather than three minutes to respond to a fire, a building and its contents were burned to the ground. Both the court of first instance and the Jamaica Court of Appeal held that in operating the go slow the brigade were not acting in the course of their employment, so that the employers could not be made vicariously liable. This was confirmed on final appeal to the Judicial Committee of the Privy Council. Here it was held that an act is deemed to have been done in the course of employment if it is either a wrongful act and authorised by the employer, or a wrongful and unauthorised mode of doing some authorised act. If however the employee's unauthorised and unlawful act could be regarded as independent and not connected with the authorised act so as to constitute a mode of doing it, the employer is not responsible. Here by operating a go slow the fire brigade were not carrying on a wrongful or authorised mode of doing an otherwise authorised act. By stopping and starting on their way to a fire this manner of driving had no connection with the authorised activity of driving to the scene of a fire as quickly as possible.

Taking industrial action therefore in furtherance of an industrial dispute, may have the effect of repudiating an essential obligation of the contract of employment, and if so unconnected with the employee's job, take him outside the course of his employment for the purpose of vicarious liability.

The extent to which an express prohibition by the employer will prevent vicarious liability will depend upon the nature of the prohibition. If it merely attempts to instruct the employee how he is to do his job, the employee may still be within the course of his employment for the purposes of vicarious liability.

> In *Rose v. Plenty* 1976 a milkman, contrary to an express prohibition, engaged a thirteen year old boy to help him deliver the milk. The boy was subsequently injured by the milkman's negligent driving and sued both the milkman and his employer. The Court of Appeal held that despite the prohibition of the employer, he remained vicariously liable as the milkman had acted within the course of his employment. Scarman L J having considered the prohibition stated that *"There was nothing in the prohibition which defined or limited the sphere of his employment, the sphere of his employment remained precisely the same as before the prohibition was brought to his notice. The sphere was as a roundsman to go the rounds delivering milk, collecting empties and obtaining payment. Contrary to instructions the roundsman chose to do what he was employed to do in an improper way. But the sphere of his employment was in no way affected by his express instructions".*

It seems therefore that only an express prohibition which effectively cuts down the 'sphere of employment' will prevent the establishment of vicarious liability. The fact that contemporary courts seem to favour the idea of a very wide sphere of employment in individual cases, severely limits the opportunity of employers to restrict liability by express instruction. It is only by deciding the authorised parameters of an individual's job, and deciding that the act complained of fell outside these parameters that vicarious liability can be successfully denied.

> In *Joseph Rand v. Craig* 1919 carters employed to take rubbish to a tip were subject to an express prohibition against tipping other than on the authorised dump. On the question of liability for unauthorised tipping the court held that as the carters were employed to transport the rubbish to and from defined places, by unauthorised tipping they had stepped outside the course of their employment and so their employer could not be held liable for their conduct.

If the act is done on the employer's premises with the employer's interest in mind, the employer may be made liable provided the act has a close connection with the employee's job.

> In *Compton v. McClure* 1975 the employer was held to be vicariously liable for the negligence of an employee who, when late for work, caused an accident when driving negligently on the factory road.
>
> Even the manager in a public house in *Stone v. Taffe* 1974 was held to be within the course of his employment when he negligently failed to ensure that a stairway was properly lighted for a customer, despite the fact that the injury occurred two and a half hours after licensed closing time.
>
> The question as to whether an employee is acting within the course of his employment while required to travel from home to a workplace other than his regular one was recently addressed by the House of Lords in *Smith v. Stages and Another* 1989. Here an action was brought on behalf of an employee, who as a passenger in the defendant's car, suffered personal injuries as a result of the negligent driving of the defendant, a fellow employee. Despite the fact that the employers neither required nor authorised the journey by car to and from their particular workplace they were joined as second defendants on a claim that they were vicariously liable for the driver's negligence. The House of Lords held that employees who are required to travel to and from non regular workplaces, and in receipt of wages for doing so, remain within the course of their employment, even if they have a choice as to the mode and time of travel. Here the employee chose to travel in his own vehicle with the employer's knowledge and so the employers were vicariously liable for his negligent driving. Employees are in the course of their employment when going about their employer's business, and this will be the case if an employee is 'on duty' on his way to and from the workplace. This would not be so in relation to an employee travelling from home to and from his regular workplace whatever the mode of transport, unless obliged by his contract of service to use the employer's transport.
>
> A number of prima facie propositions were suggested by the House of Lords in relation to the question as to whether an employee is acting in the course of his employment during travelling time. The receipt of wages would indicate that an employee was travelling in his employer's time, and acting in the course of his employment. Equally so would an employee travelling in the employer's time between different workplaces. An employee travelling in his employer's time from his ordinary residence to a workplace, other than his regular workplace, to the scene of an emergency such as a fire accident or mechanical breakdown of plant, would also be acting in the course of his employment. Deviations or interruptions of a journey undertaken in the

> course of employment unless merely incidental would normally take an employee outside the course of his employment.

While it may be reasonable for an employee to use a degree of force in protection of his employer's property, or to keep order, an employee who commits an assault which has no connection with his work will be solely liable for his conduct.

> So in *Warren v. Henleys Ltd.* 1948 the employer was held not to be vicariously liable for a physical attack by a petrol pump attendant on one of his customers. The claim that the attendant was acting within the scope of his employment was rejected, for while the attack developed out of an argument over payment for petrol, it was in reality motivated by an act of private vengeance.

It is important to draw a distinction between vicarious liability and the direct or primary liability of an employer.

> In *Carmarthenshire County Council v. Lewis* 1955 a child at a local authority nursery school wandered from the school yard onto the highway and caused the death of a lorry driver who had swerved to avoid the child. An action was brought against the council in negligence on the grounds that the child's teacher left her unattended for a short time. In fact at the relevant time the teacher was attending to the needs of another child. The court held that the teacher had in fact fulfilled the common law duty of care required of her by acting as a prudent parent would in the circumstances. Consequently there could be no vicarious liability imposed on her employer. However, the fact that the child could reach the street so easily, indicated that the council were failing in their legal duty to operate a safe system at the school, and so were held to be directly liable for their primary negligence.
>
> A further example of the distinction between the direct and vicarious liability of an employer is provided by the decision in *Nahhas v. Pier House (Cheyne Walk) Management* 1984. Here the tenant of a luxury flat deposited the key with a porter during a stay in hospital. This was the normal system operated by the owners, but unfortunately a porter, one of their employees, used the key to steal jewellery from the plaintiff's flat. In fact the porter had a long criminal record involving eleven prison terms of which his employer, the owners, were unaware. The court held that while the system of depositing keys was not negligent, the failure by the employer to thoroughly check the porter's background constituted a breach of the legal duty of care owed to the tenants which resulted in damage. Consequently the employers were liable for their primary negligence and also responsible vicariously for the criminal act of the porter carried out during the course of his employment.

Certainly to impose liability on an employer for the tortious or criminal acts of an employee under his control, there must be a connection between the act complained of and the circumstances of employment. The fact that employment gives the employee an opportunity to commit the wrongful act is insufficient to impose vicarious liability on the employer.

> In *Heasmans v. Clarity Cleaning Company* 1987 the Court of Appeal found it possible to absolve the defendant cleaning company from liability for the acts of one of their cleaners who, while employed on the plaintiff's premises, used the plaintiff's telephone to make international telephone calls to the value of £1411. The mere fact that the cleaner's employment provided the

opportunity to fraudulently use the plaintiff's telephone was not itself sufficient to impose liability on the defendant.

Loaned Employees

Occasionally the courts have been faced with the issue of vicarious liability for the tortious acts of an employee committed when he has been hired out by his primary employer to another employer.

In *Mersey Docks and Harbour Board v. Coggins & Griffith Ltd.* 1947 a crane and its driver had been hired out by one employer to another. The question before the House of Lords was which employer should be made liable for the negligent operation of the crane by the driver. Their Lordships held that while the cranedriver remained an employee of his primary employer, for the purpose of vicarious liability, responsibility depended upon whether a sufficient degree of control over his acts had passed to the primary employer. *"The workman may remain the employee of his general employer, but at the same time, the result of the arrangements may be that there is vested in the hirer a power of control over the workman's activities sufficient to attach to the hirer responsibility for the workman's acts and defaults and to exempt the general employer from that responsibility".* In this case control had passed over and consequently it was the hirer of the crane who was made liable.

A further difficulty in relation to the loaned employee is the question as to which employer is responsible if he suffers injuries due to the negligence of a fellow employee. In such cases the employee is usually advised to sue both his general employer and the employer to whom he was loaned.

This was the situation in *Thompson v. T Lohan (Plant Hire) Ltd. and J W Hurdiss Ltd.* 1987 where an action was brought by Mr. Thompson's widow alleging that her husband's death was due to the negligence of a fellow worker. Mr. Thompson, who was employed by the first defendants, (the plant owners) as a JCB driver, was killed as a result of an incident which occurred whilst he and his machine were on hire to the second defendants (the hirers). The High Court held that the claim in negligence had been proved and Mr. Thompson's employer, (the plant owners), were liable for damages. A major point of issue however, was whether the plant owners were entitled to be indemnified against liability by the hirers because of certain clauses in the hire contract to that effect. All hirings by the plant owners were made subject to the terms of the Contractors Plant Association conditions of hire, two of which were relevant in this case. Condition 8 provided that: "When a driver or operator is supplied by the owner of the plant... such person shall be under the direction and control of the hirer... Such drivers or operators shall for all purposes in connection with their employment in the working of the plant be regarded as the servant or agents of the hirer....who alone shall be responsible for all claims arising in connection with the operation of the plant by the said drivers or operators". Condition 13 went on to provide that:"During the continuance of the hire period, the hirer shall...fully and completely indemnify the owner in respect of all claims by any such person whatsoever, for injury to persons or property caused by or in connection with or arising out of the use of the plant and in respect of all costs and charges herewith whether arising under statute or common law". In the light of the above clauses the High Court held that the hirers should indemnify the plant owners against the damages and costs recovered by Mrs. Thompson. On further appeal to the Court of Appeal however it was argued that the indemnity clause was in fact inoperative as it conflicted with s.2(1) of the Unfair Contract Terms Act 1977 which states that *"A person cannot by reference to any contract term or to a notice given to persons generally or to particular persons exclude or restrict his liability for death or personal injury resulting from his negligence"*. The Court of Appeal held that as the intention of this clause was to protect the victims of negligence, there was nothing in s.2(1) to prevent a person at fault making arrangements with others to share or bear the burden of compensating those victims of negligence. The plaintiff was in no way prejudiced by the operation of the contract clauses which operated to require the hirer to indemnify the plant owner against the damages and costs recovered by the plaintiff.

The increasing practice of employees contracting out areas of work to contractors and sub contractors has important implications when determining liability for injuries caused due to negligence at the workplace.

In a recent Scottish case, *Sime v. Sutcliffe Catering Scotland Ltd.* 1990 an employee brought a claim alleging negligence by the above catering company when, carrying out her work as a canteen assistant she slipped on some food dropped by a fellow worker and suffered injury. The case was complicated by the fact that the employee was not directly employed by the catering company but by a paper manufacturer, Tullis Russell and Company. Previously the paper manufacturer had contracted out the management of the canteen to the above company, but following pressure from the trade union, had agreed to retain existing canteen staff, including the employee. It was never established whether the worker who had dropped the food was an employee of the catering company or not. The issue therefore was whether the catering company could be held liable vicariously to a worker for the possible negligent act of a worker who they did not employ. The Scottish Court of Session held that responsibility should be with the employer in control. Although not directly employed by the catering company, whether the employer relationship is *"such as to render the company liable for the negligence depends upon whether the substitute employer has sufficient power of control and supervision purely to be regarded as the effective employer at the critical time". As the "whole day to day management of the catering operation and staff was undertaken by the catering company and the canteen manager had complete control over the way in which all the canteen workers did their job"*...and *"since one of the employed persons caused the accident by being negligent in dropping food stuff onto the floor and failing to clean it up the company had to accept responsibility for that negligence"*. The fault of the injured employee was also recognised and damages were reduced by twenty five percent to reflect her contributory negligence. *"Where a person is working in or near a kitchen where a number of people are working with food or dirty dishes and where it is quite predictable that food might be spilt it is reasonably necessary that a look out be kept for any wet or slippery patches on the floor."*

Independent Contractors

Generally vicarious liability has been confined to the employer/employee relationship and where contractors are employed, responsibility for their wrongful acts is solely their own. The justification for not extending vicarious liability to employers of contractors, other than in exceptional cases, stems from the fact that the contractor is not subjected to his employer's control in the same way as an employee. One important exception, which in recent times has assumed significance, is the situation where the contractor has been employed to carry out a statutory duty imposed on the employer. This is because of the recent move towards requiring public bodies to put out many of their statutory functions for competitive tender among contractors and so the possibility of imposing liability on employers for the tortious acts of a contractor have increased significantly. The law in this area is not new.

> The case of *Hardaker v. Idle District Council* 1896 remains the leading authority in relation to the delegation of statutory duties. The council acting under a statutory power to construct a sewer, employed a contractor to carry out the work. The contractor negligently pierced a gas main and the plaintiff's property was damaged by the resultant explosion. In an action by the plaintiffs against the contractor and the council employer, the court held that in exercising their statutory power the council owed an overriding duty to the public. This duty was to construct a sewer so as not to damage the gas main and put the public at risk. The council could not discharge this duty by simply employing a contractor to carry out the work, and accordingly they remained responsible to the plaintiff for its breach.

There are then certain legal duties that cannot be delegated, and if the wrongful act of a contractor constitutes a breach of such a duty, owed by an employer to a third party, then the contractor's employer may be made vicariously liable for the default.

> In *Rogers v. Nightriders* 1983 a mini cab firm undertook to provide a hire car to the plaintiff for a journey and did so by engaging a contractor driver. The plaintiff was injured in an accident caused by the negligent maintenance of the mini cab by the contractor. In an action against the mini cab firm the court held that they were not liable as an employer could not be made vicariously liable for their contractor's default. On appeal however, it was held that as the employer had undertaken to provide a vehicle to carry the plaintiff, and since they ought to have forseen harm to the plaintiff if the vehicle was defective, they owed a duty of care to the plaintiff to ensure that the vehicle was reasonably fit. Such a duty could not be delegated to a contractor and accordingly the employers were liable for breach of the primary duty that they owed to her.

This case is a further example of the distinction that must be drawn between vicarious and direct or primary liability previously considered. By providing a negligent contractor, the employer in *Rogers v. Nightriders* had failed to fulfil a direct duty of care he owed to those he could reasonably foresee being affected.

Health and Safety and the European Community

At the beginning of the chapter, reference was made to the dramatic impact Community law has and will have on member states. All European Community member states have already, to a greater or lesser extent, legislated in an attempt to regulate the health and safety of individuals at the workplace. A fundamental aim of the European Institutions however, is under Article 100 of the Treaty of Rome to harmonise legislation throughout the Community and this most certainly applies to health and safety law, so that minimum standards are imposed for all member states. The aim is to ensure that all technical barriers to trade are lifted.

The process by which proposals in relation to workplace health and safety matters are translated into directives and then incorporated into United Kingdom law was considered earlier in Chapter 1. One of the roles of the Health and Safety Commission is, having consulted interested parties, to recommend to the Secretary of State for Employment how EC directives relating to health and safety at work may be implemented by regulations under the Health and Safety at Work Act 1974.

The Single European Act 1986 sets out the European Commission's mandate for promoting Community Health and Safety Legislation. By that Act a new Article 118A has been added to the Treaty of Rome which provides that qualified majority voting rather than unanimity is to be used for the adoption of minimum requirements for health and safety legislation. This is of course an important change in procedure, and means that despite the objections of individual member states, the majority view as to minimum health and safety standards throughout the European Community will prevail.

Article 118A provides in paragraph 1 that "*Member States shall pay particular attention to encouraging improvements especially in the working environment, as regards the health and safety of workers and shall set as their objective the harmonisation of conditions in this area, while maintaining the improvements made*".

Paragraph 2 states that *"In order to help achieve the objective laid down in the first paragraph, the Council acting by a qualified majority on a proposal from the Commission, in cooperation with the European Parliament and after consulting the Economic and Social Committee, shall adopt, by means of directives, minimum requirements for gradual implementation, having regard to the condition and technical rule obtaining in each of the Member States"*.

Community legislation on health and safety is enacted through the new 'cooperation procedure' incorporated in Article 149 of the Single European Act. Under that procedure the power of the European Parliament has been increased so that it has now two readings where it can approve, amend and reject the Common position adopted by the Council of Ministers. The process of scrutinising proposals on health and safety had been carried out by the Parliament's Environment Consumer Protection and Public Health Committee. After June 1989 responsibility for Health and Safety legislation passed to the Parliament's Social Affairs, Employment and Working Environment Committee. The main actor in the Committee debates on each particular proposal is the person the Committee appoints as its rapporteur.

By virtue of Article 118A therefore, there is now a clear and specific mechanism for introducing new law on health and safety in the Community. It should be pointed out however, that by the wording of the Article, the Commission and the Council should concern themselves with *"minimum requirement"* for health and safety legislation. Also under paragraph 2 *"such directives shall avoid imposing administrative, financial and legal constraints in a way which would hold back the creation and development of small and medium sized undertakings"*.

There is no doubt that recently there has been a dramatic acceleration in the pace of the community legislation on health and safety compared with the minimal achievement of the previous two decades. Between 1970 and 1986 only six Directives aimed specifically at promoting health and safety at work were proposed by the Commission and adopted by the Council.

(1) Council Directive for the provision of safety signs at place of work 1977.

(2) Council Directive on the protection of workers from the risks related to exposure to chemical, physical and biological agents at work 1980.

(3) Council Directive on the protection of workers from the risks related to exposure to chloride monomer 1978.

(4) Council Directive on the protection of workers from the risks of exposure at work to metallic lead and its toxic compounds 1982.

(5) Council Directive on the protection of workers from the risks related to exposure to asbestos at work 1983.

(6) Council Directive on the major accident hazards of certain industrial activities 1986.

Other Directives relevant to the protection of workers at the workplace included one in relation to accident hazards and one in relation to the classification, packaging and labelling of dangerous substances.

Despite the worthy aims of the Commission's Action Plans of 1978 and 1984 to promote a programme of health and safety measures, only moderate progress has been made. Following the Single European Act, however, there is now a new emphasis in relation to health and safety. In 1987 a third action programme for health and safety was published by the European Commission and subsequently approved by resolution of the Council of Ministers. The programme contemplates a legislative package and a large number of Directives are proposed on a number of topics such as: the organisation of safety; selection and use of plant and machinery; selection and use of personal protective equipment; revision of the safety signs directives; medical assistance on ships; protection of agricultural workers using pesticides; safety in construction; carcinogenic agents; pesticides; amendments to the asbestos directive; and amendments to the lead directive.

In December 1988 further Directives were recommended by the Commission to deal with: temporary and mobile work sites; health and safety for fishing vessels; agriculture; modes of transport; extractive industries; and nuclear plants.

Other health and safety Directives promised in the Commission's Action Programme relating to the implementation of the Community Charter of Fundamental Social Rights of Workers are: the establishment of a safety, hygiene and health agency; information for workers exposed to dangerous agents; the protection of workers exposed to physical agents; the protection of pregnant women at work; and the protection of young people.

In addition to these numerous Directives the Commission propose to issue recommendations on economic factors in process control systems, prevention of back injuries, safety in agricultural building and electricity, safety in sea fishing, prescribed occupational diseases, assessment of exposure to dangerous agents and provision and organisation of occupational health services.

The third action programme resulted in the production of a Framework Directive for the Introduction of Measures to Encourage Improvement in Safety and Health of Workers, in March 1989 which was approved by the Council for implementation by member states by January 1 1993. A number of daughter Directives were also proposed to:

1. require employers to evaluate health and safety risks;
2. introduce preventative measures and develop a preventative policy;
3. designate competent personnel or use outside agencies;
4. make arrangements for first aid, fire precautions and emergency procedures;
5. maintain records and report accidents and diseases;
6. provide information to workers;
7. consult workers or their representatives on health and safety measures;

8. provide health and safety training for workers;
9. allow workers' representatives time off with pay; and
10. allow them to receive appropriate training.

Three of the above daughter Directives have since been adopted by the Council of Ministers.

(a) *Minimum health and safety requirements for the workplace.* The Directive relates to new workplaces and provides for specified requirements relating to structural stability, fire precautions, ventilation room temperature, lighting, electrical safety etc.

(b) *Minimum health and safety requirements for use by workers of machines and equipment.* This involves providing information and consulting with employees about safety equipment and bringing the existing equipment up to minimum standards within four years.

(c) *Minimum health and safety requirements for the use by workers of personal protective equipment.* Personal protection equipment is equipment designed to be worn or held by the worker to provide protection against one or more hazards.

Further daughter Directives on the use of visual display units and the provision of minimum health and safety requirements for handling heavy loads where there is a risk of back injury will also be formally adopted by the Council for implementation in member states by January 1 1993.

While the numerous Directives impose on employers a number of specified duties which to some extent are implicit, under the broad general duties contained in the Health and Safety at Work Act 1974, legislation will still be necessary to make these specified duties explicit. Detailed regulation will be needed to specify the context of individual health and safety duties which require employees to consult with the workforce, evaluate the risks, provide adequate training and information, allocate health and safety responsibilities, cooperate with other undertakings and take necessary health and safety measures.

There are however some reservations about supplementing existing general duties, which leave employers with a wide discretion, with precise and often technical obligations in relation to some risks. Furthermore the directives do contain some duties which impose absolute requirements, which is a major departure from the general duties under the Health and Safety at Work Act which as we saw, are qualified by the expression in *"so far as is reasonably practicable"*. Nevertheless there is no doubt that far reaching though the directives may be, it could be argued that they do no more than specify in explicit terms what is already implicit in British health and safety legislation.

Assignment *The Accident*

David Hall has been employed as a machine operator by Fitters and Turners at their Stockport factory for the past six years. He is a member of the JMB, the largest trade union representing machine operators in Great Britain. As part of safety equipment supplied to him on the commencement of his employment David was supplied with a pair of work boots with a steel toe cap and a heavy tread. It was explained to David by his supervisor that all safety equipment supplied was renewable on request.

Last Tuesday afternoon a drum of oil thinner was accidently spilt onto the factory floor near to David's work station. While cleaning up operations were put into effect almost immediately, part of the factory floor was still in a highly dangerous state on the Wednesday morning. Last thing on Tuesday afternoon David had heard the works manager warn, over the firm's tannoy, of the increased risk of injury caused by the spillage and the need for increased vigilance when walking across the factory floor. Despite the warning however, when making his way to his machine on Wednesday morning, David slipped on a mixture of oil thinner and grease and landed on the base of his spine. As he was in severe pain David was immediately taken by ambulance to the local hospital. The initial medical opinion is that while the fall was not of itself serious it has further exacerbated a back condition from which David already suffered and as a consequence David may be unfit for work for a considerable period. David has an appointment to be examined by a back consultant in three weeks time.

Task

You are also employed by the JMB at their headquarters in Sheffield and specialise in advising on members legal problems. You have been called to a meeting in Stockport to discuss the legal position relating to the accident with David and his safety representative. You should be prepared to advise as to any civil or criminal proceedings that may be brought as a result of the accident and the likely outcomes.

Prepare a set of briefing notes to assist you in the meeting.

Assignment *The Faulty Trimmer*

Market Product Testing Ltd. is a marketing company specialising in assessing the market potential of products of various manufacturers. For this purpose the company employs 43 full-time interviewers who work a minimum of 35 hours per week interviewing members of the public in their homes, usually after an appointment has been made by telephone. The company has a further 67 part-time workers who telephone members of the public and occasionally act as interviewers should demand require it. Caroline is classified as a part-time employee but for the last eighteen months she has been engaged exclusively as an interviewer, invariably working for between 40 and 50 hours per week. All interviewers are under the same degree of control by the company. They are given a list of clients. Time is allocated to the interviewer for presenting the product for use by the client, followed by an interview some weeks later on its performance. While the company employs full-time staff under contracts of service, the part-time staff are classified as casual workers and are self-employed.

Last summer the company contracted with a manufacturer to test the market for electric hedge trimmers. Caroline was involved in the marketing campaign. Interviewers are under strict instructions from the company never to interfere with manufacturers products. When asked to do so by a client Caroline fitted an electric plug to the trimmer. The plug was wired wrongly by Caroline and consequently the client received an electric shock when he used the trimmer. Furthermore the client suffered injuries to his hip when he dropped the appliance on suffering the shock. The injured client has subsequently sought legal advice from his solicitor who now intends to take the matter up with the company.

Tasks

You are an administrative officer in Market Product Testing Ltd., and act as an assistant to the managing Director. He has received a letter from the solicitor whose client was injured by the hedge trimmer. The Managing Director has sent you the following memorandum.

From: Managing Director — Ref: BR/JC/2405

To: Admin. Officer — Date: 24 May 1991

There is a board meeting in two weeks time, in which there is an agenda item concerned with the employment status of interviewers. Prepare an informal report for me in which you identify the advantages and disadvantages to the company of employing all these staff as self-employed workers. Since there appears to be a strong view already within the company in favour of self-employed status for interviewers, outline in the report how this can be lawfully achieved.

Coincidentally I received yesterday a letter from a firm of solicitors who allege that we are responsible for injuries caused to one of their clients. Indicate to me in your report whether you feel that a legal claim against the company would have any merit. Could the company be made liable for any negligence it has shown, or any negligence by the interviewer in question?

1. Produce the report required by the managing director.
2. Draft a simple contract that could be used by the company for the purpose of employing interviewers on a self-employed basis.

Developmental Task

Prepare a short address to be delivered by the managing director to a meeting of the interviewers, in which he will seek to persuade them of the advantage of self-employed status.

Chapter 14

The Termination of Employment

Legal conflict between employer and employee arises most usually when the employment relationship comes to an end. Important statutory rights, such as unfair dismissal and redundancy, and common law rights, such as a wrongful dismissal all depend upon showing that the employment relationship was terminated by means of a dismissal. For this purpose therefore, it is necessary to be able to identify express and implied dismissals and distinguish them from other modes of termination of the employment relationship.

Dismissal and Notice

If an employee wishes to terminate a contract of employment he is required to comply with the employee's contractual requirement in relation to notice. Generally the length of the notice period will depend upon the nature of the employment and may increase in relation to the number of years' service. In addition, the Contract of Employment Act 1963 introduced statutory minimum periods of notice that apply where the contract is silent or provides for less favourable periods. The statutory statement of the main terms and conditions of employment supplied under s.1 of the Employment Protection (Consolidation) Act 1978 will stipulate the notice period to which the employee is entitled. Under s.49(1) of the Act, the present statutory minimum periods to which an employee is entitled are as follows.

After continuous employment for:	**Minimum notice required:**
4 weeks up to 2 years	1 week
2 years up to 12 years	1 week for each year
12 years or more	12 weeks

One further complication is that if the contract is silent as to the notice period, there is an implied term under the common law that the notice given will be reasonable and such a notice period may, in exceptional cases, exceed the statutory minimum. Certainly the seniority of the employee, the nature of his job, and the length of service could dictate that a relatively long period of notice is required.

> In *Hill v. Parsons & Company Ltd.* 1972 a senior engineer was held to be entitled to notice of six months under the common law, well in excess of the statutory rights.

There is nothing to prevent an employee from waiving his right to notice or, in fact, accepting a lump sum payment in lieu of the notice period to which he is entitled. Failure by the employer to comply with notice requirements would entitle the employee to bring an action for damages in the ordinary courts based on breach of contract. Such a claim is known as 'wrongful dismissal' referring to the wrongful manner in which the contract of employment has been terminated.

Wrongful Dismissal

Summary dismissal occurs when the contract of employment is terminated instantly without notice and it is prima facie wrongful. Such a dismissal is justifiable under the common law, however, if it can be shown that the employee is in repudiatory breach of the contract of employment because of his 'gross misconduct'. By summarily dismissing, the employer is accepting the repudiatory breach of the employee and treating the contract as discharged. Whether the alleged misconduct may be classified as gross is a question of fact and degree, but it would normally include conduct such as disobedience, neglect, dishonesty, or misbehaviour. Certainly early cases must now be viewed with caution. The summary dismissal of a housemaid in *Turner v. Mason* 1854 because she went to visit her sick mother in contravention of her employer's instructions was held not to be wrongful but would be unlikely to constitute gross misconduct in the present day.

A fundamental question that is often asked is whether the employment relationship can survive the nature of the misconduct.

> In *Pepper v. Webb* 1969 the action of the head gardener in wilfully disobeying a reasonable order was sufficient to amount to gross misconduct and provide grounds for summary dismissal, despite the contract of employment providing for three months' notice. It should be stressed, however, that the reaction of the gardener in this case represented the culmination of a long period of insolence, and the isolated use of choice obscenities by an employee to an employer may not amount to gross misconduct if there is provocation.
>
> More recently in *Denco Ltd. v. Joinson* 1991 the EAT felt that if an employee uses an unauthorised password in order to enter a computer known to contain information to which he is not entitled that of itself is gross misconduct which could attract summary dismissal. In such cases the EAT thought it desirable that the management should stress that such dishonesty will carry with it severe penalties.

The courts have recognised that a summary dismissal could occur despite the fact that an employee is already under notice of dismissal.

> In *Stapp v. Shaftesbury Society* 1982 there was held to be a summary dismissal when an employee, already serving a notice of dismissal, was sent a letter by the employer asking him to *"relinquish your duties with effect from today"*.

The remedy for a successful claim of wrongful dismissal is an action for damages amounting to the loss of wages payable during the notice period.

> In *Addis v. Gramophone Company Ltd.* 1909 the House of Lords ruled that when a servant is wrongfully dismissed from his employment, the damages for the dismissal cannot include compensation for the manner of the dismissal, for his injured feelings, or for the loss he may sustain from the fact that the dismissal in itself makes it more difficult for him to obtain fresh employment.

It seems therefore that if an employer pays the employee an appropriate lump sum on summary dismissal, which represents a full payment of pay in lieu of notice, there would be little point in bringing a claim for breach of contract as no further damages would be payable.

> In *G Cox v. Philips Industries* 1975 there was some retreat from this somewhat harsh position. Here the plaintiff was dismissed and given five months' salary in lieu of notice, the appropriate compensation under his contract of employment. He nevertheless sued for further damages for breach of contract. Prior to his dismissal the plaintiff had been demoted to a position of less responsibility and relegated to duties which were vague and inadequately expressed and this constituted a breach of his contract of employment. The High Court held that *"it was in the contemplation of the parties that such a breach of contract would expose the plaintiff to the degree of vexation which he did in fact suffer (depression, anxiety, frustration and sickness). Although it was argued by the defendants that damages for such a breach should only be awarded in funeral, wedding and holiday cases, there was no reason in principle why they should not apply to a case like the present one. Thus the plaintiff would be awarded £500".*

> In *Bliss v. South East Thames Regional Health Authority* 1985 the Court of Appeal re-emphasised the ruling of the House of Lords in *Addis v. Gramophone Company Ltd.* 1909 and reversed the decision of the High Court in the case before it to award damages to a consultant orthopaedic surgeon who had suffered frustration, vexation, and distress from the repudiatory breach of contract by his employer. *"The general rule laid down by the House of Lords in Addis v. Gramophone Company Ltd. is that where damages fall to be assessed for breach of contract rather than tort, it is not permissible to award general damages for frustration, mental distress, injured feelings or annoyance caused by the breach. Unless and until the House of Lords has reconsidered its decision in Addis, the view taken in Cox that damages for distress, vexation and frustration could be recovered for breach of a contract of employment if it could be said to have been in the contemplation of the parties that the breach would cause distress was wrong".*

> In *Stapp v. Shaftesbury Society* 1982 the court held that if there is no adequate reason which would justify summary dismissal, and if by the summary dismissal the employee as a consequence is deprived of his right to bring a claim for unfair dismissal by shortening the relevant period of continuous employment, the employee could have a remedy at common law for unfair dismissal. The measure of damages payable *"might include the loss of the right to complain of unfair dismissal which the employee would have had, had he not been summarily dismissed".*

Of course since 1971 an aggrieved employee who is qualified has the further option of complaining to a Tribunal that the instant dismissal is unfair.

In relation to breaches of discipline it is often the practice that express agreement will be reached between the employer and a trade union to identify types of conduct and classify it as 'gross misconduct' which will warrant instant dismissal.

> This was the position in *W Brooks & Son v. Skinner* 1984 where the employer had agreed with the trade union that anyone who became drunk at the firm's Christmas party, so that he was absent from the next shift, would be instantly dismissed. In accordance with the agreement the complainant was instantly dismissed and brought a claim of unfair dismissal. Agreeing

with the Tribunal the EAT held that failure to communicate to the employees the consequences of absence from work after the party, made the decision to dismiss summarily an unfair one. *"Whether or not an employer is justified in treating a particular matter of conduct as sufficient to justify dismissal must include in the particular case, that the employee knew that his conduct would merit summary dismissal. Though there is much conduct which any employee will know will result in instant dismissal, there are also instances of conduct, particularly those which have been dealt with in other ways at other times by the employer, which the employee may well consider will not merit summary dismissal."*

In the above case, therefore, it is the manner of dismissal which leads the Tribunal to conclude that the employer has acted unreasonably for the purposes of unfair dismissal. Non-compliance with disciplinary procedures in relation to dismissal is considered later in the chapter.

It may be that there are grounds for alleging that the summary dismissal of the employee is both wrongful and unfair. In such a case it would technically be possible to pursue a common law claim for wrongful dismissal based upon breach of contract in the county court and claim under statute for unfair dismissal in the Industrial Tribunal. In practice, the prospect of pursuing a speedier, less costly claim for unfair dismissal would be more attractive, particularly when you consider the various awards available and the fact that wages due for the notice period could be included in a compensatory award.

A number of cases in the 1980s culminating in *Robb v. London Borough of Hammersmith and Fulham* 1991 suggest that in cases involving a dismissal in breach of contract an interlocutory (temporary) injunction to restrain the dismissal and preserve the contract of employment so compelling the employer to go through the contractual disciplinary procedure may be the most effective remedy. Here an injunction was granted by the High Court against the employer to restrain the dismissal and treat the plaintiff as suspended on full pay until the contractual disciplinary procedure had been complied with. The employer was clearly in breach of contract and while there was no longer trust and confidence between employer and employee the injunction was workable.

In cases where a fixed term contract is prematurely brought to an end by the employer's repudiatory breach, a claim for damages for breach of contract may be the more appropriate avenue for redress, for the sum due under the unexpired term of the contract may be well in excess of the possible compensation available for unfair dismissal.

Express Dismissal

For the purposes of unfair dismissal the meaning of 'dismissal' is defined in s.55 of the EPCA 78. Section 55(2) provides that: *subject to sub-section (3) an employee shall be treated as dismissed by his employer if, but only if;*

(a) *the contract under which he is employed is terminated by the employer, whether it is so terminated by notice or without notice, or*

(b) *where under the contract he is employed for a fixed term, that term expires without being renewed under the same contract, or*

(c) *the employer terminates the contract, with or without notice, in circumstances such that he is entitled to terminate it without notice by reason of the employer's contract.*

The section envisages a dismissal arising expressly, by the employer terminating the contract, impliedly by the employee terminating the contract in response to the employer's conduct and finally a termination on the expiration of a fixed term contract of employment. Here we are concerned with an express dismissal, where an employer expressly terminates a contract of employment with or without notice. We have already said that an employer is normally required to give the employee notice in accordance with the terms of the contract or least the statutory or common law minimum period. For a dismissal with notice, therefore, there is normally no room for any misunderstanding in relation to the employer's intentions. In cases of alleged summary dismissal, however, where there is no notice, there have been claims by the employer that it was not his intention to dismiss but rather merely to discipline. While the words, "you're dismissed, fired, sacked", etc. leave little doubt as to the employer's intentions, if he uses more ambiguous language, perhaps to register his discontent with the employee, the argument that there has been no express dismissal could have some merit.

> In *Tanner v. D T Kean* 1978 the complainant had been told that he could not use the company van outside working hours. When the employer discovered that he was doing so, after abusing the employee, he said to him, "that's it, you're finished with me". The EAT held that in deciding whether the words or actions of the employer amounted to a dismissal, all the circumstances should be considered. *"A relevant and perhaps the most important question is how would a reasonable employee in all the circumstances have understood what the employer intended by what he said and did?"* Here the words spoken in the heat of the moment indicated a reprimand rather than a dismissal.

The custom and practice of the trade are also considerations to bear in mind to determine the interpretation to be placed on the language used.

> In *Futty v. Brekkes Ltd.* 1974 the Tribunal was called on to place an interpretation on the quaint language used on the Hull dock. During an altercation with his foreman the complainant fish filleter was told, "If you do not like the job, fuck off". The complainant took this as a dismissal, left, and found a job elsewhere. For the purposes of an unfair dismissal claim the employer argued in his defence that there had been no dismissal. Here the words were to be considered in the context of the fish trade, and in these circumstances were taken to mean that if you do not like the work you are doing, clock off and come back tomorrow. The custom of the fish trade was that, for a dismissal, the language used was clear and formal. The Tribunal agreed with the employer's view and held that the complainant had terminated his own employment by deciding on this occasion that he would leave and subsequently find himself alternative employment.

It should be noted, of course, that a failure to treat employees with respect could indicate a breakdown in trust and confidence so as to entitle an employee to walk out and regard himself as constructively dismissed.

Implied Dismissal

In a large number of cases it may seem superficially that the contract of employment has been terminated by the employee's conduct in 'walking out' and treating the contract as at an end. Where however, the reason for leaving was due to the conduct of the employer or those under his control, it may be that the employee could show that the employer is responsible for the contractual termination. In such circumstances an employee could argue that he has been impliedly dismissed under s.55(2)(c). Such a dismissal is commonly referred to as a constructive dismissal.

Originally the test for determining whether a constructive dismissal had taken place was to judge the reasonableness of the employer's conduct. Since *Western Excavating (ECC) Ltd. v. Sharp* 1978 however, the Courts have rejected that approach as being too vague and now the so called 'conduct test' is to be applied based upon strict contractual principles. The aim of the new test is to bring some degree of certainty to the law by requiring the employee to justify his leaving as a response to the employer's repudiatory conduct. *"If the employer is guilty of conduct which is a significant breach going to the root of the contract of employment, or which shows that the employer no longer intends to be bound by one or more of the essential terms of the contract then the employee is entitled to treat himself as discharged from any further performance."*

A breach by the employer of the express terms of the contract of employment covering such matters as wages, job location, contractual duties and job description, normally comes about when the employer unilaterally attempts to impose a change on the employee without his consent.

> In *Hill Ltd. v. Mooney* 1981 the EAT held that an attempt by an employer to unilaterally alter his obligation to pay the agreed remuneration was a breach which went to the root of the contract and consequently constituted a repudiation of it. The complainant was entitled therefore to regard himself as constructively dismissed when he resigned following the employer's decision to unilaterally change the basis upon which sales commission was payable to him. *"Although a mere alteration in the contractual provisions does not necessarily amount to a fundamental breach constituting repudiation, if an employer seeks to alter that contractual obligation in a fundamental way such attempt is a breach going to the very root of the contract and is necessarily a repudiation. The obligation on the employer is to pay the contractual wages, and he is not entitled to alter the formula whereby those wages are calculated."*

> In *Reid v. Camphill Engravers* 1990 the breach complained of was the failure of the employer to pay the statutory minimum rate of remuneration set out in the Wages Council Order. Such a breach was of a sufficiently serious nature to be repudiatory and justify a constructive dismissal when the employee resigned as a result. The issue in the case however was whether the breach, having continued for three years, had been affirmed by the employee. The EAT held that in the case of a continuing breach the employee is still entitled to refer to the initial breach to show constructive dismissal. *"In any event where an employer has a statutory obligation to make the approprite weekly payments, it is not open to an employee to agree and affirm the contract for a lower sum in wages than decreed by Parliament. In the present case therefore affirmation by the complainant could not apply."*

By demoting an employee and failing to provide him with suitable office accommodation an employer could be held to be in fundamental breach of the contract of employment. Such an employee could accept the repudiatory breach and regard himself as constructively dismissed.

> This was the case in *Wadham Stringer Commercials (London) Ltd. v. Wadham Stringer Vehicles Ltd. v. Brown* 1983 where a fleet sales director was effectively demoted to no more than a retail salesman. At the same time he was moved from reasonable accommodation to an office 8ft x 6ft with no ventilation, next to the gentleman's lavatory. As a consequence the employee eventually resigned and claimed a constructive dismissal which was unfair. The EAT agreed that there had been a fundamental breach of contract, accepted by the employee, and following *Western Excavating (ECC) Ltd. v. Sharp*, a constructive dismissal. The employer's argument that their actions were the result of economic necessity were relevant, but only in deciding the reasonableness of their conduct for the purposes of the test of fairness or for the purpose of assessing the level of compensation in an unfair dismissal claim.

The need to look for a clear breach of contractual term in applying the conduct test has encouraged both Tribunals and courts in the absence of relevant express terms to imply terms into a contract of employment. It is the need therefore to accommodate the doctrine of constructive dismissal that has encouraged judicial ingenuity in applying the business efficacy test to find implied obligations in employment contracts. An excellent example is provided by the need to maintain trust and confidence in the employment relationship.

> In *Courtaulds Northern Textiles Ltd. v. Andrew* 1979 the EAT stated that *"there is an implied term in a contract of employment that the employers will not, without reasonable and proper cause, conduct themselves in a manner calculated or likely to destroy or seriously damage the relationship of confidence and trust between the parties"*. Here a comment made to the complainant by his assistant manager that "you can't do the bloody job anyway" which was not a true expression of his opinion was held to justify the complainant in resigning and treating himself as constructively dismissed. While criticism of a worker's performance would not necessarily amount to repudiatory conduct so as to lead to constructive dismissal, here telling the employee that he could not do his job, when that was not a true expression of opinion, was conduct which was *"likely to destroy the trust relationship which was a necessary element in the relationship between the supervisory employee and his employers"*.

In many cases the employee resigns in response to an act which is the 'last straw' and the culmination of a long period of events which have caused the employee distress. In such circumstances it would be perfectly valid for a tribunal to consider whether the events, taken together, constitute a breach of the implied term of trust and confidence, and so justify a finding of constructive dismissal.

> In *Woods v. W H Car Services* 1982 this was the approach adopted by the Tribunal who, on the facts, found that events together did not amount to a breach of the implied term. On appeal and then further appeal to the Court of Appeal, the court stressed that an appellate body should only interfere with a Tribunal's decision on constructive dismissal if it is shown that the Tribunal had misdirected itself in law or that the decision was perverse and one that no reasonable Tribunal could have reached.

It is a breach of the implied obligation of mutual trust and confidence for an employer to fail to treat an allegation of sexual harassment with due seriousness and gravity, and in such a case an employee is entitled to resign and treat herself as constructively dismissed.

Similarly, failing to treat an employee fairly in relation to a disciplinary matter could constitute repudiatory conduct for the purposes of constructive dismissal.

> In *British Broadcasting Corporation v. Beckett* 1983 the complainant was a scenic carpenter who having been found guilty of an act of negligence which jeopardised the safety of others was dismissed, and then following an internal appeal, demoted. Refusing to accept the offer of a post as maintenance carpenter the complainant resigned, claiming constructive dismissal. The EAT confirmed that the imposition of a punishment *"grossly out of proportion to the offence"* can amount to a repudiation of a contract of service. Here the conduct of the employer amounted to a fundamental breach of his contractual obligations to justify a finding of constructive dismissal which was also unfair.

> In *British Aircraft Corporation v. Austin* 1978 the EAT re-stated the well known common law obligation that employers are under an implied duty to take reasonable care for the safety of their employees. *"As part and parcel of that general obligation employers are also under an obligation under the terms of the contract of employment to act reasonably in dealing with matters of safety or complaints of lack of safety which are drawn to their attention by employees."* Here the employer's conduct in failing to investigate the employee's complaint about supplying her with appropriate eye protectors amounted to a fundamental breach of her contract of employment. *"It was a serious breach which put the complainant in an unfair dilemma, either she carried on with a risk to her eyesight or she would be obliged to give up her job." This conduct was held to be sufficient to entitle the employee to leave, regard herself as constructively dismissed and seek a remedy for unfair dismissal.*

An employer is of course vicariously responsible for the actions of his employees within the scope of their employment so that if a supervisor in reprimanding an employee does so in a reprehensible manner this can be taken to be the "employers' conduct" for the purpose of constructive dismissal.

> In *Hilton International Hotels (UK) Ltd. v. Protopapa* 1990 an employee resigned when she was subjected to an officious and insensitive reprimand not justified by her conduct. The Industrial Tribunal held that she was *"humiliated intimidated and degraded to such an extent that there was breach of trust and confidence which went to the root of the contract"*. The employer nevertheless appealed against the finding of constructive dismissal arguing that the person who had carried out the reprimand, while a supervisor, had no authority to effect a dismissal. This the EAT found was an irrelevant consideration and restated the general principle that an employer is bound by acts done in the course of a supervisory employee's employment. *"Therefore, if the supervisor is doing what he or she is employed to do and in the course of doing it behaves in a way which if done by the employer would constitute a fundamental breach of the contract between the employer and employee, the employer is bound by the supervisor's misdeeds."*

In some cases, the employer's alleged repudiatory conduct relate to the way in which the employer has interpreted the express terms of the contract.

> In *Bristol Garage (Brighton) Ltd. v. Lowen* 1979 the EAT in giving business effect to a contract of employment found it necessary to imply a term limiting the effect of an express term making forecourt attendants at a petrol station responsible for a proportion of cash deficiencies. The implied limita-

> tion operated, so as to exclude losses caused by dishonesty so when the employer made a deduction for a cash discrepancy attributable to dishonesty, this was repudiatory conduct entitling the employee to resign and claim constructive dismissal.

Even where there is a well drafted mobility clause in a contract of employment, for example, 'the bank may from time to time require an employee to be transferred temporarily or permanently to any place of business which the bank may have in the UK for which a relocation or other allowance may by payable at the discretion of the bank', an employer must act reasonably when relying upon it.

> So in *United Bank Ltd. v. Akhtar* 1989 the employer was in repudiatory breach of an implied term of the contract of employment requiring reasonable notice when he sought to rely on the above clause to require a junior bank employee to move from the Leeds branch to Birmingham after giving only six days notice. As a consequence the employee who refused to move without more notice could regard himself as being constructively dismissed. Furthermore the employer's conduct in relation to the transfer could also be said to be in breach of the general implied contractual duty of trust and confidence set out by Browne-Wilkinson J in *Woods v. W H Car Services (Peterborough) Ltd.* 1982.

In cases where the employee is threatened with dismissal if he does not resign then a subsequent resignation is taken to be a dismissal. It is the threat of dismissal which causes the resignation.

> In *Sheffield v. Oxford Controls Company Ltd.* 1979 however, while such a threat had been made to the employee in question, terms of the resignation emerged which were satisfactory to him and to which he agreed. In such circumstances therefore it is not the threat of dismissal which causes the termination of the employment but rather the fact that the employee is content to resign because of the nature of the terms offered. Here therefore, there was no dismissal in law.

Having established that an employer has been guilty of repudiatory conduct for the purpose of constructive dismissal, this will normally lead to finding that the dismissal was also unfair. Fairness however, is to be judged by applying s.57(3) to the circumstances of the case and it is still open for an employer to justify the reasons for his conduct and convince a Tribunal that he had acted fairly.

Resignation

There is no dismissal if the employee expressly terminates the contract of employment by resigning. There will normally be a contractual requirement in relation to the length of notice to be given and, in addition, there is a statutory minimum period of one week where the employee has at least one month of continuous employment. Failure to comply with notice requirements is a breach of contract for which the employee could be made liable in damages. Employers rarely sue in these cases due mainly to the problem of quantifying their loss which would include the additional cost of advertising for and hiring a replacement during the notice period. The unilateral act of resigning must be distinguished from the consensual termination of employment which normally involves an exchange of consideration, e.g. a lump sum in return for the loss of the job.

Frustration

There is no dismissal for the purposes of s.55 if it can be shown that the contract of employment has been brought to an end through the operation of the common law doctrine of frustration. Frustration occurs where, due to a change in circumstances, performance of the contract becomes impossible or radically different than the performance envisaged by the parties when they made the contract. The specified events upon which a claim of frustration could be based are limited generally to long illness, and imprisonment. Certainly the distinction between the termination of a contract of employment by dismissal and termination by frustration is of critical importance.

> The view of the Court of Appeal in *London Transport Executive v. Clarke* 1981 and subsequently the EAT in *Norris v. Southampton City Council* 1984 was that frustration could arise only where there is no fault by either party. In the latter case, therefore, where the employee's misconduct made him liable to be sentenced to a term of imprisonment, the contract of employment was not frustrated but rather the employee was guilty of a repudiatory breach which, if accepted by the employer, could lead to a dismissal. Such a blatant repudiation of the contract would, of course, normally result in a finding that the dismissal was fair. These cases suggest therefore that frustration should be limited to situations where the employee is prevented through illness or accident from performing the work required of him.

> In *F C Shepherd & Company Ltd. v. Jerrom* 1986 however, the Court of Appeal considered the position of an apprentice plumber who was sentenced to Borstal training for a minimum period of six months. Failure to dismiss him in accordance with standard procedures for apprentices led the tribunal and the EAT to find that he had been constructively dismissed unfairly and so entitled to compensation. The Court of Appeal disagreed however and held that the four year apprenticeship contract had been frustrated by the six month sentence.

It is difficult in any given case to say whether the circumstances of an illness are such that it is no longer practical to regard the contract of employment as surviving. Obviously the seriousness and length of the illness are crucial factors but generally all the circumstances are relevant, including the nature of the job, the length of employment, the needs of the employer and obligations in relation to replacement, and the conduct of the employer.

> In *Notcutt v. Universal Equipment Company* 1986 the Court of Appeal considered the position of a worker who, two years from retirement and with 27 years' service, suffered an incapacitating heart attack with a medical prognosis that he would never work again. A finding that the contract was terminated by frustration meant that the employee was not entitled to sick pay during his statutory period of notice. The court held that *"there is no reason in principle why a periodic contract of employment determinable by short or relatively short notice should not in appropriate circumstances be held to have been terminated without notice by frustration, according to the accepted and long established doctrine of frustration in the law of contract. The coronary which left the complainant unable to work again was an unexpected occurrence which made his performance of his contractual obligation to work impossible and brought about such a change in the significance of the mutual obligations that the contract if performed would be a different thing from that contracted for."*

Recently the EAT in *Williams v. Watsons Luxury Coaches* 1990 provided guidance to determine whether a contract of employment has been discharged by frustration. In accordance with the House of Lords' decision in *Davies Contractors Ltd. v. Fareham UDC* 1956 the test for whether a contract has been discharged by frustration is whether, if the literal words of the contractual promise were to be enforced in the changed circumstances, performance would involve a fundamental or radical change from the obligations originally undertaken. The EAT approved of the following principles in applying the doctrine of frustration to a contract of employment in the event of dismissal:

(1) the court must guard against too easy an application of the doctrine of frustration, especially when redundancy occurs and the true situation may be a dismissal by reason of disability;

(2) although it is not necessary to decide that frustration occurred on a particular date, to decide a date is useful in helping to determine that a true frustration has occurred;

(3) there are a number of relevant factors which include, the length of previous employment, the length of foreseeable employment, the nature of the job and terms of employment, the nature, length and effect of the illness and prospect of recovery, the employer's need for a replacement, the risk of the employer acquiring statutory obligations to a replacement, the conduct of the employer, whether wages or sick pay has been paid and whether in all the circumstances a reasonable employer could be expected to wait any longer;

(4) the party alleging frustration should not be allowed to rely on the frustrating event if that event was caused by the default of that party.

Mutual Termination

Considerable support was given by the courts to the view that if the employer and employee mutually agree that the contract of employment should terminate on the happening or non-happening of a specified event, then the contract would terminate automatically on its occurrence, and there would be no dismissal for the purposes of reason. Such agreements were regarded as variations of existing contracts of employment.

In *British Leyland v. Ashraf* 1978 the employee was given five weeks' unpaid leave to return to Pakistan on condition that he expressly agreed that if he failed by a given date to return to work, "your contract of employment will terminate on that date". The EAT held that a failure by the employee to return to work on the due date amounted to a consensual termination of the contract of employment and consequently not a dismissal for the purposes of unfair dismissal.

Some retreat from the somewhat harsh conclusion was evidenced by the later decision in *Tracey v. Zest Equipment* 1982 where the EAT stressed that very clear words are required to constitute such a mutual agreement to terminate a contract of employment. Here the EAT no doubt recognised the pressure placed upon an employee to sign such an agreement as a condition of the grant of a period of leave.

The validity of automatic termination clauses must now be seriously in doubt following the judgment of the Court of Appeal in *Igbo v. Johnson Matthey Chemicals Ltd.* 1986. The case concerned a similar extended leave clause to that in *Ashraf* with a provision for mutual termination of the contract of employment in the event of non-compliance. Both the tribunal and the EAT, applying *Ashraf* held that there was no dismissal for the purposes of s.55 and, therefore, no unfair dismissal rights despite the fact that the employee had a medical certificate to explain her failure to return to work on the due date. Reaching a different conclusion the Court of Appeal held that the Tribunal and the EAT were wrong in law and that the Ashraf decision should be overruled. The conclusion was reached by applying s.140(1) of the EPCA 78 to automatic termination clauses. The section stipulates that any provision in an agreement shall be void *"in so far as it purports ... to limit the operation of any provision of this Act"*. By limiting the effect of s.55 and s.54 (the right not to be unfairly dismissed), automatic termination agreements offended s.140(1) and were therefore void. To allow reliance on such clauses would mean that, *"the whole object of the Act could be easily defeated by the inclusion of a term in a contract of employment that if the employee was late for work on any day, no matter for what reason, the contract should automatically terminate. Such a provision would virtually limit the operation of s.54(1), for the right not to be unfairly dismissed would become subject to the condition that the employee was on time for work."* While the operation of s.140 will not prevent there being a dismissal for the purposes of s.54, it is then necessary to determine whether the dismissal is fair or not in accordance with s.57.

It should be stressed that the operation of s.140 will not prevent the parties to an employment contract reaching agreement as to the termination of the contract by mutual consent not contingent upon the happening or non-happening of an event. Accordingly if the parties to a contract of employment, without duress and after taking proper advice, enter into a separate contract, supported by good consideration, with the objective of terminating the employment relationship by mutual consent, the contract will be valid and enforceable.

Such was the case in *Logan Salton v. Durham County Council* 1989. Here the complainant was a social worker who, as a result of disciplinary hearings, had been redeployed by his employer. In a statement to be considered at a further disciplinary hearing the complainant was given notice of a number of complaints against him and a recommendation that he be summarily dismissed. Prior to that meeting his union representative negotiated on his behalf a mutual agreement to terminate his employment with the Council. By that agreement the employment contract was to terminate in seven weeks' time and an outstanding car loan of £2,750 wiped out as a debt. Despite the fact that the agreement was signed by both parties, the complainant subsequently complained to an Industrial Tribunal that he had been unfairly dismissed. It was argued that a dismissal had occurred in law, for the mutual agreement to terminate was either void as an agreement entered into under duress, or void because it offended s.140(1) of the EPCA 78 because its effect was to remove statutory protection, similar to *Igbo v. Johnson Matthey Chemicals Ltd.* Both these arguments were rejected by the Industrial Tribunal and on appeal by the EAT. The EAT found that this case could be distinguished from Igbo as here there was a separate contract rather than a variation of an existing contract of employment, and the termination of employment did not depend upon the happening of some future event. Furthermore, the fact that the appellant was aware of the employer's recommendation of dismissal did not constitute duress, bearing in mind the financial inducement. *"In the resolution of industrial disputes, it is in the best interests of all concerned that a contract made without duress, for good consideration, preferably after proper and sufficient advice and which has the effect of terminating a contract of employment by mutual agreement (whether at once or at some future date) should be effective between the contracting parties, in which case there probably will not have been a dismissal."*

Unfair Dismissal

The introduction of the right not to be dismissed without good reason in the Industrial Relations Act 1971 was a recognition that an employee has a stake in his job which cannot be extinguished simply by serving contractual notice. In the same way that a tenant may acquire security of tenure in his home and resist the enforcement of a notice to quit unless it is reasonable in the circumstances, an employee, through continuous employment, can acquire security in his job. The right not to be unfairly dismissed is intended to act as a constraint on employers who feel they have the authority to hire and fire as they please. The extent to which the law of unfair dismissal achieves the objective of constraining management prerogative is arguable. Over the last twenty years unfair dismissal has developed into a highly complex area of law recognised as such as early as 1977 by Philips J in *Devis & Sons Ltd. v. Atkins* 1977, when he said, *"the expression 'unfair dismissal' is in no sense a common-sense expression capable of being understood by the man in the street"*. The present unfair dismissal law is contained in the Employment Protection (Consolidation) Act 1978, (as amended) (EPCA 78) and which, despite the vast number of reported cases on unfair dismissal, remains the primary source of the law.

Under s.54(1) in every employment to which the section applies, every employee shall have the right not to be unfairly dismissed by his employer. Having established that a prospective applicant is classified as an employee, it is then necessary to determine whether the employee is qualified to present a claim for unfair dismissal.

Qualifications

To fall within the provisions of s.54 an employee must be able to show continuous employment in a job which is not an excluded category of work. The minimum period of continuous employment is not less than two years ending with the effective date of termination. This is the date that the contract of employment actually comes to an end and if a summary dismissal is unjustified it may be necessary to add the statutory period of notice onto the date of dismissal.

A further requirement is that if on, or before, the effective date of termination, the employee has reached the 'normal retiring age' or, if more than the age of 65 (whether male or female), then there is no right to present a claim. The House of Lords in *Waite v. Government Communication Headquarters* 1983 felt that normal retiring age refers to the age that employees can normally be compelled to retire, unless there is some special reason to apply a different age in a particular case. Most emphasis has to be given to the reasonable expectations of the employees which could show that a contractually agreed retirement age has now been superseded by some different age.

In *Hughs v. DHSS* 1985 the House of Lords held that an employer can alter a normal retirement age practice by a simple announcement to that effect.

Later in the Chapter we shall discover that certain reasons for dismissal are classified by statute as automatically unfair, such as dismissal for a reason connected with trade union activities. Here a claim may be presented despite the fact that the employee has insufficient continuous employment or is over age.

> In *Discount Tobacco and Confectionery Ltd. v. Armitage* 1990 the complainant was employed as a shop manageress from February 1 1988. In May 1988, having failed to acquire a written statement of her terms and conditions of employment, she enlisted the help of her union official. A written contract of employment was then supplied to her but when it proved to contain a number of discrepancies which the complainant intended to raise, she was promptly dismissed. The reason for dismissal put forward by the employer was capability and because of her short period of employment she was not qualified to present a claim for unfair dismissal. Relying on s.58(1)(a) of the EPCA 78 however, the employee alleged that the true reason for dismissal was for membership of a trade union and the Tribunal agreed, awarding her compensation for unfair dismissal. The EAT affirmed the decision stating that for the purposes of this section there is *"no genuine distinction between membership of a union on the one hand and making use of the essential services of a union officer on the other"*. Turning to a union official for help in elucidating terms and conditions of employment is an important incident of union membership and a dismissal for that reason is covered by s.58(1).

In addition to qualifying through service, an employee must not fall within one of the excluded categories of employment.

(1) Persons employed in the police force.

(2) Share fishermen e.g. members and crew paid by a share of the profits.

(3) Employees who work ordinarily outside Great Britain.

In relation to seamen, *"a person employed to work on board a ship registered in the United Kingdom"*, they are also excluded if *"the employment is wholly outside Great Britain"*.

In *Wood v. Cunard Line Ltd.* 1990 a seaman was employed under an agreement extended into England, for employment on a British registered ship, but the ship never visited the United Kingdom. The issue was whether he was employed "wholly outside" Great Britain bearing in mind he was employed in England and spent his leave there. The Court of Appeal held that as he only worked on board the ship outside British waters he was employed wholly outside Great Britain and not qualified to bring a complaint of unfair dismissal.

(4) Employees who are employed on fixed term contracts of one year or more and have agreed in writing to exclude their rights.

(5) Employees covered by a designated dismissal procedure agreement.

(6) Certain registered dock-workers.

(7) Members of the armed forces.

The procedure involved in presenting a complaint of unfair dismissal is considered in Chapter 2. An employee must initiate proceedings by submitting an IT1 form to the Central Office of Industrial Tribunals or Regional Office of Industrial Tribunals within three months of the effective date of termination. Later in this chapter in the section on remedies, we will consider the legal position when a complaint is presented outside the time limits under s.67(2). A copy of the IT1 having been sent to ACAS, a conciliation officer is appointed to get in touch with both parties in an attempt to resolve the conflict and reach an amicable settlement. It should be stressed that in many cases an agreement is reached because of the intervention of the conciliation officer. While he is under a statutory duty to endeavour to promote a voluntary settlement of the complaint by encouraging an agreement to reinstate the employee, or make a payment of compensation, there is no requirement for the parties to cooperate or even communicate with him.

If the employee is resolved to proceed with the complaint, however, then prior to a full hearing by the Tribunal, there is a pre-trial assessment at which the details of the claim are presented. At this stage any party to the proceedings could be warned by the Tribunal that full costs may be payable if he proceeds to a full hearing. Under the Employment Act 1989 the Secretary of State has power to require that at a pre-trial review a deposit of £150 will have to be paid by a party wishing to continue with the proceedings.

If the complaint proceeds to a full hearing, the burden of proof is on the complainant to show that he has been dismissed unless that is conceded. The various forms of dismissal under s.55 and the alternative means by which a contract of employment may be brought to an end were examined earlier in the chapter. Having established that a dismissal has occurred, it then falls to the Tribunal to determine whether the dismissal is fair or unfair.

Reason for Dismissal

To assist the complainant in a claim for unfair dismissal, s.53(1) provides that an employee is on request entitled to be provided within fourteen days with a written statement giving the reasons for dismissal. The period of continuous employment to qualify for this right has been increased from six months to two years by s.15 of the Employment Act 1989. The aim of the amendment was to bring the qualifying period for the right in line with the qualifying period for bringing a complaint of unfair dismissal which was raised from six months to one year in 1979 and from one year to two years in 1985. The right to a statement of the reason or reasons applies where the dismissal is express or the non-renewal of a fixed term contract, but not if the complaint is based on a constructive dismissal. If an employer unreasonably refuses to comply with a request the employee may present a complaint to the tribunal who may declare what it finds the reasons for dismissal are and also compensate the employee with an award of two weeks' wages.

> In *Kent County Council v. Gilham and Others* 1985 the Court of Appeal held that following a request for a statement of the reason for dismissal it is acceptable for an employer to make a response which refers to earlier communications. That is, providing the covering letter specifically refers to the earlier communication, and it does contain the reason or reasons for dismissal.

The purpose of the statutory right to compel the employer to supply the employee with the reason or reasons relied on for dismissal is to enable the employee to scrutinise them in advance of the proceedings and also to tie the employer down to that reason in any subsequent proceedings. The Act requires an employer to state truthfully the reason that he was relying on in dismissing the employee so that the employee does not start with the disadvantage of not knowing the reason for dismissal if he wishes to pursue a claim for unfair dismissal.

> In *Harvard Securities plc v. Younghusband* 1990 the EAT held that whether or not the employer is telling the truth in identifying the ground relied upon

does not involve an examination of the justification for the dismissal. Here the tribunal had held that as the written reason referred to divulging confidential information, it was untrue under s.53(4) because the information in question could not in any sense be regarded as confidential. This, the EAT decided, was the wrong approach to s.53. *"There is no need under s.53 to embark upon a consideration of whether the reason was intrinsically a good, bad or indifferent one ... whether the employees were correct in describing the information in question as 'confidential' was irrelevant to the identification of the reason upon which they relied for dismissing the employee."*

In *Catherine Haigh Harlequin Hair Design v. Seed* 1990 it was held that an Industrial Tribunal has no jurisdiction to hear a complaint that the employer has not provided a dismissed employee with a statement of the particulars of the reason for dismissal unless there has been a request by the employee under s.53(1) for the particulars.

Statutory Reasons for Dismissal

The heart of unfair dismissal law is contained in s.57 and it is to this section we must devote attention. Under s.57(1) the Act clearly states that it is the employer who must show the reason or principal reason for the dismissal, and that the reason falls within one of the four categories of reasons identified in s.57(2) or is a substantial reason of a kind such as to justify the dismissal of an employee holding the position which that employee held. If the employee establishes the true reason for dismissal, and that it falls within one of the five statutory reasons identified in s.57, then the dismissal is prima facie fair. The final determination of fairness is achieved by applying the test of reasonableness contained in s.57(3). Guidance in relation to the application of s.57 was provided by Lord Bridge in *West Midlands Cooperative Society v. Tipton* 1986, who said that there are three questions which must be asked in determining whether a dismissal is fair or unfair.

(a) What was the reason (or principal reason) for the dismissal under s.57(1)?

(b) Was that a reason falling within s.57(2) or some other substantial reason of a kind such as to justify the dismissal of an employee holding the position which that employee held ?

(c) Did the employer act reasonably or unreasonably in treating that reason as a sufficient reason for dismissing the employees for the purpose of s.57(3) ?

The burden of proving, on the balance of probabilities, the real reason for dismissal, and that it is a statutory reason falling within s.57, is upon the employer. Failure to establish this true reason will make the decision to dismiss automatically unfair.

In *Timex Corporation v. Thomson* 1981, the complainant, a long serving manager, was selected for redundancy following a re-organisation of managerial posts. The reasons for his selection were lack of engineering qualifications and unsatisfactory job performance. The Tribunal concluded that the true reason for his dismissal was not redundancy but incompetence and held the dismissal to be unfair. The EAT confirmed that the Tribunal was entitled to find that they were not satisfied that the employer had put forward the true reason for dismissal. *"Even where there is a redundancy situation it is possible for an employer to use such a situation as a pretext for getting rid of an em-*

> *ployee he wishes to dismiss. In such circumstances the reason for dismissal will not be redundancy."* Here the employer had not satisfied the burden cast by s.57(1) and so the dismissal was consequently unfair.

Clearly then if the Tribunal is convinced that the reason put forward by the employer is not the true reason that was in his mind at the time of the dismissal, then it is entitled at this stage to decide that the dismissal is unfair.

> In *Price v. Gourley* 1973 the complainant worked in a cake shop and, after seven years' service, received top wages for her grade. She was dismissed and when she asked for a reason was told by the manager that it was *"just one of those things"*. At the Tribunal the employer alleged that the reason was incompetence, but as he failed to show any deterioration in her work it did seem unreasonable that it was seven years before he took any action. The true reason for dismissal the Tribunal held was simply that the employer was attempting to reduce overheads by replacing a well-paid employee with a junior on lower pay. As the alleged reason was not the true reason, and cost cutting was not a reason falling within s.57(2) or s.57(1), the dismissal was consequently unfair.

If an employer decides not to rely on a justifiable reason for dismissal and rather chooses to put forward another reason which proves to be unjustifiable, then the result may be a finding of unfair dismissal. The fact that the employer could have relied on a valid reason to dismiss will not prevent a Tribunal from making an award of compensation if the dismissal is found to be unfair.

> In *Trico-Folberth Ltd. v. Devonshire* 1989 the employer decided on compassionate grounds to withdraw a dismissal by reason of poor attendance and substitute instead a dismissal on the grounds of medical unfitness. While the original reason was perfectly justifiable the dismissal on the ground of a medical condition was unfair because of the failure of the employer to investigate and consult. The Court of Appeal confirmed that the dismissal was unfair, and whether or not the employer could have dismissed for another justifiable reason would not affect the amount of compensation awarded.

Having decided the true reason for dismissal it is then necessary for the employer to establish that it falls within the statutory reasons contained in s.57(2) or is some other substantial reason of a kind to justify dismissal under s.57(1). In practice it is rare for an employer to fail to show that the reason is categorised in the Act, so that the reason will in most cases be prima facie fair.

The reasons in s.57(2) are:

(a) *related to the capability or qualifications of the employee for performing work of the kind which he was employed by the employer to do, or*

(b) *related to the conduct of the employee, or*

(c) *was that the employee was redundant, or*

(d) *was that the employee could not continue to work in the position which he held without contravention of a duty or restriction removed by or under an enactment.*

Capability or qualification

For the purposes of this reason 'capability' is assessed by reference to skill, aptitude, health or any other physical or mental quality. The majority of cases where capability is the reason relied upon relate to incompetence or ill health. Where an allegation of incompetence is established through evidence, in determining the reasonableness of the employer's decision to dismiss it is also necessary to examine the reasons for the alleged incompetence. This could involve a consideration of the employer's appraisal processes, the amount of training and supervision required, and the extent to which employees are given the opportunity to improve their performance. Obviously there are degrees of incompetence, but even one serious lapse could be sufficient to justify a dismissal.

> In *Taylor v. Alidair Ltd.* 1978 the applicant pilot was dismissed when as a result of an error of judgment, the passenger plane he was flying landed so hard that serious damage was caused to the plane. The Court of Appeal held that *"the company has reasonable grounds for honestly believing that the applicant was not competent"*. As a result of this serious act of incompetence the belief was reasonably held, and the dismissal was consequently a fair one.

If incapability is alleged, due to the ill health of the employee, once again reasonableness of the employer's decision to dismiss must be viewed by the extent to which it is an informed judgment bearing in mind the various options available. Earlier in the chapter we considerd the extent to which a long illness can amount to a frustration of the contract of employment.

If the reason for dismissal is related to 'qualifications' of the employee this is taken to mean *"any degree, diploma or other academic, technical or professional qualification relevant to the position which the employee held."*

> In *Blackman v. The Post Office* 1974 the employee was recruited for a particular job on an established basis. A collective agreement provided that such employees' employment should only be continued if the employee passed a written aptitude test. Despite showing aptitude for the job, the employee failed the test three times. The Tribunal held that either capability or qualification could be a ground relied on for a fair dismissal.

There is no doubt however that 'qualification' has in mind matters relating to aptitude or ability so that a mere licence permit or authorisation is not such a qualification unless it is substantially concerned with the aptitude or ability of the person to do the job.

Misconduct

Misconduct as a reason for dismissal covers a wide range of circumstances including such matters as lateness, absenteeism, insubordination, breach of safety rules and immorality. Of course the gravity of the misconduct, and the steps taken by the employer to address it, are crucial factors in determining whether the decision to dismiss for misconduct is a reasonable one or not. Misconduct at work has been held to include stealing from the employer, a breach of safety instructions, refusal to obey reasonable instructions, immorality, drunkenness, and absenteeism.

Even misconduct outside of work could be classified under this head as the reason for dismissal, and provided the misconduct has some impact on the employee's job, the dismissal could be justified.

> In *Singh v. London County Bus Service Ltd.* 1976 the applicant who drove a one-man operated bus, was convicted of dishonesty committed outside the

course of his employment for which he was dismissed. The EAT held that misconduct does not have to occur in the course of work to justify a dismissal, so long as it would affect the employer when he is doing his work. For the purposes of the job, honesty was a fundamental requirement, so that an employer could fairly dismiss an employee who was found guilty of an offence of dishonesty.

Certainly, for private conduct to be used as the reason for dismissal it has to be of exceptional gravity and capable of damaging the employee's business.

In *Bradshaw v. Rugby Portland Cement Company* 1972 the applicant was dismissed following his conviction for incest. As the offence had no bearing on his work as a quarryman, and the relationship that he had with fellow workers had not deteriorated in any way, the Tribunal held that a reasonable employer would not have dismissed in the circumstances, so that his dismissal was accordingly unfair.

Redundancy

The employer may show that the reason for dismissal was that the employee was redundant. Essentially a redundancy situation arises when an employer closes part or all of his business operation, the purposes for which the employee was employed, or alternatively the requirements of the business for workers of a particular kind have ceased or diminished. For the purposes of unfair dismissal however, not only must the dismissal be by reason of redundancy but the selection of the employee in question must also be fair. A separate section devoted to unfair selection for redundancy is included later in the chapter.

Employment in contravention of the law

For the purposes of this limited category it must be shown that it would be illegal to continue to employ the employee in question. A good example is where driving is an integral part of the employee's work and he is disqualified from driving. As usual the reasonableness of the employer's decision to dismiss must be viewed in the light of the particular circumstance, not least the availability of alternative work.

In *Gill v. Walls Meat Company Ltd.* 1971 to have continued to employ the complainant, who worked on an open meat counter would have infringed Food Regulations, for he had grown a beard. Refusing to shave it off and also an offer of alternative work, the Tribunal held that the decision to dismiss was a fair one.

Some other substantial reason

This final category of reason is used to include reasons for dismissal which do not fall neatly into the previous categories. Of course it is not every "other reason" which will be included within s.57(1) so that the dismissal in *Price v. Gourley* 1973 for a cost cutting exercise was held not to be a reason of a substantial kind to justify the dismissal for the purposes of s.57(1). Nevertheless the approach seems to be that if the employer puts forward a genuine reason, which he honestly believes to be substantial, it will fall in this category.

A clash of personalities in the office was held to be a substantial reason of a kind to justify dismissal in *Treganowan v. Robert Knee & Company Ltd.* 1975. Here the complainant was dismissed because the atmosphere in the office where she worked had become so hostile that it was seriously affecting the employer's business. The prime cause of the trouble was the complainant, whose constant reference to her private life seriously upset her colleagues who felt that they could not work with her.

In *Saunders v. Scottish National Camps* 1980 the reason for dismissal relied on by the employer was that the complainant was homosexual. This reason was held to be some other substantial reason and fall within s.57(1).

Certainly the refusal of an employee to accept a reasonable alteration in terms of employment has been held to fall within this category.

Fair Dismissal

Once the employer has shown that the principal reason for dismissal is prima facie fair as included in s.57(1) or s.57(2) it is then necessary for the Industrial Tribunal to determine the heart of the issue, whether the employer acted reasonably in the circumstances.

The test of fairness is contained in s.57(3) which provides that *the determination of the question of whether the dismissal was fair or unfair, having regard to the reason shown by the employer, shall depend on whether in the circumstances (including the size and administrative resources of the employer's undertaking) the employer acted reasonably or unreasonably in treating it as a sufficient reason for dismissing the employee, and that question shall be determined in accordance with equity and the substantial merits of the case.*

Where there are multiple reasons for dismissal it must be determined which is the principal one for the purposes of applying s.57(3).

As recently as 1989 the Employment Appeal Tribunal in *Post Office Counters Ltd. v. Heavey* 1989 found it necessary to confirm that in an unfair dismissal complaint, while the burden of showing the reason for the dismissal is on the employer under s.57(2), the requirement of acting reasonably under s.57(3) is not subject to any burden of proof. It is not for the employer to "show" or for the Tribunal to be "satisfied" the employer acted reasonably in dismissing the employee. Rather the burden of proof was made neutral by the Employment Act 1980.

'Fairness' then has to be judged by the Industrial Tribunal acting as an industrial jury applying the words of s.57(3). The Tribunal is not an arbitrator and has no jurisdiction to substitute its own views of reasonableness for the employer's but must adjudicate upon what a reasonable employer would have done in the circumstances.

Useful guidelines in relation to the approach to be adopted in applying s.57(3) were provided by the EAT in *Iceland Frozen Foods v. Jones* 1982. Here Brown Wilkinson J. suggested that the approach which should be adopted by Tribunals was to start by considering the words of s.57(3) and then determine the reasonableness of the employer's conduct, not whether they believe the conduct to be fair. The Tribunal must resist the temptation to substitute its own views as to the right course for the employer to adopt and recognise that there is a band of reasonable responses to the employer's conduct. Within this 'band' reasonable employers could take different views. The role of the Tribunal is to decide whether the decision of the employer in the case before it comes within the band of reasonable responses which the employer might have adopted. If the dismissal is within the band of reasonable responses which the employer might have adopted it is fair, otherwise it is unfair. This approach to the applicant of s.57(3) has been widely adopted.

In *Rentokil v. Mackin and Another* 1989 the EAT in Scotland emphasised that the function of an Industrial Tribunal in an unfair dismissal case is to act as an industrial jury and determine whether in the circumstances the decision to dismiss falls within the band of reasonable responses which a reasonable employer might have adopted. Such a test does not mean however that such *"a high degree of unreasonableness be shown so that nothing short of a perverse decision to dismiss can be held to be unfair within the section"*. Here the EAT refused to interfere with the decision of an Industrial Tribunal that an employer had acted unfairly when he dismissed two employees who had admitted helping themselves to a milkshake while working in the kitchen of one of the employer's clients.

A decision to dismiss based purely on economic considerations may nevertheless fall within the band of reasonable response of a reasonable employer.

In *Saunders v. Scottish National Camps* 1980 the complainant, a handyman employed at a children's holiday camp, was dismissed when the employer discovered that he was a homosexual. The reason for dismissal was that the employee indulged in homosexuality and it was unsuitable to employ someone of that tendency in children's camps. Both the Industrial Tribunal and the EAT found the dismissal to be fair. They decided that a large proportion of employers in this situation would perceive that the employment of a homosexual should be restricted where there is close contact with children. This is despite the fact that such a view may not be rational or supported by evidence which is scientifically sound. There is no doubt however that the continued employment could have proved to be an economic liability for the employer, bearing in mind the views of certain parents.

If an Industrial Tribunal finds the facts and applies the relevant law in reaching a decision as to the fairness or otherwise of a decision to dismiss, then it is only in exceptional cases that an appellate body can overturn its decision on the grounds of perversity.

In *County of Hereford and Worcester v. Neale* 1986 the Court of Appeal found that the EAT had been wrong to overturn a decision of the Industrial Tribunal that a school teacher had been fairly dismissed. The reason for the dismissal was the teacher's unprofessional conduct when invigilating an 'A' level examination and while the decision to dismiss had procedural deficiencies attached to it, the Industrial Tribunal nevertheless found it to be within the band of reasonable responses open to a reasonable employer. The EAT found however that the decision to dismiss regarded in the round had *"too much haste about it, too much stubbornness and secrecy and too little concern for the appearance of fairness"* and was consequently unfair. The attitude of the Court of Appeal was that the EAT was simply substituting its own view for that of the Tribunal and that was insufficient to disturb the Tribunal's decision. To overturn a decision of an Industrial Tribunal its conclusion must offend reason and be one which no reasonable Tribunal would have reached. The response of the appellate body to it should be *"My goodness, that was certainly wrong"*.

An important issue in deciding the reasonableness of the employer's conduct is determining the date upon which fairness of the decision to dismiss is to be tested. There is case-law, notably the decision of the House of Lords in *Devis & Sons Ltd. v. Atkins* 1977 which seem to suggest that the reasonableness of the decision to dismiss should be assessed at the date when notice to terminate the employment was given and nothing that happened afterwards could have any effect upon the fairness of the decision to dismiss. While this is acceptable in relation to matters discovered after dismissal by the employer, which could support his decision to dismiss, the fact that in *West Midland Cooperative Society v. Tipton* 1986 the employer refused the employee his contractual right of appeal could be taken into account to decide the fairness of his conduct. Certainly matters which come to light during the appeal process may be taken into account in considering the overall "equity and substantial merits of the case". The House of Lords ruled in the Tipton case that a dismissal is unfair if the employer unreasonably treats the reason as a sufficient reason to dismiss or when he maintains that decision at the conclusion of an appeal process. By totally denying an employee a contractual right to appeal against a decision to dismiss, the dismissal could also be held to be unfair.

> In *Stacy v. Babcock Power Ltd. (Construction Division)* 1986 after an initial warning in November 1983, the applicant was given a notice of redundancy in February 1984 that his contract would terminate on the fourth of May 1984. The decision to dismiss by reason of redundancy was incontestably fair when given, but in April 1984 the employer secured a contract which provided new opportunities for employees to do work of the kind that the applicant had been doing, and at a nearby location. Despite these fresh employment opportunities the applicant's contract was terminated without any offer of re-engagement. On a claim for unfair dismissal the Tribunal held that the circumstances which arose after the decision to dismiss in February were irrelevant and the decision to dismiss was consequently fair. On appeal however the EAT reversed the decision and took the view that the process of dismissal was not complete until the notice had expired and a dismissal which was fair when the notice was given could become unfair by the date of its expiry. Here *"fair industrial practice would have required the respondents to offer the complainant, as a long standing employee, the opportunity of new employment before filling all the vacancies with newly recruited employees"*. Failure to offer fresh employment made the decision to dismiss unfair. Fairness in relation to redundancy selection is dealt with later in the chapter.

If the reason for dismissal is connected with the employer's belief in the culpability of an employee, then to act reasonably for the purposes of s.57(3) the employer must have made due investigation and enquiry in order to equip himself with sufficient information to arrive at an *"honest belief"* in the employee's guilt.

> In *British Home Stores Ltd. v. Burchell* 1978, Arnold J. held that an employer must have a reasonable suspicion amounting to a belief in the employee's guilt. The belief must be based on reasonable grounds and the employer must have carried out as much investigation as was reasonable in all the circumstances.

The standard of conduct required of an employer will necessarily vary with the circumstances.

> In *Ulsterbus Ltd. v. Henderson* 1989, the Northern Ireland Court of Appeal found that the Tribunal had expected too much of an employer when faced with an unfair dismissal claim by a bus conductor, who had been dismissed following an allegation that he failed to issue tickets to the value of the fares he collected from the passengers. *"What the Tribunal appears to be suggesting is that in certain circumstances it is incumbent on a reasonable employer to carry out a quasi-judicial investigation with a confrontation of witnesses and cross-examination of witnesses"*. Here the Tribunal had merely substituted its own view of fairness for that of the employers and its finding of unfair dismissal was as a consequence overturned.

There have been cases where the employer is aware that at least one of a number of employees is guilty of some act of default but even after a thorough investigation he cannot trace the culprit.

> In *Monie v. Coral Racing Ltd.* 1980 in a case involving alleged dishonesty, the employer was held to have acted fairly when he decided to dismiss both employees when only one of them may have been responsible for the guilty act.
>
> In *Whitbread & Company plc v. Thomas* 1988 the justifiability of so called 'blanket dismissals' was called in question. Here the employer's off licence, which was staffed by three part-time assistants had been plagued with stock losses for many years. Despite a number of formal warnings and a temporary transfer of all three staff to other shops, when they returned to work at the off-licence in question the losses continued. Without any suggestion of dishonesty the three staff were dismissed for failing to prevent the stock losses. The complaint of unfair dismissal was upheld by the Industrial Tribunal which felt that dismissal was not a reasonable option open to the employer. The principle relating to blanket dismissals applied in *Monie v. Coral Racing* 1980 did not apply here as the present case did not involve dishonesty. The EAT disagreed however and held that the Monie principle could apply where the reason for dismissal was capability or conduct, although such a case would be exceptional. An employer could dismiss all the members of a group where he cannot identify the individual responsible for the act when three conditions are satisfied.

(a) the act must be such that if committed by an identified individual it would justify dismissal, and

(b) the Tribunal must be satisfied that the act was committed by one or more of the group, and

(c) the Tribunal must be satisfied that there has been a proper investigation by the employer to identify the person or persons responsible for the act.

> Here then the decision to dismiss after a thorough investigation was within the band of reasonable responses open to a reasonable employer and accordingly fair.
>
> The approach to be adopted by Tribunals in relation to *"blanket dismissals"* was further considered and refined by the EAT in *Parr v. Whitbread plc t/a Thresher Wine Merchants* 1990. The case concerned the theft of £4,600 from an off-licence where the evidence suggested that one of four employees could have been responsible, but the employer had found it impossible to discover the guilty party. All four employees were dismissed and one of them, the branch manager, presented a claim for unfair dismissal. Both the tribunal and the EAT found the dismissal to be fair. The dismissal of a group of employees in such circumstances is justified provided that the employer's beliefs at the date of dismissal are based on solid and sensible grounds and the Tribunal is able to find in the evidence that:

(1) an act had been committed which if committed by an individual would justify dismissal,

(2) the employer had made a reasonable, sufficiently thorough investigation into the matter and with appropriate procedures,

(3) as a result of that investigation the employer reasonably believed that more than one person could have committed the act,

(4) the employer had acted reasonably in identifying the group of employees who could have committed the act and each member of the group was individually capable of doing so,

(5) as between the members of the group the employer could not reasonably identify the individual perpetrator.

If an employee is employed under a fixed term contract which expires this can constitute a dismissal for the purposes of the Act. A complaint of unfair dismissal would be made if such an employee is unfairly rejected when applying for a new post involving broadly similar duties. In such circumstances it would be wrong to limit the application of s.57(3) to the act of dismissal but rather the fairness of the decision not to select for the new job should also be judged.

> In *Oakley v. The Labour Party* 1988 the complainant was told that when her fixed term contract expired it would not be renewed and that following a reorganisation she could apply for a new post, which involved a broadly similar job. She complained of unfair dismissal when she was not selected for the new post. The Court of Appeal held that her interview for the new job was no more than a charade, for the employer had clearly decided beforehand that she should not be appointed. Restructuring was merely a pretext to get rid of the complainant so, inevitably, the employer's conduct was unreasonable and unfair.

Procedural Fairness

In addition to examining the reason relied upon, the process of determining the reasonableness of the employer's decision to dismiss necessarily involves a consideration of the procedure implemented by the employer in relation to the dismissal. There exists a Code of Practice drawn up by ACAS on "Disciplinary Practice and Procedures in Employment". The Code provides that employees should be fully informed of disciplinary rules and procedures and the likely consequences if the rules are broken. Also the Code identifies the essential features of a disciplinary procedure so that in cases of misconduct, the procedure should have built in a process involving formal and informal, oral and written warnings. In particular, at some point, the employee should be given the opportunity of putting his side of the case accompanied by a representative from a trade union or otherwise.

A second source of procedural standards is the increasing tendency of Tribunals to require that the process of dismissal adheres to the rules of natural justice developed and refined in administrative law.

One important point in relation to procedures is that the graver the misconduct the less requirement there would be to implement a system of warnings. Also, where warnings are given for less serious matters they should be recorded but then after a period of satisfactory conduct eventually disregarded.

The need to comply strictly with disciplinary procedures to justify a dismissal as fair was a feature of the approach of Tribunals to reasonableness in the 1970s but by the end of the decade there was a change in approach.

> In *British Labour Pump v. Byrne* 1979 the EAT formulated the *"no difference principle"* under which procedural defects could be overlooked. If,

despite the non-compliance with a disciplinary procedure, the employer could show that, on the balance of probabilities, the same course would have been adopted, the Tribunal was entitled to find the decision to dismiss a fair one. The *"no difference principle"* was subsequently approved by the Court of Appeal in *W & J Wass Ltd. v. Binns* 1982.

A change in attitude was expressed by the House of Lords in the important case of *Polkey v. A E Dayton Services Ltd.* 1987. Here, both of the previous cases and the 'no difference principle' were overruled. The basic facts of the case were that the complainant, a van driver, employed by the defendants for over four years, was without warning or consultation, handed a letter of redundancy. His claim of unfair dismissal was based on the employer's failure to observe the statutory code of practice which provides for warning and consultation in a redundancy situation. Despite there being a *"heartless disregard"* of the Code, the Tribunal, EAT and the Court of Appeal all found that the dismissal was fair. Applying the *"no difference principle"*, if a fair procedure had been adopted, the employer could still have reasonably decided to dismiss. This approach was rejected by the House of lords who held that the employer's decision to dismiss had to be judged by applying the wording of s.57(3), the test of reasonableness. There was no scope for deciding what the employer might have done had he adopted a different procedure. Where the employer fails to observe the Code, he will only be acting fairly if the Tribunal is satisfied that *"the employer could reasonably have concluded in the light of circumstances known at the time of dismissal that consultation or warning would be utterly useless"*.

The effect of Polkey then is to restore the importance of procedural requirements in relation to dismissal and to prevent an employer arguing that compliance with the procedure would have made no difference to the final outcome.

Even if the employer invokes the appropriate disciplinary procedure leading to a dismissal it must be implemented fairly and in accordance with the rules of natural justice.

In *Spink v. Express Foods Group Ltd.* 1990 prior to the dismissal of the complainant sales representative the employer had taken disciplinary proceedings against him which involved holding a disciplinary inquiry. The fact that the employer deliberately decided not to reveal the purpose of the inquiry to the complainant and the allegations against him made the proceedings and the decision to dismiss unfair. The EAT held that *"it is a fundamental part of a fair disciplinary procedure that an employee knows the case against him. Fairness requires that someone accused should know the case to be met; should hear or be told the important parts of the evidence in support of the case; should have an opportunity to criticise or dispute that evidence and adduce his own evidence and argue his case."*

Furthermore in *Louies v. Coventry Hood and Sealing Co. Ltd.* 1990 the complainants dismissal for alleged theft was found by the EAT to be unfair on the grounds that employer's belief in his guilt was based largely on the statement of two witnesses and the complainant was denied access to those documents throughout the disciplinary proceedings. *Where the essence of the case against an employee is contained in written statement by witnesses, it is contrary to the rules of natural justice and prima facie unfair for an employer to refuse to let the employee see these statements"*.

The effect of an unjustifiable delay in carrying out disciplinary proceedings could make a decision to dismiss unfair which would otherwise have been held to be fair. This would be the case even where it is shown that the complainant suffered no prejudice as a result of the delay.

> This was the decision of the EAT in *The Royal Society for the Prevent of Cruelty to Animals v. Cruden* 1986. Despite the gravity of the complainant's gross misjudgment and idleness, in this case the protracted delay in implementing disciplinary proceedings against him rendered the decision to dismiss unfair. *"s.57(3) of the EPCA 78 is concerned with whether the employer had acted fairly and not whether the employee had suffered an injustice."* In an attempt to do justice in the case however the EAT reduced both the basic award and the compensatory award to nil to reflect the complainant's grave neglect and the fact that the employer would be failing in his duty if he failed to dismiss in these circumstances.

> More recently in *Slater v. Leicestershire Health Authority* 1989 the Court of Appeal held that the fact that a manager had carried out a preliminary investigation of the applicant's misconduct and had then conducted a disciplinary hearing leading to a decision to dismiss did not of itself render the dismissal unfair. While a breach of the rules of national justice is clearly a matter to take account in determining reasonableness for the purposes of s.57(3), it is possible for the same person to conduct an investigation and still carry out a fair inquiry.

Unfair Selection for Redundancy

In cases where the reason for dismissal is redundancy then by virtue of s.57(2)(c) the dismissal will be prima facie fair. If however the circumstances of the dismissal show that the employer failed to act reasonably under s.57(3) then a redundancy dismissal would be found to be unfair and a remedy awarded.

Consequently if in a redundancy selection the employer failed to observe agreed industrial practice, this could render a decision to dismiss on grounds of redundancy unfair.

Guidance in relation to the approach to be adopted by Industrial Tribunals in determining the fairness of redundancy selections was provided by the Employment Appeal Tribunal in *Williams v. Compair Maxim Ltd.* 1982. Here the complainants had been dismissed for redundancy, the employer having failed to consult with the recognised trade union. Selection had been left to departmental managers, one of whom gave evidence that he had retained those employees whom he considered would be best to retain in the interests of the company in the long run. Length of service was not a factor taken into account. The Industrial Tribunal's finding of fair dismissal was reversed by the EAT which held the decision to be perverse. Measuring the conduct of the employer in question with that of a reasonable employer, a Tribunal taken to be aware of good industrial practice, could not have reached the decision that the dismissals were fair. The employer's decision to dismiss was not within the range of conduct which a reasonable employer could have adopted in these circumstances. While accepting that it was impossible to lay down detailed procedures for a selection process, the EAT felt that reasonable employers would attempt to act in accordance with five basic principles and should depart from them only with good reason.

(1) As much warning as possible should be given of impending redundancies to enable the union and employees to inform themselves of the facts, seek alternative solutions and find alternative employment.

(2) The employer will consult with the union as to the best means of achieving the objective as fairly and with as little hardship as possible. Criteria should be agreed to be applied in selection and the selection monitored.

(3) The criteria agreed should not depend upon subjective opinion of the person selecting but it must be capable of objective scrutiny and include such matters as attendance record, job efficiency, experience or length of service.

(4) The employer must seek to ensure that the selection is made fairly in accordance with these criteria and consider union representations.

(5) The employer should examine the possibility of finding suitable alternative employment.

The above principles, the court held, are also reflected in s.99 Employment Protection Act 1975 which applies where there is a recognised Trade Union. In addition the code of practice on redundancy as an integral part of employment law should also be taken account of by an employer wishing to act fairly. Here the dismissals were carried out 'in blatant contravention of the standards of fair treatment generally accepted by fair employers' and were consequently unfair.

> The approach adopted in Compair Maxim was applied approvingly by the Northern Ireland Court of Appeal in *Robinson v. Carrickfergus Borough Council* 1983. Here a technical officer of the council had been dismissed by reason of redundancy without warning or consultation, but because there was no agreed redundancy procedure which applied to him the tribunal had decided by a majority that his dismissal was fair. This decision was reversed by the Court of Appeal who held that by applying the Compair Maxim principles the decision to dismiss was *"outside the range of conduct which a reasonable employer could have adopted".*
>
> Also in *Grundy (Teddington) Ltd. v. Plummer* 1983 the EAT held that in deciding to dismiss two managers for redundancy without any warning, adherence to agreed selection criteria, consultation, or seeking alternative employment prospects, the employer had failed to comply with the Compair Maxim principles of good industrial practice and consequently the decisions were unfair. The argument that the EAT in Compair Maxim should not have laid down 'guidelines' as to what would constitute reasonable conduct was rejected. Equally however, a failure to comply with one of the five principles would not necessarily make a decision to dismiss unfair, for they are dealing with what a reasonable employer would seek to do if circumstances permit.

Certainly the need for consultation in a redundancy situation is one of the fundamentals of fairness and it is only in exceptional cases that a failure to consult can be overlooked.

> So said the EAT in *Holden v. Bradville* 1985. Here the employer had argued that both the need for secrecy in a company takeover and the practical difficulties involved in interviewing and consulting up to thirty three employees selected for redundancy meant that the employer could ignore the need for consultation prior to dismissal. This argument was rejected by the EAT who held that in a redundancy situation you should presume that consultation is a prerequisite to fair selection but it was up to an Industrial Tribunal to decide whether in the particular circumstances of the case before it, even without consultation, the selection is nevertheless fair. This case was not one where consultation was impracticable and nor was there evidence to

> support the view that consultation would have made no difference to the result. *"There was at least a chance that an employee could have pointed to her good performance record, her experience and her age and seniority as factors in favour of her retention, with sufficient eloquence and force to persuade the management to take her name off the redundancy list and replace it with that of one of her colleagues".*

Reinforcing the importance of the Compair Maxim guidelines, the EAT in *Graham v. ABF Ltd.* 1986 held that the more vague and subjective the criteria for selection, the more powerful is the need to consult before the employee is judged.

Under the EPCA 78 certain reasons for dismissal are categorised as automatically unfair in the absence of the employer showing that he acted reasonably in the circumstances. Under s.59 such a reason relates to redundancy. If an employee is dismissed and can show that other employees holding a similar position to his own were not dismissed, then the dismissal is unfair if the real reason for his selection for redundancy rights or the selection was in contravention of a customary arrangement or agreed procedure dealing with redundancy. Certainly for a customary arrangement to be established it must have more than a general acceptance throughout the industry but must be *"so well known, so certain and so clear as to amount in effect to an implied agreed procedure".*

> On this basis the Court of Appeal in *Bessenden Properties Ltd. v. Corness* 1974 rejected the employee's contention that a *'last in first out'* principle was universally accepted in industry and so a customary arrangement.
>
> In *Rogers & Others v. Vosper Thornycroft (UK) Ltd.* 1989 304 employees were selected for redundancy with the aim of leaving the company with a more balanced workforce. This selection process was claimed to be in breach of the customary arrangement of calling for volunteers first. The Court of Appeal held that for the purposes of s.59 a customary arrangement had to *"relate directly to the actual selection of the employee for redundancy"* and that the section only applies where actual selection of the relevant employee has itself been in breach of the customary arrangement. Calling for volunteers was not part of the selection process, rather a preliminary sifting and therefore not covered by s.59.

By complying with customary arrangements, for instance, by selecting men for redundancy on a site basis rather than considering the organisation as a whole, the employer could be acting in compliance with s.59. A claim for unfair dismissal could still have merit however, if it could be shown that the employer has nevertheless acted unreasonably under s.57(3).

It should be stressed therefore, that whether or not there are customary arrangements to be adhered to in the absence of a special reason for the purpose of s.59, a redundancy dismissal must also satisfy the test of reasonableness by virtue of s.57(3).

Dismissal on The Grounds of Pregnancy

Under s.60(1) an employee is treated as unfairly dismissed if the reason for the dismissal is that *she is pregnant or is any other reason connected with her pregnancy except either:*

(a) *that at the effective date of termination she is or will have become, because of her pregnancy, incapable of adequately doing the work which she is employed to do; or*

(b) *that because of her pregnancy she cannot or will not be able to continue after that date to do that work without contravention (either by her or her employer) of a duty restriction imposed by some other enactment.*

This ground of automatic unfair dismissal is virtually self explanatory and is intended to protect pregnant women who are dismissed often because they are entitled to maternity leave.

Once again to qualify for the right the employee has to show the minimum period of continuous employment of two years. If an employee without the necessary continuous employment is dismissed because of her pregnancy and so does not qualify to present a claim for unfair dismissal she could still claim unlawful discrimination contrary to the Sex Discrimination Act 1975. To succeed in a claim of unlawful direct discrimination the employee would have to show that in comparable circumstances a man would have received different treatment.

> In *Webb v. EMO Air Cargo (UK) Ltd.* 1990 the EAT held that when an employer dismisses an employee because she is pregnant that does not automatically amount to discrimination on the grounds of sex. Here the complainant had been recruited by a small company in July 1987 to replace another employee, an import operations clerk, who was going on maternity leave at the end of 1987. A period of six month's training had been envisaged for the complainant but after only two weeks she told the management that she thought that she was pregnant. The company then dismissed her and subsequently her pregnancy was confirmed. She complained to an Industrial Tribunal that by dismissing her they were guilty of sex discrimination under s.1(1) of the SDA 75 by giving her less favourable treatment than a comparable man. The EAT held that discrimination was not automatic when pregnancy was involved and *"unless the complainant could point to a man who would be treated more favourably, there was no question of direct discrimination"*. The test of *"whether the discrimination was on the grounds of sex or some other neutral ground, was whether she has been less favourably treated than a man was or would have been treated in comparable circumstances where those circumstances were not materially different. In the comparable circumstances a man would have been treated in the same way, the dismissal was not on the grounds of sex but on business grounds and there is no direct discrimination"*.

A recent decision of the European Court of Justice has now cast doubt on the approach adopted in Webb's case and it now seems that despite the fact that pregnancy is unique to one sex, unfavourable treatment on the grounds of pregnancy is automatically on the grounds of sex. There is no longer any need to compare the treatment of a pregnant woman with that of a hypothetical male. Such a ruling greatly strengthens the position of women so that a refusal to employ a woman because of the financial costs of the pregnancy can no longer be justified. This decision was reached in a Dutch case called *Dekker v. Stichting Vormingscentrum Voor Jonge Volwassenen (VJV Centrum)* 1991 and this interpretation of the Equal Treatment Directive should be followed by national courts in Britain.

Where an employee has sufficient continuous employment to present a claim for unfair dismissal because of her pregnancy, then the appropriate section to determine her legal position is s.60(1).

> This was confirmed in *Brown v. Stockton on Tees BC* 1988, an important decision of the House of Lords which emphasises the importance of s.60(1). Here the complainant was a care supervisor who, along with three others, was told that her employment would terminate on a given date. All four staff were given the opportunity of applying for three posts, each of one

years duration, and they all applied. The complainant who was pregnant at the time of her interview was the unsuccessful candidate and so the only one made redundant. This was despite the fact that there was no criticism of her work and one of the successful candidates had less service with the council. While she successfully claimed unfair dismissal before the Industrial Tribunal the decision was reversed by the EAT and the Court of Appeal. Both appellate bodies upheld the decision to dismiss on the grounds that the employer had acted reasonably and fairly for the purpose of s.57(3) and this was the appropriate section where the principal reason for dismissal was redundancy. The House of Lords disagreed, however, and held that the dismissal contravened s.60(1) as automatically unfair where the reason for dismissal is that the complainant is pregnant or in any other reason connected with her pregnancy. Ld Griffiths in reviewing the history of equal opportunities legislation said that *"s.60 must be seen as a part of social legislation passed for the specific protection of women and to put them on an equal footing with men"*. While recognising the inconvenience caused to employers in coping with maternity leave and security of employment, he said that *"it is part of the price that has to be paid as a part of the social and legal recognition of the equal status of women in the work place. If an employer dismisses a woman because she is pregnant and he is not prepared to make arrangements to cover her temporary absence form work he is deemed to have dismissed her unfairly. There is no reason why the same principle should not apply if in a redundancy situation an employer selects the pregnant woman as the victim of redundancy in order to avoid the inconvenience of covering her absence from work in the new employment he is able to offer others who are threatened with redundancy"*.

The exceptions in s.60(1)(a) and (b) mentioned at the beginning of this section, relate to dismissal where the employee's pregnancy makes her incapable of doing the work or there is a risk in relation to health and safety in which case a dismissal is prima facie fair. This would cover the situation where the existing job involved heavy factory work where there would consequently be a risk to the woman or her child. If however, there is a suitable vacancy which could be filled by a pregnant woman, and it is not substantially less favourable than the existing work, then a failure to offer the vacancy would make the dismissal unfair even if it is for a reason covered by s.60(1)(b). If the employer can show that there is no suitable alternative employment, or an offer of such has been unreasonably refused, then once again the dismissal is fair.

Dismissal in Connection with Business Transfer

The Transfer of Undertakings (Protection of Employment) Regulations 1981 provides some degree of protection to employees who are dismissed on the transfer of a business undertaking. Under the regulations it is provided that the dismissal of an employee before or after a relevant transfer is to be regarded as unfair if the reason is connected with the transfer. The dismissal is prima facie law however, under reg.8(2)(b) if it is for an *'economic, technical or organisational reason'* entailing change in the workforce and so regarded as *'some other substantial reason'* for the purpose of s.57(2). If the decision to dismiss is regarded as reasonable for the purpose of s.57(3) it is fair.

Guidance in relation to the interpretation of economic, technical or organisational reason was provided by the EAT in *Wheeler v Patel & J. Golding Group of Companies* 1987. Here the unfair dismissal claim by a sales assistant against the purchaser of the shop where she worked was rejected because she had been dismissed before the contractual date set for completion of the sale. In relation to the phrase an *"economic reason"* for dismissal under reg.8(2) the EAT felt that like technical or organisational reasons *"it must be a reason which relates to the conduct of the business"*. A desire to obtain an enhanced price for the business or to achieve a sale is not a reason relating to the conduct of the business. This limited meaning given to the phrase *"economic reason"* reflects the fact that if a broad literal interpretation were given to it, the majority of dismissal by transfers in such circumstances would be regarded as for an *"economic reason"*. Here the dismissal, in order to comply with the requirement of an intending purchaser, was not for an *"economic reason"*, for it did not relate to the conduct of the business, rather the vendor's desire to sell. As the vendor had not shown that the dismissal was for an economic technical or organisational reason, the unfair dismissal claim against the vendor was upheld.

A dismissal caused by or connected with the transfer of a business for the purpose of reg.8(1) will be fair if the reason for dismissal is an *"organisational one"* entailing changes in the workforce within the meaning of reg.8(2).

The changes imposed upon the complainant in *Crawford v. Swinton Insurance Brokers* 1990 on the transfer of business were held to be so radical that when she resigned as a result of them she could regard herself as constructively dismissed. From a clerk/typist who worked mainly at home, she was offered other work, with the changed function of selling insurance. The Tribunal further held however that the changes imposed were dictated by the new employer's organisational requirements, and to offer new standard conditions to existing staff was a *"change of the workforce"* for the purpose of reg.8(2). Such a finding was approved by the EAT which held that for the purpose of 8(2) there can be a *"change in the workforce"* if the same people are kept on but given different jobs. In the case of a constructive dismissal following an organisational change however, it is the Tribunal's function to *"identify the principal reason for the conduct of the employer which entitled the employee to terminate the contract and then determine whether the reason is an economic, technical or organisational one entailing changes in the workforce"*.

An important transformation of the law relating to liability for dismissals on a business transfer was brought about by the House of Lords' decision in *Lister v. Forth Dry Dock and Engineering Company Ltd.* 1989. Here the Lords held that liability for a dismissal by the vendor prior to the transfer, will pass to the purchaser, if the employee has been unfairly dismissed for a reason connected with the transfer. In order to give effect to the EEC Employee Rights on Transfer of Business Directive, Regulation 5(3) which provides that liability is to be transferred only where the employee is *"employed immediately before the transfer"* is to have the words added *"or would have been so employed if he had not been dismissed"* in the circumstances described in regulation 8(1). The effect of this change is that an employee who is dismissed solely because of a transfer is automatically passed to the transferee but if the employee is dismissed for an economic, technical or organisational reason then liability will not pass unless the employee was still employed at the time of transfer. Without such an interpretation, employees in cases like this would be left with *"worthless claims for unfair dismissal"* against an insolvent employer.

Unfair Dismissal and Industrial Action

The right to present a claim for unfair dismissal is severely restricted if at the time of dismissal the employee in question was engaged in industrial action. By virtue of s.62 the jurisdiction of a Tribunal to hear a complaint is removed if at the date of dismissal:

(a) *the employee was conducting or instituting a lock-out, or*

(b) *the complainant was taking part in a strike or other industrial action.*

unless it is shown that

(a) *one or more relevant employees of the same employer have not been dismissed, or*

(b) *any such employee has, before the expiry of three months beginning with that employee's date of dismissal, been offered re-engagement and the complainant has not been offered re-engagement.*

Provided that an employer does not discriminate between those he dismisses and those he re-engages within the minimum periods, the section effectively removes the right to present a claim if an employer decides to dismiss all those workers, who, at a given time, are engaged in a strike or other industrial action. The right to present a claim will arise once again, however, if the employer re-engages any striking workers within three months of the date of the complainant's dismissal. For this reason the complainant has a time limit of six months from the date of dismissal to present a claim.

For the purposes of the section it can be a difficult question to determine whether an employee is taking part in a strike or other industrial action.

> In *Coates v. Modern Methods and Materials* 1982 the Court of Appeal held that for the purposes of the section, an employee who stops work when a strike is called, and does not openly disagree with it, while he may be an unwilling participant, he is nevertheless taking part in the industrial action. Here the employee's fear of crossing the picket line and subsequent certified illness during the period of the strike were insufficient reasons to rebut the presumption that she was taking part in industrial action.
>
> More recently in *McKenzie v. Crosville Motor Services Ltd.* 1989 an employee and TGWU member, who had worked during a strike by TGWU members, then failed to report to work during a subsequent dispute without reason. When he was dismissed on the grounds that he was on strike, the Industrial Tribunal refused to entertain his claim of unfair dismissal deciding that it was the employee's obligation to make it clear to the employer that he was not participating in the strike, and that there was some other reasonable explanation for his absence. On appeal the EAT agreed with the Tribunal's decision, *"where an employee absents himself from work, it is incumbent upon him, as an implied contractual obligation, to provide his employer with information and a reason for his so doing. Where strike action is taking place, in addition to this normal obligation it falls to the employee to maintain contact with the employer so as to establish that he is not away from work as a result of withholding his labour"*. The burden of disassociation, therefore, is entirely on the employee.

"Relevant employees" are defined as those employees at the establishment who were taking part in the strike at the date of the complainant's dismissal. It does not include, therefore, those

employees who have participated in the strike and then returned to work before that date, so the fact that they are not dismissed does not entitle the dismissed employees to present a claim.

In deciding whether a Tribunal has jurisdiction under s.62(2) to entertain a complaint of unfair dismissal, the time at which it has to be shown that one or more employees who took part in a strike were not dismissed, is the conclusion of the relevant hearing at which the Tribunal determines whether it had jurisdiction. So held the Court of Appeal in *P & O European Ferries (Dover) Ltd. v. Byrne* 1989. Consequently if the identities of the strikers who had not been dismissed are revealed during the proceedings, an employer can absolve himself of liability by simply dismissing them. An employer who, by mistake, fails to dismiss all the strikers in these circumstances will still be able to shelter behind s.62, therefore, if the mistake is revealed before the conclusion of the proceedings and those strikers employed are summarily dismissed.

> The full impact of s.62 was demonstrated by the Court of Appeal in *Power Packing Casemakers Ltd. v. Faust and others* 1983. Here the employees had been operating a voluntary overtime ban in pursuance of wage negotiations. When threatened with dismissal, all except three employees agreed to work overtime. The three were promptly dismissed and their complaint of unfair dismissal was upheld by an Industrial Tribunal. This was despite the fact that they were taking industrial action, for the Tribunal felt that s.62 was inapplicable as the men were not in breach of their employment contracts. The EAT disagreed however, stating that the Tribunal had no jurisdiction to hear the complaint as the men were taking part in *"other industrial action"* within the meaning of s.62. The Court of Appeal held on further appeal, that industrial action whether in breach of contract or not, if it has the object of applying pressure or disrupting the employer's business, must in accordance with s.62 remove the jurisdiction of the Tribunal, unless the employees could show that they had been subject to discriminatory treatment.

By pursuing a form of industrial action which does not constitute a breach of employment contracts, the employees in the above case were nevertheless effectively stripped of their statutory right to present a claim for unfair dismissal.

In cases where an individual worker is dismissed for misconduct during a period of industrial action, then it is only by applying the basic principles of unfair dismissal law that the fairness of the decision to dismiss can be determined.

> In *McClaren v. National Coal Board* 1988 following an alleged assault by the complainant on a working miner, his employer decided to report the matter to the police rather than implement the normal disciplinary procedure at the colliery. When convicted of an offence, the decision was taken to dismiss the complainant. On a complaint of unfair dismissal, the Tribunal found that normally the failure to give the complainant a chance to put his side of the case would render the dismissal unfair but not so in the circumstances of industrial warfare. Both the EAT and the Court of Appeal disagreed however, and held that *"standards of fairness are immutable"*. *"No amount of heat in industrial warfare can justify failing to give an employee the opportunity of offering an explanation"*.

Remedies for Unfair Dismissal

To seek a remedy for unfair dismissal a complaint must be presented to an Industrial Tribunal within the stipulated time limits. The Act provides that a Tribunal will not have jurisdiction to hear a complaint unless it is presented within three months beginning with the "effective date of termination". The expression "effective date of termination" means for most purposes the date that the employment actually terminates. The Act further provides however, that a Tribunal may hear a complaint presented outside the time limits if it is satisfied that it was not reasonably practicable to present the claim in time. The exercise of this discretion by Tribunals has been the issue in a number of cases.

> In *Palmer and Saunders v. Southend on Sea Borough Council* 1984 the Court of Appeal held that in construing the expression 'reasonably practicable', the best approach is to read 'practicable' as the equivalent of 'feasible' and to ask *"was it reasonably feasible to present the complaint to the Industrial Tribunal within the relevant three months"*. Also the court stressed that the issue is one of fact for the Industrial Tribunal and it is seldom that an appeal from its decision will lie.

In some cases it could be argued that the reason for the delay in presenting the claim was due to the time involved in investigating facts which give rise to the belief that the dismissal is unfair.

> In *Churchill v. Yeates & Son Ltd.* 1983 the reason relied on by the employer for dismissal was redundancy, but subsequently the applicant discovered that someone else was doing his old job. In addition to alleging that the process of dismissal was unfair because of lack of consultation or warning, etc., the applicant presented his claim for unfair dismissal out of time when he discovered that someone else had been engaged to do his job. The Tribunal ruled that as the claim of unfairness based on the true reason for dismissal was not related to unfairness due to the process of dismissal, it was reasonably practicable for the applicant to present his claim within the time limits. This somewhat harsh decision was reversed by the EAT who held that *"ignorance of a fact, the existence of which is fundamental to the right to claim unfair dismissal, can amount to circumstances which render it not reasonably practicable for a complaint of unfair dismissal to be presented within the three month limit"*. This is the case even if there are other grounds which could have formed the basis of a timely complaint. Here the new factual allegation challenged the honesty and genuineness of the reason for dismissal given by the employer and was fundamental to the success or failure of the claim.

The fact that an applicant relied on bad advice from a skilled advisor is not an excuse to present a claim out of time.

> In *Riley v. Tesco Stores Ltd.* 1980 the reason that the dismissed employee put forward for not presenting an unfair dismissal claim within the three month period was that she had relied on the advice of a skilled advisor. Following a dismissal for alleged theft from her employer, she was advised by the Citizens Advice Bureau that she could not proceed with her complaint of unfair dismissal until after the criminal proceedings had run their course. Almost ten months after the effective date of termination, when she was acquitted of the charge against her, she presented a claim for unfair dismissal which both the Tribunal and EAT held could not be heard as it was out of time. Having engaged a "skilled advisor" it was reasonably practicable for her to present the claim within the three month time limit. This decision was upheld by the Court of Appeal who found that if a claim is presented out of time due to ignorance of rights it is the role of the Tribunal to consider the circumstances of the mistaken belief and any explanation for it, including advice taken, and then ask whether the ignorance or mistake is reasonable. If

either the applicant or his skilled advisor was at fault or unreasonable, then it was reasonably practicable to present the claim in time.

In *Jean Sorelle Ltd. v. Rybak* 1991 the bad advice was given by an employee of the Industrial Tribunal and the EAT found that as a consequence it was not reasonably practicable for the employee to present the claim within the time limit.

In cases where the claim is not presented in time due to the negligence of an advisor it may be possible for an aggrieved employee to maintain an action in damages against the advisor for the lost opportunity of securing a remedy for unfair dismissal.

In *Siraj-Eldin v. Campbell Middleton Burness & Dickson* 1989 the Court of Session held that to succeed in a claim for damages in negligence against solicitors who failed to present an unfair dismissal claim in time, an employee had to show that the complaint had some substance, and possessed more than nuisance value. If, in examining the complaint, the court feels that no reasonable Tribunal could have concluded on the evidence that dismissal was not a reasonable option, then the employee will not have suffered loss in being denied the opportunity of presenting his claim.

Where redundancy is the reason relied on for dismissal and an employer subsequently appoints a replacement for the job in question, this may provide the complainant with evidence that this was not the true reason for dismissal.

In *Machine Tool Research Association v. Simpson* 1988 the complainant, aware that staff reductions were planned, accepted the decision that she was dismissed by reason of redundancy. Subsequently, however, when she discovered that in fact she had been replaced, she had good reason to doubt that redundancy was the true reason for dismissal and presented a claim for unfair dismissal but, unfortunately, some three days outside the statutory three month time limit. Both the Industrial Tribunal and the EAT felt that the Tribunal had jurisdiction to hear the complaint, as it had not been reasonably practicable for the applicant to present the claim in time. The Court of Appeal agreed and held that it was not reasonably practicable to present a complaint where during the three month limitation period there were crucial or important facts unknown to the applicant which subsequently become known and gives rise to a genuine belief that he may have a claim. To establish that it was not reasonably practicable to present the claim in time, the applicant must satisfy three stages of proof.

(a) It was reasonable for him not to be aware of the relevant fact which would help establish the claim.

(b) Knowledge of the fact has been reasonably gained in the circumstances and that knowledge is crucial in promoting the belief that the applicant may have a substantive claim.

(c) Acquisition of that knowledge must be crucial to the decision to bring a claim.

Reinstatement or Re-engagement

If a complaint of unfair dismissal is successful, the Tribunal has authority to make an order for reinstatement or re-engagement or make an award of compensation. Irrespective of whether he has requested the remedies on his IT1, the Tribunal is obliged to explain the remedies of reinstatement and re-engagement to a successful complainant and discover whether he wishes to apply for such an order.

An order for reinstatement requires the employer to treat the complainant in all respects as if he had not been dismissed. By such an order, the employer would be required to make good any arrears of pay or any rights or privileges which would have accrued but for the dismissal. If the employee would have benefited from improvements in terms and conditions but for the dismissal, then the order must reflect the improvement from the date it was agreed. In exercising its discretion to make an order of reinstatement the Tribunal must take account of:

(a) the wishes of the complainant;

(b) whether it is practicable for an employer to comply with such an order; and

(c) whether the complainant contributed to the dismissal and whether it would be just to make such an order.

If the Tribunal decides not to make an order for reinstatement it must then consider the possibility of re-engagement. An order of re-engagement requires the employer, his successor, or an associate to employ the complainant in comparable work, or other suitable employment, and on making such an order the Tribunal must specify the terms upon which the re-engagement is to take place. Such terms include the identity of the parties, the nature of the employment, remuneration, an amount payable for arrears of pay, rights and privileges restored, and the date the order must be complied with.

For re-engagement the Tribunal must take account of the following considerations:

(a) the wishes of the employee;

(b) whether it is practicable for the employer to comply with an order for re-engagement; and

(c) where the employee contributed to some extent to the dismissal and whether it would be just to order re-engagement and if so, on what terms;

and except where the Tribunal takes account of contributory fault, re-engagement should be ordered on terms as far as reasonably practicable as favourable as an order for reinstatement.

> In *Nairne v. Highland & Islands Fire Brigade* 1989 the complainant was found to be unfairly dismissed because of a procedural irregularity, in that the purpose of a disciplinary interview had not been made clear to him, and he was never warned that he could be dismissed. This was despite the fact that the reason for dismissal was justifiable. The employee in question was a fire officer, who for the second time had been found guilty of a drink/driving offence and as a result had been disqualified from driving for three years. It was a contractual requirement of his job that he was able to drive and it was unreasonable to employ a substitute driver for a three year period. The finding of unfair dismissal was affirmed on appeal and the extent of the employee's contributory fault increased from 25% to 75%. Such a high degree of contributory fault and the fact that there was no suitable alternative job available made this an unsuitable case to order re-engagement.

If a Tribunal decides not to make either order it must make an award of compensation. But even if either order is made, a Tribunal has no power to ensure that it is complied with. Failure to comply or fully comply with an order of reinstatement or re-engagement can only lead to an award of compensation subject to the maximum limit.

> In *Artisan Press v. Strawley and Parker* 1986 after finding that the complainants had been unfairly dismissed from their jobs on security staff because of membership of an independent trade union, the Tribunal ordered that they should be reinstated. The employer purported to re-employ them, but in fact their job duties differed significantly and rather than security, the new jobs involved cleaning with minor security functions. A further complaint of non-compliance with the reinstated order was upheld, the Tribunal awarding sums of £18,367 and £20,080 respectively. On an appeal against the amount of the additional awards, the EAT refused to accept the employer's argument that a distinction should be drawn between non-compliance with an order of reinstatement and failing to comply fully with such an order. *"Under s.69(2) 'reinstatement' means treating the employee as if he had not been dismissed. If the employee is reinstated, but on less favourable terms, then he has not been reinstated in accordance with s.69(2)."* Here the amount of the awards would not be interfered with.

> In *O'Laoire v. Jackel International Ltd.* 1990 the Court of Appeal held that if a reinstatement order under s.69 is not complied with, whether wholly or in part, the complainant's only remedy is to apply to the Tribunal for an award of compensation under s.71 and such an order is subject to the maximum limit laid down in s.75. The earlier decision of the EAT in *Conoco (UK) Ltd. v. Neal* 1989, that the monetary provisions of a reinstatement order were enforceable through a separate cause of action in the County Court was wrong and would be overruled.

Regardless of the loss therefore, which could include substantial arrears of wages, if the employer refuses to re-employ, the complainant's compensation is limited to the statutory compensation in force at the time, the basic compensatory and additional awards. In practice few orders for reinstatement or re-engagement are made and fewer still are not complied with. The main redress for unfair dismissal remains to secure an award of compensation.

Compensation

Under s.72 an order for compensation as redress for unfair dismissal may consist of a basic award, a compensatory award, an additional award and where the dismissal related to the membership or non-membership of a trade union, a special award.

Basic award

The basic award is payable in all cases of unfair dismissal irrespective of loss and is based upon the complainant's continuous employment and average week's wage. It should be noted however that if it can be shown that the complainant contributed to the dismissal through his own fault, or has unreasonably refused an offer of reinstatement, the amount of the basic award can be reduced by a just and equitable proportion. The computation of the basic award is the same as for a redundancy payment, so the present maximum is £5,940.

The amount of the basic award is calculated by reference to the period the employee has been continuously employed, ending with the effective date of termination. By reckoning backwards from the effective date of termination the number of years employment can be determined allowing:

(a) one and a half weeks' pay for each year of employment in which the employee was not below 41 years of age;

(b) one week's pay for each year the employee was not below 22 years of age;

(c) a half week's pay for each year of employment between 18 and 21 years of age.

To calculate the basic award therefore it is necessary to determine the employee's gross pay up to a maximum of £184, his length of service up to a maximum of 20 years and his age. The maximium amount of a "week's pay" was raised from £184 to £198 by the Employment Protection (Variation of Limits) Order 1991. The maximum award payable therefore is for an employee who is dismissed after 20 years' service, over the age of 41, with a gross wage in excess of £198. He will be entitled to a basic award of 20 x 11/2 x £198 = £5,940.

In many cases the employee's period of continuous service will cover more than one age rate barrier. In such circumstances it is necessary to calculate the entitlement at the relevant rate, e.g. for an employee who is made redundant at the age of 44 who, after 15 years' service has a gross wage of £160, is entitled to

3 years x 11/2 x £160	£620
plus	
12 years x 1 x £160	£1,920
	=£2,540

A disturbing rule for employees close to retirement is that on the effective date of termination, for each month that an employee is over the age of sixty four, the amount of the basic award is reduced by one-twelfth for each complete month worked. The justification for this is that the point of the basic award is to compensate the employee for the loss of accrued redundancy rights which, of course, are not payable on retirement.

If the employee is entitled to a redundancy payment because of an unfair dismissal by reason of redundancy, the basic award is reduced by the amount of the redundancy payment. Since both awards are calculated in the same way, in most cases the redundancy payment will reduce the basic award to nil.

Finally there is one case where there is a minimum basic award payable regardless of the calculation and that is where the dismissal is connected with trade union membership within s.58 or s.59(a). The minimum payment is £2,650 but even that sum could be reduced because of contributory fault.

Compensatory Award

In assessing the amount of the compensatory award, up to the present maximum of £10,000 under the Unfair Dismissal (Increase of Compensation Limit) Order 1991, a Tribunal must have regard to the loss sustained by the complainant in consequence of the dismissal. If there is no loss, then no compensatory award is payable.

> Such was the position in *Isleworth Studios Ltd. v. Richard* 1988 where the complainant was unfairly dismissed when his fixed term contract was prematurely brought to an end. The fact that during the unexpired term of the contract the complainant went on to earn £10,000 in excess of what he would have earned in his former employment meant that he had suffered no loss.

The amount of a compensatory award should take account of any failure by the employee to mitigate his loss, for instance by refusing an offer of suitable alternative employment. The Court of Appeal held in *Babcock Fata v. Addison* 1987 that any money paid in lieu of notice should be deducted from a compensatory award as should any ex gratia payment made. Heads of compensation that are assessable include the loss of fringe benefits attached to the job, expense incurred in seeking alternative work, net wages lost up to the hearing, estimated future earnings, the termination of continuous employment which necessarily limits future rights and the loss of pension rights. The compensatory award, like the basic award, may be reduced because of the complainant's contributory fault.

Under the Industrial Tribunals (Interest) Order 1990 provision is made for interest to be payable on any sums *"payable by virtue of a relevant decision of a Tribunal"* with effect from *"a calculation day"* which is defined as *"the day immediately following the expiry of the period of forty two days beginning with the relevant decision day".*

Additional Award

If the Tribunal makes a reinstatement or re-engagement order with which the employer fails to comply, the Tribunal will make an additional award unless it was not practicable to comply with the order. The additional award is between 13 and 26 weeks pay subject to the maximum of £198 per week.

Special Award

The special award may be payable if the dismissal is in connection with membership or non-membership of a trade union. The amount of a special award is one week's pay multiplied by 104 or £13,180 whichever is greater, up to a maximum of £26,290.

Interim Relief

If the dismissal is in connection with trade union membership or participating in trade union activities, an application may be made for interim relief within seven days of the dismissal, supported by a signed certificate from a trade union official that there are reasonable grounds to believe that this is the true reason for dismissal. A Tribunal satisfied that there are reasonable grounds can order that the employment should continue until the final hearing.

All compensation is of course payable by the employer but either the complainant or the employer can join as a party to the proceedings, a specified person who could be made to contribute the whole or a portion of the compensation payable. This would be the case where it could be shown that the employer was induced to dismiss the employee by pressure being placed by a trade union, for instance the threat of industrial action, and the reason for the pressure was that the complainant was not a member of a trade union.

The statutory remedies of reinstatement, re-engagement and compensation are the intended redress for a victim of unfair dismissal. Certainly the possibility of obtaining an injunction to restrain a dismissal in breach of a contract of employment is now extremely unlikely.

> In *Alexander v. Standard Telephones and Cables Ltd. and Wall* 1990 the common law rule that the courts will not grant an injunction which will have the effect of compelling specific performance was re-emphasised, the High Court indicating a solitary exception where it can be shown that the employer has not lost confidence in the employee in question. Since this will rarely be the case in a dismissal situation, the prospect of an injunction to restrain a dismissal must now be highly unlikely.

Assignment *Unfair Dismissal*

For the purpose of this assignment you are to assume the role of Sarah Maxwell, a newly appointed legal advisor employed at the regional office of ACAS in the North East of England. One of the main functions of your job is to assess the legal position and advise conciliation officers when complaints of unfair treatment are presented to the Industrial Tribunal. Complaints of unfair dismissal have been presented in relation to the following areas of conflict.

1. The first dispute involves a Mr. Simmonds who was employed by Hennessy, a transport company from 1978 to May 1991 as a HGV driver at their Gateshead depot. All drivers at the Gateshead depot are members of the Transport and General Workers Union. Mr. Simmonds, unhappy at the attitude of the TGWU shop steward of the depot, left the union in March 1991. Although there is no closed shop at the depot the other drivers threatened to strike if Mr. Simmonds was not sacked or moved elsewhere. In April 1991 the Transport Manager at the company's head office in Newcastle upon Tyne instructed Mr. Simmonds by letter that he must either rejoin the TGWU or work under similar conditions from the Middlesbrough depot where union membership is not an issue. Mr. Simmonds replied by letter in late April stating that the company had no right to move his place of work, particularly to pacify militant trade unionists, and that he was left with no option but to tender his resignation. Mr. Simmonds employment terminated at the end of May. In early June Mr. Simmonds started proceedings alleging unfair dismissal.

2. Tom, Bill and Harry have been employed for many years as store keepers by Brightsides plc, a large central heating company with a national reputation. The men work at the company's Darlington depot and between them man the store on a shift system eighteen hours a day, six days a week. For some time the store at its Darlington depot has been plagued by serious stock losses and despite extensive efforts to identify the cause of the culprit or culprits the management have been unable to do so. All three storekeepers have received both oral and written warnings and earlier in the year were temporarily transferred to other depots in the North East for a six week period. There was no evidence during that period of losses at any depot including Darlington. Now that Tom, Bill and Harry have returned however, following a stock check last week the stock losses at Darlington are more serious than ever. The three men have been dismissed with wages paid in lieu of notice and were told that the reason for dismissal was their failure to prevent the stock losses. All three have presented individual complaints alleging unfair dismissal.

3. Major Homes Ltd. is a large construction company specialising in private housing developments mainly in the north east of England but more recently, throughout England and Wales. On 5 May 1991 the company's personnel manager for the North East reports to the management that David Allgood the site manager on a Major Homes Development in Durham has been charged with assault occasioning actual bodily harm for which he is to be prosecuted in the near future. It is alleged that following a heated argument between Mr. Allgood and Jimmy Power (a labourer employed by Major Homes) in a public house, Allgood attacked Power and physically assaulted him. The argument apparently concerned Mr. Power's entitlement to overtime pay from the com-

pany. Foreseeing the possibility of further conflict between the two, the management decide to transfer Mr. Allgood to a site in South Wales and they inform him of their decision to take effect from 1 June 1991. Allgood objects to the transfer in vain and not wishing to work away from the North East finds no alternative but to fail to report for work on 1 June 1991 despite having nine years loyal service with the company. His request for a hearing to put his side of the case is also rejected by the company on the grounds that this procedure only applies where there has been a dismissal rather than a resignation. A further request on 7 July 1991 by Allgood's solicitor for a hearing to deal with the issue, is also rejected by letter on 26 August 1991 following Allgood's conviction for assault on 20 August 1991. On 3 September 1991 Allgood's solicitor presents a complaint on his behalf alleging unfair dismissal.

Task

In the role of Sarah Maxwell your task is to prepare reports on the above scenarios in which you (a) assess the legal position and (b)bearing in mind the likely outcome of an unfair dismissal claim, make constructive suggestions as to how to resolve the conflict.

Chapter 15

Redundancy Payments

The right to a redundancy payment for workers dismissed because there is no longer a demand for their services was first introduced in 1965 under the Redundancy Payment Act. The 1965 Act represented a major statutory intervention in the individual employment relationship, for while redundancy/severance payments have always been contractually agreed, the Act made the state redundancy payment a statutory requirement for qualifying employees. It was the first example of any state provision for compensation for workers who lost their jobs through no fault of their own. The complex provisions of the Act are now found in Part VI of the Employment Protection (Consolidation) Act 1978.

The object of redundancy provision is to compensate a worker for the loss of a long term stake he has in his job. In the mid 1960s it was thought that the provision of lump sum severance payments to redundant employees would encourage a shake out of underemployed labour in industry generally, with less risk of industrial action. It was also thought that such payments would encourage mobility of labour to accommodate technological advances. Under the original scheme every employer made contributions to the Redundancy Fund and until October 1986 received a rebate of 35% for every payment made. As from October 31 1986 however, the rebate was abolished except for those employers who employ less than ten employees. Industrial Tribunals have jurisdiction over disputes relating to entitlement and the amount of any redundancy payment and also where the complaint is one of unfair dismissal due to unfair selection for redundancy. It should be recognised that between 1965 and 1971 disputes in relation to redundancy provided the main work of Industrial Tribunals in industrial conflict. When the right not to be unfairly dismissed was introduced in 1971 however, employees were more likely to argue not that they had been dismissed by reason of redundancy, but rather that they had been dismissed unfairly and so entitled to increased compensation.

Qualifying Workers

To qualify for a payment under the present scheme it is necessary to have worked as an employee for the same employer for at least sixteen hours a week for an unbroken period of two years after the age of 18, ending on the relevant date. Earlier in Chapter 11 we considered the distinction between employment and self employment so that in *Hellyer Bros. v. McCleod* 1987 when the court held that trawlermen were not to be regarded as employees, their claim to a redundancy payment failed. Certain categories of employees are excluded from making a claim:

(1) Persons who have attained retirement age which under s.16 of the Employment Act 1989 is 65 for both men and women.

(2) Persons employed under a fixed term contract of two years or more who agree in writing to exclude their rights to a payment provided they do so before the expiration of the term.

(3) Share fishermen, i.e. paid by a share of the profits.

(4) Crown employees.

(5) Persons ordinarily employed outside Great Britain unless on the date of dismissal for redundancy they are in Great Britain following the employer's instructions.

(6) Persons who are covered by a redundancy agreement approved by the Secretary of State.

(7) Certain registered dockworkers.

(8) Certain National Health Service employees.

(9) "Office holders" who are not employees.

(10) Domestic servants in a private household who are close relatives of the employer.

Dismissal

To qualify to make a claim for a redundancy payment, an employee must have been dismissed by reason of redundancy, laid off or kept on short time. The definition of dismissal for this purpose is set out in s.83(2) of the EPCA 78 in broadly similar terms to the definition of dismissal under s.55 for the purposes of unfair dismissal. An employee is treated as having been dismissed by his employer if:

(a) the contract is terminated by the employer, by notice or without notice, or

(b) the employee was employed under a fixed term contract which has now expired and not been renewed, or

(c) the employee terminated the contract with or without notice in circumstances such that he is entitled to terminate it without notice by reason of the employer's conduct.

The Act further provides under s.93 that there is a deemed dismissal because of the employer's act or some event affecting him, for example the employer's death, dissolution of a partnership, or winding up of a company.

> In *Brown v. Knowsley BC* 1986 the applicant having been employed in a college of further education under a number of fixed term contracts was offered a one year temporary contract from 1 September 1983, stipulated to last as long as funds from the Manpower Services Commission were provided for the course she taught. On 3 August 1984 she was given written notice that as the MSC funding had ceased, her employment terminated on 31 August 1984. The applicant's claim for a redundancy payment was rejected by the tribunal who found there to be no dismissal but rather a discharge of the contract by performance. The EAT agreed that there had been no dismissal, and held that the contract was terminable on the happening or non-happening of a future event, in this case the withdrawal of funding by the MSC.

If an employee leaves prematurely in a redundancy situation without waiting to be dismissed, then this will prejudice the success of a claim.

> In *Morton Sundour Fabrics v. Shaw* 1966 the employee in question, having been warned of the possibility of redundancy, left to take other employment. The court held that as he had not been dismissed, he was therefore not entitled to a redundancy payment.

> In *Birch v. University of Liverpool* 1985 the Court of Appeal held that there was no dismissal when employees, who were told that staff reductions were necessary, then applied for and were given early retirement. This constituted a mutual termination of their contract rather than dismissal for the purposes of redundancy.

Even when notice of dismissal by reason of redundancy has been served, if employees subsequently accept an offer of voluntary early retirement, as an alternative to redundancy, they would not be entitled to a redundancy payment.

> This was the controversial decision of the EAT in *Scott v. Coalite Fuels and Chemicals Ltd.* 1988. By reaching an agreement as to a voluntary termination of employment, the nature of an earlier notice of dismissal was consequently changed so that the tribunal was entitled to find that there had been no dismissal for the purpose of redundancy. The EAT found support for the decision from *Birch v. University of Liverpool* but of course a major distinction between the two cases is that in Birch there had been no dismissal.

> In *Mowlem Northern Ltd. v. Watson* 1990 a foreman employee was given notice that his employment would terminate by reason of redundancy on a given date when his contract came to an end. Without prejudicing his right to a redundancy payment the employee was offered the chance to work temporarily beyond the date that the redundancy notice expired in the hopes that this would lead to an offer of further permanent employment. The employee took up the offer but after a few months resigned and claimed the redundancy payment. The employer's decision to withhold the payment was upheld by the Industrial Tribunal who felt that the subsequent termination of employment was not by reason of redundancy. On appeal however the EAT held that *"there is nothing in statute to preclude the employer and employee from postponing the date by mutual agreement until the happening of an agreed event"*. The idea of offering temporary employment in the hope that something permanent might arise was *"a thoroughly sensible arrangement and there was nothing in law preventing it"*. An employee should in such circumstances retain the right to a redundancy payment.

If an employee succumbs to pressure to resign in a redundancy situation, the resignation could still be treated as a dismissal for the purposes of redundancy.

> In *Caledonian Mining Co Ltd. v. Bassett* 1987 a sympathetic approach was taken by the EAT to employees who in a redundancy situation had written to their employer terminating their employment. The men had originally been told that manpower on their site would be reduced, and asked whether they would be interested in alternative employment. Despite an expression of interest by the men, the employer did not respond and failed to offer alternative work. The men did receive an offer from the National Coal Board which they accepted. This led to the letter of termination which the employer argued constituted a resignation, and as there had been no dismissal

in law there was no right to a redundancy payment. The EAT agreed with the tribunal however and held that the men had been encouraged to resign and take another job with the intention of avoiding redundancy payments. The true position here was that the employer had caused the men to resign, and in reality the employer was terminating the contract. Accordingly the employees were dismissed in law and entitled to a redundancy payment.

The Act itself recognises that it may be in the employee's interest to leave prematurely in a redundancy situation and still qualify for a payment. Under s.85 if an employee has already received notice of dismissal, he may, during the obligatory period of that notice, serve his own notice to terminate the contract earlier than the employer's notice. Provided the employee's notice is served during the obligatory period which is the minimum period of notice required by statute, basically one week for each year's employment up to twelve, then the employee will not lose his right to a redundancy payment. If the employee's notice is served outside the obligatory period it will be interpreted as a resignation and no redundancy claim can be made. Also, as a response to the employee's notice, the employer can, under s.85, serve a second notice requiring the employee to withdraw his notice. Failure to comply could lead to an employee losing the right to the whole or part of the payment.

A s.83 'dismissal' could be either express or implied so that a unilateral variation of the contract of employment to which the employee does not assent could constitute a repudiatory breach and entitle an employee to leave and regard himself as constructively dismissed.

In *Marriott v. Oxford District Coop Society Ltd.* 1969 a foreman supervisor was told by his employer that the position of foreman was no longer required and that his wage would be reduced by £1 per week to reflect his loss of status. The employee continued to work under protest for three weeks before terminating his employment by notice, claiming redundancy. The Court of Appeal held that there had been no true consent to the contractual variation, and the contract of employment had been terminated by reason of redundancy so that the employee was entitled to a redundancy payment.

Earlier in Chapter 12 the fluid nature of the contract of employment was discussed, particularly in relation to contractual variation. While the express terms of the contract of employment could provide for a change in contractual duties, there is also a degree of managerial discretion or prerogative to effect changes in work patterns. It could be therefore that a reorganisation of the working day, a requirement to adapt to new working methods or a change in the place of employment, even without express authorisation in the contract of employment, could nevertheless be justified on the grounds of efficiency, and so would not constitute a breach of the contract of employment.

Lay off and short time

In cases where there is a cessation or diminution in work requirements the employer may respond by laying off staff or putting them on to short-time. In the absence of a contractual right to do so, such action could of course, constitute a breach of contract enabling the employee to regard himself as constructively dismissed and so entitled to claim redundancy or unfair dismissal. For a lay off or short-time of four consecutive weeks or an aggregate of six or more weeks in a period of thirteen weeks, s.88 provides that an employee can serve notice that he intends to make a claim for a payment. For this purpose "lay off" occurs where no work and no wages are provided and short-time means that an employee earns less than one half his wages in any given week. In such a situation an employee could then serve notice to terminate the contractual relationship altogether and so qualify for a redundancy payment. This is subject to the employer's right to serve a counter notice within the time limits, which will defeat the claim if the employer can show that there is a reasonable prospect of work in not later than four weeks time, for at least thirteen weeks, without the possibility of lay off or short-time working. The onus is on the employer to establish through evidence the likelihood of the period of employment, and failure to do so will mean that the employee is entitled to a redundancy payment.

Redundancy Dismissal

The right to a redundancy payment arises when a qualifying employee has been dismissed by reason of redundancy or is laid off or kept on short time for the purposes of s.88. The reason for dismissal must therefore be redundancy, a presumption of which arises in favour of the applicant unless the contrary is proved. It is for the employer to rebut the presumption of redundancy on the balance of probabilities by showing that the dismissal was for some reason other than redundancy. In s.81(2) the Act provides that there is a dismissal by reason of redundancy if it is attributable wholly or mainly to:

(a) the fact that his employer has ceased or intends to cease, to carry on the business for the purposes of which the employee was employed by him, or has ceased, or intends to cease, to carry on that business in the place where the employee was so employed, or

(b) the fact that the requirements of that business for employees to carry out work of a particular kind, or for employees to carry out work of a particular kind in the place where he was so employed, have ceased or diminished or are expected to cease or diminish.

In paragraph (a) the Act envisages redundancy arising because the business is closed or it is intended that it will be. Such a closure could relate to the whole business or just a part of it and be permanent or temporary. In addition paragraph (a) provides that redundancy could arise if the business is closed in the place where the employee works. If, however, the employee's contract provides that he could be required to move to a new work location, and the employer attempts to trigger the clause, then there is no redundancy. Even without an express clause there is an implied term in the contract of employment that the employee may be moved to a new work location within reasonable commuting distance from home.

The requirements of the business for employees of a particular kind will have ceased if they are replaced by independent contractors. To replace an employee with a self-employed person will be a dismissal by reason of redundancy and the dismissed employee will be entitled to a payment. This will also be the case where it is the employee himself who is being reinstated on self-employed status. Liability to make redundancy payments could be one of the costs of an employer transferring work from employees to independent contractors, but as we saw earlier in Chapter 11, it may be that there are financial benefits in the long run. Such benefits would include the loss of future rights to redundancy payments and possible unfair dismissal rights and lower National Insurance contributions.

The fact that the dismissed employee has been replaced by another employee will not normally lead to a finding of redundancy for it cannot be said that the requirements of the business for an employee have ceased or diminished. There would be a redundancy, however, if it could be shown that the replacement employee was moved because of a reduction in requirements. Here an employee is being dismissed to make way for an employee who would otherwise be surplus to requirements and so the dismissed employee is entitled to a redundancy payment.

In situations where the employee's skills have become outdated because of changes in working methods to which he cannot or is not prepared to adapt, there have been conflicting views as to whether, if he is dismissed, it is by reason of redundancy or incapability.

In the history of the law of redundancy there are early examples of the courts being called upon to draw a distinction between diminishing requirements for an employee because of a reduction in a particular kind of work carried on, and diminishing requirements for an employee due to his failure to adapt to new working methods.

> In *North Riding Garages Ltd. v. Butterwick* 1967 a workshop manager with thirty years experience was dismissed following a takeover and reorganisation of the business. The manager found it difficult to adapt to new methods which had been introduced, in particular coping with costs estimates. The repair side of the workshop for which he had been responsible was deliberately run down and the sales side increased. Following his dismissal a new workshop manager was engaged. The Tribunal upheld the employee's claim for a redundancy payment deciding that the presumption of redundancy had not been rebutted. On appeal, however, it was held that there had been no change in the requirements of the business to carry out a particular kind of work, for there was still a need for a workshop manager. It was the employee's personal deficiencies which caused the dismissal rather than redundancy. *"An employee remaining in the same kind of work was expected to adapt to new methods and higher standards of efficiency, unless the nature of the work he was required to do was thereby altered so that no requirement remained for employees to do work of the particular kind which was superseded."*
>
> *"Personal deficiencies"* was again the reason put forward by the employer for dismissal in *Hindle v. Percival Boats* 1969. The claimant, a highly skilled woodworker with twenty years boat-building experience was dismissed for being *"too good and too slow"* when fibreglass became the main material for boat-building rather than wood. He claimed a redundancy payment on the grounds that his dismissal was attributable wholly or mainly to a reduction in the employer's requirements for woodworkers. A majority of the Court of Appeal held that there was no dismissal by reason of redundancy, for the true reason for dismissal was that the claimant was too slow and his continued employment uneconomical. In the dissenting judgment, however, Lord Denning, M R, placed great emphasis on the statutory presumption of redundancy. *"Redundancy payment is compensation to a man for the loss of the job; and a man should not be deprived of it merely because the employer thinks or believes that he is being dismissed for a reason other than redundancy."*

The contemporary approach to change seems to be that so long as the job function remains, there is no redundancy. If an employee is given a very wide job function, that is likely to mean where there are technological or social changes in the way that a job is performed, that does not make it a different kind of work for the purposes of redundancy.

In cases where the reason for dismissal is redundancy, but the employer was entitled to terminate the contract by reason of the employee's misconduct, the right to a redundancy payment will be lost. Obviously if the reason for dismissal is misconduct then the question of a redundancy payment does not arise, so the section seems to be designed to cover the situation where redundancy is the reason given for the dismissal, but it transpires that there was good cause to dismiss for misconduct. If the employee has already served notice of the "obligatory period" for redundancy, and the employee is dismissed for gross misconduct during that period, the employee can still apply to the Tribunal which can award all or part of the redundancy payment. Furthermore, if the misconduct takes the form of strike action during the "obligatory period" any dismissal for that form of "misconduct" will not operate to disqualify the redundancy payment. If, however, the strike takes place before the notice of dismissal for redundancy, and the employee participates, that would be classed as misconduct so as to disqualify a redundancy claim under s.82(2).

> Some guidance in relation to the operation of the section is provided in *Bonner v. H Gilbert Ltd.* 1989. Here the applicant was given notice that his employment would terminate on 13 February 1987 for redundancy, but in fact he was dismissed on 13 January 1987 for alleged dishonesty. The case falls squarely under s.82(2) but the issue was whether the employer was entitled to terminate the contract because of the employee's conduct. The EAT held that the Tribunal was wrong in applying the unfair dismissal test of reasonableness to the employer's decision to dismiss for misconduct. Rather, the contractual approach adopted in *Western Excavating v. Sharp* 1978 for the purposes of constructive dismissal should be applied. The employer's burden was *"to show that the employee was guilty of conduct which was a significant breach going to the root of the contract or which showed that the employee no longer intended to be bound by one or more of the essential terms of the contract".*

As we noted earlier, due to the fact that the possible compensation payable for unfair dismissal is well in excess of the State redundancy payment it may be that an applicant is more likely to pursue a claim for unfair dismissal rather than a redundancy payment. Redundancy is of course one of the specific reasons identified in s.57 EPCA 78 as a prima facie fair ground for dismissal. If redundancy proves not to be the true reason relied on for dismissal then we saw in Chapter 15 that a Tribunal is entitled to find that the dismissal is unfair.

Suitable Alternative Employment

If, before employment terminates, the employer makes the employee an offer either to renew the contract of employment or re-engage the employee under a new contract which constitutes suitable alternative employment, then provided the new contract is to commence within four weeks of the previous one terminating, an unreasonable refusal to accept such an offer will mean that the employee will not be entitled to make a claim for a redundancy payment. Failure to take up an offer of a new contract on identical terms and conditions of employment therefore would normally constitute an unreasonable refusal to accept re-engagement and, as a consequence, an employer will lose the right to make a claim for payment. If the offer is of alternative employment, it is necessary to determine its suitability in relation to the previous employment. For the new employment to be "suitable" it must be substantially similar to the previous job and not employment of an entirely different nature at the same salary. The question is one of fact and degree and one which the Tribunal must examine in the light of the particular circumstances of the case including such matters as the nature of the work, the rates of pay, the place of work, the new status, and fringe benefits. Personal factors affecting the employee may also be considered such as social and family links, accommodation, and the children's education.

> In *Devonald v. J D Insulating Company Ltd.* 1972 the applicant was required to move from a factory in Bootle to another in Blackburn. He refused, and on his claim for redundancy the tribunal held that suitable alter-

native employment had been offered as he was already required under his present employment to do outside contract work.

In practice the question as to whether the alternative employment is suitable or not will be considered at the same time as the issue as to whether it is reasonable to refuse it or not. While it is reasonable to refuse unsuitable work, it is unreasonable to refuse suitable alternative employment.

In *Fuller v. Stephanie Bowman Ltd.* 1977 the applicant typist refused to move from Mayfair to a new office in Soho. She found the move distasteful, particularly as the new office was above a sex shop. The tribunal found that the refusal to move was unreasonable in the circumstances, as it was based on undue sensitivity and the claim for redundancy consequently failed.

The decision of the EAT in *Gloucestershire County Council v. Spencer* 1985 supports the view that it is for management to set the appropriate standard of work to be achieved. Here the number of cleaners at a school had been reduced from five to four and the hours of work of the remaining employees cut by forty five minutes. The employer recognised that standards would drop, but maintained nevertheless, that the new terms constituted an offer of suitable alternative employment. This offer was rejected by the remaining cleaners on the grounds that they felt they could not continue to do a satisfactory job. The Industrial Tribunal agreed and found that while the alternative jobs were 'suitable' within the meaning of the section, the employees' refusal to accept the new terms was not unreasonable as they could not do the new jobs adequately in the time allotted. The EAT held that the Tribunal was in error, for the standard of work set by the management, cannot be reasonably objected to by employees as a ground for refusing to work. Accordingly the offer of suitable alternative employment had been unreasonably rejected and the applicants were not entitled to redundancy payments.

If an employee accepts an offer of alternative employment on different terms and conditions, he is entitled to a trial period under s.84(3). The length of the period is four weeks, but if the new job requires retraining, the parties can specify a longer trial period in writing. If, for any reason, during the trial period the employee gives notice to terminate his employment, or the employer terminates for a reason connected with the change to the new job, then the employee is treated as dismissed from the date that the previous contract terminated. To determine his rights to a redundancy payment it is then necessary to examine the original reason for dismissal, whether the offer of alternative work was suitable, and whether the termination by the employer reasonable. In cases where the offer of new employment involves changes in employment terms, which would otherwise constitute a repudiatory breach, then under the common law, an employee who nevertheless accepts the new job for a period could still change his mind and resign claiming constructive dismissal. In such circumstances therefore, there is a common law trial period which on its expiration, can be extended further by the statutory trial period under s.84(3).

Redundancy on a Business Transfer

To secure the right to a redundancy payment where an employee is dismissed on the transfer of a business undertaking the employee must establish that he is qualified to claim and that he is dismissed by reason of redundancy within the definition. For transfers of a commercial venture covered by the Transfer of Undertakings (Protection of Employment) Regulations

1981 an employee's contract is automatically preserved with the transferee employer so that rights in relation to redundancy are preserved with the new employer.

The effect of the Regulations is that where a relevant transfer is made the employee's contract continues with the new employer so that there is no dismissal and consequently no redundancy. Regulation 5(3) of the 1981 Regulations states that a transfer of liability to the transferee employer will only occur where the employee was employed in the undertaking *"immediately before the transfer"*. If an employee is dismissed because of the transfer then liability in relation to him is passed automatically to the new employer. If however an employee is dismissed because of an organisational economic or technical reason under regulation 8(1) then liability will not pass unless he was still employed at the time of the transfer.

Those employees who are subsequently dismissed by the transferee employer will have the right to a redundancy payment if the dismissal is by reason of redundancy.

Dismissal could even be constructive, as for instance where the transfer employer unilaterally attempts to impose radical changes in terms and conditions of employment on the employee. It is still open to the employer of course to make an offer of suitable alternative employment to the employees which, if unreasonable refused will prejudice his right to a payment.

In cases where the Regulations do not apply, because the transfer is not of a commercial venture, redundancy rights are covered by section 94 of the EPCA 78. Under section 94, on a relevant change in ownership, if the employee continues to be employed by the new employer then then there is no right to a redundancy payment and continuity of employment is preserved. If an employee is made an offer of alternative employment by the new employer which is suitable but unreasonably refused under the s.82 the employee may lose the right to a payment. Where alternative employment is offered either by the old employer or the new employer then the employee is entitled to have a trial period of four weeks (or longer if agreed) in the new job. The employee has then the option of either accepting the new employment, or terminating the contract in which case he will be regarded as having been dismissed on the date the previous contract came to an end for the reason which applied then. It may then be necessary, for the purpose of redundancy entitlement, to decide whether the new employment was in fact an offer of suitable alternative work.

Redundancy Procedure

The Employment Protection Act 1975, ss.99-108, contains a number of rules relating to the procedure to be invoked in a redundancy situation where an independent trade union is recognised in relation to the class of employees involved. The primary duty imposed on the employer under s.99 is to consult with trade union representatives. If an employer proposes to dismiss 100 or more employees as redundant within 90 days or less or 10 or more employees within 30 days then he must consult within the 90 or 30 day periods respectively. In other cases the employer must consult at the earliest opportunity. For the purposes of the consultation the employer is required to disclose to the trade union representative:

(a) the reasons for the disposals;

(b) the numbers and descriptions of employees whom it is proposed to dismiss as redundant;

(c) the total number of employees of any such description employed by the employer at the establishment in question;

(d) the proposed method of selecting the employees who may be dismissed; and

(e) the proposed method of carrying out the dismissals with due regard to any agreed procedure including the period over which the dismissals are to take effect.

The employer is further obliged to consider any representations made by the trade union representatives, respond to them, and give reasons if they are rejected.

If an employer fails to comply with the consultation requirements then the trade union could seek a remedy by presenting a complaint to an Industrial Tribunal. The Tribunal can make a declaration as to non-compliance and also make a protective award requiring the employer to pay the specified employees their wages for the "protected period", specified not to exceed the consultation period to which they were entitled, 90, 30 or 28 days. An employer who fails to comply with a protective award can be required to do so on an individual complaint to a Tribunal by an employee.

The duty to consult under s.99 is an obligation which must be complied with even where it is obvious that nothing can be achieved.

> In *Sovereign Distribution Services Ltd. v. Transport & General Workers Union* 1989 the EAT found that the Industrial Tribunal had rightly made a protective award against an employer who had failed to consult the recognised trade union over redundancies as required by s.99. The purpose of the section is to ensure consultation takes place even where the employer thinks that to consult will achieve nothing. *"The statutory duty to consult in many cases provides the only opportunity for employees through their recognised trade unions, to be able to seek to influence the redundancy situation and to put forward other ideas and other considerations, not only as to the overall decision but also as to the individuals who should be made redundant and other material aspects."*

Whether or not there is an independent trade union involved, the Act also requires an employer to notify the Secretary of State in writing of proposed redundancies. The notification period is at least 90 days if it is proposed to dismiss 100 or more employees within 90 days or less, or 30 days if it is proposed to dismiss 10 or more employees within a 30 day period. Copies of the notice must be given to trade union representatives where there is a recognised independent trade union. Failure to notify the Secretary of State can lead to a fine on summary conviction.

The law relating to the process by which a redundancy situation is dealt with is supplemented by codes of practice. The ACAS code on discipline and dismissal includes a section on redundancy. The matters dealt with by the code include consultation, selection procedures, alternative employment, appeal procedure and redundancy counselling. Codes of Practice do not constitute rules of law but their importance was re-emphasised by the House of Lords in *West Midlands Cooperative Society v. Tipton* 1986.

The ACAS Code stresses the need for the fullest consultation between employers and employees or trade unions in advance of a redundancy situation. They should produce agreed selection and appeal procedures. Failure to warn and consult may of course render a redundancy dismissal unfair. For the purpose of selection, the Code advocates objective criteria including skill, age, length of service, standard of performance and future requirements for employees.

Finally, mention should also be made of the fact that an employee with two years' service who is given notice of dismissal by reason of redundancy has the right, during the notice period, to be given reasonable time off during working hours, to look for new employment or make arrangements for future training. The employee is also entitled to be paid at the appropriate rate during the period of absence and can present a claim to a tribunal if his rights are denied.

Redundancy Calculation

If an employee believes that as a qualifying worker he has been dismissed by reason of redundancy, the onus is upon him to make a claim to his employer for a redundancy payment. If the employer denies the claim or simply refuses to make a payment, the remedy of the employee is by way of complaint to an Industrial Tribunal. The time limit for such a complaint is six months from the relevant date of termination unless within that time the employee has presented the claim to his employer in writing. Even then the Tribunal has power to extend the time limit by up to a further six months if it is satisfied that it is just and equitable in the circumstances. If a redundancy payment is made (otherwise than in compliance with an order of the Tribunal specifying the amount), then an employer is guilty of an offence if he fails without reasonable excuse to give the employee a written statement indicating how the payment was calculated. The sum is calculated in the same way as a basic award by reference to the age of the claimant, the length of continuous employment and the weekly pay of the claimant.

Amount of the payment

Age (inclusive)	Amount of week's pay for each year of employment
18-21	½
22-40	1
41-65	1 ½

Given that the aim of the payment is to provide a lump sum for the employee while he is seeking new employment, the fact that he will soon qualify for state retirement pension is also a factor in calculating the amount. Accordingly, for each month that the claimant is over sixty-four at the relevant date, the amount is reduced by one twelfth.

Section 16 of the Employment Act 1989 (EA 89) equalises the age at which men and women cease to be entitled to a statutory redundancy payment and in so doing brings the age limits on entitlement to redundancy payment into line with those on the right to claim unfair dismissal. The tapering provision which previously started at 64 for men and 59 for women and which had the effect of reducing the redundancy payment by one twelfth for each month of employment beyond those ages, will in future apply to both men and to women. An employer will be excluded from the redundancy payment scheme where there is a normal retiring age of below 65 for employees holding the position which he held, applicable to both men and women alike, and the employee has reached that age. If the normal retiring age is over 65, or is different for men and women, or there is no normal retiring age, the age limit for entitlement will be 65.

Another feature of the calculation is the fact that each year the maximum week's pay is adjusted to reflect the current average wage which is presently £198. Consequently the present maximum redundancy payment is 20 years x 1 ½ (for employment between the ages of 41-65) x £198 = £5,940. For employees in a weekly fixed rate then the contractual rate is the current average wage. In cases where the wage does vary, however, a week's pay is calculated by reference to the average hourly rate of remuneration over the last twelve weeks of employment.

> In a complex decision relating to the calculation of an average week's wage for the purpose of redundancy entitlement, the House of Lords held in *British Coal Corporation v. Cheesbrough* 1990 that in calculating an employee's average rate of remuneration, work in overtime hours must be treated as if they had been done in normal working hours and the remuneration reduced accordingly. Where however an employee's contract provides for bonus payment only for work done during normal working hours, the overtime hours worked should not be treated as if they would attract bonus payments.

While the payment is made by the employer, originally he was entitled to claim a rebate from the Redundancy Fund financed by weekly levies from employers. Under the Employment Act 1988 the Redundancy Fund was abolished.

Assignment *Len the Printer*

Len is 47 and for the last 23 years has been employed as a printer by Fulton Printers Ltd., a small printing and typesetting business located in Bradford. For the last fourteen years Len has been foreman printer and his present gross wage is £187 per week. Since 1984 the management of the business has been effectively in the hands of Tim Fulton, the eldest son of the company's founder. Tim is concerned that the business has become less profitable as a whole and for some time has maintained only a steady turnover with a general increase in wage levels. On the printing side, old fashioned machinery and outdated methods contribute to a nett loss making exercise. Tim has convinced his fellow directors, his father included, that the printing side of the business should be terminated. Typesetting on the other hand, which is more lucrative, is to be substantially developed with investment in new technology. The business will then become a specialist typesetter, servicing printing firms throughout the Bradford area. Len is told the news on his 48th birthday in a personal letter from Tim. As a loyal servant of the business, Len is offered, in Tim's words "the opportunity to meet the challenge of retraining as a typesetter on his present wage and so secure his future with the business". The letter goes on to point out that "the only alternative is to leave and take your chances in the job market". Len is aware that his employment prospects as a printer are not good but is uncertain whether he can cope with what is effectively a different job requiring different skills. He is also concerned that his employer does not operate a redundancy scheme with its employees.

Tasks

You are employed by the Union of British Printworkers, at their headquarters in Birmingham, where you deal with employment problems being experience by union members.

Len is a member of the union, and he has written to it seeking help in relation to his situation at Fultons. The letter has been passed to you from your senior, for immediate attention. In it Len writes:

"I really don't know whether I have actually been made redundant at my place of work, and whether I am entitled to a redundancy payment. I have wondered about taking up the company's offer and retraining, but my worry is that I might find myself unable to cope with new demands, and have to leave anyway. I suppose if this happened I would lose any rights to a redundancy payment."

1. Produce notes on Len's redundancy dilemmas, to be attached to the file that has been opened for Len, in which you
   (a) identify whether if he leaves Fultons it will be by reason of redundancy;
   (b) state whether he is entitled to redundancy payment if he does leave through redundancy;
   (c) explain whether Len is correct in his view that by leaving after retraining he will lose his rights to redundancy pay, and
   (d) calculate the redundancy payment Len would receive if he were regarded as a redundant worker.

2. Write a reply to Len in which you clearly but briefly explain to him, in simple terms, his legal position. The letter will incorporate your findings which have been recorded on the entry you have made to the file. Len's address is 18 Ulverston Terrace, Bradford, West Yorkshire.

Developmental Task

Undertake a role play exercise in which you simulate an interview between Tim and Len, with yourself as Len's representative. The aim of the interview is to allow full and frank exchange of views regarding Len's position.

Chapter 16

Business Property (Tangible)

The Nature of Property

Most businesses own a wide range of property. This property is likely to take many different forms and perform a variety of functions. A glance at the balance sheet of any business will reveal the major types of property - or assets - commonly used by the trading organisation.

Under the heading *'fixed assets'* are found those items of property of a relatively permanent character which are acquired for use in the business. These may be tangible assets such as plant and machinery, vehicles and premises, or intangible assets such as patents, trademarks and goodwill. The balance sheet will also show the *'current assets'* of the business which will include raw materials, work in progress, stock, debtors and cash.

The legal rules which regulate the ownership, use and disposal of these different forms of business property vary according to the nature of the property itself and the legal category into which it placed.

The ownership of property brings with it certain legal rights and duties. These rights include the right to use and enjoy physical possession of the property, to consume it, after it, destroy it or dispose of it by transferring ownership of it to another person by way of gift or sale. An owner must also bear the risk of loss or damage to his property by accident or liability arising because of the use to which the property is put. A prudent owner will usually safeguard against these risks by taking out adequate insurance. In this chapter it is proposed to consider some of the main rights and duties which arise in relation to tangible business property, in particular business premises. In the final chapter we will examine the law relating to intangible business assets such as copyright and patents. A useful starting point for both chapters is to set out a formal classification of property under English law. From this model it is possible to identify the types of property which are of significance in the business world. You must appreciate however that English property law has developed over hundreds of years so that the legal terminology may well be unfamiliar to you.

The Classification of Property

Most legal systems distinguish between two main types of property, movable and immovable. This distinction is based upon the nature and characteristics of the property itself. Movable property includes goods and chattels, shares, debts and cheques; while immovable property is land and the things which go with land such as buildings and rights of way.

The English legal system unfortunately does not adopt this approach and, for historical reasons, makes a primary distinction between real and personal property. Real property is simply freehold land and we all will consider the rights of the freeholder later. All forms of property other then freehold land are categorised as personal property.

The historical reason for the distinction between real and personal property is that, in the early days of the common law, a form of legal action known as *a'real'* action could be used by an owner of freehold land if he had been wrongfully dispossessed of the land. If the real action was sucessful the common law courts could order that the true owner be entitled to recover the land wrongfully taken. This remedy was not available to an owner of any other type of property, not even to a holder of leasehold land, and such owners could only take an action in court to recover damages or financial compensation from the person who had taken their property because the court had no power to order the restoration of their property to them. Thus real property was that property which could be recovered by taking a *'real'* action in the courts and all other property was classified as personal property. The classification survives today even though the powers of the courts have changed over the centuries and it is now perfectly possible for a court to make an order restoring personal property to its true owner.

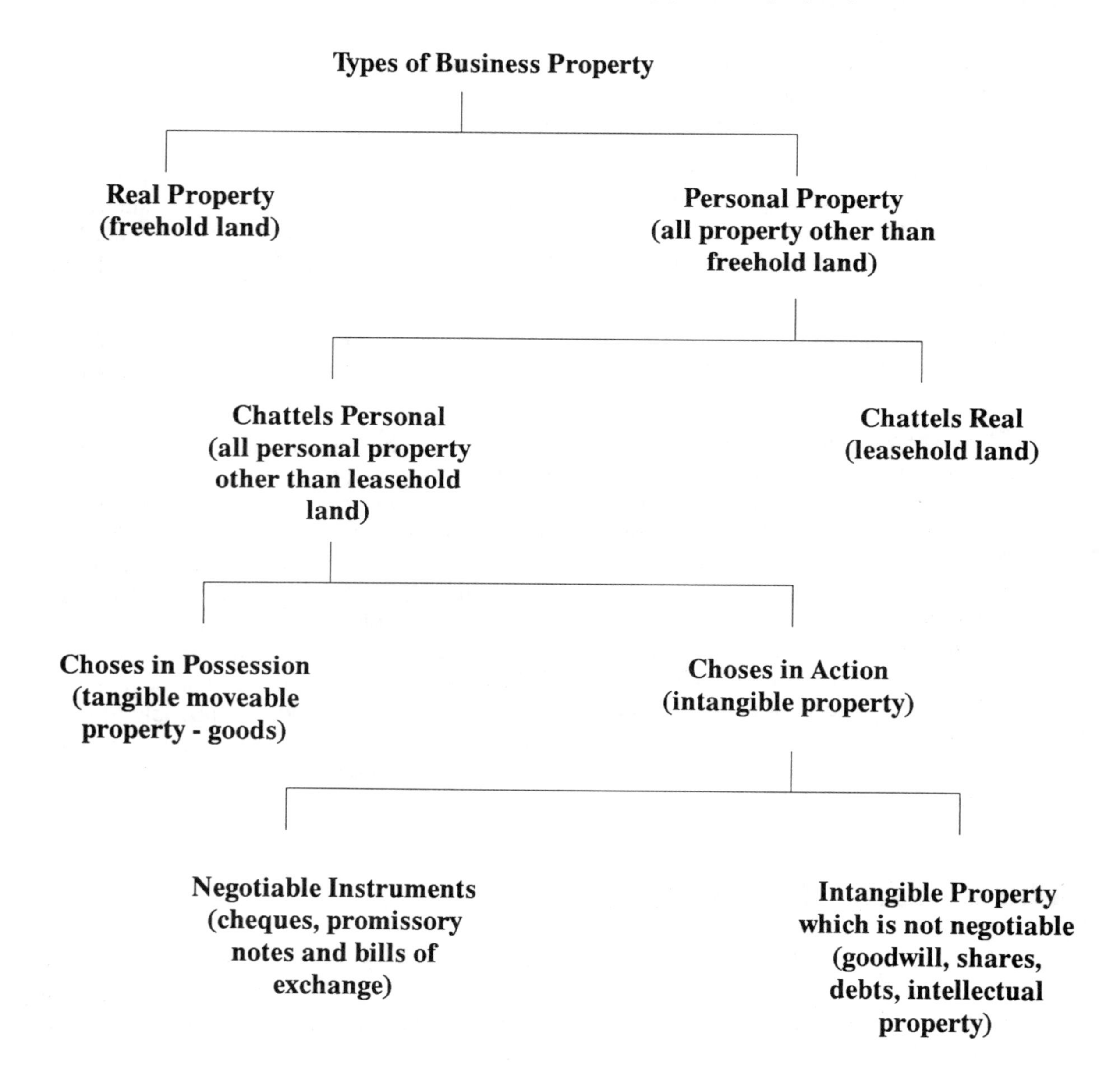

Fig. 16.1 Classification of Business Property

Chattels real and chattels personal

All types of personal property are known as *chattels*. *Chattels* is an old English word, meaning goods, derived from the word for cattle, which were in those days the most valuable form of personal property. Land and buildings held under the terms of a lease are chattels real. They are the form of personal property (chattels) most closely resembling freehold land (real property) and derive their name accordingly. The holder of leasehold land has a form of personal property despite the fact that it may be a valuable interest in land.

All other forms of personal property are known as chattels personal. Chattels personal are those forms of property, tangible and intangible, which other systems would classify as movable property, such as plant and equipment, vehicles, patents and debts.

A further division or classification of chattels personal is made between *'choses in possession'* and *'choses in action'* depending on whether they are tangible or intangible.

Choses in possession and choses in action

Choses is a French word meaning things. *Choses in possession* or things in possession therefore are items of physical movable property for instance 'goods' within the meaning of the Sale of Goods Act 1979 such as books, machinery, cars or desks.

Choses in action or things in action differ from choses in possession in that they have no physical existence. Choses in action are intangible forms of personal property such as goodwill, patents and debts, the rights in which can only be asserted by taking legal action.

There may be some physical or tangible evidence of the existence of the property rights in question but the rights themselves are intangible. For example, a share certificate is a tangible piece of paper, but its value lies in the legal rights which it represents, rights to vote at meetings of the company, rights to receive dividends and rights to share in the ultimate division of the property of the company on winding up once prior claims have been met.

Negotiable instruments such as cheques, bills of exchange and promissory notes are choses in action which represent the right to receive the payment of sums of money. The law relating to the ownership and possession of choses in action in the subject matter of the next chapter. Here we will confine ourselves to a consideration of the tangible assets of a business in particular what is often regarded as the most significant asset of a business, the land from which it operates.

Land

Land is the most permanent and often the most valuable asset which a business can own. For legal purposes, the buildings and other fixtures such as fences and trees on the land are treated as being part of it, and thus the ownership of business premises is regarded by the law as the same thing as the ownership of the land on which those premises stand. The airspace above and the soil below the land are also treated as being part of the land.

The premises from which businesses operate may be owned by the business outright. This is referred to as freehold ownership. On the other hand the premises may be rented from some other person or organisation. This is referred to as leasehold ownership. Technically all land in England and Wales is owned by the Crown and individuals or business organisations may hold an *'estate'* in land. The expression "estate in land" refers to the measure of a person's interest in land from the point of view of time.

Under s.1 of the Law of Property Act 1925, only two legal estates can exist in land: the fee simple absolute in possession (the freehold estate); and the term of years absolute (the leasehold estate).

Freehold Land

The *fee simple absolute in possession* in the freehold estate in land which effectively represents absolute ownership. This expression 'fee' refers to the fact that the estate is inheritable; 'simple' means that there are no restrictions on who may inherit; 'absolute' refers to the fact that the grant is unconditional and 'in possession' means that the grant is to take effect immediately.

The freehold owner is entitled to immediate possession of his land and this entitlement cannot be brought to an end except by the owner himself. He is entitled to pass on his ownership by sale to another or by inheritance to any of his heirs.

The only practical effect of the Crown's technical ownership of land is that the land will pass to the Crown as *'bona vacantia'* in the unlikely event that the freehold owner dies without any next of kin whatsoever and without a will giving the property to a named beneficiary.

For all practical purposes the freeholder is the absolute owner of the land and consequently the purchase of the freehold estate will normally necessitate the payment of a substantial sum of money to the vendor. The money can of course be raised by using the land as security to negotiate a business mortgage and repaying the capital sum plus interest to a lender (mortgagee) over a number of years. Nevertheless a lender will still require that a significant proportion of the cost must be funded by the prospective purchaser. Additionally, while it is usual to equate freehold with absolute ownership, you should also appreciate that even a freeholder is subject to many common law and statutory restrictions in relation to his freedom to use the land for his own purposes. Some of the following restrictions apply equally to the holder of leasehold land (considered later in the chapter.)

Rights and restrictions regarding landholding

(a) the right to develop the land

A landowner is subject to the control of the local planning authority under the Town and Country Planning Act 1971 in relation to any proposed development of the land. Planning permission is required for any material alterations to buildings on land or the use to which they are put. If an individual is considering acquiring a piece of land, there is a means by which he can obtain outline planning permission for any proposed development to ascertain whether full planning permission is likely to be granted.

If an owner carries out development without permission, the local planning authority may serve an *enforcement notice* on him requiring the works to be removed or the new use to be discontinued. If the enforcement notice is not complied with the authority may enter the land and restore it, charging the cost to the owner and alternatively, or in addition, may take proceedings in the Magistrates' Court against the owner. The Magistrates may impose a fine of £1,000 and a further penalty of £50 per day thereafter while the contravention continues.

Under the Building Act 1984, formerly the Building Regulations 1965 and 1976, plans for the construction of new buildings or for the structural alteration of existing buildings must be approved by the local authority. The purpose of the Building Regulations is to ensure that building construction is carried out in accordance with good building and design principles.

Building inspectors may inspect the building works as they continue in order to see that the approved plans are adhered to.

(b) the right to retain ownership

Wide powers are conferred on local authorities and other bodies with regard to the compulsory purchase of land. A freeholder can be required to sell his interests in the land to a body exercising compulsory purchase powers, usually in order to facilitate some development scheme. An owner can, of course, object to a compulsory purchase in order and then a Public Local Inquiry will have to be held to consider the views of those affected. Such inquiries are conducted by an inspector who will recommend a course of action to the appropriate Minister (the Secretary of State for the Environment) and his decision is final.

(c) the right to natural resources

An owner has full mineral rights, however by statute certain natural mineral resources such as gas, oil and coal belong to the government or one of its agencies. Thus coal is in the ownership of British Coal, a state corporation.

(d) the right to water

The owner of land adjoining a river enjoys certain common law rights. These riparian rights as they are known, allow him to take water for ordinary purposes connected with the land. The right however is substantially modified by the Water Resources Act 1963, which operates a licensing system for the extraction of water.

(e) rights in relation to the use of land

As a general proposition a landowner, subject to planning control, can use the land as he likes. However the ability of the businessman to operate any business he chooses is subject to a number of restrictions. Such restrictions may arise by means of express or implied agreement. Whether an individual occupies premises as a freeholder business or a tenant there could be some restriction on his rights to use the property for business purposes.

In a business lease we shall see that the deed creating it will contain a number of covenants. A covenant is simply a contractual term contained in a deed. One such covenant will normally restrict business use, and this could come in a positive or negative form. It could restrict the tenant from carrying on a particular business or using the property for a particular purpose, for instance carrying on the business of a retail travel agent. Alternatively the covenant could prevent the tenant from carrying on a particular form of trade or any activity causing a nuisance or annoyance, such as a public house. Both the landlord and tenant have bound themselves personally by the covenants in the lease and will retain this contractual liability throughout its term. A covenant restricting business use will also be enforceable against a sub tenant or an assignee of the business lease, by the original landlord or even a new landlord who has purchased the freehold estate.

Restrictive covenants may also apply to a freeholder. Such restrictive covenants could originate from a transaction under which one landowner, Smith sold part of his land to a purchaser, Jones. In the deed conveying the land to Jones, Smith may for the benefit of land retained by him, have extracted a promise from Jones not to use the land for anything except residential purposes. Thus if Jones now attempts to break the covenant by setting up a business, Smith can seek an injunction to prevent him. Of course it is not always the seller who abstracts the promise, it could be the purchaser who imposes a restriction on the seller. A major feature of such covenants is that they will become attached to the land which carries the burden and enjoys the benefit so that successive holders of the land may be bound by them.

> Recently in *C & G Homes Ltd. v. Secretary of State for Health* 1990 the issue before the Court of Appeal was whether the acquisition and use by the Health Secretary of two adjoining houses on a private housing estate in Bath as accommodation for four former mental patients contravened a restrictive covenant to use the houses as private dwellings. The court held that while the houses were being used as dwellings they were not "private dwelling houses" within the terms of the covenant for the occupiers were neither owners, tenants or members of the Health Secretary's, family but remained patients in NHS care. *"the use of these houses seemed to be that of a hospital annex or mental health hostel. Praiseworthy though that no doubt was, it was not a use which would be regarded as a normal use of a private dwelling house."*

Where the character of a neighbourhood changes or it becomes obvious that the covenant impedes some reasonable use of the land it is possible to apply to the Lands Tribunal which has power to modify or discharge the covenant.

The freedom to use premises for business purposes is also subject to constraints imposed by the criminal and civil law. An occupier of land may be restrained by injunction from using his property in such a way as to cause a nuisance to his neighbours, adjoining occupiers or to the public as a whole.

> In *Halsey v. Esso Petroleum* 1961 the plaintiff was the owner of a house on a residential estate and the defendant owned and occupied an oil storage depot on the river bank nearby. On various occasions noxious acid smuts were emitted from metal chimney stacks at the depot which caused damage to the plaintiff's washing, and the paint work of his car. There was also a particularly pungent oily smell from the depot of a nauseating character but which was not a health risk. Further cause for complaint was the noise emitted from the boilers during nightshift which varied in intensity but at its peak reached 63 decibels causing the plaintiff's windows and doors to vibrate. The noise was exacerbated by the arrival of heavy tankers at the depot, sometimes in convoy and as many as fifteen in one night. It was on the basis of these complaints that the plaintiff brought an action alleging nuisance and claiming damages and injunctions to restrain the activity. The Court held that:
>
> 1. The acid smuts emitted from the chimneys constituted the crime of public nuisance and as the plaintiff had suffered special damage in relation to his motor car he could recover damages for the tort of private nuisance.
> 2. Acid smuts which arise from a non natural use of land and then escape to adjoining land and cause damage will also give rise to strict liability in tort based on the principles laid down in the case of *Rylands v. Fletcher* 1868
> 3. Injury to health is not a necessary ingredient in the cause of action and since the particularly pungent smell from time to time emitted from the depot went far beyond a triviality, and was more than would effect a sensitive person, it was an actionable nuisance.
> 4. The noise from the boilers at night disturbed the resident's ordinary comfort and use of their property as did the noise from the vehicles and both would constitute a private nuisance.

5. Injunctions and damages were awarded to restrain the unlawful activities to the extent that they constituted an actionable nuisance.

Activities on land have also been made unlawful by statute and may constitute a statutory nuisance. From the 1st January 1991 a range of provisions formerly contained in the Public Health Act 1936 and the Public Health (Recurring Nuisances) Act 1969 cease to have effect and are replaced and extended by the Environmental Health Act 1990. Under s.79(1) a list of circumstances may amount to a statutory nuisance including emissions of smoke, gas, fumes, dust, steam, smells or other effluvia and noise from premises which are prejudicial to health or a nuisance. Detection and enforcement of the law is in the hands of local authorities, in particular environmental health officers. They are charged with the duty of inspecting their areas and also investigating complaints with the aim of preventing and eliminating statutory nuisances. Their powers extend to serving abatement notices on individuals or organisations requiring the abatement, prohibition or restriction of the nuisance and the execution of works or the taking of other necessary steps. Contravention of a notice or failure to comply with its terms is a criminal offence and could lead to a prosecution in the Magistrates Court and a fine of up to £2000 for each offence.

(f) the right to freedom from unlawful interference

Interference with the right of an owner of land to enjoy quiet possession of his land may be actionable under the civil law as the tort of trespass. Any person who, without lawful authority, enters or remains upon the land of another, or places or throws any physical object on to such land, is a trespasser. An occupier of land may use reasonable force, if necessary, to eject a trespasser, but only after asking him to leave and allowing him a reasonable opportunity to do so. An occupier of land may also sue a trespasser for damages and does not have to prove that he suffered any loss as a result of the trespass. He may apply for an injunction in order to prevent the continuation or repetition of the trespass. As previously illustrated in *Halsey v. Esso Petroleum* 1961 an owner or occupier of land may also be able to sue in the torts of nuisance or *Rylands v. Fletcher* either for an injunction or for damages in circumstances where his enjoyment of his own land is interfered with as a result of activities carried on by his neighbours which amount to an unreasonable or unlawful use by his neighbours of their land.

Acquisition of Land

The acquisition of land involves the transfer of property rights in land which is usually achieved by the formal process of conveyancing. Contracts for the sale or other disposition of land made before 27 September 1989 are governed by the requirements of s.40 Law of Property Act 1925. There does not have to be a formal written contract in order to comply with s.40, but rather written evidence which supports the existence of the contract. This must be signed by the party against whom it is to be used as evidence (or his agent) and contain details of the essential terms of the contract. The essential terms which the document must contain are:

(a) the names of the vendor and purchaser;

(b) the identity of the land;

(c) the price to be paid by the purchaser.

Now following the Law of Property (Miscellaneous Provisions) Act 1989 for contracts made after 27 September 1989 s.40 of the Law of Property Act 1925 is repealed totally. Under s.2 of the 1989 Act a contract for the sale or other disposition of an interest in land can only be made in writing, signed by the parties and incorporating all the terms which the parties have expressly agreed in one document or, where contracts are exchanged, in each. It is no longer possible therefore to have an oral contract for the sale of land evidenced in writing and a failure to comply with s.2 will make the contract invalid.

The process of conveyancing

The process of conveyancing is concerned with the legal mechanism for the sale or purchase of land or of an interest in land. The process is basically the same for all land regardless of the purpose for which it is used, be it a private house, an office, a factory or farmland. There may be some variation in the detail of the process, however, depending upon (a) whether the freehold or the leasehold estate is being transferred and (b) whether the title to the land is registered at the Land Registry, or is unregistered. We need not examine the detail of these variations and shall simply consider the basic process in outline.

This process is divided into two stages - the periods *before* and *after* an exchange of contracts.

Prior to an exchange of contracts

A person who wishes to sell land may either advertise the property himself or employ an estate agent to act on his behalf in negotiating the sale. When a purchaser is found, an agreement will be made in principle for the sale of the property at an agreed price, and it is then that the vendor and the purchaser will instruct their respective solicitorsof licensed conveyancers. At this stage the transaction is 'subject to contract'.

As previously stated from 27 September 1989 a contract for the sale of land is only valid if it complies with s.2 of the Law of Property (Miscellaneous Provisions) Act 1989. In fact both the purchaser and vendor will not usually wish to be legally bound until a formal exchange of contracts has been made. This is because the purchaser will have to conclude his financial arrangements and fully investigate the property before he commits himself, and the vendor may wish to arrange the purchase of a new property to take effect at the same time as his sale is completed. All correspondence passing between the parties or their representatives will be marked with the words 'subject to contract' but following s.2 of the 1989 Act this expression is of less significance.

The following matters will need to be dealt with before an exchange of contracts can take place.

(a) **Draft contracts**

The vendor's solicitor will obtain the title deeds relating to the property and, using information gathered from the deeds and from the vendor himself, will draw up a draft contract with an identical counterpart which will be submitted to the purchaser's solicitor for approval.

(b) **Enquiries and searches**

The purchaser's solicitor will make investigations about the property by:

(i) visiting the property and inspecting it;

(ii) sending a standard form of preliminary enquiries containing questions about physical and legal aspects of the property to the vendor's solicitor;

(iii) making enquiries to the Local Authority to discover what information it has relating to it or to proposals which may affect it, for example demolition orders or road improvement schemes;

(iv) making a search in the Register of Local Land Charges to determine whether any matter registered there affects the property.

(c) **Finance**

Prior to an exchange of contracts the purchaser will wish to conclude his financial arrangements so that he can satisfy himself that once he is legally bound he is able to raise the full amount of the purchase price. The majority of domestic purchases are made with the aid of a building society mortgage, and it is at this stage in the process that confirmation is required from the mortgagee that the necessary funding will be available to finance the purchase. The purchase of business premises is often funded, at least partly, by a mortgage also, but from a commercial bank rather than a building society. The nature of a mortgage, and the rights and obligations of the mortgagor and the mortgagee are considered later in the chapter. Before lending money on the security of a mortgage, the mortgagee will wish to be satisfied firstly that the borrower has the ability to repay. He will do this by enquiring of the employer of a private individual borrower, or assessing the accounts of a business borrower covering the last three financial years. Secondly he will wish to be sure that the property itself is sufficiently valuable to provide full security in the event of default by the borrower. This will usually be done by instructing an independent surveyor to give a valuation of the property.

(d) **Survey**

A contract for the sale of land is governed by the common law principle *'caveat emptor'* or 'let the buyer beware'! There are no statutory implied terms of quality or fitness for purpose. The purchaser takes the property as he finds it and must therefore satisfy himself about its physical condition and the state of any buildings before an exchange of contracts with the vendor.

A purchaser will usually employ a surveyor to act on his behalf in inspecting the property in order to find out whether there are any structural defects or other problems such as dry or wet rot, rising damp or woodworm. If any problems of this nature are detected while the purchase is 'subject to contract', the purchaser is free to look for another property, or to re-negotiate the price. If the defects become manifest after he has purchased, he will not usually be able to sue the vendor because of the *'caveat emptor'* rule.

Where the purchaser is financing the purchase with a loan on the security of a mortgage of the property, the mortgagee will usually arrange a survey himself, at the purchaser's expense, before agreeing to advance the money. If the mortgagee is a building society, then under the Building Societies Act 1986, it must arrange a survey for the purposes of valuation. As we have seen, a surveyor, acting for a building society in these circumstances owes a duty to the borrower to take reasonable care in carrying out a visual inspection of the property.

In *Yianni v. Edwin Evans & Sons* 1981 the plaintiffs were buying a house for £15,000 with the aid of a £12,000 building society mortgage. The building society instructed the defendant surveyors to carry out a valuation of the property. After an inspection of the house the defendants reported to the building society that in their opinion the house was adequate security for a loan of £12,000. The plaintiffs completed the purchase of the property and soon afterwards discovered serious cracks in the foundations. They sued the defendants for £18,000 which was the estimated cost of repairing the foundations. The Court held that the defendants owed a duty of care to the plaintiffs and that they were liable to pay the £18,000 damages in the tort of negligence for a breach of that duty of care.

Exchange of contracts to completion

Once the parties are satisfied that all the preliminary matters outlined above have been satisfactorily sorted out, they will be clear to enter into a legally binding contract. They will sign identical counterparts of the formal contract and the purchaser's solicitor will deliver his client's signed part along with a deposit representing 10% of the purchase price to the vendor's solicitor. In exchange he will receive the vendor's signed part of the contract. At this point the parties are legally bound by the contract. It will usually be a matter of three or four weeks before the sale is finally completed. The 10% deposit paid by the purchaser on exchange is a sign of his good faith and will be forfeited if he subsequently withdraws from the contract without justification.

Once contracts have been exchanged, the purchaser has an insurable interest in the property and should take out a policy of insurance immediately. He will not however, be in full possession of the property until completion takes place.

In the time before completion, the purchaser's solicitor will examine the title deeds to the property and investigate the vendor's title in order to be absolutely certain that the vendor is able to give full ownership to the purchaser without any possibility of a claim by any other person. For this purpose the purchaser's solicitor also makes further searches in central registers. It is possible for a person with legal rights over the property, such as a second mortgage, to protect his rights by registering them in a central register. The effect of such a registration is that the person to whom the property is conveyed will take subject to those rights unless they are discharged before completion by the vendor, for example by redeeming the second mortgage out of the proceeds of sale.

The purchaser's solicitor prepares the formal deed of conveyance in readiness for completion. Following the Law of Property (Miscellaneous Provisions) Act 1989 certain formalities for the creation and execution of deeds have been abolished. Under s.1 there is no longer a requirement that a deed made by an individual must be made by sealing the document. A valid deed must be signed and witnessed and make it clear that it is intended to be a deed.

Where the vendor conveys the land to the purchaser as a 'beneficial owner' the following covenants are implied by s.76 the Law of Property Act 1925:

(i) that the vendor has a good right to convey the property;

(ii) that the purchaser will enjoy quiet possession of the property;

(iii) that the property will be free from claims or demands by any other person;

(iv) that the vendor will, if necessary, at a future date, remedy any defect in the present conveyance.

Completion of the transaction

On the day of completion the purchaser will pay the balance of the purchase price (90%) to the vendor in return for the title deeds to the land, including the conveyance to himself, and the keys to the property. The property now fully belongs to the purchaser and he may take up possession.

Leasehold Land

Where a business operates from premises which are rented, the occupier will be a tenant and own a leasehold estate in the land. The landlord will be the owner of the freehold estate. A leasehold estate (or 'term of years absolute') is created when a freeholder grants a lease to a tenant for a certain term. This will include a lease for a time period which is fixed, for example a seven year lease. Alternatively the term of the lease could be made certain by the service of a notice to quit, for instance a monthly tenancy. The lease gives the business tenant the right to occupy the land and premises to the exclusion of all others (including the landlord) in return for the payment of rent. When the period of the lease comes to an end the landlord is entitled, at common law, to regain possession of his property. By Act of Parliament, however, the tenant will usually have the right of security of tenure. This right to stay in possession will override the landlord's common law right to regain possession, and will enable the tenant to extend his period of occupation by virtue of a new lease on terms which are reasonably equivalent to the terms contained in the original lease.

The terms of a business lease

A business lease will normally be granted by deed and will contain the rights and obligations of the landlord and the tenant in the form of covenants. A covenant is simply a contractual promise made in a deed.

Leases of business premises will usually contain the following covenants:

(a) **By the tenant**

- (i) to pay rent and rates (there may also be a rent review clause under which the amount of the rent may be increased from time to time);
- (ii) to keep the premises in a good state of decorative repair;
- (iii) to permit the landlord to enter the premises from time to time in order to view the state of repair;
- (iv) not to carry out alterations to the premises without the landlord's consent;
- (v) not to assign, sublet or otherwise part with possession of the premises;
- (vi) not to use the premises for any purpose other than that stated in the lease.

(b) **By the landlord**

- (i) not to interfere with the tenant's quiet enjoyment of the property;
- (ii) to insure the premises;
- (iii) to keep the main structure and exterior of the premises in good repair.

The covenants of a business lease may be positive, for instance to pay rent or negative for example not to sublet. They are enforceable by means of an action for damages, or in some cases an injunction to prevent a breach or specific performance, for instance to require a landlord to fulfil a repair obligation. A business tenant may also have a number of important rights conferred by statute. Under the Landlord and Tenant Act 1927 the right of a tenant to claim compensation for improvements made to the premises was first introduced and under the Landlord and Tenant Act 1954 Part II security of tenure was first recognised. It is of crucial importance therefore in determining the rights of a business tenant to ensure that the tenancy in question falls within the protection of the 1954 Act.

The Act applies to tenancies where the property comprised in the tenancy is or includes premises occupied by the tenant for the purposes of his business. It must be emphasised that the Act is limited to tenancies only and would not cover a mere licence.

> In *Addiscombe Garden Estates Ltd. v. Crabbe* 1958 following the analysis of a document which was referred to as a licence, the court concluded that it was in fact a lease. This conclusion was reached on the basis that the content of the document was written in the form of a lease rather than a licence. Included in the document were terms referring to repair, quiet enjoyment, and re-entry. The Court held that the relationship of the parties was determined by the law and not by the label which the parties chose to put on the document.

> Alternatively in *Shell-Mex and B.P. Ltd. v. Manchester Garages Ltd.* 1971 the plaintiffs allowed the defendant garage company occupation of a filling station under a licence agreement. One clause of the licence required the defendants not to impede the plaintiffs rights of possession and control of the premises. The Court held that this clause showed that the transaction constituted a licence and not a tenancy and represented a genuine management agreement not covered by the 1954 Act.

A business tenant must also show that the occupation of the premises is for the purpose of a business carried out by the tenant.

> In *Hancock and Willis v. GMS Syndicate Ltd.* 1982 the tenant took an assignment of additional business premises but then subsequently ceased to require them. To provide an income from the premises therefore, the tenant granted an exclusive licence of them to a printing company but retained use of the wine cellar for monthly staff lunches. The Court held that the 'thread of continuity' had been broken and as the tenant had ceased to occupy the premises for the purposes of a business carried out by them they were not entitled to renew the lease.

Additionally, the occupation of premises must be for business purposes. Business is defined as to include *a trade, profession or employment or any activity carried on by a body of persons whether corporate or unincorporate.* For a body of persons therefore, corporate or unincorporate, *'any activity'* may be regarded as a business for the purposes of the Act.

> In *Westminster Roman Catholic Diocese Trustee v. Parkes* 1978 occupation of premises as a community centre in connection with a church was held to be a business and come within the Act's protection. This was in accordance with the decision in *Addiscombe Garden Estates Ltd. v. Crabbe* 1958 where the activity of a member's tennis club was held to be within the Act.

As far as operating a business from home is concerned, the question as to business purposes is decided by examining the extent of business activity.

> In *Royal Life Saving Society v. Page* 1978 a partner in a firm of seafood importers who interviewed business clients at home, kept business documents and a business phone there, was held to operate a business for the purposes of the Act.

If the business is being operated in breach of a use covenant then the Act does not apply unless the immediate landlord or his predecessor in title has consented to the breach or the immediate landlord has acquiesced in its continuance.

In *Bell v. Alfred Franks and Bartlett Company Ltd.* 1980 the tenant used a garage for business purposes in contravention of a covenant that it was to be used for a car only. As there was no evidence of consent or acquiescence on the part of the immediate landlord then the 1954 Act was inapplicable and a notice to quit which had been served was valid and effective.

In *Nozari - Zadeh v. Pearl Assurance* 1987 the landlord claimed that a business tenancy of restaurant premises in London was not protected by the 1954 Act because the business was not carried out by the tenant but rather by a number of companies controlled by him. As a consequence the tenant failed to satisfy the requirement of occupying the premises for the purposes of a business carried out by him. The argument by the tenant that the companies were his "alter ego" and occupation by them was equivalent to occupation by him was rejected by the Court of Appeal which held that the tenancy did not come within the protection of the 1954 Act.

Certain tenancies are excluded from the Act including those of agricultural holdings, licensed premises, service tenancies and those of a term less than six months. Furthermore the Act provides that the County Court can authorise contracting out of its provisions on an application by both the landlord and tenant.

If a tenancy is protected by the 1954 Act then it can only be terminated by the landlord in accordance with the provisions of the Act and will not end automatically on the expiration of the term. The procedure for termination involves the service of a statutory notice by the landlord which if countered by the tenant could lead in the absence of agreement to a final determination by the County Court. As a general rule the tenant is entitled to a new tenancy, on fair terms, unless the landlord establishes a statutory ground of opposition.

Landlord's grounds for opposing a new tenancy

The alternative grounds upon which a landlord can rely to oppose a tenant's application to the court for a new tenancy are set out in s.30 of the 1954 Act.

S.30(1) (a) Breach of a repairing obligation

Relying on this ground the landlord must prove that in view of the state of repair of the premises resulting from the tenant's failure to observe a repairing obligation under the current tenancy, a new tenancy ought not to be granted. To grant possession on this ground the court must be satisfied that the breach of the repairing covenant is a serious one. This was the case in *Lyons v. Central Commercial Properties Ltd.* 1958 where the court held that the breach of a repairing covenant was of such a serious nature that the tenant ought not to be granted a new tenancy.

S. 30(1) (b) Persistent delay in paying rent

Here the landlord must prove that in view of the tenant's persistent delay in paying rent due under the current tenancy, a new tenancy ought not to be granted. Here again the court must be satisfied that the delay is a serious one, either over an extended time period or consist of a number of separate delays.

In *Hurstfell v. Leicester Square Property Co.* 1988 the Court of Appeal held that this ground had not been established in relation to a tenant who in the past had been guilty of persistent delays but because of his recent good record had convinced the court that there would be no recurrence of late payment.

S. 30(1) (c) Other substantial breaches

In this case the landlord must prove that the tenant ought not to be granted a new tenancy in view of other substantial breaches of obligation under the current tenancy or for any other reason connected with the tenant's use or management of the holding.

Again the important question for the court to determine is the seriousness of the breach and whether the tenant has any proposals for its remedy. In relation to "any other reason connected with the tenant's use or management of the holding" an illegal use of the premises would certainly amount to such a reason.

> In *Turner & Bell v. Searles Ltd.* 1977 the tenants were found to be using the premises unlawfully by parking coaches in breach of planning law, having had an enforcement notice served upon them. As it was clear that the tenants intended to continue the illegal use under a new tenancy, the landlord was held to be entitled to possession under s.30(1) (c).

S. 30(1) (d) Provision of suitable alternative accommodation

Relying on this ground the landlord must prove that the tenant ought not to be granted a new tenancy as the landlord is willing to provide him with suitable alternative accommodation. The question of deciding whether the alternative accommodation offered is suitable is to be determined by reference to all the circumstances, and in particular whether any goodwill attaching to the premises will be preserved.

S. 30(1) (e) Letting or disposing of the property as a whole

Here the landlord may object to the granting of a new tenancy in a case where the current tenancy was created by a sub-letting of only part of the premises let under a superior tenancy, and the interest of the tenant's immediate landlord is to terminate in the near future. The ground relied on is that the superior landlord requires possession of the premises as he might reasonably be expected to re-let the property as a whole or dispose of the property as a whole. To succeed on this ground the superior landlord would have to show that the re-letting value of the property as one unit is much higher than if re-let in separate parts.

S. 30(1) (f) Demolishing or reconstructing the premises

The objection of the landlord in this case is that the tenant ought not to be granted possession because the landlord intends, on the termination of the tenancy to demolish or reconstruct the premises, or a substantial part of them, or to carry out substantial work of construction on them and he could not reasonably do this work without obtaining possession of the premises.

> In *Betty's Cafe v. Phillips Furnishing Stores* 1959 it was held that the relevant intention of the landlord has to be established at the date of the court application. This intention must be proved to be a fixed one evidenced by positive steps to secure its implementation, e.g. planning applications, building contracts and building plans.

For the purposes of reconstruction the intention to carry out substantial work must be shown.

> In *Atkinson v. Bettison* 1955 installing a new front to a shop was held to be insufficient to constitute reconstruction whereas in *Joel v. Swaddle* 1957 changing the identity of a small shop into a large hall intended to be an amusement arcade was held to constitute reconstruction.

Certainly the expression "reconstruction" envisages rebuilding work and a demolition of part so that reconstruction as opposed to construction can take place.

In *Botterill and Another v. Bedfordshire C.C.* 1984 the council landlord opposed the renewal of a lease of four acres of land to a gun club by relying on s.30(1)(f). The substantial work of reconstruction planned by the council was to remove top soil, deposit waste and then plant some trees. The Court of Appeal held that landscaping of this nature could not constitute a substantial work of reconstruction under the Act and a new tenancy was ordered.

In *Edwards v. Thompson* 1990 the Court of Appeal held that the landlords intention to reconstruct a smithy as part of a larger scheme of residential development had not been sufficiently established in relation to the development as a whole. A new tenancy of the smithy was ordered for a term of one year.

Under the provisions of the 1954 Act, the fact that the landlord required possession of only part of the premises for only a short period would not prevent him from obtaining possession. This position was altered by the Law of Property Act 1969 which provides that the landlord cannot establish his need for possession under the 1954 Act if:

(a) the tenant is willing to have a term included in the new tenancy conferring a right of access on the landlord sufficient to enable him to carry out the work; or

(b) the tenant is willing to accept a new tenancy of an economically separable part of the holding and the landlord is able to carry out the works by having possession of the remainder.

S.30(1)(g) The Landlord intends to occupy for his own purposes

Here the ground is that the tenant ought not to be granted a new tenancy because the landlord intends to occupy the premises for the purpose of a business to be carried on by him therein or as his residence. For the purpose of showing intention the same factors to establish proof applicable to s.30(1)(f) are relevant.

In *Lightcliffe & District Cricket and Lawn Tennis Club v. Walton* 1978 the landlord, a farmer, relied on s.30(1)(g) to resist the tenant's application for a new tenancy of a piece of land. However the fact that the farmer failed to show through clear evidence his plans for making use of the land, convinced the court that his application should be rejected and a new tenancy was granted to the tenant.

In *Skeet v. Powell-Sheddon* 1988 the Court of Appeal held that a landlord who proposed to run a hotel business without occupying the premises but as a business partner through the management of her husband and daughter, could still be described as intending to occupy the premises for the purposes of a business to be carried on by her.

A statutory limitation on the landlord relying on the s.30(1)(g) ground is that it cannot be relied on if the landlord's interest was purchased or created within the five years previous to the termination of the tenancy and throughout that five year period there had been a tenancy or succession of tenancies of the holding.

Proof of any of the seven alternative statutory grounds may be sufficient to enable the landlord to recover possession of the business premises and successfully oppose the tenant's application for a new tenancy. It should be stressed however that grounds 30(1) (d), (f) and (g) are absolute in that if they are proved by the landlord then the court must grant him possession. The remaining grounds 30(1) (a), (b), (c) and (e) are discretionary and even if proved by the landlord the court nevertheless has a final discretion to determine whether a new tenancy is granted.

The court application and the new tenancy

It should be stressed that in the majority of cases and usually as the result of a compromise, agreement is reached as to the grant and/or terms of the new tenancy without the need for court intervention. In the event of failure to reach agreement however, a court application will proceed. The court must determine two distinct issues. Firstly, whether the tenant is to be granted a new tenancy and if this is so, then to determine its content.

The first issue, of course is determined by the court deciding whether the landlord has satisfied the s.30 ground relied on.

Having decided that a new tenancy is to be ordered, the court is faced with the second issue, its content. In the absence of agreement the Act confers a wide discretion on the courts in this matter. The subject matter of the new tenancy, is generally that part of the premises occupied by the tenant for the purpose of the business under the original tenancy. So far as the length of the new tenancy is concerned, its duration is to be such, up to a maximum of 14 years, as the court considers reasonable in all the circumstances. It is unlikely that the new tenancy will be granted for a term which exceeds the original tenancy and factors such as the landlord's intention to demolish or redevelop in the future are relevant to decide its length. In *Betty's Cafe v. Phillips Furnishing Stores* 1959 the renewed lease with a 14 year term was reduced to five years on appeal after considering the length of the original lease.

The rent payable under the new tenancy is that amount, having regard to the terms of the tenancy, that a willing lessor might reasonably expect to let the property at, on the open market.

> In *O'May v. City of London Real Property* 1982 the Court confirmed that the onus is on the party seeking a departure from the status quo. Here the landlord attempted to insert a service charge into a three year term in return for a rent reduction. The Court held that the charge was an unacceptable burden in comparison with the reduced rent and should not be permitted. The attempt to impose a service charge for common parts, lifts, etc., was an attempt to shift a burden which normally fell on the landlord.

The courts are concerned to ensure that if there is a variation in the lease there is a sufficient reason for it. Also there is a concern that a change in rent will adequately compensate the tenant for any variation in the lease. The objective is simply to achieve a fair and reasonable balance between the parties.

Compensation for improvements

During the term of a business tenancy it is likely that the tenant, or his predecessors in title will carry out improvements to the property. These improvements will ultimately benefit the landlord, since they will increase the potential letting value of the property when the letting under which they were carried out comes to an end. The Landlord and Tenant Act 1927 provides for compensation to be paid to the tenant by the landlord in such circumstances, subject to certain requirements being satisfied, and certain conditions being fulfilled.

In order to obtain compensation it is not enough that the tenant has simply carried out the improvements. He must in addition have followed the statutory procedure laid down in the 1927 Act. Under this procedure the tenant must first have served notice on the landlord of his intention to carry out improvements, accompanied by a specification and plan of the works to be carried out. The landlord then has 3 months to serve a notice of objection. If he fails to do so then the improvement is regarded as being authorised. In any event no objection can be served if the improvement is being carried out in pursuance of a statutory obligation. If the landlord does serve a notice of objection during the statutory time period the tenant can apply to the court for a certificate that the improvement is a proper one.

Once the certificate is granted, and the court may in granting it impose conditions and modify the specification or plans, the improvement becomes an authorised one. The claim for compensation must be made by the tenant in the prescribed form and include the date the work was carried out, its costs, details of the work and the amount now being claimed by the tenant. The claim must be served on the landlord within strict time limits on the termination of the tenancy. The Act provides for a further payment of compensation for disturbance where the landlord has been given possession because of reconstruction or carrying on a business himself. The amount of compensation is three times the rateable value and six times if the tenancy has lasted for fourteen years or more.

> In *Department of the Environment v. Royal Insurance* 1987 the fact that the tenant had occupied the premises one day short of the fourteen years meant that there was no entitlement to the larger sum. The practical difference for the tenant was £161,665 compensation rather than £333,330.

Business Premises and Liability

In Chapter 13 we considered the extent to which an employer in control of work premises may be made liable for injuries caused to workers both under common law negligence and the Health and Safety at Work Act 1974. Occupiers of business premises whether freeholders or business tenants have further duties placed upon them to ensure the safety of all lawful entrants by virtue of the Occupiers Liability Act 1957 and in some cases an obligation to take reasonable care extends to uninvited visitors under the Occupiers Liability Act 1984.

Under the Occupiers Liability Act 1957 an occupier of business premises owes the common duty of care to all his lawful visitors and that is to take such care as in all the circumstances is reasonable to provide for their safety. Notice that the duty is owed by the occupier, the person in control of the premises and he would certainly include the owner in possession or a business tenant or licensee. The business landlord however is regarded as the occupier in relation to parts of the premises which remain under his control, e.g. entrance hall, lifts, forecourt or other common parts. Also if the landlord is under an obligation to repair, he may under s.4 Defective Premises Act 1972 be made liable for injuries that occur as a result of his failure to fulfil a repair obligation. Where the premises are let therefore, both the landlord and the tenant may be regarded as occupier of the premises for different purposes under the Act.

> In *Ferguson v. Welsh and others* 1988 an employee, Mr. Ferguson, sustained serious injuries when engaged on demolition work on a site owned by the District Council. Having invited and accepted a tender to do the demolition work from Mr. Spence, an approved contractor of the council, the council were unaware that the work had been subcontracted to Mr. Ferguson's employers, the Welsh brothers. This was despite the fact that the original invitation to tender expressly prohibited subcontracting without the council's approval. Mr. Ferguson's claim for damages against his employers, the Welsh brothers, for breach of statutory duty was upheld in the High Court. Whether the council as occupier of the premises owed Mr. Ferguson a duty of care under the 1957 Act was only finally resolved in the House of Lords. Their Lordships held that despite the express prohibition on subcontracts,

Mr. Ferguson was nevertheless a lawful visitor of the council. "The contractor engaged by the council was placed in control of the site for demolition purposes and to one who had no knowledge of the council's policy of prohibiting subcontracts, that would indicate that he was entitled to invite whomsoever he pleased onto the site for the purposes of carrying out the demolition. Moreover having put the contractor into occupation of the premises and thus into a position to invite the subcontractors and their employees onto them for the purpose of demolishing the building, the council must be taken to have invited the appellant in for that purpose so as to create a duty of care." The House of Lords therefore confirmed that for the purposes of liability there may be different occupiers of the premises. In this case however the council although occupiers were not in breach of the common duty of care when the injury occurred as a result of the unsafe system of work adopted by subcontractors.

The obligation of the occupier in the above circumstances is to take reasonable care in entrusting the work to an independent contractor and under s.2(4)(b) of the 1957 Act takes such steps as he reasonably ought in order to satisfy himself that the contractor was competent and that the work had been done properly. Certainly the occupier will have acted reasonably if he selected a reputable organisation to do work on the premises rather than a local handyman.

In *O'Connor v. Swan & Edgar* 1963 the plaintiff was injured by a fall of plaster when she worked as a demonstrator on the first defendant's premises. The fall of plaster was due to the faulty workmanship of the second defendants who had been engaged as contractors to work on the premises. The court held that as the first defendants had acted reasonably in entrusting the work to a reputable contractor then as an occupier he had satisfied the duty of care which was owed. The second defendants however were held liable in the tort of negligence for faulty workmanship.

Following the Unfair Contract Terms Act 1977 it is no longer possible for an occupier of business premises to exclude the common duty of care in relation to his visitors. To fulfil the duty owed it is necessary to ensure that premises are indeed reasonably safe or alternatively ensure that visitors are safe by giving adequate warning of any dangers. The 1957 Act mentions two categories of visitor in particular, children and independent contractors. It says that in relation to child visitors an occupier must be prepared for them to be less careful than adults. This suggests that for instance that an occupier of retail premises to which the public have access will owe a higher standard of care towards children than adults. The requirement of parental control however is a significant factor in establishing liability for injury caused to child visitors.

In *Simkiss v. Rhondda B.C.* 1983 a seven year old suffered injury when she fell 30 or 40 feet after sliding on a blanket down a steep slope owned by the council. The High Court found the council liable for breach of the common duty of care in failing to either ensure that the mountainside was safe for children to play on or alternatively fencing it off. The Court of Appeal took a different view of the matter however and pointing out that adults would have realised that the mountainside must have been an obvious danger, the council was entitled to assume that parents would have warned their children of the danger. In reversing the decision of the High Court, the Court of Appeal stressed that the council's duty of care was not broken by failing to fence the mountain. To require a local authority to fence every natural hazard under its control would impose too onerous a burden.

Not only children but independent contractors are also singled out for mention in the Act. Such persons engaged to carry out specialist work should be aware of the risks inherent in their own trades.

> This is reflected in *Roles v. Nathan* 1963 where, despite being warned of the danger, two chimney sweeps carried on working on a boiler and were killed by carbon monoxide poisoning entering from the ventilation system. The employer/occupier was held in the circumstances not to be liable. Ld. Denning M.R. stated that *"when a householder calls in a specialist to deal with a defective installation on his premises he can reasonably expect the specialist to appreciate and guard against the dangers arising from the defect".*

> In *Rae (Geoffrey) v. Mars (UK)* 1990 an experienced surveyor was instructed to survey business premises and given the assistance of a graduate trainee by the defendant to show him round. The surveyor fell and suffered severe injuries when entering a printing ink store, the floor of which was three feet below the level of the door. No warning of the danger had be given by the trainee. In an action for damages under the Occupiers Liability Act 1957 to court held that notwithstanding his specialist expertise the surveyor like all visitors should have been given a warning of the exceptional nature of the hazard and the occupiers were accordingly in breach of their duty under s.2. By failing to switch on his torch however, while entering the store room, the surveyor was also at fault and the damages awarded were reduced by one third to reflect his contributory negligence.

In determining liability for breach of the common duty of care all the circumstances must be considered not least the premises in question.

> The court found no breach of duty in *Hogg v. Historic Buildings and Monuments Commission for England* 1988 when an employee at Pendennis castle had fallen while descending some external steps due to the presence of a rainwater gully. Recognising that building standards in 1540 would not conform to present day requirements the court held that the antiquity of the building was a factor in determining whether s.2 was fulfilled. Hadrians Wall was not to be judged by the standards of Haringay Town Hall.

In relation to invited visitors it was not until 1972 that the courts finally recognised that in some circumstances an occupier of business premises could be found liable in damages for injuries caused to a child trespasser.

> In *British Railways Board v. Herrington* 1972 British Rail had negligently failed to maintain fencing which ran between their railway track and a park frequently used by children. A six-year old climbed through the fence, wandered onto the track, and suffered severe injury on the electrified rail. The House of Lords held the Board liable in negligence to the child trespasser. The Court stated that, *"... if the presence of the trespasser is known or ought reasonably to be anticipated by the occupier then the occupier has ... a duty to treat the trespasser with ordinary humanity".* Among the factors to be taken into account in such cases are the degree of potential harm faced by the trespassers, the financial resources of the occupier and, in the case of children, whether the premises act as an allurement. In this case the Board were aware of a known and potentially lethal danger particularly to children. The standard of care required of an occupier in these circumstances was to *"act as a conscientious humane man, with his knowledge, skill and resources,*

> *could reasonably be expected to act".* British Rail had not fulfilled this duty and were liable for damages.

It should be noted that the duty owed to a trespasser is a restricted duty and much less than the standard of care owed to a lawful visitor. In addition, the court pointed to the economic resources of the occupier as a factor to determine whether he had acted reasonably. The rule in *British Railways Board v. Herrington* had been applied in later cases.

> In *Pannett v. McGuinness Ltd.* 1972 a demolition contractor was made liable for injuries caused to a five-year old trespasser by an unguarded fire. This was despite the fact that the contractor, aware of the danger, had posted workmen to guard the fire. The fact that the workmen were absent when the injury occurred meant, as far as the injured child was concerned, nothing was done to safeguard him.

> In *Umek v. London Transport Executive* 1984 a canteen assistant employed by the defendants was killed when she crossed the railway tracks and was struck down by a train. The station subway was out of action due to flooding and the staff foreman had roped it off and put up a notice stating that staff should use the footbridge rather than cross the tracks. The plaintiff ignored the notice to her cost and her personal representatives subsequently brought on an action in negligence against the LTE. The claim alleged that train drivers should have been warned of the potential hazard of staff walking across the line. The High Court agreed that failing to warn was indeed negligent, given the fact that the LTE were aware that staff were crossing the tracks. The plaintiff as a trespasser was owed the common duty of humanity which had been broken by the defendants. As the plaintiff was 75% to blame for the accident however, damages would be reduced by that amount to reflect the contributory fault.

In an attempt to clarify the rules relating to the liability of an occupier towards trespassers the Occupiers Liability Act 1984 was passed. The Act replaces the common law, which includes the rules laid down by the House of Lords in Herrington's case, 1972.

Under the 1984 Act the occupier will owe a duty to trespassers if:

(a) he is aware or ought to be of danger; and

(b) knows or has reasonable grounds to believe that the trespasser is or may be in the vicinity of danger; and

(c) may reasonably be expected in all the circumstances to offer some protection to the trespasser against the danger.

Having established the existence of a duty the Act goes on to provide that the duty extends to taking such care as in all the circumstances is reasonable to see that the trespasser does not suffer injury by reason of the danger concerned. It is also provided that the duty may in an appropriate case be discharged by warning.

Whether the objective of clarification has been furthered by converting the law into a statutory form is to be doubted for the existence of a duty of care will still demand a consideration of *"all the circumstances"* to determine whether the trespasser deserves protection. This may well involve a consideration of the circumstances identified in Herrington's case such as the resources of the occupier, the extent of likely harm, the frequency of trespass etc. In addition the 1984 Act has confined itself to personal injury and so the common law is still relevant if the claim involves damage to the property of the trespasser.

Land as Security

The value to a business of its freehold or leasehold land extends beyond the intrinsic value of such property as a place from which the business is conducted, or a resource in the production process. The business may also use the land as a means of raising finance by obtaining a loan secured by a mortgage of the land.

A mortgage is simply a transaction under which a borrower, the mortgagor in return for a loan from the lender, the mortgagee gives security in the form of property which is usually land. Domestic mortgages are most commonly created when a building society, bank, insurance company or local authority lends money towards the purchase of a home. For business premises a commercial mortgage will usually be arranged through a mortgage broker with a bank or finance company. In the business context the mortgage transaction can provide the means by which either:

(a) commercial premises are acquired from which the business activity is carried on, or

(b) additional funds are raised to finance business activity.

To create a formal or "legal" mortgage of a freehold or leasehold two methods are available under the Law of Property Act 1925. The first method involves the transfer of a lease (usually for 3000 years) from the mortgagor to the mortgagee subject to a clause that the lease is to terminate when the loan is repaid. This is called a provision for cesser on redemption. If the property to be mortgaged is leasehold then a sub lease is granted for a shorter period than the original lease. While the lease is merely notional and no rent is payable under it, it does provide a means by which the mortgagee can if necessary enforced his security. The second method available is simpler, more popular with institutional lenders and is known as the "charge" method. Here the mortgagor charges his land with the repayment of the debt by the means of a short deed expressed to be a charge by way of legal mortgage. The main difference between a charge and a mortgage is that under the charge the borrower retains ownership in the property and the lender is given certain rights over it. Under the mortgage however some ownership of the property is transferred to the lender for the purposes of providing security for the loan.

An alternative to the legal mortgage is the less formal "equitable" mortgage. An equitable mortgage arises where no mortgage deed is executed and the borrower merely deposits the title deeds of the property with the lender. While there is no transfer of ownership to the lender under such an arrangement the borrower is effectively prevented from selling or remortgaging the land. A weakness of the equitable mortgage is that if a subsequent legal mortgage were to be created over the land, that mortgage would take preference if the mortgagee had no knowledge of the equitable mortgage.

Where a legal mortgage is created, this must be done by deed. The deed must comply with the Law of Property Act 1925 and the Law of Property (Miscellaneous Provisions) Act 1989. The mortgage deed will set out the rights and obligations of the mortgagor and mortgagee, which will usually include the following:

The rights of the mortgagor

(a) **The right to redeem the mortgage** - the mortgage deed will provide for the repayment of the amount borrowed (the capital sum) with interest by instalments over a definite period of time which is usually a number of years. The mortgagor has the right to be discharged from his obligations under the mortgage deed once the capital sum has been repaid with interest; and he has the right to make a full repayment at any time, even before the date specified in the mortgage, and thereby redeem his property. Generally the courts have sought to protect the right of the mortgagor and have not allowed mortgage terms which unreasonably prevent or postpone the mortgagor's right to redeem the mortgage.

In *Fairclough v. Swan Brewery Co. Ltd.* 1912 a twenty year mortgage term postponed the right to redeem for nineteen years and forty six weeks. This postponement was held to make the mortgage virtually unredeemable and so declared void.

(b) **The right to enjoy the use of his land** during the repayment period, without any interference by the mortgagee, so long as he (the mortgagor) is fulfilling his obligations under the mortgage and repaying the instalments as they fall due. In these circumstances the mortgagor has full use of his property though there may be some restrictions, for example on structural alterations or leasing without the consent of the mortgagee since these could affect the value of the security.

The rights of the mortgagee

The principal right of the mortgagee is to the repayment of the capital sum with interest in accordance with the terms of the mortgage. If the mortgagor defaults in his obligation to repay, the mortgagee can rely on one or more of the following rights.

(a) **The right to sue the mortgagor.** The mortgagor is under a contractual obligation to repay the full amount of the loan with interest. If he is in arrears he may be sued personally by the mortgagee for the full amount and not merely for the outstanding instalments. Usually however, the mortgagee will prefer to enforce his rights against the property because the mortgagor is not likely to be able to satisfy a judgment debt if he is in such financial difficulty as to be unable to repay the mortgage instalments.

(b) **The right to take possession of the property** if the mortgagor defaults in the repayment of the loan. This right will be contained in the mortgage deed and will usually be exercised by the mortgagee as a preliminary step, prior to exercising a power of sale, in order to obtain vacant possession of the property.

(c) **The power of sale.** This power may be exercised by the mortgagee where at least two months' interest is overdue and where he has served notice on the mortgagor requiring him to repay the mortgage debt in full and the mortgagor has failed to do so within three months. The mortgagee may then sell the property over the head of the mortgagor, take out all sums due to him from the proceeds of sale and pay any remaining monies back to the mortgagor.

(d) **Foreclosure.** This amounts to the transfer of the mortgaged property to the mortgagee absolutely and may only be done by an order of the court, which is obtained in two stages.

The first stage involves an application to the court, where the mortgagor is substantially in arrears, for an order requiring him, within a specified time, to repay the loan and redeem the mortgage.

If the mortgagor fails to redeem the mortgage, the second stage involves a further application to the court for a final order of foreclosure terminating the mortgagor's right of redemption and transferring the ownership of the land absolutely to the mortgagee.

Tangible Property other than Land

Choses in possession

Earlier in this chapter it was noted that choses in possession are items of personal property which have a physical existence and can be touched or moved. In other words they are goods. Chapters 8 and 9 deals with the legal rules relating to contracts for the sale of goods and other contracts involving the transfer of ownership of goods from one party to another. The detailed regulation of such transactions simply reflects the fact that the production and distribution of goods is the lifeblood of the majority of business organisations in the commercial world.

We shall now consider the legal consequences, both under the criminal law and under the civil law, of the unlawful interference by one person with the goods of another.

Criminal liability for interference with goods

A person who interferes with the property of another may be liable, under the criminal law, to punishment in the form of a fine, or imprisonment, or both. The main offences relating to such interference are contained in the Theft Act 1968 and the Criminal Damage Act 1971.

Theft

By section 1 of the Theft Act 1968 a person is guilty of theft if he dishonestly appropriates property belonging to another with the intention of permanently depriving the other of it.

'Property', for the purposes of this offence, is defined in s.4 of the Act to include "money and all other property, real and personal, including things in action and other intangible property", although the section goes on to exclude land from the definition except in one or two specified instances. Theft, like most other criminal offences, contains two main elements:

(a) the mental element or guilty mind, called 'mens rea'

(b) the physical element or guilty act, called 'actus reus'.

The guilty act is the 'appropriation'. This involves taking or otherwise assuming the rights of an owner of property belonging to another. The mental element of the offence is the dishonesty of the accused, and his intention to permanently deprive the owner of his property. Without an intention to permanently deprive the owner of his property the offence is not committed. The dishonest borrowing of property belonging to another is not theft, but a separate offence is created by the Theft Act 1968, s.12, of taking a conveyance such as a motor car without lawful authority and this offence may be committed without an intention to permanently deprive the owner of his conveyance.

Criminal damage to property

By section 1 of the Criminal Damage Act 1971 a person who without lawful excuse destroys or damages any property belonging to another, intending to destroy or damage such property or being reckless as to whether any such property would be destroyed or damaged is guilty of an offence.

Property, for the purposes of this offence, is defined by the Act as *"property of a tangible nature, whether real or personal, including money'.'* Because of the nature of the offence, choses in action are not included in the definition, although clearly land and buildings are included as well as goods and money. The guilty act which constitutes the offence is the damage or destruction caused to another's property. If this is done by fire then the offence is known as arson. The mental element is the intention of the accused or his recklessness as to whether the property is damaged or destroyed.

Civil liability for interference with goods

The civil law remedies available to a person whose goods have been wrongfully interfered with are contained in the Torts (Interference with Goods) Act 1977. The Act applies to goods, which are defined by s.14 to include *"all chattels personal other than things in action and money"*. The Act therefore applies to choses in possession but not to choses in action.

Section 1 of the Act defines 'wrongful interference with goods' to mean conversion of goods,trespass to goods,negligence so far as it results in damage to goods and any other tort so far as it results in damage to goods.

Conversion of goods

Conversion of goods is the denial of an owner's title to goods. Such a denial may take the form of wrongfully taking them away from the owner, keeping them, destroying them or disposing of them to a third party.

Trespass to goods

Trespass to goods is denying the owner of goods the right to possession of them by wrongfully removing them or damaging them without depriving the owner of them completely.

Negligence

Negligence involves a failure to take reasonable care which results in foreseeable damage to the goods.

The remedies available under the Act are contained in s.3 which provides for

(a) damages alone; or

(b) damages in addition to an order for specific delivery of the goods. An order for specific delivery is discretionary and may be refused, or if granted, may be subject to conditions imposed by the court; or

(c) an order that the defendant pay the value of the goods to the plaintiff instead of specific delivery.

Assignment *The Wandering Child*

Fiona Berry and John Cheng are business partners who run a number of travel agency related outlets in Lancashire. One such agency Fiesta Travel is situated in premises in Bolton held on a 21 year lease with a break clause and rent reviews at seven year intervals from North Western Properties Ltd. The lease has now run for six years and despite repeated requests by Fiona, the landlords seem reluctant to fulfil their clear repairing obligation in relation to the plaster work on the ceiling of the main office which is in a dangerous state of disrepair. A further cause for anxiety is the condition of the electrical wiring in the building, which again falls within the landlords responsibility.

Concerned at the time it takes for the landlord to respond to a request to repair, Fiona decided to hire Gerry, a local odd job man, to carry out wiring work in the premises. In addition, North Western Properties finally responded to the request for repairs to the ceiling by hiring Joplings, a well known building contractor to carry out the work. Unfortunately because of pressure of work, Joplings decide to sub contract the work to Tom and Jim, a couple of lads who are "quick and cheap and can manage small jobs".

The events of the last two weeks have driven Fiona to despair! The first replastering work while completed in good time has not been a success. Firstly Sheila, a prospective customer suffered head injury caused by a fall of plaster when she was glancing at travel brochures in the premises. Furthermore Jim in carrying out the replastering work sustained a violent electric shock when he touched exposed electric cables to a light fitting which Gerry had not properly insulated. The icing on the cake was an incident yesterday. Wayne, a six year old on the premises with his parents there to book a holiday, wandered through a door marked 'private' apparently in search of toilets. He fell down the steps inside the door leading to the cellar and suffered a broken arm. The stairs were not lit.

Fiona and John feel that they may face potential legal claims for these incidents and fix an appointment with Masters & Milburn a local firm of solicitors to seek legal advice. On the morning of their appointment the couple receive a letter from North Western Properties indicating that it is exercising its option to discontinue the business lease by virtue of the break clause. The couple bring the letter with them to the solicitors. Despite their problems they don't wish to leave the Bolton Premises.

Task

You are working for Masters and Milburn as part of a work experience programme and have been asked to interview Fiona and John and to follow up the interview with a written report to one of the senior partners Janet Stephenson. You need to include in the report your assessment of the legal position in relation to liability and the termination of the business lease. Your task is to produce the report for Ms Stephenson. The report should clearly state the legal arguments both for and against the likelihood of Fiona and John incurring liability for the injuries to Sheila and Wayne.

Development Task

Look at the kinds of warning notices displayed in commercial premises and places such as building sites. Using your knowledge of the law concerning occupiers liability and exclusion clauses consider how for the notices you have looked at are lawful.

Chapter 17

Business Property (Intangible)

Choses in action

In the last chapter it was seen that choses in action are forms of personal property which have no physical existence, although they may be evidenced by some physical thing such as a share certificate or a mortgage deed. The essential characteristic of a chose in action is that it is a property right which can, if necessary, be asserted by taking legal action in the courts.

Examples of choses in action which are important in a business context include the following:

(a) debts owed to a business;

(b) shares held in a business;

(c) business goodwill;

(d) intellectual property, such as patents, copyright and trademarks; and

(e) negotiable instruments, such as cheques and bills of exchange.

The nature of choses in action

Because of the intangible nature of this form of property the law has recognised that in some cases special protection is needed to prevent infringement of the owner's rights in relation to it. This can be seen particularly in respect of intellectual property.

The legal nature of various forms of intangible property are considered below:

(a) debts

A debt is a legal right to receive payment. In a business context this will usually involve the right to payment for goods and services provided to a customer. The business owns the right to payment. This creates an asset, which appears in the balance sheet. As an item of business property a debt can be sold. Some organisations actually specialise in purchasing debts, at a discount. Unless they are in need of immediate funds businesses will not usually sell their debts. However where a debtor is in financial difficulties, and the chances of enforcing the debt through court action are small the business may be glad to cut its losses and sell the debt at a heavy discount. Debt recovery presents a major problem for all businesses, especially small businesses which have limited funds available to them, and can easily experience cash flow difficulties. It is not unusual for small organisations with a full order book but with many outstanding debts to go under as a result of such difficulties.

(b) shares

Shares are issued to members of a company according to their capital contributions, and represent their stake in the ownership of the company. Shares usually carry voting rights as well as the right to share in the profits of the company by way of dividends. The characteristics of shares are more fully examined in Chapter 3.

(c) business goodwill

Business goodwill is the term used to describe the most fundamental asset of any business organisation, its reputation. The reputation of any business operating in a market is measured by the extent to which its goods or services have achieved public respect. This respect is normally built up over a number of years so that a regular custom develops to ensure a steady level of business. To obtain a good reputation it is necessary for a business to recruit a skilled and loyal workforce and in many cases maintain a high level of research and development into its products. A number of factors contribute to establishing and maintaining the goodwill of a business including its marketing strategy, custom, workforce and future plans for the goods and services it provides. The tort of passing off, discussed below, is the legal means by which a business can protect its goodwill in circumstances where another trader, misrepresenting his goods or services as those of the plaintiff, attempts to cash in on the goodwill of the plaintiff's business.

There is normally no need to place a monetary value on businesses goodwill and therefore it will not usually appear in the assets column of the Balance Sheet when yearly accounts of a business are drawn up. Unlike tangible assets however, if it is lost it cannot be easily replaced. The necessity to value goodwill arises when there is a change in the ownership of the business. On the introduction of a new partner into a partnership it may be necessary to value the goodwill to determine his or her capital contribution. If a business is sold as a going concern then the amount by which the purchase price exceeds the value of the tangible assets of the business represents the value of the goodwill.

(d) intellectual property

(e) negotiable instruments

These two aspects of intangible property are dealt with in detail below.

Intellectual Property

The law of intellectual property is concerned broadly with the protection of ideas and information in a commercial context. The protection conferred on the owner of intellectual property usually takes the form of an exclusive right to exploit the ideas or information in the market place, in most cases for a limited period of time, coupled with a range of remedies to enable him to enforce his right in the event of infringement. This enables him, in effect, to curtail the activities of competitors who are unable to engage in specific types of conduct relating to the subject matter of his rights without his consent. The effective monopoly conferred by the ownership of intellectual property can clearly be an extremely valuable business asset. This asset may be exploited directly by the business as part of its ordinary commercial activity or by licensing others to use it in their business in return for licence fees or royalties.

In order to gain legal protection, some forms of intellectual property need to be registered. Patents, registered trade and service marks and registered designs come within this category. Others, such as copyright and the unregistered design right automatically qualify for protection

	Copyright	Patents	Registered design	Unregistered design right	Products (protection of topography) Regulations 1987	Registered trade marks and service marks	Common law trade marks and service marks: passing off
Rights protected	literary dramatic musical and artistic work, sound recordings, films, broadcasts, cable programmes, published editions, computer software	inventions: processes or products with industrial application	features of shape configuration pattern or ornament applied to an article by an industrial process to give visual appeal	any aspect of the shape or configuration of all or part of an article other than surface decoration– includes purely functional design	computer chips layout of semiconductors	emblems, symbols, logos etc connecting goods or services with their producer or supplier	goodwill of a business
Need for registration	no	yes	yes	no	no	yes	no
Duration of protection	lifetime of author plus 50 years	20 years	renewable five year periods, maximum 25 years after 1.8.89 maximum15 years before 1.8.89	lesser of 15 years from creation or 10 years from marketing	lesser of 15 years from creation or 10 years from marketing	unlimited where mark is in use in trade	unlimited
Availibility of licence as of right to competitor	no	licence as of right during last four years except for pharmaceutical patents compulsory licence where patent unreasonably underused	compulsory licence where design unreasonably underused	licence as of right during last five years	no	no	no
First ownership	author or his employer	inventor or his employer	designer or commissioner or designer's employer	designer or commissioner or designer's employer	designer or commissioner or designer's employer	registered proprietor	owner of the business

Figure 17.1 Comparison of major forms of intellectual property

without the need for registration. Where registration is required, this can be a time consuming and costly exercise involving the services of specialist agents, and in some cases substantial renewal fees are payable in order to maintain the registration.

At this point it may be noted that there is an inherent tension between the monopoly of exploitation conferred by intellectual property rights on the one hand, and the aims of competition policy, as embodied in competition law on the other, so that for example in cases relating to trade within the European Community, the provisions in the Treaty of Rome governing the free movement of goods (articles 30-36) and competition (articles 85-90), have been used in some situations to limit the effect of national intellectual property rights.

One feature of UK law which attempts to deal with the possible abuse of monopoly power in this context is the availability in some cases of compulsory licences and licences as of right to competitors. Under the Patent Act 1977, for example, licences as of right are available during the last four years of the twenty year term, and compulsory licences may be granted by the Comptroller General of Patents Designs and Trademarks on grounds set out in s.48. These are broadly based on the unreasonable underuse of the patent by the patentee. Under the Copyright, Designs and Patents Act 1988, anti competitive licensing conduct in relation to copyright (s.144), or the unregistered design right (s.238), may give rise to compulsory licensing powers. This can occur where the Monopolies and Mergers Commission have reported that the conduct is operating against the public interest, following a reference made under the Fair Trading Act 1973 or the Competition Act 1980. Similar powers arise under s.11A of the Registered Designs Act 1949 and s.51 of the Patents Act 1977.

A comparison of some of the features of the major forms of intellectual property is contained in Figure 17.1.

Patents

The grant of a patent gives to the patentee a twenty year monopoly in the exploitation of a process or a product, in return for clear and complete disclosure of the invention.

The principal objectives of the patent system are threefold. Firstly, to reward the creative effort of the inventor. This aim was made clear in the judgment of the European Court of Justice in *Centrafarm v. Sterling Drugs* 1974:

> *"the patentee, to reward the creative effort of the inventor, has the exclusive right to use an invention with a view to manufacturing industrial products and putting them into circulation for the first time, either directly or by the grant of licences to third parties; as well as the right to oppose infringements."*

Secondly, as an incentive to innovation and increased economic activity; and thirdly as a means of making known to others in industry full information about the latest technical advances.

A patent for the UK may be registered either at the British Patent Office in London or at the European Patent Office in Munich. An application to the European Office, which was created by the European Patent Convention 1973, may result in the grant of identical patents covering each of the signatory states. It is also possible to obtain a single priority date for patents covering a number of other countries worldwide under the Patent Cooperation Treaty 1970, although separate applications must then be pursued in each country. The Patent Act 1977 was introduced in order to bring the UK system for granting patents into line with the European system as contained in the 1973 Convention.

In order to qualify for the grant of a patent, s.1 of the Patent Act 1977 provides that an invention must:

(a) *be novel,*

(b) *involve an inventive step,*

(c) *be capable of industrial application, and*

(d) *fall outside the categories of excluded subject matter.*

In order to satisfy the requirement of novelty under s.2 the invention must not be part of the *"state of the art"* at the time at which the patent application is made. The state of the art includes *"any matter (whether a product, a process, information about either, or anything else) which has at any time been made available to the public (whether in the United Kingdom or elsewhere) by written or oral description, by use, or in any other way."* Prior public disclosure by the inventor or any other person, for example by publication of an article in a periodical, will therefore defeat an application for a patent.

> In *Windsurfing International v. Tabur Marine* 1985 an application relating to a windsurfer included a feature described as "a pair of circuate booms". This referred to the wishbone shaped grip which is held by the user whilst wind-surfing. Evidence showed that prior to the application an amateur had used in public a model which he had made with a pair of straight booms which flexed into arc shapes when used. The Court of Appeal held that the wish-bone feature was part of the state of the art, and the requirement of novelty was not satisfied.

An invention will be taken to involve an inventive step, under s.3, if, having regard to the state of the art, it is not *"obvious to a person skilled in the art."* Obviousness will defeat the requirement of an inventive step. Obviousness is judged by the standards of the notional skilled technician who is familiar with the state of the art but is himself lacking in inventive ability.

The invention will be taken to be capable of industrial application, under s.4, if it can be made or used in any kind of industry, including agriculture. If it has no known practical application, or if it doesn't actually work, then no matter how interesting it is, it is probably not patentable. Methods of treatment of the human or animal body by surgery or therapy, or of diagnosis practised on the human or animal body are deemed to be incapable of industrial application by s.4(2). Clearly it would be against the public interest if new medical techniques were not available for the benefit of all.

Certain things are specifically excluded from patent protection under s.1(2) and s.1(3). These include discoveries, scientific theories or mathematical methods not associated with practical applications; literary, dramatic, musical or artistic works or computer programs which attract copyright protection; plant and animal varieties and essentially biological processes for the production of plants and animals although some protection is given in the case of plant varieties by the Plant Varieties and Seeds Act 1964; and inventions which encourage offensive, immoral or anti-social behaviour.

Where an invention is made by an employee at the workplace, the approach of the common law was that it is the property of his employer. Thus in *Patchett v. Sterling* 1955 Lord Simonds stated:

> *"It is an implied term of the contract of service of any workman that what he produces by the strength of his arms or the skill of his hand or the exercise of his inventive faculty shall become the property of the employer."*

The scope of this principle has been limited by s.39 of the Patent Act 1977, under which the employee is entitled to the rights in his own invention unless either the invention might reasonably be expected to result from the carrying out of his duties or at the time of the invention he has a special obligation to further the interests of the employers undertaking because of the nature of his duties and the particular responsibilities which flow from them. The employer will be entitled to the patent rights where the employee is employed to use his skills to solve technical problems or is employed in a research and development capacity or in a senior managerial position. Otherwise they will belong to the employee.

> In *Reiss Engineering Co. v. Harris* 1985 the defendant was employed to sell valves and deal with customer problems in the first instance. He was not required to deal with serious technical problems as these were referred to the Swiss company who supplied the technology to the plaintiff. After receiving notice of redundancy but before his employment had terminated, the defendant invented a new valve. His employers claim that they owned the invention was rejected because the defendant was not employed to design or invent, nor could an invention reasonably be expected to result from his normal duties.

Where an invention made by an employee belongs to an employer under s.39, the inventor may have a statutory right to compensation under s.40(1). This arises where the patent is of "outstanding benefit" to the employer and it is just that compensation should be awarded. Where the patent belongs to the employee the employer is entitled to use it only if he has a licence from the employee or where it has been assigned to him by the employee. In such cases the employer will have paid for the licence or assignment, but nonetheless, the employee may be entitled to compensation under s.40(2) where the consideration which he received is inadequate compared to the benefit derived by the employer from the patent, and where it is just that compensation should be paid. This is an example of a statutory exception to the normal rules relating to consideration in the law of contract.

The protection conferred by the grant of a patent lasts, subject to the payment of renewal fees, for twenty years from the date of filing the application. The process of registration can be lengthy - up to four and a half years from application. The exclusive rights of exploitation vesting in the patentee may of course be assigned or licensed to others contractually, or exercised by the patentee himself. In any event, during the last four years, licenses as of right may be obtained by competitors on terms as to payment or otherwise which will be settled by the comptroller general of patents, or by the courts. In addition, once a patent has been granted for three years, the comptroller has power to grant compulsory licences on grounds set out in s.48 of the 1977 Act, again on terms which will be settled by him. The grounds are broadly based on underuse of the invention, for example resulting in an undersupply to the UK market or to export markets of the product.

Infringement of a patent may arise directly, for example where the infringer produces or uses a patented product, or indirectly, for example where the infringer supplies another person with the means of putting the invention into effect, in each case without lawful authority. Remedies for infringement, under s.61, include an injunction; an order for delivery up and destruction of any infringing product; damages; an account of profits and a declaration.

Trade Marks, Service Marks and Passing Off

A trade mark or service mark is an emblem symbol or logo which is designed to establish a connection between goods or services and their producer or supplier. The use of such a mark is one of the means whereby a business establishes product identity with the aim of encouraging brand loyalty among consumers and enhancing business goodwill.

English law recognises two types of trade or service marks, those which are registered under the Trade Marks Act 1938 as amended by the Trade Marks (Amendment) Act 1984 and those which, although unregistered, are recognised at common law. The former are protected by legal action for infringement under the 1938 Act and by the common law tort of passing off. The latter are protected by a passing off action only. There are a number of other significant differences between common law and registered trade marks which may be mentioned at this stage:

(a) a registered trade or service mark relates to particular categories of goods or services in which the proprietor of the mark actually trades. If a competitor uses the same mark on different categories of goods or services there is no infringement under the 1938 Act, but there may be passing off at common law if damage can be proved;

(b) a distinctive trade or service mark may be registered prior to the acquisition of a reputation connected with it whereas at common law the mark is protected only on evidence of an established reputation;

(c) a trade or service mark which is not distinctive, for example because it consists of words which are obviously and solely descriptive of the product, is incapable of registration. Such a mark may qualify for common law protection where the words can be shown to have acquired a 'secondary meaning' as for example in the case of *Reddaway v. Banham* discussed below; and

(d) a registered mark may be assigned or licensed to another and thereby become divorced from the goodwill of the business in respect of which it was acquired. Unregistered marks are inseparable from the goodwill of the business which they represent.

Registered trade and service marks

Under the Trade Marks Act 1938, s.68(1), a **trade mark** is defined as:

> *"a mark used or proposed to be used in relation to goods for the purpose of indicating a connection in the course of trade between the goods and some person having the right ... to use the mark".*

A **service mark** is similarly defined in relation to a mark showing a connection with the provision of services. The expression mark is also defined in s.68(1) as including *"a device, brand, heading, label, ticket, name, signature, word, letter, numeral, or any combination thereof."* The "get-up" or shape of goods or of their container has been held not to be capable of registration as a trade mark:

> In Re: *Coca-Cola Co's Applications* 1986 the House of Lords held that the Coca-Cola Company were not entitled to register as a trade mark the distinctively shaped bottle in which their products had been marketed worldwide since the early 1920's on the grounds that a mark must be something distinct from the thing being marked, and a bottle is a container and not a mark.

A register of trade and service marks is maintained at the Patent Office by the Comptroller General of Patents Designs and Trade Marks. The register is open to public inspection under s.1 of the 1938 Act and is being computerised following the Patents, Designs and Marks Act 1986 so as to make the process of searching and obtaining copies of entries quicker and less costly. The register is divided into two parts, Part A and Part B.

Under s.3 of the 1938 Act the mark cannot be registered in general, rather it must be registered in connection with particular goods or services, or classes of goods or services. There are in fact thirty four separate classes of goods and eight classes of services defined in Schedule 1 of the Act. Under s.4 registration in Part A gives the proprietor an absolute monopoly in the use of the mark in that he has the exclusive right to use it in relation to the goods or services specified. There are no defences to an action for infringement of a Part A mark, once infringement is proved. In the case of a Part B registration, however, the monopoly in the use of the mark is limited in that the infringer can invoke a defence under s.4 if he can show that his use of the mark is not likely to mislead the public as to the identity of the producer or supplier.

In order to be registered in Part A, a trade or service mark must be distinctive. The purpose of the mark is to distinguish the goods or services of one business from those of another. The requirement of distinctiveness will be fulfilled if the mark contains or consists of one of the five categories of "essential particulars" set out in s.9. These are:

(a) the name of a company, firm or individual represented in a special or particular manner;

(b) the signature of the applicant;

(c) invented words;

(d) words, having no direct reference to the character or quality of the goods or services, which are not geographical names or surnames; or

(e) any other distinctive mark upon evidence of its distinctiveness.

In order to secure registration in Part B of the register it is not necessary to come within one of these categories, it is sufficient, under s.10, that the mark is "capable of" distinguishing the proprietor's goods or services from those of other businesses. A new mark which is not distinctive would be registered under Part B until it established a wide reputation in connection with the proprietor's goods or services, upon evidence of which it could be registered on Part A.

The Registrar will refuse to register a mark which is deceptive at the time of the application. Where, for example, there has been prior registration of the same or a confusingly similar mark for the same categories of goods or services, s.12 prevents registration. Similarly under s.11 where there has been prior use of an unregistered mark, if registration would give rise to reasonable doubt as to the source of the product, leading to a real and tangible danger of confusion.

> In *Mitsubishi v. Fiat* 1987 the plaintiffs manufactured cars and used the word 'Lancia' as a trade mark. They sought to prevent the defendants from registering 'Lancer' as a name for one of their cars. While the words sounded similar the two trademarks looked completely different. The Court of Appeal, which took the view that in the case of important or expensive purchases the sound of the words is likely not to play a significant role, held that there was no risk of confusion between the two trade marks and that the defendants could register 'Lancer' as a trademark.

The Registrar will refuse, under s.11, to register a mark containing matter which is contrary to law or morality or is a scandalous design. In addition he has an overriding discretion, under s.17(2), to refuse an application or accept it subject to conditions.

> In *Edwards Application* 1945 the Registrar refused to register "Jardex" as a trademark for a poisonous disinfectant because a meat extract was already registered as "Jardox". Although s.12 was inapplicable as the goods were not of the same class or category, registration was refused under s.17(2) on the grounds that possible confusion in use could have serious consequences.

Infringement of a registered trade mark or service mark occurs under s.4 where a similar or identical mark is used by another trader without authority in relation to goods or services in the same category. We have already noted the difference between Part A marks and Part B marks in connection with infringement. Infringement also occurs where the mark is used to "import a reference" to the registered proprietor or his goods, for example in comparative advertising in which the plaintiff's goods, referred to by their trade mark, are characterised as inferior to the defendant's goods. Remedies for infringement include an injunction and an account of profits or damages. It is a criminal offence under s.60 of the 1938 Act to represent that a mark is registered when in fact it is not, and under s.58 fraudulently to apply a mark to goods, labels, packaging or advertising materials where the mark is identical or similar to a registered trade mark.

Passing off

The tort of passing off is designed to protect the goodwill of a business and to enable it to defend its common law rights in respect of unregistered trade or service marks. Goodwill, which is a type of intangible property, was defined by Lord Macnaghten in *I.R.C. v. Muller & Co. Margarine Ltd.* 1901 as *"the benefit and advantage of the good name, reputation and connection of a business. It is the attractive force which brings in the custom."* In *Star Industrial Co. Ltd. v. Yap Kwee Kor* 1976 Lord Diplock stated:

> *"A passing off action is a remedy for the invasion of a right of property ... in the business or goodwill likely to be injured by the misrepresentation made by passing-off one person's goods as the goods of another. Goodwill, as the subject of proprietary rights, is incapable of subsisting by itself. It has no independent existence apart from the business to which it is attached."*

The tort of passing off is committed where one business represents its goods or services, either innocently or intentionally, to be those of another. The basic principle was stated in *Perry v. Truefitt* 1842 by Lord Langdale:

> *"A man is not to sell his own goods under the pretence that they are the goods of another man."*

This may occur, for example, where the defendant simply lies about the origin of his product.

> In *Lord Byron v. Johnson* 1816 the defendant advertised that certain poems which he had published were written by the plaintiff. In fact they were written by someone else. It was held that he was liable in the tort of passing off.

Liability extends well beyond this, so that for example, the use by a trader of a term which accurately describes the composition of his own goods might nevertheless amount to passing off if that term is understood in the market in which the goods are sold to denote the goods of a rival trader.

> In *Reddaway v. Banham* 1896 the plaintiffs manufactured camel hair belting bearing a design consisting of an image of a camel and the words 'Camel Hair Belting'. The defendants also manufactured camel hair belting bearing the words 'camel hair belting' for sale in the same market in which the plain-

tiff's product was well established. The defendants were held to have passed off their goods as the goods of the plaintiff because, although camel hair belting was accurately descriptive of the goods, the words had acquired a secondary meaning under which customers within that market understood them to be goods of the plaintiff.

The essential elements of an action in passing off were identified by Lord Diplock in *Erven Warnink B.V. v. J. Townend & Co. (Hull) Ltd.* 1979. He said that there are:

> *"five characteristics which must be present in order to create a valid course of action for passing off: (1) a misrepresentation (2) made by a trader in the course of trade, (3) to prospective customers of his or ultimate consumers of goods or services supplied by him, (4) which is calculated to injure the business or goodwill of another trader (in the sense that this is a reasonably foreseeable consequence) and (5) which causes actual damage to a business or goodwill of the trader by whom the action is brought or will probably do so."*

The facts of *Warnink v. Townend* were that the dutch plaintiffs manufactured a drink called 'advocaat' which had acquired a substantial reputation in Britain as a distinct and recognisable beverage, having been marketed here for many years. The essential ingredients of advocaat were the spirits, egg yolks and sugar. From 1974 a drink called "Keeling's Old English Advocaat", which was a mixture of dried egg powder and Cyprus sherry, was made and marketed by the defendants in England, where it captured a substantial share of the plaintiffs market. The House of Lords held that the plaintiffs were entitled to protection from the deceptive use of the name advocaat by the defendants, and granted an injunction preventing its use by them.

In order to show that there has been a misrepresentation by the defendant, the plaintiff must establish that his goods have acquired a reputation in the market and are known by some distinguishing feature. This feature may be a name, such as advocaat or camel hair belting, a symbol or logo in the nature of a common law or registered trade mark, or some other feature, such as the appearance or packaging of the goods. The misrepresentation occurs when the distinctive feature is adopted in relation to the product of the defendant and as a result customers in the market are deceived or are likely to be deceived into buying the product believing it to be the plaintiffs. As to the degree of likelihood of deception, the requirement will not be fulfilled if, in the words of one judge, *"only a moron in a hurry would be misled"*. On the other hand, in a case where it is demonstrable that the public has been or will be deceived, it is no defence to argue that they would not be deceived if they were *"more careful, more literate or more perspicacious."*

In *Reckitt & Colman Products Ltd. v. Borden Inc.* 1990 the plaintiffs had, since 1956, sold lemon juice under the brand name Jif in plastic squeeze containers made in the shape, colour and size of natural lemons. No other trader in the UK sold lemon juice in a similar container until the defendants launched such a product. The trial judge found that although a careful shopper would realise the defendants lemon was not that of the plaintiffs, since it was merely a question of reading the label, the evidence nevertheless established conclusively that the introduction of the defendants lemons would result in many shoppers buying them in the belief that they were purchasing the plaintiffs' lemons, as the lemon shape was the crucial point of reference for the shopper who paid little attention to the labels. Accordingly, the judge granted an injunction to restrain the defendants from marketing their product "in any container so nearly resembling the plaintiffs' Jif lemon shaped container as to be likely to deceive without making it clear to the ultimate purchaser that it is not of the goods of the plaintiffs". The defendants appealed and the House of Lords held, on the basis of the judge's finding of fact, that the elements of passing off had been established and the injunction should remain in place.

In *McDonald's Hamburgers v. Burgerking (UK)* 1986 the defendants advertised their "whopper" hamburger stating "It's Not Just Big, Mac" and "Unlike some Burgers, its 100 per cent, pure beef, flame grilled, never fried, with a unique choice of toppings." The plaintiffs were granted an injunction on the grounds that, reading the advertisement, the public would be likely to be deceived into thinking that the burger was an improvement of their 'Big Mac' burger, available at the defendants premises.

The element of damage will usually be proved by evidence that the plaintiff's potential customers have been or are likely to be diverted to the defendant. Where there is no damage, actual or anticipated, the action will fail.

In *Wombles v. Womble Skips* 1977 the owners of the copyright in the Wombles books and children's television series were unable to obtain an injunction against a company that hired out 'Wombles' rubbish skips because the essential elements of passing off had not been established. They were unable to demonstrate that they had suffered or were likely to suffer, any damage as a result of the defendant's activities. Uncle Bulgaria was not best pleased!

The remedies available in a passing off action are damages for the loss which the plaintiff has suffered, or an account of the profits which the defendant has made as a result of the passing off. In addition the court may grant an injunction to restrain the defendant from continuing his unlawful activities.

Designs

The protection of industrial designs, since the coming into force of the Copyright, Designs and Patents Act 1988, arises either by registration under the Registered Designs Act 1949, (as amended by the 1988 Act), or without registration by virtue either of the 'unregistered design right' created by the 1988 Act or, in the case of computer microchips, by the Products (Protection of Topography) Regulations 1987. The unregistered design right in effect replaces the protection previously conferred by the Copyright Act 1956 on industrial drawings, and thereby reduces the scope of protection available for industrial designs.

Registered designs

A design which gives visual appeal to mass produced goods may be registered under the Registered Designs Act 1949. This gives protection for a period of five years, renewable on payment of renewal fees for further five year periods up to a maximum of 25 years in total if registered after the 1988 Act, or 15 in total if registered before.

A design is not registrable under the 1949 Act where the ultimate appearance of the article is not material to the consumer, for example in the case of a waste disposal unit which, when installed, will be hidden from view. An unregistered design right may however arise in respect of purely functional articles of this nature, where aesthetic considerations are not normally taken into account by a purchaser.

In order to qualify for registration, the design must come within the definition of a design in s.1(1) of the 1949 Act, which states:

> *"In this Act "design" means features of shape, configuration, pattern or ornament applied to an article by any industrial process, being features which in the finished article appeal to and are judged by the eye, but does not include -*
>
> *(a) a method or principle of construction, or*
>
> *(b) features of shape or configuration of an article which*
>
> *(i) are dictated solely by the function which the article has to perform, or*
>
> *(ii) are dependant upon the appearance of another article of which the article is intended by the author of the design to form an integral part".*

In *Interlego AG v. Tyco Industries Inc.* 1988 the Privy Council had to rule upon a case governed by the pre 1988 Act law, under which the plaintiff claimed copyright protection for the design drawings of Lego bricks. Copyright could be claimed pre 1988 if the artistic work in question as not a design capable of registration under the 1949 Act. The plaintiff argued that the design of the bricks was purely functional and therefore incapable of registration due to the wording of s.1(1)(b)(i). The Privy Council held that the designs were capable of registration under the 1949 Act and consequently were not protected by copyright. The design of the bricks was not purely functional as they clearly had eye-appeal as well as significant features in terms of outline and proportion which were not dictated by function.

The so called *must match* exception contained in S.1(1)(b)(ii) was newly introduced by the 1988 Act, and applies to situations where the design of the article must match that of another article of which it is intended to form an integral part. This covers such items as replacement body panels for motor vehicles, the designs of which are not capable of registration. As we shall see such articles are also outside the protection of the unregistered design right.

In order to be registrable, the design must be new. This requirement of novelty will not be satisfied if a substantially similar design is registered in pursuance of a prior application or has already been published in the UK.

The original ownership of a design is vested in its author under s.2, except in two cases. First, where the design is created pursuant to a commission for money or money's worth, in which case the person commissioning it is treated as the original owner. Second, where the design is created by an employee in the course of his employment, his employer is treated as the original owner. Under s.2(4), where a design is generated by computer in circumstances where there is no human author, the person by whom the arrangements necessary for the creation of the design are made is taken to be the author.

The registration of a design gives the registered proprietor the exclusive right, under s.7, to make or import articles of that design for sale, hire or business use and to sell, hire or offer to sell or hire them. Any person who does any such act without the authority of the proprietor, or makes anything to enable such articles to be made will be liable for infringement. This liability is strict and arises without the need to prove copying. Remedies for infringement of a registered design include an injunction and damages, although under s.9 damages cannot be awarded against a defendant who neither knew nor had reasonable grounds for supposing that the design was registered. Section 9 further provides that merely marking the article "registered" will not constitute reasonable grounds unless this is accompanied by the design number.

Unregistered design right

The unregistered design right was created by Part III of the Copyright, Designs and Patents Act 1988. The 1988 Act, in s.51, withdrew copyright protection from most functional industrial designs. Prior to this, although artistic copyright could not subsist in manufactured articles as such, prior drawings of such articles had copyright protection as artistic works provided they were not registerable under the Registered Designs Act 1949.

As we saw in the case of *Interlego AG v. Tyco Industries Inc.* 1988 this put design owners into a surprising position of having to argue that their designs did not qualify for registration under the 1949 Act, in order to claim the considerably better protection offered by the law of copyright. This anomalous situation was the subject of much criticism, not least by the House of Lords in *British Leyland Motor Corporation v. Armstrong*, a decision which took away that protection in relation to the design of spare parts for cars.

> In *British Leyland Motor Corp. Ltd. v. Armstrong Patents Co. Ltd.* 1986 the defendant, without having seen the plaintiff's design drawings, copied spare parts for its cars by a process of reverse engineering, which simply involved copying the shape and dimensions of the original articles. The House of Lords held that this infringed the plaintiffs copyright in the design drawings since, by s.48(1) of the Copyright Act 1956, 'reproduction' of the artistic work included converting it into three dimensional form. However, the plaintiff's rights were, in their lordships' opinion, subordinate to the competing entitlement of car owners to access to a free market in spare parts in order to keep their cars in working order. Accordingly the plaintiff was not entitled to enforce its copyright in a manner so as to maintain a monopoly in the supply of spare parts for its vehicles, and the defendant was free to manufacture without licence.

Copyright as a means of protecting functional industrial designs was, as previously noted, substantially withdrawn by s.51 of the 1988 Act. and replaced by the unregistered design right.

The unregistered design right arises in respect of an 'original design' under s.213 of the 1988 Act. Designs covered by the section are defined in s.213(2) and (3) which state:

"(2) *In this Part "design" means the design of any aspect of the shape or configuration (whether internal or external) of the whole or part of an article.*

(3) *Design right does not subsist in -*

(a) *a method or principle of construction,*

(b) *features of shape or configuration of an article which -*

(i) *enable the article to be connected to, or placed in, around or against, another article so that either article may perform its function, or*

(ii) *are dependant upon the appearance of another article of which the article is intended by the designer to form an integral part, or*

(c) *surface decoration."*

The exceptions contained in s.213(3)(b), the so-called *must-fit* and *must-match* exceptions, are a significant extension of the consequences of the decision in *British Leyland v. Armstrong* 1986.

The *must-fit* exception in s.213(3)(b)(i) clearly applies to spare parts, such as exhaust systems, engine parts etc., and probably goes a good deal further. For example it could apply to fixing devices, or accessories for an electric drill. The *must-match* exception in s.213(3)(b)(ii) applies to spare parts such as vehicle body panels, the shape of which is integral to the appearance of the vehicle as a whole.

An unregistered design right does not subsist, by s.213(3)(c), in surface decoration. This is not excluded from copyright protection by s.51, and may also be protected by registration as *"features of pattern or ornament"* under the 1949 Act.

The unregistered design right arises when the design has been recorded in a design document or when an article has been made to the design. A design document, by s.263(1), means any record of a design, whether in the form of a drawing, a written description, a photograph, data stored in a computer or otherwise. The right belongs to the designer unless it was created in pursuance of a commission, in which case it belongs to the person who commissioned it. Where the design was created in the course of the designer's employment, the right belongs to the employer.

The design right expires fifteen years from the end of the calendar year in which the right arose, or, if sooner, ten years from the end of the calendar year in which articles made to the design were first available for sale or hire. During the last five years of the design right term, any person is entitled to a licence as of right upon terms which, in the absence of agreement, will be settled by the comptroller.

The owner of the unregistered design right has, by s.226, the exclusive right to reproduce the design for commercial purposes, either by making articles exactly or substantially to the design, or by making a design document for the purpose of enabling such articles to be made. Any person who, without authority, engages in any of these activities is liable for primary infringement. Secondary infringement arises where an infringer who knows or has reason to believe that an article is an infringing article, imports it into the UK, has it in his possession for commercial purposes, sells or hires it, or offers or exposes it for sale or hire in the course of a business.

Remedies for infringement include an injunction, an order for delivery up of infringing articles or moulds or tools for making them, an account of profits, or damages. Additional damages may be awarded for flagrant infringement under s.229(3). No damages, however, will be awarded for innocent primary infringement, although the other remedies are available. In a case where a licence as of right would have been available at the time of infringement, a defendant who undertakes to take such a licence will not be subjected to an injunction, an order for delivery up, or an award of damages in excess of double the amount of royalties which would have been payable if such a licence had been granted.

Products (Protection of Topography) Regulations 1987

The 1987 regulations were introduced under the enabling provisions of the European Communities Act 1972 in order to implement an EC directive. Their purpose is to confer protection, which bears some of the features of the unregistered design right, upon the creator of the patterns of circuitry and layout of semiconductor products such as the computer microchip. A semiconductor product is defined in r.2(1) as:

> *"an article the purpose of which is the performance of an electronic function and which consists of two or more layers, at least one of which is composed of semiconducting material and in or upon one or more of which is fixed a pattern appertaining to that or another function."*

The 'topography right' subsists in the arrangements of the layers of a semiconductor product, and in the pattern on the surface of the layers. Under r.3, the topography must be original in order to qualify for protection. Like the unregistered design right, the duration of protection is the lesser of fifteen years from the end of the calendar year in which the topography is created, or ten years from the end of the calendar year in which it is first marketed.

Ownership of the topography right, which arises automatically without the need for registration, confers a monopoly in the commercial exploitation of the semiconductor product. This vests in the designer unless it was created in pursuance of a commission, in which case it belongs to the person who commissioned it. Where the topography was created in the course of the designer's employment, the right belongs to the employer. There is no provision for the grant of licences as of right in the topography regulations.

Copyright

Copyright is an important form of intellectual property, the ownership of which gives rise to a range of exclusive rights in relation in relation to the copyright work. The effect of these rights is to enable their owner to prevent others from using the copyright work in a number of different ways. The Copyright Designs and Patents Act 1988, which came into effect on 1st August 1989, applies to all copyright works made on or after that date. Works made prior to that date are governed by previous legislation, such as the Copyright Act 1956 or earlier Acts, which will continue to have practical importance for many years to come having regard to the duration of copyright protection. In this text, however, it is proposed to deal only with the main features of the 1988 Act.

Copyright arises automatically without the need for registration or other formality. It is, however, common to see published work carrying the copyright symbol ©. Whilst this is not necessary in order to obtain copyright protection in the UK, the use of the symbol in conjunction with the name of the copyright owner and the year of first publication has three purposes. First it confers protection under the terms of Universal Copyright Convention 1952 in a number of other countries, including the USA, without the need for any other formality. Second, it raises a number of presumptions under s.104, s.105 and s.106 as to the authorship of the work, ownership of the copyright and date of first publication. These presumptions may of course be rebutted by appropriate evidence to the contrary. Third, it serves as a reminder of the rights of the copyright owner, and a warning against infringement.

Copyright work

The range of subject matter which attracts copyright is set out in s.1 of the 1988 Act, which states:

> *"1(1)Copyright is a property right which subsists ... in the following descriptions of work -*
>
> *(a) original literary, dramatic, musical or artistic works,*
>
> *(b) sound recordings, films, broadcasts or cable programmes, and*
>
> *(c) the typographical arrangements of published editions."*

It may be noted that in order at attract copyright there must actually be a work. The law of copyright does not protect ideas as such, rather the embodiment or expression of the ideas in a work.

	Literary work	Dramatic and musical work	Artistic work	Sound recording	Film	Broadcasts and cable programmes	Published editions
Nature of work	any work which is written, spoken or sung (other than dramatic and musical work) including tables, compilations and computer programmes	dramatic work includes dance and mime (recorded in any form) musical work consists of music without words (literary work) or actions (dramatic work)	graphic work (painting, diagram, chart etc) photograph, sculpture, collage (all irrespective of artistic quality) architectural work and works of artistic craftsmanship	recording of sounds or of literary dramatic or musical work from which the sounds may be reproduced	recording on any medium from which a moving image may by any means be produced	transmission of information (eg tv or radio programme or teletext) by wireless telegraphy (broadcast) or by a non-wireless cable programme service (cable programme)	typographic arrangement (layout) of published edition of literary, dramatic or musical work
First ownership	author (creator of the work), or, if made in the course of employment, the author's employer			person undertaking arrangements necessary for making sound recording or film		person making broadcast or providing cable programme service	publisher
Duration of protection	50 years from end of year of author's death, or, 50 years from end of year of death of last surviving joint author, or, where author unknown, 50 years from end of year in which first made available to the public, or, where computer generated, 50 years from end of year in which the work was made. Parliamentary copyright: 50 years for Acts and Measures Crown Copyright 125 years or 50 years from first commercial publication.			end of 50th year from making, or end of 50th year from release if release within 50 years of making		end of 50th year from first transmission	end of 25th year from first publication

Figure 17.2 Copyright : subject matter, first ownership and duration

> In *Green v. Broadcasting Corp of New Zealand* 1989 the plaintiff, Hughie Green, claim for damages from the defendant for infringement of his copyright in the scripts and dramatic format of the television show Opportunity Knocks. The defendant had broadcast a similar show in New Zealand with the same title and without the authority of the plaintiff. Although no scripts were produced in evidence, the plaintiff's evidence was that he wrote the scripts of the show, such as they were, by having the same form of introduction for each competitor, using the same catch phrases throughout the show like "For so-and-so, Opportunity Knocks", "This is your show, folks, and I do mean you", "make your mind up time" and using the 'clapometer' to measure audience reaction to competitors' performances. The Privy Council acepted that the evidence established the existence of scripts, but concluded, in the absence of precise evidence as to what they contained, that they did no more than express a general idea or concept for a talent quest and therefore were not the subject of copyright.

The requirement of originality in s.1(1)(a) in relation to literary, dramatic, musical or artistic works was explained in *London University Press v. University Tutorial Press* 1916 by Peterson J as follows:

> *"The word original does not in this connection mean that the work must be the expression of original or inventive thought. Copyright Acts are not concerned with the originality of ideas, but with the expression of thought, and, in the case of literary work, with the expression of thought in print or writing. The originality which is required relates to the expression of the thought. But the Act does not require that the expression must be in an original or novel form, but that the work must not be copied from another work - that it should originate from the author."*

Literary work is defined in s.3(1) as:

> *"any work, other than dramatic or musical work, which is written, spoken or sung, and accordingly includes:*
>
> *(a) a table or compilation, and*
>
> *(b) a computer programme"*

Literary work is one of the most important categories of copyright work, embracing a wide range of subject matter such as textbooks, novels, newspaper articles, poems, plays, song lyrics, letters, essays, scripts, speeches, bus timetables, instructions, databases and computer programs. Where the work consists of the spoken word, copyright does not arise unless and until the work is recorded. The recording, which may be by writing, tape, film or any other means, will trigger the creation of copyright in favour of the speaker, or his employer, whether or not the speaker has authorised the recording. This also applies in the case of original dramatic or musical work which is spoken or sung.

Dramatic work encompasses not only drama but also works of dance and mime. In *Green v. Broadcasting Corp of New Zealand* 1989, discussed above, the plaintiff's argument that his use of a number of catch phrases in the presentation of each Opportunity Knocks show gave rise to the subsistence of copyright in the format of the show as a dramatic work, was rejected by the Privy Council. Lord Bridge stated that *"a dramatic work must have sufficient unity to be capable of performance and ... the features claimed as constituting the 'format' of [the plaintiff's] show, being unrelated to each other except as accessories to be used in the presentation of some other dramatic or musical performance, lack that essential characteristic."*

Musical work is defined in s.3(1) as:

> *"a work consisting of music, exclusive of any words or action intended to be sung, spoken or performed with the music".*

This refers to the music only; song lyrics being literary work and accompanying action being dramatic work. Where these three elements are the creation of different authors, the duration of copyright in each will vary according to the lifespan of the individuals concerned.

Artistic work is widely defined in s.4 and falls into two categories. The first includes graphics, paintings, drawings, diagrams, maps, charts, plans, engravings, etchings, lithographs, woodcuts, photographs, sculptures and collages, all of which attract copyright regardless of artistic quality. In the second category come architectural structures, buildings or models and works of artistic craftsmanship, all of which must display some degree of artistic merit in order to come within the definition.

In addition to literary, dramatic, musical and artistic works, copyright subsists in sound recordings, including records cassettes and compact disks; films and videos; broadcasts; cable programmes and the typographical layout of published editions.

Authorship and ownership of copyright

The first ownership of copyright in a work is the author of it, under s.11(1). Where a literary, dramatic, musical or artistic work is made by an employee in the course of his employment, however, his employer is the first owner of the copyright, subject to any agreement to the contrary.

In the case of literary, dramatic, musical or artistic work, the author, under s.9(1), is the person who creates the work. Where such work is computer generated, the author is taken to be the person by whom the arrangements necessary for the creation of the work are undertaken.

In relation to other types of copyright work, s.9(2) provides that the author shall be taken to be:

> *"(a) in the case of a sound recording or film, the person by whom the arrangements necessary for the making of the recording or film are undertaken;*
>
> *(b) in the case of a broadcast, the person making the broadcast ...;*
>
> *(c) in the case of a cable programme, the person providing the cable programme service in which the programme is included;*
>
> *(d) in the case of the typographical arrangements of a published edition, the publisher."*

Like any other form of property, copyright can be dealt with by way of sale purchase or gift, or devolve as part of a deceased person's estate on death. The copyright owner has, in effect, a number of separate rights. These rights can be divided up, and dealt with separately. Take, for example, the case of an author who has written a novel. A number of different rights in his original literary work could be assigned to separate purchasers. Thus he could sell the right to publish in hardback to A, in paperback to B, the french translation rights to C, spanish to D, the film rights to E and the right to publish in comic strip form to F. Further subdivision along these lines, or in terms of time period, or geographical area, are also possible. Such possibilities are recognised by s.90(2) which states:

> *"(2) An assignment or other transmission of copyright may be partial, that is, limited to apply -*

> *(a) to one or more, but not all, of the things the copyright owner has the exclusive right to do;*
>
> *(b) to part, but not the whole, of the period for which the copyright is to subsist."*

Under s.91, future copyright can be assigned in whole or in part before the work comes into existence. Where this is done, for example as part of an agreement to publish work which has not yet been written, copyright vests in the assignee as soon as it comes into being.

Any assignment of copyright, in whole or in part, existing or future, will not be effective unless the assignment is in writing, and signed by or on behalf of the assignor.

Duration of copyright

Copyright in literary, dramatic, musical or artistic work expires, under s.12 fifty years from the end of the calendar year in which the author dies. In the case of joint authorship the fifty year period is counted from the end of the year in which the last of the joint authors dies. Where the work is of unknown authorship, copyright expires fifty years from the end of the year in which it is first made available to the public. In the case of computer generated work, the fifty year period begins at the end of the year in which the work is made.

Copyright in a sound recording or a film expires, under s.13 fifty years from the end of the year in which it is made, unless it is released during that time, in which case copyright expires fifty years from the end of the year in which it is released. In the case of broadcasts and cable programmes, copyright expires fifty years from the end of the year of first transmission, while copyright in the typographical arrangement of a published edition expires twenty five years from the end of the year in which the edition was published.

Infringement of copyright

Infringement of copyright occurs where a person does something in relation to a copyright work, without the authority of the copyright owner, which is an *"act restricted by copyright"* under s.16(1), and which falls outside the scope of *"acts permitted in relation to copyright works"* within sections 28-76 of the 1988 Act. In defining acts restricted by copyright, the performance of which will amount to primary infringement, s.16(1) sets out the rights associated with copyright ownership. These are, in effect, two sides of the same coin. Section 16(1) states:

> *"The owner of the copyright in a work has ... the exclusive right to do the following acts in the UK -*
>
> *(a) to copy the work;*
>
> *(b) to issue copies of the work to the public;*
>
> *(c) to perform, show or play the work in public;*
>
> *(d) to broadcast the work or include it in a cable programme service;*
>
> *(e) to make an adaptation of the work or do any of the above in relation to an adaptation;*
>
> *and those acts are referred to as the 'acts restricted by the copyright'."*

Infringement may take the form of doing an act restricted by the copyright, or authorising another person to do such an act.

In *CBS Songs Ltd. v. Amstrad Consumer Electronics plc* 1988 the plaintiff sued for damages and an injunction to prevent the sale of twin deck tape recording machines by the defendant, on the grounds that the tape to tape facility on the machines was likely to encourage home taping and copying of copyright material. The House of Lords dismissed the plaintiff's argument that the defendant had authorised infringement, or was a joint infringer with any person who used the machines for taping copyright material, and the claim failed as the machines were perfectly capable of lawful use.

The Act takes a broad view of the scope of primary infringement. This is reflected in s.16(3) which states:

"References to the doing of an act restricted by the copyright in a work are to the doing of it -

(a) in relation to the work as a whole or any substantial part of it, and

(b) either directly or indirectly"

Whether the defendant has copied a *substantial part* of the plaintiff's work is a question of degree depending on the particular facts of the case. In *Ladbroke v. William Hill* 1964, Lord Reid stated that the question *"depends much more on the quality than on the quantity of what he has taken"*. Where the plaintiff's work is highly original, the taking of a fairly small part of it may be held to be substantial. On the other hand where the plaintiff's work, although original, is rather commonplace, the taking of a greater part of it quantitatively may still not be substantial.

Where there is a claim of infringement based on copying, the plaintiff must prove that the defendant's work is taken from the work of which he is the copyright owner. The claim will fail, therefore, if the defendant can show either that both pieces of work were derived from a common source, or that he produced his work independently. Where the two works are substantially similar, and it is shown that the defendant had access to the plaintiff's work or the opportunity to become familiar with it, the Court will infer copying in the absence of evidence to the contrary.

In *Francis Day & Hunter Ltd. v. Bron* 1963 the plaintiff owned the copyright in a musical work 'In a Little Spanish Town', composed in 1926 and exploited extensively by way of sheet music, broadcasting and gramophone records. The song retained its popularity over the years and a number of recordings of it were made. In 1959 the defendant published a song 'Why', which, the plaintiff alleged, reproduced a substantial part of its work. The plaintiff claimed that the first eight bars of the chorus of Spanish Town had been reproduced consciously or unconsciously in the first eight bars of Why. The judge, Wilberforce J, accepted the defendant's evidence that he had not consciously copied the plaintiff's work. He found that the first eight bars of the chorus of Spanish Town constituted a substantial part of the whole tune and that there was a considerable degree of similarity between those eight bars and the first eight bars of Why, though there were differences enough to take into account when considering whether Why could be an independent creation. In considering whether there had been unconscious copying, he stated: *"The final question to be resolved is whether the plaintiff's work has been copied or reproduced, and it seems to me that the answer can only be reached by a judgment of fact upon a number of composite elements: The degree of familiarity (if proved at all, or properly inferred) with the plaintiff's work, the character of the work, particularly its qualities of impressing the mind and memory, the objective similarity of the defendant's work, the inherent probability that such similarity as is found could be due to coincidence, the existence of other influences upon the defendant composer, and not least the quality of the defendant's own evidence on the presence or otherwise in his mind of the plaintiff's work."* In a decision which was subsequently confirmed by the Court of Appeal, the judge held that there was insufficient evidence upon which to find unconscious copying, and the plaintiff's claim failed.

It may be noted that in addition to a range of civil remedies for infringement, including damages, an injunction, an order for delivery up and a right in limited circumstances to seize infringing copies and other associated articles, the 1988 Act creates a number of criminal offences, under s.107, for activities in the course of a business, which amount to infringement.

In any action for infringement of copyright, it is a defence to show that the activities of the defendant come within the scope of acts permitted in relation to copyright works. These are contained in s.28 to s.76 of the 1988 Act, and include, for example, fair dealing with a literary dramatic musical or artistic work for the purposes of research or private study under s.29, fair dealing for the purposes of criticism or review of the work under s.30, non reprographic copying for the purpose of instruction or any copying for the purpose of examinations under s.32, things done for the purposes of parliamentary or judicial proceedings under s.45 and a range of other acts.

Moral rights

The 1988 Act created, for the first time in UK copyright law, the so called rights of *paternity* and *integrity* in favour of the author of copyright work, and a right of *privacy* in favour of a person commissioning a film or photograph for private and domestic purposes. The rights of paternity, integrity and privacy all subsist for the duration of the copyright under s.86, and can be enforced by an action for breach of statutory duty under s.103. They are personal to the author and cannot be assigned, although they may be waived either by contract or in a signed document, and they devolve as part of the author's estate after his death.

The right of paternity is a right to be identified as the author of a literary, dramatic, musical or artistic work or the director of a film whenever the work is being published commercially, performed in public or broadcast. The right of paternity does not come into effect unless it is asserted either by a term in the assignment of copyright, or in a signed written notice.

The right of integrity is a right which arises, without the need to assert it, in favour again of an author or film director. It is a right not to have the work subjected to derogatory treatment. For these purposes, under s.80(2):

"*(a) 'treatment' of a work means any addition to, deletion from or alteration to or adaption of the work, other than -*

(i) a translation of a literary or dramatic work, or

(ii) an arrangement or transcription of a musical work involving no more than a change of key or register; and

(b) the treatment of a work is derogatory if it amounts to distortion or mutilation of the work or is otherwise prejudicial to the honour or reputation of the author or director".

The right of privacy was introduced in the 1988 Act to counterbalance the abolition of the rule previously contained in s.4(3) of the Copyright Act 1956 that copyright in commissioned photographs belonged to the person who commissioned them. Under the 1988 Act copyright in such works belongs to the photographer. However, where a person commissions a film or a photograph for private and domestic purposes, he has the right, under s.85(1), not to have the work exhibited in public or broadcast, and not to have copies of the work issued to the public.

Negotiable Instruments

The most important types of negotiable instruments are bills of exchange and cheques, although many others may be encountered in the commercial world, such a promissory notes, bank notes, bankers' drafts, treasury bills and dividend warrants. For the business community the cheque is the most commonly used method of payment, and an appreciation of the rules concerning the use of cheques is of prime importance. All negotiable instruments have the following special characteristics, which are not shared by other choses in action, and are referred to collectively as negotiability.

The characteristics of negotiability are:

(a) ownership is transferred by delivery alone if the instrument is payable to bearer, or by endorsement and delivery if payable to order;

(b) a transferee taking in good faith and for value who is a 'holder in due course' acquires a good title despite any defects in the title of the transferor;

(c) the holder of a negotiable instrument can sue on it in his own name whether or not he is a party to it;

(d) on assignment of the instrument there is no need to notify the person who will eventually have to pay out on it.

Bills of exchange and cheques

A bill of exchange is *"an unconditional order in writing, addressed by one person to another, signed by the person giving it, requiring the person to whom it is addressed to pay on demand, or at a fixed determinable future time, a sum certain in money to, or to the order of, a specified person, or to bearer"*. The person who gives the order, or draws up the bill, is known as the *drawer*. The person who is ordered to pay is known as the *drawee*, and the person to whom payment is to be made is known as the *payee*.

A cheque is *"a bill of exchange drawn on a banker payable on demand."*

By combining the two definitions, a cheque may be defined as an unconditional order in writing, signed by the person giving it (the drawer or customer), requiring the banker to whom it is addressed (the drawee) to pay on demand a sum certain in money to, or to the order of, a specified person (the payee), or to bearer.

Cheques are widely used in the commercial world because, as an alternative to cash, they are much more convenient both in terms of the security risks involved in carrying around large sums of cash and because they provide a record of payment for accounting purposes and evidence of payment for legal purposes.

Cheques are not, however, legal tender and there is no obligation to accept a cheque in payment of a debt. A person or organisation who is owed money can refuse to accept a cheque and insist on payment in cash. In order to encourage the use of cheques and to make them more acceptable in the ordinary course of business, banks issue bankers cards to their customers which effectively guarantee that a person accepting a cheque up to the value of £100 will be paid by the bank.

Bills of exchange are used mainly in the field of foreign trade and they can be used as a means of allowing a buyer time to pay for the goods. A bill of exchange may look like this:

Durham October 10th, 1991

£5,000

Six months after date pay C Ltd. (payee) the sum of five thousand pounds.
(signed) A. Ltd. (drawer)

To B Ltd. (drawee)
Paris France

Where A Ltd. sells goods to the value of £5,000 to B Ltd. in France, and A Ltd. owes £5,000 to C Ltd. who is also in France, A Ltd., by drawing a bill of exchange on B Ltd. is effectively instructing B Ltd. to pay C Ltd. the money A Ltd. owes C Ltd., and is avoiding the necessity of physically transporting those sums of money back and forwards to France.

Negotiation - the transfer of ownership

The method of transferring ownership of negotiable instruments is known as negotiation and its form depends upon whether the instrument is made payable to bearer, or to order. For the purposes of simplicity we shall refer here only to cheques, although what is said will also apply to bills of exchange generally.

A cheque payable to bearer is negotiated by simple delivery. Thus if a cheque is drawn in favour of *"John Smith or bearer"* and John Smith hands over the cheque to Tom Brown in settlement of a debt, ownership of the cheque is transferred to Tom Brown by the act of handing it over without any other action being taken.

A cheque payable to order is negotiated by indorsement and delivery.

An indorsement is simply the signature of the payee on the back of the cheque. If a cheque is drawn in favour of *"John Smith or order"*, to negotiate the cheque to Tom Brown, John Smith must sign the back of the cheque and then hand it over to Tom Brown. Whether the cheque will be a bearer cheque or an order cheque in the hands of Tom Brown will depend upon the form of the indorsement. If John Smith signed his name on the back of the cheque without naming a new payee this is known as an *indorsement in blank* and has the effect of converting the cheque into a bearer cheque. If, on the other hand, John Smith has named a new payee by writing *'Pay Tom Brown or order'* or simply *'Pay Tom Brown'* on the back of the cheque and then signed it, this is known as a *special indorsement* and the cheque remains an order cheque.

Effect of forged or unauthorised signature

The general rule is that a forged signature is *wholly inoperative*. Where a signature is forged or unauthorised, it is as though that signature was not there at all on the cheque. As there can be more than one signature on a cheque, it is necessary to distinguish the consequences of forgery of particular signatures.

Forgery of the drawer's signature

Since a cheque is an unconditional order in writing *'signed by the person giving it'*, where the signature of the drawer is forged, and therefore wholly inoperative, the document is not a cheque or a bill of exchange. It is therefore entirely worthless, and no-one can acquire any rights under it.

Forgery of an indorsement

order cheques

Where a cheque is drawn payable to order, the payee must indorse it before he can negotiate it to someone else. Similarly, where a cheque has been negotiated and, by special indorsement, is made payable to another person, known as the indorsee, that other person must himself indorse the cheque before he can negotiate it further. In each case, because the cheque is an order cheque, the indorsement is essential if the negotiation is to transfer ownership validly.

Where an essential indorsement on an order cheque is forged, no subsequent party can acquire ownership of the cheque. For example, A draws a cheque on B bank in favour of C or order. C indorses it and negotiates it to D. A thief steals the cheque, forges D's indorsement and negotiates it to E. E indorses the cheque and negotiates it to F.

A ——→ C ——→ D // E ——→ F

There is a break in the chain and D is the true owner. D can recover the cheque from F, suing in tort if necessary.

Whilst title does not pass under a forged indorsement, persons subsequent to the forgery may have certain rights as between themselves so that in the example above F could sue E.

bearer cheques

In the case of bearer cheques an indorsement is not essential to valid negotiation because ownership of a bearer cheque passes by delivery alone. Therefore if an indorsement on a bearer cheque is forged, the forgery does not affect the subsequent negotiation of the cheque.

Rights of the holder in due course

We noted earlier that one of the characteristics of a negotiable instrument was that in certain circumstances the person receiving the instrument can acquire a better title to it than the person who transferred it to him. This rule applies to a person who receives a cheque or bill of exchange as a *holder in due course.*

A holder in due course is one who has taken a cheque:

(a) complete and regular on the face of it;

(b) before it was overdue (i.e. in circulation for 10 days or more);

(c) without notice that it had been previously dishonoured, if that is the case;

(d) in good faith and for value;

(e) without notice of any defect in the title of the person who negotiated it to him.

A holder in due course can sue, in his own name, any or all of the parties to a cheque. This does not apply, however, in relation to an order cheque which bears a forged essential indorsement because no party subsequent to the forgery can acquire title to the cheque, and therefore no such party can be a holder in relation to the cheque.

Crossed cheques

The object of crossing a cheque is to convey instructions to the banker as to the manner of payment. Cheques can be crossed simply by drawing two parallel lines across the face of the cheque.

The effect of crossing a cheque is that it must be paid through a bank account. The payee or bearer will not be able to obtain cash for it across the counter in a bank. This provides some safeguard in the case of stolen cheques because a thief will not wish to be traced by putting a cheque through his account and because the processing of the cheque will allow a time delay during which the cheque could be stopped.

General crossing

Two parallel lines are drawn across the face of the cheque. The words *and company* in full or abbreviated may be written between the lines but this is not essential. The effect of a general crossing is that the cheque is payable only through a bank account. The cheque cannot be paid over the counter.

Special crossing

The name of a particular bank or branch is written between the parallel lines. The effect of a special crossing is that the cheque must be paid into the named bank or branch.

Not negotiable

The words *not negotiable* may be written between the parallel lines. The effect of these words is to remove the characteristics of negotiability from the cheque. Although it is still transferable, the holder of such a cheque can obtain no better title to it than the person from whom he took it. There can be no *holder in due course* in relation to a cheque with a not negotiable crossing.

Account payee

This crossing does not prevent the cheque from being transferred or from being negotiable. It is an instruction to the banker who may be liable in negligence if he collects the money for some account other than that of the person named as payee.

In order to maximise security when payment is being made by cheque, a combination of crossings may be used. Many banks supply cheque books with pre-printed crossings on request to their customers.

Transfer of intangible property

Unlike negotiable instruments, ownership of most types of choses in action cannot be transferred by delivery alone. A formal assignment of the benefit of most intangible property rights is required in order for the transfer of ownership to be fully effective.

If, for example, A owes B £500 and B wishes to transfer the right to receive that money to C, B will have to make a formal assignment of the debt to C. This must comply with s.136 of the Law of Property Act 1925, which provides that an assignment of a debt or chose in action will transfer to the assignee all the rights of the assignor if:

(a) the assignment is absolute and not merely partial;

(b) it is in writing and signed by the assignor;

(c) written notice is given to the debtor or other person liable on the chose in action.

In the example B must sign a document assigning the debt to C and give written notice of it to A in order to comply with s.136.

Assignment *What's in a Name?*

In the last fifteen years Ricca has become a household name in fabrics and furniture design. To have Ricca furnishings in your home is for many people the mark of success.

When the young designers Richard and Catherine Bratton formed their Ricca company in 1969 they had no idea that their up-market products would become the basis of a £50 million business by the mid nineteen eighties, or that their distinctive style and Ricca logo would become internationally known.

In 1984 when the company went public, it was already an organisation employing four hundred staff at its main premises in Derby. You work in its small legal department at Derby, as an assistant to one of the two company lawyers, Michael Richardson. Your department deals with a wide range of legal matters, and at the moment you are working on three separate issues which Michael has asked you to look over, prior to discussing them with him. These issues are briefly described below.

The Ricca name and logo. A newly formed company that is competing in the same market as Ricca, is regarded by the Ricca board of directors has having unreasonably infringed Ricca's business interests, by incorporating in the name of Reeca Ltd., and selling a range of furniture described as the 'Celeste range'. Ricca produced a range called 'Celestial' a term which the company has registered as a trade mark. The two furniture ranges are of a different style however, and whilst the logo of each company is a design based upon the letter 'R', which incorporates a similar typeface, the Ricca logo is circular, whereas the Reeca logo is triangular.

The design director. Following an internal disagreement with other members of the board, the design director, Milos Kasna left the company earlier this year and set up his own business designing and printing fabrics. His company is already selling fabrics which are based upon a design started by Mr. Kasna after he resigned from the company, while he was still working out his notice. Additionally he is selling a fabric which he designed for Ricca four years ago, but which the company stopped producing after one year because of poor sales.

The lease. Part of the Derby premises, housing the furniture division of the company, is held on a ten year lease which is due to expire in eight months time. There is evidence that the landlord, wishes to expand his business, which adjoins the furniture division and may oppose the renewal of the lease.

Tasks

1. Examine the situations involving the competition from Reeca Ltd. and Milos Kasna's new company, and produce a brief report for Michael Richardson which advises him of Ricca's legal rights, and how the company should proceed.

2. Produce a paper to be tabled at the next meeting of the board of directors, which outlines the rights of the company in relation to the renewal of its business lease.

Index